Security in Computing Systems

Joachim Biskup

Security in Computing Systems

Challenges, Approaches and Solutions

 Springer

Prof. Dr. Joachim Biskup
Fakultät für Informatik
Technische Universität Dortmund
August-Schmidt-Str. 12
44227 Dortmund
Germany
joachim.biskup@cs.uni-dortmund.de

ISBN 978-3-540-78441-8   e-ISBN 978-3-540-78442-5

Library of Congress Control Number: 2008937819

ACM Computing Classification (1998): H.1.1, E.4, E.3, D.4.6, K.6.5

Cover design: KünkelLopka GmbH, Heidelberg, Germany

Printed on acid-free paper

9 8 7 6 5 4 3 2 1

springer.com

Preface

This monograph on *Security in Computing Systems: Challenges, Approaches and Solutions* aims at introducing, surveying and assessing the fundamentals of security with respect to computing. Here, "computing" refers to all activities which individuals or groups directly or indirectly perform by means of computing systems, i.e., by means of computers and networks of them built on telecommunication. We all are such individuals, whether enthusiastic or just bowed to the inevitable. So, as part of the "information society", we are challenged to maintain our values, to pursue our goals and to enforce our interests, by consciously designing a "global information infrastructure" on a large scale as well as by appropriately configuring our personal computers on a small scale. As a result, we hope to achieve secure computing: Roughly speaking, computer-assisted activities of individuals and computer-mediated cooperation between individuals should happen as required by each party involved, and nothing else which might be harmful to any party should occur.

The notion of security circumscribes many aspects, ranging from human qualities to technical enforcement. First of all, in considering the explicit security requirements of users, administrators and other persons concerned, we hope that usually all persons will follow the stated rules, but we also have to face the possibility that some persons might deviate from the wanted behavior, whether accidently or maliciously. So, in order to achieve security, we have to protect our activities and cooperations against threatening "attackers". Surely, however, as in everyday life, we also have to rely on trust in some partners. Otherwise, we would end up with staying in complete isolation and doing nothing. Second, since we have delegated a number of actions still increasing to computers, the components of a computing system themselves appear as subjects: we have to decide which components are to be trusted and which ones are to be considered as potential attackers. Additionally, while attacks are performed by technical components, usually under outside control, security enforcement also has to be achieved by use of technical components, preferably under our own control or under the control of trustworthy persons. Finally, we are left with a central problem of computer science: how to design, implement and verify trusted components which will enforce our security requirements technically when running in a potentially hostile environment?

So far, we do not have easy and final answers, and probably we shall never get them. Social communications are in principle open to all kinds of both pleasant and frightening events, and so are the corresponding technical interactions within computing systems. Thus, in both domains, achieving security appears to be a never-ending task. Nevertheless, people have obtained great insight into social communication and organization over centuries and even millenniums, resulting in the concepts of fundamental human rights and individual self-determination within the framework of a balance of power in democratic societies. Clearly, insight is not enough: it also has to be realized. Correspondingly, over only the last few decades, computer science has collected basic knowledge about computing systems, resulting in a largely accepted body of essentials of secure computing and an impressive collection of applicable security mechanisms. Again, knowledge has to be materialized within actual computing systems.

In this book, we concentrate on the essentials of secure computing and a collection of the most promising security mechanisms. We have a reader in mind who knows about computer science and engineering, and who is able and willing to study details which are beyond the scope of this introduction and survey in more specialized texts. We present our view of the fundamental knowledge about security in computing systems, leaving more practical instructions for specific situations open either to the experience of the reader or, again, to other texts.

The material of this book is organized into four cross-referencing parts: challenges and basic approaches; fundamentals of information flow and inference control; security mechanisms, with an emphasis on control and monitoring on the one side and on cryptography on the other side; and implementations. Though we have made every effort to make the text readable in sequential order, the reader should be aware that getting a deeper understanding probably requires one to follow the cross-references back and forth.

Part One, on "Challenges and Basic Approaches", starts with a more detailed elaboration of the notion of security in computing systems, emphasizing, among other things, the larger socio-technical context of security. Then, we identify information flow between senders and receivers as a fundamental abstraction of computing. This abstraction allows us to express security requirements in the form of interests of participants affected by information flows, and to face the inevitable trade-offs in this realm. Finally, we outline a view of computing systems and their vulnerabilities that should help the reader to see various security requirements and mechanisms within a broader technical context.

Part Two, on "Fundamentals of Information Flow and Inference Control", examines the basic abstraction in more depth. We first clarify the impact of and the relevant relationships between the following notions: messages transmitted between parties, inferences made by some party, and the resulting information gain and knowledge. In doing so, we also outline appropriate formalizations in order to lay the foundations for algorithmic treatments. We are then prepared to understand inference control as a basic goal of engineering security in computing systems. Sequential programs, parallel programs, (logic-oriented) information systems in general and statistical databases in particular are inspected in turn to determine whether and how we can algorithmically enforce security by inference control. Finally, we exhibit the close connection between the following events: on the one side, the possibility of making nontrivial inferences and thus the possibility of an information flow from one party to another, and on the other side, the possibility of interference by one party with another. Though many security requirements ultimately refer to the permission or the prohibition of information flows or interferences, their strict algorithmic enforcement turns out often to be limited for reasons of computational intractability or even non-computability. As a conclusion, we learn that for practical purposes, we must look for less ambitious though still effective approaches.

Part Three, on "Security Mechanisms", provides a structured introduction to these approaches. We first identify three key ideas, and for each of them we sketch some related mechanisms. To briefly summarize, redundancy allows one to detect failures and attacks or even to recover from such unfortunate events, isolation prevents unwanted information flows or interferences, and indistinguishability makes maliciously planned observations appear random or uniformly expected and thus useless. In most practical situations, however, these key ideas have to be suitably combined in order to obtain overall effectiveness. Additionally, at run time, we nearly always have to properly identify or at least suitably classify agents and to authenticate them, and at design time, security administrators have to specify their security policies, which decide which agents are permitted to gain access to or are prohibited from gaining access to which operations on which objects. There are two classes of techniques to combine these basic ideas.

The techniques of control and monitoring work roughly as follows: identifiable agents can get access rights granted and revoked, and access requests of agents are intercepted by control components that decide on allowing or denying the actual access. Additionally, the recordable activities of all agents are audited and examined for possible "intrusions", i.e., whether they appear "acceptable" or "violating".

The techniques of cryptography are based on secrets generated and kept by agents, rather than on identities. Such a secret can be exploited as a cryptographic key: the key holder is distinguished in being able to execute a specific operation in a meaningful way, while all other agents are not. This extremely powerful paradigm can be used in many ways, in particular as follows. For encryption, only the key holder can compute the plaintext belonging to a given ciphertext. For authentication and non-repudiation, only the key holder can compute a digital signature for a given message. Beyond these standard applications, there is a wealth of further possibilities, including anonymization, secret sharing and zero-knowledge proofs. Leaving technicalities aside, modern cryptography can be characterized as enabling cooperation under limited trust. Speaking more technically, cryptography allows one to reduce complex security requirements to an appropriate management of secrets.

Most real-life applications demand an appropriate combination of instantiations of both classes. Apparently, the secrecy of cryptographic keys has to be enforced by access control; and, often, identities used for control and monitoring are best authenticated by cryptographic means.

It is less obvious, but most important for the development of future interoperable systems built from autonomous agents, that access rights conceptually bound to specific agents can be managed by certificates and credentials, i.e., by digitally signed digital documents which refer to an agent by merely using a suitable reference (called a public key) to his secret cryptographic key.

Finally, in Part Four, on "Implementations", we briefly review some selected implementations of security services. In particular, we show how basic and composite security mechanisms, as described in preceding chapters, have been put together to comply with the architecture of specific applications and meet their requirements. Taking suitable abstractions of UNIX, Oracle/SQL, CORBA, Kerberos, SPKI and PGP as examples, these applications include an operating system; a database management system; middleware systems, with distributed client–server systems as a special case; and a file and message system.

At the end of each chapter, we give some bibliographic hints. Faced with the huge number of contributions to the diverse topics of security in computing, we have made no attempt to cover the relevant literature completely. Rather, these hints reflect only the limited experience and background of the author.

As stated before, the presentation of all this material concentrates on the essentials of secure computing and a collection of the most promising security mechanisms; in most cases we leave out many formal details and full proofs, as well as practical advice about commercially available systems.

Nevertheless, throughout the chapters, where appropriate, we introduce formalizations. We strongly believe that security, like other branches of computer science and engineering, needs precise formalizations and thorough formal verifications based on them, including proofs in the style of mathematics. This belief is in accordance with some highly ranked requirements of governmental security evaluation criteria. However, full formalizations would be beyond the scope (and a reasonable size) of this monograph, and the state of our knowledge often does not allow one to treat practical systems in a purely formal way.

Furthermore, relevance for practical purposes is intended to be achieved by preparing readers to engineer their specific computing systems from the point of view of security. This includes answering the following groups of related questions, all of which are discussed in the text.

The first group is concerned with the fundamental notion of security:

- What and whose security interests should be enforced?
- How to balance conflicting interests?
- What requirements result from legitimate security interests?

The second group deals with the core of the engineering of systems:

- What technical mechanisms support or enforce what security requirements?
- How can various security mechanisms be composed together?
- What organizational structures are needed to embed technical security mechanisms?

Finally, the third group assesses the achievements of security technology:

- How do you convince yourself and others about what kind and degree of security a specific security design and its implementation satisfy, and how do you verify this?
- What assumptions about trust and attacks, at the level of individuals and organizations as well as at the technical level, does the above conviction or verification rely on?

At this point, after having surveyed the amount of exciting material presented in this monograph (and many further publications) and after having advertised the readers' anticipated benefit, a reminder to be modest is due:

Security deals with ensuring that computing systems actually do what various autonomous users expect them to do, even if some components or partners misbehave, either unwillingly or maliciously.

Thus the reader should always be aware of the intrinsic difficulties to be overcome.

A Guide to Reading and Teaching with this Book

I have written this rather voluminous text in the style of a monograph, to be read and studied by researchers, developers, academic teachers and advanced students interested in obtaining a comprehensive and unified view of security in computing systems. The text is not necessarily designed for teaching, though it is suitable.

Holding a volume like this, some readers might want to concentrate on specific aspects of the whole picture, rather than sequentially follow the full presentation. Moreover, some readers might wonder how to extract background material for a course on security, whether introductory or more specialized. In the following, I shall give some hints for selecting appropriate parts from the book.

Regarding *concentrating on specific aspects* I can recommend that you use the book as follows, among other possibilities:

- For managers and non-specialists in security, the following parts of the book provide a (mostly informal) overview of the *Essentials of Security*, including the requirements and options for technical enforcement:

Part One:	Challenges and Basic Approaches (Chapters 1–3)
Chapter 6:	Key Ideas and Examples
Chapter 7:	Combined Techniques
Chapter 8:	Techniques of Control and Monitoring: Essentials
Sections 17.1–3:	UNIX Operating System, Oracle/SQL Database Management System and CORBA Middleware (only selections, as case studies)
Chapter 10:	Elements of a Security Architecture (introduction only)
Section 10.1:	Establishing Trust in Computing Systems
Section 10.2:	Layered Design (introduction only)
Chapter 12:	Techniques of Cryptography: Essentials (without Sections 12.7–8 and 12.9.4)
Sections 17.4–6:	Kerberos, Simple Public Key Infrastructure (SPKI/SDSI) and Pretty Good Privacy (PGP) (only selections, as case studies)

- For actual or prospective specialists in security with background knowledge, the following parts provide a (nearly) self-contained introduction to *Control and Monitoring*:

Chapter 6:   Key Ideas and Examples
Chapter 7:   Combined Techniques
Chapter 8:   Techniques of Control and Monitoring: Essentials
Chapter 9:   Conceptual Access Rights
Chapter 10:   Elements of a Security Architecture
Chapter 11:   Monitoring and Intrusion Detection
Sections 17.1–3, 5:   UNIX Operating System,
                        Oracle/SQL Database Management System,
                        CORBA Middleware and
                        Simple Public Key Infrastructure (SPKI/SDSI)

- For actual or prospective specialists in security with background knowledge, the following parts provide a (nearly) self-contained introduction to *Cryptography*:

Chapter 6:   Key Ideas and Examples
Chapter 7:   Combined Techniques
Chapter 12:   Techniques of Cryptography: Essentials
Chapter 13:   Encryption
Chapter 14:   Authentication
Chapter 15:   Anonymization
Chapter 16:   Some Further Cryptographic Protocols
Sections 17.4–6:   Kerberos,
                        Simple Public Key Infrastructure (SPKI/SDSI) and
                        Pretty Good Privacy (PGP)

- For actual or prospective researchers with background knowledge, the followings parts provide an introduction to *Inference Control*:

Chapter 2:   Fundamental Challenges
Chapter 4:   Messages, Inferences, Information and Knowledge
Chapter 5:   Preventive Inference Control

- For experienced readers with solid knowledge, the following parts provide a framework proposal for *Security Engineering*:

Chapter 1:   Introduction
Chapter 7:   Combined Techniques
Chapter 10:   Elements of a Security Architecture
Chapter 17:   Design of Selected Systems:
                        UNIX Operating System,
                        Oracle/SQL Database Management System,
                        CORBA Middleware,
                        Kerberos,
                        Simple Public Key Infrastructure (SPKI/SDSI) and
                        Pretty Good Privacy (PGP

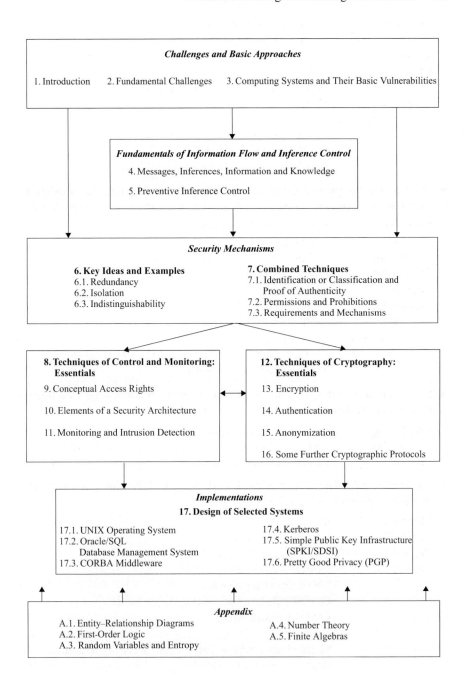

Fig. 0.1. Dependency diagram, indicating roughly the mutual impacts of the topics treated in this book

Regarding *extracting background material for teaching*, I have experience in using the material for courses, which might have the following titles:

- Security: Challenges and Approaches;
- Security by Control and Monitoring;
- Security by Cryptography;
- Inference Control;
- Models and Architectures of Secure Computing Systems.

Evidently, these courses correspond closely to the reading recommendations. The first course is suitable for students in their third year; the remaining courses are recommended for students in their fourth or fifth year. Depending on the context of the curriculum and the assumed background knowledge of the students, I have always presented and discussed some appropriate material from the following sections:

Section 1.2:	Fundamental Aspects of Security
Section 2.2:	Security Interests
Section 7.2:	Permissions and Prohibitions
Section 7.3:	Requirements and Mechanisms

Clearly, I also invite you to profit in other ways from this monograph, while still hoping for patient readers who aim to learn from and evaluate my attempts to provide a broad perspective on security. For the purpose of achieving this goal, you will find some assistance:

- First, where appropriate and convenient, throughout the monograph I have provided layered *overviews* which concentrate on the essentials or summarize background material presented in different places. In particular, these overviews emphasize how the numerous topics treated fit together. Although the topics have been arranged in a sequence for presentation in a text, it is important to keep in mind that only well-designed combinations of them can achieve the goals of security.

- Second, I have prepared a *dependency diagram*, indicating roughly the mutual impacts of the material on the level of chapters. This dependency diagram should also be helpful for finding appropriates ways to select material for reading and teaching. This dependency diagram is printed on page xiii.

- Third, I have assembled a comprehensive *index* spanning about 25 pages, which I hope will be fruitfully employed for identifying the numerous mutual impacts of specific topics. Besides this, the index helped me (hopefully successfully) to keep the terminology and notation sufficiently coherent, while collecting together results from numerous and diverse subfields of computer science.

- Fourth, I have included an *appendix* gathering together important concepts from selected fields of computer science and mathematics used in the monograph. More specifically, basic concepts and notations of conceptional modeling, logic, probability, integers and algebra are presented.

- Finally, I have provided a rich list of *references*, which, however, necessarily remains incomplete. Nevertheless, I strongly recommend you to study the references given whenever you are more deeply interested in a topic introduced in this monograph.

Acknowledgments

The selection and organization of the material covered, as well as the presentation, is based on my experiences in teaching and research in security over the last twenty years, though these years have been shared with similar activities in the field of information systems too.

I gave my first lecture on a topic in security in the winter semester of 1982/83, and my first publication in this field is dated 1984. Since then, I have been involved in security not only through teaching in the classroom, through my own research and through supervising diploma and doctoral theses, but also through various other activities.

Most notably, I have been a member of the IFIP Working Group 11.3 on Database Security from the beginning, have become a steering committee member of ESORICS (European Symposium on Research in Computer Security), participated in the EU-funded projects SEISMED (Secure Environment for Information Systems in Medicine) and ISHTAR (Implementing Secure Healthcare Telematics Applications in Europe), and (formally) supervised and (actually) learnt from my colleagues' activities in the EU-funded projects CAFE (Conditional Access for Europe) and SEMPER (Secure Electronic Market Place for Europe). Moreover, I have been supported by several grants from the German Research Foundation (Deutsche Forschungsgemeinschaft or DFG), among others, within the framework of the Priority Program (Schwerpunktprogramm) "Security in Information and Communication Technology" and the Research Training Group (Graduiertenkolleg) "Mathematical and Engineering Methods for Secure Data Transfer and Information Mediation".

I gratefully acknowledge challenging and fruitful cooperation with all the students and colleagues I have met at the many opportunities that presented themselves. Today, I cannot clearly distinguish what I have learnt about security from each of these individuals. But I am pretty sure that I gained many worthwhile insights and help from all of them: thank you so much, dear students and colleagues!

This monograph has a predecessor which remains uncompleted so far and perhaps for ever. Its story originates in 1997, when I started the task of elaborating selected parts of my lectures and integrating these parts into a common, comprehensive framework. In spring 2002, these lecture notes already amounted to 434 pages, still leaving many unwritten holes. Though I made progress, constantly but slowly, I never managed to carefully write down all the details presented in the lectures. But, in any case, the project of producing such a comprehensive work appeared to become unrealistic, ending up with too many pages, potentially inconsistent, which were likely to find too few readers.

So, I very much appreciated the suggestion from Springer-Verlag to plan a volume like the present one. Since then, and with much helpful support from the publisher, I have finally completed this monograph.

Thank you again to all who have assisted and supported me, both during the early stages and during the recent years.

Joachim Biskup

ISSI – Information Systems and Security
Fakultät für Informatik
Technische Universität Dortmund

Table of Contents

Part One
Challenges and Basic Approaches

1 Introduction

In this introductory chapter, we first briefly review security considerations for housing as a model for computing systems. We then abstractly declare the fundamental aspects of security in computing as a paradigm for the rest of the monograph. Subsequently, we identify the broader social and political context of security in computing, tentatively sketch a general definition, and treat selected aspects of the design and life cycle of secure computing systems.

1.1 The Need for Security

Computing has become part of everyday life. Traditional forms of human interactions have been converted to computer-assisted or computer-mediated versions, and entirely new options for cooperation and communication have evolved. As in any sphere of life, so in computing: individuals, as well as groups and organizations, are concerned about security. Usually, our intuitive understanding of security is quite mature but often also dazzling and delusive. Security in computing can greatly benefit from our experiences in other fields, though the innovative sides of computing often demand original solutions. Additionally, since computing means employing formalisms, security in computing requires precise and formalized procedures. Having the similarities and differences of computing and other fields in mind, we start by making some idealized observations about security in housing, whereby a home, considered as a living space, might correspond roughly to a computing system.

In a home, an individual or a group such as a family creates a region of self-determination, aiming at preserving

- *freedom from injury*;
- *confidentiality* of actions, writing and correspondence; and
- *availability* and *integrity* of property.

The individual discretionarily regulates *admission* to the home, either opening the door for other occupants, wanted visitors and authorized service staff or refusing to see others. The individual enforces his regulations by employing a lock as a further technical protection aid. The lock should be operable only with suitable keys, and the keys should not be forgeable, neither by chance nor by exhaustive trial. Finally, in order to ensure the intended protection, the individual carefully stores and manages the keys.

The overall success of the regulations and protection mechanisms relies on numerous assumptions, which are hardly fully satisfied in practice. For example:

- The door provides the only possibility to access the home (for instance, you cannot enter through the windows).
- The manufacturers and the dealers of the door, lock and keys have followed the expected rules and do not misuse the individual's trust in them (for instance, none of them has kept a duplicate of a key).
- The individual never loses any of the keys, nor gives any untrusted person an opportunity to make a duplicate.
- If the individual entrusts a key to a neighbor for emergency use, then this neighbor acts only in the individual's interests.
- Officials such as the police respect privacy within the protected realm of the home.
- Criminals either are deterred by the protections, or fail to force the door.

Just guarding the borderline of the home, however, is not sufficient for security. The individual additionally takes care of security *inside*, for example in order to provide a protected living environment for children. On the one side, children are offered opportunities to develop freely, but on the other side all these opportunities should be childproof, i.e., the children's carelessness or awkwardness, hardly predictable in detail, should not endanger them. Besides arranging for the home to be suitable for children, the individual essentially relies on the manufacturers to meet the security specifications for their goods. Children should be able to leave and reenter the home, possibly under supervision, but they should never succeed in completely disabling the borderline protection.

There are many further security considerations. As an example, the individual might care about the danger of fire:

- First of all, as *preventive* measures, all rules of fire protection are followed while planning and erecting the home, preferably using refractory building materials.
- Additionally, to *limit the fire damage* in case the prevention should fail, fire extinguishers or other firefighting equipment are installed, and all people involved are trained to operate them appropriately.
- Finally, to *compensate the losses* caused by a fire or by firefighting, the individual takes out fire insurance.

All such measures require additional *expenditure* of money. In general, the individual will allow costs according to his advisors' *risk assessment*, which will evaluate at least the following points: the vulnerabilities to fire, the events leading to a fire and the probabilities of their occurrence, the effectiveness of security measures, and the impacts of an actual fire.

So far, all considerations have been made from the point of view of the individual supposed to be the *owner* of the home. In general, however, many other *parties* are directly or indirectly involved, for instance other occupants, financiers, neighbors, the local community, the fire department, the state and possibly many others.

All parties might have their specific *security interests*, partially matching the owner's interests but potentially also *conflicting* with them. In the end, they all together should aim at *multilateral* security, balancing all interests and the affordable costs.

In modern housing, it is a naive simplification to assume that there is just one door on the borderline between the home and the environment. There are several further *connections* between the two sides, in particular water pipes, sewers, power cables and telecommunication lines. Like the door, all these connections enable parties inside and outside to *cooperate* deliberately. And even if there are no permanently materialized connections, the crucially needed cooperations are implemented on a case-by-case basis, say by transporting wrapped goods through the door or exploiting wireless telecommunication. As for people passing the door, independently of the kind of materialization, for all cooperating *transactions* across the connections, the owner has to set up security regulations or, if appropriate, agree on regulations with the respective parties outside, and effectively enforce these regulations, preferably by the use of technical aids.

Going one step further, the individual might be the owner of a *mobile* home. Then there are additional challenges. At any site, the home owner and the site administrator, as well as further parties involved, have to negotiate the specific connections between the mobile home and the environment, the regulations for the wanted transactions, and their enforcement. As in the immobile case, the two sides might have specific and potentially conflicting security interests. However, whereas in the immobile case the parties are more or less known to each other, in the mobile case the parties may appear as strangers to each other, having no obvious reason for mutual *trust* at the beginning. Nevertheless, both sides might want to cooperate but only if they can preserve their mutual security interests.

Roughly summarizing, security for housing deals with the home on the inside and its connections to the environment to enable cooperation with the outside world, balances the differing interests of various parties, anticipates threats, and installs and operates affordable technical protection aids.

The mobile-home situation, with all its sophisticated ramifications or alternatives left open here, can be used as a powerful model for considerations about security in computing systems. Another promising model is the commercial procedure for trading, where two or more parties exchange goods, including currency. Clearly, however, any example has its limitations, and will fail to capture all aspects of the new field of computing, which is characterized by its (Turing-)universality, enormous speed and worldwide connectivity, among many other features.

The examples mentioned above come from established and well-understood fields for which we have good experience in security that is exploitable for computing. These fields also, increasingly, emerge as part of computing: electronic commerce is already in operation; so-called "computing nomads" travel around using their mobile laptops as universal working tools; and visionaries are starting to create "ubiquitous computing", where homes and computing equipment are closely intertwined.

1.2 Fundamental Aspects of Security

Assuming a rough and intuitive understanding of security, as sketched above, and a general background knowledge about computing systems, we now declare what we regard as the fundamental aspects of security in computing. We intend to use this declaration as a paradigm for the rest of the monograph, without always explicitly mentioning this intention, and we also recommend that this declaration is followed in practical work.

In its present form, the declaration remains highly abstract and general. We argue that, in principle, for each concrete computing system or meaningful sub-system, the declaration should be suitably refined and implemented. Being highly ambitious and demanding, however, the declaration will often be only partially implemented – in this monograph, for reasons of space limitations, and in practical applications, for reasons of a lack of knowledge, time or other resources.

- *Security* should be designed as a comprehensive property of a computing system (usually distributed) that is embedded in an environment.
- The design should reflect the *interests* of all actively or passively involved *participants*. In particular, *conflicts* must be appropriately balanced.
- Interests are often determined by more fundamental *values*, including freedom from injury and self-determination, secrecy and property rights, as well as social participation, living space, and law enforcement.
- A participant, or his representative, should specify *security requirements* by identifying the requested *informational activities* and the suspected *threats*. Suspected threats should be determined with regard to the participant's accepted interests and requested activities.
- Mainly but not exclusively, threats might be directed against the following *security goals*, interpreted as *interests*:
  - *availability* of data and activities;
  - *confidentiality* of information and actions;
  - *integrity* of the computing system, i.e., correctness of data concerning contents and the unmodified state of data, programs and processes;
  - *authenticity* of actors, including later
  - *non-repudiation* of their actions.
- *Security mechanisms* might aim at
  - *preventing* security violations;
  - *limiting* the damage caused by violations while they are occurring; and
  - *compensating* their consequences.
- Security mechanisms should be evaluated as to whether, or to what extent, they *satisfy* the security requirements.
- The *assumptions* underlying the evaluation should be explicitly identified, in particular regarding the *trust* assigned to participants or system components.
- The *expenditure* for the security mechanisms selected should be justified by the *risks* recognized.

1.3 Informational Assurances

Security in computing should be *multilateral*, respecting and enforcing the balanced interests of *all* participants concerned. Computing has evolved into an integral and inseparable part of everyday life. Accordingly, individuals are not left alone to negotiate their interests; instead, modern democratic societies are increasingly setting up a social and juridical framework for regulating computing, including many aspects of security. In the following, we outline the current development of an "information society" and its framework for "informational assurances".

1.3.1 The Information Society

The *information society* comprises all individuals who participate in or are affected by computing, as well as public institutions, of any level, and private companies, of any size. These individuals, institutions and companies are tied together by a historically achieved and developing framework of informational and other rights and interests, which in some instances might be shared or in other circumstances might be in conflict.

Seen from the perspective of this discussion, the information society is technologically based on public or private telecommunication services, on which computerized networks of all kinds of computers are run, ranging, for example, from personal computers, through office workstations with local or specialized global servers, to powerful mainframe computers. Such networks are used for a wide variety of purposes, in particular to exchange raw data, such as electronic mail; to provide informational services of all kinds, such as daily news, video entertainment, event and transportation schedules, and database records; and to support informational cooperation such as home banking, electronic commerce and certification of digital documents.

Additionally, the information society needs a further foundation, namely a coherent and balanced system of informational rights and socially agreed and legally founded rules, as well as mechanisms that support the participants in enforcing their issues. We call such a system "informational assurances".

1.3.2 A General Framework

Dealing with *informational assurances*, we have to consider the full complexity of the information society with all its interdependences and feedback loops. In particular, we have to cope uniformly with all the items that are indicated by keywords in Figure 1.1, without visualizing all the subtle relationships among them.

Informational assurances, in a narrower sense, comprise the informational rights, the social and legal rules, and the enforcing technical security mechanisms.

By the very nature of the information society, nearly *every* individual, group, public institution, civil association or private company has to be treated as a *partic-*

participants

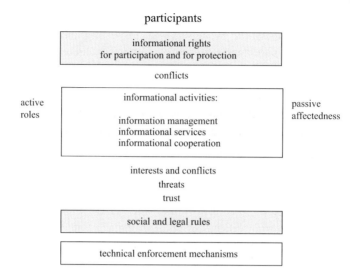

Fig. 1.1. Informational assurances

ipant. A participant may play an active role, or might be only passively affected by the actions of other participants. In general, every participant will be concerned in many ways.

Informational *rights* always arise with a double meaning. On the one hand, a participant is entitled to behave according to the chosen designation: he has all civil rights to *participate* in the activities of the information society and to take advantage of them. On the other hand, a participant who is an individual enjoys fundamental human rights, including privacy in the sense of informational self-determination, and all participants are the object of all kinds of *protection* that a state offers: in any case, informational activities should not be harmful to them. Therefore many informational activities should be *both* enabled *and* restricted by law and its enforcement.

On the basis of general informational rights about *participation*, a participant can actively pursue his specific informational needs and wishes. The participant's demands may be concerned with a wide range of *informational activities*, which can be roughly classified as follows:

- *information management* as such (meaning that the participant is providing or collecting and processing any kind of data that seems relevant to his participation);
- *informational services* (meaning, for example, that the participant is asking for or delivering press services, electronic entertainment, database retrieval, etc.), or
- *informational cooperation* (meaning that the participant is involved, for example, in some role in electronic commerce, electronic voting, document certification, etc.).

Once a participant is involved in some informational activity, actively or passively, he is following several *interests*, which may vary considerably depending on the specific situation. The security *goals* commonly cited for defining computer security, namely *availability, confidentiality, integrity, authenticity* possibly with *non-repudiation*, and others, should be understood first of all as specific interests of participants within an informational activity.

Both general rights, on the basis of which participants are involved in some informational activity, and the specific interests of the participants involved may turn out to be conflicting. Indeed, they will be in conflict most of the time. The *conflicts* arise from the various active roles and types of passive affectedness in an informational activity.

A conflict may result in *threats* to rights or interests. In fact, in the case of conflicting issues, one participant following his issue appears as threatening the conflicting issues of another participant. Additionally, we are also faced with threats resulting from the accidental or malicious *misbehavior* of some participant. Such a troublemaker may be involved intentionally in an informational activity, or may come more or less from outside, for instance misusing some computing facilities that are available to him because of general rights of participation.

Although there are, in general, unavoidable conflicts and threats, informational activities, seen as purposely arising interactions of participants, must be somehow based on *trust*. Ideally, a participant would prefer to trust only those other participants whom he can exercise some kind of control over. Practically, however, the case of having direct control over others rarely occurs. Basically, there are two ways of solving this dilemma. In the first way, the assistance of further participants as (*trusted*) *third parties* is required. They are intended to act as some kind of notary or arbitrator, who is to be trusted by the original, possibly mutually distrusting participants. In the second way, the trust is shifted to some technical equipment or, more precisely, to the people delivering that equipment.

For any kind of trust, we need some *social and legal rules*. They are required either to establish trust, as, for example, in the case of a notary or a technical control board, or to deter misbehavior or, if that fails, to deal with the consequences of misbehavior. Such rules have to be enforced somehow. In hopefully rare cases, this task is the role of law courts.

For the routine cases of everyday life in the information society, however, it appears desirable to shift most of the enforcement burden directly onto technical mechanisms. By the design and tamper-resistant construction of such *technical security enforcement mechanisms*, it should be technically infeasible to violate the rules or, otherwise, the mechanisms should effectively provide sufficient documented evidence against a violator.

It is worthwhile to elaborate how the *political aspects*, dealing on one side with informational rights and on the other side with the social and legal rules for trust, are intimately intertwined with the *technical aspects*, comprising on the one side informational activities and on the other side technical mechanisms to enforce rules.

1.3.3 Privacy and Informational Self-Determination

In most cases, informational rights are based on traditional fundamental human and civil rights. These traditional rights are reinterpreted and concretized with respect to the new technical possibilities for informational activities. Some of these new possibilities, however, may not be appropriately captured by the traditional rights. In these cases, the fundamental human and civil rights have to be augmented by additional, newly stated informational rights. In this subsection we consider the traditional idea of privacy and the new postulate of informational self-determination as a prominent example.

Fundamental human rights include the idea of the unconditional *dignity of man* and, accordingly, the protection of personal self-determination, which can only be partly restricted on the basis of laws. Democratic societies have elaborated this guideline into a sophisticated *personal right*, which nevertheless might vary from country to country. Sometimes the protective side of the personal right is summarized as a famous quote from the nineteenth century that each citizen has "the right to be let alone", meaning that others, in particular the government, have to respect the citizen's *privacy*. However, the enabling side also is important, roughly captured by the right of "the pursuit of happiness". A framework from sociology appears to be helpful for providing a modern reinterpretation of these traditions, in particular because it is reasonably close to some concepts of computing. In this framework, individuals act in social roles. Basically, a *social role* is determined by two aspects:

- a *mode of behavior*, i.e., a template for more or less uniformly executed sequences of actions; and
- a *group of persons*, with respect to whom or together with whom an individual applies a mode of behavior.

In this view, an individual is seen as an actor involved in a large variety of different roles, which might overlap or follow each other in time. As a highly simplified example, in Figure 1.2 some social roles of the author are listed by referring to a mode of behavior and a group of persons, using designators taken from everyday usage. Of course, all individuals together are seen to form a net of dynamically proceeding role-based interactions.

Informational self-determination then basically means the following:

- An individual can determine by himself which personal *information* he is willing to *share* with group members in a specific social role.
- An individual can *select* his social *roles* under his own responsibility.
- Others respect the intended *separation of roles*, refraining from unauthorized information flows between different roles.

This wording emphasizes that informational self-determination, first of all, deals with the individual's right to control his personal information rather than to keep personal data absolutely secret. Ideally, and positively expressed, an individual should keep overall control of all the personal information that that individual

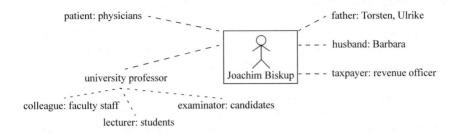

Fig. 1.2. Visualization of an individual and his social roles

has revealed in acting in various roles. In negative terms, the many group members whom an individual interacts with in different roles should not exploit their specific knowledge for unintended purposes; in particular, they should not gather all their information into one "personal profile". Clearly, as usually, these postulates might be in conflict with other rights and interests.

While *privacy* and its specific refinement into *informational self-determination* are social, juridical and political notions referring to human individuals, computing ultimately consists of data processing. Accordingly, the postulates for the support of individuals have to be appropriately translated into rules for the protection of personal data. Here the term *personal data* means any data about the personal or factual circumstances of a *specific* or *determinable* individual, called the *person concerned*. Thus privacy in the context of computing should be enforced by rules about processing personal data, including all phases of processing, ranging from data collection, through data exploitation of any kind, to long-term storage and transmission to other sites. In order to meet their goals, such *protection rules for personal data* should be governed by the following general guidelines:

- [*based on permission*] Personal data should be processed (whether by computing or other means) only on the basis of a permission expressed in a law or with the explicit consent of the person concerned.
- [*need-to-know*] Whenever achievable, processing personal data should be restricted to actual needs, preferably by avoiding the collection of personal data at all or by converting it into nonpersonal data by anonymization.
- [*collected from the source*] Whenever reasonable, personal data should be collected from the person concerned.
- [*bound to original purpose*] Personal data should be processed only for the well-defined purpose for which it was originally collected.
- [*subject to inspection*] A person concerned should be informed about the kind of processing that employs his personal data.
- [*under ongoing control*] "Wrong" personal data should be corrected; "no longer needed" personal data should be deleted.
- [*with active support*] Agents processing personal data are obliged to actively pursue the privacy of the persons concerned.

1.3.4 Enforcement of Informational Self-Determination

The notion of informational self-determination and the corresponding protection rules for personal data have been developed with an emphasis on defending individuals against the assumed overwhelming informational power of public institutions and private companies. The basic goals require that, in principle, each individual should freely decide on whom he gives what part of his personal data to and on what kind of processing of his personal data he is willing to agree to. Accordingly, an individual should retain full control over the processing and dissemination of his personal data. However, this principle is called into question by

- conflicting social goals,
- technical difficulties, and
- the lack of effective and efficient technical security enforcement mechanisms.

Examples of *conflicting social goals* are public security, law enforcement, national defence, the operation of social and health services, scientific research, freedom of the press, participation in public decision, and trade interests. Basically, legislators have dealt with such conflicts in two ways: a basic *privacy act* simply declares that some agencies or institutions are exempted from the principle, or the basic law refers to additional *sector-specific privacy laws*, each of which regulates the conflicts in some restricted domain. (Critics, however, argue that there are too many global exemptions, and that sector-specific laws do not cover all relevant domains and lack coherence.)

Technical difficulties are grouped mainly around the following four observations. First, once an individual has disclosed some personal data (understood as knowledge about him), voluntarily or under legal compulsion, this data (understood as digits) is processed within a computing system that is under the control of someone else. Although, ideally, a subject is entitled to control his data (knowledge), this data (digits) is not physically available to that subject but only to those agents against whom, among others, his privacy should be protected. Second, the correlation between data as knowledge and its encoding as digits is inherently difficult to monitor. In some cases it is even deliberately blurred, for instance by cryptographic encipherment. Third, digital data can be easily duplicated and may be spurious. Fourth, much data (considered as knowledge) is not merely personal but deals with *social relationships* with other individuals within the real world, for instance data about matrimonial and that person's children, or about medical treatment. Accordingly, within a computing system, this data (as digits) is not unambiguously connected to a personal file but may be spread across the files of all persons involved, or the data may be disguised as pointers or related technical concepts.

Basically, the first observation (about external control) is treated by penalties and some supervision, the second (about data and knowledge) by a sophisticated though not technically elaborated definition of "personal data" (as any data about circumstances relating to a specific (identified) or determinable (identifiable) person), and the third (about duplication and spuriousness) by a technical addendum to the basic privacy laws. Such an addendum states some high-level, declarative behavior rules for well-controlled data processing. The fourth observation (about data dealing with *social relationships*) has been solved the worst, and in fact it may also be seen as resulting from another kind of conflict between social interests. Whereas the original concern emphasize the potential conflicts between a weak individual and a powerful institution, the conflicts inherent in social relationships may also arise between individuals of about equal strength. The more everyday life and computing are integrated, the more these conflicts become challenging, too. Moreover, even without any conflicting interests, the problem of how to represent real-world relationships within the formalism of a computing system has been intensively studied in the field of data modeling but has not generally been solved.

The *lack of technical security enforcement mechanisms* for the principle of informational self-determination is mainly due to the problems already discussed: without a socially agreed settlement of conflicts, we cannot construct a fair technical security enforcement mechanism; the postulated ideal control and the actual physical control are separated; the semantics of digitally stored data with respect to the outside world are rarely captured algorithmically; and the physical possibilities for manipulating and duplicating digital data cannot be fully controlled using only traditional data-processing techniques but very much require us to employ new technologies such as cryptography.

1.3.5 Legislation

Informational rights are encoded in laws, ordinances or related documents, such as directives of the European Union. Recently, an increasing number of fields of life in the information society have been legally regulated. In each particular case, some balance is stated between enabling and encouraging widespread exploitation of computing on the one side and restriction of activities and protection of citizens on the other side. Here we give only some prominent examples:

- *Privacy acts* detail the principles of informational self-determination. In most cases, but with many variations, these laws first declare a general and protecting forbiddance, and then allow processing of personal data under specifically listed conditions, including referencing subsidiary sector-specific privacy laws for special application fields.
- *Telecommunication and services acts* enable the public and commercial exploitation of informational activities, in particular when based on the Internet, and lay foundations for legally binding transactions in public administration and private commerce. For the latter purpose, the proper usage of digital signatures is encouraged.
- *Intellectual property acts* support and extend the traditional concept of authors' (or their publishers') copyright in texts or images to all kinds of electronic multimedia objects, the contents of which can be understood as intellectual value produced and then owned by the originator.

- *Criminal acts* identify definitely offending behavior within computing systems and thereby aim at restricting malicious computing under the threat of penalties.

1.3.6 Security Evaluation Criteria and Security Agencies

Ideally, *developers* of computing systems aim at offering technical security enforcement mechanisms, and *consumers*, i.e., owners, administrators and more generally all affected participants of computing systems, specify their security requirements. *Security evaluation criteria* are official documents intended to assist developers and consumers to reliably match offers and requirements. Such criteria are developed and published by national *security agencies*. Additionally, these agencies act as *evaluators*: a developer can submit a product as a *target of evaluation* to an agency, and the agency examines the *security functionality* offered by the product and determines the *assurance level* that it achieves, i.e., a measure of the evidence that the product actually has the claimed properties.

Security evaluation criteria and security agencies evolved as governmental attempts to establish some of the *trust* needed for a framework of informational assurances, basically by setting up rules of secure computing and serving as independent evaluators. About 20 years ago, when the seminal *Trusted Computer System Evaluation Criteria* (TCSEC), known as the *Orange Book*, was issued by the US Department of Defense, these attempts started with quite a narrow view, which was dominated by military needs and an emphasis on strict confidentiality (against the assumed enemy) in more or less centralized (operating) systems. Since then, various improvements have been developed, thereby broadening the scope of application and interests and adapting to the rapid development of highly distributed open computing systems, which are now being marketed and employed worldwide. The *Information Technology Security Evaluation Criteria* (ITSEC), jointly published about ten years later by some European countries, was an important step towards civil applications and internationality. Currently, the combined experience is gathered in the *Common Criteria for Information Technology Security Evaluation* (CC), a version of which has also become an *ISO standard*. An evaluation of a product using the Common Criteria is supposed to be accepted in all countries that support the Common Criteria.

In practice, evaluations tend to be rather expensive and often of limited value, as critics argue, for several reasons, including the following: the criteria are seen to be biased and not to fully capture the notion of multilateral security; component products (which are too small) are evaluated rather than a whole computing system; and it is difficult to appropriately treat the rapid development of product versions and the open world of possible environments. Nevertheless, the information society needs to improve informational assurances, and today the above criteria and the supporting security agencies are the best available state-offered link between informational rights, as expressed in legislation, and the products actually marketed.

Concerning content, the Common Criteria now cover a wide scope of security in computing, simultaneously constituting a reference for security in computing systems and a voluminous administrative handbook for preparing actual evaluations. Basically, the criteria describe two orthogonally seen aspects, namely security functionality and assurance, which are classified in fine granularity. On this basis, the criteria also present *protection profiles*, which are both described generally and exemplified. At the top level of the classification of the *security functionality*, the following nine items are listed (which are described further in this monograph):

- *Audit*, as the basis of monitoring and analyzing the behavior of participants;
- *Communication*, with an emphasis on providing evidence for sending and receiving of messages;
- *User Data Protection*, with an emphasis on enforcing availability, integrity and confidentiality of the users' objects;
- *Identification and Authentication*, for enforcing authenticity with non-repudiation and accountability;
- *Privacy*, including non-observability, anonymity, pseudonymity and unlinkability;
- *Protection of the Trusted Security Functions*, which deals with the installation, administration and operation of security mechanisms, i.e., how security mechanisms are securely protected in turn;
- *Resource Utilization*, including fault tolerance, priorization and scheduling;
- *Target of Evaluation Access*, including log-in procedures;
- *Trusted Path/Channel*, dealing with the physical link between a (human) participant and the (processor of the) technical device employed.

For *security assurance*, the Common Criteria define seven *evaluation assurance levels* (EALs):

- functionally tested (EAL1);
- structurally tested (EAL2);
- methodically tested and checked (EAL3);
- methodically designed, tested and reviewed (EAL4);
- semiformally designed and tested (EAL5);
- semiformally verified design and tested (EAL6); and
- formally verified design and tested (EAL7).

Furthermore, the Common Criteria treat the following top-level *assurance classes* (the key words of which are described further in this monograph):

- Configuration Management,
- Delivery and Operation,
- Development,
- Guidance Documents,
- Life Cycle Support,
- Tests, and
- Vulnerabilities.

For each of the subclasses of the assurance classes, appropriate assurance levels are required.

Finally, a *protection profile* comprises generic requirements for a well-defined application field, listing advisable security functionality and assurance that are intended to be reusable in many concrete applications. The following examples are fully specified: *Commercial Security 1 – Basic Controlled Access Protection*, as a baseline set for protection of systems running in a closed, non-hostile and well-managed environment; *Commercial Security 3 – Role-Based Access Protection*, for more sensitive environments; and *Network/Transport Layer Packet Filter Firewall*, for establishing a controlled point of defence and audit at the borderline of a local network with its services and the outside global network.

1.4 Notions of Security

Evidently, the notion of security has many facets, which might depend on the point of view of a specific investigation, the levels of abstraction under consideration, or even social agreements or personal opinions. In any case, it appears demanding to treat security in computing systems as a *comprehensive* property that takes care of many aspects with mutual impacts. Accordingly, in this monograph we refrain from attempting a single concise, authoritative definition. Rather we refer the reader to:

- the full material of this monograph and other work;
- the *fundamental aspects of security*, declared as a paradigm in Section 1.2;
- the *general framework of informational assurances*, introduced in Section 1.3;
- the *security evaluation criteria*, sketched in Section 1.3.6;
- a tentative *outline of a formal theory*, developed below in Section 1.4.1; and
- an *elementary practical checklist* for evaluations, also presented below, in Section 1.4.2.

1.4.1 Outline of a Formal Theory

Any formal notion of security in computing systems should comply with the framework of informational assurances sketched in Section 1.3. In particular, the formal considerations about the security of the technical components of the systems or its subsystems should refer to more comprehensive reasoning about all relevant aspects. And the formalism should comply with the diversity of *interests* of the *participants* involved and cover the anticipated *threats*. The commonly used security goals – availability, confidentiality, integrity, authenticity including non-repudiation, confidentiality and others – merely express such interests in a high-level declarative way, and, accordingly, these goals have to be substantially refined in accordance with the participants' potentially different views of a specific informational activity.

Basically, our tentative approach results from capturing the process of designing a system that can be claimed to be secure. At the beginning of this process, the *par-*

ticipants in an informational activity are supposed to form a (usually fictitious) *community*. Each participant, or an appropriate group of them, expresses their specific needs and wishes with regard to the computing system to be designed. Even at this level of abstraction, some *conflicts* between the participants' demands, and with respect to informational (or other) rights, may arise. After appropriately resolving these conflicts, all further steps are based on the fundamental assumption that the intended purposes of the system are legitimate and consistent. Accordingly, on this level, we tentatively define:

> A computing system is *secure*
> iff it satisfies the intended purposes
> without violating relevant informational (or other) rights.

Then, in further refinement steps, all the concepts have to be detailed and formalized: the concepts already introduced, as well as further ones such as the participants' *interests* and the anticipated *threats*, and the *trust* in subsystems that the participants are willing to grant. In general, all concepts are considered to be *distributed*. Finally, at the end of the process, all notions in the extended definition set out below should be meaningful. Roughly speaking, this definition says that the final system meets the intended purposes, even if it is *embedded* in adverse *environments*, and it "does not do anything else" that has been considered to be harmful and has been explicitly forbidden therefore. A little more precisely, but still subject to major improvements, we consider the following:

Let

P	be the set of *participants* in the community,
$Req = (Req_p)_{p \in P}$	be a family of (sub)specifications for services (for the intended purposes),
F	be a *computing system* (to be designed and finally implemented),

and, for each participant $p \in P$, let

Req_p	be the subspecification *required* by participant p,
F_p	be the subsystem of F that is *trusted* by participant p,
$Environment_p$	be a set of (potentially) adverse *environments*,
$Forbidden(E)$	be for each $E \in Environment_p$, a set of services declared to be *forbidden* for the environment E,

such that

$$Threat_p = (E, Forbidden(E))_{E \in Environment_p}$$

> denotes the *threats* anticipated by participant p,
> each of which consists of an adverse environment and
> a corresponding family of forbidden services
> (that p wants to avoid).

Then we define, still tentatively:

The system *F securely implements* the required services *Req*
for the community *P* under the threat model,
given by F_p and *Threat$_p$* for all $p \in P$
iff

[*reliable correctness*]
for each $p \in P$ and each environment $E \in Environment_p$
the combined system of F_p and E satisfies all required services $RS \in Req_p$, and

[*confinement*]
for each $p \in P$ and each environment $E \in Environment_p$
the combined system of F_p and E does *not* satisfy
any forbidden service $FS \in Forbidden(E)$.

Obviously, it is not at all clear how to elaborate soundly all technical details of such a definition, and the present state of knowledge and practice is far away from dealing with such a notion of security in realistic examples. Nevertheless, we argue that this attempt highlights the ultimate goal accurately.

1.4.2 A Practical Checklist for Evaluations

Though theory is indispensable to achieving a high degree of security, for many practical purposes some more directly applicable advice is helpful, too. In many practical situations, an owner or administrator of a computing system has to evaluate a statement such as "this particular system is *secure*". In a first step, a comprehensive view of the circumstances visualized in Figure 1.3 is needed; in particular one must provide answers to the following questions:

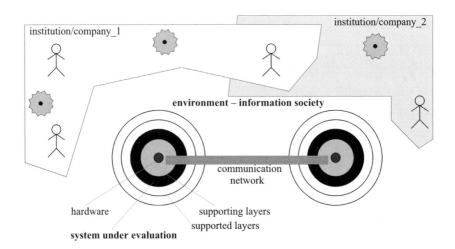

Fig. 1.3. Visualization of a comprehensive view for the purposes of a security evaluation

- On what other *components*, in what layers, is the system based?
- In what *environment* is the system embedded?
- In what *institution* or *company* is the system used?

In a second step, some more refined issues have to be investigated for the *actual version* (*configuration*) of the system and the *actual* circumstances:

- [*security policy*] Are the security requirements explicitly expressed?
- [*authorization*] Is every access, i.e., every execution of an operation by a subject on an object, preceded by an explicit permission, say by granting a corresponding access right or a suitable cryptographic key?
- [*control*] Is such a permission controlled before execution, explicitly by checking access rights or implicitly by the need for a suitable cryptographic key?
- [*authenticity*] Is the authenticity of all items checked before the execution?
- [*monitoring*] Can intrusions that occur despite the above, i.e., violations of the security policy, be detected, though potentially only afterwards, and can any resulting damage be limited or compensated?
- [*total coverage*] Do the security mechanisms cover local accesses to the components of the system and its basis and its environment, global accesses to remote components, and the transfer of messages between all local and global components?

1.5 The Design Cycle for Secure Computing Systems

Security is a comprehensive property of a computing system. Accordingly, in general, security can be achieved to a satisfactory extent only if it is taken into consideration from the very beginning of the *design cycle*. In rare exceptions, *add-on* security mechanisms for already existing systems might also be fully successful. However, experience mostly reports substantial difficulties in achieving security afterwards for systems initially constructed without security in mind. Nevertheless, in practice, adding some degree of security to an existing system might be better than just doing nothing to enhance security.

Hence, in general, it is essential to include security considerations at all stages of the design cycle, whatever concrete method of *software engineering* is employed. Here we shall only discuss briefly the impact of compositionality and refinement, outline some general construction principles, and present an introduction to risk assessment.

1.5.1 Compositionality and Refinement

Ideally, a computing system is developed by employing some software engineering method. Such a method usually distinguishes several abstraction layers, which include at least a specification layer and an implementation layer. In the implementation layer, the computing system finally constructed can be very large, comprising many and diverse components. The resulting complexity of the implementation often challenges an evaluation of whether the security requirements are actually satisfied. This challenge can be potentially mastered if design and implementation follow appropriate rules of *compositionality* and *refinement*, as sketched in the following.

One common kind of *compositionality* deals with one specific layer, aiming at deriving a security property of a large complex component from the (supposedly) already known properties of its constituent parts. Ideally, we would like to have the following inductive situation:

- There are some more or less simple *basic components*, the (functional and security) properties of which are well understood.
- There are some *composition operators* that can be used to combine already existing components into a *compound component* whose properties can be determined from the properties of its components.
- Only systems or components that are inductively constructed from basic components by composition operators are considered.

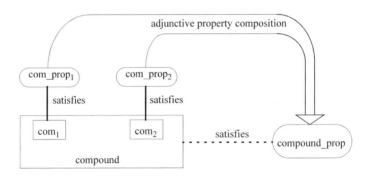

Fig. 1.4. One composition step

Figure 1.4 visualizes one composition step in more detail. There are two (more basic) components com_1 and com_2, which satisfy the properties com_prop_1 and com_prop_2, respectively. The (less basic) component *compound* results from applying a suitable (functional) composition operator (not explicitly shown in the figure) to com_1 and com_2. For determining properties, adjunctive to the (functional) composition operator, there is a *property composition* operator that constructs some property *compound_prop* from com_prop_1 and com_prop_2. In order to be useful in the overall design cycle, the adjunctive property composition operator should deliver a property that will actually be of interest: at best, the strongest postcondition for the result of the functional composition; more realistically, for instance, the (possibly adjusted) conjunction of the properties of the arguments. Given this situation, *compound* is required to satisfy *compound_prop*. As a special case, if we are dealing with only one (possibly adjusted) property, for instance expressing some confidentiality interest, for both the components and the compound, the requirement of compositionality demands just that that property is preserved under functional composition. Instead of composition operators we could, more generally, also consider *composition relations*.

Refinement deals with the translation between two adjacent layers, aiming at realizing components in a higher layer (seen as a specification) with components of the lower layer (seen as an implementation). Basically, with regard to the functional options specified in the higher layer, a refinement determines some details that were previously left open. Such decisions about the details can have double-edged effects. On the one side, some functional options may be excluded (in the case *trace refinement*). Therefore, one might expect that the implementation will behave in a more *confined* way concerning security, but, unfortunately, the implementation may possibly also allow an observer to make more *inferences*. On the other side, some functional options may be elaborated by differentiating possibilities (in the case of *action* and *data refinement*). Therefore, the implementation may be richer and, accordingly, the implementation might be subject to new *vulnerabilities*. Ideally, we would like to have the following situation:

- In the higher layer, there are *specifications* (of the wanted computing system or of components), and the properties of the specifications are well understood.
- There are *refinement operators* that can be used to translate a specification into an *implementation* whose properties can be determined from the properties of the specification.
- Only systems or components that are constructed by appropriate refinement operators applied to suitable specifications are considered.

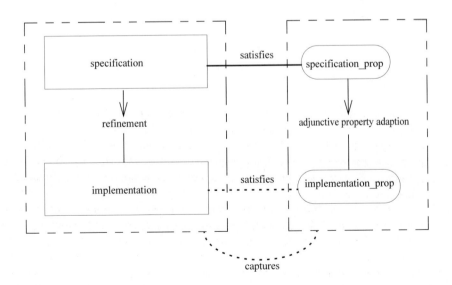

Fig. 1.5. One refinement step

Figure 1.5 visualizes one refinement step in more detail. In the higher layer, there is a component *specification* that satisfies the property *specification_prop*. The component *implementation* in the lower layer is related to *specification* by the *refinement* relation, preferably as a result of applying a corresponding refinement operator. Adjunctive to the (functional) refinement relation, there is a *property adaption* relation, which again should deal with properties that are of interest. The property *implementation_prop* is related to *specification_prop* with respect to property adaption, again preferably as a result of applying a corresponding property adaption operator. Given this situation, *implementation* is required to satisfy *implementation_prop* and, additionally, the refinement instantiation under consideration is required to "capture" the property adaption instantiation. Here, the meaning of "capture" is roughly the following: the security achievements in the higher layer can be improved in the lower layer but must not be impaired.

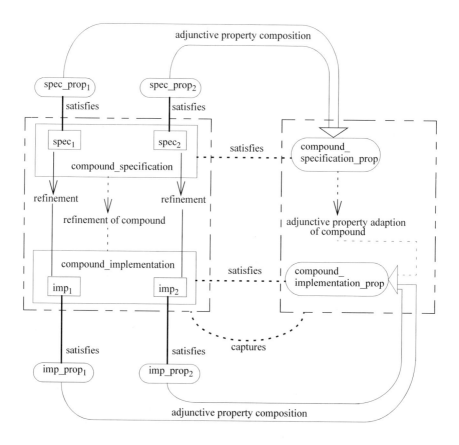

Fig. 1.6. Compositionality of refinement and compositions

Additionally, we would like to exploit compositionality and refinement together. Therefore, the operators and relations involved have to be appropriately *compatible*. For instance, we might wish to proceed as follows, and as visualized in Figure 1.6. First, in the specification layer, a major component is built from more basic specification components, thereby achieving compositionality. Then, the more basic components are refined into implementations. Finally, these implementations are composed in the implementation layer in order to obtain a major component in the implementation layer, again thereby achieving compositionality.

If this procedure is followed, the achievements of compositionality in the two layers and of refinement should be *compatible* in the following sense: the final *compound_implementation* should refine the final *compound_specification*, and this refinement instantiation should "capture" the corresponding property adaption instantiation. Additionally, in order to make these requirements meaningful, the property of the final *compound_implementation* considered should be simultaneously constructed according to an adjunctive property composition in the implementation layer and an adjunctive property adaption between the layers. Such a compatibility has also been called *compositionality (of refinement and compositions)*.

Unfortunately, the ideals sketched here are rarely achievable. In fact, research has indicated that compositionality (in any sense) and refinement with regard to security properties are usually difficult to realize in practice. Often the crucial point is what we have called *confinement* in Section 1.4.1, i.e., ensuring that a compound or refined component does not enable definitely unwanted functionality. Nevertheless, for some special situations, the goals have been achieved.

1.5.2 Construction Principles

The following general *construction principles* are widely accepted though they are at times expressed with some variation.

The principle of *open design* demands that the design and the actual implementation of security mechanisms may or even must be made public. The reasoning behind this principle is that strong security cannot be based on the supposed ignorance of potential attackers: they could perform better than expected. Additionally, publication enables a large community of affected or otherwise interested people to contribute to an independent, unbiased and thorough investigation of the actual achievements. The insight behind the principle can be summarized by the slogan "no security by obscurity".

It is important to note that this principle does not exclude the possibility that participants may control their security interests by keeping private secrets such as cryptographic keys; for cryptography, the principle requires only that cryptographic protocols and algorithms are freely distributed for inspection.

The principle of *fail-safe defaults* demands that any informational activity within a computing system is forbidden unless it has been explicitly permitted.

This reasoning is based on the experience that failures are always unavoidable to a certain extent: these are the cases that should be covered by the default rule.

However, the following warning is due: even this rule does not necessarily ensure something like perfect security (or the illusion thereof). For example, during operation, permissions might be granted inadequately, an attacker might succeed in circumventing the default rule itself, or an attack might interrupt the availability and integrity of the whole system, including the component for enforcing the default rule, just by cutting off the power supply.

Moreover, this principle should not exclude a reasonable provision for *emergency cases*, for instance in the case of hospital information systems, that would allow someone to override standard prohibitions by exceptional permissions.

The principle of *fine granularity* demands that elementary, independent (abstract) activity classes are defined as units of control. The reason is that during operation, actual permissions can be granted according to the following *administrative principles*: the principle of *need-to-know* or, better and more generally, of *need-to-act*, requires that permissions are granted only if they are strictly needed for the grantee's role; and the principle of *complete mediation* insists that permissions are granted to well-defined *single* activity executions (rather than allowing any sequence of executions over a long period of time once some initial action has been allowed). Clearly, these administrative principles can only be followed if the technical prerequisites have been implemented beforehand at construction time.

The principle of *economy of mechanisms* aims to put the main burden of security enforcement on technical mechanisms that (end) users will preferably invoke automatically, or at least by use of a routine in a user-friendly fashion. The reason is that clumsy or time-consuming procedures would not be accepted by the direct participants and would therefore not be applied at all.

This rule, however, does not mean that security should come for free: usually, strong security requires additional expenditure on the computing system, substantial organizational effort in administration and also disciplined behavior of the users.

The principle of *complexity reduction* demands that the security mechanisms are appropriately concentrated, on reasonably small and manageable components. The reason is that for a large computing system as a whole, a detailed evaluation or even a formal verification of security properties can rarely be performed. The hope is to make (relatively) small security components definitely trustworthy, and to let these trustworthy components enforce the security requirements of the overall system, even if other components behave faultily or even maliciously.

It is important to note that this rule does not necessarily require one to have just one *security kernel*, as proposed for single-machine operating systems. Rather, for multilateral security, each participant involved might wish to control his own personal security component. For instance, an individual (end) user applying cryptography to enforce his particular interests might want to concentrate all secret key-related operations on a *personal computing device* (a separate computer, typically only occasionally connected to the rest of the system).

1.5.3 Risk Assessment

When one is designing a secure computing system, the final costs of achieving security can impact crucially on the decisions. In particular, the *expenditure* for the selected security measures should be justified by the recognized *risks*. *Risk assessment* is an often painful and controversial social process, managed towards reaching conclusions that are based on financial figures.

This process suffers from inherent difficulties. Most importantly, it translates the *multilateral* and potentially conflicting and essentially different viewpoints and interests of participants into one linear scale of amounts of money, thereby making items originally considered as basically different seem easily comparable. As a further consequence, since during the translation various parameters have to be estimated, small and often not convincingly justifiable variations of parameters might result in the inversion of relationships between summary figures.

Nevertheless, the purpose of risk assessment, of coming up with *documented decisions*, is highly worthwhile, and its basic terminology is clearly helpful. At this point, we shall only outline our interpretation of some basic notions. A warning is appropriate: unfortunately, these notions are used with variations, and even in this monograph some terms are overloaded and their meaning depends on the concrete context.

In the first step, the basic *assets* of the computing system (to be designed or already in operation) and of its affected environment are listed, including, among other things, the hardware and software, the information persistently stored, the informational activities offered, and the human individuals concerned.

Next, a survey of *vulnerabilities* with regard to the security *interests* considered is prepared: basically, for each listed asset, (ideally) all possible ways in which an interest might be negatively affected are documented. Once the possibilities have been identified, they are weighted with their estimated *probability of occurrence*. Clearly, such estimations have to take (planned or existing) *countermeasures* into account, including *technical security enforcement mechanisms*. In this context, a *threat* might be seen roughly as a relationship of the following kind: an originator or a cause is assumed to actually exploit a vulnerability of an asset, with some positive probability that must be taken as serious for the overall investigation.

Countermeasures give rise to actual, definite *costs*. Each serious vulnerability, if actually exploited in an *attack*, results in some *loss*, which must again be estimated in terms of *costs*. The overall *risk* (which is left despite the countermeasures) is then the probability-weighted sum of the estimated costs of losses. Thus the overall risk denotes costs that are likely to occur.

Finally, the overall costs of countermeasures on the one side and the overall risk on the other side are evaluated concerning *affordability* and *acceptance*.

In general, some comparison is necessary: some (planned or already existing) situation is related to some advocated alternative situation, and the resulting costs and risks are compared. Then, typically, the alternative situation is preferred if its increase in the definite costs of the countermeasures is justified by its reduction of the likely overall risk.

Risk assessment, even if only rudimentarily performed, requires appropriate tools to assist one in completely covering the possible situations and to manage the highly structured data needed.

For example, a tool can maintain a *threat matrix* of the following kind: each listed asset corresponds to a row, each of the interests considered corresponds to a column, and an entry describes the identified vulnerabilities of an asset with regard to an interest, together with the estimated probabilities. Another tool might add countermeasures as a fourth category, resulting in a representation of the *threat–countermeasure relationships*.

Typically, however, the items in the categories are not independent, and not all combinations are meaningful. Additionally, countermeasures might be targeted in turn, resulting in some kinds of higher-order threat. Hence far more sophisticated techniques from the discipline of knowledge representation are desirable, such as refinement hierarchies, and/or-trees and full conceptual modeling.

1.6 The Life Cycle of Secure Computing Systems

Typically, a concrete operational computing system is subject to ongoing adaptations, modifications and corrections. For example, *adaptations* are required by new versions of the underlying layers, *modifications* arise by addition of new features and *corrections* fix reported flaws. All these changes can affect the security properties of the system. Therefore, during the full *life cycle* of the system, the administrator has to maintain the security properties as an invariant and, if possible, should also strengthen them.

Managing computing systems is a complicated task, which can be partially assisted by various tools. Invariantly ensuring the expected security properties, as (hopefully) initially assured, is an additional challenge, for which, in general, supporting tools are mandatory.

At least in theory, such a tool should have at least the following features. First, the tool should document the current security *requirements*, the current *evaluation* of how the requirements are satisfied by the current *version*, and the current underlying *assumptions*. Second, for modifications of the system, the tool should *incrementally analyze* the new situation on the basis of the documented knowledge about the current situation, thereby avoiding the need to start all investigations from the beginning.

However, practice is far away from such idealizations. Nevertheless, basically, the administrator has no other options than to approximate the ideals as best he can.

1.7 Bibliographic Hints

Faced with the huge number of contributions to the diverse topics of security in computing, throughout this monograph we deliberately refrain from attempting to cover the relevant literature completely. Rather, the hints that we give only reflect the limited experience and background of the author.

The various facets of security are captured in several textbooks about security: Hoffman [257] and Hsiao/Kerr/Madnick [260] provide early attempts at a broad view of security. The seminal book of D.Denning [163] is still highly worthwhile to study. More recent presentations originate, for example, from Amoroso [14], Pfleeger [394], Gollmann [234], Anderson [16], Eckert [180], Pieprzyk/Hardjono/ Seberry [395] and Bishop [57]. Stajano [460] discusses security for ubiquitous computing. Informative collections of computer-related risks and actually harmful incidents are described and collected by Neumann [370, 371]. Avizienis/Laprie/ Randell/Landwehr [21] provide a comprehensive taxonomy of dependable and secure computing.

Besides general treatments of security, there are also many more focused elaborations of it, for example for network security by Cheswick/Bellovin [131], Garfinkel/Spafford [216] and Stallings [462, 463], and for database security by Castano/Fugini/Martella/Samarati [118] and, more recently, by Bertino/Sandhu [51]. Moreover, cryptography not only is a fundamental technique of security, but can also be seen as a scientific discipline in its own right. Accordingly, cryptography has its own tradition in publications. Comprehensive presentations include the work of Stinson [470], Menezes/van Oorschot/Vanstone [347], Schneier [437] and Salomaa [419], as well as the most fundamental treatments presented by Goldreich [226, 228, 229]. More detailed hints in relation to specialized topics and cryptography are provided at the end of the respective chapters.

The research literature on security is partly presented in specialized conferences and journals, but is also widely spread over other sources that have a broader scope than just security. Examples of specialized conferences include the *IEEE Symposium on Security and Privacy* (since 1980), the *European Symposium on Research in Computer Security* – ESORICS (since 1990), and the *ACM Symposium of Computer and Communication Security* – CCS (since 1993); there are many further events that are devoted mainly to specific subfields of security (or purely to cryptography). Important specialized journals are *Computers and Security* (since 1982), *Journal of Computer Security* (since 1992), *ACM Transactions on Information and System Security* (since 1998), *International Journal of Information Security* (2001) and *IEEE Transactions on Dependable and Secure Computing* (since 2004). The *Computer & Communication Security Abstracts* (since 1992) gather together abstracts from numerous sources.

The exposition of security given in this introductory chapter is based on the author's view of the general experience, as expressed in the work mentioned above and many other sources too. Some parts of the chapter are based on more specific contributions. Informational assurances are discussed by Fiedler [207] and Biskup

[65]. The view of privacy is inspired by Bull [109], a sentence of the German Constitutional Court [110] and the directives of the European Commission [191, 192, 193], but the concrete legislation might be different in particular countries. Important security evaluation criteria are issued by the US Department of Defense [167] as the "Orange Book", by the European Communities [194] as ITSEC, and by a worldwide consortium [141] as the Common Criteria.

Specific attempts towards an appropriate notion of security include the proposals of Dierstein [170], Parker [384], Biskup [62], Biskup/Bleumer [64] and Rannenberg [403]. Lampson [308] considers the notion of confinement. Examples of recent contributions to compositionality and refinement originate from Abadi/ Lamport [2], Canetti [115], Mantel [330, 331], Backes/Pfitzmann/Waidner [25], Santen [433] and Alur/Grosu/Lee/Sokolsky [12]. The construction principles are inspired by Saltzer/Schroeder [421]. Risk assessment is treated by, for example, Barber/Davey/et al. [438, 266] for health-care systems, using the CRAMM tool [146], and discussed by Eloff/Labuschagne/Badenhorst [189].

The notion of security is closely related to the notion of *dependability*. Avizienis/Laprie/Randell/Landwehr/et al. [21, 311] provide introductions to the corresponding discipline.

2 Fundamental Challenges

Security in computing systems aims at supporting participants in enforcing their interests in the presence of potential or actual threats, preferably by exploiting technical mechanisms of computing. In this chapter, we first identify *information flow* between senders and receivers as a fundamental abstraction of computing, which is based on *message transmissions* and additional *inferences*. Then we outline how we can *detect* modified message transmissions by making appropriate provisions, and how we can *recover* from such modifications by performing inferences. Within this framework, finally, we discuss the various *interests* of participants, together with their *conflicts* and inevitable *trade-offs*.

2.1 Information Flow from Senders to Receivers

We treat the following event as fundamental in computing: some *information flows* from a *sender* over a *channel* to a *receiver*. In basic cases, and in many different forms, this event occurs just by the sender transmitting a meaningful *message* to the receiver, as visualized in Figure 2.1. However, information flow arises by additional means too: the receiver of a message can exploit a priori knowledge about the behavior of the sender to *infer* informative conclusions that are not explicitly expressed in the message.

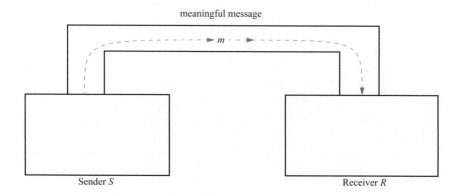

Fig. 2.1. Transmission of a meaningful message

2.1.1 Message Transmission

In programming, a simple kind of *message transmission* is captured by the execution of an *assignment* statement, syntactically expressed, for instance, as R:=S. Semantically, the current content *m* of the part of memory denoted by the program variable *S* is transmitted to the part of memory denoted by the program variable *R*. If the program variables *S* and *R* refer to single memory cells, then the transmission can be handled directly by the hardware. However, if *S* and *R* denote compound structures such as arrays or records, then they refer to some collections of cells, and accordingly the assignment statement usually has to be first translated into a sequence of elementary hardware commands.

In other words: the program variable *S* acts as a sender and the program variable *R* acts as a receiver, and we might say either that *S* *writes* into *R* or that *R* *reads* from *S*, or that some other mechanism *pushes* the transmission, depending on how the transmission is controlled.

For distributed computing systems, for example, the intended transmission control might be expressed using the following methods:

```
sender::send_data(receiver,message)
receiver::receive_data(sender,message)
receiver::send_request(sender,method,descriptor)
sender::receive_request(receiver,method,descriptor)
```

If the sender *S* wants to push the transmission of the message *m* to the receiver *R*, then *S* calls S::send_data(R,m). On execution, the core message *m* is wrapped with data about the sender and the receiver, and then the triple (S,R,m) is transported. If *R* is ready to accept, then *R* calls R::receive_data(sender, message). On execution, the assignments sender:=S and message:=m are performed. The overall transmission is visualized in Figure 2.2.

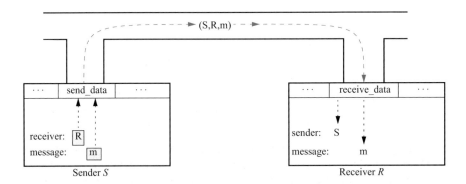

Fig. 2.2. Transmission of a meaningful core message *m* in a distributed system, pushed by the sender *S*

However, if the receiver R wants to push the transmission, a somewhat richer protocol is needed. First, the receiver R calls

```
R::send_request(S,send_data,d),
```

leading to the quadruple $(R,S,send\_data,d)$ being transported over the channel. At the other site, the sender S then calls

```
S::receive_request(receiver,method,descriptor),
```

leading to the local assignments

```
receiver:=R, method:=send_data and descriptor:=d
```

being performed. Subsequently, the sender determines the requested core message m from the description d, and the protocol proceeds as in the first case. The overall procedure is visualized in Figure 2.3.

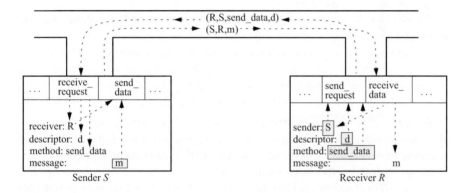

Fig. 2.3. Transmission of a meaningful core message m in a distributed system, pushed by the receiver R

Clearly, there are many other examples and variations of message transmission, possibly requiring far more sophisticated protocols with further interactions. For example, within the framework of database transactions, a transaction scheduler, a version control and a crash recovery manager are additionally involved. In dealing with the security of an abstract message transmission, all aspects and side effects of the concrete implementation have to be taken into consideration, guided by the following summarized insight gained from the above examples:

- Message transmission can be implemented in several essentially different ways.
- The requested transmission of the core message might be implemented by a protocol that comprises the transportation of auxiliary messages, possibly even in the reverse direction and between further agents.
- The impact of the participant pushing the transmission is important.

2.1.2 Inferences

A transmitted message, seen as a string (of letters and, ultimately, of 0's and 1's), is not necessarily *meaningful* concerning content for a receiver or any other *observer*. It may happen and can even be sensible that an observed string appears random and without information. In such cases, from the point of view of the observer, the message transmission has not caused an information flow. In many other cases, however, an observer succeeds in assigning a meaning to the observed string, roughly in the following sense: he determines an assertion expressing the truth of some aspect of his considerations. If, additionally, the observer has newly learnt this truth, then the message transmission has caused an *information flow* from the observer's point of view.

Hence, the observation of the same message can be seen as a random event by one observer and interpreted as an information flow by another. Actually, as explained below, a sender can deliberately exploit this property of message transmission by appropriately enabling an information flow only for the designated receiver.

Information flow is based not only on pure message transmissions but also on additional means. Most importantly, an observer can infer further assertions from the messages observed and from additional a priori *knowledge* about the behavior of the sender or other aspects under consideration. Roughly outlined, we have the following notion of *inferences* in mind here:

- The observer expresses all his knowledge and experience as sentences (in some appropriate language), supposed to be true. The collection of the resulting sentences is taken as a *presupposition*.
- This presupposition somehow describes the *possible worlds*, as seen from the observer's point of view: (conceptually) the observer evaluates to be possible exactly those overall situations for which the presupposition is true. In general, the presupposition is not strong enough to identify just one world and to exclude all others. Rather, the observer is left with some uncertainty about which of the possible worlds is the actual one.
- Then, a (further) assertion is an *implication* of the presupposition, if the assertion is true in all worlds possible under the presupposition. In particular, in some sense the knowledge explicitly expressed by an implied sentence is already implicitly contained in the knowledge represented by the presupposition.
- Then making inferences means determining implications.

Summarizing, we suggest the following general description of *information flow* based on message transmission, as visualized in Figure 2.4:

1. Observing a message: consider a string m.
2. Assigning meaning: determine a sentence Δ_m.
3. Expressing knowledge: form presupposition Π as a collection of sentences.
4. Testing novelty: infer whether Π implies Δ_m.

5. Updating the knowledge: if novel (not implied), add Δ_m to Π and reorganize, resulting in Π_{new}.

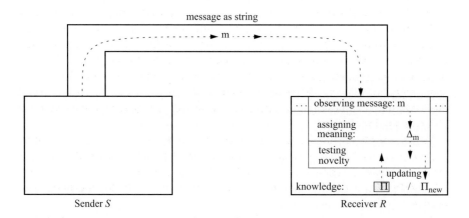

Fig. 2.4. General description of information flow based on message transmission

Having many different variations and instantiations, this general description appears to be quite fruitful for studying both security attacks and technical counter-measures. Here we shall give only a simple abstract example. Suppose an observer has a priori knowledge and experience of a sufficiently rich fragment of arithmetic, and he accesses a satisfiable linear equation

$$\alpha \cdot x + \beta \cdot y = \gamma \text{ with two variables } x \text{ and } y. \qquad (2.1)$$

So far, the observer cannot solve the equation. Rather, the observer is led to evaluate any "arithmetic world" that assigns a random value to the variable x as possible. Similarly, he is uncertain about the assignment to the variable y.

If the observer now gets a message which he can interpret regarding content as an independent satisfiable linear equation

$$\alpha' \cdot x + \beta' \cdot y = \gamma' \quad \text{with the same variables } x \text{ and } y, \qquad (2.2)$$

then he can solve the resulting system of two linear equations, i.e., he can calculate the uniquely determined values assigned to x and y as ξ and ζ, respectively. Speaking in terms of inferences, the observer thereby infers the assertions "$x = \xi$" and "$y = \zeta$" as implications of the presupposition, including the first equation, together with the second equation.

From the point of view of this observer, receiving the second equation causes an information flow: before, for each of the variables, the observer regards any value as possible; afterwards, he can infer the actual values.

We can use this example to explain how a sender can make provision for a message transmission to result in an information flow only for the designated receiver. Suppose the sender envisions a future need to transmit two numbers ξ and ζ to a specific receiver. As a preparatory step, the sender somehow takes care that only the receiver, and no one else, learns the first equation (2.1). Afterwards, if the need arises, the sender transmits the second equation (2.2) to the receiver. Now the receiver can infer the values ξ and ζ from the two equations (2.1) and (2.2) available to him. If any other participant observes the transmission, whether accidently or purposely, then that participant knows only the second equation (2.2), and in general, for this participant, the observation does not cause any information flow with respect to a single variable. However, concerning the joint values of the variables, an information flow occurs even for this participant, since he can exclude all value pairs that do not satisfy the second equation (2.2).

In this example, the first equation serves as a *key* for the information to be communicated by the transmission of the second equation. Those participants who know the key can infer the full information about the values of the variables. For others who possess neither the key nor other appropriate a priori knowledge, all values appear equally possible. Note that the second qualification is crucial: if, for example, somebody knows a priori or successfully guesses the value of one of the variables, then he can infer the value of the other variable just by substituting the already known or guessed value into the observed equation and then solving the resulting linear equation with the other variable.

In order that an observer can actually exploit the option to infer implications, the observer needs sufficient *computational means*, i.e., he needs an algorithm that actually computes the wanted implication in feasible time and with feasible other resources.

Summarizing, the discussion indicates the following:

- A message transmission does not necessarily cause an information flow for any observer.
- Sometimes an observer has to infer implications in order to let a message transmission appear as an information flow from his point of view.
- For such an inference, the observer can exploit a priori knowledge such as a previously acquired key.
- For an actual inference, the observer needs appropriate computational means.

2.1.3 Inspections and Exception Handling

A message transmission can be disturbed, garbled or forged in many ways. Accordingly, senders are concerned that their message actually reaches the receiver without modification, and receivers are aware that an observed message might not be exactly the message that was sent, or that the observed message might contain a false sender specification. A receiver therefore tries to *inspect* a received message to determine whether it originated from the indicated sender in the present form. Thereby, in some sense, the receiver has to make appropriate inferences as follows:

- On the basis of the message considered and additional knowledge, the receiver aims at inferring suitable implications in order to *detect* whether or not the core message and the sender specification are correct and unmodified.
- In the negative case, the receiver aims additionally at inferring further implications that might enable appropriate *exception handling*, say by reconstructing the original message or tracing back the root cause.

If the receiver has "no additional knowledge" at all, then his task is hopeless: the receiver cannot distinguish the correct and modified cases. Thus, beforehand, the sender or another participant acting on the sender's behalf has to provisionally provide the additional knowledge required for detecting modifications and handling them. Alternatively, cooperating senders and receivers can jointly agree on such provision.

Among the endless variety of disturbance, garbling, forgery or other unfortunate intervention in a message transmission, some kinds have attracted special attention. Here we briefly introduce the main ideas, following the coarse structure of the layered design of computing systems.

In the *data layer*, a message is treated as a string over some alphabet, and ultimately as a *bit string*. While being transmitted, some single bit or short substring might be modified; this is most likely to occur because of physical or technical shortcomings of the channel. Typically, a single "1" is changed into a "0" or vice versa, or a short substring bursts into only 1's or only 0's. Usually, the receiver treats such events as accidental *technical errors*.

In the *transport layer*, a message is considered to be composed of larger units, such as *blocks* when the core message is moved intermediately to or from persistent memory, or *packets* when the core message is transferred from one location to another. During the transmission of such blocks or packets, some units might be lost, unexpectedly added, incorrectly addressed or delivered, interchanged, or otherwise unfortunately affected. Often, a receiver treats such events not only as accidental *technical errors* but also as potentially deliberately performed *attacks*.

In the *application layer*, the message is considered as a whole, in particular with regard to meaningful content. While being transmitted, the message might leave the realm controlled by the sender, and then the original message might be replaced by another message. The difference between the original and the replaced message might be arbitrarily large, ranging from a single bit, through some blocks or packets, to the whole message. Moreover, it might also happen that there was not an original message at all. Usually, a receiver treats such events as deliberate *forgeries* with regard to content.

All kinds of modification can overlap, coincide or interfere. For example, a forgery with regard to content in the application layer might also suffer from technical errors in the lower layers, or the combined effects of several technical errors in the lower layers might look like a forgery in the application layer.

Participants counteract the different kinds of modification and their causes with different precautions, hopefully ensuring the needed inferences as a basis for suitable exception handling. Again, here we only outline the main ideas, which are elaborated further throughout the monograph.

Data Layer. In the *data layer*, the string representation of messages is augmented by *redundancy*. More specifically, the sender uses more bits for the representation of letters than are strictly required to distinguish between different letters of an alphabet Σ. There are then fewer letters to be represented than the number of different bit strings of the selected length available. Accordingly, an *encoding* function *encode*: $\Sigma \to \wp\{0,1\}^*$ can map each letter $\omega \in \Sigma$ on a non-empty, non-singleton set $\Omega \subseteq \{0,1\}^*$ such that these sets are pairwise disjoint. Additionally, for each letter $\omega \in \Sigma$, one element *select_encode*(ω) of the corresponding set Ω is selected as a distinguished code string. Obviously, there is a partial inverse *decoding* function *decode*: $\{0,1\}^* \to \Sigma$ where

$$decode(\,y) = \omega \quad \text{for all bit strings } y \in encode(\omega). \tag{2.3}$$

On the basis of an appropriate construction of such functions, senders and receivers can agree on the following protocol:

- Instead of a letter $\omega \in \Sigma$, a sender always transmits the distinguished bit string *select_encode*(ω).
- A receiver first checks whether he has observed one of the distinguished bit strings.
- In the positive case, the receiver *assumes* an unmodified transmission and computes the pre-image *decode*($\,y$) of the observed bit string y.
- In the negative case, the receiver has *detected an error* and *attempts* to *correct the error*, again by computing the pre-image *decode*($\,y$).

In this protocol, we see the added redundancy as some auxiliary objects that allow one to infer, under suitable assumptions, that an error has occurred, and possibly to correct it. Here, the suitable *error assumption* states the following: an originally sent distinguished bit string *select_encode*(ω) might be modified, but only such that the receiver can still observe an element of the set *encode*(ω).

Clearly, the overall quality of the protocol depends crucially on the choice of the encoding function, on the error assumption capturing the real circumstances and on efficient algorithms for the functions *select_encode* and *decode*. The discipline of coding theory has discovered a large body of successful insight into this topic.

Transport Layer. In the *transport layer*, again *redundancy* is added, here typically by duplicating the items. For example, when a block is to be persistently stored on a disk, a copy is held in a physically separate memory as long as the block is useful for the application. Similarly, when a packet is to be transferred, the sender keeps a copy until he gets an acknowledgement of receipt. In the case of a fault, the copies can be used for recovery purposes, in these examples by reconstructing the block on the disk and by resending the packet, respectively.

Again, the participants involved have to follow *fault-tolerant protocols* agreed beforehand comprising appropriate provision, fault detection and recovery. And the overall quality is determined by appropriate fault assumptions and the effectiveness and efficiency of the algorithms implemented. The discipline of fault-tolerant computing has supplied sophisticated procedures for this purpose.

Application Layer. In the examples discussed so far, the added redundancy is exploited to correct errors or to recover from faults. In principle, any participant who can access the auxiliary objects can perform such exception handling. This feature is explicitly undesired or even intolerable in the *application layer* when dealing with forgeries. In general, a receiver should still be able to *detect* a *forgery* with regard to content, but should be strictly prevented from "successfully correcting" it.

For example, the following would be unacceptable: after receiving a presumably forged message that means a legally binding contract or a sum of digital money, the receiver just arbitrarily "corrects" the digital document. In fact, such a "correction" would be indistinguishable from a forgery itself. Hence, in this context, the designated sender has a distinguished position: if a participant detects that a message supposedly originating from the designated sender does not look as expected with regard to content, then only the designated sender should be able to reproduce the originally wanted state.

The requirements outlined above can indeed be satisfied by a special kind of redundancy. Thereby, by exploiting modern cryptography, the designated sender generates an auxiliary object as a piece of evidence (an exhibit) that indicates that he is the producer of the message, and then he appends this object to the message. This *cryptographic exhibit* must, essentially, rely on a property specific to only the designated sender (in order to prove that he is the distinguished originator), and it must depend on the specific message (in order to distinguish it from a forgery).

Technically, the specific property of the sender is materialized by a secretly generated and confidentially kept cryptographic *authentication key* ak_S, (preferably) only known to the sender. By applying an *authentication* algorithm *Aut* (preferably essentially injective), the sender employs the authentication key to generate a cryptographic exhibit $red_{S,m} = Aut(ak_S, m)$ for any of his messages m.

The designated receiver has to be equipped with a matching *test key* tk_S, which he employs in an *authenticity verification* algorithm *Test*. This algorithm enables the receiver to check whether a message m with an appended cryptographic exhibit *red* originates from the claimed sender S without modification. Therefore, in addition to some further important conditions, (ideally) the following strong *correctness property* should hold for the two algorithms:

$$Test(tk_S, m, red) = true \text{ iff } red = Aut(ak_S, m), \tag{2.4}$$

for all messages m and objects *red*.

The overall quality of such algorithms depends crucially on actually distinguishing the designated sender as the holder of the authentication key from all other participants, and on the effectiveness and efficiency of the implementation. The discipline of cryptography has produced highly successful and often astonishing solutions to this and many other problems that arise when participants want to cooperate under conditions of limited trust.

Overall Architecture. Summarizing the above discussion and examples, we now present a general descriptive and operational framework underlying *inspection* and *exception handling*, and visualize it, appropriately simplified, in Figure 2.5:

- A message transmission can be accidently disturbed or deliberately distorted, with the effect that the receiver observes a modified or even forged message.
- As a provision against such unfortunate events, senders generate redundancy in the form of *auxiliary objects*, in particular:
  - additional (check) bits for encoding,
  - copies for fault-tolerant computing, and
  - cryptographic exhibits for authentication.
- Participants agree on protocols to exploit the redundancy, in particular:
  - to detect and correct errors for decoding,
  - to detect and recover from faults for fault-tolerant computing, and
  - to detect forgeries for authenticity verification.
- At least conceptually, the exploitation of this framework relies on implications that the receiver infers from the message observed, the generated redundancy, and further knowledge and experience, mainly captured by the protocols.

Clearly, like the general description of information flow based on message transmission, the framework presented here for inspection and exception handling can also have many diverse variations and instantiations. We argue, however, that these two approaches, alone or together, can be seen as a common idea underlying many specific security mechanisms.

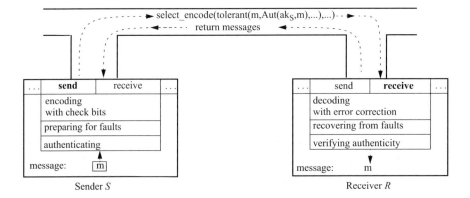

Fig. 2.5. General framework for inspection and exception handling

2.1.4 Control and Monitoring

Message transmission over a channel offers the possibility to *intercept* messages, i.e., some participant diverts the message traffic to his realm, considers each passing message in relation to some particular goal, possibly modifies it, and either forwards it to the designated receiver or decides to do something else. Clearly, such a participant might appear as a threat to the sender and the receiver. However, a whole class of security mechanisms based on the features of interception are suitable for *confining* the informational activities of participants. Usually, such a confinement is intended to restrict the senders and to protect the receivers. Here we only sketch two examples.

An *access control* component can be seen as such a confining participant. Conceptually, it is located between the active subjects (participants) of a computing system and the objects that these subjects potentially want to access. Thus the subjects are seen as senders, and the objects as receivers. Whenever a subject (participant) wishes to actually invoke an operation at an object, say reading its content, modifying it by writing or executing some other method, the subject sends an appropriate message to the object, the content of which means the required operation. These messages are intercepted by the access control component, which then decides about the request, on the basis of some security policy.

Fully permitting a request basically means forwarding the message to the selected object (which then executes the required operation); denying the request roughly means stopping the message, adding a notification and sending it back to the sender (thereby prohibiting the execution of the required operation). In this way, the access control component restricts the subjects, since not all their access requests are actually granted, and at the same time it protects the objects against undesirable accesses.

In a centralized system, there is usually a single access control component, which has to cover all accesses. In distributed client–server systems, each node has its own access control component: each message containing a client–server request is first controlled at the sender's node in order to restrict the sender's activities, and then independently controlled again at the receiver's node in order to protect the receiver's objects (resources). In networks, borderlines of local subnets are similarly controlled by *firewalls*: here, outgoing or incoming messages are usually seen as packets, the headers (and sometimes also the bodies) of which are evaluated to decide whether the packets should be forwarded or rejected, according to some security policy.

Beyond permitting or denying accesses, such intercepting *control components* can additionally *monitor* the message traffic and analyze it in order to *detect* ongoing attacks, or *intrusions*. Such violations of the security requirements attempt to circumvent the direct control, say by performing a malicious sequence of operations each of which in isolation is not forbidden, or by exploring and misusing flaws in the system. The discipline of control and monitoring has developed many helpful architectures and effective facilities for all kinds of the tasks sketched.

2.2 Security Interests

In any computing system some kind of message transmission is offered as an informational service, and various more advanced informational services based on that service are usually provided. When dealing with security, each of the participants involved should express their *interests* with respect to the specific *service* under consideration, and sometimes also with respect to extended informational activities. Some interests mainly expect *reliable correctness*, i.e., correct execution of the specified service even in the presence of threats, and maybe also additional evidence for actual executions. Other interests mainly require *confinement*, i.e., that nobody can misuse the service for unwanted effects. *Threats* might have various originators or causes, these being among others:

- the interest holder himself;
- participants directly involved in the service;
- participants who have implemented the service;
- other participants who are authorized to share the computing system;
- intruders from outside; or even
- manufacturers, vendors and administrators.

Originators might threaten the service

- harmlessly and accidently, or
- maliciously and deliberately.

And *causes* might range from

- improper requirements, through
- faulty implementations or
- wrong administration, to
- unfortunate external events.

Clearly, these general distinctions are not sharp but need to be refined for any specific service and related to each other. In the following, we survey exemplarily the commonly identified interests in relation to our basic abstraction, namely information flow based on message transmission. Thereby, we also discuss and refine the more fundamental list of interests often used to define security: *availability, confidentiality, integrity,* and *authenticity* with *non-repudiation*.

2.2.1 Availability

Whenever the service of message transmission is useful for an application at all, there are participants who claim an interest in *availability*. These participants expect that a called message transmission will indeed be executed, with the actual parameters provided and at the wanted time. This interest might also be expressed gradually: preferably, the actual service execution should take place; otherwise, some *exception handling* should allow a substitutional activity or at least raise an appropriate notification.

2.2.2 Integrity: Correct Content

Typically, a transmitted message is meaningful because it refers to some content with respect to the outside world or the computing system itself. For example, messages to or from a database often reflect assertions about the world modeled by the database schema. If the database is a stock inventory, then the database should assert the *correct* current state of the stock. This kind of *integrity* as *correct content* should be maintained under all update operations and, accordingly, also messages containing query answers should enjoy this kind of integrity with regard to content.

Obviously, the wanted relationship between the formal database and the real world cannot be fully enforced by formal or even algorithmic means. Rather, more modestly, we have to monitor *semantic constraints* (often called *integrity constraints*), which are reasonable invariants for the database. Then, for update messages, the original service of message transmission is extended by the automatic enforcement of semantic constraints. Similarly, in a computer-assisted fund transfer system, messages reflect "real" cash flows, which are to be monitored with respect to various integrity conditions. For instance, a condition might express that the sum of all accounts maintained should remain invariant, unless some amount of money is explicitly inserted or withdrawn.

2.2.3 Integrity: Unmodified State

In order that a received message is correct concerning content, it must not be modified during the transmission, i.e., the receiver must see exactly what the sender has produced. For long-distance transmissions, neither physical effects on the channel nor other participants at the mediating net nodes should alter the message. If the transmission is executed with a delay in time, in particular if the message is temporarily stored in a database file, then the initial memory state must persist. The interest in *integrity* as the *unmodified state* of a message is visualized in Figure 2.6.

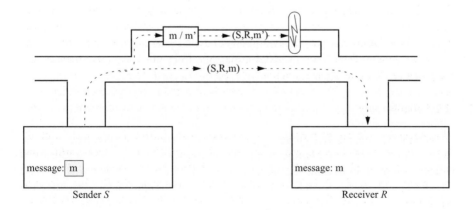

Fig. 2.6. The interest in integrity as the unmodified state of a message

Extending our reasoning beyond messages, a participant usually also requires integrity of the programs and processes underlying the service, since otherwise the expected results will rarely happen. In particular, the program actually started has to be identical to the specified program (neither modified nor substituted, whether accidently or maliciously), and the process actually running has to execute the specified program (and not accidently or maliciously exchange its code).

The interest in integrity as unmodified state is comprehensive and far-reaching: it comprises all items of the computing system, including the translations between upper and lower layers, ultimately referring to physical memory and transmissions.

2.2.4 Integrity: Detection of Modification

If *integrity* as unmodified state cannot be fully satisfied, we might restrict our interest by insisting that any *modification* can be *detected* as such. Additionally, sometimes but not always it is reasonable to expect that a detected modification will be *corrected*, i.e., that the original state is *recovered*. Such an extended interest in detection of modification meets closely the corresponding requirements for availability.

2.2.5 Authenticity

The interests in availability and integrity mentioned so far refer to the service as a whole, here, as an example, message transmission, or to a meaningful state of some of its components, here, as an example, transmitted data, programs or processes. The further interests refer mainly to the participants involved.

The interest in *authenticity* requires the correctness of the sender of a message, as visualized in Figure 2.7. Typically, the interest holder is the receiver, who wants to ensure that a received message, explicitly or implicitly containing a claim about its sender, has actually been sent by the indicated participant.

2.2.6 Non-Repudiation

Often, the receiver has an extended interest beyond pure authenticity: he not only wants to ensure that he has received a message from the correct sender, but also wants to prove to third parties that he has received a particular message from a specific sender. Thereby, the receiver's interest is directed to forcing the sender *not to repudiate* the message in a dispute later on (and to recognize the content as an obligation, for example).

Obviously, any participant acting as a potential sender has the reverse interest: he wishes to restrict the enforcement of non-repudiation to those messages that indeed originate from him. In other words, neither the receiver nor anybody else should be able to falsely claim the participant as the originator of a message not sent by him. The interest in non-repudiation is closely related to classical expectations about handwritten signatures.

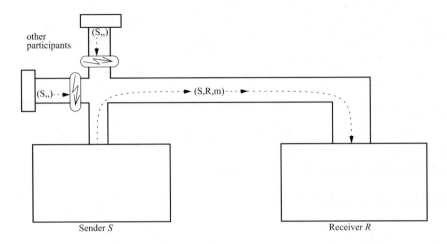

Fig. 2.7. The interest in authenticity as correctness of the sender

2.2.7 Confidentiality

Usually, the sender knows (the content of) the message that he is sending, and often requires that the message is carefully directed exclusively to the designated receiver. This interest in *confidentiality* aims at the correctness of the receiver, as visualized in Figure 2.8. Nobody else should get the message, and nobody else should be able to read the message during the transmission or to infer its content by other means.

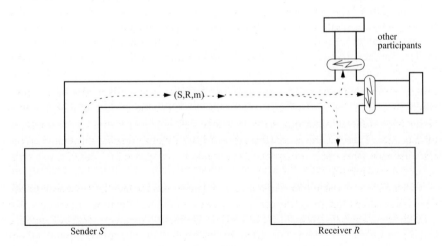

Fig. 2.8. The interest in confidentiality as correctness of the receiver

The actual instantiation of the interest in confidentiality might vary considerably among the participants directly involved in an application or otherwise concerned. For example, for a computing system that is embedded into a hierarchical organization, managers might express confidentiality requirements aimed at preserving (intellectual or other) property. As far as personal data is considered, however, the persons concerned will wish to control the usage of their data, according to the principle of informational self-determination, with the aim of preserving their privacy. In such cases, conflicts quite often arise.

In order to enforce strict confidentiality, aimed at whatever right, it is mandatory to control not only the pure messages but also the potential inferences based on them, i.e., to control the enabled information flow.

2.2.8 Non-Observability

The interest in confidentiality can be strengthened to a requirement to keep the full *activity* of message transmission or parts of it *non-observable* by third parties. The strongest form is that nobody apart from the directly involved sender and receiver can detect that a deliberate message transmission is taking place. A more modest form might require only that an observer of message transmissions cannot determine the corresponding pairs of senders and receivers, except for the respective participants of course.

2.2.9 Anonymity

The interest in *anonymity* can be understood as a special form of non-observability, of particular importance for *digital payment systems* in *electronic commerce*, and more generally for all kinds of *credential-based access control* to resources of any kind. The fundamental requirement is that participants can act as senders of messages without revealing their identity, but only proving their eligibility for the interaction under consideration, say spending a digital coin or accessing a digital service. Thereby, participants can interact anonymously with others in a computing system in a similar way to what they do in the traditional world, where people often use bills and tickets without exhibiting their identity. In the informational services and interactions of the near future, both example applications will tend to be combined: a participant requests a specific digital service and pays for it with digital money, with an interest in anonymity, i.e., without being identifiable as a specific individual.

Clearly, in such systems, the service provider might have conflicting interests, in particular in non-repudiation, in order to ensure that the provider will eventually be paid.

Also, an interest in anonymity often arises in the context of *scientific* or *administrative databases*. If a citizen is asked for personal data or, because of an overriding interest, obliged by law to reveal some such data, then the individual's right of informational self-determination can sometimes be respected by requiring that the personal data is used only in an anonymized form, i.e., the individual concerned appears as an anonymous sender of appropriately modified data originally considered as personal.

Clearly, again other interests might be in conflict, for instance the interest in integrity as correctness with regard to content.

2.2.10 Accountability

There are many more possible interests originating from special situations, additional obligations of participants or even properties of security mechanisms. In the following, we discuss only a few of them.

The administrator of a computer system is responsible for ensuring the expected functionality. In general, this obligation also includes support of the accepted interests of the users. In computing, as in any other field, the administrator should be prepared to deal with misbehavior or even attacks on the system, and with violations of interests. There is then an interest that some informational activities in the system, in particular pushing a message transmission or another service, can be traced back to specific individuals, in order to hold them responsible for the consequences. This interest in *accountability* lays the foundations for deterring misuse or pursuing attackers.

2.2.11 Evidence

The next interest often arises in the context of accountability, and it can also be interpreted as a security mechanism. If a sender transmits a message to a receiver, possibly assisted by further agents, then all interacting participants might have an interest in getting pieces of *evidence* (exhibits) for their contribution. Later on, such exhibits could be exploited in any dispute about the actual events. For example, the sender can ask the transmitter for an exhibit of pushing a message transmission, and the transmitter can ask the receiver for an exhibit of delivery (acknowledgement of receipt).

2.2.12 Integrity: Temporal Correctness

Some interests are meaningful only if many participants send messages to each other, assisted by transmitters, over a longer period of time. The interest in *integrity* as *temporal correctness* can then become important. For example, the receiver might require that all the messages originating from a specific sender reach him in the correct sequence, i.e., the sequence in which they were sent. Another interest of a receiver might be to get messages delivered without substantial delay or, more modestly, to be able to decide whether a received message is *reasonably fresh*.

2.2.13 Separation of Roles

The interest in *separation of roles* usually arises only in the case of computing systems offering many diverse message transmissions or other informational activities. Additionally, typically, the senders and receivers represent individuals acting on behalf of an organization. Under these circumstances, over time, a particular individual may behave in several different social roles, to be kept strictly separated.

For example, in public administration, messages might contain personal data. Then the informational self-determination of the persons concerned often requires that there is no information flow between administrative roles, in particular that personal data collected in one role is processed only for that role's well-defined purpose. Other examples occur whenever an individual has both administrative and supervising obligations which should not be executed simultaneously on the same subject.

2.2.14 Covert Obligations

The list of potential special interests appears to be endless, in particular if more advanced informational activities or even collections of them are considered.

The compound interest in *covert obligations* is a further example. Here the content of a message is interpreted as an obligation of the sender to the receiver. At the time of receipt, the receiver sees only the message, and cannot determine the obligation, which is wrapped in some way, by himself. However, later on, owing to some further event, the receiver should be able to reveal the obligation, and then the sender should indeed recognize it. This situation might arise when a tender is submitted and later opened.

The overall compound interest in covert obligations comprises an interest in confidentiality concerning the obligation in the first stage, and an interest in non-repudiation in the second stage.

2.2.15 Fair Exchange

The interest in *fair exchange* is also a compound one. During many informational activities in *electronic commerce*, participants agree to simultaneously exchange digital documents or goods. As in traditional trading, each participant aims at getting the expected item from the other side whenever he delivers the item offered by himself.

2.2.16 Monitoring and Eavesdropping

Fundamental human rights demand the confidentiality of private messages, whether they are letters, phone conservations or emails. However, governmental security agencies sometimes have a conflicting interest in *monitoring* and *eavesdropping*, i.e., in observing selected message transmissions and determining the content and meaning of the messages sent. Usually, in order to allow law enforcement in the case of extremely dangerous criminal acts or for the purpose of national security or related goals, the responsible agencies have restricted rights to pursue these interests under some specific rules and conditions.

2.3 Trade-Offs

In general, a computing system is embedded in an environment, it is actively used by many and various participants, other participants might be passively affected, and, additionally, diverse further participants might assist in producing, administering or maintaining the system. In summary, a large number and a great variety of individuals are involved, and their *interests* vary considerably, potentially leading to partial or total mutual *conflicts*, to be balanced under *trade-offs*.

The reasons for accepting trade-offs are deep and, basically, inevitable. In the information society, an increasing part of individual and social life is supported by or even shifted to computing systems, thereby formalizing previously intuitive behavior. Accordingly, not only the functional aspects but also the conflicts and trade-offs of social communications and interactions are translated into the formalizations underlying the computing systems. In fact, once formalized, conflicts and trade-offs are often expressed more concisely and recognized as more challenging than before.

Roughly outlined and simplified, whereas in traditional life individuals can solve difficulties case by case, exploiting personal insight and taking responsible decisions, formalization and computing require us to develop general, algorithmic solutions beforehand, ideally covering all possible cases. Clearly, traditional life is not so easy, but it is regulated by a social and juridical framework too, and computing usually lacks total coverage of all cases. But there is a difference: legal rules are purposely subject to later disputes and detailed interpretation in law courts, whereas ideally, though it is rarely achievable, computing should unambiguously enforce rules by technical mechanisms, avoiding violations from the beginning.

In the following subsections, we concentrate on three aspects concerning trade-offs. First, we treat the trade-offs between the autonomy of individual participants and their cooperation. Second, we deal with the trade-offs between unavoidable threats and indispensable trust. Third, we discuss the trade-offs between confidence and provision. These considerations relate to the achievable degree of security and the required expenditure.

2.3.1 Autonomy and Cooperation

In any society, interaction and communication between participants are performed in the context of fundamental values, which determine normatively the allowance of more specific goals and interests. The fundamental *values* as a whole are already conflicting: some emphasize *autonomy* of individuals, whereas others require *cooperation* between them. For example, freedom from injury and self-determination, secrecy, and property rights primarily support an individual's autonomy, whereas social participation, rights to living space and law enforcement favor cooperation.

Obviously, such conflicts are inherited by more specific goals and interests. More specifically, a security interest can be seen to express a preference towards

Table 2.9. Interests and their support for autonomy or cooperation: + means roughly that the interest emphasizes the property at the head of the column; − means roughly that the interest conflicts with the property; • means roughly that the interest also supports the property

Interest	Autonomy	Cooperation
availability	•,+	+,•
integrity: correct content	•	•
integrity: unmodified state	•	•
integrity: detection of modification	+	•
authenticity	+	•
non-repudiation	•,+	+
confidentiality	+	•
non-observability	+	•
anonymity	+	•
accountability	−,•	+
evidence	•,+	+
integrity: temporal correctness	+	•
separation of roles	+	•
covert obligations	+	•
fair exchange	+	•
monitoring and eavesdropping	−	+

either autonomy or cooperation, or might appear to be balanced. In the following, we tentatively and exemplarily outline some general observations, which are summarized in Table 2.9.

The interests in *confidentiality*, *non-observability* and *anonymity* are often founded on the value of informational self-determination and, accordingly, these interests accentuate autonomy. Insisting on autonomy, a participant in a computing system will usually pursue such interests against other participants, who will be seen as potential opponents or even attackers.

Those participants, however, will agree on a cooperation only if their possibly conflicting interests are adequately dealt with too, in particular their interests in the *availability* of the informational activity used for cooperation, as well as their interests in *non-repudiation*, *accountability* and *evidence*. In fact, the latter goals might support the conflicting autonomy of the participants, enabling them to successfully settle disputes later on.

Although at first glance such discrepancies appear to be technically intractable, the discipline of modern cryptography offers a wide range of astonishing, powerful solutions not only for this conflict but also for many others.

The different interests in *integrity* often aim equally at cooperation and autonomy. On the one side, cooperation relies on messages that are correct regarding content, are unmodified and arrive in time. On the other side, a participant wishes to autonomously detect violations. The interest in *authenticity* is similarly balanced: cooperation requires reliable authenticity verification, but a participant wishes to perform the tests autonomously.

The interest in *monitoring* and *eavesdropping* is in direct conflict with the interests of confidentiality, non-observability and anonymity, and clearly restricts the autonomy of individuals in favor of other overwhelming values, which are ultimately aimed at social cooperation.

In general, the interest in *accountability* also conflicts with confidentiality, non-observability and anonymity. However, if participants wish to cooperate in an informational activity, they essentially rely on a duly administrated computing system. In particular, they expect that violating behavior will be detected and effectively counteracted. If it is restricted to this goal, honest participants will accept accountability, regarding it as helpful for their interest in cooperation.

The interests in *separation of roles*, *fair exchange* and *covert obligations* arise only in the context of advanced cooperation. In some sense, they aim at strengthening the autonomy of participants affected by the misbehavior of others.

2.3.2 Trust and Threats

Computing systems support cooperation between participants. While interacting and communicating, one participant might see another participant both as a wanted partner and as a potentially *threatening* opponent, as, for example, in the case of fair exchange. However, if the fear of attacks finally prevailed, then no cooperation would be successfully completed, and participants would remain in unproductive isolation.

Hence, in any case, at least some limited *trust* has to be assigned to some participants involved. Likewise, components of a computing system might fail, but a user has to trust at least some components in order to exploit the potential of the system.

Concerning the trade-offs between trust and threats, the crucial points of *multilateral security* are summarized by the following requirements, which can rarely be fully satisfied in practice:

- The trust needed should be minimized while simultaneously maximizing the achievable functionality, thereby facing the potential threat from the untrusted parts.
- Each participant should autonomously assign trust at their own discretion.
- As far as possible, assigned trust should be justified, and the assigning participant should have the power to verify the trustworthiness and to control the actual behavior of the trusted realm.

In both practical situations and theoretical investigations, trust is often introduced as an *assumption*, hopefully founded on an approximate satisfaction of the ideals summarized. Minimizing trust then means reducing the needed assumption to a reasonable and manageable fraction of the overall considerations.

In fact, many technical security enforcement mechanisms can be seen as an attempt to concentrate trust into a small part of the whole system, preferably under the direct control of the interest holder concerned. For example, *cryptographic* mechanisms concentrate trust into correctly and confidentially generated and stored private (secret) *keys* which allow the key holder a distinguished behavior, and mechanisms for *access control* concentrate trust into small *kernels*, which unavoidably intercept all requests.

2.3.3 Confidence and Provision

Security requirements should be enforced by appropriate security mechanisms. Such mechanisms aim at preventing violations, limiting damage and compensating the consequences. The expenditure should relate to the recognized risks. In order to meet these goals, security administrators have to take informed and justified decisions for each particular case. Often they can select from a range of options, depending on whether they prefer a more confident and optimistic view or a more provisional and pessimistic view.

In a *confident* and *optimistic* approach, the administrator chooses relatively weak security mechanisms, roughly expecting the following: at relatively low cost, only slightly affecting the standard operations, most of the anticipated threats are effectively covered, but exceptional violations (hopefully rare) might still be possible; such violations will, hopefully, manageable or acceptable, though potentially at high cost.

In a *provisional* and *pessimistic* approach, the administrator selects relatively strong security mechanisms, roughly expecting the following: at relatively high cost, greatly affecting the standard operations, all anticipated threats are effectively covered.

If different options are actually available, then the trade-offs should be evident:

- cheap versus expensive;
- basically unaffected standard operations versus an essential security overhead;
- approximate versus complete coverage of threats;
- toleration versus strict avoidance of exceptional violations.

Here we can roughly sketch three examples. In the first example, optimistically, we audit all activities and, taking random samples or in cases of suspicion, analyze the audit trail for violations only afterwards; pessimistically, all requests for activities are fully controlled and decided in advance.

In the second example, in the case of a network, optimistically, the validity of digital credentials is just assumed in offline mode and only afterwards, in cases of suspicion is the validity further verified in online mode at a central certificate repository; pessimistically, every decision based on digital credentials is preceded by an online verification at a central repository.

In the third example, in the case of trading, optimistically, cooperating participants issue exhibits by themselves, which are subject to later evaluation by a trusted third party only in the case of disputes; pessimistically, every trade is mediated and supervised by a trusted notary.

2.4 Bibliographic Hints

The presentation in this chapter is mostly based on the general literature listed in Section 1.7. Selected topics in this chapter are treated further in more detail in other chapters, where additional bibliographic hints are provided.

3 Computing Systems and Their Basic Vulnerabilities

Security is a comprehensive property of a technical system that operates in a larger social and political context. After all, in order to achieve security in computing systems, we have to understand the fundamentals of the *computing technology*, including the hardware, vertically layered software, horizontal distribution and telecommunication, and to identify their basic *vulnerabilities*. Additionally, as far as possible, security should be based ultimately on *technical security enforcement mechanisms* that have been implanted into the system. In this chapter, we outline computing technology as it stands without security mechanisms, describe the basic vulnerabilities and discuss the options for constructing security mechanisms by exploiting the technology itself. This outline, which is partly visualized in Figure 3.1 and briefly summarized in Table 3.4 on page 62, is meant to be exemplary and by no means exhaustive. Finally, we also discuss how the limitations of (general) computability and efficient computability affect security considerations.

3.1 Architecture

Typically, a computing system is built in *vertical layers*: founded on hardware, which consists of electronic and thus physical devices, several virtual layers of software subsystems are implemented, providing functionality in increasingly more sophisticated forms. These forms of functionality have to be translated stepwise back into machine programs, i.e., software that can be directly executed by a hardware device. The basic options for translation are compiling and interpreting. Roughly sketched, *compiling* statically converts a full program in a higher layer into a program in the supporting lower layer, and the resulting program can then be used in the supporting layer, either by a further compilation, by interpretation (usually repeated) or, in the case of a machine program, by direct physical execution (again usually repeated) on a hardware device. In outline, *interpreting* seemingly executes a program on a virtual machine, but in fact, interpreting dynamically translates single statements of a program in a higher layer stepwise into statement sequences or, more generally, (small) programs in the supporting layer, where the results of the translation are immediately executed in turn, either by further interpretation or directly, depending on the layer.

Figure 3.2 shows a typical example of such a vertically layered design. In the figure, only one hardware device is explicitly shown; other hardware devices on more or less remote sites are connected by appropriate (tele)communication lines.

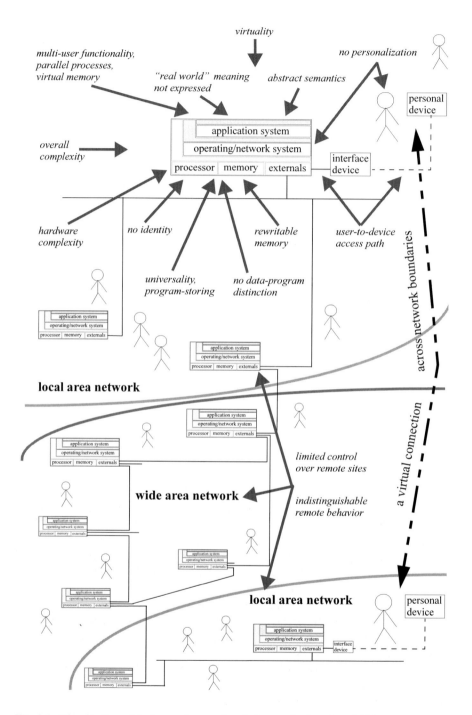

Fig. 3.1. Visualization of features of computing that cause basic vulnerabilities

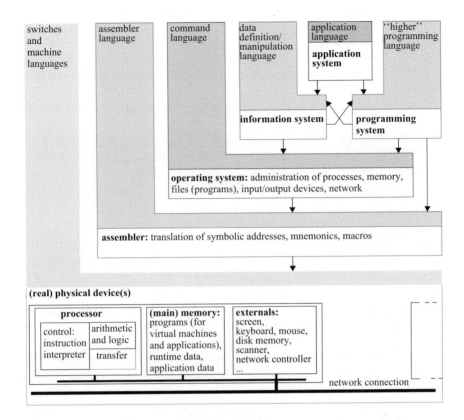

Fig. 3.2. Layered design of a computing system

Accordingly, there is also a *horizontal distribution* into several, in fact often numerous connected components, each of which is again vertically layered. In some sense, the Internet is one huge computing system. Moreover, in order to make the physical distribution transparent, a further hierarchy of virtual layers is maintained. Along this hierarchy, application statements referring to the overall distributed system are translated into local actions and additionally needed physical communication actions related to remote sites. Additionally, components interact with human individuals as users and are then often operated in the context of a larger organization. Finally, components might also be *embedded* into a non-computing mechanical or natural environment by means of sensors and controllers. In that case, the computing system appears as part of an even larger technical or even socio-technical–natural system.

The paradigm of *virtuality* is extremely powerful for elaborating functionality. However, it also exposes a fundamental vulnerability: the security achieved in a specific virtual layer is in fact virtual too, i.e., it can potentially be undermined by the translation process back to the machine layer, and it can potentially be circumvented by participants operating on lower layers. In general, the translation process has been designed and implemented over the years by many individuals and groups, such that no single person has complete knowledge of or even control over its totality. Moreover, in most cases, at least some selected participants must operate on lower layers, for instance in order to administer, maintain and supervise the system.

Virtuality and distribution, individually and even more together, allow extraordinary and maybe even overwhelming *complexity*, leading to a further vulnerability: in principle, every item in the overall structure of a computing system could interfere with any other. Unfortunately, however, in general, no single participant is aware of all items and their details.

3.1.1 Physical Devices

At the bottom of the layered design, there is the *hardware*, i.e., the physical devices that directly execute machine programs. Typically, these devices are universal, program-storing machines, built according to the von Neumann architecture and as powerful as abstract Turing machines. *Universality* here means that, in principle, if somebody provides a suitable program, any computable task can be performed. And the term *program-storing* refers to the fact that arbitrary programs can be stored in the machine memory and later be executed.

Universality and program-storing make hardware overwhelmingly powerful but also vulnerable: if an adversary succeeds in storing a malicious program and then in executing it, then the machine performs the will of the adversary, as expressed in the program, and, at least in principle, any will that is computable at all can be imposed on the machine in this way. The whole fancy world of *viruses*, *worms*, *Trojan horses* and other malicious *computing creatures* can be seen as exploiting just this vulnerability. As a countermeasure, some facilities to master or even to restrict universality and program-storing can be provided. However, then the crucial problem of *multilateral* security is who has the power over such countermeasures: individual participants as owners of their subsystems, some software providers, or even hardware manufacturers?

At the core of a piece of hardware, there is a *processor* with at least some built-in memory, which is manufactured as a mass product. Traditionally, a single processor instance does not have an obvious *identity*, i.e., it is indistinguishable from any other instance of the same product. Accordingly, one instance of a processor can be freely substituted by another instance, and without further provision in the virtual layers, observers have no means of recognizing any difference. This feature, together with universality and program-storing, makes computing vulnerable to various kinds of *masquerades*, i.e., an attacking participant might successfully create the illusion to a victim that the victim is operating on or communicating with a specific machine but in fact he is not. The possibility of masquerades clearly endangers all efforts at achieving *authenticity* of messages or information. As a countermeasure, recent proposals suggest that some worldwide unique *identifier*

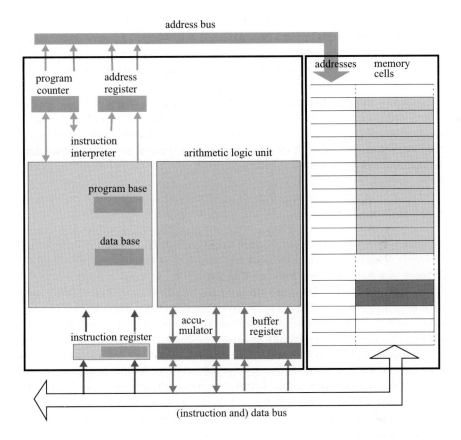

Fig. 3.3. Internal structure of a processor and its memory

should be artificially implanted in processor instances in a physical tamper-resistant way, and that this identifier should be automatically added to messages where and when potentially needed. However, at the same time, implanted unique identifiers and their automatic usage can make any kind of *anonymity* impossible.

Many applications require the origin of messages to be traced back to responsible individuals, i.e., *authenticity* and *non-repudiation* should ultimately refer to humans. Therefore, in addition to identifying hardware instances, some unforgeable and tamper-resistant binding between a hardware instance and an identifiable individual could be seen as desirable. As a further vulnerability, traditional hardware does not provide any kind of *personalization* of hardware instances as a means for such a binding. However, if it did, say by *biometrics*, anonymity would be even more severely endangered, and individuals would be faced with many problems related to hardware instances that are delegated, lost and found, stolen, or acquired by extortion or physical violence.

A closer look at the internal structure of a *processor* and its usage of *memory*, as sketched in Figure 3.3, reveals some further vulnerabilities or refined versions of those already described. In the following, we list only three of them as examples.

First, the distinction between a program and the manipulated data is only given implicitly by the context, which is manifested mainly by the (current value of the) *program counter* and the addressing mechanism. Any stored program is vulnerable to being (accidently or maliciously) *modified* by some process that treats the *program (code)* as data. In fact, such a process can even execute the modified program itself. Then, the program is *self-modifying* under execution. Furthermore, these observations extend also, if applicable, to *runtime objects* such as the *stack* or *heap* maintained during program execution. Basically, *buffer overflow attacks* exploit these features.

Second, more generally, any data (or instructions) contained in a memory cell can be *arbitrarily* manipulated by any program execution *writing* into that cell. Thus the *integrity* of data (and the instructions of a program) is vulnerable to unintended *modification*, whether accidently or maliciously.

Third, in order to execute a program, it must first be appropriately stored in memory and then appropriately started by setting the program counter to the start address. Typically, program starts are managed by *interrupt routines*, which, more generally, allow one to intervene in the control flow of a single program and thereby enable interaction with parallel outside events. Interrupt routines are programs by themselves and thus subject to all of the vulnerabilities discussed before.

Modern hardware usually has some fairly rudimentary built-in countermeasures. Basically, while in principle preserving universality, program-storing and the possibilities underlying the more specific vulnerabilities just mentioned, these countermeasures aim at tamper-resistant restriction of the usage of these features to well-controlled *modes*, with regard to executing instructions as well as to using the contents of memory cells.

There are numerous further kinds of vulnerability. Some of them result again from the extraordinary *complexity* of even a single piece of modern hardware, which will have been designed and manufactured by an extremely complicated process. An inventive intruder might detect functionalities that have never been foreseen or realized for normal usage but could be misused for attacks, including exploiting them to use *covert channels*, i.e., some hidden *information flow* that is somehow modulated onto observable events within the hardware, in particular concerning the actual behavior in *real time*. Other vulnerabilities stem from physical effects such as electromagnetic radiation that allow observations that are not captured by the conceptual design. Moreover, the physical *access path* employed as the channel between the input/output device for the user, say a keyboard and a screen, and the processor together with the main memory is a special point of vulnerability: all security-relevant messages from and to the user, including passwords and more sophisticated items for ensuring the authenticity of the person acting, could be very worthwhile for an attacker, and therefore this access path must be protected from unintentional leakage and malicious interference of any kind.

3.1.2 Virtual Vertical Layers

Any functionality of a computing systems is founded on the physical devices. Accordingly, strictly speaking, the virtual layers do not enhance the theoretical computational power but only enhance its usability. Practically, however, the enhancements result in a new quality of service, which then lets new vulnerabilities be seen. Nevertheless, it must be emphasized again that all countermeasures in a virtual layer, like any normal functionality, are translated in some way to the bottom hardware layer. In order to be effective, the countermeasures should be appropriately physically founded there.

The layer of the *operating system* typically introduces *multi-user functionality* with the management of (virtual) *parallel processes* and *virtual memory*, thereby interacting with more or less autonomous external input–output devices, additional storage devices, and devices of remote components. The basic new vulnerabilities arise from allowing several users or several tasks from one user to work on the same hardware, thereby *sharing* the processor and the memory. Then, sharing might result in unwanted *interference*, or, seen otherwise, in unwanted *information flow*. Some examples of more refined vulnerabilities are the following. Concerning memory, the *working spaces* of processes might overlap, or real memory might subsequently be allocated to different processes, allowing a process to observe *unerased data* of the preceding usage. Concerning processes, virtual independent processes might access *state information* of other processes and thus not be confined to the explicitly programmed interactions. Furthermore, inappropriately controlled *race conditions* might cause unexpected behavior.

Layers for general-purpose higher *programming systems* offer theoretical universality in a more human-manageable form. As a result, programmers working with advanced programming systems are, hopefully, very prolific in implementing new services for users. Unfortunately, malicious participants might also be more productive in preparing attacks. Ideally, the *abstract semantics* of the programs written in a higher programming language is well defined, say using a *virtual machine*, and this virtual machine is correctly implemented, allowing exactly what is expected and nothing else. In practice, however, there might be gaps and flaws, which can cause unwanted effects or can be purposely exploited. Usually, higher programming languages discipline programmers to employ well-structured control flows and data, and thus the verification of security properties tends to be more manageable. On the other hand, vulnerabilities might also arise from the abstract semantics failing to capture all security-relevant aspects, for instance measurable *real time*.

Layers for *special-purpose systems*, such as database management systems or more general *information systems*, and final *application systems*, often deal with activities and data that have a direct *meaning* with respect to the real world outside. For instance, a medical record administration system deals with medical treatments and the persons involved, and, in particular, with the personal medical data of patients. This *real meaning*, however, is often not explicitly and fully expressed in the programs themselves, which at first glance just express manipulations of abstract data. Vulnerabilities then arise from failure to capture all security-relevant aspects in additional documents. Clearly, the vulnerabilities of general-purpose systems mostly apply also to the special-purpose case. In particular, often the latter systems are theoretically as powerful as the former ones and are thus *universal*, but in some hidden form, allowing a more or less crude *simulation* of arbitrary computations.

The general recommendation for countermeasures against these and other vulnerabilities is to employ the best features of *software engineering*, in particular *compositionality* and *refinement*, whenever possible and as far as possible. Thereby, the wanted security properties should be comprehensively stated, capturing all relevant aspects, and later verified for the final implementation. Another helpful concept of software engineering is *object-orientation*. Thereby, the possible usage of a virtual object is clearly defined by the *methods* that are declared for that object's class, and thus the normal usage is also accordingly restricted, provided the implementation actually achieves the intended *encapsulation*, i.e., the implementation of the object can be accessed only by an implementation of any of its methods.

3.1.3 Virtual Digital Objects and Implementing Bit Strings

In the virtual layers, participants may deal with *objects* of any kind. Examples are programs, files, messages, documents such as medical records or scientific publications, and music and video items. When translated back to the hardware layer, all of these objects are implemented just by *bit strings*. A basic vulnerability then becomes visible: a bit string as such does not have an identity, it can be easily duplicated, and afterwards no difference between the original bit string and its duplicate is observable (except that the original and duplicate are stored in different places). Thus, while in the higher layers participants often have an idea of a uniquely *identified* or at least *identifiable* object in mind, in the bottom layer there are just bit strings that are suitably physically represented, without any possibility of distinguishing between the original and a duplicate.

This basic vulnerability could be exploited in many ways, in particular by challenging intellectual rights. For instance, in an application-oriented upper layer designed for electronic commerce, objects might be seen as *commercial goods*, owned by somebody. That owner also usually has the right to produce *copies* and to sell them individually. Then, each copy has a financial value in itself. Accordingly, if some unauthorized participant copies such an object, there is a financial loss for the owner. Another example from electronic commerce is *digital coins*, which are intended to be used like real cash. However, the coin objects are also represented just by bit strings, and thus are vulnerable to *double spending*, i.e., transferring the economic value expressed by the coin not merely once but repeatedly.

There have been various attempts to invent cryptographic countermeasures. Basically, these attempts aim to attach additional data to the instances of virtual objects in order to make them identifiable, or least distinguishable from each other. Additionally, where appropriate and achievable, the additional data can allow some *personalization* of the copies, i.e., a binding between a copy and a responsible individual. For instance, such a personalization might express a statement of the form "this copy has been produced for the person identified as follows: ...". Such attachments of any kind must be (at least) "unforgeable", "non-separable" and "non-erasable". Clearly, the enlarged objects can still be easily duplicated as bit strings. Then, however, the copies also carry the added information, thereby assisting efforts to detect and prosecute unauthorized duplication.

3.1.4 Horizontal Distribution

Horizontal distribution introduces further vulnerabilities, due mainly to *limited control* over remote sites. If a participant, or an administrator acting on behalf of a group of participants, wants to protect a local subsystem with respect to the local interests, then he ideally, and hopefully also actually, more or less has control over his site, its hardware and the virtual layers on top of it (clearly subject to all of the vulnerabilities discussed above, in particular those that are related to multi-user functionality). But beyond the physical borderline of the local site, the local administrator has no actual power over what is going on in the rest of the system. Without any provision such as agreed protocols, theoretically the rest of the system could be arbitrarily malicious, though in practice this will rarely be the case.

Additionally, while a local participant can locally observe incoming messages, in principle he cannot be sure about the actual *remote activities* that caused any observation. Thus a local participant usually has to rely on selective *trust* in his remote partners, the available a priori *knowledge* and the actual local observations in order to derive the best achievable *inferences* from these items. The vulnerabilities are obvious: the actual behavior could be any of the behaviors that, on the basis of these inferences, appear possible but indistinguishable, including an attacking behavior.

Attacking behavior might have numerous disguises and aim at various purposes. Most generally, beyond the borderline of local power and control, remote participants might *eavesdrop*, thereby challenging confidentiality, and they might *intercept*, *read*, *modify*, *redirect* or *replay* messages originating from other participants, or *forge* messages, or just *produce* their own messages at their discretion, thereby threatening all kinds of security interests. In particular, remote participants might try to produce large numbers of messages that cannot be processed in time with the available resources and thus cause an overload, resulting in the unavailability of sites for the normal functionality, i.e., from the sites' clients point of view, a *denial of service*.

Horizontal distribution often comes along with *openness* in various forms. For instance, the concrete forms of interaction are not fixed but dynamically negotiated, following some protocols that allow substantial variations. Vulnerabilities arise from the difficulty in analyzing the actual form at run time. Furthermore, the actual participants are often neither predetermined and registered beforehand nor otherwise known by identity. Accordingly, remote users appear as *strangers*, and local decisions about their local permissions must be negotiated on the basis of dynamically exhibited properties. The exhibition of such properties is vulnerable to *lies* and *forgeries*, among other attacks. As a countermeasure, digitally signed *credentials* issued by trusted participants have been proposed in order to guarantee that the claimed properties hold in reality. As usual, there might be trade-offs with other interests, for example, a request to show personal properties might be in conflict with the interest in confidentiality.

Table 3.4. Brief summary of features of computing and basic vulnerabilities

Feature	Basic vulnerability
virtuality	"virtual security" corrupted or circumvented in supporting layers
overall complexity	no global, complete understanding; unexpected interferences
universality, program-storing	imposed (malicious) "computable will"
processors without identity	masquerades
devices without personalization	masquerades, repudiated human–device binding
no data–program distinction	program (self-)modification (buffer overflow attacks)
rewritable memory	program and data modification
hardware complexity	hidden functionality, covert channels
user-to-device access path	exposed attack target
multi-user functionality, parallel processes and virtual memory	unintended interferences by resource sharing
abstract semantics of virtual layers	incorrect translation, non-captured but security-relevant aspects
"real-world" meaning not expressed	unperceived attack possibilities
seemingly restricted functionality	universality by simulation
(identifiable) virtual digital objects represented by bit string	unauthorized copying (double spending of coins)
limited control over remote sites	remote activities only derivable by inferences
indistinguishable remote behavior	eavesdropping, message manipulation and forgery, (malicious) message production

3.1.5 Personal Computing Devices

As discussed before, some basic vulnerabilities arise from the lack of personalization and from the unrestricted (in principle) possibilities of interference between components of a large computing system. As a countermeasure, some proposals have suggested that each participating individual should possess and employ a *personal computing device*. Such a device is no more than a universal, program-storing computer like any other piece of hardware, but it is in a small-size box suitable for being carried about everywhere. The basic idea is to *personalize* such a device for its owner, to concentrate in that device all of the data and functionality that are crucially needed to technically enforce the owner's security interests, and otherwise to restrict its functionality appropriately in order to reduce its vulnerabilities. Whenever there is a functional need, the personal computing device is connected to the rest of the overall system, say using the Internet. Otherwise, as a default, the device remains physically isolated.

In particular, such personal computing devices are useful for employing *cryptography*. The cryptographic *keys* to be kept secret are generated, stored and exploited for cryptographic operations only within the device; thus, the crucial secret information never explicitly flows beyond the borderline of the device. Moreover, once correctly initialized, the hierarchy of its virtual layers can be specially protected against unintended interference. Thus the owner has a reasonable assurance that the versions of the operating system and of application systems originally installed are indeed in operation, i.e., the corresponding programs have not been modified.

Clearly, the problems with personalization mentioned before also apply to personal computing devices. Moreover, these devices might still be subject to the general vulnerabilities and would then be a highly worthwhile target from the point of view of attackers.

3.2 Complexity of Computations

Security can be studied from the perspective of "attackers" who intentionally look for vulnerabilities in order to pursue malicious goals (or who accidently just perform operations affecting a vulnerability), or from the point of view of a "defender" who attempts to defend a computing system against *all possible* (malicious or accidental) exploitations of vulnerabilities. In the latter case, security has to deal somehow with "all possibilities". Then, in many cases, all possible information flows based on observed messages, and, especially, all possible actual behaviors of remote participants have to be determined, i.e., the defender has to derive *inferences*.

Unfortunately, however, it is well known that the general *inference problem* is undecidable and thus not fully tractable by computing. Consequently, as an implanted part of a computing system, any *technical security enforcement mechanism* is in principal restricted in its functionality. Hence, for practical purposes, explicit dynamic considerations of inferences are usually completely avoided by excluding beforehand crucial cases on the basis of a static analysis at design time, or the general notion of an inference is replaced by an appropriate computable approximation. In the latter case, we are often left with search problems, which might be practically infeasible, in the sense that their worst-case runtime complexity is exponential or even worse. Then again, static avoidance and dynamic approximation are the usual remedies.

At first glance, and actually in many concrete situations, the attacker is in a better situation: the attacker might be happy with deriving only some specific inferences that can actually be computed in particular cases. However, sometimes the attacker can also be faced with the general limitations of *computability* and *efficient computability*. In fact, a whole class of *cryptographic* security mechanisms is based on the limitations of efficient computability, which can be roughly outlined as follows. The defender prepares an appropriate provision that forces any potential attacker to computationally solve a practically strictly infeasible problem in order to be successful. Here, "practically strictly infeasible" is formalized by saying, roughly, that any *probabilistic Turing machine* is likely to need at least exponential time for any successfully attacking computation. It is important to note that such a condition expresses a lower bound for the problem under consideration. Unfortunately, so far computer science has provided only limited knowledge about lower bounds, and often the existence of a lower bound has only been convincingly conjectured but not mathematically proven.

3.3 Bibliographic Hints

Essentially, this chapter outlines the author's view of the common knowledge about computing technology. Individual readers might prefer to consult their favorite textbooks to find their own perspective, and thus we list just a few examples.

Tanenbaum/et al. [472, 473, 474, 475, 478] treat nearly the full range of the vertical layers and the horizontal distribution. The presentations of Hennessy/Patterson [254, 385], Tanenbaum [472] and Oberschelp/Vossen [375] concentrate on the lower layers. Tanenbaum/Woodhull [473, 474, 475], Silberschatz/Galvin/Gagne [447] and Stallings [461] provide an introduction to operating systems and their network components. Tanenbaum/van Steen [478] and Coulouris/Dollimore/Kindberg [143] survey distributed systems from a more general perspective. Date [152], Ullman/Widom [489] and Elmasri/Navathe [188] treat database management systems, as do Weikum/Vossen [497] and Lewis/Bernstein/Kifer [315], with an emphasis on transaction processing. General programming languages are captured by Bauer/Wössner [33], Sehti [440] and Mitchell [358], and programming methodologies and software engineering are considered by Gries [240] and Bjorner [83].

The more theoretically inclined fields of computability and computational complexity are surveyed from different points of view by Hopcroft/Motwani/Ullman [258], Rogers [413], Wegener [496], and Börger/Grädel/Gurewich [98].

Part Two
Fundamentals of Information Flow and Inference
Control

4 Messages, Inferences, Information and Knowledge

People employ computing systems for "information processing". Accordingly, in Chapter 2 we introduce the fundamental challenges of security in terms of *information flows*, which are based on *message transmissions* and *inferences*. More specifically, in Section 2.1 we outline and visualize two important patterns for treating security in computing systems: Subsection 2.1.2, with Figure 2.4, presents a general description of information flow based on message transmission and involving inferences, and Subsection 2.1.3, with Figure 2.5, provides a general framework for *inspection* and *exception handling*, involving inferences again. Seen from the point of view of *security interests*, as described in Section 2.2, the description in Subsection 2.1.2 is mainly used for enforcing *confidentiality* and related security interests, whereas the framework in Subsection 2.1.3 is used mainly for dealing with *integrity* and *authenticity* and related security interests, comprising, in particular, *availability*. Clearly, several interests might be important simultaneously, and thus the former and the latter pattern are often relevant at the same time.

In this chapter, we inspect more closely the relationships between four basic terms, namely *messages*, *inferences*, *information* and *knowledge*, and thereby lay the foundation for studying many dedicated security mechanisms within a general perspective. In particular, we present a general model for information flow control and *inference control*, suitable for various examples stemming from sequential or parallel programming and information systems.

4.1 A General Perspective

Roughly summarized, an *observer* of a *message* or other *event* achieves an *information gain* if that observer can convert his *a priori knowledge* into strictly increased *a posteriori knowledge* when adding the *meaning* of the message or event and making all possible *inferences*. Such a gain might remain merely *potential* or might be *actually* realized, depending on the fundamental computational capabilities and the available computational resources of the observer.

This general perspective resumes the visualization given in Figure 2.4 and is depicted more generally in Figure 4.1. The perspective emphasizes the crucial distinction between just observing a *message* or event on the one hand and gaining *information* on the other hand. The difference might depend on various circumstances, which include the extent of the following features:

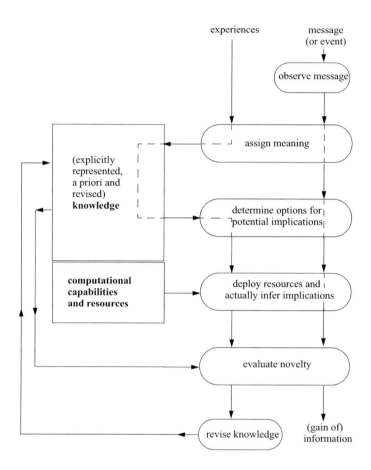

Fig. 4.1. A general perspective of messages, inferences, information and knowledge, and the impact of an observer's computational capabilities and resources

- The observer selects a *framework for reasoning* as the pertinent *communicative context* or *universe of discourse*.
- The observer interprets an observation within the selected framework, and thereby assigns a *meaning* to the observation.
- The observer has some *a priori knowledge* related to the meaning of the observation. For example, this knowledge might result from a common understanding of the situation considered, explicit declarations for the computing system involved, previous experiences or observations, or secrets deliberately distributed beforehand (as cryptographic keys).
- The observer employs a declarative notion of *logical implication* that is applicable to the selected framework, and thus he can potentially reason about the fictitious *implicational closure* of his a priori knowledge and the added meaning of

the observation. For example, if all items are formalized by first-order logic sentences, then the standard logical implication is defined in the Tarski style in terms of interpretations (models) of formulas. However, an observer might prefer to exploit other approaches as well, including those that deal with *probabilities*, *vagueness*, *uncertainty*, *preferences* and related notions.

- The observer *computationally infers* selected or even all implications, and evaluates actual inferences concerning *novelty*. In order to do so, the observer must *deploy* the *computational resources* available to him. However, the observer remains inevitably restricted by the fundamental limitations exhibited by computability theory and complexity theory. In particular, the following results are relevant: standard logical implication in first-order logic is an undecidable but still recursively enumerable (semi-decidable, recognizable) problem, and standard logical implication in propositional logic is closely related to the corresponding satisfiability problem, which is NP-complete and thus is expected to be solvable only in exponential time in the worst case.
- The observer treats the newly inferred implications as the *information gained* from his observation (and the other features used). Furthermore, the observer aims to appropriately *revise* his previous *knowledge* in order to reflect the recent gain, thereby getting *a posteriori knowledge*.

These and related features appear in various forms. Before considering specific instantiations, we shall add some further brief general comments.

First, the notion of *knowledge* allows the following complementary interpretations. An observer's knowledge determines those "worlds" that the observer sees as "possible", but all of them remain *indistinguishable* to him; complementarily expressed, the observer's knowledge leaves the observer *uncertain* about which one of the indistinguishable *possible worlds* is the actual *real world* (which is thought of as basically hidden and as revealing some of its aspects by observable messages or events). The first interpretation emphasizes that an observer might reason only with purely abstract ideas, whereas the second interpretation suggests the materialized existence of a "real world". The pertinent interpretation is irrelevant to most applications.

Second, there are two particularly interesting cases for the *information gain* based on an observation:

- The *a priori knowledge* and the *a posteriori knowledge* might be *identical*: the knowledge has remained invariant; the observer has learnt nothing novel; and the set of possible worlds has not changed.
- The *a posteriori knowledge* determines exactly one possible world: the knowledge has become complete, and the observer has learnt any property that is expressible in the selected framework.

Third, these cases, as well as further ones, might be identified in the layer of *potential* implications or in the layer of *actual* inferences. Clearly, provided that actual inferences are *correct*, an increase in *actual* knowledge must somehow be reflected in the potential layer. However, the converse is definitely not true, since it

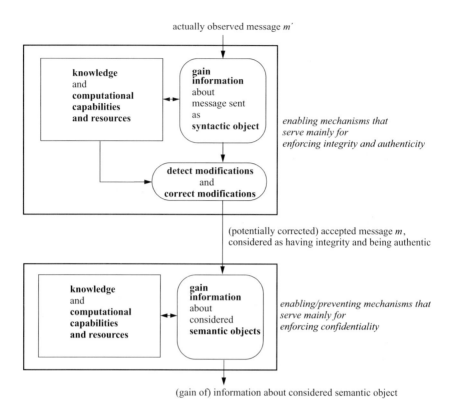

Fig. 4.2. Gaining information for inspection of syntactic message objects and exception handling, and for enabling/preventing information flow concerning semantic objects

might well happen that an increase in *potential* knowledge cannot be detected by means of *actual* inferences, owing to computational limitations. In fact, the security mechanisms of large parts of cryptography exploit just this insight of computing theory and complexity theory. It is important to note that in the context of *preventing* an unwanted gain of information, security mechanisms should be based on problems that are computationally infeasible for "nearly" *all* instances rather than for "worst cases" only. As a side note, the condition of correctness of inferences is sometimes referred to as assuming a *rational observer*, while abstracting from computational limitations, i.e., identifying potential implications with actual inferences, is sometimes denoted by assuming an *omnipotent observer*.

Finally, the general perspective depicted in Figure 4.1 suggests a further distinction. While an observed message *m* is seen as a *syntactic object* (an uninterpreted *bit string*), the assigned meaning *y* is treated as a *semantic object* (some interpreted item, such as a number). Then, the semantic object and the current knowledge together might contain some information about possibly other *semantic objects x* which are the real focus of a consideration.

The difference between the syntactic object and the assigned semantic object is particularly important in the context of enforcing *confidentiality* when using the general description of information flow. However, in the context of enforcing *integrity* and *authenticity* when using the general framework for inspection and exception handling, this difference is often deliberately not made, since the observer is wondering about the bit string actually sent (in contrast to the observed string) and thus wants to make inferences about it just as a string.

If an application requires the enforcement of both kinds of security interest, then both the general framework for inspection and exception handling and the general description of information flow are exploited, as roughly visualized in Figure 4.2. First, the observed message m' is inspected for possible modifications and – if applicable and achievable – corrected into an accepted message m, assumed to have integrity and be authentic. Subsequently, this message is evaluated for the information contained about some semantic objects under consideration.

In the first step, typically, the mechanisms used for gaining information are unconditionally *enabling*, i.e., all participants should be able to successfully achieve the relevant goals. In the second step, however, some distinction is typically necessary: the *designated receiver* should be provided with appropriate (a priori) knowledge beforehand in order to *enable* him to actually gain the pertinent information, whereas other *unauthorized* observers should be *prevented* from achieving this goal, by a lack of appropriate knowledge or sufficient computational capabilities and resources.

4.2 Simple Mathematical Models

For any instantiation of the general perspective, a deep and thorough investigation of its possible achievements requires a precise mathematical model. In this section, we discuss a variety of simple mathematical models and their potential for selected classes of applications:

- *Algebra*-oriented models introduce a first level of formalization, linking the (actual) gain of information to (algorithmically) solving sets of equations.
- *Logic*-oriented models provide further means to formally express sentences supposed to be true, or even to formally denote the modalities of an agent's knowledge or belief about such sentences. These models link the (actual) gain of information to (algorithmically) inferring logical implications. In this context, we see solving equations as a special case of determining implications. In both cases, some "implicit information" is converted into "explicit information".
- *Probability*-oriented models add the further aspect that alternatives might be weighted by their likelihood. Then, the (actual) gain of information is linked to (algorithmically) determining conditional a posteriori probability distributions.
- Clearly, there are further kinds of models, and advanced applications might demand sophisticated combinations of several features.

4.2.1 Inversion of Functions and Solving Equations

We start with an elementary algebra-oriented *functional* model that already allows several interesting special cases. Using this model, an application is mathematically described as follows:

- The *framework for reasoning* is given by a function $f : D \to R$ with a domain $D = dom(f)$ containing at least two elements, range $R = range(f)$, and an abstract assignment $x \to f(x)$ of function values to arguments. The observer is assumed to *know* this framework *a priori*, possibly except for some crucial *parameter* that a designated participant keeps secret in order to act as a distinguished observer.
- The observer receives a message m, seen as a *syntactic object* in the form of a bit string. Then the observer interprets m as a *semantic object* $y \in R$, generated by the sender by applying the function f to some semantic object $x \in D$ that is the real focus of the consideration.
- Accordingly, the message m is seen as possibly containing information about some (hidden) *semantic object* $x \in D$ such that $f(x) = y$.
- The observer aims at gaining this information, i.e., the observer tries to invert the function f for the given range value y; equivalently expressed, he attempts to find the set of solutions of the equation $f(z) = y$ for the unknown variable z.

(Everywhere) Injective Functions. Suppose that for each $y \in R$ there exists a unique $z \in D$ such that $f(z) = y$. The sought information is then an immediate implication of the framework known a priori and the interpretation of the observed message as a function value. Thus, in principle, the observer can *potentially* gain *complete* information about the hidden object. However, the *actual* gain depends on the observer's possibilities to actually compute the unique solution of the given equation.

Nowhere Injective Functions. Suppose that for each $y \in R$ there exist at least two different domain values $z_1 \in D$ and $z_2 \in D$ such that $f(z_1) = f(z_2) = y$. Then, even in principle, the observer cannot gain the sought information completely, since under the given assumptions, the observer cannot *distinguish* the candidate domain values. However, the observer can still possibly gain some *partial information* as follows.

The observer's *a priori knowledge* includes the fact that the hidden object x must be an element of the domain D. On the basis of his interpreted observation, his *a posteriori* knowledge comprises the implication that

$$x \in \{ z \mid f(z) = y \} \subseteq D.$$

If the inclusion is strict, i.e., $\{ z \mid f(z) = y \} \neq D$, then the observer has *potentially* gained novel *partial* information. For, in principle, on the basis of his observation, the observer can now *exclude* the possibility that the hidden object x is an element of the difference set $D \setminus \{ z \mid f(z) = y \}$. Again, the *actual partial* gain depends on the observer's possibilities to actually compute the relevant items.

Arbitrary Functions. In general, a function might be neither everywhere injective nor nowhere injective. The potential for gaining information then depends on the inversion properties of the range element $y \in R$ considered, case by case. More specifically, given the interpretation $y \in R$ of an observed message, the observer might first aim at determining the *pre-image* $\{ z \mid f(z)=y \}$. There are then four cases:

- *Complete* (potential) information gain: the pre-image contains exactly one element x, i.e.,

  card $\{ z \mid f(z)=y \} = 1$, and accordingly $\{ z \mid f(z)=y \} = \{x\}$.

- *Partial* (potential) information gain: the pre-image contains at least two (indistinguishable) elements but does not comprise the full domain D, i.e.,

  card $\{ z \mid f(z)=y \} > 1$ and $D \setminus \{ z \mid f(z)=y \} \neq \emptyset$.

- *No* information gain: the pre-image is equal to the full domain D, i.e.,

  $\{ z \mid f(z)=y \} = D$.

  In this case, the interpreted observation does not narrow the a priori knowledge about the domain D of the function f.

- *Framework not applicable*: the pre-image is empty, i.e.,

  $\{ z \mid f(z)=y \} = \emptyset$.

  In this case, the interpreted observation does not fully fit the framework. This might be an interesting insight in its own right, constituting a gain of information for a different framework, but not for the framework modeled by the function f.

Again, the *actual* gain depends on the observer's possibilities of actually computing the relevant items. Basically, this means that effective techniques and efficient algorithms to *solve* the *equation* considered are crucial for an actual information gain.

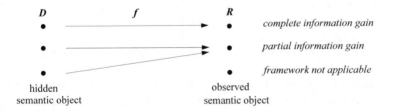

Fig. 4.3. A framework of reasoning, exemplifying three cases regarding information gain

Figure 4.3 depicts a simple example where all cases occur, except the third one of "no information gain" that happens iff the function considered is *constant*. In the following we present several more concrete examples, taken from group theory, number theory and the theory of relational databases.

First, we consider a nontrivial *group* $(G, \bullet, e)$, where G is the underlying set of group elements, $\bullet : G \times G \to G$ is the binary *group operation*, and e is the neutral element. The group inversion function is denoted by

$$^{\text{inverse}} : G \to G, \text{ where } x^{\text{inverse}} \bullet x = e \text{ for all } x \in G.$$

The group properties ensure the *solvability of equations*: every equation of the form $k \bullet x = y$, where two of the items are given, has a unique solution for the third item. Observing the result $y \in G$ of an application of the group operation enables a *partial information* gain about the arguments, since

$$G \times G \setminus \{ (k,x) \mid k \bullet x = y \} \neq \varnothing;$$

in fact, the pre-image of y contains exactly as many elements as G.

If we fix the first (or, similarly, the second) argument of the group operation to some parameter $k \in G$, we obtain a family of functions, each of the form $\bullet_k : G \to G$, where $\bullet_k(x) = k \bullet x$. Now suppose that an observer sees the result $y \in G$ of an application of a parameterized function. We can then distinguish two cases. If the observer knows the pertinent parameter k, then he can gain *complete information* about the remaining argument, since $\bullet_k(x) = y$ implies that

$$k^{\text{inverse}} \bullet y = k^{\text{inverse}} \bullet (k \bullet x) = (k^{\text{inverse}} \bullet k) \bullet x = e \bullet x = x.$$

Otherwise, if the observer does not know the pertinent parameter k, we have

$$\{ x \mid \text{there exists } k \in G : k \bullet x = y \} = G,$$

and thus the observer gains *no information* about the remaining argument. The various situations are shown in Figure 4.4 for the group based on addition modulo 3.

	remaining argument x		
	0	**1**	**2**
0	⓪	1	2
parameter k **1**	1	2	⓪
2	2	⓪	1

observation: $y = 0$
pre-image: $\{(0,0),(2,1),(1,2)\}$
remaining argument
for known parameter $k=1$: 2
set of possible remaining arguments
for unknown parameter: $\{0,1,2\}$

Fig. 4.4. Options for information gain based on observing the result of a group operation

Many *cryptographic mechanisms* exploit an appropriate group setting. In particular, the additive and multiplicative structures on *residue classes* modulo some cardinal n are used, where the *additive structure* forms a group for any modulus, whereas the *multiplicative structure* does so only for a *prime* modulus. Note that for $n = 2$ the additive structure coincides with the Boolean XOR operation, i.e., for all $k, x \in \{0,1\}$, we have $k + x \bmod 2 = k$ XOR x.

On the basis of such structures, more advanced cryptographic constructions aim at providing families of parameterized functions that are injective and additionally have a property called *one-way with trapdoor*. This property says roughly that the values of the function can be efficiently computed but the *pre-images* can not, except when the observer knows the pertinent parameter that serves as the "trap-door". Hence, knowing this parameter enables an *actual* complete information gain, whereas, otherwise, the complete information gain remains *potential*. The *RSA functions* $RSA_{p,q,d}^{n,e}$ and the *ElGamal functions* $EG_a^{p,g,A}$ are well-known examples.

Second, we outline a construction to *control* the "amount" of information gain enabled. Intuitively, an observer can gain "much" information if the pre-images of observed semantic objects are *small*; at the best, these are singleton sets for an injective function. The observer can gain only "a small amount of" information if the pre-images are *large*; at the worst, for a constant function, there is one pre-image that is identical to the domain. Hence, if a designer wants to enable an infor-mation gain that corresponds to pre-images of some fixed cardinality c, if this is inevitable with some exceptions, then he has to define a partition of the domain D all classes of which have this cardinality c, and to determine a function that induces such a partition by means of its pre-images.

This task is easily done as follows, for example. Let $D = \{0,1,\ldots,m\}$ such that $c \cdot n = m+1$, and define $f : \{0,1,\ldots,m\} \rightarrow \{0,1,\ldots,n-1\}$ by $f(x) = x \bmod n$. Then each pre-image looks like $\{a, a+n, a+2 \cdot n, \ldots, a+(c-1) \cdot n\}$. Figure 4.5 shows an example for $m+1 = 12$, $n = 3$ and $c = 4$.

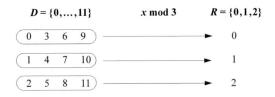

Fig. 4.5. Control of information gain by means of the cardinality of pre-images

Finally, we briefly mention an example from the field of *relational databases*. We suppose a *database schema* that is declared by two relation schemes $R(A,B)$ and $S(B,C)$, where R and S denote relation symbols, and A, B and C denote attributes (column names). A *query* is then syntactically given by a *relational expression* over the schema, and the semantics of a query is a function that maps *database instances* of the form (r,s), where r and s are relations fitting the schema, onto some output relation t. Figure 4.6 visualizes the schema, an instance and the query results for the relational expressions

R join S, project$_A$ (R) and project$_B$ (R),

for computing the *natural join* of the instance relations r and s, and the *projections* of the instance relation r on the attributes A and B.

One can easily observe that in general the *natural join* is not injective, owing to *dangling tuples* that do not find a matching tuple in the other relation. Accordingly, seeing the output relation enables only a *partial* information gain about the (stored

r	A	B		s	B	C		r joins s	A	B	C		project$_A(r)$	A		project$_B(r)$	B
	a	b_1			b_1	c			a	b_1	c			a			b_1
	a	b_2															b_2

Fig. 4.6. A relational database with query results, exemplifying a dangling tuple and duplicate removal

but kept hidden) instance. However, if the mutual *inclusion dependencies (referential constraints)* for the join attribute B are enforced as declared invariants, then dangling tuples cannot occur, the join becomes injective and a *complete* information gain is enabled.

Regarding the *projections*, in general they are not injective either. One reason for non-injectivity is the occurrence of *duplicates* that are removed before outputting the result. However, if a *key constraint* for the projection attribute B (a *functional dependency* $B \rightarrow A$) is enforced as a declared invariant and, additionally, the corresponding attribute value assignment is known as part of the framework, then duplicates cannot occur and the original relation r (but not the relation s) can be uniquely reconstructed from an observed projection result. Thus, a *complete* information gain about the projected relation is then enabled.

4.2.2 Projections of Relations

The elementary functional model can be restated as a special case of a more general *relational model*. The restatement is based on identifying a function $f: D \rightarrow R$ with its associated graph

$$F = \{ (x, f(x)) \mid x \in D \} \subseteq D \times R,$$

which is a binary relation between elements of D and R. The generalization results from considering an arbitrary relation. Using the generalized relational model, an application is mathematically described as follows:

- The *framework for reasoning* is given by a relation

  $Rel \subseteq D_1 \times D_2 \times \ldots \times D_k$ over some universe $U = D_1 \times D_2 \times \ldots \times D_k$,

  and an abstract assignment

  $(x_1, x_2, \ldots, x_k) \rightarrow \chi_{Rel}(x_1, x_2, \ldots, x_k) \in \{false, true\}$

  of Boolean values to arguments for the associated characteristic function χ_{Rel}. Furthermore, two *projections* of the relation are identified: one projection $proj_{In}(Rel)$, containing at least two elements and corresponding to the *domain* of a function, specified by an index set $In \subseteq \{1, 2, \ldots, k\}$, and another projection $proj_{Out}(Rel)$, corresponding to the *range* of a function, specified by an index set $Out \subseteq \{1, 2, \ldots, k\}$. The observer is assumed to *know* this framework *a priori*, possibly except some secretly kept *parameter*.

- Additionally, the observer might have the further *a priori knowledge* that only tuples of some specific subset *Embed* $\subseteq U$ can actually occur. Thus the framework could be refined by considering *Rel* $\cap$ *Embed* rather than just *Rel*.
- The observer receives a message m, seen as a *syntactic object*, in the form of a bit string. Then the observer interprets m as a *semantic object* y that is supposed to be an element of the projection $proj_{Out}(Rel)$. Furthermore, the sender is assumed to have generated y as the *Out* projection of some tuple $t \in Rel$. The real focus of the consideration is then the *In* projection x of that tuple t.
- Accordingly, the message m is seen as possibly containing information about some (hidden) *semantic object* $x \in proj_{In}(Rel) \cap \{ z \mid (z,y) \in proj_{In,Out}(Rel) \}$.
- The observer aims at gaining this information, i.e., the observer tries to determine the *In pre-image* $\{ z \mid (z,y) \in proj_{In,Out}(Rel) \}$ of the relation *Rel* for the given element y of the *Out* projection.

Again, given the interpretation $y \in proj_{Out}(Rel)$ of the observation, there are several cases:

- *Complete* (potential) information gain: the *In* pre-image contains exactly one element x, i.e.,

  card $\{ z \mid (z,y) \in proj_{In,Out}(Rel) \} = 1$,

  and accordingly

  $\{ z \mid (z,y) \in proj_{In,Out}(Rel) \} = \{x\}$.

- *Partial* (potential) information gain: the *In* pre-image contains at least two (indistinguishable) elements but does not comprise the full *In* projection $proj_{In}(Rel)$ of the relation R, i.e.,

  card $\{ z \mid (z,y) \in proj_{In,Out}(Rel) \} > 1$ and

  $proj_{In}(Rel) \setminus \{ z \mid (z,y) \in proj_{In,Out}(Rel) \} \neq \varnothing$.

- *No* information gain: the *In* pre-image is equal to the full *In* projection $proj_{In}(Rel)$, i.e.,

  $\{ z \mid (z,y) \in proj_{In,Out}(Rel) \} = proj_{In}(Rel)$.

  In this case, the interpreted observation does not narrow the a priori knowledge about the *In* projection of the relation *Rel*.

- *Framework not applicable*: the *In* pre-image is empty, i.e.,

  $\{ z \mid (z,y) \in proj_{In,Out}(Rel) \} = \varnothing$.

  In this case, the interpreted observation does not fully fit the framework. This might be an interesting insight in its own right, constituting a gain of information for a different framework, but not for the framework modeled by the relation *Rel*.

As in the functional model, the *actual* gain depends on the observer's possibilities to actually compute the relevant items.

An important example of the relational model is about expressing the semantics of a *programming language* in terms of relationships between initial and final program states, and investigating the information gain about selected parts of the initial state enabled by observing some aspects of the final state. More specifically, but grossly simplified, we suppose that the *syntax* of the programming language allows one to specify a well-formed *program P* with a fixed set of static variables *Var*, each of which has the same type *Value*. Thus, in particular, a *state σ* of a *program execution* describes a current assignment of values to variables, i.e., $\sigma \in State = Value^{Var}$. The set of states can also be seen as a cartesian product $Value \times Value \times \ldots \times Value$, where each component corresponds to one of the variables in *Var*. Then, the *semantics sem(P)* of the program *P* is given as a binary relation on states, i.e, by

$$sem(P) \subseteq State \times State = (Value \times \ldots \times Value) \times (Value \times \ldots \times Value).$$

An element $(\sigma_{init}, \sigma_{fin})$ of this relation indicates that the initial state σ_{init} can be transformed into the final state σ_{fin} by a *possibly nondeterministic* or *probabilistic* execution of the program *P*, assumed always to be halting.

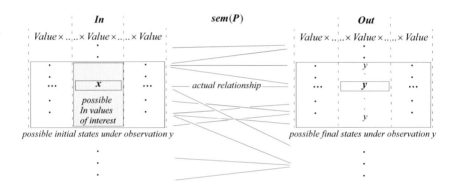

Fig. 4.7. Information gain about possible *In* values of interest as a result of an observation of an *Out* value *y*, based on the semantics of a program *P*

The further formalization is straightforward, as visualized in Figure 4.7. The *aspect* of an observation about some part of a *final state* is described by the set *Out* $\subseteq Var$ of accessible variables, corresponding to specific components of the *second* half of the cartesian product, and an *actual* observation is given by the observed assignment of values to those variables, i.e., by some

$$y \in proj_{Out}(sem(P)).$$

Correspondingly, the *selected parts* of interest about the *initial state* are described by a set *In* $\subseteq Var$ of variables, corresponding to specific components of the *first* half of the cartesian product. With this notation, the task of gaining information about the value *initially* assigned to these components amounts to determining the possible *In* values of interest, i.e.,

$$\{ z \mid (z,y) \in proj_{In,Out}(sem(P)) \}.$$

In slightly more general terms, given the semantics of the program, the task is basically to transform an (observed) *postcondition*, expressed in terms of an *Out* value, into a *weakest precondition* about *In* values of the (hidden) initial state.

Many further examples arise from *coding theory*, which deals with *error detection* and *error correction* in the *data layer* and thus with the *integrity* of messages. Accordingly, the distinction between an observed message and its intended meaning is not made, as depicted in the upper part of Figure 4.2.

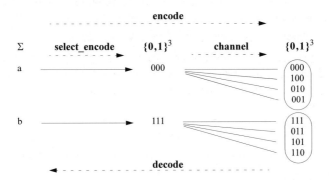

Fig. 4.8. Decoding as information gain about a message sent as a syntactic object, enabled by encoding by means of adding redundancy in order to prepare for an assumed channel behavior

Figure 4.8 shows a simple situation, which enables *error correction*, understood as *information gain* about the (hidden) actually sent message based on the (visible) received one. Suppose a sender wishes to communicate one of the symbols of the alphabet $\Sigma = \{a,b\}$ over a channel that may distort a message but only in a predictably limited way. The prediction postulates the *1-bit error assumption*: whenever it transmits a bit string of length 3, the channel erroneously modifies at most one bit. This is formalized by a relation $channel \subseteq \{0,1\}^3 \times \{0,1\}^3$.

Rather than communicating a symbol directly, the sender first employs a redundancy-adding function $select\_encode: \Sigma \to \{0,1\}^3$ that makes the two function values differ in all three bits. In more general terms, by defining

$select\_encode(a) = 000$ and $select\_encode(b) = 111$,

we ensure that any pair of function values has a *Hamming distance* of 3. When, now, either 000 or 111 is transmitted according to the postulated relation *channel*, then as a composed effect of *select_encode* and *channel*, the observer sees either an element of the 1-bit neighborhood of 000 or an element of the 1-bit neighborhood of 111.

In more general terms, the composition of *select_encode* and *channel* is captured by the set-valued function $encode: \Sigma \to \wp\{0,1\}^3$. The set values of *encode* form a partition of $\{0,1\}^3$ into non-empty, pairwise disjoint neighborhoods of those elements that are distinguished as values of *select_encode*. Information gain considered as error correction is then performed by decoding any element of a neighborhood into its distinguished element, i.e., the function $decode : \{0,1\}^3 \to \Sigma$ is derived as $decode(y) = x$, for any observable bit string $y \in encode(x)$.

4.2.3 Determination of Equivalence Classes

So far, the underlying alternatives for the semantic item under consideration have been treated as identifiable objects. In some applications, however, the interest of an observer might be directed toward some specific *properties* of the semantic items rather than on their *identity*. In this case, all objects that share the same properties can be seen as *equivalent* and, accordingly, the observer's goal might only be a gain of information about the *equivalence class* of the hidden semantic object.

4.2.4 Impact of Message Sequences

An observer might receive a *sequence* of messages, all of which are supposed to refer to the *same* semantic object x. From each individual message, the observer can possibly gain some partial information about this object. Additionally, the observer can try to *combine* the information gains in order to determine the hidden object x as precisely as possible. In order to exemplify the impact of combining the information gained from a message sequence, we shall only sketch, for the sake of simplicity, a straightforward extension of the elementary functional model. Using the resulting model, an application can be mathematically described as follows:

- The *framework for reasoning* is given by a sequence of functions $f_i : D \to R$ with a domain $D = dom(f_i)$ containing at least two elements, range $R = range(f_i)$, and abstract assignments $x \to f_i(x)$ of function values to arguments. The observer is assumed to *know* this framework *a priori*, except for some secretly kept *parameters*.
- The observer receives a sequence of messages m_i, seen as *syntactic objects*, in the form of bit strings. Then the observer interprets m_i as a *semantic object* $y_i \in R$, generated by the sender by applying the function f_i to a single semantic object $x \in D$ that is the real focus of the consideration.
- Accordingly, the messages m_i are seen as possibly containing information about some (hidden) *semantic object* $x \in D$ such that $f_i(x) = y_i$.
- The observer aims at gaining this information, i.e., the observer attempts to find the set of solutions of the *set* of equations $f_i(z) = y_i$ for the unknown variable z.

Again, there are several cases. If the set of equations has a unique solution, then the observer (potentially) gains *complete* information. If there are at least two (indistinguishable) solutions but the set of solutions is strictly included in the domain D, then the observer (potentially) gains *partial* information. Otherwise, if there is no solution at all, the framework is *not applicable*.

These cases can easily be rephrased in terms of equivalence classes, as explained in the following. Intuitively, each function f_i is assumed to capture some *property* of the elements in the underlying domain D. Formally, each function f_i determines an *equivalence relation* $\sim_i \subseteq D \times D$, defined by $(z_1, z_2) \in \sim_i$ iff $f_i(z_1) = f_i(z_2)$. Accordingly, the domain D is partitioned into disjoint *equivalence classes*, which are just the non-empty pre-images of elements in the range R:

$$Par(f_i) := \{ \, \{ z \mid f_i(z) = y \} \mid y \in R \, \} \setminus \{ \emptyset \} \subseteq \wp D.$$

Combining the information gains from the semantic objects y_i then means taking the intersection of the corresponding classes, i.e., determining

$$\{ z \mid f_1(z) = y_1 \} \cap \dots \cap \{ z \mid f_n(z) = y_n \}$$

after n observations. A *complete* (potential) information gain then corresponds to an intersection that is a singleton set $\{x\}$ containing the unique solution of the equations involved. And a *partial* (potential) information gain corresponds to an intersection containing at least two elements but not the full domain.

A further rephrasing indicates that dealing with sequences of messages just means exploiting the elementary functional model for an appropriately composed function, namely the product function $f = (f_1, f_2, \dots, f_n)$, which is defined componentwise by

$$f(z) = (f_1(z), f_2(z), \dots, f_n(z)).$$

A pre-image of this product function is just the intersection of the pre-images of the components. Accordingly, the best case (concerning information gain), of the product function f being *injective*, is reflected by the fact that the (classwise-taken) intersection of the partitions $Par(f_1), Par(f_2), \dots, Par(f_n)$ contains only singleton sets. And the worst case, of the product function f being *constant* (and thus providing no information gain at all), is characterized by the fact that the intersection of the partitions just contains D as a single element.

As a kind of repeated warning, we emphasize that *actual* information gains depend on the observer's possibilities to actually compute the relevant items, in this case the intersections of the pertinent pre-images. And we restate that the skill of solving sets of equations is crucial.

In a simple example from number theory, the first function f_1 is the *integer division* by a fixed cardinal n, $f_1(x) = x$ div n, and the second function f_2 is the attached *remainder function*, $f_2(x) = x$ mod n. Each cardinal x can then be reconstructed from the two function values by means of $x = (x$ div $n) \cdot n + x$ mod n. Figure 4.9 visualizes this setting for the divisor $n = 3$ and the domain $\{ 0, 1, \dots, 11 \}$: the intersection of any two pre-images from the first and the second function contains exactly one element.

Another well-known class of examples from algebra arises when observations yield a *set of linear equations*, where all operations are done in a field. In particular, but not exclusively, statistical databases and cryptography exploit such settings. A more concrete case is sketched in Subsection 2.1.2; more detailed cases are presented in, for instance, Section 5.5 and Section 16.3.

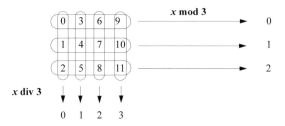

Fig. 4.9. Observation of integer division and remainder enables complete information gain

A further example is taken from the field of relational databases: a first non-injective query (a view) can be *complemented* by another query such that both queries together are injective. As a consequence, an observer seeing the answers to both queries can gain *complete* information about the stored database instance.

4.2.5 Implications in Classical Logics

In algebra-oriented models, the framework of reasoning is typically specified in a semi-formal style, based on commonly used conventions about the underlying algebraic structures. In particular, the supposedly known description of an abstract assignment of function values to arguments usually relies on some informally given assumptions. A *classical logic* provides means to fully formalize a framework of reasoning, but also requires one to do so. Thus, on the one hand a classical logic is powerful and flexible, but on the other hand it might turn out to be painful to handle. In the following, we roughly outline the logical approach.

The *syntax* of a logic specifies which *atomic formulas* can be formed, and how to inductively compose further formulas, typically by using *propositional operators* such as "and", "or" and "not", or *first-order operators* such as "for all x" and "there exists x". The *semantics* of a logic is defined in terms of interpretations. Each interpretation assigns a truth value, either `false` or `true`, to every atomic formula. This assignment is then inductively extended to those composed formulas that are considered as sentences (which do not contain a free occurrence of a variable). The *pragmatics* of a logic deals with how to express possible facts of a "real world" by sentences of the logic. Figure 4.10 visualizes how a logic is exploited to set up a framework for reasoning and to gain information from observations.

In this figure, for the sake of simplicity, we assume something like a given "reality", a fragment of which is seen as the "world" we are interested in. Basically, this world is given by a set of "actual facts", i.e., by what is really the case. We might think about other facts that do not hold in reality. The syntax of a logic should be expressive enough to denote each possible fact by a sentence, guided by the pragmatics. Furthermore, there is a (human) observer who somehow knows certain "actual facts", by "experience" or by "observations".

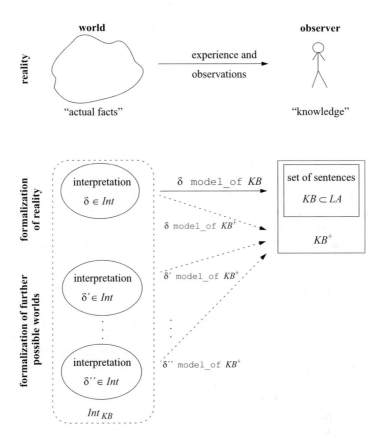

Fig. 4.10. A logic-oriented framework for reasoning

The observer's knowledge is then mathematically represented by a *knowledge base KB*, which is a subset of the "language" *LA* consisting of all well-formed *sentences*. Thus some or even all "actual facts" of the "world" in "reality" are captured by pragmatically appropriate sentences. In such a representation, the *explicit* knowledge is fully formalized, i.e., there are no further assumptions. However, there might be further implicit knowledge. The knowledge base *KB* uniquely determines its *implicational closure KB$^+$* consisting of all logical implications of *KB*. Thus the observer's *implicit* knowledge is represented by *KB$^+$*. In general, there might be many different knowledge bases that share the same implicational closure, and (algorithmically) inferring implications might turn out to be computationally infeasible.

The *syntactic* representation of an observer's knowledge as a set of sentences *KB* is complemented by a corresponding *semantic* representation. First, under suitable assumptions, the "world" in *reality* is captured by a *distinguished interpretation* $\delta \in Int$, where *Int* denotes the class of all *interpretations*. This interpretation δ

assigns the truth value `true` to exactly those sentences that pragmatically correspond to the "actual facts", and assigns `false` to all other sentences (those that correspond to possible facts that do not hold in "reality"). In this way, all sentences of
the observer's syntactic knowledge base *KB* are assumed to be *semantically true*
under the distinguished interpretation δ, or, equivalently expressed, the interpretation δ is seen as a *model* of the set of sentences *KB*, i.e., δ `model_of` *KB*, and thus
also δ `model_of` KB^+. This assumption also entails that the knowledge base *KB* is
consistent.

Second, in general, there are further interpretations, examples of which are
denoted by δ′ and δ″ in the figure, that are models of KB^+ as well but do not
exactly capture the "world" in "reality" and thus are essentially different from δ.
However, from the observer's point of view they appear as equally *possible*, since
the available knowledge base *KB* does not allow the observer to *distinguish*
between the intended interpretation δ and the further ones that make KB^+ true.

This kind of ambiguity should not arise if the observer's knowledge base *KB* is
pragmatically complete, i.e., it captures all "actual facts" of the "world" in "reality": *KB* should then be *syntactically complete* (in the sense that for all sentences,
KB^+ contains either the sentence or its negation) and *semantically complete* (in the
sense that all models of KB^+ are essentially the same, up to isomorphisms). Otherwise, some "actual fact" will not be reflected in the formalization, leading on the
syntactic side to a sentence such that neither the sentence nor its negation is logically implied by the knowledge base, and on the semantic side to essentially different models of the knowledge base that assign different truth values to some
sentence.

Summarizing and further exploiting a classical logic-oriented model, we may
describe an application mathematically as follows:

- The *framework for reasoning* is given by a logic and a consistent but not yet
  complete knowledge base $KB \subset LA$ of the selected logic. The observer is
  assumed to *know* this framework *a priori* (possibly, but rarely in practice, except
  for some secretly kept parts).
- The observer receives a message *m*, seen as a *syntactic object* in the form of a
  bit string. The observer then interprets *m* as a *sentence* $y \in LA$, corresponding to
  an "actual fact" of the "world" in "reality".
- Accordingly, the message *m* is seen as possibly containing information about
  this (hidden) world that is (conceptually) formalized by the distinguished interpretation δ.
- The observer aims at gaining this information, i.e., in semantic terms, the
  observer tries to determine the class of interpretations that are a model of his a
  priori knowledge base *KB* and the given sentence *y*. Equivalently, in syntactic
  terms, the observer aims at determining the implicational closure of *KB* and *y*.
  Clearly, instead of seeking information about the full distinguished interpretation or the full implicational closure, respectively, we could restrict our attention
  to some aspect of the respective semantic or syntactic item.

Similarly to the algebra-oriented models, given the knowledge base KB and the interpretation $y \in LA$ of the observation, there are several cases:

- *Complete* (potential) information gain: there is a unique interpretation δ, up to isomorphisms, that is a model of $KB \cup \{y\}$, and this interpretation is then the distinguished one. Equivalently, $KB \cup \{y\}$ is now *syntactically complete*.
- *Partial* (potential) information gain: there are still at least two essentially different (but indistinguishable) interpretations δ' and δ'' that are a model of $KB \cup \{y\}$; however, there is also an interpretation δ''' that is a model of KB but not of $KB \cup \{y\}$, and thus this model has been *excluded* from being the distinguished one.
- *No* information gain: any interpretation that is a model of KB is a model of $KB \cup \{y\}$; equivalently, the knowledge base KB *logically implies* the added sentence y. In this case, the interpreted observation does not narrow the a priori knowledge.
- *Framework not applicable*: there is no model at all for $KB \cup \{y\}$; equivalently, $KB \cup \{y\}$ is *inconsistent*. In this case, the interpreted observation does not fully fit the framework. This might be an interesting insight in its own right, constituting a gain of information for a different framework.

Again, the *actual* gain depends on the observer's possibilities to actually compute the relevant items. Basically, this means that effective techniques and efficient algorithms to infer the *logical implications* considered are crucial for an actual information gain.

As a simple example, we shall formalize the *addition* for residue classes modulo 2, or, equivalently, the Boolean *XOR* operation, that yields the result

$$y = k + x \bmod 2 = k \text{ XOR } x.$$

We first introduce *propositional atoms* (*symbols*) of mnemonic form v_i, where v is either the first argument k, the second argument x or the result y, and i is a domain/range value, i.e., either 0 or 1. Assigning `true` to the atom v_i is intended to mean that "variable v has value i". This meaning is then captured by an a priori knowledge base KB with two *propositional formulas*. The first formula represents the function table:

$$[[k\_0 \land x\_0] \Rightarrow y\_0] \land [[k\_0 \land x\_1] \Rightarrow y\_1] \land$$
$$[[k\_1 \land x\_0] \Rightarrow y\_1] \land [[k\_1 \land x\_1] \Rightarrow y\_0] .$$

The second formula ensures that each variable has a unique value:

$$[k\_0 \Leftrightarrow \neg k\_1] \quad \land \quad [x\_0 \Leftrightarrow \neg x\_1] \quad \land \quad [y\_0 \Leftrightarrow \neg y\_1] .$$

If an observer sees a function value, then he adds the corresponding atom to the knowledge base and determines the pertinent logical implications. For instance, after the value $y = 1$ has been observed, the atom y_1 is added, and then the updated knowledge base $KB \cup \{y\_1\}$ logically implies $[k\_0 \land x\_1] \lor [k\_1 \land x\_0]$.

If the observer also knows the parameter k, then, for example, the atom k_1 may be added as well, and the updated knowledge base $KB \cup \{y\_1, k\_1\}$ logically implies x_0, and thus the observer gains complete information about the hidden second argument.

A slightly more involved example deals with the semantics of a *programming language* in terms of *preconditions* and *postconditions*. Consider the following program fragment, where all variables have type $\{0,1\}$ with addition modulo 2:

```
y := a + x;
if y=1 then z := 0 else z := 1
```

In an execution, we distinguish three points of time, namely *pre* (before the first statement), *med* (after the first statement but before the second statement) and *post* (after the second statement). Accordingly, extending the preceding example, we introduce variables of mnemonic form v_{time}_i, where *time* denotes either *pre*, *med* or *post*. The a priori knowledge base *KB* then contains all formulas needed to express the function table and the uniqueness conditions.

If, for instance, an observer then sees the value 1 of the variable z at time *post*, the *postcondition* z_{post}_1 holds. Assuming the semantics expressed in terms of logic as well, the a priori knowledge base, the semantics of the second statement and the postcondition together logically imply the intermediate assertion y_{med}_0. In turn, the a priori knowledge base, the semantics of the first statement and the intermediate assertion together logically imply the *precondition*

$$[a_{pre}\_0 \wedge x_{pre}\_0] \quad \vee \quad [a_{pre}\_1 \wedge x_{pre}\_1],$$

which constitutes the gain of information from the postcondition.

4.2.6 Logics of Knowledge and Belief

A classical logic provides a syntax and a corresponding semantics to fully formalize a framework of reasoning. However, we still speak about the "knowledge" of an observer on a meta-level: this knowledge is captured by informally considering a set of sentences as representing it, or, equivalently, by referring to the corresponding set of interpretations. There are no dedicated syntactic features to easily express that, for example, "observer A knows y" within such a logic.

Moreover, besides knowledge, we might also want to express the "belief" of an observer. Roughly outlined, the difference between knowledge and belief is the following: what is "known" is supposed to be "actually true", whereas what is only "believed" might turn out to be "actually false".

Modal logics of *knowledge* and *belief* are designed to express the specific knowledge and the specific belief, respectively, of a particular observer. Basically, the *syntax* is extended by *modal operators* for expressing statements of the form "observer A knows y" and "observer A believes y", respectively, for each identified observer A. The *semantics* is revised accordingly: instead of considering each interpretation individually, *Kripke structures* are employed.

A *Kripke structure* comprises a whole family of interpretations and, additionally, for each identified observer A, there is a specific binary relation R_A on these interpretations, called A's *indistinguishability* or *possibility relation*. The basic intuitive idea behind the relation R_A is that it captures the fact that observer A cannot "distinguish" any two R_A-related interpretations, or that observer A holds any two R_A-related interpretations to be "equally possible" from his specific point of view.

Given a Kripke structure and that an interpretation δ of it has been fixed, a modal expression of the form "observer A knows y" or "observer A believes y", respectively, has a truth value `true` assigned inductively to it iff all interpretations δ' that are R_A-related to δ assign `true` to the (inductively simpler) expression y. The difference between knowledge and belief is then reflected semantically by imposing different properties on the *indistinguishability relations*: for knowledge, these relations must be *reflexive, symmetric* and *transitive*, whereas for belief, they must be only *serial, transitive* and *euclidean*.

The distinction between knowledge and belief can also be reflected syntactically by specifying appropriate axioms. For example, the property of reflexivity corresponds to an axiom (or axiom scheme) which requires that any implicational formula expressing "if observer A knows y, then y" is always true. This axiom is usually referred to as ensuring *true knowledge*. In contrast, the property of seriality corresponds to a weaker axiom (or axiom scheme) which requires that any formula expressing "observer A does not believe both y and *not y*" is always true. This axiom is usually referred to as ensuring *consistent belief*.

As on the semantic side, knowledge and belief also share some syntactically expressed axioms. For example, the properties of symmetry and transitivity, and of being euclidean, respectively, lead to the following requirement: any implicational formula expressing "if observer A does not know/believe y, then that observer knows/believes that he does so" is always true. This axiom is usually referred to as capturing *negative introspection*.

The advantage of fully formalizing knowledge or belief, or several variants of such modalities, is that any item of interest is then syntactically expressed and therefore prepared for algorithmic treatment, at least in principle, although this is subject to the fundamental limitations of computability or computational feasibility.

4.2.7 Probability-Oriented Models

Pure algebra-oriented models and pure logic-oriented models treat "knowledge", "events" and related items by a strict *either–or evaluation*: each (statement about an) item is *evaluated* to be *either* false *or* true. Some applications, however, suggest that we should refine the framework by allowing more general weights. In addition to some other approaches such as *fuzzy logic*, *probability theory* provides sophisticated and well-understood means to do so.

Usually, a *probability*-oriented model extends an underlying algebra-oriented or logic-oriented model by *weighting* each relevant item with a real number that is interpreted as a *probability*, i.e., roughly speaking, as the *likelihood* that the pertinent item will actually be selected from a predefined range of possibilities. For the purpose of normalization, each weight is taken from the interval [0..1], and all weights over a predefined range add up to 1. Then, restricting ourselves to the case of a finite predefined range of possibilities, a weight 0 corresponds roughly to an evaluation to false, and a weight 1 corresponds roughly to an evaluation to true. In technical terms, *random variables* are exploited to denote a range of possibilities together with their probabilities, in order to capture the relevant events of an application under consideration.

As a simple example, we reconsider the *group* based on *addition* modulo 3 as shown in Figure 4.4. We distinguish three kinds of event: selection of a parameter k; selection of a remaining argument x; and computing the sum modulo 3 of the selected parameter and the selected argument and making the result y observable. Each kind of event can be described as a random variable, for instance as follows:

- The parameters $k = 0$, 1, 2 are selected with equal probabilities of 1/3 each, i.e.,
  $Prob_K(0) = Prob_K(1) = Prob_K(2) = 1/3$.
- The remaining arguments $x = 0$, 1, 2 are selected with probabilities
  $Prob_X(0) = 1/4$, $Prob_X(1) = 1/4$ and $Prob_X(2) = 1/2$,
  independently of the selection of the parameter.
- The observable results $y = 0$, 1, 2 occur with the following derived probabilities:
  $Prob_Y(0) = Prob_K(0) \cdot Prob_X(0) + Prob_K(2) \cdot Prob_X(1) + Prob_K(1) \cdot Prob_X(2) = 1/3,$
  $Prob_Y(1) = Prob_K(1) \cdot Prob_X(0) + Prob_K(0) \cdot Prob_X(1) + Prob_K(2) \cdot Prob_X(2) = 1/3,$
  $Prob_Y(2) = Prob_K(2) \cdot Prob_X(0) + Prob_K(1) \cdot Prob_X(1) + Prob_K(0) \cdot Prob_X(2) = 1/3.$
  Thus, observable events appear as random in this example.

Seeing a result y, an observer might aim to gain information about the hidden remaining parameter x by calculating the *conditional probabilities* of a further *random variable* that captures the events "selection of a remaining argument x under the condition that y has been observed". As shown in Section 12.6, the pertinent *a posteriori probabilities* can be determined from the *a priori probabilities* of the two selections using *Bayes' Theorem*. In this example, however, there is *no information gain*, since the a priori probabilities coincide with the a posteriori probabilities, as proved in Section 12.6 within a broader context.

4.3 Inference Control

In the preceding sections, we outline a general perspective on information gain about a hidden item of interest, resulting from considering implications of a priori knowledge and suitably interpreted observations about that item, and we sketch some increasingly complex mathematical models for this perspective. Additionally, we emphasize the distinction between potential and actual information gain, which depends on the computational capabilities and resources available to algorithmically infer the pertinent implications. In this section, we introduce inference control as a security mechanism. More specific instantiations of inference control are presented in the next chapter. Moreover, as argued at the end of this section, large parts of cryptography can be seen as dealing with inference control too, and employing access rights should be guided by inference control as well.

Roughly summarized, *inference control* serves the following purposes:

- For enforcing a specific *security interest*, e.g., confidentiality or integrity,
- and targeting a specific *participant* of a computing system and the suspected *threats*,
- the participant's options for *information gain* are controlled, i.e., the pertinent abstract logical implications or actual inferences are suitably *enabled* or *prevented*.

In the following, we concentrate on the aspect of *prevention*. But it is always important to keep in mind that the controlled computing system should enable at least some useful service, since otherwise we could just get completely rid of it.

In general, a potentially threatening and thus controlled participant cannot be forced to ignore observations or to refrain from inferring implications. Accordingly, inference control has to ensure that explicitly permitted or inevitably accessible observations are not harmful even if a (potentially malicious) participant tries their best to act as a "rational" and maybe even "omnipotent" observer. There are two basic approaches to achieving this goal, *dynamic monitoring* and *static verification*, which might also be suitably combined:

- While the computing system is running, *dynamic monitoring* inspects each relevant event as it occurs, case by case, concerning potential or actual harmful inferences, in each case *before* the event can actually be observed by the controlled participant, and if necessary *blocks* a critical observation. In doing so, dynamic monitoring keeps track of the actual history of *previous observations*, whether explicitly enabled or only assumed to have taken place.
- Before the computing system is started, *static verification* makes a *global* analysis of all possible runs of the computing system and the corresponding potential sequences of events observable by the controlled participant, and inspects them as a whole and *in advance* concerning potential or actual harmful inferences. If necessary, a planned computing system is modified in such a way that all critical observations are *blocked* right from the beginning, without further monitoring at runtime.

These basic approaches can be rephrased briefly in terms of programming: inference control in the form of *dynamic monitoring* supervises a running *process* and possibly *interferes* with the execution, as visualized in Figure 4.11; inference control in the form of *static verification* examines a *program* as a text and possibly *modifies* the text, as visualized in Figure 4.12. In addition to their particular components, both approaches have to use the applicable *semantics* of the programming system and the actual or assumed *a priori knowledge* of the controlled participant.

Furthermore, both approaches need a specification of the security requirements, i.e., a *security policy* that captures the pertinent notion of harmfulness.

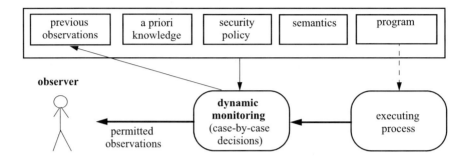

Fig. 4.11. Inference control by dynamic monitoring of a process that executes a program (considered as a text)

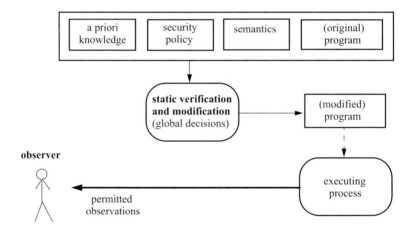

Fig. 4.12. Inference control by static verification and modification of a program (considered as a text)

Regarding *computational complexity,* there are at least the following trade-offs between the basic approaches. On the one side, dynamic monitoring requires a high *runtime* effort, including keeping track of previous observations, but *only situations that actually occur* must be handled. On the other side, static verification puts a heavy burden on an administrator at *design time*, leaving nothing to do at run time, at the price that *all possible* situations must be analyzed. Both approaches demand an algorithmic treatment of implication problems that might turn out to be, in general, computationally *unsolvable* and thus can only be *approximated* at best. Unfortunately, any correct approximation might result in more *blockings* than strictly needed.

Regarding *cooperativeness*, in principle dynamic monitoring is expected to enable more observations, since it considers specific situations rather than all of them. However, case-by-case decisions might slow down the system in an unacceptable way. Then, if the system is forced to meet real-time requirements, further approximations beyond those due to general unsolvabilities might be needed, resulting in additional blockings.

Regarding *blockings*, both basic approaches can employ the following kinds of technique, which allow many variations and combinations:

- An observation evaluated to be harmful is made *invisible*, or an underlying event may even be totally *suppressed*. In terms of programming, such a goal can be achieved by *refusing* to execute a crucial statement or to return a crucial output value, or by suitably modifying a program (considered as a text), respectively.
- An observation evaluated to be harmful is *substituted* by another one held to be harmless.

A further distinction is whether the observer is *notified* of a blocking, either explicitly or implicitly by some reasoning. Clearly, in some situations, recognizing a blocking might constitute harmful information too. For example, if a Boolean return value is *substituted* by its dual value, then the modification must not be communicated. However, if data that identifies human individuals is substituted by randomly generated pseudonyms, then the modification is obvious anyway and thus can be communicated. Regarding an explicitly notified *refusal*, we have to take care about the observer's options to determine the reason for the refusal, and on the basis of that to find out about the hidden event.

Any techniques employed should be carefully designed regarding cooperativeness: in general, the computing system should still be useful for a controlled participant. Thus, in particular, refusals should not occur when they prevent the system being used for its intended purposes, and substitutions should not affect the intended purposes in an irresponsible way.

The above introduction indicates that inference control is a highly ambitious goal, the costs of which cannot always be afforded, and that it might even be beyond the present state of our knowledge. However, security interests taken seriously, such as confidentiality and integrity, demand not only control of messages but also control of information and thus of inferences. This discrepancy between demands and skills is often solved pragmatically along the lines surveyed in Chapter 7 and presented in more detail in subsequent chapters. In particular, using application-oriented and informal reasonings, the consideration of whether an information gain or not should be enabled can be reduced to the specification of a subject's *permissions* and *prohibitions* to access the objects of a computing system. Then, the permissions and prohibitions are expressed either by setting appropriate *access rights* or by generating and distributing appropriate cryptographic *keys*.

4.4 Bibliographic Hints

The notions of "information" and "knowledge" are fundamental to science as a whole, including philosophy and the social sciences, and accordingly there is a great variety of approaches, explications and theories related to these notions and the underlying phenomena. Besides science, the arts contribute to an understanding of these ideas as well, as might do other human activities. Hence, it is well beyond the scope of this monograph (and beyond the experience of the author) to comprehensively survey the relevant literature, and so we shall completely refrain from giving general references.

The minor fraction of insight presented in this chapter has been selectively gathered and abstracted from work on security and from the mathematics that that work is based on. The literature is overwhelmingly rich, and so we only indicate a few examples of textbooks that might be helpful in deepening readers' understanding of the mathematical models.

Grimaldi [242] gives a broad introduction, emphasizing finite structures. Lidl/ Niederreiter [321] provide a background for algebra-oriented models specialized to finite fields, Gathen/Gerhard [217] treat algorithmic aspects of algebra, and Raghavarao [401] and Beth/Jungnickel/Lenz [52] provide an introduction to combinatorial structures useful for designing settings that lead to solvable equation systems.

Abiteboul/Hull/Vianu [6] describe the foundations of databases, and Brachman/ Leveques [99] provide an introduction to knowledge bases. Nerode/Shore [368] present a broad perspective on logic and its applications. Robinson/Voronkov [412] have gathered together the state of our knowledge regarding inference systems. Ebbinghaus/Flum [179] and Libkin [320] concentrate on a special variant of logic where, on the semantic side, the interpretations considered are required to be finite. Blackburn/Rijke/Venema [84] deal specifically with modal logic, as do Fagin/ Halpern/Moses/Vardi [198], with an emphasis on understanding and applying the notion of knowledge. Feller [202], Kallenberg [289] and many others as well present probability theory. Texts on coding theory and on cryptography, listed elsewhere in the book, are relevant as well.

The impact of inference control on security issues was identified in the seminal textbook of D.Denning [163]. Later publications that devote an important amount of space to inference control include the book by Bishop [57]. Farkas/Jajodia [199] provide a short introduction to inference control, with many references to original contributions. Further, more specific bibliographic hints are given in other chapters where concrete inference mechanisms are presented.

5 Preventive Inference Control

In general, *inference control* deals with both enabling and preventing information gain that is based on abstract logical implications or actual inferences from observations. In this chapter, we concentrate on security mechanisms for *preventing* a participant of a computing system from gaining specific information about *hidden* parts of the system behavior from observing selected *visible* parts. We examine some examples of basic constructs of computing systems regarding their potential for information gain, and how to *block* actual exploitation in order to meet some *confidentiality* requirements. The constructs examined include expressions (over some data types); assignments and procedure calls; sequential and parallel control structures; real execution time; and database query answering, including statistical queries. Finally, within a trace-based model, we consider formalizations of *noninterference* that capture the duality between preventing *information gain* for the sake of *confidentiality* and preventing *causality* for the sake of *integrity*.

5.1 Inference Control for Sequential Programs

Sequential programs appear in numerous forms, and in each case the actual particularities should be carefully examined. Roughly summarized, using sequential composition or guarded commands such as conditionals or repetitions, a *sequential program* is formed from elementary assignments and procedure calls, where an assigned value arises from accessing a variable or, more generally, from evaluating an expression. More specifically, for the purpose of an introductory exposition, we consider the following partially overlapping main constructs:

- declaration of *typed identifiers* and generation of corresponding *program variables*, whose current values constitute a (*storage*) *state* of an execution;
- a *state transition*, caused by *generating* a new program variable or *destroying* an existing one, or by *assigning a value* to a program variable, which includes *passing an actual parameter* during a *procedure call*;
- *control* of the execution sequence according to the *sequential composition* of commands, or by *guarded commands* such as a *conditional* or a *repetition*;
- evaluation of an *expression* that may occur in an assignment, as an actual parameter or as a guard;
- computation of a *function* value needed during the evaluation of an expression, where the function is implicitly given by a fundamental type or has been explicitly declared.

In order to determine the potential for information gain and to control them, we shall adapt the mathematical models introduced in Section 4.2. The control mechanisms explored can be seen as instantiations of the general structure of inference control presented in Section 4.3. Given the complexity of sequential programs that we have sketched, a precise computational analysis of the potential for information gain will often be infeasible or even impossible. Accordingly, when designing a preventive mechanism for sequential programs, we shall *approximate* the general notion of *information gain* by an observer in the following ways:

- Rather than explicitly dealing with *observers*, we determine the pertinent *carriers* of data and information: accordingly, we shall often speak about *data flow* and *information flow* from one carrier to another, implicitly meaning that a fictitious observer *could* exploit the observation of the receiving carrier to gain information. Subsection 5.1.1 provides an extended example, Subsection 5.1.2 develops the notion of information flow in more detail, and Subsection 5.1.3 discusses the related computational challenges.
- Rather than distinguishing the four identified cases (complete gain, partial gain, no gain, and not applicable) for each individual observation, we aim at uniformly *blocking* complete or partial information gain for all anticipated situations. Subsection 5.1.4 exemplifies a formal definition of blocking.
- Rather than dealing with the precise details of the objects themselves, we attach abstracting *labels* to them: each such label denotes concisely a particular aspect of the information considered. Subsection 5.1.5 introduces a formal notion of such labels, and Subsection 5.1.6 presents some helpful properties of labels.
- Rather than explicitly tracing the exact proliferation of information gain during a stepwise program execution, we often just assume the *transitivity* of information flows (between carriers, and abstracted by labels). On the basis of this assumption, the preventing mechanism operates *compositionally* according to the syntactic structure of a program. Subsection 5.1.7 and Subsection 5.1.8 present some selected proposals for dynamic monitoring and static verification, respectively.

5.1.1 An Example

We now exemplify some of the constructs and approximations mentioned above by considering the executions of a procedure that is declared as follows:

```
procedure flow(
    in      init, guard, x, y: integer;
    out     result:           integer);
    local  help:              integer;
begin
    help := 2;
    help := help + init * init;
```

```
    if guard ≥ 0
    then help := help + x
    else help := help + y
    fi;
    result := help
end flow
```

We are interested in the gain of information enabled about the actual parameter values of the input variables init, guard, x and y, passed *before* the execution of the body, when the value of the output variable result is observed *after* the execution. Additionally, treating all variables as carriers, we shall also inspect various examples of information gain that may arise during subparts of the executions.

First, the assignment command help := 2 does *not* enable any information gain, since the constant value 2 is part of the declaration supposed to be known a priori.

Second, the assignment command help := help+init*init is executed in three substeps. The first substep evaluates the subexpression init*init by computing the fundamental multiplication function and then delivers an unidentified product value. Observing this product value enables a nearly complete information gain about the actual parameter value of init passed, since the latter value is either the negative or the positive square root of the product value.

The next substep determines the final value of the full expression help+init*init by computing the fundamental addition function for the arguments declared, and then delivers an unidentified sum value. This sum value depends formally on both arguments. However, the first argument is known a priori to be always the constant value 2, and thus observing this sum value enables a complete information gain about the second argument, and, by *transitivity*, a nearly complete information gain about the value of init passed as well.

The third substep, finally, assigns the sum value to the local variable help. This final assignment can be understood as an explicit, direct *data flow* of the sum value into that variable. Accordingly, observing help enables the information gain mentioned above about the value of init passed.

Summarizing, the complete assignment command help := help+init*init can be seen as causing an *information flow* from the carrier init to the carrier help.

Third, we examine the branches of the guarded command individually, and then analyze the impact of selecting one of them.

The execution of the assignment command help := help+x in the positive branch evaluates the expression help+x, then delivers an unidentified sum value and, finally, assigns this sum value to the reused local variable help. If the command is inspected separately, observing the sum value enables an information gain about neither the previous value of help nor the value of x.

However, an observer can achieve a partial information gain about the pairs of these values. Furthermore, if the observer knows one of the argument values a priori, then the sum value uniquely determines the other argument value. By *transitivity*, the same reasoning applies for the value of help after the execution. Summarizing, the complete command is better seen as causing some *information flow* from the carriers help and x back to the carrier help.

Still assuming that the positive branch is selected, the execution of the body is equivalent to the execution of the following command sequence:

```
help    := 2;
help    := help + init * init;
help    := help + x;
result  := help
```

The final step of this sequence can be understood as a direct, explicit *data flow* from the local variable help to the output variable result. By *transitivity*, the full sequence can be regarded as causing an *information flow* from the carriers init and x to the carrier result.

If the negative branch is selected, then all considerations apply similarly for the alternative command sequence.

For the complete guarded command

if guard ≥ 0 **then** help := help + x **else** help := help + y **fi**

the branch, with its command, is selected by the actual parameter value of the input variable guard. In general, observing the value of help after this command is executed does not enable an information gain about the guarding variable. However, with some additional a priori knowledge, such a gain might indeed be possible.

For example, consider the a priori knowledge that

the value of help is 2,
the value of x is greater than or equal to 8, and
the value of y is less than 8.

Then, observing the value of help after the execution offers the possibility of gaining partial information about the value of guard according to the following equivalences:

the observed value of help is greater than or equal to 10 *iff*
the value of guard is greater than or equal to 0;

the observed value of help is less than 10 *iff*
the value of guard is less than 0.

Summarizing, the guarded command is better seen as causing some *implicit information flow* from the carrier guard to the carrier help, besides those information flows identified before, namely either from the carriers help and x or from the carriers help and y. In total, it is even better to suppose an information flow to help from all variables mentioned, namely guard, help, x, and y.

Whenever we summarize a consideration, we basically list those carriers that are better seen to be the *senders* of some data or information flowing to a *receiving* carrier. Such a summarizing list can be dynamically attached to the receiving carrier as some kind of *label* that concisely represents the *approximated* flows.

5.1.2 A Classification of Information Flows

The above example suggests that we should distinguish the following kinds of *information flow*:

- A *direct* information flow – actually, a direct *data flow* or, in other words, a direct *message transmission* – arises when a value is explicitly transported from an (identified or unidentified) variable to another one, provided that the value is not known a priori to be a specific constant. Such direct information flows originate from assignment commands, from passing actual parameters or from providing arguments for the computation of a function.
- An *indirect* information flow might arise from the arguments to the value of the computation of a function.
- A *transitive* information flow arises from combining two "matching" information flows. Such transitive information flows originate from command sequences and from nested expressions.
- An *implicit* information flow arises when a guarded command has an impact on the control. Typically, the information flows from the constituents of the guarding expression into the selected branch; more concretely, for example, this may be the flow into the carriers that get a value assigned there.

These distinctions are complemented by another one that refers to the reachability or actual reaching of a command that might cause an information flow:

- An information flow is said to be *formally declared* if the pertinent command is part of the program (seen as a text) under consideration.
- An information flow is said to be *realizable* (or *existential*) if the pertinent command is reachable for at most one execution with appropriate input values.
- An information flow is said to be *realized* (or *occurring*) if the pertinent command is actually reached during an execution.

Reconsidering the guarded command within the example procedure flow, we can easily observe that the information flow caused by the assignment command in either branch is not only formally declared but also realizable. During each particular execution, however, only exactly one of them is realized.

5.1.3 Computational Challenges

The main computational challenge for inference control is to analyze the highly involved interplay of the various features summarized in Subsection 5.1.2 above. In the following, we outline some selected difficulties, some of which appear even for a single feature.

Regarding *direct* flows, we emphasize the condition that the transmitted data must *not* be a known constant. In general, however, whenever expressive means to declare functions are available, we are faced with the *constantness problem* for programs that describe functions, which is well known to be undecidable for universal programming languages, owing to *Rice's Theorem*.

Regarding *indirect* flows, we have already discussed the general difficulties in Chapter 4. As in the constantness problem, most of the other relevant *decision problems* for programs are, in general, computationally unsolvable as well.

Regarding *transitive* flows, we observe that the "matching" condition is most crucial. For example, consider the following sequence, where g is a Boolean guard:

```
if g then help := x; if not g then y := help
```

For some executions, the first command may cause a flow from x to help, and similarly, for some executions, the second command may cause a flow from help to y. However, there are no executions such that both flows occur, and, accordingly, there is never a transitive flow from x via help to y. In order to recognize this fact, one must detect that the two guards are complementary (which is easily seen in this example but undecidable in general).

Another difficulty is depicted abstractly in Figure 5.1 using the relational model. Concerning the relation $Rel_2 \subseteq V \times R$, an observation of $y \in R$ enables a partial information gain about the pertinent intermediate value $v \in V$, since the pre-image excludes one of the possible values in V. Similarly, concerning the relation $Rel_1 \subseteq D \times V$, each single value of the pre-image excludes one of the possible elements of D. However, taking the pre-images together, i.e., considering the pre-image of the pre-image of the observation y, we get the full domain, and thus there is no gain of information concerning the composed relation $Rel_1 \circ Rel_2$.

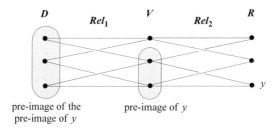

Fig. 5.1. A relation Rel_1 and a relation Rel_2 that enable information flows separately, but whose composition $Rel_1 \circ Rel_2$ does not

Regarding *implicit* flows, we show here an example procedure whose execution causes implicit flows without any direct flows:

```
procedure implicit(
    in     x:   boolean;
    out    y:   boolean);
    local  z:   boolean;
```

```
begin
  y := false;
  z := false;
  if x then z := true fi;
  if z then y := true fi
end implicit
```

There are no direct flows, since all assignments are with constants. Moreover, within the command guarded by x, there is no assignment to y. Nevertheless, the body is semantically equivalent to the assignment command y := x, and thus the body causes a flow from x to y that results from the following interplay:

an implicit flow from x to z by the guarded command **if** x **then** z := true;
an implicit flow from z to y by the guarded command **if** z **then** y := true;
a transitive flow by sequencing the implicit flows.

The completeness of the information gain is supported by the finiteness of the type boolean, which enables an exhaustive distinction of all values by appropriately employing guarded commands.

A further example shows an intricate interplay between *implicit flows* and the *constantness problem*:

```
procedure difficult(
  in      x:  integer;
  out     y:  integer);

  function f(z: integer) : integer;
  { f computes a total function, as implemented by the body;
      f returns the output value 0 on the actual input parameter value z=0}
  begin ... end;

begin
  if f(x) = 0
  then y := 1
  else y := 2
  fi
end difficult
```

We distinguish two cases for the locally defined function: either the function constantly returns 0, or there exists an actual input parameter value $z \neq 0$ such that the function returns a different value. In the former case, the body of the procedure is semantically equivalent to the assignment command y := 1, which does not cause any information flow. In the latter case, an observation of the output value y enables a partial gain of information about the actual parameter value x, by excluding either the value z or the specially treated value 0. Thus an information flow occurs iff the locally defined function is non-constant, which in general is an undecidable property.

Regarding *formally declared* flows, we basically have to check each syntactic construct of a programming language for whether it *possibly* enables an information flow, and to recognize instantiations of any enabling construct in a concrete program. While the former task requires a somewhat involved examination by a human investigator, in most cases the latter task can be efficiently automated as part of the syntax analysis.

Regarding *realizable* flows, we recall that the *reachability problem* for commands is well known to be undecidable in general; in fact, it is a generalization of the *halting problem*. Accordingly, the *realizability problem* for information flows is undecidable as well. This computational limitation substantially constrains the static-verification approach for inference control, whereas the dynamic-monitoring approach is not affected.

Regarding *realized* flows, we just note that for the static-verification approach this notion is meaningless, whereas for the dynamic-monitoring approach the detection of this property is immediate.

5.1.4 An Adapted Relational Model for Carriers and Blocking

We generalize the considerations exemplified above by adapting the *relational model* (dealing with projections of relations), where the relations studied arise from the semantics of some programming constructs. Basically, each such relation *Rel* can be regarded as an instantiation of the following abstract form:

- *Rel* relates input objects taken from a domain D to output objects taken from a range R, i.e., $Rel \subseteq D \times R$.
- Each input object $x \in D$ consists of a *visible part* x_{vis} and a *hidden part* x_{hid} such that $x_{vis} \in D_{vis}$ and $x_{hid} \in D_{hid}$, i.e., $D \subseteq D_{vis} \times D_{hid}$, and, accordingly, $Rel \subseteq D_{vis} \times D_{hid} \times R$. We consider each of the three components D_{vis}, D_{hid} and R as a *carrier*.

We then define the notion that the relation *Rel* complies with the prevention goal in the following way:

Rel is said to *block any information gain* about D_{hid} from observing R while knowing D_{vis} iff

for all (known, visible input parts) $x_{vis} \in D_{vis}$,
for all (syntactically possible outputs) $y \in R$:
either the framework is *not applicable* or *no information gain* is possible, i.e.,

either $\varnothing = \{ z \mid (x_{vis}, z, y) \in Rel \}$

or $\varnothing \neq \{ z \mid (x_{vis}, z, y) \in Rel \} = \{ z \mid \text{exists } a : (x_{vis}, z, a) \in Rel \}$.

This definition treats a relation *Rel* that arises from programming constructs that are only *partially defined* as follows. It is possible that an execution starting with x_{vis} may not halt; there is then no output at all and, accordingly, speaking about "observing an output" is meaningless. However, this case should depend only weakly on the hidden input part: in terms of the opposite case, if x_{vis} leads to a halting situation (in this case, whatever the actual observation y is like), the set of possibly employed hidden input parts is always the same, namely

$\{ z \mid \text{exists } a : (x_{vis}, z, a) \in Rel \}$.

Accordingly, the very fact of an actual observation enables the implication that the actual hidden input part x_{hid} is an element of this set. This implication may constitute a gain of information or not, depending on the a priori knowledge about the set

$$\{ \ z \mid (x_{vis}, z) \in D \ \}.$$

Figure 5.2 visualizes an example where a gain of information is achieved by excluding an element of D_{hid} from being the actual element.

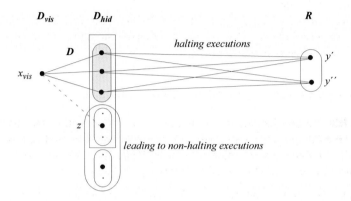

Fig. 5.2. A visible input part x_{vis} that leads to two possible observations y' or y'' after halting with the *same* hidden input parts, and that allows at least one further hidden input part z according to D: a halting observation excludes z as an actual hidden input part

Under the simplifying assumptions that $D = D_{vis} \times D_{hid}$ and that any input from D leads to a halting execution and, accordingly, to some observation $y \in R$, we can express a *violation* of the prevention goal in a slightly more manageable form:

Rel does *not* block any information gain about D_{hid} from observing R while knowing D_{vis} iff

there exist
(a known, visible input part) $x_{vis} \in D_{vis}$,
(possible outputs) $y' \in R$ and $y'' \in R$ with $y' \neq y''$ and
(possible hidden input parts) $z' \in D_{hid}$ and $z'' \in D_{hid}$ with $z' \neq z''$ such that:
  $(x_{vis}, z', y') \in Rel$, and
  $(x_{vis}, z'', y'') \in Rel$, but
  $(x_{vis}, z', y'') \notin Rel$
(which excludes z' under the observation of y'').

If, additionally, *Rel* is the graph of a *totally defined* function $f : D_{vis} \times D_{hid} \to R$, then a *violation* is expressible as follows:

f does *not* block any information gain about D_{hid} from observing R while knowing D_{vis} iff

there exist
(a known, visible input part) $x_{vis} \in D_{vis}$,
(possible outputs) $y' \in R$ and $y'' \in R$ with $y' \neq y''$ and
(possible hidden input parts) $z' \in D_{hid}$ and $z'' \in D_{hid}$ with $z' \neq z''$ such that:
$$f(x_{vis}, z') = y', \text{ and}$$
$$f(x_{vis}, z'') = y''$$
(which excludes z' under the observation of y'').

A straightforward approximate attempt to avoid any such violations is to ensure that executions do *not* depend *at all* on the hidden input part; i.e., any kind of involvement of a hidden input part – even if the involvement is only a formal one without any immediate actual impact – is eliminated right from the beginning.

5.1.5 Introducing Labels

In general, a sequential program comprises many *carriers* of information, which include, in particular, the generated *program variables* and suitable representations of the *control* of the execution sequence. Accordingly, for such a program, many different instantiations of the adapted mathematical model are relevant. Following the above straightforward approximate attempt, a *preventive* mechanism of *inference control* basically implements a strategy that is composed of actions of three kinds:

- It keeps track of which carrier is dependent on which carriers.
- It compares the identified "dynamic" dependence with a static policy specification of the permitted dependency.
- In the case of a violation, it reacts suitably.

More formally, we suppose a set $Car = \{c_1, \ldots, c_n\}$ of carriers, and we then consider the *power set lattice* $(\wp\, Car, \subseteq, \cap, \cup)$. The set inclusion relation $\subseteq$ is a finite partial order on $\wp\, Car$ such that for any two sets of carriers X and Y, the $\subseteq$-infimum is $X \cap Y$ and the $\subseteq$-supremum is $X \cup Y$. The elements of the power set lattice, i.e., the sets of carriers, are employed as *labels* (also known in some contexts as *security levels* or *security classifications*) as follows:

- [policy specification] Each carrier $c \in Car$ is assigned a *static label* $sl(c) \in \wp\, Car$ (also known in some contexts as a *clearance*) that *specifies* that the carrier c is *permitted* to depend on all carriers of $sl(c)$ but not on any other ones. In other words, the only *permitted information flows* into c are those that originate from the carriers of $sl(c)$.
- [approximated information content] Each carrier $c \in Car$ is assigned a *dynamic label* $dl(c) \in \wp\, Car$ (also known in some contexts as a *(dynamic) classification*) expressing that the carrier c is supposed to *actually depend* only on carriers of $sl(c)$ but not on any other ones. In other words, all (possibly virtually) *realized information flows* into c originate from $sl(c)$, and thus $sl(c)$ can be seen as a concise representation of an approximated *information content* of the carrier c.

Clearly, during dynamic monitoring or in the course of static verification, the dynamic labels are repeatedly determined according to the progress of the actual execution or the verification analysis, respectively.

Given the static and dynamic labels, a *preventive* mechanism of *inference control* proceeds roughly as follows. For each event to be controlled, the mechanism

- computes the expected effect of the event on the dynamic labels of the carriers, on the basis of the current dynamic labels, and then
- checks whether, for each carrier c, the new dynamic label $dl(c)$ is included in its static label $sl(c)$, i.e., whether $dl(c) \subseteq sl(c)$, and finally
- reacts accordingly; i.e., if the expected effect of the event violates the dominance by the static label declared by the policy specification, then the event is treated as *prohibited* and appropriately *blocked*; otherwise, the event is treated as *permitted*, and the dynamic labels are updated as expected for the event.

Such a mechanism enforces the *control invariant* "for each carrier c: $dl(c) \subseteq sl(c)$" under all executions. Accordingly, the mechanism complies with the policy specification iff the dynamic labels correctly approximate the information content of carriers and thereby appropriately capture the (possibly virtually) realized information flows.

The approach sketched so far can be easily generalized and thereby adapted for a wide range of applications: rather than considering the power set lattice with respect to carriers for the labels and the computation of the expected effects of events, we can employ *any* other finite lattice in just the same way. Given any finite lattice $(SL, \leq_{SL}, inf_{SL}, sup_{SL})$, we can readily interpret the components as follows:

- An element l of the underlying finite domain SL of *labels* or *security levels* denotes a particular *aspect of information* whose flow is under control.
- The binary relation $\leq_{SL}$ is a *partial order* on the domain SL. This relation allows us to *compare* some of the aspects with respect to a kind of "inclusion" or "relative strength" or any other suitable focus of interest. When we form a partial order, some aspects may be *incomparable*, but, according to transitivity, if a first and a second aspect are related and, additionally, the second aspect is related to a third one, than the first one is related to the third one as well. Thus labels are used under the assumption that information flows can be treated as *transitive*.
- Moreover, for each pair of labels $l_1 \in SL$ and $l_2 \in SL$, the partial order allows an *infimum* (*greatest lower bound*) $inf_{SL}(l_1,l_2)$ and a *supremum* (*least upper bound*) $sup_{SL}(l_1,l_2)$ that capture the *common part* of the aspects represented by l_1 and l_2, and the *accumulation* of these aspects, respectively. Allowing infimums and supremums often enables a concise representation of the expected effect of an event with regard to information flows. Note that the partial order $\leq_{SL}$ and the functions inf_{SL} and sup_{SL} are formally related; in particular,

$$l_1 \leq_{SL} l_2 \quad \text{iff} \quad l_1 = inf_{SL}(l_1,l_2) \quad \text{iff} \quad l_2 = sup_{SL}(l_1,l_2).$$

There are numerous examples of definition of a finite lattice of labels for the sake of controlling information flows. We shall mention only a few of them.

In order to capture the *origins* (or *sources*) of information, we can employ the *power set lattice* with respect to carriers, $(\wp Car, \subseteq, \cap, \cup)$, introduced above as the starting point of the current discussion.

In order to simply *characterize* information concerning the interest in *confidentiality* as either *permitted* or *prohibited*, or in other terms as either "open" or "secret", we can let the former term precede the latter one. More generally, we can use a *finer characterization* concerning the interest in confidentiality with more than just two linearly ordered terms, for example by assigning the labels "open", "confidential", "secret" and "top secret", which are supposed to be *linearly ordered* as they are listed. Figure 5.3 shows graphical representations as Hasse diagrams.

Fig. 5.3. The Hasse diagrams of two linearly ordered sets of characterizations concerning the interest in confidentiality

In order to describe information by *subject matter*, we can select a set KW of predefined *keywords* and employ the *power set lattice* with respect to the keywords, $(\wp KW, \subseteq, \cap, \cup)$; for example, the information units of this book may be labeled by a subset of the keyword set

$$KW = \{\text{avail(ability)}, \text{conf(identiality)}, \text{int(egrity)}, \text{auth(enticity)}\}.$$

Figure 5.4 shows a graphical representation as a Hasse diagram.

Having already defined two lattices

$$(SL1, \leq_{SL1}, inf_{SL1}, sup_{SL1}) \text{ and } (SL2, \leq_{SL2}, inf_{SL2}, sup_{SL2})$$

capturing two aspects of interest, we can deal with both aspects jointly by employing the *product lattice* with domain $SL1 \times SL2$ where all operations are taken componentwise; in particular

$$(l_1, l_2) \leq_{SL1 \times SL2} (l_1', l_2') \text{ iff } l_1 \leq_{SL1} l_1' \text{ and } l_2 \leq_{SL2} l_2'.$$

In some situations, we might want to start with an *arbitrary* relation $Rel \subseteq SL \times SL$ over some finite domain SL of labels such that the relation reflects some grading relationships between the aspects represented by the domain elements. In that case, we can always *embed* the relation Rel into a suitably constructed lattice. Such a lattice and the corresponding embedding can be constructed stepwise, roughly as follows:

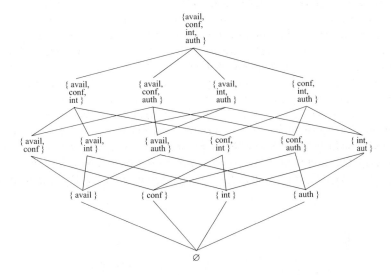

Fig. 5.4. The Hasse diagram of the power set lattice over the keyword set $KW =$ {avail(ability), conf(identiality), int(egrity), auth(enticity)}

- Replace *Rel* by its reflexive and transitive closure *Rel**.
- Contract each maximal set of mutually related elements to a single element.
- Complete the resulting relation by adding missing infimums and supremums.

Figure 5.5 provides a simple example.

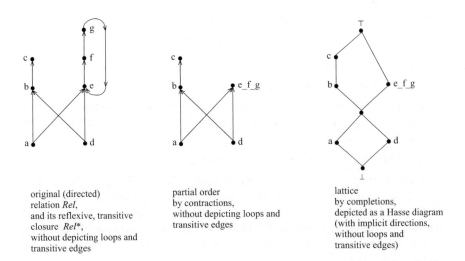

original (directed)
relation *Rel*,
and its reflexive, transitive
closure *Rel**,
without depicting loops and
transitive edges

partial order
by contractions,
without depicting loops and
transitive edges

lattice
by completions,
depicted as a Hasse diagram
(with implicit directions,
without loops and
transitive edges)

Fig. 5.5. Embedding a relation into a lattice by employing contractions and completions

5.1.6 Carriers, Labels and Expressions

Given a set of carriers *Car*, the power set lattice ($\wp\,Car, \subseteq, \cap, \cup$) is of particular importance, since it provides a means to capture the *origins* (or *sources*) of information. Moreover, in some situations the elements of this lattice can be employed as provisional labels that are subsequently transformed into labels expressing a more special interest. Such situations can be formally described as follows.

Suppose that ($SL, \leq_{SL}, inf_{SL}, sup_{SL}$) is any other finite lattice. We then consider a function that maps each carrier c to some label l of SL, intuitively giving some *meaning* to the content of the carrier c:

means: $Car \rightarrow SL$.

Furthermore, we extend this function to a function on $\wp\,Car$, intuitively by aggregating the accumulated contents of a set of carriers with the help of the supremum function sup_{SL}:

$$means: \wp\,Car \rightarrow SL \quad \text{with} \quad means(X) := sup_{SL}\{\,means(c)\,|\,c \in X\,\}. \quad (5.1)$$

This extension provides a useful *embedding* of the power set lattice with respect to carriers into the other lattice. More specifically, the following properties hold:

$$\text{If } X \subseteq Y, \text{ then } means(X) \leq_{SL} means(Y), \text{ and} \quad (5.2)$$

$$means(X \cap Y) \leq_{SL} inf_{SL}\{\,means(X), means(Y)\,\}. \quad (5.3)$$

Hence, under the embedding, the supremums are strictly preserved, by the definition (5.1), and the infimums are correctly approximated, by the property (5.3). In general, however, the infimums are not strictly preserved. Figure 5.6 shows a counterexample: for the lattices depicted and the embedding denoted by m, we have

$$m(\{a,b\} \cap \{a,c\}) \neq inf(\,m(\{a,b\})\,,\,m(\{a,c\})\,).$$

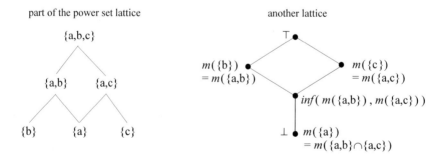

Fig. 5.6. An embedding of the power set lattice with respect to carriers that does not strictly preserve infimums

In a more special but often relevant situation, we might want to embed the power set lattice with respect to carriers into the simplest linear order on two characterizations (say, "open" and "secret", as shown in Figure 5.3) as follows. The carriers themselves are characterized as either "open" or "secret". In this way, the carrier set Car is partitioned into two disjoint subsets O and S such that $Car = O \cup S$ and $O \cap S = \varnothing$. If we define $means: Car \rightarrow \{open, secret\}$ accordingly, i.e.,

$$means(c) = \begin{cases} open & \text{if } c \in O \\ secret & \text{if } c \in S \end{cases}, \tag{5.4}$$

we obtain the following useful property for the extended embedding:

$$X \subseteq O \quad \text{iff} \quad means(X) = open. \tag{5.5}$$

Other situations, however, might require more sophisticated tools than just assigning labels of some lattice to carriers. For example, suppose that the events to be controlled can be treated as function applications which are followed by storing the result in a carrier. The effect of the first part of such an event can be described in more detail by an *expression* that takes the input carriers as arguments. This expression can be represented by its *syntax tree*, where the inner nodes denote the functions applied and the leaf nodes refer to the input carriers. The effect of the second part of the event could then be described by assigning the pertinent expression (or syntax tree) to the result carrier.

Obviously, if we use expressions as labels, we achieve a higher expressiveness, but at the price of possibly losing the computationally helpful algebraic properties of lattices. We, finally, observe that labels taken from the power set lattice with respect to carriers just abstract from full expressions (or syntax trees) by reducing an expression to its set of arguments (or a syntax tree to its set of leaves).

5.1.7 Examples of Dynamic Monitoring

In this and the next subsection, we present some selected variations of the general strategy for a *preventive* mechanism of *inference control*, which is based on enforcing a *control invariant* requiring that the *dynamic labels* of *carriers* are always dominated by their respective *static labels*. The variations apply to progressively more structured programming languages, ranging from (abstract versions of) machine languages to high-level procedural languages. The impact of the structures becomes relevant mainly when *implicit information flows* due to guarded commands are approximated. Moreover, for less structured languages we might prefer dynamic monitoring, in the hope of compensating for the missing structural declarations by more runtime data. Finally, the variations also differ in their reaction to an expected violation of the pertinent control invariant.

Monitoring Machine Programs with Refusing Abortions. The first variation has the following features:

- We consider a low-level elementary *machine language*.
- The only guarded command is an unstructured *conditional jump* instruction.
- The control of the execution sequence is represented by a *program counter pc*.
- The set of *carriers* comprises the program counter *pc* and the set of (program) variables (storage locations).
- The power set lattice ($\wp\,InVar, \subseteq, \cap, \cup$) with respect to the set *InVar* of input (program) variables is used for labels.
- Inference control is realized by *dynamic monitoring* of program executions.
- The reaction to a violation is to *refuse* further execution, i.e., to *abort* it, and to *notify* the user accordingly.

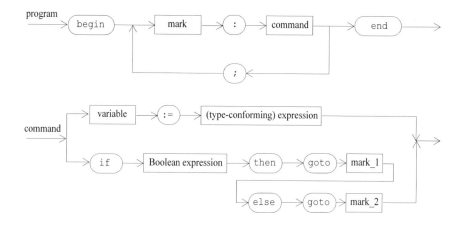

Fig. 5.7. A syntax diagram for a "machine language" with unstructured conditional jump instructions, to be dynamically monitored

More specifically, we consider a very simple "machine language", whose syntax is shown by the syntax diagram in Figure 5.7 and can be sketched as follows:

- $x_1, x_2, \ldots$ are input (program) variables of type integer.
- $r_1, r_2, \ldots$ are additional local (program) variables of type integer or Boolean.
- y is the output (program) variable, of type integer.
- A command is either a well-formed *assignment* of the form

$$u := \text{expression}(w_1, \ldots, w_n) \tag{5.6}$$

  or a well-formed unstructured *conditional jump* of the form

$$\texttt{if expression}(w_1, \ldots, w_n) \texttt{ then goto mark\_1 else goto mark\_2.} \tag{5.7}$$

- A program is a sequence of marked commands, bracketed by a `begin`–`end` pair, with "`;`" used as a delimiter. Furthermore, any mark (jump goal) specified in a conditional jump should actually occur as the prefix of some command.

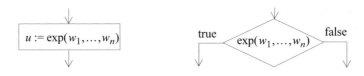

Fig. 5.8. Flow diagrams for "assignment" and unstructured "conditional jump"

The *semantics* of this "machine language" is defined along the usual lines. The execution of a program P is started by initializing the input variables $x_1,\ldots,x_k$ that occur to some actual parameters (integer values) $a_1,\ldots,a_k$, and the local variables $r_1,\ldots,r_m$ that occur and the output variable y to the value 0. Afterwards, the program P is executed stepwise by evaluating the respective expression and taking the action that it denotes, visualized as flow diagrams in Figure 5.8. If the last command of the program is reached, the current value assigned to the output variable y is considered to be the result of the execution. Accordingly, the semantics $|P|$ of a program P can be defined more formally as

$$|P| : \mathbf{Z}^k \longrightarrow partial \rightarrow \mathbf{Z},$$

$$|P|(a_1,\ldots,a_k) = \begin{cases} \text{final value of } y & \text{if the program halts,} \\ \text{undefined} & \text{otherwise.} \end{cases}$$

Regarding the *policy specification* for expressing *permitted information flows*, *static labels* are declared only for the program counter pc and the output variable y. Given a program P, the static labels are taken according to a partition of the set $InVar = \{x_1,\ldots,x_k\}$ of the input variables occurring in P into two disjoint subsets O and S such that $InVar = O \cup S$ and $O \cap S = \emptyset$, the intention being as discussed in Subsection 5.1.6. Accordingly, in order to permit only information flows from the "open" input variables in O, the static labels are defined as follows:

for the program counter, $sl(pc) := O$;
for the output variable, $sl(y) := O$.

The related *control invariant* and the *control postcondition* enforce the intention:

for the program counter, the control invariant $dl(pc) \subseteq sl(pc) = O$ is aimed at selecting an execution path that depends only on the "open" input variables;

for the output variable, the control postcondition $dl(y) \subseteq sl(y) = O$ is aimed at finally returning a result value that depends only on the "open" input variables.

Regarding the approximations of *information content* and the *reaction* to a policy violation, *dynamic monitoring with refusing abortions* proceeds by modifying the usual semantics, as sketched for a program P in the following:

- On interpreting the prefix `begin`, the usual initialization of the program variables is complemented by an initialization of the *dynamic labels* for all carriers:

for each input variable, $dl(x_i) := \{x_i\}$;
for each local variable, $dl(r_i) := \varnothing$;
$dl(y) := \varnothing$;
$dl(pc) := \varnothing$.

- On interpreting an *assignment* of the form "$u := \text{expression}(w_1,\ldots,w_n)$", the usual evaluation of the expression and storing of the result value are complemented by updating the dynamic label of the variable u on the left-hand side:

$dl(u) := dl(w_1) \cup \ldots \cup dl(w_n)$.

- On interpreting a *conditional jump* of the form "if expression($w_1,\ldots,w_n$) then goto mark_1 else goto mark_2", the usual control actions performed by manipulating the program counter are wrapped as indicated by the following instructions:

$dl(pc) := dl(pc) \cup dl(w_1) \cup \ldots \cup dl(w_n)$;		/ *update dynamic label of pc*
if $dl(pc) \subseteq sl(pc)$		/ *check control invariant for pc*
then	**if** expression($w_1,\ldots,w_n$)	/ *execute wrapped command*
	then goto mark_1	
	else goto mark_2	
	fi	
else	$y := \text{mum}$;	/ *react to violation by "refusal"*
	halt	/ *and abort execution*
fi		

- On interpreting the postfix end, the usual halting of the execution is preceded as indicated by the following instruction:

if $dl(y) \subseteq sl(y)$	/ *check postcondition for y*
then $y := \text{mum}$	/ *react to violation by "refusal"*

Under dynamic monitoring, the usual semantics $|P|$ of a program P is modified to a *monitoring semantics* of the form $\|P\| : \mathbf{Z}^k \;-\!\!\text{partial}\!\rightarrow \mathbf{Z} \cup \{\text{mum}\}$. If all details of the above sketch are carefully and appropriately elaborated, the following theorem can be justified.

Theorem 5.1   [monitoring with refusing abortions]

Let P be a program, and let $|P|$ denote the usual semantics, and $\|P\|$ the monitoring semantics. The following properties then hold:

1. If $\|P\|(a_1,\ldots,a_k) \neq \text{mum}$, then $\|P\|(a_1,\ldots,a_k) = |P|(a_1,\ldots,a_k)$.
2. If the actual parameter lists $(a_1,\ldots,a_k)$ and $(b_1,\ldots,b_k)$ coincide for all "open" input variables in O, then $\|P\|(a_1,\ldots,a_k) = \|P\|(b_1,\ldots,b_k)$; more specifically, the control of the monitoring semantics selects the same execution path, and if applicable, the execution is aborted in the same step.

Sketch of Proof: The first property is a consequence of the following behavior of the monitoring semantics: in each step, either the execution comprises the usual semantics, or the execution is immediately aborted on a violation, after assigning mum to the output variable y.

The second property can be verified indirectly, by assuming that different execution paths could be selected and considering the first differing step. This step is then preceded by a conditional jump that causes the different selections. Thus, for this conditional jump, the guarding expression must contain a variable w_i that is evaluated differently. Furthermore, by the coincidence of the "open" input parameters and by following the same sequence of assignments up to that point, the last assignment to that variable w_i must depend on a "secret" variable, which then contributes to the dynamic label $dl(w_i)$. However, this leads to an abortion during the wrapping of the conditional jump under consideration, which contradicts the assumption. ❏

Clearly, monitoring with refusing abortions is rather restrictive and appears to be of mainly theoretical interest. The basic approach might be applicable to controlling unknown *mobile code* on the basis of some accompanying security assertions that can be reflected by the policy specification.

Monitoring Machine Programs with Non-Notified Skipping. The second variation has the following features:

- We consider an elementary *machine language* for straight-line programs with a restricted option of forward jumps.
- The only guarded command is a structured *conditional jump* instruction.
- The control of the execution sequence is represented by a *program counter pc*.
- The set of *carriers* comprises the program counter pc and the set *Var* of (program) variables (storage locations).
- The embedding of the power set lattice $(\wp\, Var, \subseteq, \cap, \cup)$ into the linear order on the two characterizations in the set $SL = \{\text{open}, \text{secret}\}$ is used for labels.
- Inference control is realized by *dynamic monitoring* of program executions.
- The reaction to a violation is to *skip* an assignment, *without notifying* the user accordingly. In some sense, the user is *misled* or *told a lie* about the treatment of the program.

More specifically, we consider a "machine language" whose syntax is shown by the syntax diagram in Figure 5.9 and can be sketched as follows:

- $x_1, x_2, \ldots$ are (program) variables of type integer.
- A command is either a well-formed *assignment* of the form

$$u := \text{expression}(w_1, \ldots, w_n) \tag{5.8}$$

or a well-formed structured *conditional jump* of the form

$$\text{if expression}(w_1, \ldots, w_n) \text{ then compound command fi,} \tag{5.9}$$

where a compound command is a sequence of commands with ";" used as a delimiter.
- A program is a compound command, bracketed by a begin–end pair.

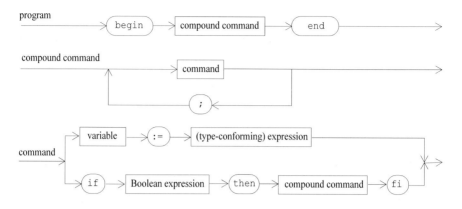

Fig. 5.9. A syntax diagram for a "machine language" with structured conditional jump instructions, to be dynamically monitored

Again, the *semantics* of this "machine language" is defined along the usual lines. The execution of a program P is started by initializing the variables $x_1,\ldots,x_k$ that occur to some actual parameters (integer values) $a_1,\ldots,a_k$. Afterwards, the program P is executed stepwise by evaluating the respective expression and taking the action that it denotes, visualized as flow diagrams in Figure 5.10. Owing to the structured form of the conditional jump instructions, only forward jumps can occur. When the last command of the program is reached, the current values assigned to the variables are considered to be the result of the execution. Accordingly, in this variation. the semantics $|P|$ of a program P can be defined more formally as

$$|P| : \mathbf{Z}^k \longrightarrow partial\rightarrow \mathbf{Z}^k,$$

$$|P|\,(a_1,\ldots,a_k) = \begin{cases} \text{final value of } (x_1,\,\ldots,\,x_k) & \text{if the program halts,} \\ \text{undefined} & \text{otherwise.} \end{cases}$$

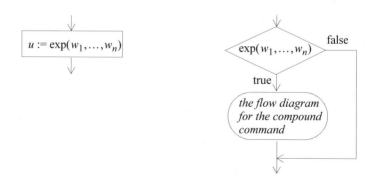

Fig. 5.10. Flow diagrams for "assignment" and structured "conditional jump"

Regarding the *policy specification* for expressing *permitted information flows*, *static labels* are declared for all program variables. Given a program P, the static labels are assigned according to a partition of the set $Var = \{x_1,\ldots,x_k\}$ of the variables occurring in P into two disjoint subsets O and S such that $Var = O \cup S$ and $O \cap S = \varnothing$, with the intention being discussed in Subsection 5.1.6. Accordingly, in order to permit only information flows into an "open" variable of O originating from the "open" variables, the static labels are defined as follows:

for an "open" variable $x_i \in O$, $sl(x_i) := \text{open}$;

for a "secret" variable $x_j \in S$, $sl(x_j) := \text{secret}$.

The related *control invariant* enforces the intention, but in this variation only the "open" variables need explicit care:

for an "open" variable $x_i \in O$, the control invariant $dl(x_i) \leq_{SL} sl(x_i)$ is aimed at assigning a value to x_i only if that value depends only on the "open" variables.

Regarding the approximations of *information content* and the *reaction* to a policy violation, *dynamic monitoring with non-notified skipping* proceeds by modifying the usual semantics, as sketched for a program P in the following:

- On interpreting the prefix `begin`, the usual initialization of the program variables is complemented by an initialization of the *dynamic labels* of the program counter pc and of the variables $x_i \in Var$:

  $dl(pc) := \text{open}$, and
  furthermore, a stack for saving and restoring values of $dl(pc)$ is initialized;

  for each variable, $dl(x_i) := sl(x_i)$, but note that in this variation the dynamic labels of the variables are never updated (and thus their role could be replaced by the initial values, i.e., the static labels).

- On interpreting an *assignment* of the form "$u := \text{expression}(w_1,\ldots,w_n)$", the usual evaluation of the expression and storing of the result value are executed only under the condition that the control invariant would not be violated under the (suppressed) update of the dynamic label of u; otherwise, these actions are simply skipped.
  Thus the usual actions are wrapped as indicated by the following instructions:

  ```
  if      sup_SL(dl(pc),dl(w_1),...,dl(w_n)) ≤_SL sl(u)   / check control invariant
  then    u := expression(w_1,...,w_n)
  else    skip
  ```

- On interpreting a structured *conditional jump* of the form "`if` expression($w_1,\ldots,w_n$) `then` compound command `fi`", the usual execution control action — by manipulating the program counter according to the value of the guarding expression — is complemented by wrapping the execution of the compound command roughly as follows.
  Before the execution, the current value of the dynamic label of the program counter is pushed on the stack, and a new value is computed as the supremum of the current value and the values of the dynamic labels of the variables occurring

in the guarding expression; in order to take care of *implicit information flows*, this new value is used *during* the monitored execution of the compound command (as long as it is not incremented by a nested structure).

After the execution, the dynamic label of the program counter is reset by popping it from the stack.

Thus the usual actions are modified as indicated by the following instructions:

if	expression($w_1, \ldots, w_n$)	/ *usual execution control*
then	*push* $dl(pc)$;	/ *save dynamic label of pc*
	$dl(pc) := sup_{SL}(dl(pc), dl(w_1), \ldots, dl(w_n))$;	
		/ *compute new dynamic label of pc, for controlling implicit flows*
	execute the compound command under monitoring;	
	pop $dl(pc)$	/ *restore dynamic label of pc*
else	**skip**	

• On interpreting the postfix **end**, the usual halting of the execution is performed.

Expressed more intuitively, the dynamic monitoring can operate in two modes. The "open mode" is used when $dl(pc)$ = open: assigning a value to an "open" variable is then permitted only if the pertinent expression does not contain a "secret" variable; otherwise, it is skipped. The "secret mode" is used when $dl(pc)$ = secret: assigning a value to an "open" variable is then always skipped.

In the variant of dynamic monitoring sketched above, the usual semantics $|P|$ of a program P is modified to a *monitoring semantics* of the form

$$\|P\| : \mathbf{Z}^k \xrightarrow{partial} \mathbf{Z}^k.$$

If all details of the sketch are carefully and appropriately elaborated, the following theorem can be justified.

Theorem 5.2   [monitoring with non-notified skipping]

Let P be a program, and let $|P|$ denote the usual semantics, and $\|P\|$ the monitoring semantics. The following property then holds: if the actual parameter lists $(a_1, \ldots, a_k)$ and $(b_1, \ldots, b_k)$ coincide for all "open" variables in O, then the output lists of $\|P\|(a_1, \ldots, a_k)$ and $\|P\|(b_1, \ldots, b_k)$ do so as well.

Sketch of Proof: Given two such actual parameter lists, the selected execution paths can differ only in subpaths that have been executed in "secret mode". These subpaths do not change "open" variables. Moreover, an assignment to an "open" variable with an expression containing a "secret" variable is always skipped.   ❏

5.1.8 Examples of Static Verification

In this subsection, we sketch two further variations of the general strategy for a *preventive* mechanism of *inference control*. Both variations fully employ the structures of high-level procedural programming languages in order to deal with *implicit information flows* due to *guarded commands*. As exemplified before, on the one hand the mechanisms must *approximate* the information flow from the argument components of the guard into the carriers manipulated in the pertinent scope of the guard. Owing to the structures used, this scope can easily be determined syntactically. On the other hand, once this scope has been left, the impact of the guard should be reset appropriately in order to avoid unnecessary restrictions.

The two variations are examples of *static verification* of a program (considered as a text), and they are integrated into the functional analysis of the program, on the basis of compositional semantics. One variation uses *procedural semantics* and thus can be supported by the pertinent *compiler*. The other uses *axiomatic semantics* and thus can be supported by tools for *program verification* in terms of preconditions, invariants and postconditions. In both cases, we need to identify appropriate *carriers* of the information concerning the *execution control*, which of course must remain fictitious for a static analysis.

For the compiler-supported procedural approach, the progressively more complex *syntactical subparts* of a program are considered as some kind of carriers. For the verification-tool-supported axiomatic approach, an appropriately selected abstraction of the *program counter* is used.

Compiler-Based Verification of Structured Programs. This third variation has the following features:

- We consider a high-level *procedural programming language*.
- The guarded commands are structured *conditionals* and *repetitions*.
- The fictitious control of the execution sequence is represented by the *syntactical subparts* of a program.
- The set of *carriers* comprises these syntactical subparts (execution control) and the set of (program) variables (storage locations).
- The power set lattice ($\wp\, Var, \subseteq, \cap, \cup$) with respect to the set *Var* of (program) variables is used for labels.
- Inference control is realized by *static verification* of a program (considered as a text).
- The reaction to a violation is to *refuse* an execution.

More specifically, we consider a grossly simplified version of a typical procedural language, whose syntax is shown by the syntax diagram in Figure 5.11 and can be sketched as follows:

- $x_1, x_2, \ldots, y_1, y_2, \ldots$ and $z_1, z_2, \ldots$ are typed (program) variables, where x_1, $x_2, \ldots$ and $y_1, y_2, \ldots$ are declared as formal parameters and $z_1, z_2, \ldots$ are declared as local variables of a procedure; each variable v has an elementary type with extension (domain) D_v.
- A command is one of the following well-formed alternatives:
  - an *assignment* to a variable, with an *expression* to be evaluated and assigned;
  - a *sequence* of commands, bracketed by a begin–end pair, with ";" used as a delimiter;
  - a structured *conditional*, used as a *conditional forward jump* or a two-sided *alternative*;

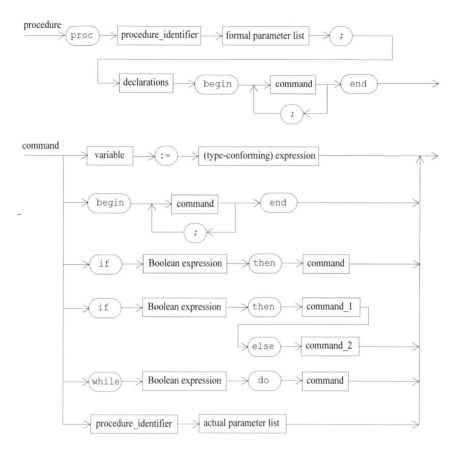

Fig. 5.11. A syntax diagram for a procedural language with structured conditionals, repetition and procedure calls, to be statically verified

- a *repetition* where the guard occurs in front of the body, i.e., a `while` instruction;
- a *procedure call* supplying a list of appropriate *actual parameters*.

• A *procedure* (declaration) comprises an identifier, a *formal parameter* list, *local declarations* and a *body*. A body is a *sequence* of commands where all variables that occur must be formal parameters or locally declared (and thus "global variables" are forbidden for the sake of a compositional verification). A *formal parameter* is either a pure *argument parameter* that must not occur as the left-hand side of an assignment, or, if preceded by the keyword `var`, a pure *result parameter* or a combined *argument/result parameter*.

• A *program* is just a procedure, which might contain nested local procedures.

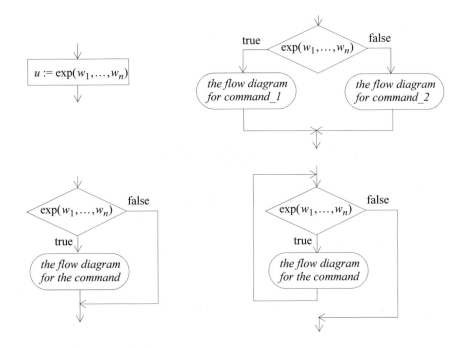

Fig. 5.12. Flow diagrams for "assignment" and the structured commands of "conditional jump", "two-sided alternative" and "`while` repetition"

The *semantics* of this procedural language is defined basically along the usual lines. The execution of *calling a procedure P* is started by *passing* the actual parameters and, additionally, to avoid unforeseen *side effects*, by automatically *initializing* each pure result parameter and each local variable with an appropriate constant. Afterwards, the body of the procedure P is executed stepwise by evaluating the respective expression and taking the action that it denotes. Figure 5.12 visualizes these actions for an *assignment* and for the *structured commands* as flow diagrams.

If the last command of the called procedure is reached, then the execution control returns to the calling procedure, whereby the values currently assigned to the *argument/result* and *result parameters* are considered to be the result of executing the call. Since "global variables" are forbidden, there are no further side effects.

For a procedure P, let $x_1, \ldots, x_m$ be the formal argument parameters, $y_1, \ldots, y_n$ the formal argument/result or result parameters and $z_1, \ldots, z_k$ the local variables. The semantics $|P|$ of the procedure P can then be more formally defined as

$$|P| : D_{x_1} \times \ldots \times D_{x_m} \times D_{y_1} \times \ldots \times D_{y_n} \; -partial \rightarrow \; D_{y_1} \times \ldots \times D_{y_n} \, ,$$

$$|P| \, (a_1, \ldots, a_m, b_1, \ldots, b_n) = \begin{cases} \text{final values of } y_1, \ldots, y_n & \text{if the procedure halts,} \\ \text{undefined} & \text{otherwise.} \end{cases}$$

Regarding the *policy specification* for expressing *permitted information flows*, *static labels* are declared for all variables. Given a procedure P, the labels are taken from the *power set lattice* $(\wp Var, \subseteq, \cap, \cup)$ with respect to the set of variables $Var = \{x_1, \ldots, x_m, y_1, \ldots, y_n, z_1, \ldots, z_k\}$, where some restrictions apply. The intention of declaring the static label $sl(v) = V \subseteq Var$ for a variable $v \in Var$ is to permit only information flows into v that originate from the variables in V. Accordingly, the following restrictions apply:

- a formal *argument parameter* x_i must get $\{x_i\}$ as its static label;
- a formal *result parameter* y_j might get a static label V_j such that

$$y_j \notin V_j \subseteq \{x_1, \ldots, x_m, y_1, \ldots, y_n\},$$

  not containing any other pure result parameter as well;
- a formal *argument/result parameter* y_j might get a static label V_j such that

$$y_j \in V_j \subseteq \{x_1, \ldots, x_m, y_1, \ldots, y_n\},$$

  not containing any pure result parameter.

Fig. 5.13. A syntax diagram for an integrated declaration of the type and static label of a variable

Figure 5.13 indicates how the declaration of the type and the static label of a variable can be integrated. As an example, we consider the following procedure (declaration) that serves to return the maximum of the argument parameters x_1 and x_2 by use of the result parameter y:

```
proc max(  x₁ : integer flow {x₁} ;        / argument parameter
           x₂ : integer flow {x₂} ;        / argument parameter
    var    y : integer flow {x₁, x₂} );    / result parameter
begin
   if   x₁ > x₂ then   y := x₁ else   y := x₂
end
```

In order to enforce the intention of the static labels, the *control invariant* concerning the variables, $dl(v) \subseteq sl(v)$, is complemented by additional *control conditions* concerning the compositional syntactical structures. Roughly summarized, during the *syntactical analysis*, all expressions and commands are assigned a *dynamic label* (shown by a numbered box in Figure 5.14), and for all commands an appropriate *control condition*, basically expressed in terms of the dynamic labels (shown by a circle in Figure 5.14), is generated and then verified.

This process starts at the leaves of the pertinent syntax tree by defining the dynamic label of an occurrence of a *variable* as the respective static label, which is

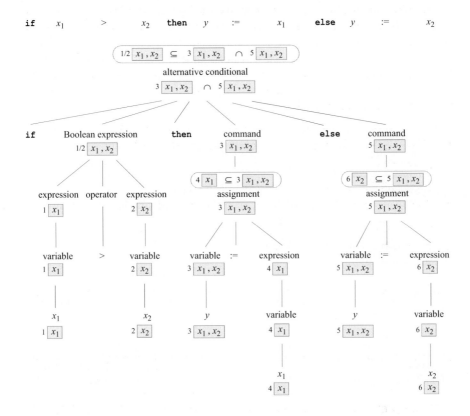

Fig. 5.14. An example of a compiler-based verification, by defining dynamic labels (numbered boxes) and generating control conditions (circles) in a bottom-up process

declared in the corresponding `flow` clause, and by defining the dynamic label of an occurrence of a *constant* as the least label, i.e., as the empty set. Afterwards, dynamic labels are defined stepwise in a bottom-up fashion by appropriately propagating the already available data up the syntax tree, in order to approximate the relevant *information content*.

Figure 5.14 shows the verification process for the example procedure. Table 5.15 specifies the general rules for inductively defining the *dynamic labels* and generating the *control conditions* to be verified. These rules comply with the following guidelines:

- As before, the information flow caused by evaluating a functional *expression* is approximated by the $\subseteq$-supremum of the labels of the arguments.
- For an *assignment*, including a *procedure call* which is treated like a multiple assignment to argument/result and result parameters, the control condition requires that the label of the receiving carrier dominates the label of the data to be transported.

Table 5.15. Inductive definition of dynamic labels and control conditions for the syntactic constructs of a procedural language

Expression/command e / C	Assigned dynamic label $dl(e) / dl(C)$	Generated control condition
constant: $e \equiv const$	$\varnothing$, i.e., least element	
variable: $e \equiv v$	$sl(v)$, i.e., static label	
functional expression: $e \equiv f(w_1, \ldots, w_n)$	$dl(w_1) \cup \ldots \cup dl(w_n)$	
assignment: $C \equiv u := e$	$dl(u)$	$dl(e) \subseteq dl(C)$
sequence: $C \equiv \text{begin } C_1, \ldots, C_m \text{ end}$	$dl(C_1) \cap \ldots \cap dl(C_m)$	
conditional jump: $C \equiv \text{if } e \text{ then } C_1$	$dl(C_1)$	$dl(e) \subseteq dl(C)$
alternative: $C \equiv \text{if } e \text{ then } C_1 \text{ else } C_2$	$dl(C_1) \cap dl(C_2)$	$dl(e) \subseteq dl(C)$
repetition: $C \equiv \text{while } e \text{ do } C_1$	$dl(C_1)$	$dl(e) \subseteq dl(C)$
procedure call: $C \equiv P(a_1, \ldots, a_m, b_1, \ldots, b_n)$	$dl(b_1) \cap \ldots \cap dl(b_n)$	for $x_i \in sl(y_j)$: $dl(a_i) \subseteq dl(b_j)$ for $y_i \in sl(y_j)$: $dl(b_i) \subseteq dl(b_j)$

- For a *guarded command*, the control condition requires that an *implicit flow* of the information represented by the label of the guarding expression is permitted for *all* assignments in the scope of the guard.
- In order to generate a condition referring to *all* constructs constituting a *composed* command, whether this is a *sequence* or an *alternative*, the assigned label is computed as the $\subseteq$-infimum of the contributing labels.

The only *reaction* to a detected policy violation is to provide the reason for the violation, and to refuse the actual execution of such a violating procedure.

If all details of the above sketch are carefully and appropriately elaborated, a theorem of the following form can be justified.

Theorem 5.3   [compiler-based verification]

Let P be a procedure with a totally defined semantic function $|P|$. If P satisfies all generated control conditions, then the following property holds: for any execution of the calling of P, any *realized information flow* from a variable v to a variable w is *permitted* according to the declaration of the static label of v, i.e., all other information gains are *blocked* in the sense of Subsection 5.1.4.

Idea of Proof: By a structural induction, one can show that the verified control conditions imply the implicitly treated control invariant concerning the variables, which in turn are proved to correctly approximate all realizable (and thus all realized) information flows. ❑

The compiler-based approach sketched above has great potential regarding further advanced programming constructs, provided that all constructs considered are compositionally structured and carefully avoid unforeseen side effects.

Axiomatically Based Verification of Structured Programs. The fourth variation deals with programs of roughly the same kind as those treated by compiler-based verification. Rather than employing operational semantics, this variation is based on *axiomatic semantics*. This variation has the following features:

- We consider a high-level *procedural programming language*.
- The guarded commands are structured *conditionals* and *repetitions*.
- The fictitious control of the execution sequence is represented by the *syntactical subparts* of a program. Within the annotating assertions (preconditions and postconditions), the execution control is captured by two specific *control variables* that can be seen as abstract versions of a *local program counter* and a *global program counter*.
- The set of *carriers* comprises the two control variables (execution control) and the set of (program) variables (storage locations).
- The power set lattice ($\wp\,Var, \subseteq, \cap, \cup$) with respect to the set *Var* of (program) variables is used for labels.
- Inference control is realized by *static verification* of a program (considered as a text).
- The reaction to a violation is to *refuse* an execution.

For the sake of brevity, we consider only a fragment of the procedural language introduced above. This fragment comprises *assignments*, the two-sided *alternatives* used as *conditionals*, and while *repetitions*. The *semantics* is the same as before, but is now supposed to be *axiomatically* specified by statements about the *state transitions* that are caused by executing a program or, more generally, any command.

In this context, a *state s* is given by the values assigned to the (program) variables in *Var*, and can be described by *assertions* expressed in the language of some suitable logic. If C is a command and A_{pre} and A_{post} denote assertions, then

$$\{A_{pre}\}\ C\ \{A_{post}\}$$

is a convenient shorthand for a statement about state transitions, roughly saying the following (ignoring non-halting or undefined computations):

> For all states s, if A_{pre} (annotated as a *precondition*) is true for the state s *before* the execution of the command C, then the assertion A_{post} (annotated as a *postcondition*) is true for the new state s' *after* the execution of the command C.

The semantics is then defined as the inferential closure of some *axioms* in the form of such statements under some *inference rules* for such statements.

Regarding the *policy specification* for expressing *permitted information flows*, *static labels* are declared for all variables. Given a procedure *P*, the labels are taken from the *power set lattice* ($\wp \, Var, \subseteq, \cap, \cup$) with respect to the set of variables. The intention of declaring the static label $sl(v) = V \subseteq Var$ for a variable $v \in Var$ is to permit only information flows into *v* that originate from the variables in *V*. This intention is captured by the *control invariant* concerning the variables, $dl(v) \subseteq sl(v)$.

An *axiomatically based verification* of a procedure or a command aims at proving the control invariant to be a postcondition for some precondition. In order to do so, we need some extensions of the axiomatic framework:

- A state also comprises an assignment of *dynamic labels* to variables.
- Furthermore, besides the (program) variables, the specific *control variables* *local* and *global* are introduced.
- The language for assertions offers means to express properties of extended states. As a convention, such assertions are written as a conjunction of three parts, each of them dealing with a separate aspect:
  - *AV* is an assertion about the program variables only.
  - *AL* is an assertion about the control variable *local*, whose dynamic label represents the *implicit flows* from the guards of conditionals and of repetitions.
  - *AG* is an assertion about the control variable *global*, whose dynamic label represents the *implicit flows* from the guards of repetitions beyond their execution.
- For each construct of the programming language, an approximation of the *information flow* caused is captured by an *axiom* or an *inference rule* concerning statements about transitions from one extended state into a succeeding extended state under the execution of the construct. In the following, we only briefly consider the three constructs of the selected fragment.

Concerning an *assignment* of the form $u := e$, where *e* denotes an expression of the form "expression($w_1, \ldots, w_n$)" with a derived dynamic label $dl(e) := dl(w_1) \cup \ldots \cup dl(w_n)$, there is an *assignment flow axiom*

$$\{ AV [\, dl(u) \, / \, dl(e) \cup dl(local) \cup dl(global)] \wedge AL \wedge AG \} \quad u := e \quad \{ AV \wedge AL \wedge AG \}.$$

This axiom captures both the flows from the expression and the implicit flows from the guards whose scopes extend to the execution of the assignment under consideration, by saying roughly the following:

if *before* the execution of the assignment the modified assertion $AV [\ldots / \ldots]$ about the program variables holds, where the modification $[\ldots / \ldots]$ replaces the dynamic label $dl(u)$ by the $\subseteq$-supremum of the dynamic labels of the expression *e* and the two control variables,

then the assertion *AV* holds *after* the execution for the new extended state, whereas any assertions *AL* and *AG* about the control variables remain invariant.

Concerning a two-sided *alternative* of the form if e then C_1 else C_2, where e again denotes an expression and C_1 and C_2 are the nested commands in the scope of the guarding expression e, there is an *alternative flow rule*, which has three premises and one conclusion:

$$\{ AV \wedge AL' \wedge AG \}\ C_1\ \{ AV' \wedge AL' \wedge AG' \}$$
$$\{ AV \wedge AL' \wedge AG \}\ C_2\ \{ AV' \wedge AL' \wedge AG' \}$$
$$AV \wedge AL \wedge AG \Rightarrow AL'\ [\ dl(local)\ /\ dl(e) \cup dl(local)\ ]$$

$$\overline{\{ AV \wedge AL \wedge AG \}\ \text{if } e \text{ then } C_1 \text{ else } C_2\ \{ AV' \wedge AL \wedge AG' \}}$$

This rule captures the *implicit flow* from the guarding expression e by manipulating the control variable *local* with the substitution $[\ dl(local)\ /\ dl(e) \cup dl(local)\ ]$; this manipulation can be reset after the execution of either branch of the alternative. As expressed by the first two premises, both branches are uniformly treated, assuming both of them to be realizable.

Concerning a *repetition* of the form while e do C, where e again denotes an expression and C is the nested command in the scope of the guarding expression e, there is a *repetition flow rule*, which has three premises and one conclusion:

$$\{ AV \wedge AL' \wedge AG \}\ C\ \{ AV \wedge AL' \wedge AG \}$$
$$AV \wedge AL \wedge AG \Rightarrow AL'\ [\ dl(local)\ /\ dl(e) \cup dl(local)\ ]$$
$$AV \wedge AL \wedge AG \Rightarrow AG'\ [\ dl(global)\ /\ dl(e) \cup dl(local) \cup dl(global)\ ]$$

$$\overline{\{ AV \wedge AL \wedge AG \}\ \text{while } e \text{ do } C\ \{ AV \wedge AL \wedge AG' \}}$$

This rule captures the *implicit flow* from the guarding expression e by manipulating the control variable *local* with the substitution $[\ dl(local)\ /\ dl(e) \cup dl(local)\ ]$ and, additionally, the control variable *global* with the substitution $[\ dl(global)\ /\ dl(e) \cup dl(local) \cup dl(global)\ ]$. Whereas the former manipulation can be reset after the execution of the body C, the latter one must not be reset: the dynamic label of the control variable *global* keeps the information related to the guard that the repetition has been successfully completed without running into a *non-halting* loop.

If all details of the above sketch are carefully and appropriately elaborated and extended for the remaining constructs, a theorem of the following form can be justified.

Theorem 5.4   **[axiomatically based verification]**

Suppose that for a procedure P, the following statement about state transitions and the following formula can be inferred:

$$\{\ true \wedge dl(local) \subseteq \varnothing \wedge dl(global) \subseteq \varnothing\ \}\ P\ \{\ AV \wedge dl(local) \subseteq \varnothing \wedge AG'\ \}$$
$$AV \wedge dl(local) \subseteq \varnothing \wedge AG' \Rightarrow \text{for all } v \in Var\colon dl(v) \subseteq sl(v)$$

The following property then holds: for any execution of the calling of P satisfying the precondition of the statement about state transitions, i.e., outside the scope of any information-carrying guard, any *realized information flow* from a variable v to a variable w is *permitted* according to the declaration of the static label of w, i.e., all other information gains are *blocked* in the sense of Subsection 5.1.4.

Idea of Proof: By a structural induction, one can first show that the assignment flow axiom and the flow rules for the structured commands correctly approximate all realizable (and thus all realized) information flows. The statement about state transitions then describes a postcondition for any execution of the calling of the procedure outside the scope of any information-carrying guard. By the supposed validity of the formula, this postcondition implies the control invariant.   ❑

Like the compiler-based approach, and with the same provisions, the axiomatically based approach sketched above has great potential as well. However, whereas compiler-based techniques are highly efficient, axiomatically based verifications tend to be tedious and too complex for large application programs. On the other hand, integrated axiomatically based tools for both functional and information flow analysis could support more detailed and more exact approximations of information flows.

5.1.9 Resetting and Downgrading Dynamic Labels

Assuming information flow to be always *transitive* considerably simplifies the analysis of programs and their executions. Moreover, if dynamic labels are used, the transitivity assumption often justifies the convenient approximation of an information flow by the *supremum* of the supposed current information contents of the pertinent sources. However, then the information content of a carrier appears to *monotonically increase* over time, becoming more and more *sensitive* and thus giving rise to more and more *blockings*. In some situations, this monotonic increase might indeed be *realized*, and then the blockings are actually necessary; but in other situations, the monotonic increase might simply be an unwanted consequence of too liberal approximations, and then it is better if the blockings are avoided.

In the exposition given so far, basically two techniques for soundly *resetting* the *dynamic label* of a carrier have been employed:

- Whenever a *program variable* is assigned a new value, the previously held value is supposed to be lost. Accordingly, the dynamic label of the variable is redefined as the label that has been computed for the new value on the basis of the evaluated expression. As a special case, if the expression is just a constant, then the new label is the least element of the lattice employed, and thus the dynamic label is completely reset. This special case includes the mandatory initialization of local variables when a procedure call is started.
- Whenever a *structured command* is properly left and control continues the execution outside the scope of the guarding expression, then the dynamic label of the pertinent version of a *control variable* can be reset to its value before the structured command was entered. In fact, the impact of structures is just to offer this possibility.

Unfortunately, there seem to be no further generally applicable techniques for *forgetting information*. Thus, a *security officer* either accepts potentially unnecessary blockings or aims at finding a sharper approximation of the information content considered, by use of a case-by-case analysis, or he explicitly and discretionarily decides to ignore a (potential) information flow.

Interventions of the latter kind, known as *downgrading*, have been proposed with diverse appearances. In essence, the dynamic label of a carrier is deliberately decreased to a lower level that balances conflicting requirements concerning *confidentiality* and *availability*. On the one hand, the downgraded label is still high enough to reflect (and thus forbid) the potential practical exploitation of the carrier's theoretical information content; on the other hand, the downgraded label is low enough to avoid unwanted blockings. Accordingly, a responsible officer should exercise informed downgrading, following some rules of good practice that lead to acceptable compromises for a specific application.

The concept of downgrading is part of the *decentralized label model*. The main emphasis of this model is on providing each individual *owner* of some information with a flexible and expressive means to specify the allowed receivers, when the execution of a program is shared. Roughly outlined and considerably simplified, in this model a *label* is a set of *policies*, each of which consists of an *owner* and a list of *readers*, where owners and readers are supposed to be identifiable *principals*, i.e., each label has the following form:

$$\{ (owner_1 : reader_{1,1}, \dots), \dots, (owner_k : reader_{k,1}, \dots) \}.$$

Assigning such a label to a *carrier* (e.g., an input channel, an internal program variable or an output channel) or to some *data* (e.g., the result of evaluation of an expression) means the following: the respective information content is permitted to be *transferred* to a principal *prin* iff that principal is a *grantee* of *all* policies in the label, i.e., iff

$$prin \in \{owner_1, reader_{1,1}, \dots \} \cap \dots \cap \{owner_k, reader_{k,1}, \dots \}.$$

Intuitively, *all* principals acting as an owner of some information have to agree to a transfer, where an owner is always supposed to agree to a transfer to himself.

While information is being processed during the execution of a program, the static label of the receiving carrier must always be *at least as restrictive* as the dynamic label of the transferred data, in the sense that each grantee for the receiving carrier is a grantee for the transferred information as well. Moreover, while (in intuitive terms) information is flowing, the labels assigned to a piece of information might become more and more restrictive: any deposit of a piece of information in a labeled carrier possibly *excludes* additional principals from accessing this (copy of the) information.

However, in order to maintain the needed *availability* of information, any of the owners might independently want to dynamically relax the exclusions by somehow *downgrading* (*declassifying*) their part of the label, or, more precisely, by generating a copy of the information with a label that is less restrictive with respect to this owner's grantees.

An owner can achieve this goal provided that he is a member of the specific *authority set of principals* on behalf of which the program execution is performed, and the program contains a suitable command that is dedicated to such a relaxation. With these provisions, when the dedicated command is executed, a copy is generated with a new label where this owner's part is modified as described in the command, but the policies of all other owners remain unchanged. Thus a strict relaxation is only achieved as far as is permitted by the other owners' policies.

5.1.10 The Programming Language Jif

The features of the decentralized label model presented above and further features have been implemented in the programming language *Jif* (*Java Information Flow*), which is an extension of (a sublanguage of) *Java*. Jif provides inference control by *static verification* of labeled programs as an extension to type checking, by analyzing the main constructs of Java for all kinds of information flows, including those caused by exceptions, and verifying the pertinent control conditions. The feature of downgrading, however, demands some limited *dynamic monitoring*, which also extends to granting authorities along chains of procedure calls, or dealing with additional runtime labels.

5.2 Inference Control for Parallel Programs

Many applications run programs that employ not only the constructs of sequential programming but also additional constructs for the *parallel* execution of several threads. Moreover, these threads have to coordinate their actions and to synchronize at specific points of their execution. Coordination and synchronization introduce new kinds of *implicit information flows*.

Intuitively, if one thread can only proceed if another thread has completed some specific actions, then the latter thread appears like a guard for the former one. Accordingly, the additional constructs of parallel programming and their interaction with the constructs of sequential programming have been studied.

We merely exemplify these considerations by use of a simple parallel program:

```
x,y,z: boolean;
s:      semaphore;

begin
   z:= false;
   cobegin
      thread_1:   read(x);
                  if x then signal(s)
   ||
      thread_2:   y := false;
                  wait(s);
                  y := true
   coend;
   z:= y
end
```

After the first command, on **cobegin**, the execution splits into two independent threads; afterwards, on **coend**, the threads *synchronize* and the execution continues as a single thread.

The threads share a *semaphore* s, which can hold non-negative integer values and is implicitly initialized with 0. This semaphore offers two operations:

- wait(s) *suspends* the execution of the thread until the value of the semaphore is set to a positive value by another thread, and then decrements s and *resumes* the execution;
- signal(s) simply increments the value of s.

By accessing only the program variable y, an observer of thread_2 can possibly infer the value of x read by thread_1: since the assignment y:=true is guarded by the semaphore, which in turn is in the scope of the guard x in the conditional, observing the value true for y implies that x has been given the value true as well.

Similarly, by accessing only the program variable z, an observer can possibly infer the value of x, too: since thread_2 terminates only if thread_1 signals the semaphore and the synchronization occurs only if both threads terminate, observing the value true for z implies that x has been given the value true as well.

Generalizing, inference control has to consider the following features and their interaction with sequential constructs: semaphores and synchronizations act as *guards* for the subsequent commands and might cause *non-halting computations*.

5.3 Inferences Based on Covert Channels

Usually, the semantics of sequential or parallel programs is defined in terms of an abstraction designed to appropriately model the behavior of real computing devices. Inference control – as presented so far – refers to the pertinent abstraction. Accordingly, inference control correctly captures only those information flows that can be described in terms of the abstraction, but fails to deal with potential further flows over *covert channels*.

An important example of this discrepancy results from the treatment of *time*. Typically, an abstraction for *sequential programs* implicitly or explicitly postulates that state transitions or other events occur at discrete points in time, which are linearly ordered. The length of the time span between two successive points in time is not important for the semantics, and thus is ignored.

However, when a program is executed on a specific computing device, then *real time* is involved. Moreover, an observer might have a priori knowledge about the real time consumed by particular instructions, and might be able to measure how real time elapses between some visible aspects of the functional behavior. Then, the additional data with respect to real time might suffice for inferring some details of the hidden aspects that would remain undetectable otherwise.

As a simple example, consider *dynamic monitoring* with *non-notified skipping*. While the statement of Theorem 5.2 suggests the absence of an information flow in the abstract setting, nevertheless the sketch of the proof indicates that an observer might be able to distinguish *different* subpaths in "secret mode" by measuring a different behavior with respect to real time. In contrast, *dynamic monitoring* with *refusing abortions* appears to be resistant to a corresponding inference: statement 2 of Theorem 5.1 suggests the absence of an information flow both in the abstract setting and for a specific implementation in real time.

Abstractions for *parallel programs* usually postulate more advanced abstractions about time that, in particular, provide means to reason about the *joint occurrence* in time of some event for two or more agents involved. Still, these abstractions do not deal with real time but typically only replace a global linear sequence of discrete points in time by a collection of local sequences where some partial relationships between their elements are assumed, owing to joint events.

As a further example, a sender and a receiver might also purposely establish a covert *timing channel*, generically outlined as follows. At agreed points in *real time*, the sender *signals* a bit of information by either generating a jointly observable event or not, for example by either *locking* a *shared resource* or not, or by either causing heavy *paging traffic* or not, or by use of any other distinguishable alternative behavior.

On the one hand, in general, when using a covert channel of this kind, the malicious users can achieve only a limited *data rate* and *reliability*. But, on the other hand, a *security officer* charged to detect and analyze all relevant vulnerabilities might only rarely obtain exact estimates about the achievable properties, given only incomplete and imprecise knowledge of the real and often not fully documented circumstances.

In general, covert channels for inferring or signaling information might arise from any kind of *unexpected observations* an "attacking user" could invent, or any *unexpected usage* of a shared computing system, respectively. In preparing against an unwanted exploitation of covert channels, a responsible security officer is challenged by the vagueness and openness of "unexpected behavior".

Accordingly, the literature, and this text as well, can only provide hints about the kinds of "unexpected behavior" that have already been experienced, including the following classes of examples, out of an in principle never-ending list of further possibilities:

- *Timing channels* exploit observable differences in behavior in real time.
- *Energy consumption channels* exploit the fact that (hidden) different behaviors are related to observable differences in energy consumption. Similarly, other *physical effects* such as measured electromagnetic fields could be exploited.
- *Storage channels* exploit the status of shared storage containers.
- *Exception-raising channels* are based on observable parts of the exception handling within some protocol, where an exception is either triggered as an observable event within a specific context or not. Observe that a security protocol might *refuse* to execute a specific request and then react with a corresponding *notification* as an observable event.

There is no universal countermeasure against detected covert channels. An obvious piece of advice is to "close a covert channel" by explicitly taking care that originally distinguishable events become *indistinguishable* for the suspected observer. Examples include the following:

- making the real execution time independent of some crucial input values, by performing *dummy operations* if necessary;
- decoupling consumers of shared resources, by assigning predetermined access times;
- unifying protocol executions, by eliminating case-dependent exceptions.

Clearly, achieving indistinguishable behavior often has the price of degraded performance, and then a suitable compromise between the conflicting interests of confidentiality and availability must be found.

5.4 Inference Control for Information Systems

Preventive inference control can be performed in different layers of a computing system, including the layer of *application systems*. *Information systems* of all kinds are typical examples. *Shared* by many and diverse clients, they often challenge the *security officer* with a trade-off between *availability* and *confidentiality*: for any particular client, on the one hand, the system should return useful answers to queries issued by the client according to that client's legitimate purposes and needs, and on the other hand, the system should hide any further information that it keeps available for other clients.

In this section, we outline a generic framework for *dynamic monitoring* of query sequences, based on a simple *logic-oriented, model-theoretic* approach to *complete* information systems. This approach comprises the following items, which basically instantiate the components "program", "semantics" and "execution process" shown in Figure 4.11:

- The *information system* maintains two kinds of data, a statically declared *schema* and a currently stored *instance*. A schema captures the universe of discourse for the intended application and formally defines the set of all conforming instances. An instance is an *interpretation* δ which assigns a truth value to every sentence q of some logic, i.e., to all sentences that are expressible in the universe of discourse. More formally, we assume that a "well-behaving" binary Boolean operator model_of is defined such that δ model_of q denotes the pertinent truth value. As an example, in classical *propositional logic*, an interpretation δ specifies a truth value for each propositional variable, and the operator model_of evaluates a propositional sentence q in the usual way, namely bottom-up, by applying the function tables of the propositional connectives.
- A (closed) *query* q is just a sentence in the pertinent logic.
- Given an instance δ and a query q, the ordinary *query evaluation* of the information system returns the pertinent truth value false or true, i.e.,

$eval(\delta,q) := \delta$ `model_of` q.

- Equivalently, and more conveniently for this exposition, the ordinary *query evaluation* either confirms the queried sentence or returns its negation, i.e.,

  $eval^*(\delta,q) :=$ `if` δ `model_of` q `then` q `else` $\neg q$.

- An *observer* might be a single client or a group of clients expected to collaborate. An observer can issue any *query sequence* $Q = \langle q_1,q_2,\dots,q_i, \dots \rangle$. Given an instance δ, the system's ordinary query evaluation returns the corresponding sequence $\langle eval^*(\delta,q_1),eval^*(\delta,q_2),\dots,eval^*(\delta,q_i), \dots \rangle$.

As indicated in Figure 4.11, dynamic monitoring requires further components, namely "security policy", "a priori knowledge", "previous observations" and the central component for the "case-by-case decisions" on permitting observations. The overall instantiation is visualized in Figure 5.16.

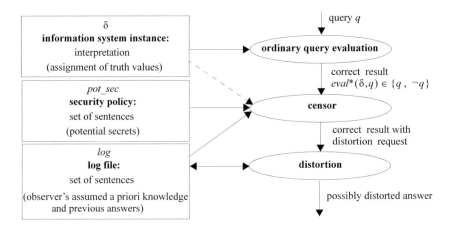

Fig. 5.16. Inference control by dynamic monitoring of query sequences, based on a logic-oriented model of information systems

A *security policy* is specified as a set $pot\_sec = \{ps_1,\dots,ps_k\}$ of sentences, in this context called *potential secrets*. Intuitively, declaring a sentence ps_i as a potential secret requires the following:

> The observer, supposed to be *rational* and *omnipotent* (not restricted concerning computational capabilities and resources), should not be able to infer that ps_i is true in the stored instance δ, even if this is actually the case, i.e.,

> from the observer's perspective the system's behavior can always be rationally explained on the basis that ps_i is false.

In other words, the observer should never be able to distinguish the actually stored instance δ from some conforming instance δ' that makes ps_i false, and this *indistin-*

guishability should be achieved under all circumstances considered. A more formal definition is given below.

The circumstances include the situation where the observer is supposed to be *aware* of the security policy, i.e., following a very conservative approach to enforcing confidentiality, the observer is seen as *knowing* the set of sentences whose potential truth the system is directed to keep secret.

Additionally, the observer is assumed to have some *a priori knowledge* that is captured by a consistent set *prior* of sentences. Furthermore, when issuing a query sequence, the observer is considered to retain all *previously returned* answers. Accordingly, the system maintains a *log file* called *log* that always contains a set of sentences and reflects the system's view of the observer's knowledge: *log* is initialized with the a priori knowledge *prior* and suitably updated after each of the observer's queries is processed.

The "case-by-case" decisions are taken in two steps. First, a *censor* inspects whether the ordinary answer would be harmful with respect to the security policy, and possibly investigates further issues. Second, if and as requested by the censor, the ordinary answer is *distorted*. Basically, two kinds of distortion are offered, refusals or lies, employed differently in various more specific methods:

- Using a *refusal*, for example by returning the special answer mum, the system *notifies* the observer that it has classified the query as harmful. Of course, the observer must not be able to exploit this notification to violating the security policy in any way. It turns out that the system does not need to memorize the refusals in the log file.
- Using a *lie* (also called a *false answer*), i.e., by returning the *negation* of the (correct) ordinary answer – clearly without a notification – the system aims at hiding a potential secret that is actually true or at preparing to achieve this goal for succeeding queries. Of course, the observer must not be able to exploit the lie to detect an inconsistency or to violate the security policy in another way. A returned lie is also stored in the log file.
- In a *combined* method, both kinds of distortion are used, depending on the specific situation.

Figure 5.17 shows the different behaviors for a simple example with a query sequence of length 2. In the following we present the censors of the methods in more detail, define a formal notion of *preserving confidentiality* which combines aspects of the algebra-oriented and logic-oriented models outlined in Section 4.2, state that the methods indeed satisfy the requirements, and justify this statement.

Refusal Method. On each query q, the refusal censor checks whether adding the correct ordinary answer or the false answer to the current log file *log* would be harmful with respect to any potential secret *ps* in the security policy *pot_sec*, i.e., the censor requests that the ordinary answer is distorted into a refusal expressed by mum iff

(exists ps)[$ps \in pot\_sec$ and [$log \cup \{q\}$ implies ps or $log \cup \{\neg q\}$ implies ps]].

universe of discourse:	propositional atoms			$\{\,p\,,\quad q\,,s1\,,s2\,,\quad s3\,\}$
information system instance:	interpretation	δ	:=	$\{\,p\,,\neg q\,,s1\,,s2\,,\neg s3\,\}$
security policy:	potential secrets	pot_sec :=		$\{\,s1,s2\,,s3\,\}$
	true potential secrets			$\{\,s1,s2\,\}$
a priori knowledge:		$prior$	:=	$\{\,p\Rightarrow s1\vee s2\,,\ p\wedge q\Rightarrow s3\,\}$

query	ordinary answer	refusal method	lying method	combined method
p	**p**	**p** correct answer	**¬p** lie protects disjunction of potential secrets	**p** correct answer
q	**¬q**	**mum** refusal protects false potential secret **s3**, due to false answer	**¬q** correct answer	**¬q** correct answer, since false answer does not have to be considered

Fig. 5.17. Two queries, the ordinary answers and the possibly distorted answers obtained with three distortion methods for a propositional information system

Inspecting the correct answer enforces the invariant that the log file never implies any of the potential secrets. This property and the property that the log file always contains only sentences that are true with respect to the information system instance form the *control invariant*. These properties must be required as a *precondition* too.

Additionally, inspecting the false answer is necessary in order to avoid *meta-inferences* of the following kind: "On observing a mum, the only reason for the refusal could be that the correct answer would reveal some potential secret, and thus this potential secret is true in the information system instance". In other terms, the observer should not be able to tell for what reason the censor requires a refusal.

Lying Method. On each query q, the lying censor checks whether adding the correct ordinary answer $eval^*(\delta,q)$ to the current log file log would be harmful with respect to the *disjunction* of all potential secrets, i.e., the censor requests that the ordinary answer is distorted into its negation iff

$$log \cup \{\, eval^*(\delta,q)\} \text{ implies } ps_1 \vee \ldots \vee ps_k\,.$$

Thus the lying method does not need to inspect the false answer but always has to protect the pertinent disjunction, even if this disjunction itself has not been declared a potential secret.

Requiring the *precondition* and enforcing the *control invariant* that the log file never implies this disjunction are necessary in order to avoid a *hopeless situation* of the following kind. Suppose the system allows the observer to know (or to believe) that the disjunction $ps_1 \vee \ldots \vee ps_k$ is true in the information system instance. The observer could then start querying the potential secrets ps_i in turn. Clearly, the system must always lie, and thus the observer gets the answers $\neg ps_1, \ldots, \neg ps_k$, leading to an inconsistency which would imply any sentence and thus any potential secret.

Combined Method. On each query q, the combined censor decides between three alternatives. If both adding the correct ordinary answer $eval^*(\delta,q)$ and adding the false answer $\neg eval^*(\delta,q)$ to the current log file log would be harmful, then the censor requests that the ordinary answer is distorted into a *refusal*, thereby escaping a seemingly hopeless situation. If only the correct ordinary answer would produce harm and not its negation, then the censor requests the system to *lie*, i.e., to distort the ordinary answer into its negation. Otherwise, i.e., if the correct ordinary answer does not produce harm, then the censor allows the system to return the correct answer. In doing so, the censor enforces the *control invariant* that the log file never implies any of the potential secrets, which is required as a *precondition* as well.

For any method, the security requirements can be more formally captured as follows. The method is said to *preserve confidentiality* iff

for each finite prefix of each query sequence Q,
for each information system instance δ,
for each security policy *pot_sec*,
for each a priori knowledge *prior*
  such that the respective precondition is satisfied by δ, *pot_sec* and *prior*,

  for all potential secrets $ps \in pot\_sec$,

  there exists an information system instance δ', satisfying the precondition as well,

  such that (i)   the returned (possibly distorted) answer sequences
              under δ and δ' coincide
              (and thus δ and δ' are indistinguishable), and

          (ii) $eval^*(\delta',ps) = \neg ps$
              (and thus $\neg ps$ appears to be possible).

Theorem 5.5   [preservation of confidentiality]
The refusal method, the lying method and the combined method always preserve confidentiality under the respective precondition.

Sketch of Proof: Suppose that, for some suitable parameters, the method has been executed, and consider a specific potential secret ps. The precondition and the control invariant ensure that, afterwards, the current log file does not imply this potential secret ps. By the standard definition of "logical implication" in terms of interpretations (instances), there exists an instance δ' that makes all sentences in the log file true but the potential secret ps false. Thus δ' satisfies property (ii).

Property (i) can be verified by an inductive argument, which depends on the respective method, and basically uses the following key observations. Concerning the refusal method, the censor decides in an *instance-independent* way, owing to the symmetric treatment of the correct and the false answer. Concerning the lying method, the possibly added lies have not been harmful, and now appear as true in the alternative instance δ'. Concerning the combined method, the refusal condition is *instance-independent* and, furthermore, any non-refused answer has not been harmful, and now appears as true in the alternative instance δ'.   ❏

Similar results can be obtained when the generic framework is varied in several different ways: we might want to express the security policy in terms of *secrecies* (pairs of *complementary sentences*) equally protecting both alternatives; weaken the *awareness* assumption; include *open queries*; and consider *incomplete informa- tion systems* as well, using a *proof-theoretic* approach.

Though, at first glance, all these results suggest positive solutions to the task of inference control, they also indicate the intrinsic limitations: within the framework presented, effective censors need to decide on *logical implications* and thus have to be based on algorithmic *theorem proving*. Unfortunately, however, logical implica- tion is undecidable in general, and theorem proving for decidable cases tends to be of high computational complexity. Moreover, the framework requires a complete formalization of all relevant aspects using the pertinent logic, which is impossible in general, and puts a heavy burden on a security officer in the manageable cases.

5.5 Inference Control for Statistical Information Systems

In this section we consider a specialized kind of *information system* and the dedi- cated usage of such systems for *statistical* purposes. For the sake of a simple expo- sition, an information system is modeled as an instance r of a relation scheme $R(K, V)$, where the attribute K is declared as a *key* and the attribute V is seen as some dependent *property* whose values are taken from the set of real numbers.

As a typical example, for each tuple (k, v) in the instance r, the key value k is an abstract identifier uniquely denoting a human *individual*, and the associated property value v expresses the yearly income of the denoted individual. Clearly, an income value constitutes *personal data* in the sense of the legislation about *infor- mational self-determination*, provided the pertinent individual can be determined. Hence, for enforcing *privacy*, access to such an information system must be regu- lated according to the *protection rules for personal data*. This requirement also applies if the information system is used for statistical purposes, for example for calculating the mean income or median income regarding some sample sets of individuals: the *statistician*, and further receivers of his results as well, must not be able to infer the income of any particular individual from the answers to statistical queries.

Obviously, we are faced with a potential *conflict* of *interests*: on the one hand, the statistician is interested in the *availability* of statistically aggregated data, and on the other hand, the individuals concerned are interested in the *confidentiality* of their personal data. Unfortunately, in general there are no simple means to resolve the conflict. For, roughly summarized, even if the system *refuses* to give answers to immediately harmful queries, such as queries related to samples of a size too small for hiding, a (maliciously acting) statistician might design sufficiently long query sequences that would enable him to set up a solvable system of equations whose solution reveals some particular personal data.

In the following two subsections, we shall present some illustrative examples. Accordingly, countermeasures must not only suitably restrict the sample sizes and the overlap (intersections) of samples but also carefully limit the number and the kinds of queries.

An alternative to refusals explores *lying* in the form of replacing the correct property values by (statistically) distorted values, for example by adding some random "noise", in such a way that the answers to the anticipated statistical queries are not "essentially affected", while successful calculations for "noise removal" are prevented. The subtle considerations necessary for this approach are beyond the scope of this monograph.

5.5.1 The Summation Aggregate Function

In this subsection, we present some examples showing how classical insight into the solvability of linear equations over the real numbers can be exploited to circumvent restrictions that lead to *refused answers*.

In the first example, we suppose the following situation:

- We fix an instance r of an information system publicly known to contain exactly N tuples whose key values form the set of identifiers $\{1,\dots,N\}$, without loss of generality.
- A query q somehow determines a *sample* set of identifiers, denoted by $sample(r,q)$.
- The query language is closed under Boolean combinations; for example, given the queries q_1 and q_2, the query $q_1 \vee \neg q_2$ determines the sample set

$$sample(r, q_1 \vee \neg q_2) = sample(r,q_1) \cup (\{1,\dots,N\} \setminus sample(r,q_2)).$$

- The statistical *aggregate function* is *summation*: on input of a query q, the system returns the result

$$sum(r,q) = \sum_{\substack{k \in sample(r,q)}}^{(k,v) \in r} v, \qquad (5.10)$$

i.e., the summation (in the real numbers) over the property values v associated with the identifiers k determined to belong to $sample(r,q)$.
- For some suitable threshold parameter $t < N/2$, the system *refuses* the answer to a query q iff

$$\text{card } sample(r,q) < t \quad \text{or} \quad \text{card } sample(r,q) > N - t, \qquad (5.11)$$

that is, iff the cardinality of the sample set is either too small or too large.

As shown in the following, under weak additional suppositions, the statistician can circumvent the *size restriction* expressed by the refusal condition (5.11) by exploiting the answers to an appropriately designed sequence of permitted queries.

In particular, by circumventing the restriction for a query q with card $sample(r,q) = 1$, the statistician can determine the exact property value associated with the uniquely determined key value k, and thus infer the personal data of the individual denoted. The circumvention proceeds as explained roughly in the following:

- Suppose the system refuses a query q according to the known condition (5.11).
- Supposing, additionally, a suitably small threshold t and some helpful a priori knowledge about the situation, the statistician selects a query $q_{tracker}$ such that

$$2 \cdot t \leq \text{card } sample(r, q_{tracker}) \leq N - 2 \cdot t , \tag{5.12}$$

and submits the queries $q_{tracker}$ and $\neg q_{tracker}$, which are both correctly answered.
- On the basis of the closure property, the statistician submits the queries

$$q_1 \equiv q \vee q_{tracker} \text{ and } q_2 \equiv q \vee \neg q_{tracker}$$

and observes the reaction of the system.
- In case 1, if the system correctly returns both answers, the refused result $sum(r,q)$ can be derived by solving the *linear equation*

$$sum(r,q_1) + sum(r,q_2) = sum(r,q_{tracker}) + sum(r,\neg q_{tracker}) + sum(r,q).$$

Moreover, we note that in this case the sample set is too small.
- In case 2, if the system refuses the answer to q_1 (and similarly if the system refuses the answer to q_2), the sample set for q is too large and thus the sample set for $\neg q$ is too small. The statistician then applies the circumvention for $\neg q$: since case 1 holds for $\neg q$, the statistician succeeds in inferring $sum(r,\neg q)$. The refused answer $sum(r,q)$ can then be derived by solving the *linear equation*

$$sum(r,q) + sum(r,\neg q) = sum(r,q_{tracker}) + sum(r,\neg q_{tracker}).$$

The strength of this circumvention profits from a powerful query language that offers the possibility to perform arbitrary Boolean operations on sample sets, leading to short, simulating query sequences.

In a second, slightly artificial example, we suppose a different situation, where queries have a special syntactic form and are additionally dynamically monitored regarding the *overlaps* (intersections) of their sample sets:

- Again, we fix an instance r of the information system publicly known to contain exactly N tuples whose key values form the set of identifiers $\{1, \ldots, N\}$, without loss of generality.
- A query $q \equiv (k_1, \ldots, k_{size})$ directly specifies a sample set of different identifiers, i.e., $sample(r,q) = \{k_1, \ldots, k_{size}\}$, where the cardinality $size \geq 2$ of all sample sets is a fixed system parameter.
- The statistical *aggregate function* is *summation*, as before.
- The system accepts any query of the fixed sample cardinality $size$, which should be chosen appropriately. Furthermore, for some overlap parameter $over$, the system accepts only query sequences $q_1, q_2, \ldots$ such that

	value v_1	value v_2	value ... v_i	value ... v_{size}	value v_{size+1}	answer
query q_1	0	1	... 1	... 1	1	ans_1
query q_2	1	0	... 1	... 1	1	ans_2
.	.	.	.	.	.	.
.	.	.	.	.	.	.
query q_i	1	1	... 0	... 1	1	ans_i
.	.	.	.	.	.	.
.	.	.	.	.	.	.
query q_{size}	1	1	... 1	... 0	1	ans_{size}
query q_{size+1}	1	1	... 1	... 1	0	ans_{size+1}

Fig. 5.18. Coefficient matrix of the set of linear equations for the unknowns $v_1, \dots, v_{size+1}$ resulting from the query answers

$$\text{for all } i \neq j: \text{ card } sample(r,q_i) \cap sample(r,q_j) \leq over. \tag{5.13}$$

Whenever a query violates the acceptance conditions, the system *refuses* the correct answer.

Despite the restriction expressed by the overlap condition (5.13), under weak additional suppositions, the statistician can exploit carefully designed query sequences to reveal all N property values, needing only $O(N)$ permitted queries. The additional supposition required and the design of these queries depend on the strength of the overlap condition.

If the overlap condition holds trivially, i.e., if $over = size$, then under the supposition that $N \geq size + 1$, the exploitation proceeds as follows:

- The statistician selects any $size + 1$ different key values; without loss of generality, these may be just the key values $1, \dots, size + 1$.
- For each of these key values i, the statistician submits the query q_i that comprises all selected key values except i, i.e.,

$$q_i \equiv (1, \dots, i-1, i+1, \dots, size+1),$$

which is correctly answered by $ans_i = sum(r, q_i)$.

- The property value v_k associated with the key value k can then be computed as

$$v_k = \left(\frac{1}{size} \sum_{i = 1, \dots, size + 1} ans_i \right) - ans_k. \tag{5.14}$$

This claim can be justified by inspecting the coefficient matrix of the set of *linear equations* for the unknowns $v_1, \dots, v_{size+1}$ resulting from the query answers, as depicted in Figure 5.18. More precisely, in the right-hand side of (5.14), we can equivalently replace the summation over all rows (corresponding to the known queries) i by a summation over all columns (corresponding to the unknown property values) j, straightforwardly simplify the terms and, finally, employ the definition of ans_k:

$$\left(\frac{1}{size}\sum_{i=1,\,...,\,size+1} ans_i\right) - ans_k = \left(\frac{1}{size}\sum_{j=1,\,...,\,size+1} size \cdot v_j\right) - ans_k$$

$$= \sum_{j=1,\,...,\,size+1} v_j \quad - \overset{j \neq k}{\underset{j=1,\,...,\,size+1}{\sum}} v_j \quad = v_k\,.$$

For the strongest overlap condition, i.e., if $over = 1$, under the supposition that $N \geq size \cdot (size - 1) + 1$, the exploitation proceeds as follows:

- Depending on the parameters $size$ and $over = 1$, the statistician determines $t = size \cdot (size - 1) + 1$ and constructs a matrix

$$E_{size,1} = [e_{i,j}] \quad \text{of size } t \times t \text{ over } \{0,1\},$$

  with the following properties and interpretations:

  1. Each row i has exactly $size$ many 1's, to determine a query.
  2. Each pair of different rows i_1 and i_2 has exactly one 1 in common, to ensure an overlap $over$ of 1.
  3. The matrix has a nonzero determinant, to enable a unique solution of the corresponding set of *linear equations*.

- For each row i, the statistician submits the query q_i that comprises all key values j such that $e_{i,j} = 1$; this query is correctly answered by

$$ans_i = sum(r, q_i) = \overset{e_{i,j}=1}{\underset{j=1,\,...,\,t}{\sum}} v_j\,.$$

- Now, as before, the property values involved can be computed by solving the set of equations for the unknowns $v_1, \ldots, v_t$ resulting from the query answers.

The construction of a suitable matrix is known from the discipline of combinatorics. We exemplify such a construction for $size = 3$ and thus $t = 7$ (and $over = 1$), yielding a *finite projective plane* with seven points $1, \ldots, 7$ and seven lines $q_1, \ldots, q_7$, as depicted in Figure 5.19. Here, each line q_i has three points (line q_6 looks like a circle); each pair of two different lines has exactly one point in common.

Summarizing, the attempts considered above to confine a statistician working with the aggregate function *summation* by restricting the sizes and overlaps of the sample sets queried could succeed only if, additionally, the number and kind of permitted queries were suitably restricted. Moreover, the suitability of such a restriction essentially depends on the specific situation; in all cases presented, however, the whole instance can be *universally* compromised by a sequence of queries whose length is linear in the number of tuples.

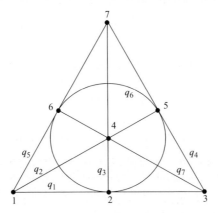

Fig. 5.19. A visualization of a finite projective plane with seven points and seven lines

5.5.2 Selector Aggregate Functions

One might wonder whether the disappointing insight summarized above is essentially caused by the choice of the aggregate function: summation, and related functions as well, straightforwardly suggest that one should set up linear equations in the real numbers and solve them. Unfortunately, similar results hold for another class of interesting aggregate functions, called *selector functions*, such as *maximum*, *minimum* and *median*, though an attacking statistician might have to expend some more effort and the success might only be *selective*, in the sense that some confidential property values can be inferred but not necessarily all of them.

As an example, we reconsider the situation examined above for summation, now regarding an *arbitrary* selector function:

- We fix an instance r of an information system publicly known to contain exactly N tuples whose key values form the set of identifiers $\{1,\ldots,N\}$, without loss of generality.
- To simplify the considerations, we additionally assume that the instance is *injective*: if, for different key values $k_1 \neq k_2$, the tuples (k_1, v_1) and (k_2, v_2) are in the instance r, then the associated property values are different as well, i.e., $v_1 \neq v_2$.
- A query $q \equiv (k_1, \ldots, k_{size})$ directly specifies a sample set of different identifiers, i.e., $sample(r,q) = \{k_1, \ldots, k_{size}\}$, where the cardinality $size \geq 2$ of all sample sets is a fixed parameter.
- The statistical *aggregate function* is any *selector function* sel that, on input of a sample set (of cardinality $size$), returns just one of its elements.
- The system accepts any query of the fixed sample cardinality $size$, which should be chosen appropriately. Furthermore, for the overlap parameter $over = 1$, the system accepts only query sequences $q_1, q_2, \ldots$ such that

$$\text{for all } i \neq j: \text{card } sample(r,q_i) \cap sample(r,q_j) \leq 1. \tag{5.15}$$

Whenever a query violates the acceptance conditions, the system *refuses* the correct answer.

Regardless of the concrete selector function, under the supposition that $N \geq size^2$, a statistician might always circumvent the restrictions to compromise at least one of the property values, as outlined roughly in the following:

- Depending on the parameters $size + 1$ and $over = 1$, the statistician determines $t = (size + 1) \cdot size + 1 = size^2 + size + 1$ and constructs a matrix

$$E_{size+1,1} = [\, e_{i,j}\,]_{1 \leq i \leq size^2 + size + 1,\, 1 \leq j \leq size^2 + size + 1}$$

of size $t \times t$ over $\{0,1\}$, as depicted in Figure 5.20, with the following properties:

1. Each row i has exactly $size + 1$ many 1's.
2. Each pair of different rows i_1 and i_2 has exactly one 1 in common.

- The statistician then deletes one row of $E_{size+1,1}$, say row 1, and all columns j where the selected row has a 1, i.e., without loss of generality, the last columns $size^2 + 1, \ldots, size^2 + size + 1$. The result is a matrix

$$F = [\, e_{i,j}\,]_{2 \leq i \leq size^2 + size + 1,\, 1 \leq j \leq size^2}$$

of size $(size^2 + size) \times size^2$ over $\{0,1\}$, for which the following derived properties hold:

1. Each row i has exactly $size$ many 1's (since exactly one 1 is deleted).
2. Each pair of different rows i_1 and i_2 has at most one 1 in common.

Figure 5.20 visualizes the construction by showing the remaining part in gray.

- For each row i of the matrix F, the statistician submits the query q_i that comprises all key values j such that $e_{i,j} = 1$; this query is correctly answered by

$$ans_i = sel(\, sample(r,q_i)\,). \tag{5.16}$$

- Now, the statistician has obtained $size^2 + size \geq size^2 + 1$ property values, all of which originate from the set $\{v_1, \ldots, v_{size^2}\}$. Accordingly, at least two of the values obtained must be equal, say the value v returned by both the query q_{i_1} and the query q_{i_2}. Since the overlap is restricted to 1 and the instance is assumed to be injective, the statistician can determine the unique key value k such that (k,v) is an element of the instance r, thereby revealing a piece of information that should be kept confidential.

Most notably, the inference exploits only the generic property of any selector function that it returns a value from the finite argument, together with the combinatorial "pigeonhole" construction, to produce more selections than a suitable finite set has elements. If a specific selection function is considered, such as the maximum or median, more efficient inferences are possible by using more special properties.

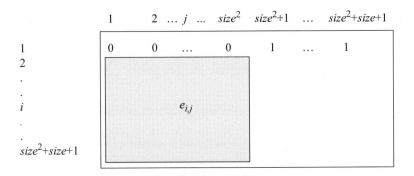

Fig. 5.20. Format of the matrix $E_{size+1,1}$ and of its submatrix F, shown in gray

5.6 Inference Control for Mandatory Information Systems

In Section 5.4, we outline a generic framework for *dynamic monitoring* of query sequences issued to a logic-oriented information system, aiming at enforcing a discretionary security policy for the sake of *confidentiality*. In Section 5.5, we introduce the more specific situation of statistical information systems, where the security policy declares all personal data to be kept confidential. Both in the generic situation and the more specific situation exemplified, we could alternatively follow the approach of *static verification* and *modification*. At design time, the verification would inspect the original instance to determine whether there is a permitted query sequence under which some harmful inference could occur, and the modification would remove such possibilities by replacing the original instance by an alternative *inference-proof* instance, which (hopefully) would still satisfy the *availability* needs.

In this section, we treat an example of the approach of static verification. The static approach is motivated by the following observations about the *schema* of an information system: the schema is already declared and published at design time before any (end)user appears, and the schema carries important and possibly crucial information that all users can later exploit as part of their *a priori knowledge*.

Moreover, at design time, a *security officer* might not be able to identify the prospective individual users, and thus might prefer to express his security policy in terms of a partially ordered set of *labels* or *security levels*, as introduced in Subsections 5.1.5-6. The usage of labels leads to the *mandatory* or *organization-oriented* approach to access rights management, as discussed further in Section 9.8.

A major goal of this approach is to consistently regulate permissions and prohibitions such that essentially only *unidirectional* information flows occur, where the label of the sender (source) must be dominated by the label of the receiver (sink). However, in order to fully achieve this goal, the security officer has to take care that the assigned labels correctly and completely reflect the *inferences* potentially made by a receiver. In particular, the static assignments should comply with the following informally expressed property of being *inference-proof*:

> If the label assignments permit access to entities or their relationships,   (5.17)
> then they also permit access to all inferable entities and relationships.

5.6.1 A Labeled Information System with Polyinstantiation

Our example of static verification is based on a simplified metamodel for *object-oriented* information systems, leading to a straightforward *logic-oriented* formalization. The metamodel comprises *classes* and their declared *attributes* in the schema layer; and *objects*, (plain) *data*, and *valuations* of an object by unique data according to its attributes in the instance layer. Each object must be an *instance of* a class; the direct instance objects of a class form its direct *extension*. Moreover, there is a *subclass/superclass hierarchy* between classes: a subclass *inherits* the attributes of all its superclasses, and a subclass *forwards* its instance objects to all its superclasses. Figure 5.21 visualizes the core of the metamodel by use of an ER model.

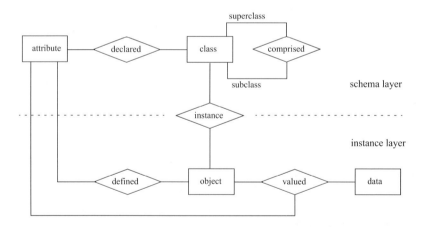

Fig. 5.21. ER model of a simplified metamodel for object-oriented information systems

We can obtain a logic-oriented formalization by introducing a suitable *predicate symbol* for each *entity* class and each *relationship* class; for conciseness, we just reuse the identifiers used in the ER model. Then, the *semantic constraints* for the metamodel, expressed informally so far, can be captured by (the implicit closure under universal quantification of) implicational formulas (rules), as outlined and explained in the following:

- [typed relationships] Each entity (term) occurring in a relationship (non-unary atom) is properly *typed* according to the pertinent entity class (unary predicate symbol). As an example, the rule

  `declared(a,c)` $\Rightarrow$ `attribute(a)` $\wedge$ `class(c)`

  expresses the instantiation of this requirement for the `declared` relationships.
- [acyclic hierarchy] The subclass/superclass hierarchy between classes is transitive, antisymmetric and irreflexive, which can be expressed by suitable rules.
- [inherited attributes] An attribute *a* declared in a class *c* is inherited by all subclasses *sc* of class *c*, expressed by the rule

  `declared(a,c)` $\wedge$ `comprised(sc,c)` $\Rightarrow$ `declared(a,sc).`

- [complete attribute declarations] An attribute *a* defined for an object *o* must be declared in some class *c* that the object *o* is an instance of, and vice versa, expressed by the combined rules

  `defined(a,o)` $\Longleftrightarrow$ ($\exists$c) `[declared(a,c)` $\wedge$ `instance(o,c)].`

- [forwarded class extensions] An object *o* that is an instance of a class *c* is an instance of all superclasses *sc* of class *c* as well, expressed by the rule

  `instance(o,c)` $\wedge$ `comprised(c,sc)` $\Rightarrow$ `instance(o,sc).`

- [no free objects] Each object *o* is bound as an instance of some class *c*, expressed by the rule

  `object(o)` $\Rightarrow$ ($\exists$c) `[instance(o,c)].`

- [complete valuations] Each attribute *a* defined for an object *o* must be valuated by some data item *d*, expressed by the rule

  `defined(a,o)` $\Rightarrow$ ($\exists$d) `[valued(a,o,d)].`

- [unique attribute values] Each valuation of an attribute *a* for an object *o* has a unique data item *d*, expressed by the rule

  `valued(a,o,d`$_1$`)` $\wedge$ `valued(a,o,d`$_2$`)` $\Rightarrow$ d$_1$=d$_2$.

Now that each of the constructs, i.e., entities and relationships, has been captured by an atomic formula and appropriately constrained by the rules, we can extend the metamodel to include *labels* (*security levels*).

Conceptually, we introduce *labels* as a new kind of entity that can participate in `classified` relationships with the original constructs. Formally, these relationships are captured by using a new unary predicate symbol `label` and associating an original *n*-ary predicate symbol `construct` (except for `attribute` and `data`) with a new (n+1)-ary predicate symbol `construct`^{clas}, where the additional entry is instantiated with a label intended to classify the (sensitivity of the) instantiation of the original entries. Figure 5.22 visualizes and exemplifies the extension of the metamodel and its formalization.

The extended metamodel is further described by additional *label constraints*, which can again be captured by (the implicit closure under universal quantification of) *implicational formulas* (*rules*), as outlined and explained in the following:

labeled construct

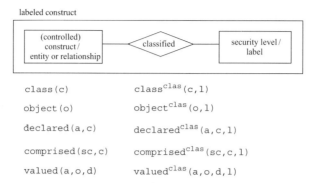

class(c)	class^{clas}(c,1)
object(o)	object^{clas}(o,1)
declared(a,c)	declared^{clas}(a,c,1)
comprised(sc,c)	comprised^{clas}(sc,c,1)
valued(a,o,d)	valued^{clas}(a,o,d,1)

Fig. 5.22. Labeled constructs in the extended metamodel with classifications

- [complete labeling] Each original construct must be labeled, expressed by the rule template

```
construct(termlist) ⟹
(∃l)[construct^clas(termlist,l) ∧ label(l)],
```

which is understood to be exemplified for each applicable construct.
- [no artificial constructs] Conversely, for all applicable constructs except valuations, only originally present entities and relationships appear in labeled extensions, expressed by the rule template

```
construct^clas(termlist,l) ⟹
[construct(termlist) ∧ label(l)],
```

which must not be exemplified for the valued predicate.
- [polyinstantiated attributes] Though originally attribute values were required to be unique, i.e., an object (identifier) could serve as a *key* for a valuation, the metamodel now offers the option that different attribute values may occur for the same object but different labels. However, the attribute values must be still unique for each label, i.e., an object (identifier) and a label *together* form a key for a valuation. These constraints are expressed by the rules

$$valued^{clas}(a,o,d,l) \Rightarrow (\exists d_0)[valued(a,o,d_0) \wedge label(l)]$$

and

$$valued^{clas}(a,o,d_1,l) \wedge valued^{clas}(a,o,d_2,l) \Rightarrow d_1 = d_2 .$$

The reasons for permitting *polyinstantiated* attributes are not obvious, and in fact they are controversial. The main argument in favor sees polyinstantiation as a solution to the following obvious conflict:

- From a purely functional point of view, the *key constraint* regarding objects should be enforced as an invariant under all updates, rejecting any insert command that would result in a violation.

- From the point of view of the *mandatory* approach to access rights management aiming at unidirectional information flows, a user attempting a violating insertion must not be informed about a rejection if that user is not permitted to learn the underlying information, i.e., the existence of a conflicting construct.

Polyinstantiation solves the conflict by relaxing the key constraint as specified above, leading to the following practical behavior. When a violating insertion is requested, the system rejects the request and *notifies* the requestor accordingly, whenever the requestor is permitted to access the already existing valuation causing the violation; otherwise, the system polyinstantiates the valuation *without* any notification.

Unfortunately, however, once polyinstantiation has been accepted, many challenges arise: all operations for the original metamodel must be appropriately extended to handle polyinstantiated valuations, including the full query and update facilities with optimizations, and transaction management with versioning, and the underlying semantic justifications for the extended operations must be convincingly expanded as well. Unfortunately, apparently, no proposed framework for doing so has been commonly accepted.

5.6.2 Inference-Proof Label Assignments

Given an assignment of labels taken from a finite *lattice* $(SL, \leq_{SL}, inf_{SL}, sup_{SL})$, in order to satisfy the required property (5.17) of being *inference-proof*, two more refined metarules must be verified, one regarding the *instantiation* of constructs and another regarding the *existence* of constructs. In both cases, the permission to access a construct is represented by a label, i.e., for an inspected label l, all constructs whose labels are ($\leq_{SL}$-)dominated by l are permitted to be accessed. Accordingly, the metarules express that whenever *all* constructs appearing in the premises of a rule are permitted to be accessed, i.e., the *supremum* of their labels is dominated by l, so are all constructs appearing in the conclusion, i.e., their supremum is dominated by l as well; equivalently, the supremum with respect to the conclusion is dominated by the supremum regarding the premises.

More specifically, the metarules to be verified demand the following:

- Regarding *instantiation*, for each valid rule expressible in the metamodel of the form

$$p_1(\ldots, x_{1,i}, \ldots) \wedge \ldots \wedge p_n(\ldots, x_{n,i}, \ldots) \Rightarrow q(\ldots, y_j, \ldots),$$

where all variables y_j in the conclusion occur among the variables $x_{k,i}$, the following rule, expressible in the extended metamodel with labels, holds as well:

$$p_1^{clas}(\ldots, x_{1,i}, \ldots, l_1) \wedge \ldots \wedge p_n^{clas}(\ldots, x_{n,i}, \ldots, l_n)$$
$$\wedge\ q^{clas}(\ldots, y_j, \ldots, l)$$
$$\Rightarrow$$
$$l \leq_{SL} sup_{SL}(l_1, \ldots, l_n).$$

- Regarding *existence*, for each valid rule expressible in the metamodel of the form

$$p_1(\ldots,x_{1,i},\ldots) \wedge \ldots \wedge p_n(\ldots,x_{n,i},\ldots)$$
$$\Rightarrow$$
$$(\exists\ldots y_j \ldots)[q_1(\ldots,y_{1,j},\ldots) \wedge \ldots \wedge q_m(\ldots,y_{m,j},\ldots)],$$

where all existentially quantified variables y_j occur among the variables $y_{k,j}$, and all variables $y_{k,j}$ in the conclusion occur among the variables y_j and $x_{k,i}$, the following rule, expressible in the extended metamodel with labels, holds as well:

$$p_1^{clas}(\ldots,x_{1,i},\ldots,l_1) \wedge \ldots \wedge p_n^{clas}(\ldots,x_{n,i},\ldots,l_n)$$
$$\Rightarrow$$
$$(\exists\ldots y_j\ldots)(\exists la_1)\ldots(\exists la_m)$$
$$[q_1^{clas}(\ldots,y_{1,j},\ldots,la_1) \wedge \ldots \wedge q_m^{clas}(\ldots,y_{m,j},\ldots,la_m)$$
$$\wedge\ sup_{SL}(la_1,\ldots,la_m) \leq_{SL} sup_{SL}(l_1,\ldots,l_n).$$

5.7 Noninterference in Trace-Based Computing Systems

The challenges of inference control arise whenever several participants *share* a computing system. For simplification, in the following we assume just two participants, the first one *cleared* (permitted) only to handle events *classified* by the *label* o(pen), and the second one cleared to handle events that are classified either by the label *o* or by the label *s(ecret)*, where the linearly ordered labels $o < s$ form a very simple *lattice*. The fundamental issue of inference control is then to *confine* the participant cleared by *o* to the events classified by *o*, even if this participant might be a *rational* and *omnipotent* reasoner who *knows a priori* the overall specification of the system.

Intuitively and neutrally expressed, this goal is achieved if there is no *interference* between occurrences of events classified by *s* and events classified by *o*. Thus, in terms of *confidentiality* regarding the events classified by *s*, there should be no *information flow* "from *s* to *o*", and in terms of *integrity* regarding the events classified by *o*, there should be no *causality* "from *s* to *o*". In other words, but still in need for further clarification, on the basis of the permitted observations, the participant cleared by *o* should have the "informed illusion" of employing the computing system as a single user, being "sufficiently" *virtually isolated* from the other participant, neither learning anything "interesting" and new about him nor being in any way "essentially" affected by him.

Conceptually, an *event* within a computing system can occur as one step in the execution of a program, i.e., as one activity of a *process* (or thread). In fact, a process generates a sequence of events called a *trace*; a program statically describes the set of its dynamic and possibly *nondeterministic* executions, i.e., a set of *traces*. Additionally, like the external outputs produced by the execution of the program, the *external inputs* can be seen as events as well. Finally, a shared computing system, statically described by the programs to be potentially executed and the potential external inputs, can be characterized by the actually possible *interleavings* of the input traces and the traces that are dynamically generated by the processes. In this context, an interleaving of two or more traces is the result of merging the events of those traces into one trace.

Hence, abstracting from the generators of events, (the behavior of) a (shared and possibly nondeterministic) computing *system* can be fully modeled as a set of traces. Moreover, by classifying the underlying events by the labels o and s, we can distinguish which participant is *permitted* to directly observe which events. The *confinement problem* then demands a *static verification* that the required noninterference actually holds. In the following, we outline and discuss this fairly general approach more formally. We start by specifying the underlying notion of a system and the classification by labels more precisely:

- *Event* is a finite set of (symbols for) *events*. This set is disjointly partitioned into the *input events In*, the *encapsulated events Ca* and the *output events Out*, i.e.,

  $Event = In \cup Ca \cup Out$.
- *Trace* is the set of words over *Event*, denoting the corresponding sequences of events, i.e.,

  $Trace = Event^{*}$.
- *Sys* is a *prefix-closed* set of traces, describing all (initial parts of) possibly *nondeterministic* behaviors of a computing system, including its external inputs and outputs, i.e.,

  $Sys \subseteq Trace$, and

  if $\sigma \in Sys$ then each prefix of σ is an element of *Sys* as well.
- *class* provides a *classification* of all events (in the spirit of the *mandatory* approach to access rights management), assuming $o < s$, i.e.,

  $class : Event \rightarrow \{o, s\}$.
- For $E \subseteq Event$, we define the *restriction* on a label l, i.e., on either o or s, as

  $E|_{l} = \{ e \mid e \in E \text{ and } class(e) = l \}$;

  we canonically extend this definition for $\sigma \in Trace$ and $T \subseteq Trace$ as follows:

  $\sigma|_{l}$ is the restriction of the trace σ to the events in $Event|_{l}$,

  obtained by deleting all occurrences of events that are in $Event \setminus Event|_{l}$, and

  $T|_{l} = \{ \sigma|_{l} \mid \sigma \in T \}$,

  again obtained by deleting all occurrences of events that are in $Event \setminus Event|_{l}$.

5.7.1 Noninterference Properties

To study formalized versions of noninterference, we consider the *permitted view* of the participant cleared by o on the system *Sys*, i.e., the restriction

$Sys|_{o} = \{ \sigma|_{o} \mid \sigma \in Sys \}$.

Seeing $|_o$ as a function of the form

$$|_o : Sys \to Sys|_o \subseteq Trace,$$

we investigate the (potential) *gain of information* about the (hidden) events classified by s, as obtained by this user from observing a specific trace $\psi \in Sys|_o$. As discussed in Subsection 4.2.1, on the basis of a priori knowledge, the user will determine the *pre-image*

$$\{ \xi \mid \xi \in Sys \text{ and } \xi|_o = \psi \},$$

and by comparing his observation with the *possible causes* determined, the user is able to find out what (hidden) events classified by s have *possibly* occurred, i.e., the restriction of the pre-image on the label s,

$$\{ \xi|_s \mid \xi \in Sys \text{ and } \xi|_o = \psi \},$$

called the *s-pre-image*.

Clearly, if the *s*-pre-image contains exactly one trace, then the user achieves a *complete* information gain about the hidden events, and thus the wanted confinement is violated. So the problem remains of which pre-images containing more than one element should be considered harmful regarding noninterference and which ones harmless. Somewhat surprisingly, there are several reasonable answers, the relationships between some of which are not obvious. For the purpose of inspecting four selected answers, in the following we consider only *s-ambiguous* systems for which the function $|_o$ is *nowhere injective* and thus all pre-images contain *at least two* traces.

To obtain a first answer, recall the similar situation for inference control in informations systems presented in Section 5.4. There, for each sentence to be kept confidential, the pre-image of an answer sequence is required to contain an "indistinguishable instance" that makes the sentence false. In the present context, an analogue of "making a crucial sentence false" could be "making a crucial event not happen".

In this analogy, noninterference means that the pre-image of the observed $\psi \in Sys|_o$ contains the trace ψ itself; equivalently, the *s*-pre-image contains the empty trace, indicating that the observation possibly results from a system trace where no events classified by s occur at all. Intuitively, if, from the point of view of an observer cleared by o, no activity classified by s is *indistinguishable* from some "real" activity classified by s, then we might postulate the desired noninterference. Formally summarizing and equivalently rephrasing the first answer, we can require the *noninference* property for *s*-ambiguous systems:

$$\text{For all traces } \sigma \in Sys, \text{ we have } \sigma|_o \in Sys \text{ as well.} \qquad (5.18)$$

We make two side notes. On the one hand, such a postulate still accepts a *partial* information gain in the sense of Subsection 4.2.1. On the other hand, if an *s*-pre-image was a singleton containing just the empty trace, then even the complete information about the "absence of activity" classified by s would be revealed.

A second answer can be seen as an adaption of the case where "no information gain" holds for a constant function in the general functional model. Basically, in this case an observation might be the result of any hidden behavior whatsoever. The adaption to the present context defines the meaning of "whatsoever" by the restriction $Sys|_s$, which describes all actually possible activities classified by s. More formally, we can require the *separation* property for s-ambiguous systems:

For all traces $\psi \in Sys|_o$, and for all traces $\xi \in Sys|_s$, $\quad$ (5.19)

for each trace σ that is an arbitrary interleaving of ψ and ξ,

we have $\sigma \in Sys$ as well.

Further answers explore the partitioning of $Event = In \cup Ca \cup Out$ into input events, encapsulated events and output events. Then, for example, we might be interested in ensuring that the restrictions of traces on o do not depend on the *input events* classified by s. In such a system, the *interface* for input events classified by s could not be misused to transmit some information to an observer of the system cleared only by the label o. In some sense, an "attacking" or "subverted" participant having access to that interface could not exploit the system as a *covert channel*. Seen as an adaption of the case "no information gain" recalled above, in this example the meaning of "whatsoever" refers only to all actually possible input activities classified by s, rather than to the full activities as before.

More formally, as a third answer, we can require the *(input-)nondeducibility* property for s-ambiguous systems, which should in fact be "s-input-ambiguous":

For all traces $\psi \in Sys|_o$, and for all traces $\xi \in Sys|_s$, $\quad$ (5.20)

there exists a trace $\sigma \in Sys$ such that $\sigma|_o = \psi$ and

σ restricted to the events in $In|_s$ equals ξ restricted to the events in $In|_s$

(obtained by deleting all occurrences of events that are not in $In|_s$).

Obviously, nondeducibility is a weakened version of separation; in particular, it is not required that all interleavings between the observation ψ and the inputs ξ actually occur in Sys.

A fourth answer strengthens the emphasis on the special role of input events classified by s in two ways: it does *not* leave open (1) which input sequences classified by s actually occur, and (2) which interleavings between the observation and the (hidden) inputs actually occur. Rather, this answer requires the following: (1) all syntactically possible traces ξ_{in} of (hidden) input events actually occur, and (2) for each such trace ξ_{in}, all interleavings with the observation ψ actually occur, either directly, or indirectly by a further suitably "correcting" interleaving with a trace of encapsulated and output events classified by s. More formally, as the fourth answer, we can require the *(interleaving-based) generalized noninterference* property for s-ambiguous systems:

$$\text{For all traces } \psi \in Sys|_o \text{, and for all traces } \xi \text{ over } In|_s, \qquad (5.21)$$
$$\text{for all interleavings } \tau \text{ of } \psi \text{ and } \xi,$$
$$\text{there exists a trace } \sigma \in Sys \text{ such that}$$
$$\sigma \text{ restricted to the events in } Event|_o \cup In|_s \text{ equals } \tau$$
$$\text{(and thus, in particular, } \sigma|_o = \psi \text{ and } \sigma \text{ restricted to } In|_s \text{ equals } \xi\text{).}$$

Each of the outlined properties of *noninference* (5.18), *separability* (5.19), *nondeducibility* (5.20) and *generalized noninterference* (5.21), and many further ones suggested in the literature as well, gives a particular answer to the question of which situations should be considered to be harmful when some part of a computing system should *not interfere* with another part. Accordingly, a *security officer* has to carefully investigate case by case which answer is appropriate for a specific application. Moreover, two issues regarding the *static verification* of the selected answer are important:

- Can a verification of the selected property be performed *compositionally*, as sketched in Subsection 1.5.1? Unfortunately, some of proposed properties do not possess compositionality, and some others do so only under suitable conditions. Grossly simplified, noninference and separability are composable, nondeducibility is not, and generalized noninterference is composable only in special cases.
- How can one actually prove the selected property for a *component* (or for the full system)? Referring to the possibly infinite set of all traces that constitute the component investigated, the purely declarative style of the property definitions seems to hinder the practical verification of nontrivial examples. Fortunately, however, in many examples a security officer can successfully apply a proof technique known as *unwinding*, to be explained in the following.

5.7.2 Verification by Unwinding

A noninterference property requires the *closure* of a set of traces, i.e., whenever some trace is in the set, some further traces of a specific form are as well. Basically, the specific form expresses the desired richness of a pre-image regarding a restricted trace observed by a participant cleared by *o*. The desired richness formalizes what should be *indistinguishable* for the participant, and thus limits the participant's options for information gain.

To verify such a closure property, one can exploit the inductive flavor of traces understood to be generated stepwise by some state-based execution mechanism. Then, like in other approaches to inference control, the required *global* confidentiality property is reduced to a *local invariant* governing each single step of the overall generation process, together with a suitable precondition. In mathematical terms, we can employ the inductive word structure of the possible traces.

More specifically, the "unwinding" proof technique for the static verification of a closure property proceeds as follows:

- First, we aim at identifying a local invariant for one execution step in the form of *unwinding conditions*. Intuitively, the unwinding conditions ensure that the pertinent indistinguishability relation between traces remains invariant for each single step, i.e., the occurrence of a further event e.
- Then, we prove the identified invariant to be sufficient for the closure property, possibly after strengthening it appropriately, establishing an *unwinding theorem*.
- On the basis of these prerequisites, we inspect the particular system to be verified to find out whether it satisfies the unwinding conditions and thus, by the unwinding theorem, the closure property.

In the following, we demonstrate the unwinding proof technique by a simple example. We consider the *noninference* property (5.18). For this property, two traces σ_1 and σ_2 of a system are required to be *indistinguishable* to a participant cleared by o or, in other words, *equivalent* regarding o, if the permitted views on those traces coincide; i.e., more formally,

$$\sigma_1 \sim_o \sigma_2 \text{ iff } \sigma_1\big|_o = \sigma_2\big|_o . \tag{5.22}$$

The unwinding condition of *local observance* treats one line of activity: given a previously executed trace σ (the current state) of the system, if σ has an extension in the system by a crucial event e classified by s, then σ and the extended trace σe (the successor state) are indistinguishable. By the properties of equality and the restriction function $\big|_o$, the unwinding condition of local observance obviously holds in any system (and thus is not particularly helpful in this simple example).

The unwinding condition of *transition consistency* imposes a constraint on a system regarding the extension of indistinguishable traces: if two previously executed traces σ_1 and σ_2 are (inductively) assumed to be indistinguishable, then either the two extended traces $\sigma_1 e$ and $\sigma_2 e$ are not in the system, or both are in the system and then are indistinguishable as well.

To derive the noninference property from these unwinding conditions, we proceed by an induction on the length of a trace. To start with, we just observe that the projection of the empty trace yields the empty trace itself. Then we consider any nonempty trace σ of the system with prefix τ and last event e. The system being prefix closed, τ is a trace of the system, and thus, by the induction hypothesis, $\tau\big|_o$ is a trace of the system as well. Since $\tau \sim_o \tau\big|_o$, by transition consistency, $\tau\big|_o e$ is a trace of the system too. Now, in accordance with the unwinding condition of local observance,

$$\sigma\big|_o = \tau e\big|_o = \tau\big|_o e\big|_o . \tag{5.23}$$

Thus $\sigma\big|_o$ is equal to either $\tau\big|_o e$ or $\tau\big|_o$; in both cases, $\sigma\big|_o$ is an element of the system.

Finally, let the particular system *Sys* be described by a regular expression over the two events o and s, which, for conciseness, are identified with their classifications, such that $Sys = (s\ s^*\ o + o)^*$. Each trace is generated as a finite sequence of either a nonempty repetition of the secret event s immediately followed by the open event o or of the open event o alone. An accepting finite state automaton is shown in Figure 5.23. Clearly, in this simple example we can see directly that *Sys* has the noninference property, since any occurrence of the secret event s can be dropped by the construction of the defining regular expression. Following the unwinding proof technique, we can also easily verify the unwinding condition of transition consistency: two traces are indistinguishable if they have the same number of occurrences of the open event o; the option of extending them by a further event does not depend on the occurrences of the secret event s.

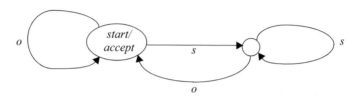

Fig. 5.23. An accepting finite state automaton for the system *Sys*

5.8 Bibliographic Hints

Basically all textbooks on security in computing systems cover at least some aspects of inference control, in particular the seminal textbook by D.Denning [163] and the book by Bishop [57]. The aspects presented in this chapter are mainly based on or inspired by the following selected references.

Cohen [139, 140] develops and studies an abstract model for sequential programs, strongly emphasizing the impact of a priori knowledge. Jones/Lipton [281] deal with computational challenges. D.Denning [160] discusses the usage of labels. Compiler-based verification of structured programs is first proposed by D.Denning/P.Denning [161], whereas axiomatically based verification is introduced by Andrews/Reitman [17]. Myers/Liskov [360] resume work on the usage of labels for the programming language Java, as part of a more ambitious project on language-based security, dealing in particular with downgrading.

Dynamic controlled query evaluation by refusal and lying has been pioneered by Sicherman/de Jonge/van de Riet [445] and Bonatti/Kraus/Subrahmanian [93], and later further elaborated by Biskup/Bonatti [66, 69, 74, 75, 78]. Biskup/Wiese [82] propose a static variant, generating an inference-proof instance. Biskup/Embley/Lochner [79, 80] consider special, optimized cases for relational databases. Biskup/Weibert [81] extend the theory to incomplete information systems. Related work has been contributed, for example, by Brodsky/Farkas/Jajodia [106] and Dawson/De Capitani di Vimercati/Lincoln/Samarati [154, 155].

Inference control for statistical database queries has been studied extensively; examples of important contributions are the work of Chin/et al. [132, 133], D.Denning/Schlörer/et al. [162, 164] and Traub/et al. [483]. Leiss [313] summarizes most of the early work. More recently, for example, Wang/Li/Wijesekera/Jajodia [494] adapt the basic techniques to more advanced information systems, and Domingo-Ferrer/et al. [176] gather together further advances.

Olivier/von Solms [377] and Cuppens/Gabillon [147] treat inference-proof label assignments. Moreover, several kinds of polyinstantiation have been proposed and further investigated: for example, Jajodia/Sandhu [273, 427] treat polyinstantiation for multilevel relational databases, Lunt/D.Denning/et al. [166, 329] employ polyinstantiation in SeaView, Winslett/Smith/Qian [501] propose semantics for polyinstantiation based on believing and seeing, and Cuppens/Gabillon [147, 148] discuss polyinstantiation and cover stories further; Castano/et al. [118] provide an early overview.

Noninterference properties have been studied within various models, starting with deterministic state-based systems and later with nondeterministic trace-based systems. Introducing the concept of noninterference for deterministic state-based systems, Goguen/Meseguer [237, 238] pioneer the topic. Then, for example, Haigh/Young [244], Foley [213] and Jacob [271] contribute further, Bieber/Cuppens [54] survey and compare several formalizations, and Rushby [415] elaborates the evolving theory. Regarding nondeterministic trace-based systems, Sutherland [471] proposes the property of nondeducibility, McCullough [337, 338] suggests generalized noninterference and identifies non-compositional cases, McLean [344, 345] considers separability and studies compositionality further, and O'Halloran [376] adds noninference.

Mantel [330, 331, 332] performs a systematic comparison of these and further concepts, identifying more elementary properties from which all variants can be composed. Our exposition has been inspired by this work. There are many further contributions; for example, Focardi/Gorrieri [211, 212] and Ryan [416] provide extensive studies in the framework of process algebras such as CSP, and Gray [239] includes probabilities, as does Santen [433] in more recent work.

Finally, Hughes/Shmatikov [262] propose a modular specification framework for information-hiding properties.

Part Three
Security Mechanisms

6 Key Ideas and Examples

This chapter opens the part of the monograph that provides a structured introduction to *technical security enforcement mechanisms*. For the structure we have in mind, we first identify three *key ideas*:

- *Redundancy* enables one to infer needed information, to detect failures and attacks and even to recover from such unfortunate events.
- *Isolation* prevents unwanted information flows or interference.
- *Indistinguishability* makes maliciously planned observations appear random or uniformly expected and thus useless.

For each of the key ideas, we shall sketch some important examples. In most practical situations, however, the key ideas have to be suitably combined in order to obtain overall effectiveness. Such combinations and additional concepts are treated in the next chapter.

6.1 Redundancy

As a provision against unfortunate events that challenge mainly the *availability* but also the *integrity* and *authenticity* of services, a participant may add *redundancy* to an object under consideration. In particular, a sender may add redundancy to a message before transmitting it. Later, following protocols agreed beforehand, the same or another participant can exploit the redundancy to detect failures and attacks and possibly even to recover from them. In particular, after observing a message, a receiver can infer *implications* about the presumable actual behavior of the sender or any interference stemming from an attacker.

Redundancy can be added to any kind of object, including messages to be transmitted over a channel, data to be persistently stored in memory, programs to be executed on demand and processes actually running. There are two basic forms of redundancy: the considered object, or a suitable part of it, is *duplicated* or even *multiplied* more times, or in addition to the considered object, some further *auxiliary objects* are constructed.

Afterwards, by inspecting the potentially corrupted state of the object under consideration together with the added redundancy, in the best case a participant might be able to infer the original state of the object, thereby ensuring its full *availability* and its *integrity as unmodified state*. In other cases, the participant might still infer that the inspected state differs from the original state, thereby ensuring *integrity as detection of modification*, or the participant might infer statements about the *authenticity* of the object, including either a confirmation of the claimed originator of the object or evidence of a forgery.

In this section, we survey some important examples that range from physical measures over various protocols for virtual layers to cryptographic methods. For each example, we describe the kind of added redundancy and the protocols that exploit that redundancy to detect a modified state and for recovery and exception handling, depending on the particular situation. However, most of the descriptions will be very sketchy, pointing to more elaborate treatments in other parts of this monograph or just leaving the reader to consult appropriate specialized literature.

6.1.1 Spare Equipment and Emergency Power

All computing is founded on *physical* activities, performed by the *hardware* equipment, consuming electrical *energy*. Thus, to maintain continuous service in the case of a hardware *failure* or a power interruption, additional *spare equipment* and *emergency power* must be devised.

Regarding spare equipment, as an extreme option, a complete duplicate hardware configuration may be kept in reserve. In most cases, however, only some critical parts are held in a local stock, in order to be able to immediately replace a failed part without waiting for external delivery. More generally, hardware maintenance for service-critical systems is organized by use of a layered *contingency plan*, ranging from a few locally kept parts to comprehensive stocks run along established supply chains.

Furthermore, provisions are needed to *restart* a crashed system after repair with the same software configuration and a well-defined *recovery state*. Again, as an extreme option, the whole computing system, including the software may be permanently run in parallel such that on the failure of the currently productive system, basically only a switch to the reserve system is needed. In this extreme case, not only the static parts of a computing system are replicated but also the dynamic parts, including duplicate or even *multiple execution* of processes.

Regarding emergency power, the options differ according to the time requirements for keeping the system operational. At the one extreme, if permanent service is crucial, for example for surgery equipment in a hospital, an independent *emergency generator* is provided. At the other extreme, a suitable *battery* is installed just to save the transitory part of the current system configuration, for example the contents of hardware registers, into durable storage. Again, in all cases, carefully designed *exception handling* to switch from normal operational mode to the *emergency mode* is crucial to making the emergency power effective.

6.1.2 Recovery Copies for Data and Programs

Once the hardware and electrical energy are reliably supplied, we have to take care of the "soft" parts in a corresponding way. However, in principle, the task of keeping data and programs in reserve is much easier, since in the end these items are only *bit strings* and thus can be easily *duplicated* and saved in independent storage, preferably also in several different locations. In general, again a layered *contingency plan* is advisable, ranging from *short-term* copies of main-memory contents saved on an operational hard disk, through *medium-term* copies of the contents of operational hard disks saved on a backup hard disk, to *long-term* copies held on completely separated devices and in separate places, for example magnetic tapes relocated in a suitable strongroom in some safe place sufficiently far away from the operational system.

The contingency plan should be largely automated, guaranteeing the generation of the backup copies independently of human interaction as far as possible. Often, backup data is constructed in an *incremental* way, copying only those parts modified since the last backup.

An additional issue for automation is a *recovery scheme* to reset the data or program configuration to a well-defined previous state by transferring saved copies back to the operational system. As an example, database management systems offer this functionality for the contents of the database as part of their *transaction* management. Since in some situations the recovery of a previous data state might be too costly or inconvenient for other reasons, more advanced systems might even follow a *compensation scheme* that transforms a corrupted data state into an acceptable data state, suitably mixed from previous, current and freshly computed data.

6.1.3 Deposit of Secrets

A highly important special case of maintaining recovery data arises in *cryptography*. Nearly all cryptographic mechanisms are based on some randomly generated *secret*, a cryptographic *key*, as explained further in Chapter 12. The actual holder of such a key is *distinguished* to perform some operation in a meaningful way, whereas all other participants are not. Clearly, if the designated holder loses the key, then that person is not distinguished any longer, unless he can access a safely *deposited copy* of the key. Similarly, if the designated holder accidently becomes incapable of acting, for example if that person passes away, or if he disappears voluntarily, no other participants can substitute for him regarding the pertinent operation, unless they can determine a copy from safely deposited shares of the key, for example as explained in Section 16.3.

More generally, key-based cryptography needs to be complemented by suitable *key-recovery* schemes and *key-escrowing* schemes to guarantee the availability of the service enabled by the pertinent key under all anticipated circumstances. A major concern is to minimize the *trust* to be assigned to the participants involved.

6.1.4 Switching Networks with Multiple Connections

Extending the considerations from a local to a distributed computing system, we observe two opposing facts. On the one hand, distribution often comprises *replication* of components and thus naturally leads to redundancy. As an example, a distributed database management system might offer a sophisticated replication scheme for the database contents, aimed at providing local replicates of appropriate views of the database contents at all participating sites, for the sake of both efficient local computing and independence of connectivity to a central site.

On the other hand, additional points of *failure* might arise if the successful cooperation of two remote participants depends crucially on a single network component, whether this is a physical line or a mediating network server. Accordingly, most (global) networks are designed to provide a high degree of redundancy regarding both lines and servers. In particular, *routing* is a major task, of selecting ways of transporting messages through a network that are available and are efficient overall.

6.1.5 Fault-Tolerant Protocols

In all layers, ranging from local processes through network services to final applications, *fault-tolerant protocols* are based on appropriate redundancy. The recovery schemes mentioned above, in particular database transaction management and network routing, are specific examples. In fact, fault-tolerant computing is a discipline of computer science in its own right. A major goal of this discipline is to keep a computing system operational under an anticipated class of *failures*, in modern terms, to support the "survivability".

The techniques applied are protocols to achieve this goal automatically, preferably without the direct intervention of humans. Within these protocols, the redundancy provided is employed in three basic ways:

- To *infer* a hidden original state from observations and auxiliary redundancy and to reconstruct it accordingly (e.g., the coding protocols for detecting or correcting transmission failures regarding bit strings, already mentioned in Subsection 2.1.3 considering the data layer, examined in Subsection 4.2.2 from the point of view of inferences, and treated further in Subsection 6.1.6).
- To *abort* a failing operation and to *restart* it from a saved or reconstructed previous state, or even to *redo* a completed operation if inputs later discarded have been used, or the results appear suspicious, or similar reasons apply (e.g., the abort/commit and redo protocols for database transactions, and the acknowledge and resend protocols for network messages, also already mentioned in Subsection 2.1.3 considering the transport layer).
- To take a *majority vote* regarding the actual outputs of computations performed independently and in parallel, directed toward achieving the same result.

The last way, of majority voting, is most appropriate if there is no agent or component that has full control over the overall situation, for whatever reason. We shall briefly describe two example situations, which have many variations.

First, suppose that we have a specification of a complex embedded service that is crucial for the overall effectiveness of its environment. Given an initial implementation, we might be concerned about its absolute correctness regarding the specification. Even worse, we might wonder whether the implementers might have found the specification not to be totally well-defined for some special cases. In this situation, in principle, we should reinspect the specification and then (formally) verify the implementation. In practice, however, on the basis of the state of art and science of programming, in the end probably nobody would be willing to guarantee the service without some reservations.

In order to reduce the remaining *risk* of an actual failure, we might order two further totally independent implementations, performed by different teams, preferably based on different programming tools, maybe even coded in different languages and, finally, executed on different hardware. Then, these three implementations of the same service are run in parallel, and whenever the service has to provide some value or some decision to its environment, the results computed by the three independent processes are compared. If the results are equal, the common result is seen as correct; if two of them agree but the third one differs, then a "majority vote" applies; otherwise, when all three mutually disagree, apparently some additional exception handling is mandatory.

Clearly, at additional cost, we could expand the scheme of parallel redundant computation with majority voting to more than three components, suitably taking care of the conflicting situation of equal votes for an even number. In general, however, two independent components would not be too helpful, except for raising a warning when different results were produced and calling an additional exception handling.

Second, suppose that we have a distributed computing system of four agents A_i. Each of them can locally compute a value a_i in a perfect way. Then, on the basis of a communication network enabling a directed connection between each pair, each agent should tell its value to the other agents such that, ultimately, each agent knows the vector of all values. Unfortunately, however, it might happen that some of the agents are partially or even fully *corrupted* or, equivalently, the outgoing connections might arbitrarily distort the values to be transmitted. So, after a first round of messages sent, each agent has received some value from each of the other agents but this value might be an "arbitrary lie" or otherwise incorrect. Without further assumptions, since nobody can force an agent (and its outgoing connections) to operate honestly and correctly, the situation is hopeless.

However, a strong majority of honest and correct agents can still achieve the subgoals that they ultimately know the other values correctly and possibly detect the occurrence of a corruption regarding a small minority. To succeed, the first round must be complemented by suitable further rounds and a final majority vote, as proposed by the *Byzantine agreement* protocols.

In the simple example sketched above, let us assume that only one agent is corrupted. In the second round, each agent has to communicate the local result of the first round, i.e., the vector of all received values including the agent's own one, to each of the other agents. But, again, the sole corrupted agent might produce arbitrary values. As the result of the second round, each of the three honest and correct agents has three vectors.

A careful analysis shows the following about the components of these vectors. Regarding the component for an honest and correct agent, at least two values will agree, and thus at most one differs, and the value supplied by the majority is the correct one. Regarding the component for the corrupted agent, all three values might be different, then revealing a corruption.

Summarizing this example, the Byzantine agreement protocol sketched adds sufficient redundancy to the first round by forwarding received values once again, such that under the *failure* assumption that at most one agent out of four is corrupted, the remaining at least three honest and correct agents can still learn their values.

Among many other techniques, the discipline of fault-tolerant computing deals with Byzantine agreement protocols for more general situations and other failure assumptions, identifying bounds for the size of a majority needed to be successful. For instance, the example sketched above suggests that in general, more than two-thirds of the participants must behave honestly and correctly.

6.1.6 Error-Detecting and Error-Correcting Codes

As already mentioned in Subsection 2.1.3 considering the data layer and examined in Subsection 4.2.2 from the point of view of inferences, by adding redundancy to a bit string before a transmission, a sender can enable the receiver to detect and sometimes even to correct some kinds of failure during the transport. In this situation, a *failure* assumption is often expressed in terms of *bursts*, which are erroneously generated long(er) sequences of either 0's or 1's, for example indicating logically a physical problem in the transmission line, or in terms of k-of-m *bit errors*, where at most k bits of a formatted bit string of length m have accidently been distorted from 0 to 1 or from 1 to 0.

The well-established discipline of *coding theory* provides a rich variety of solutions. Though the basic approach is quite simple, the actual protocols are mostly highly sophisticated. To explain the basic approach, suppose both the sender and the designated receiver know that either a single 0 or a single 1 will be transmitted. Obviously, a *failure* assumption of a 1-of-1 bit error cannot be successfully treated: on receiving a bit, say a 1, the receiver cannot tell whether the 1 was actually sent or the 1 was produced from a 0 by an error.

So the participants agree that either 10 or 01 will be sent, where the first bit can be interpreted to correspond to the originally agreed information, and the second bit to constitute the added redundancy (known as a *parity bit*). If, now, a 1-of-2 bit error actually occurs, the receiver sees either 11 or 00, both of which are different from the agreed strings, and thus the receiver can *detect* the trouble. The receiver still cannot decide which of the bits has switched, since the *Hamming distance* between the observed string and each agreed string, i.e., the number of differing positions, is 1. Thus, to *correct* a 1-of-n bit error, additional redundancy is needed, resulting in a Hamming distance of at least 3 between two agreed strings. Now, for $n = 3$, agreeing on the strings 100 and 011 would enable the receiver to find the position of a switch of 1 bit, by decoding the received string into the uniquely determined agreed string that has the least Hamming distance.

More generally, coding theory has systematically developed efficient procedures to encode an agreed set of messages in a redundant way, by employing longer bit strings than needed to distinguish the messages, such that any *failure* according to a pertinent assumption can be efficiently detected or even corrected by a corresponding decoding procedure. In particular, efficiency is an important concern, directed toward avoiding a costly explicit and exhaustive search to find the agreed bit string with a minimal Hamming distance and the error positions.

6.1.7 Cryptographic Pieces of Evidence

As already discussed in Subsection 2.1.3 considering the application layer, some situations require redundancy to be added as *cryptographic pieces of evidence* (*cryptographic exhibits*) for the sake of *authentication*. Unlike the situation for coding, the particular challenge is to enable the successful generation of an exhibit exclusively for a *distinguished* holder of a *secret*, employed as an *authentication key*. In particular, nobody (except the key holder) should succeed in performing an "error correction", i.e., *forging* an exhibit. However, dependent on the concrete mechanism, an "error detection", i.e., the detection of a forgery attempt, might be possible for others as well.

This possibility holds for all cryptographic mechanisms implementing *digital signatures*. In this case, the distinguished holder of the authentication key publishes a matching *test key*, suitable for *verifying*, for any claimed exhibit (presumable digital signature) added to a message, whether the message is authentic or not, i.e., whether the exhibit has been computed by means of the pertinent authentication key. Other cryptographic mechanisms for authentication, however, require a knowledge of the secret to perform a successful verification, and thus restrict the verification to those participants who share the secret. A simple example of this case is briefly explained in Subsection 6.3.1 (there emphasizing indistinguishability).

The approaches used in employing cryptographically produced redundancy for the sake of authentication are introduced more comprehensively in Subsection 12.4.2, examined further in Section 12.7 and treated fully in Chapter 14. The more general discussions in Section 7.1 are highly relevant as well. Moreover, some other cryptographic mechanisms exploit redundancy too. For example, as described further in Subsection 12.4.5, *one-way hash functions* can be seen to provide a redundant *fingerprint* or *digest* of a message. After its generation, the fingerprint is separated from the message and used as some kind of substitute for the message. Later on, a claimed matching of the message with its redundant substitute can be verified by freshly recomputing the fingerprint and comparing the fresh one with the old one.

6.2 Isolation

As a protection against unwanted information flows or interferences that challenge mainly the *confidentiality* or the *integrity* and *authenticity* and also challenge the *availability* of services, a participant may *isolate* the services considered from other parts of the computing system. The isolation can be *physical*, using separated physical devices for the services considered. Or the isolation may be only *virtually* achieved in higher layers of the computing system, for example by exploiting encapsulation in object-oriented design, by fencing services with control components that intercept and evaluate incoming and outgoing messages, or by cryptographic methods.

In general, any virtual isolation has to be appropriately founded on a physical isolation. For instance, virtual encapsulation and control components should be based on physical hardware support in order to prevent circumvention, and the secret keys needed for cryptographic methods should preferably be stored in physically isolated memory.

In this section, we survey some important examples that cover the range of possibilities indicated above. Where appropriate, we shall also discuss the relationship between physical and virtual isolation. Figure 6.1 roughly visualizes the placement of selected isolating mechanisms within the overall architecture of a distributed computing system.

The selections refer only to mechanisms that require explicit *access decisions* at runtime, indicated in the figure by an occurrence of "?", in order to enable the restricted usage of the isolated components according to declared *permissions*. Virtual cryptographic isolations employing more implicit access decisions based on the distribution of secret keys are not shown in the figure, but nevertheless are equally important.

6.2.1 Spatial Separation and Entrance Control

The simplest approach to isolation is to *spatially separate* an autonomously operated, *stand-alone* computing system in a dedicated closed room with locked doors (and windows), together with an effective *entrance control* enabling only *authorized individuals* to enter and then to (unrestrictedly) use the system. This simple approach, however, may suffer from serious threats to the underlying interests, based on the following events, for example:

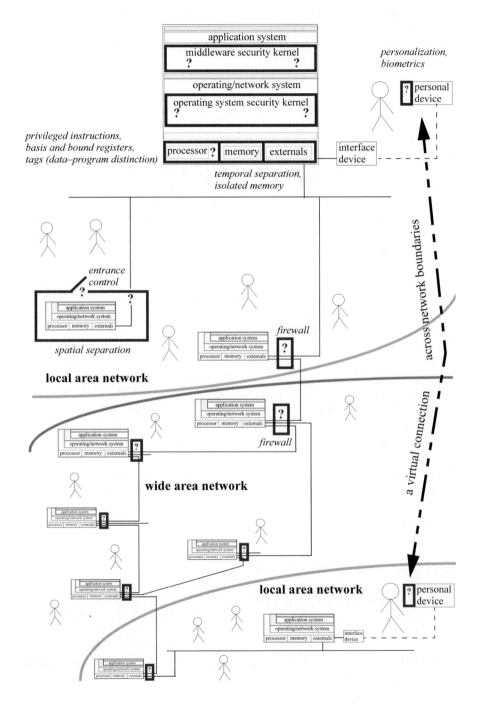

Fig. 6.1. Features of computing, and isolating mechanisms requiring explicit access decisions

- The selection of the (unrestrictedly) authorized individuals might not match the interests, owing to organizational weaknesses or unresolved conflicts.
- If two or more individuals are designated as authorized, they might (unrestrictedly) interfere and collaborate.
- An (unrestrictedly) authorized individual might misuse the trust for unexpected and unwanted goals.
- The entrance control might fail, and some unauthorized individual might succeed in entering and then (unrestrictedly) exploiting the system.

These and similar problems arise mainly from the *all-or-nothing effect*: either an individual can enter the room and then employ the system arbitrarily, or an individual must stay away and cannot use the system at all. Accordingly, any mechanism with an all-or-nothing effect should be supplemented by further, more finely granulated measures.

The concerns mentioned do not fully apply in one important special case: here, there is exactly one authorized individual, seen as the system's *owner*; the system is confined to a fixed collection of well-defined services in a *tamper-resistant* way; and these services exclusively support the *interests* of the owner. Substituting the locked room by other appropriate physical protections, these conditions could be met if the participant possesses a tamper-resistant *personal computing device*, always carefully prevents its loss, and prevents damage or other harm to it, and only employs it responsibly for his personal goals.

In the general case, and in this special case as well, further threats may arise when more comprehensive services are wanted. The complete spatial separation is then at least partially or temporarily interrupted in order to connect to a larger system. This problem always arises when the following fundamental conflict takes effect: on the one hand the requirement to isolate a local component, and on the other hand the need or wish to cooperate with other components, and ultimately to be connected to the whole Internet.

6.2.2 Temporal Separation and Isolated Memory

Several participants can share a computing system in two ways regarding time, either *strictly in sequence* or *overlapping in time*. In both cases, the participants might interfere, possibly without intent, when the processes executed on behalf of them access commonly used memory. Thus, to prevent unwanted interference, careful isolation of the parts of memory employed is required.

If sharing is done strictly in sequence, isolation is achieved by completely *erasing* all memory contents after finishing a job. In this context, "erasing" means that an agreed *normal state* of the memory, and more generally of the whole system, is reestablished. This normal state is maintained as an *invariant* of any usage of the computing system: it holds before and after any usage and, accordingly, a usage leaves no traces.

If sharing is done so that there is overlapping in time, the notion of a normal state must be adapted and additional measures are necessary. Basically, the adaptation restricts the erasure to the parts of the memory actually employed, in general including the *central registers* of a processor.

The additional measures ensure that the allocated *process spaces* (containing programs to be executed, runtime stacks for managing procedure calls, heaps for dynamically generated objects, etc.) always remain strictly isolated, i.e., one process can never access memory locations currently reserved for a different process. In order to ground these measures on physical tamper-resistant mechanisms, modern (hardware) processors offer dedicated features of memory protection and privileged instructions.

6.2.3 Memory Protection and Privileged Instructions

Memory protection aims at physically restricting memory accesses with respect to addresses and the mode of the operation requested. Roughly outlined, this protection mechanism ensures the following behavior of the processor's instruction interpreter.

If, on behalf of a process *proc*, during the instruction cycle, the next instruction must be fetched from a memory location identified by *address* or a machine instruction of the kind *instr* = [*operation* , *address*] is considered, then the request is actually executed iff a specific *protection condition* is satisfied, and otherwise some error handling is triggered. Such a protection condition might depend on the process, the activity requested and the address referred to. Basically, there are two different approaches, which offer many variations and combinations.

Basis Register and Bound Register. The first approach to memory protection is visualized in Figure 6.2. This approach employs two special registers, called the *basis register* and the *bound register*, which might contain memory addresses and are used as follows.

Whenever a process is started and gets an address space allocated, the address *basis* of the first memory cell allocated is loaded into the basis register, and, correspondingly, the address *bound* of the last memory cell allocated is loaded into the bound register.

Afterwards, while the process is running, the contents of these registers serve to guarantee that requested memory accesses either fall into the specified range or are rejected. More specifically, supposing relative addressing, first the specified relative address is added to the contents *basis* of the basis register, and then the sum *target* is intermediately stored in the address register designated to select the pertinent physical memory cell. Before the selected cell is accessed, however, the target address is compared with the contents *bound* of the bound register: the requested access is performed only if $target \leq bound$. If all addresses are non-negative, then this mechanism enforces the protection condition $basis \leq target \leq bound$, for all memory locations actually accessed.

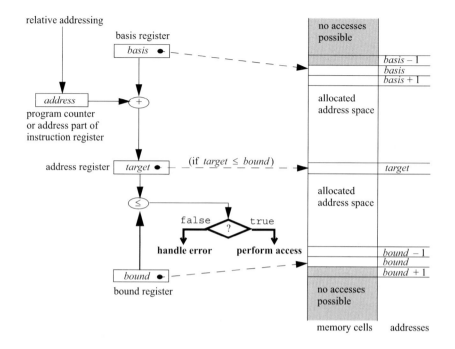

Fig. 6.2. Memory protection by basis register and bound register

Memory Tags. The second approach to memory protection is visualized in Figure 6.3. This approach employs short physical extensions of memory cells, called *memory tags*, which might contain annotating *tags* and are used as follows.

At design time, the possible usages of a memory cell's contents are classified. Each class is given an identifying tag that can be stored in a memory tag in order to declare the expected usage of the associated memory cell. Typically, there are 2^n classes, which can be denoted by bit strings of length n, distinguished by the properties of the activating item (in particular, the processor state), the process on behalf of which the request is executed, and the operation demanded by an instruction. Examples include the following:

- *read* access to an executable *instruction* (fetching into the instruction register) by any *user process* or by special *operating system processes*;
- *read* access to *arbitrary data* (loading into a data register) by any *user process* or by special *operating system processes*;
- *write* access with *arbitrary data* (storing from a data register) by any *user process* or by *special operating system processes*;
- *read* access to *data of a specific type* (e.g., integer, string, address or pointer), which has to be suitably recognized by the context or other means;
- *write* access with *data of a specific type* (e.g., integer, string, address or pointer), which has to be suitably recognized by the context or other means.

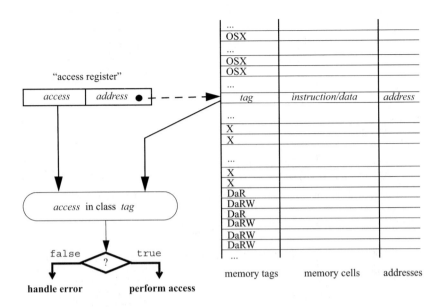

memory tags	memory cells	addresses

Fig. 6.3. Memory protection by tags (of length 2 in binary representation) for four classes, denoted by the mnemonics OSX (operating system instruction load), X (application system instruction load), DaR (data read) and DaRW (data read or write)

In the simplest variation, there are only two classes, distinguishing between accesses to instructions and arbitrary data, denoted by tags of length 1. More advanced variations might also distinguish between the usual data types of a programming language or even support suitably customized application types.

At the time of loading of some content into the memory for later usage, or alternatively when preparing for such a loading, each memory tag is assigned a tag according to the intended usage of the associated memory cell's contents.

Afterwards, while the loaded content is actually being used, for each request to access a memory cell, the wanted (kind of) access is compared with the stored tag: the requested access is performed only if the access is in the class denoted by the tag. Accordingly, this mechanism enforces a *protection condition* that any actual access to a memory cell must conform to a previously declared intention.

The basic approach of memory tags offers many variations, in particular concerning the size of the "cell" that is associated with a memory tag and the number of usage classes. Clearly, these parameters determine the resulting overhead in terms of additionally needed memory and additional operating time. For example, suppose that the memory consists of m cells, each of which can store exactly 1 machine word, and that there are 2^n classes. Then we need $n \cdot m$ extra bits of memory, and the conformance check is performed for any instruction cycle at least once in the fetch phase, and possibly once again in the remaining phases when data is handled.

Alternatively, if a coarser granularity of cells is selected, considering "cells" that contain $k > 1$ machine words, then a tagged memory for m machine words requires only $n \cdot m / k$ extra bits of memory and the conformance checks might be relaxed, but more sophisticated control semantics are needed or a less strict protection is achieved.

Summarized Comparison. The two basic approaches achieve memory protection quite differently and in different layers, namely by controlling physical cell addressing and the (semantic) usage of cell contents, respectively. Table 6.4 summarizes and compares the achievements of the two approaches. If both kinds of control are required, the approaches can even be suitably combined.

Table 6.4. Physical memory protection: basis register and bound register compared with memory tags

	Basis register and bound register	**Memory tags**
Extra memory	2 registers	linear in the size of memory
Operational overhead	assigning the registers; calculating and comparing addresses during memory accesses	assigning the memory tags; checking conformance during memory accesses
Abstraction layer of separated items	dynamically allocated address spaces	instances of types known to the processor
Granularity	more coarse (according to the memory requirements of dynamically generated, active items)	more fine (according to the size of instances of static types)
Protection goal primarily achieved	isolation of active items for avoiding unintended sharing of memory	isolation of instances of types for avoiding unintended usage
Coordination with higher layers	relative addressing, as usually employed	mapping of more application-oriented types to usage classes denoted by tags
Deployment	widespread, mostly together with other mechanisms of indirect addressing	seldom, mostly only in a simple variation

Privileged Instructions. The mechanisms for memory protection presented must be supported by further measures to control the initializing assignments to the registers or memory tags, respectively. Therefore, such assignments can be activated only by *privileged instructions*, whose usage is restricted in turn. In general, these instructions are enabled only for processes that execute dedicated security programs or dedicated parts of the operating system, and are not available for user processes.

In order to enforce such a restriction, appropriate higher-order protection mechanisms are tamper-resistantly implanted into the hardware, typically by entering suitable microprograms in physically isolated, non-rewritable special memory. These mechanisms include the option to operate the processor in different (security or protection) *states* or *modes* that determine which privileged instructions are executable. Clearly, the state transitions must be protected, too.

Figure 6.5 visualizes the interaction of memory protection, privileged instructions, processor states and protected state transitions in a simplified schematic way. The memory cells can be manipulated by the usual instructions for user processes, whereas the basis register, the bound register and the memory tags are accessible by privileged instructions only. The availability of either kind of instruction is determined by the processor state, which is materialized by the contents of a processor *state register*.

This register contains one bit encoding either "operating system" or "user process". If the register is set to "operating system", then all instructions are executable, including the privileged ones; if the register is set to "user process", then only instructions for user processes are executable, and any attempt to call a privileged instruction immediately triggers an error handling. Finally, state transitions are performed by a dedicated circuit that can only be directed by privileged instructions or by the error handling.

6.2.4 Separate Process Spaces

Once physical memory protection is provided, virtual *process isolation* can be achieved in the *operating system* layer roughly as follows.

- First, as already mentioned in Subsection 6.2.2, each process has an exclusive *process space* allocated to it, for any kind of data needed for the execution. The memory protection mechanism must comprise the management of *virtual memory* and thus be effective along the full storage hierarchy, including all *caches*.
- Second, the process management that switches the processor between processes must ensure that inevitably shared resources such as *central registers* are reset to *normal states*.

These issues are examined further in Subsection 10.2.4, where the employment of a *microkernel* is advocated.

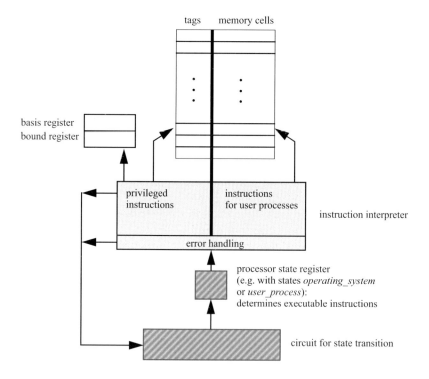

Fig. 6.5. Memory protection with higher-order protection mechanisms (an arrow roughly means "may manipulate")

6.2.5 Object-Oriented Encapsulation

Programming languages support several aspects of isolation, which are useful in particular for engineering software in the application layer. Considering for example *locality* and *encapsulation*, we can recognize some common underlying ideas.

In principle, we could write programs where, at every place, any operation could be executed on any data item, and subsequently control may be passed to any place. However, for disciplined engineering, we should refrain from doing so, and modern programming languages guide or even force programmers to work in a structured way to avoid arbitrary interference between activities in any two places. In other words, various parts of a program are separated from each other, each part suitably *isolated* on the one hand and *accessible* in a controlled way on the other hand. This feature and related ones are surveyed in Subsection 10.2.7. In the following, we only sketch an aspect of *object-oriented programming*.

A programmer should not write commands for directly manipulating "raw data", for instance "bit by bit". Instead, the programmer should first describe the concepts he has in mind by a *class declaration* (an abstract data type), which includes an abstract specification of internal states and of the methods for changing a current state. Later, whenever needed, the programmer is allowed to *create* a new *instance object* of the declared class. Each such object *encapsulates* the details of its implementation, and, accordingly, the object can be manipulated only indirectly, by calling one of its declared methods.

6.2.6 Security Kernels

If, for the sake of protection, an item is separated from its environment, it nevertheless should remain useful, and thus other items must be appropriately granted some controlled access. The overall management of separation combined with controlled access turns out to be a challenging task if there are many and diverse items. A commonly employed solution is to combine and concentrate the control activities within a dedicated component.

Roughly outlined, first, separation is generically organized by establishing an *interface* that must be used for *any* interaction between the items considered. Then, a preferably small (and thus hopefully verifiably correct) *kernel* is devised to control and monitor each actual interaction, for example by *intercepting* each call across the interface and deciding on either forwarding, rejection or modification.

Specifically for the operating system layer, this approach is described further in Subsection 10.2.4. Much more generally, the combined techniques of *control and monitoring* as a whole – which together with cryptography, in the view presented in this monograph, establish the overall scope of security mechanisms – can be seen as a sophisticated elaboration of the solution sketched. These techniques are introduced in Subsection 7.2.2 within the broader framework of Chapter 7; their essentials are summarized in Chapter 8, and Chapters 9–11 present important details.

6.2.7 Stand-Alone Systems

We could attempt to physically implement the desired *isolation* of a local computing system by operating it in a *stand-alone* mode, without any outside connections. Recalling previous discussions, in particular having in mind today's overall situation of *distributed computing* as visualized in Figure 6.1, this approach will be acceptable only in special cases.

Moreover, this approach could turn out to be an illusion, since for configuring the system, including installing the software, some temporary connections appear to be inevitable; at least the programs and the data must be input somehow.

Nevertheless, for special purposes and under a suitable relaxation together with compensating control, "nearly" stand-alone systems might still be helpful. A particular advantage is that only limited dynamic control and monitoring are needed once the system has been successfully initialized.

6.2.8 Separate Transmission Lines

Sharing a computer *network* usually offers a great advantage for all participants involved. However, the *endusers* of a computer network rely in some way on services that are not under their control but are operated by other participants. In the absence of sufficient *trust* in the operators of the network, two or more endusers might agree on a special requirement to keep their communication in physical isolation.

They then need physically separated *transmission lines*, used exclusively according to their agreement and under the full control of themselves or trusted agents. In most practical situations, however, such an extreme measure will not be affordable. Moreover, it will not be necessary, since *virtual isolation* by *cryptographic mechanisms* usually satisfies the protection requirements much more flexibly and at much lower cost.

6.2.9 Security Services in Middleware

If the communication services of computer networks are extended to the services of *middleware*, enabling shared distributed applications on the basis of a federated object system, total physical isolation of some participants regarding the remaining ones appears to contradict the whole approach. Accordingly, any mechanism for enforcing isolation has to achieve the goal virtually, by cryptography as well as by control and monitoring.

This reasoning is discussed more generally in Chapter 10, which presents the elements of a security architecture with an emphasis on distributed systems. The pertinent issues regarding middleware are specifically surveyed in Subsection 10.2.6 and discussed in further depth in Section 10.3, leading to the evolving amalgam of cryptography with control and monitoring, the techniques of *certificates and credentials* introduced in Subsection 7.2.2.

6.2.10 Firewalls

In many situations, isolation is not designed to be total and unconditional. Rather, it is devised with some relaxation and a compensating mechanism of control and monitoring. To follow this approach, a suitable interface must be identified or additionally established, where the generally desired isolation may be partially suspended under well-defined conditions.

Firewalls are a particular example, typically placed at the physical borderline between a local area network and the surrounding wide area network. At this borderline, there is a "natural interface" according to the *ISO/OSI model* for networks, which captures the full range of layers from physical lines up to applications. We treat firewalls in Section 10.4 as part of our broader view of a security architecture in Chapter 10.

6.2.11 Cryptographic Isolation

As mentioned before in Subsection 6.1.7, described further in Section 6.3 below and in Subsection 7.2.2, and fully discussed in Chapter 12 regarding the essentials and in the Chapters 13–15 regarding important details, *cryptography* achieves *virtual isolation* by making the holder of a secret *distinguished* among all other participants in the following sense.

The holder of the *secret*, called a *cryptographic key*, is enabled to perform some operation successfully, whereas all other participants will fail. This description applies for a rich variety of operations, including *decrypting* an encrypted bit string and thus assigning meaning to a purposely scrambled message, and generating a *cryptographic piece of evidence* or, in particular, a *digital signature*.

6.3 Indistinguishability

As a provision against maliciously planned observations that challenge mainly the *confidentiality* of information and actions or the *anonymity* of acting participants, and may challenge further interests as well, a participant or a group of participants may blur their specific informational activities by making them *indistinguishable* from random or uniformly expected events. As a result, an unauthorized observer cannot infer the details or even the occurrence of a specific activity.

Basically, as already indicated, indistinguishability can be achieved in two forms. On the one side, some explicit *randomness* is generated, and then the specific activity considered has this randomness *superimposed* on it such that the activity appears (sufficiently) random itself. Many cryptographic protocols follow this approach: the secret key is randomly selected from a very large number of possibilities, and the randomness of the secret key is transformed into (some sufficient degree of) randomness of the activity that is protected by the cryptographic protocol. On the other side, a suitably designed *standardized behavior*, possibly consisting just of dummy activities, is foreseeably produced, and then the specific activity considered is hidden among the foreseeable behavior, for instance by replacing one of the dummy activities.

In this section, we give some examples of both forms. All examples are related in some way to *cryptography*, mostly used as part of a more complicated protocol.

6.3.1 Superimposing Randomness

As discussed in Subsection 6.2.11, explained more thoroughly in Chapter 12 and detailed further in Chapters 13–16, *cryptography* employs secret keys to *virtually isolate* participants from each other. The holder of a *secret key* is designated to perform a specific operation as intended (thus, in this context, that agent is a *distinguished* participant), whereas all other participants will not succeed. In order to protect against clever guessing or an exhaustive search, a secret key must appear like a *randomly* selected element of a *large* collection of possibilities. In the best cast, the key is a *truly random* string of sufficient length, or at least is generated by using a truly random string as a *seed*.

Truly random strings are *indistinguishable* in the sense that they cannot be separated apart according to any general "meaningful property": roughly restated in terms of a paradox, although each random string is specific, nevertheless they all look like the same (think about lottery numbers). This kind of indistinguishability is used as a paradigm of cryptography as follows: superimposing the randomness of a key, and possibly further randomness, on an object under consideration results in a changed appearance of this object that then appears as it were random itself. In the following, we outline this paradigm by means of four examples.

Encryption. The intention of an *encryption algorithm* is to employ an *encryption key* to make any specific *ciphertext* appear random, except to the designated holder(s) of the matching secret *decryption key*, who should be able to recover the pertinent plaintext from a ciphertext. As a result, from the point of view of a non-designated observer of a ciphertext, the possible plaintexts cannot be distinguished: any of them could have led to the observed ciphertext, or at least no one of them can be "determined" to be the pertinent one.

A simple concrete example is shown in Figure 6.6 (and treated in more depth in Section 12.6 and Section 13.2). There are two possible plaintexts, 0 and 1, for example denoting the invisible events "loss" and "win", arising with probability q and $(1-q)$, respectively. Furthermore, as a source of *randomness*, there are two equally distributed keys, 0 and 1, each of which is used with probability 1/2, independently of the plaintext.

The *randomness* of the keys is then *superimposed* on the plaintexts, making the ciphertexts appear random as well. For example, this claim can be justified as follows:

$$Prob[y = 0] = Prob[x = 0] \cdot Prob[k = 0] + Prob[x = 1] \cdot Prob[k = 1]$$

$$= (q + (1 - q)) \cdot \frac{1}{2} = \frac{1}{2}.$$

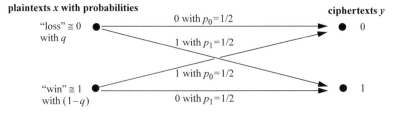

Fig. 6.6. Superimposing the randomness of keys on plaintexts, making ciphertexts appear random too, and letting hidden plaintexts be indistinguishable on the basis of an observed ciphertext

The effect of superimposing randomness can, alternatively, be described in terms of a mental experiment. Suppose you wish to construct an efficient *accepting device* that can discriminate (hidden) plaintexts on the basis of observing (visible) ciphertexts. Clearly, in this example, such a device cannot exist, since an observed ciphertext does not contain any information about the specific plaintext from which the ciphertext has been generated, and thus this plaintext and the alternative one remain completely *indistinguishable*. In other examples, we might be content with acceptors that achieve only a negligible effectiveness. A more formal exposition of this kind of reasoning is presented in Section 13.11.

Authentication. Besides other properties, in order to prevent *forgeries* by *substitution attacks*, an *authentication algorithm* should achieve the following. The algorithm employs a secret *authentication key* such that any specific *cryptographic piece of evidence* (*cryptographic exhibit*) appears random, except to the designated holder(s) of the *authentication key*. As a result, from the point of view of a non-designated observer of a (known or maliciously intercepted) cryptographic exhibit belonging to a specific object, the possible cryptographic exhibits cannot be distinguished regarding their acceptance as evidence for *other* objects: for any other object, any of the possible cryptographic exhibits will still be seen as a candidate, or at least no one of them can be "determined" as the pertinent one.

A simple concrete example is shown in Figure 6.7 (and treated in more depth in Section 12.7 and Section 14.2). There are two possible objects, 0 and 1, for example again denoting the events "loss" and "win", respectively. Furthermore, as a source of *randomness*, there are four equally distributed keys, 00, 01, 10 and 11, each of which is used with probability 1/4, independently of the object.

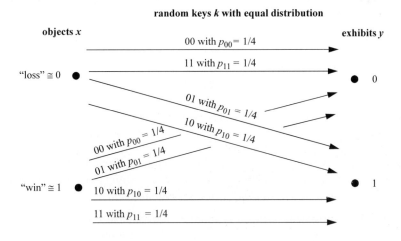

Fig. 6.7. Superimposing the randomness of keys on objects, making cryptographic exhibits appear random too, and letting possible cryptographic exhibits be indistinguishable regarding their acceptance for other objects on the basis of an observed exhibit

The *randomness* of the keys is then *superimposed* on the objects, making exhibits appear random as well, even if one exhibit has been observed. This claim may be informally justified as follows. Suppose the exhibit 0 for the event "loss" is known. Then, either key 00 or key 11 has been secretly used. These keys still map the event "win" onto either exhibit, 0 or 1, which are thus *indistinguishable* regarding their acceptance on the basis of the pertinent secret key.

One-Way Hash Functions. A one-way *hash function* is intended to generate *cryptographic pieces of evidence* (*cryptographic exhibits*) for a participant who knows an object. Usually, a hash function is not keyed, and thus it must appropriately comprise *randomness* itself. As a result, from the point of view of an observer who sees only a hash value, this hash value appears random. Accordingly, the possible objects that could have led to the observed hash value basically remain *indistinguishable* to this observer, with the following exception.

The observer can tentatively try to compute hash values of possible objects and compare those values with the observed value, thereby expecting to find mismatches and thus to exclude the objects considered from having led to the observed hash value. This and other properties of one-way hash functions are treated in more depth in Subsection 12.4.5.

Secret Sharing. A protocol for *secret sharing* aims at generating a number of *shares* of some *secret* such that sufficiently many shares together permit the secret to be reconstructed, whereas each individual share, or even any insufficient collection of shares, appears random. As a result, from the point of view of an observer who does not see sufficiently many shares, all values of the set from which the secret has been chosen are *indistinguishable*. In this case, the *randomness* is introduced by means of the share generation algorithm. A prominent example is treated in more depth in Section 16.3.

6.3.2 Hiding among Standardized Behavior

Randomness achieves indistinguishability by *uniformity*: on the basis of an observation, each possibility of a range of hidden options appears to be equally likely, and the observer does not have any means to gain information about the option actually valid. Alternatively, or in combination with randomness, we can also produce uniformity by following a *standardized behavior*. In the extreme case, a standardized behavior always looks the same, though some invisible differences still arise. In the following, we exemplify the paradigm of hiding actual differences among standardization, which is treated in more depth in Chapter 15.

Non-Observable Activities. In the first example, a participant performs a standardized behavior by apparently doing the same at all predefined points in time, always according to a publicly known protocol. However, at the discretion of the participant, the standardized behavior might hide actual differences in the intention or purpose of the participant's activity. As a prominent instantiation, a participant might want to hide the points in time at which he is *sending* a message to somebody according to his informational needs. Therefore, the participant pretends to be *uniformly active*, sending a message of the same length to some fixed intermediate address at every agreed point in time as follows.

On the one hand, if he needs to communicate with some partner, the participant

- prepares a corresponding document,
- appropriately adds the final destination of the communication,
- pads the document with some additional material until it has the expected length (or, if necessary, first splits the document and then pads the last fragment),
- envelops all data,
- waits for the next agreed point in time, and
- then sends the final message to the intermediate address used as a postbox.

On the other hand, at all other points in time, if no "real activity" is due, the participant just sends a *dummy message* of the expected length (to be discarded by the postbox owner).

A "real activity" and a "dummy activity" are then *indistinguishable* to an observer who only monitors the outgoing message traffic, without being able to inspect the contents, and thus the "real activities" can be considered as *non-observable*, since they are hidden among the standardized behavior.

Brokers and Blackboards. In the instantiated example above, the participant employs a sort of fixed intermediate postbox in order to hide the final destinations of communications. More generally, we might want to hide not only destinations but also sources or even the corresponding pairs. Basically, this goal can be achieved by the uniformity of the standardized behavior of *brokers* or *blackboards*.

A *broker* acts as a mediator between possible senders and possible receivers of messages. As described above, a sender first envelops a document and then sends it to the broker, who unpacks the document and forwards it to the final receiver. From the perspective of an observer who sees only the message traffic of a sender, all messages appear to go uniformly to the broker and thus are *indistinguishable* regarding the final destination. Correspondingly, from the perspective of an observer who sees only the message traffic of a receiver, all messages appear to come uniformly from the broker and thus are *indistinguishable* regarding the original source. Clearly, the broker is a more powerful observer, since he can – and must – still see the pertinent pairs of senders and receivers. However, if a chain of brokers is suitably employed, no single broker can gain this information.

A *blackboard* acts similarly to a broker, except that a received and unpacked message is uniformly published on a commonly accessible reading medium (rather than forwarded). The expected receivers can then search the published documents according to their wishes.

Group Activities. A *group* of participants might authorize its members to act on behalf of the community but without revealing the actor's *identity* to observers outside the group. For example, in some context, each group member should be able to produce an accepted cryptographic exhibit such that a normal verifier cannot trace back the responsible individual. Thus all group members are *indistinguishable* to such a verifier.

This requirement alone could be satisfied by letting all group members share a secret as an authentication key. On the basis of a more sophisticated key generation and distribution scheme, cryptography can do even better: there are cryptographic protocols that additionally enable some designated insiders to identify an individual producer of a cryptographic exhibit.

6.4 Bibliographic Hints

Most of the material in this chapter is the author's view of selected common background knowledge regarding computing in general and the field of security in computing systems in particular. Thus the textbooks listed at the end of the introductory Chapter 1 provide further aspects and different views. To understand the broad view presented here, the comprehensive taxonomy of dependable and secure computing prepared by Avizienis/Laprie/Randell/Landwehr [21] is also highly worthwhile.

Most of the topics discussed are treated further in subsequent chapters, where more specific bibliographic hints are given. In the following we list mainly a few selected references with respect to topics not covered elsewhere.

Jalote [277] provides an introduction to fault-tolerant computing. Avizienis/et al. [20] review the achievements of fault-tolerant computing in 1995, after 25 years of research. Butler/et al. [113] report on more recent challenges and efforts regarding increasingly complex systems. In relation to more specialized topics, Goloubeva/ et al. [235] examine how to achieve hardware fault tolerance by use of software, and Lewis/Bernstein/Kifer [315] and Weikum/Vossen [497] survey database transactions. Tanenbaum/van Steen [478] consider fault-tolerance in distributed systems. Berlekamp [42], Blake/Mullin [85], Pless [396] and Hoffman/et al. [256] present algebraic approaches to coding theory. A general background on hardware organization is supplied by Hennessy/Patterson [254]. Feustel [206] discusses the special issue of tagged memory.

7 Combined Techniques

Usually, the key ideas for technical security enforcement mechanisms, *redundancy*, *isolation* and *indistinguishability*, have to be suitably combined in order to obtain overall effectiveness concerning security. In this chapter, we provide an introduction to such combinations and, additionally, consider two further important concepts: at run time, we nearly always have to properly *identify* or at least suitably *classify* agents and *authenticate* them, and at design time, security administrators have to specify their *security policies* in terms of which agents are *permitted* or *prohibited* to gain access to which operations on which objects. Then, there are two classes of techniques for combining the three key ideas and the two additional concepts:

- *Control* and *monitoring* works roughly as follows. Identifiable agents can have *access rights* granted and revoked, and access requests of authenticated agents are intercepted by *control components* that decide on allowing or denying an actual access on the basis of valid access rights. Additionally, the recordable activities of all agents are *audited* and examined with regard to possible *intrusions*.
- *Cryptography* is based on secrets generated and kept by agents: the secrets are exploited as cryptographic *keys*. Such keys distinguish the key holder so that that agent is enabled to execute a specific operation in a meaningful way, in contrast to all other agents. This extremely powerful paradigm can be used in many ways, including *encryption*, *authentication* and, in particular, *digital signatures*, *anonymization*, *secret sharing* and *zero-knowledge proofs*.

Most real-life applications again demand that instantiations of both classes are combined appropriately. Evidently, the secrecy of cryptographic keys must be enforced by access control, and often identities used for control and monitoring are best authenticated by cryptographic means.

A further combination can be seen as constituting an evolving third class of techniques that will be very important for the development of future interoperable distributed systems built from autonomous agents:

- *Certificates* and *credentials*, which are digitally signed digital documents and are also referred to as *digital legitimations*, conceptually bind *properties* that are relevant for access decisions to specific agents, which are denoted only by *public keys*. Here, a public key is understood as a suitable reference to a *private* (*secret*) cryptographic *key* held by the agent considered.

Such properties can be directly identifying, otherwise characterizing or, more generally, only in some way *classifying*; as a special case, they may express the status of being a grantee of *access rights*. A client addressing a remote server then shows such documents together with a service request, and the server decides on the request by relating its local security policy to the documents exhibited and other available documents.

For conciseness of the presentation, we shall treat this third class as a variant and offspring of the first one, while referring to the cryptographic ingredients of the second one where needed.

7.1 Identification or Classification, and Proof of Authenticity

In the introductory exposition of this chapter we speak about generic *agents*; in other contexts, we refer to *participants, subjects, entities* or related terms. Any such term denotes somebody or something that is capable of acting and thus is considered as a target of security concerns. When we are dealing with such a concern on an intuitive level, the intended meaning of the term is assumed to be sufficiently clear, as, for example, in the treatment of permissions and prohibitions in Section 7.2 below. However, more concrete technical considerations usually require more sophisticated differentiations, which are highly relevant to achieving security.

More specifically, the technical notion of a *participant* (or an agent, etc.) should refer to a well-defined application context; it usually depends on the *vertical system layer* under consideration, ranging, for example, from "human individual" through "physical computing device" to "(virtual) process"; and it might additionally vary with the *horizontal distribution* of the system. Some common features are roughly summarized as follows, and discussed further in the remainder of this section:

- A participant has an *identity*, reflected by an *identifying name* (or *identifier*).
- Besides the identifying name, a participant has further *properties* or *attributes* that might be relevant to the security concerns.
- Typically, each participant is *connected* to a chain or an otherwise structured set of other participants that *act on behalf* of the original participant, where the connections are employed for *communication* between the participants involved.
- Each individual participant has some natural or given *peculiarities* that can be employed to effectively recognize that participant, i.e., to distinguish that participant from all others or to relate the participant's current *appearance* to a claimed identifying name.
- A recognizer needs an *internal representation* of the participant's expected peculiarities, to be matched with an appearance actually shown.

The *identification* of participants or their *classification* according to properties, and the recognition of participants, i.e., a *proof of the authenticity* of an appearance, are particularly important for the following goals:

- to *authenticate* a participant *before* permitting a *requested action* or *while* exchanging *messages*, and
- to hold a participant *accountable* for some observed action *after* the fact.

7.1.1 Some Idealized Non-Computerized Situations

The aspects sketched and related above are well known in the non-computerized world, which can thus serve to indicate worthwhile concepts. Furthermore, the procedures invented for computing should at least be compatible with the (possibly adapted) regulations established in the embedding non-computerized world.

Before beginning the technical discussions for computing systems, we shall briefly review some simplified and idealized non-computerized situations. We first consider a mother and her child. Shortly after birth and in the course of a year, respectively, they start denoting each other by locally meaningful names (the given first name or, often, a related pet name, and "mama", respectively), and each of them learns an internal representation of the other. Whenever they meet in person afterwards, they immediately recognize each other and thus are ready to interact, for example by addressing each other or one serving the other, without any preliminaries.

The mother might introduce a relative whom is known to her to the child, and, vice versa, a sufficiently grown-up child might introduce a friend who is already known to the child to the mother. Like the mother and the child, the person introduced is perceived as having a unique identity, represented by an identifying name that serves its purpose for the relevant scope of the extended family and friends.

The person introduced is recognized by specific peculiarities that distinguish that person from any other person, at least within the relevant scope and usually even beyond. More specifically, the person introduced is mentally recognized by means of an internal representation of his specific peculiarities, which (presumably) is different from the internal representation of any other relevant person's peculiarities.

A stranger might introduce himself to the mother, to the child or, directly or indirectly, even to the whole family. This stranger does so by specifying his name and showing certified documents that relate that name to a representation of some observable peculiarities, for example a photograph or a handwritten signature, and are issued by some trusted authorities. Again, this representation can be checked for a match with the directly visible peculiarities themselves.

After the introduction, the person introduced might from then on be identified by the name used during the introduction, or given a new local name. Moreover, the certified documents used for the introduction might be employed further for repeated recognitions, or a new local agreement about other peculiarities to be shown for recognition might come into operation, together with an internal representation and a corresponding matching procedure.

The persons involved might also want to cooperate not only face-to-face but also remotely by exchanging letters. For the needs of the transport and delivery service contracted to deliver the letters, the persons have to refer to each other by means of globally identifying compounds of a name and an address, and they have somehow to trust the selected service organization concerning aspects of availability such as timely handling, the integrity of letters and the confidentiality of contents. Furthermore, the persons must recognize and authenticate the actual (invisible) sender of a delivered (observable) letter by means of a peculiarity that can be inspected remotely, for example a handwritten signature, or an included token attributable to the claimed sender only.

7.1.2 Local Identifiers

In this subsection, we sketch the typical situation in a local computing system. We coarsely distinguish the following kinds of participants and objects and outline the respective connections, as visualized in Figure 7.1:

- a *human individual*,
- a (physical) *personal computing device*,
- a (physical) *interface device*,
- a *physical computing device* (with a *processor* as its main component, and running an *operating system* and other *system software*),
- a *process*,
- an *operating system kernel*,
- a (physical) *storage device*, and
- a (virtual application) *object*.

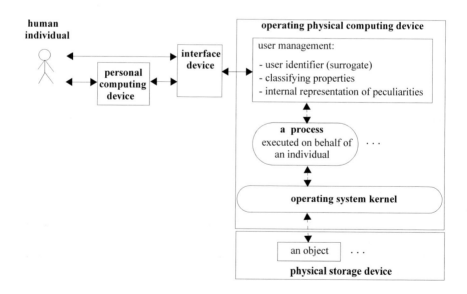

Fig. 7.1. Simplified view of participants and their connections in a local computing system

We first observe the following differences. Human individuals have a natural, biologically materialized and socially accepted *identity*; in particular, each individual is considered to be distinguishable from all other potential human participants in the real world. Physical devices are manufactured as mass products and thus only have an inorganically materialized identity, which can be supplemented for practical purposes by an additionally given artificial term such as a serial number. But processes are only virtual, non-materialized concepts that get their identity solely by discretionary attribution. A similar remark applies to application objects.

Before a *human individual* can use a computing system, in particular a *physical computing device*, the system requires an *introduction* and *registration* of this individual as a *user*. For this purpose, the system maintains a local *user management* component. This component internally denotes any registered user by an *identifying name*, i.e., a local *user identifier* (*username*), and the overall system employs the identifier as an internal *surrogate* for the external human individual represented.

After registration, an individual has to initialize each system access by specifying the local user identifier, and then, in normal mode, the system performs all actions on behalf of the human individual by *processes mastered* by the pertinent identifier. For special purposes, the system might offer some suitably restricted further actions that are implemented by processes under a different *mastership*. In turn, whenever a process needs to read from or write to a storage device, any such storage manipulation is mediated by the *operating system kernel*.

Summarizing, we make another observation. On the one hand, on a conceptual level, a human individual is seen to perform a computing action on a virtual object. On the other hand, in an actual implementation, there is a chain of connected items: the individual who has a biological and social identity – the physical interface device – the physical computing device – a virtual process – the operating system kernel – the physical storage device – the storage representation of the virtual object. Basically, along this chain, the conceptual action is fragmented into a series of messages between neighboring items, from the origin to the target and the full way back.

Accordingly, in order to enforce the conceptual perception that an individual is permitted (or prohibited) to perform an action on an object, the "natural identity" of a human individual must be appropriately reflected along this chain, ensuring that the *messages* involved are directed as expected. In particular, at least the following *connections* must fit the requirements:

- between the human individual and the interface device, either directly or with the help of a secure *personal computing device*;
- between the interface device and the physical computing device (with an initializing user process): a secure *physical access path*;
- between one process and another local process: secure *process communication*;
- between a process and the local storage: a secure *operating system kernel*.

In this context, the notion of a "connection" is mainly a fiction, which is implemented by appropriately related individual messages. Similarly, the more general notion of a *user session* is a fiction as well. Concerning security, it is crucial that an actual implementation correctly reflects the pertinent fiction over the time span under consideration, i.e., that the implementation realizes the conceptual *tranquility assumption*, which is inherent in the notion of a connection or session. In more practical terms, for any implementation, the following issues must be treated:

- *frequency* of control: only initially, repeatedly for each sensitive action, permanently for each individual message or otherwise;
- *scope* of control: for specific kinds of actions, for complex transactions (*single sign-on*) or otherwise.

7.1.3 Global Identifiers

A *horizontally distributed* system raises additional challenges. In such a system, human individuals might want to establish and maintain (necessarily fictitious) *end-to-end* (*peer-to-peer*) *connections*. However, the individuals are only registered with their respective local systems, and they need the support of network services that transport messages between local systems by means of possibly many intermediate systems. Figure 7.2 shows a simplified situation.

Accordingly, as far as global identification is wanted, a participant must obtain a *globally distinguishable identity*, which is then reflected by a globally applicable scheme of assigning a *global user identifier*. In particular, human individuals registered with one local system must be *introduced* to another cooperating system, and physical devices must be introduced to *remote systems* as well. For the latter goal, the identity of the device must be established by artificial terms, for example dynamically assigned *IP numbers* or statically implanted and tamper-resistant *serial numbers* for processors.

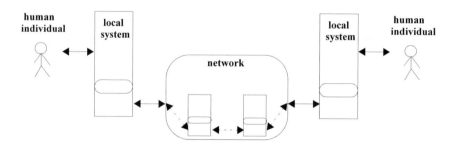

Fig. 7.2. Simplified view of an end-to-end connection in a global computing system

7.1.4 Interoperable Classification

In several situations, global identification appears neither wished, nor easily achievable, nor actually useful. The wish might be in conflict with the interest in *anonymity*. The achievement of global identification would depend on a worldwide unconditionally *trusted authority* that would provide the organizational background for managing global identifiers, but there might be participants who would at least partially object to submitting to the authority's rules. The usefulness of global identification assumes that knowing the identity of a remote partner in a cooperation is helpful for the intended activity, but when one is cooperating with a stranger for a limited purpose, some dedicated *properties* of the stranger might be more important than the identity.

Whenever global identification is not appropriate, a participant might still be classified with respect to *properties* that are shown. For example, in a university environment, an activity might be permitted for a student and prohibited for a staff member, or vice versa. Accordingly, in this context, the status, for example student, staff, faculty or something else, is decisive, but not the exact identity. Like an identity, a property must be appropriately denoted inside the system, and the selected denotation must be properly processed so that it captures the intended meaning.

In a local system, an administrator can easily declare the processable denotations and define their local semantics. In a global and horizontally distributed system, however, the interoperable interpretation of properties and their denotation constitute a great challenge. For example, a participant might claim to be a "student" when addressing a remote computing system of a university abroad; that system then has to decide whether the participant's status, communicated by the denotation "student", indeed corresponds to the local understanding of somebody learning and researching at a high-level educational institution. As for global identifiers, *trusted authorities* are needed to assist in assigning properties and using appropriate denotations across local system boundaries.

If a computing system treats participants according to their shown properties, the system neither registers its users in advance nor maintains *persistent* internal *surrogates* for them. Whenever a participant addresses the system like a *stranger*, merely by communicating some of its properties, and the system permits the request, the system dynamically creates a *transitory* internal representation of the *requestor* for the period of the requested activity. Clearly, as before, during this period the system has to take care of the pertinent chain of connected participants.

7.1.5 Provisions for Authentication and Proof of Authenticity

Whenever a participant addresses a system, the participant must be appropriately identified by a suitably agreed or introduced identifier, or at least classified by some declared properties. Additionally, the system has to *recognize* the participant in the following sense: the system has to decide whether the claimed identifier or properties actually belong to the addressing participant, whose *appearance* is manifested only by some communicated data. Clearly, just taking the data concerning the identifier or the properties is not enough: anybody who knows this data could *impersonate* the proper holder.

Hence, on the one hand, the addressing participant must communicate some additional *redundant* data that serves as pieces of *evidence* (*exhibits*) for the participant's claim, and on the other hand, the system must maintain some *verification data*, employed for a *matching procedure* (a *verification algorithm*, *test method*, …), visualized in simplified form in Figure 7.3.

On the basis of the communicated exhibits and the local verification data, the matching procedure aims at providing a *proof of the authenticity* of the addressing participant, i.e., at recognizing that the participant is the claimed one. If the procedure succeeds, the appearance of the participant is accepted, and all further actions are mastered by the pertinent internal surrogate; otherwise, if the procedure fails, some exception handling is necessary. In principle, but hopefully only in rare cases, such a matching procedure might deliver incorrect results: *false positives* by accepting the shown exhibits of a cheating participant, and *false negatives* by rejecting the shown exhibits of the proper holder.

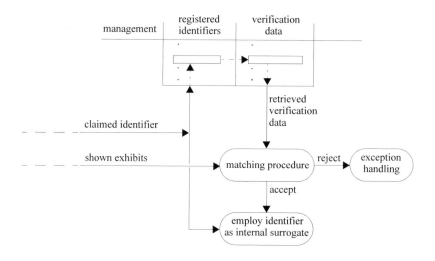

Fig. 7.3. Matching of communicated exhibits with local verification data

In order to avoid incorrect results, an (honest) participant and a recognizing system have to prepare carefully by agreeing on the participant's *peculiarities*, from which exhibits can be derived, and on the corresponding verification data. We first list some options for the peculiarities of *human individuals*:

- *individual knowledge*: password, passphrase, PIN (personal identification number), personal data, historic data, … ; (discretionarily selected) cryptographic key, random number (nonce), … , if cryptography is used;
- *physical possession*: smartcard, personal(ized) computing device, … ;
- *biological characteristics* (*biometrics*): fingerprints, eye pattern, genetic code, speech sound, … ;
- *individual* (*reproducible*) *behavior*: pattern of keyboard striking, … .

For *physical devices*, examples of exploitable peculiarities include the following:

- tamper-resistant, physically implanted serial number;
- tamper-resistant, physically implanted cryptographic key;
- discretionarily selected cryptographic key;
- random number.

In each case, the participant must provide suitable verification data to the anticipated recognizing system in advance, and generate suitable exhibits for each access later on, in such a way that the agreed matching procedure works effectively, as expected. In some sense, the verification data functions as the system's *internal representation* of the participant's peculiarities.

However, in general, the verification data should be *neither* just a copy of (a digital encoding of) the peculiarities *nor* a copy of the derivable exhibits themselves. For, otherwise, any malicious agent that managed to access these copies could *impersonate* the proper holder, and this includes the recognizing system itself. For the same reason, often a much stronger *unforgeability property* is desirable:

$$\text{Knowing the verification data alone} \qquad (7.1)$$
$$\text{should } not \text{ enable one to produce any matching exhibits.}$$

Basically, *cryptography* can contribute to (partially) achieving this property in various ways, for example as roughly outlined in the following:

- By applying *encryption*, any verification data suitable for any peculiarities can be persistently stored in encrypted form, such that only the recognizing system, which holds the (secret) decryption key, can actually exploit the verification data.
- By applying asymmetric *cryptographic authentication*, a participant's given peculiarity can be made to consist of a private (secret) *authentication* or *signature key*, and the corresponding public *test key* serves as the verification data, which effectively accepts exhibits produced by the private key.
- By applying a collision-resistant *one-way hash function*, a (digital encoding of any) peculiarity is mapped to a *hash value* serving as stored verification data. Later on, the peculiarity can be shown as an exhibit, whose hash value is recomputed and compared with the stored value.

However, in general, these contributions of cryptography alone are *not* sufficient to ensure an overall effective authentication. For each particular approach, there are many further issues to be solved, including the following.

The first issue arises when one is preparing for later authentications: how can a participant convince a remote recognizer that some proposed verification data is actually related to the participant's identity and peculiarities? In general, the participant and the recognizer have to rely on a *trusted authority* as a third party that *certifies* the relationship considered, as indicated in Figure 7.4.

Fig. 7.4. The role of a trusted authority

The second issue arises whenever repeated accesses might occur: how can a recognizer convince himself that shown exhibits are *fresh*, rather than maliciously *replayed* from a previous intercepted communication. In general, the freshness of a message can be assumed only on the basis of additional provisions. One possibility is the usage of *timestamps*, supposing sufficiently well synchronized clocks.

Challenge–response procedures offer another option, as outlined in Figure 7.5. Typically, the recognizer *challenges* the participant to acknowledge the receipt of a freshly generated *random value*, called a *nonce*, and the participant generates exhibits of receipt by means of his peculiarities and sends these exhibits as a response.

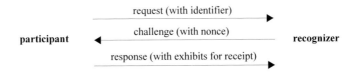

Fig. 7.5. Messages sent in a simple challenge–response protocol

The third issue, sketched in Figure 7.6, concerns the supposed connection from one participant to another one acting as a recognizing system: how can the participant avoid being connected to a malicious *man-in-the-middle* attacker and showing him sensitive data such as unprotected verification data or reusable exhibits, thereby enabling a later impersonation? In general, *mutual identification* and *mutual authentication* are the proposed remedies. However, establishing the necessary initializing provisions constitutes a great challenge, usually solved by *trusted authorities* again.

Fig. 7.6. Attack by redirecting an assumed connection to a "man-in-the-middle"

A further issue is protection against malicious *guessing* or *probing* of acceptable exhibits. First of all, exhibits must be generated such that they appear as if they are randomly selected out of a sufficiently large space of possibilities. If cryptography is used, this requirement demands, in particular, suitably selected and sufficiently long *cryptographic keys*. If *passwords* or similar (digital encodings of) peculiari- ties are used, similar precautions are due; in particular, the items actually used should not be an element of a small semantically determined subset of the syntacti- cally possible items.

For example, if passwords can be formed from 12 characters, then a participant should not select a friend's first name: an attacker might exploit a small dictionary of common names, trying each of them until an acceptance is obtained. Notably, this *dictionary attack* also succeeds if the recognizing system stores the hash val- ues of passwords or employs a related protection mechanism. Figure 7.7 visualizes the general situation and the recommended selection of an exhibit.

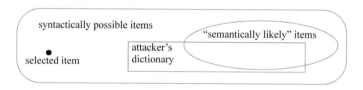

Fig. 7.7. Recommended selection of exhibits from outside the expected attack dictionaries

7.2 Permissions and Prohibitions

Participants employ a computing system for informational activities, pursuing their own individual obligations, tasks and interests as well as supporting cooperation with other participants. Whereas individual wishes and needs often require the *iso- lation* of services and their resources, at least virtually, common activities require *sharing*. Both aspects are implicitly covered by a *security policy* that describes which identifiable or at least classifiable participants are permitted or prohibited to employ which operational options.

Here we refer to an *operational option* as any abstract informational activity, concretely offered service or possibly executable method invocation on an object, depending on the level and the details of the consideration. If a *permission* for an operational option is restricted to a single participant, some kind of isolation concerning all the other participants is required. Conversely, if a *prohibition* for an operational option is declared with regard to specific participants, again a corresponding isolation is required. However, if a permission is granted equally to several participants, some kind of sharing is wanted.

Permissions and prohibitions, i.e., a concretely instantiated security policy for a computing system (or only an application), are treated in several layers, most importantly including the following ones:

- The participants by themselves, or some distinguished participants acting on behalf of the others, *specify* and *declare* the wanted permissions and prohibitions.
- The declarations are then (hopefully) appropriately *represented* by the means of the computing system and inside it.
- The representations are (hopefully) efficiently *managed* there, both for *decisions* on actual requests for an operational option and for *updates*.
- The decisions are effectively *enforced*, i.e., (hopefully) exactly those requests are successfully executed that have been declared permitted, and, accordingly, none of those that have been declared prohibited.

Taking the full range of layers into account, it appears reasonable to integrate the treatment of permissions and prohibitions closely with the purely functional aspects. More specifically, the declarations should refer to the kind and granularity of the operational options under consideration, for example of functional objects and their methods. And, as far as possible, the basic functionality, possibly together with suitable extensions, should be exploited for the internal representation, management and enforcement of the declarations.

As an example, we sketch the situation for an application of a relational database management system. The security policy, in the form of wanted permissions and prohibitions, is specified during the conceptual design phase, which is devoted to documenting the basic entity and relationship classes, their dependencies and usages, and further aspects of the application. The declarations of both the application database schema and the security policy are expressed by using the system's data definition language, resulting in the respective relational (tabular) internal representations.

Afterwards, these representations are managed in more or less the same way, and also query processing and the taking of access decisions are basically uniformly treated, and so are updates with regard to application data on the one side and updates with regard to permissions and prohibitions on the other side.

7.2.1 Specification

A specification of permissions and prohibitions for operational options can be seen as an instantiated *security policy*, which should reflect the pertinent requirements of a specific application. In accordance with general *construction* and *administrative principles*, the following guidelines for such security policies are useful:

- alignment with the *environment*,
- *least privileges* according to *need-to-know* or *need-to-act*,
- *separation of roles*,
- *purpose binding*,
- *separation of privileges*.

Computing systems, and thus the operational options offered, are usually embedded in an *environment*, for example an organization. In this case, the *organizational structures* on the one hand and the *security policy* on the other hand should be well *aligned*, for obvious reasons. Given the structures, one might want to declare a matching security policy for the computerized part of the overall tasks. However, vice versa, it might turn out that computerization and its specific security requirements demand that the old structures are adapted too.

In whatever environment, participants often act in a specific *social role* or according to a specific job description. The specific task then requires the availability of operational options. Clearly, a participant should be given the needed permissions, but in general only those permissions, i.e., the *least privileges* that are sufficient. Thus permissions and prohibitions should be declared according to the administrative principles of *need-to-know* and, more generally, *need-to-act*. Furthermore, if a participant is involved in several roles sequentially or in parallel, then the respective actions should be suitably *separated*, i.e., guaranteed to cause no unintended information flow or interferences.

Information or other resources are often made available to a participant who actually needs them for acting in a specific role. Then, forwarding the resource and thereby granting permission to use it are *bound* to a specific *purpose* that is in the scope of the receiver's role. If the receiver is strictly confined to that role, purpose binding is achieved on the receiver's side. However, once the resource (or a copy of it) is under the control of the receiver, that receiver might deviate from his role, and then the purpose binding might be violated too. Thus we would like to constrain a permission by a purpose-specific *condition*.

Some operational options should not be permitted to a single individual but rather to a group of them, who have to cooperate in order to use those options. Such a group can be either statically fixed, or dynamically arranged by gathering together a threshold number of candidates. In all cases, the *separation of privileges* achieved should prevent or at least impede misuse of permissions.

7.2.2 Representation, Management and Enforcement

A declared security policy, i.e., the permissions and prohibitions for operational options as wanted by peers, has to be appropriately represented, managed and technically enforced inside the computing system. As already announced in the introduction to this chapter, we distinguish three classes of techniques: control and monitoring, cryptography, and certificates and credentials, as an evolving amalgam. In the following, we present only simplified models or interpretations of these classes; these are expanded in more detail in other parts of the monograph.

Local Control and Monitoring. Figure 7.8 shows a generic model of local *control and monitoring*. In a purely functional view, there are participating *subjects* who make requests to access controlled *objects*, with the aim of changing their internal states, triggering further requests, generating and returning results, or performing other suitable actions. For security, however, subjects and objects are separated by a control and monitoring component that cannot be bypassed.

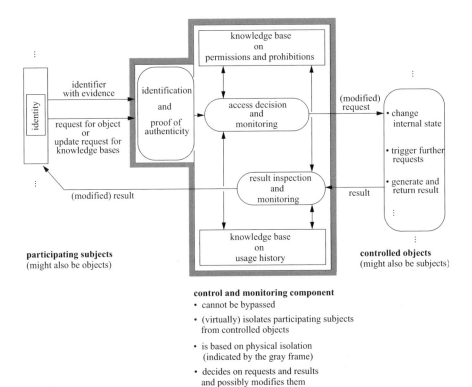

Fig. 7.8. A generic model of local control and monitoring for enforcing permissions and prohibitions

Now, a subject's *request* is intercepted and underlies an *access decision*: the request is either denied or forwarded to the object, possibly in a modified form. Correspondingly, a returned *result* is either discarded or forwarded to the subject, again possibly suitably modified. Ideally, one also would like to *inspect* the object's internal state transition and other actions after the fact once again and to possibly undo them, but the sophisticated transaction mechanisms needed are rarely feasible.

Access decisions and result inspections are founded on appropriate knowledge bases. A *knowledge base* on *permissions* and *prohibitions* represents internally the peers' specification of a security policy. In particular, previously declared *access rights* for subjects are stored and managed there. If required by the security policy, another *knowledge base* on the *usage history* may allow decisions and inspections to be made in a way that depends on previous computing activities. This knowledge base on the usage history also serves for *monitoring* all actions within the system, in particular for *auditing* and *intrusion detection*.

The control and monitoring component always has to relate the presumable sources of incoming requests, i.e., the subjects actually acting, to internal surrogates of potential subjects as used in the knowledge bases. In the most common case, *identities* are employed. Subjects are known under an (at most locally unique) *user identifier* that serves as an internal *surrogate*. Accordingly, access rights are expressed in terms of identities. A request is accompanied by the requestor's identifier, and appropriate exhibits of authentic usage of the identifier. On the control side, *identification and authentication* are then performed.

The generic model has numerous variations and different instantiations. In concrete approaches, some subcomponents may be only rudimentary or even missing, the conceptual knowledge bases are often only implicit and hidden in other features, and implementations might be either centralized or distributed.

Cryptography. Figure 7.9 shows a generic interpretation of *cryptography* for enforcing permissions and prohibitions. Again, in a purely functional view, there are participating *subjects* who make requests to access *objects* with the aim of performing some actions. But cryptography neither exploits identities for security nor actually separates the objects from the subjects. Rather, when cryptography is used, the permitted and prohibited operational options of a subject are determined by the *secrets* that are available to that subject. Such a secret is commonly called a cryptographic *key*. A subject's request is performed as intended only if the subject can exhibit a key that is specific to the request. Otherwise, the request might still access the pertinent object but the result is in general not "meaningful", though it may possibly be "harmful".

Under this interpretation of cryptography, a cryptographic mechanism conceptually substitutes for the *control* component: basically, a request is always "tentatively performed", but if the pertinent key is not provided, the "raw" result does not satisfy the expected properties.

For example, without a matching *decryption key*, a read access to an encrypted text still returns a string but not the original plaintext. However, if the read access

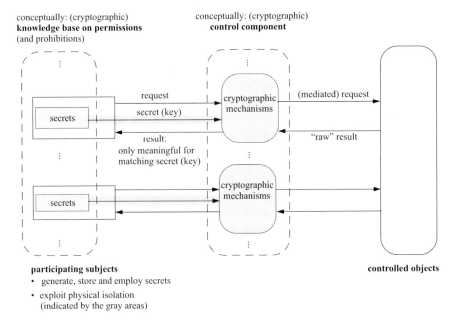

conceptually: (cryptographic)
knowledge base on permissions
(and prohibitions)

conceptually: (cryptographic)
control component

cryptographic
mechanisms

secrets

request

secret (key)

(mediated) request

result:
only meaningful for
matching secret (key)

"raw" result

cryptographic
mechanisms

secrets

participating subjects
- generate, store and employ secrets
- exploit physical isolation
  (indicated by the gray areas)

controlled objects

Fig. 7.9. A generic interpretation of cryptography for enforcing permissions and prohibitions

is extended to a write access, the encrypted text might be destroyed and thus the access might be harmful, clearly even without the pertinent key. As another example, the possession of a *signature key* enables the key holder to generate a string as a digital signature for a digital document such that afterwards the document can be recognized as originating from the key holder. Any other participant, who will not hold the specific signature key, can still produce some string and claim it to be good as a signature, but nobody else should accept this claim.

As outlined above, cryptography discriminates participants by their possession of secret keys (rather than by identities), and accordingly the stored secrets conceptually constitute the system's *knowledge base* on *permissions*. In some sense, a secret functions like an access right. However, there are also important differences. Most notably, a subject might generate and store his secrets at his own discretion, though he can also get a shared secret granted. In all cases, the secret holder has to appropriately protect his secrets, in particular when using them. For this purpose, control and monitoring, as introduced earlier, are usually exploited, based on physical isolation of the secrets.

The interpretation of cryptography given above leaves room for many refined considerations, in particular about how to implement a security policy that is specified in terms of abstract permissions and prohibitions by an actual *distribution* and *management* of secret *keys*. Moreover, not all aspects of cryptography are captured by this somewhat restricted interpretation.

Certificates and Credentials. One distinction between control and monitoring on the one hand and cryptography on the other is expressed in terms of what enables a subject to get a request permitted: either the subject's authenticated identity together with related access rights or the possession of secret keys, respectively. However, the distinction appears less strict if the overall design is considered: an identity can be exploited only after a successful authentication, which, in turn, often requires personal secrets (e.g. passwords or signature keys) to be employed; and a secret can be exploited only after a successful access, which, in turn, is often bound to an identity. Accordingly, both approaches are usually combined appropriately.

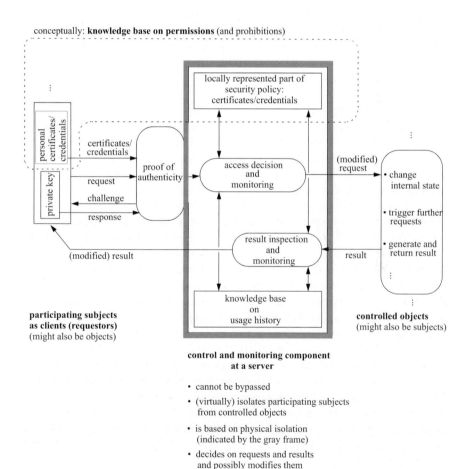

Fig. 7.10. A simplified model of certificates and credentials for enforcing permissions and prohibitions

Figure 7.10 shows a simplified model of an evolving combination that is based on *certificates* and *credentials* and designed for distributed systems. Basically, inspired by cryptography, this combination replaces identities by references to secret keys, and, adapting control and monitoring, it intercepts requests and takes explicit access decisions.

More specifically, a participating subject is conceptually represented by a *surrogate* that is generated as a matching pair of a *private* (*signature*) *key* and a *public* (*verification*) *key*, as invented for public key cryptography. The subject keeps the private key (often also called the *secret key*) strictly confidential and uses it for *digitally signing* digital documents; all participants consider the public key as an abstract reference to the subject, and they can exploit the public key to *verify* digital signatures that have been issued by use of the matching private key.

Permissions (and to some extent also *prohibitions*) on operational options are expressed with respect to the surrogates only, in general without referring to identities. Direct permissions or other information from which permissions might be derived are encoded in digital documents that refer to a public key, i.e., the surrogate of some participating subject, as the *grantee*. The *issuer* of such a document digitally signs it, in order to protect against forgeries. Depending on the exact flavor of the content, the digital document is called a *credential* (in particular, for direct permissions) or a *certificate* (in particular, for properties which only later can be converted into permissions). Thus credentials and certificates can be seen as implementations of (direct and indirect, respectively) *access rights*. Then, the totality of all such digital documents conceptually constitutes a *knowledge base* on *permissions* (and *prohibitions*). Usually, however, the documents are appropriately distributed among the participants, such that a requestor often has to accompany a request by (copies of) those credentials that can support a positive *access decision*.

In principle, certificates and credentials need no further protection besides valid digital signatures. However, digital documents can be easily *duplicated* and then potentially misused by a violator. Such a violator might try to *masquerade* as the subject who is represented by the public key in a document. Thus, usually in a *challenge–response* procedure, a requestor typically has to authenticate himself by proving the possession of the matching private key.

Also, for certificates and credentials, there are many variations that are mainly devoted to highly distributed applications that enable "strangers" to cooperate as clients (requestors) and servers, sometimes even *anonymously*, though in all cases practical experience is still limited. For wide acceptance, a *public key infrastructure* (*PKI*) is needed, in particular for guaranteeing the expected properties of digital signatures, and appropriate *revocation* services for certificates and credentials have to be provided.

7.3 Requirements and Mechanisms

In this section, we relate *security requirements* to *security mechanisms* for enforcing them. Regarding security requirements, we treat the major *security interests* in the sense of Section 2.2:

- *availability*: requested data or action returned or executed, respectively, in a timely manner;
- *integrity*: an item's state unmodified, or its modification detectable;
- *authenticity*: claimed origin of data or action recognized as correct;
- *non-repudiation*: correct origin of data or action provable to third parties;
- *confidentiality*: information kept secret from unauthorized participants;
- *non-observability and anonymity*: activities kept secret;
- *accountability*: activities traceable to correct origin.

Regarding security mechanisms, on the one hand we consider the following *key ideas* as introduced in Chapter 6:

- *redundancy*: adding additional data or resources to enable needed inferences, detect failures and attacks, or recover from them;
- *isolation*: separating items to disable information flows and interferences;
- *indistinguishability*: hiding data or activities by letting them appear to be random samples of a large collection or to appear as uniformly expected.

On the other hand, we consider *combined techniques* in the sense of Subsection 7.2.2, which are discussed in more detail in the rest of this monograph:

- *local control and monitoring*: this is *identity*-based, using identification, proof of authenticity, permissions as access rights, control of intercepted requests and results, and monitoring of overall behavior;
- *cryptography*: this is *secret*-based, using encryption, (cryptographic) authentication including digital signatures, anonymization, randomness, one-way hash functions, timestamps, and more advanced protocols built from these blocks;
- *certificates and credentials*: these are *property*-based, using features of local control and monitoring applied to requests that are accompanied by digitally signed assignments of security-relevant properties to public keys.

We have attempted to give some general hints regarding which requirement can be *satisfied* by which mechanism. These hints are organized in tabular form in Table 7.11 and Table 7.12, where for each pair of an interest and a key idea or combined techniques, the pertinent entry provides the following information:

- A statement briefly summarizes a major contribution, or a secondary contribution that arises in the context of another interest.
- An empty entry indicates that, in general, the mechanism does not contribute to the requirement.

As a disclaimer, we emphasize that these hints are grossly simplified and do not cover all contributions, and thus they can serve only for an initial orientation.

Table 7.11. Interests and enforcing mechanisms (part 1)

Interest	Redundancy	Isolation	Indistinguishability	Control and monitoring	Cryptography	Certificates and credentials
Availability	provisionally multiplying (sub)objects or generating auxiliary objects to reconstruct lost or corrupted objects	attributing distinguishing identifiers or characterizing properties confining threatening operations in the context of integrity		granting access rights for enabling permitted operations (and confining them as far as they are threatening) detecting and reconstructing losses and corruptions while intercepting requests and results	generating and distributing secrets (keys) for enabling permitted operations	issuing documents about properties for enabling permitted operations (and confining them as far as they are threatening)
Integrity	provisionally generating auxiliary objects to detect modifications	confining operations on objects to dedicated purposes generating distinguishing secrets	making exhibits appear randomly selected for preventing forgeries	specifying prohibitions for rejecting or confining threatening operations	detecting unwanted modifications of objects	specifying prohibitions for rejecting or confining threatening operations
Authenticity	adding exhibits derived from a distinguishing secret	attributing distinguishing identifiers generating distinguishing secrets	making exhibits appear randomly selected for preventing forgeries	recognizing a requestor by identification and proof of authenticity	recognizing a requestor or actor by verifying cryptographic exhibits	challenging a requestor and verifying cryptographic exhibits in responses

Table 7.12. Interests and enforcing mechanisms (part 2)

Interest	Redundancy	Isolation	Indistinguisha-bility	Control and monitoring	Cryptography	Certificates and credentials
Non-repudiation	adding cryptographic exhibits in the form of digital signatures derived from a distinguishing secret	generating distinguishing secrets	making exhibits appear randomly selected for preventing forgeries		proving an actor responsible by verifying cryptographic exhibits in the form of digital signatures	assigning provable responsibility to issuers of documents by verifying cryptographic exhibits in the form of digital signatures
Confidentiality		confining operations on objects to dedicated purposes	making data appear randomly selected from a large collection of possibilities	specifying prohibitions for rejecting or confining threatening operations	prohibiting gain of information by encrypting data	specifying prohibitions for rejecting or confining threatening operations
Non-observability/anonymity			hiding activities in a large collection of possibilities	untraceably mediating requests and results	superimposing randomness	issuing documents about properties referring to public keys (rather than identities)
Accountability	adding cryptographic exhibits in the form of digital signatures or similar means derived from a distinguishing secret	attributing distinguishing identities generating distinguishing secrets		logging and analyzing intercepted requests and results	proving an actor responsible by verifying cryptographic exhibits in the form of digital signatures or similar means	logging and analyzing intercepted requests and results

7.4 Bibliographic Hints

On the one hand, the basic material of this chapter might be seen as "common knowledge" of the community formed by researchers and practitioners in the field of security in computing systems. Accordingly, in other work the material might remain implicit, or specific parts might be treated in a more advanced and technically deeper form. The latter also applies for this monograph: for each of the concepts discussed, other chapters contain more detail and also provide appropriate references to important publications, which are not repeated in this section.

As an exception, we supplement the bibliographic hints about cryptographic authentication given in Chapter 14 by the following examples of important contributions to further aspects of authentication. Burrows/Abadi/Needham [111] introduce a logic of authentication, known as BAN logic, to reason formally about the achievements of cryptographic authentication protocols. Lampson/Abadi/Burrows/Wobber [309] study authentication in distributed systems. Abadi/Gordon [3] propose the spi calculus for evaluating cryptographic protocols. Abadi [5] surveys and examines these and further approaches from a general perspective. Bolle/Connell/Pankanti/Senior [97] survey the usage of biometrics.

On the other hand, however, this chapter presents a specific view of how the individual mechanisms contribute to an acceptable degree of overall security. Necessarily, so does any survey about security, either implicitly or explicitly. In particular, each of the textbooks listed at the end of Chapter 1 expresses an opinion about this issue.

In fact, this issue has raised ongoing controversies, with views ranging from strongly emphasizing control and monitoring to greatly favoring cryptography. The author's message should be clear: in general, we have a crucial need for both techniques, and an amalgam of them leading to certificates and credentials as well; for more special situations, the decisions about the most appropriate mixture should be taken case by case.

8 Techniques of Control and Monitoring: Essentials

8.1 Requirements, Mechanisms and their Quality

In order to meet security requirements, the participants, or the *security officers* acting on behalf of the participants, have to specify security policies at design time, in terms of which agents are permitted or prohibited to perform which operations on which objects. Within the computing system, the *permissions* and, if applicable, *prohibitions* actually declared are persistently represented and managed by a *knowledge base*.

For the techniques of *control and monitoring* and similarly for the variant of *certificates* and *credentials*, as introduced in Section 7.2 and visualized in Figure 7.8 and Figure 7.10, respectively, this conceptual knowledge base on permissions and prohibitions is implemented in some suitable way and then employed to take explicit *access decisions* for dynamically evolving access *requests*. As a prerequisite, the requesting *subjects* on the one side and the controlled *objects* on the other side must be *isolated* from each other such that each request has to be *completely mediated* by some appropriate interface. At this interface, the *control* and *monitoring component intercepts* every request and then decides whether and to what extent the requested access is actually enabled. Furthermore, requests to *update* the knowledge base on permissions and prohibitions are intercepted as well, in order to decide whether and to what extent the requested *control operations* on the knowledge base are actually enabled.

In order to take meaningful access decisions, the control and monitoring component must *recognize* a requesting subject as a participant that is entitled to be permitted or prohibited to act, either by an *identifier* or by appropriate *properties*. In each case, the claimed identifier or properties must be verified by a *proof of authenticity*, in order to avoid *impersonation*.

Finally, despite all efforts, the preventive control mechanisms might fail to achieve the intended goals. Thus prevention should be complemented by additional *monitoring* mechanisms that observe the actual behavior of participants, and evaluate it as either acceptable or violating.

8.2 Essential Parts

In this section we outline further the six essential parts of any instantiation of the techniques of *control and monitoring*, which we have already mentioned above:

- declaration of permissions and prohibitions,
- control operations,
- isolation, interception and mediation of messages,
- proof of authenticity,
- access decisions, and
- monitoring.

Furthermore, we shall briefly discuss where to place and how to justify a *root of trust* for the overall design. More detailed discussions of selected topics are presented in Chapter 9, surveying *conceptual access rights*, Chapter 10, treating the elements of a *security architecture*, and Chapter 11, introducing *monitoring* by logging and intrusion detection with reactions.

8.2.1 Declaration of Permissions and Prohibitions

In order to express *permissions* and *prohibitions*, we need first of all to conceptualize and denote their carriers, i.e., the *subjects* that are intended to be confined. Furthermore, for the sake of convenience or other reasons, we might want to treat *collectives* of subjects in a uniform way. Complementarily, we have to conceptualize and denote the targets of permissions and prohibitions, i.e., the *objects* that the subjects may access or not. Again, objects might be collected into *classes*, *domains* or related *aggregates* for uniform treatment. Finally, the kinds of *access* offered might vary, from a simple selection between generic *reading* and *writing* to a sophisticated distinction between many application-specific *methods*. Again, we usually abstract from concrete accesses and instead refer to their (*operational*) *modes*, possibly shared by several accesses.

In simple situations, a permission or a prohibition can be *directly* expressed by explicitly naming the respective subject, object and operational mode. In general, however, we might prefer to specify the needed items in a more *indirect* way, employing a wide range of techniques of computer science, in particular those developed for programming languages and knowledge engineering. In such cases, a careful distinction between the syntactic expressions and their intended semantics is crucial. In particular, the syntactic means provided to deal with *structures* in collectives of subjects (e.g., *hierarchies*), aggregates of objects (e.g., *complex compositions*) and modes of access (e.g., further *method invocations*) must be suitably handled at the semantic level. Moreover, any more general techniques for deriving implicit properties of the items considered from explicit properties might be exploited, ranging, for example, from simple *inheritance* rules according to structural relationships to suitably restricted *first-order logic reasoning*.

In simple approaches, either only permissions or only prohibitions are explicitly expressed, whereas, by default, the complementary notion is defined as the absence of the explicit one. In more advanced approaches, however, both permissions and prohibitions are explicitly expressible, which then demands the *resolution of conflicts*. Such conflicts might arise in particular from two or more derivations that are based on different explicit declarations.

Finally, in all cases, the declaration of permissions and prohibitions must be *complete* in the sense that for each actual access request, a *well-defined decision* can be taken. More specifically, at least conceptually, we need a function `decide` that for any actual parameters of a request returns a definite answer as to whether the request should be accepted or denied. To summarize, the following *completeness property* is required:

> For any request of a subject s to access an object o in an operational mode m, (8.1)
> the declared permissions and prohibitions entail
> a unique and definite access decision.

8.2.2 Control Operations

On a first level, the permissions and prohibitions for the functionality of a system, i.e., the possible functional accesses, are considered. On a second level, we must treat the permissions and prohibitions for the *control operations* that manipulate the first-level functional permissions and prohibitions, including *granting* and *revoking* of *functional* permissions and prohibitions. Moreover, we can also provide more advanced control operations, for example for *transferring* or *delegating* permissions and prohibitions to declare functional permissions and prohibitions. Clearly, in general, we could also define further levels of control.

For each system, we also need to define which subjects may grant permissions and prohibitions initially or by means of some special qualifications. Examples range from postulating a (nearly) omnipotent *administrator*, often known as the *root* or *superuser*, permitted to manage any kind of permissions and prohibitions, to assigning each subject that generates a new object the *ownership* of the creation, coupled with the permission to manage the permissions and prohibitions for it. There are also many further combinations and variations of these examples.

In general, the granting of permissions should be done with great care. In an extreme case, if owing to extensive grantings every subject was ultimately permitted to arbitrarily access every object, the whole attempt at control would be useless. Accordingly, an administrator or owner planning some control operations might first want to *analyze* the potential consequences regarding which subjects can eventually acquire which permissions. More generally, for any *control state* resulting from control operations, we might want to perform such an analysis. Unfortunately, however, depending on the control operations supported and the expressiveness supplied for permissions and prohibitions with respect to them, such an analysis can turn out to be computationally infeasible or even impossible. Thus, we can only postulate a weak form of an *analysis property*:

> For any control state resulting from control operations, (8.2)
> the analysis problem regarding
> which subjects can eventually acquire which permissions should be
> computationally feasible or at least admit a computational approximation.

8.2.3 Isolation, Interception and Mediation of Messages

The effective enforcement of declared permissions and prohibitions relies on a system *architecture* that strictly *isolates* subjects from objects, at least virtually, and respecting the fact that some entities might act both as a subject and as an object depending on the current context. More specifically, a subject should not be able to directly access any object. Rather, at least conceptually, the architecture should provide a means by which a subject can send a message containing an *access request* such that any such message will be intercepted by a separating *control and monitoring component*. After intercepting a message, the control and monitoring component mediates the request, basically in three steps: *identification* and *proof of authenticity*, *access decision* and forwarding, and further *monitoring*. To summarize, admitting only carefully designed exemptions, the following architectural *complete mediation property* is required:

$$\text{Each request of a subject to access an object} \qquad (8.3)$$
$$\text{is intercepted and mediated by a control and monitoring component.}$$

8.2.4 Proof of Authenticity

While declared permissions and prohibitions refer to well-conceptualized *subjects*, the control and monitoring component must relate the sender of any request message, i.e., an actual *requestor*, to a pertinent subject. More specifically, given a request message, the control and monitoring component must *recognize* the requestor as one of the conceptualized subjects, being aware of the possibility of a maliciously cheating agent that might aim to pretend to be somebody who it is actually not. Clearly, in general, the requesting agent must provide some further *evidence* regarding itself, and the control and monitoring component can then base a *proof of authenticity* on both the freshly communicated evidence and suitably maintained permanent *verification data*. In most cases, *cryptography* contributes in an essential way to the design and the implementation of the pertinent procedures. To summarize, and extending the preceding reasoning to the target objects, independently of the techniques exploited, the following *authenticity property* is required:

$$\text{Any mediation of an access request} \qquad (8.4)$$
$$\text{is based on a proof of authenticity of the requestor and,}$$
$$\text{as far as needed, of the target object as well.}$$

8.2.5 Access Decisions

Once a requestor has been recognized as a conceptualized subject, the control and monitoring component takes an *access decision* by evaluating the request with respect to the previously declared permissions and prohibitions. At least conceptually, the declarations can be seen as constituting a knowledge base, from which the access decision is derived as a logical consequence. Depending on the complexity of the conceptual *knowledge base on permissions and prohibitions*, such derivations might vary from simple lookup procedures to highly sophisticated reasoning. Such reasoning might additionally consider the dynamic evolution of the controlled system, as conceptually represented by a *knowledge base on the usage history*. Clearly, in this case such a knowledge base must be appropriately maintained by logging all relevant events. To summarize, we postulate the following *architectural requirement*:

> The control and monitoring component maintains suitably isolated   (8.5)
> knowledge bases on permissions and prohibitions and on the usage history.

8.2.6 Monitoring

Additional monitoring might be necessary or at least useful for several reasons. First, an accepted and forwarded request might produce some *results* that should be *inspected* afterwards to determine whether they are evaluated as permitted or prohibited. Insofar as the results are to be *returned* to the original requestor, the inspection might retain all or some parts of them, i.e., totally block the forwarding to the requestor or suitably modify the results before forwarding. Insofar as an internal state of an accessed object might have been changed or further requests to other objects might have been triggered, the options for undoing such effects depend strongly on additional mechanisms such as *transactions*, seen as atomic actions that can be finally either completely committed or aborted. In the latter case, the effect should be (largely) *indistinguishable* from the situation where the access has not occurred at all.

Second, and complementary to access decisions and result inspection, the control and monitoring component can analyze all messages, whether containing requests or returned results, and possibly further audit data regarding an *intrusion defense policy*. At least conceptually, such an additional policy assists in classifying the activities actually occurring as either semantically *acceptable* or *violating*.

Most notably, though the notions of permissions and prohibitions should be semantically related to the notions of acceptable behavior and violating behavior, respectively, in general they will not fully coincide, owing mainly to the at least partially inevitable shortcomings of the preventive access control mechanisms, or even purposely for the sake of efficiency.

In fact, the latter case might arise as follows. If access control is designed according to a purely *provisional* and *pessimistic* approach aimed at totally preventing any violating behavior, the actual implementation might turn out to be inefficient, requiring too much overhead and thus causing a substantial and unaffordable delay in executing actual accesses. In this case, a (more) *optimistic* approach might be preferred: for the sake of efficient runtime enforcement, a relaxed notion of permission is employed, at the price of potentially enabling some violating behaviors, but in the hope of detecting such unfortunate events after the fact by additional monitoring, which may spend some more time on analyzing the actual activities. Clearly, a system administrator should carefully evaluate the trade-off between security and functional efficiency sketched above by means of a thorough *risk assessment*. To summarize, we postulate the following architectural *monitoring requirement*:

Complementarily to access decision and result inspection,   (8.6)
the control and monitoring component audits and analyzes all activities
regarding potential violations defined by an intrusion defence policy.

8.2.7 Root of Trust

We might imagine an ideal world where all subjects behave as expected, all informational devices actually operate as completely specified on the basis of a careful and well-understood design, and correct and complete knowledge is available whenever needed. In the real world, however, such an imaginary scenario is not met with at all; in fact, in some sense, the discipline of security in computing systems aims at managing the imperfections we all know about. In particular, in this discipline we face potentially maliciously behaving subjects, failing implementations of inadequate designs, and decision making regarding remote subjects whose appearance is constituted by some communicated messages only.

Although every effort should be made to firmly ground the management of imperfection on technical mechanisms, there always remains the need to base at least small parts of an overall computing system on *trust*. In this context, trust in a technical part usually means, or at least includes the requirement, that the participant controlling that part is trusted. Moreover, as security is a *multilateral* property that respects potentially conflicting *interests*, trust is essentially context-dependent, i.e., subjectively assigned by one participant but refused by another one.

Dealing with control and monitoring, the issue of trust often arises when the following problems are investigated:

- Does the *control and monitoring component* as a whole actually work as expected, intercepting and suitably mediating each access request? In particular, does the component support *availability* by accepting permitted requests, and does it preserve *integrity* and *confidentiality* by denying prohibited accesses?
- Do participants permitted to execute *control operations* behave appropriately and honestly when granting, revoking, transferring or delegating permissions?
- Do shown *evidence* and maintained *verification data*, as needed for a *proof of authenticity*, reflect the actual *peculiarities* of remote communication partners?

8.3 Bibliographic Hints

Basically, all textbooks on security in computing systems contain introductory sections on control and monitoring; see Subsection 1.7. More specific references for special topics are given as bibliographic hints at the end of the next three chapters.

9 Conceptual Access Rights

Permissions and prohibitions in computing systems are commonly called (positive or negative) *access rights*. At least conceptually, such access rights are maintained by an appropriate *knowledge base*. As with any other knowledge base, its *static aspects*, usually referred to as the *information schema*, determine the structures that can be used to represent the intended permissions and prohibitions, and its *dynamic aspects* give rise to the available *operations*, which in this case comprise at least the following ones:

- *taking an access decision* on the basis of the information represented in the knowledge base, including *solving conflicts* between permissions and prohibitions;
- *updating* the knowledge base by inserting new data on permissions or prohibitions, and by modifying or deleting already existing data, possibly including cascading effects;
- *analyzing* an instance of the knowledge base concerning the actual achievement of security during its further dynamic development, including determining the possible future instances under updates and investigating the impact of these instances on security goals such as availability, confidentiality and integrity.

A central distinction between the various approaches to access rights management considers who is in charge of setting up permissions and prohibitions, and what kind of options the agents in charge actually have. In practice, this distinction often includes the frequency with which the knowledge base on permissions and prohibitions is exploited for access decisions. Basically, there are two different lines:

- In *discretionary* or *participant-oriented* approaches, in principle, the *individual participants* are supposed to be responsible for the objects they are working with and, accordingly, they are enabled to declare permissions and prohibitions at their *discretion*. However, in order to achieve overall security, clearly these approaches have to follow some agreed rules too. In particular, the responsibilities have to be consistently determined, and, usually, besides individual participants, there are also more powerful system administrators. Though it is desirable to submit every individual request to an explicit access decision, in practical discretionary approaches the controls are sometimes less strict, mainly owing to preferring supposed efficiency to security.

- In *mandatory* or *organization-oriented* approaches, in principle, a (fictitious) administrator of the *organization* that is running the computing system is supposed to *mandatorily* regulate the permissions and prohibitions in an a priori consistent way. The regulations might aim at strictly controlling either the *information flow* between objects and agents or their *integrity*, or both. However, in order to be manageable in practice, some aspects of the regulations are usually handled by several special participants who are *trusted* to follow the overall rules. For mandatory approaches, it is crucial that every request is effectively submitted to a controlling access decision.

9.1 Conceptual Models of Discretionary Approaches

In *discretionary approaches*, the expressiveness for declaring access rights can vary substantially, from a simple explicit lookup representation of the wanted access decisions to highly sophisticated means to provide explicit data and rules from which access decisions are implicitly inferred. In this section, we conceptually outline the options for the static aspects.

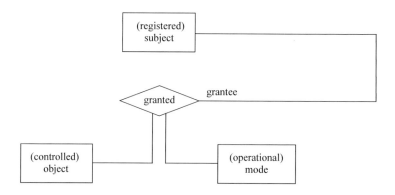

Fig. 9.1. ER model of the ternary relationship class *granted* for permissions

In *lookup representations*, there is at least a ternary relationship class *granted*, as indicated in Figure 9.1. A relationship of the form (*subject, object, mode*) specifies the following items:

- an identifiable and registered *subject* that is a participant seen as a grantee;
- a controlled *object* that is a possible operand of an access request;
- an (operational) *mode* that signifies a set of operations on the object.

Such a relationship is intended to represent that the *subject* is permitted to perform any operation of the specified *mode* on the *object*.

A relationship class *granted* can be immediately implemented as a database relation with three attributes (columns). Figure 9.2 displays an instance where an agent *user* is a registered subject; the package *application* is seen both as a registered subject and a controlled object; the flat files *data_file* and *recovery_file* are controlled objects; and *execute*, *read* and *write* are modes. The intended meaning of the instance shown is the following:

- (subject) *user* is permitted to perform on *application* (as an object) operations of mode *execute*, on (object) *data_file* operations of mode *read* and on (object) *recovery_file* operations of mode *write*;
- *application* (as a subject) is permitted to perform on (object) *data_file* operations of the modes *read* and *write*, and on (object) *recovery_file* operations of mode *read*;
- by default, any other access request is considered to be prohibited.

Granted	Subject	Object	(Operational) Mode
	user	application	execute
	user	data_file	read
	user	recovery_file	write
	application	data_ file	read
	application	data_ file	write
	application	recovery_file	read

Fig. 9.2. An instance of the relational implementation of the relationship class *granted*

Given a relational instance of the relationship class *granted*, an *access decision* is taken by means of a simple lookup of the tuple that corresponds to the request. In doing so, the function mode assigns to each operation (symbol) that might occur in an access request an appropriate (operational) mode:

```
function decide(subject, object, operation): Boolean;
return (subject, object, mode(operation)) ∈ Granted.
```

Updates are done by explicitly inserting, modifying or deleting tuples.

A relationship class *granted* can equivalently be formalized as an *access control matrix* or as a directed, labeled *access control graph*. For an *access control matrix*, each subject s that occurs determines a row, each object o that occurs determines a column, and the matrix entry at the crossing point contains the set of all modes m that are permitted for s on o, i.e., all m such that $(s,o,m) \in$ *Granted*.

An *access control graph* has a node for each subject s and object o that occur, and a tuple $(s,o,m) \in$ *Granted* is represented by a directed edge from s to o with label m. In most cases, the access control matrix is fairly sparse, i.e., most matrix entries are the empty set (of modes). Thus implementations usually exploit a space-efficient representation of either compressed rows or compressed columns:

- The row of subject s is given by a *privilege list* or *capability list*

  $Cl(s) := \{ [o,m] \mid (s,o,m) \in Granted \}$.
- The column of object o is given by an *access control list*

  $Acl(o) := \{ [s,m] \mid (s,o,m) \in Granted \}$.

Figure 9.3 shows the instance of Figure 9.2 in the equivalent forms mentioned.

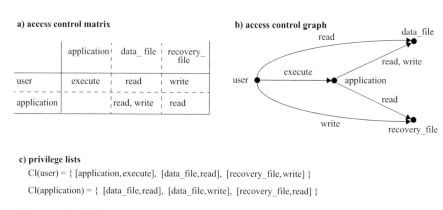

a) access control matrix

	application	data_file	recovery_file
user	execute	read	write
application		read, write	read

b) access control graph

c) privilege lists

Cl(user) = { [application, execute], [data_file, read], [recovery_file, write] }

Cl(application) = { [data_file, read], [data_file, write], [recovery_file, read] }

d) access control lists

Acl(application) = { [user, execute] }

Acl(data_file) = { [user, read], [application, read], [application, write] }

Acl(recovery_file) = { [user, write], [application, read] }

Fig. 9.3. An instance of the relational implementation of the relationship class *granted* shown as an access control matrix, an access control graph, privilege lists and access control lists

While in the simplest case the knowledge base on permissions and prohibitions on the one hand and the access decisions on the other hand are basically the same, advanced situations require more sophisticated knowledge base structures to algorithmically infer decisions. We shall discuss the following features:

- A *privilege* is an aggregate of a controlled object and an applicable operational mode.
- A privilege can be granted to different kinds of *grantees*, which might also be *collectives*. A collective can be a *group*, understood as a set of equally treated participants, or a *role* which can be roughly interpreted as a collection of simultaneously needed privileges.
- The *grantor* of a privilege can have an impact on access decisions or updates.
- Each controlled object can be assigned an *owner*, who is primarily responsible for discretionary permissions and prohibitions.

- We can define *structural relationships* on controlled objects, such as the *part_of relationship*, and *specializations* of the object class, in particular the subclass of executable *programs*. Similarly, we can define structural relationships and specializations for grantees and grantors.
- A program, seen as static text, is executed by a dynamically generated *process* that in turn is *mastered* by an individual participant, on behalf of whom the instructions of the program are processed.
- We can introduce *inclusion relationships* for the class of operational modes, and we can specialize modes into *functional* and *administrative* ones.
- The grantor of a privilege can impose *constraints* on its usage, in particular *temporal conditions* or conditions referring to the *computing history*.
- The grantor of a privilege can select the intended semantics of a later *revocation*, in particular concerning cascading effects, by using the *issue time*.
- So far, privileges have been regarded as permissions or *positive access rights*, together with a default rule for prohibitions. Additionally, one might consider *negative privileges* or *negative access rights* that are interpreted as explicit prohibitions.

There are numerous variations and combinations of these features, in each specific case requiring appropriate representation structures and procedures for access decisions. Not all combinations are useful or manageable. In fact, in practice, mostly only a core functionality is provided, dealing with *grants* of *privileges* concerning operational *modes* on controlled *objects* to *grantees* by *grantors*, together with some application-dependent extensions.

9.1.1 Refining the Granted Relationship

Figure 9.4 refines the basic `granted` *relationship* modeled in Figure 9.1 and introduces the features of privileges, grantees, collectives, grantors and owners.

Privilege. A programmer declares, for a data type, or depending on the programming paradigm, for a class, the structural properties of a data element or object, respectively, as well as the available operations. Accordingly, a data element or object and its *operations* (*methods*) are often seen as an aggregated entity. For the purpose of access control, several closely related operations are usually treated in the same way and therefore are uniformly signified by an *operational mode*.

Then, a data element or *object o* and a *mode m* are again seen as an *aggregated entity* [*o,m*] called a *privilege*. For any application, the definable privileges basically determine the *granularity* of access right specifications: a *fine* granularity supports detailed and gradual policies, whereas a *coarse* granularity tends to result in simple all-or-nothing policies.

Grantee. A *privilege* is *granted* to a *grantee*. To establish such a relationship, one needs syntactic means to insert a corresponding fact (using the relational implementation, just the corresponding tuple) into the knowledge base. Often, the keyword `grant` is used. In classical access control, grantees are registered and

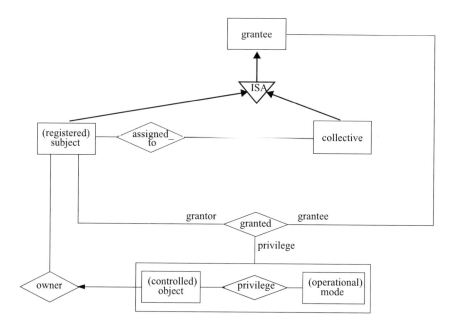

Fig. 9.4. Refined and augmented ER model of the relationship class *granted* for permissions, exploiting some of the more common differentiating features

identifiable participants, or collectives of them. However, in more recent approaches, a grantee can also be a more abstract entity that is characterized only by particular properties. Once a `granted` relationship has been inserted into the knowledge base in favor of a grantee, and as long as this insertion is considered to be valid, the participant(s) denoted can employ the privilege granted.

Collective. A *collective* is an abstraction that serves for sound management of privileges. Considered as grantees, collectives can be granted privileges, without being able to act on their own. Rather, acting subjects are independently *assigned* to a collective, thereby acquiring the privileges of the collective.

Grantor. Sometimes it is important for access decisions or updates to know who has declared a `granted` relationship, i.e., who has acted as the *grantor*. Then the knowledge base has to represent relationships of the form (*grantor, grantee, object, mode*). The additional item of the grantor is often used during later revocations and for resolving conflicts between permissions and prohibitions. Moreover, the grantor item is also useful for accountability.

Owner. Typically, objects have a *lifespan*: they are created, then possibly repeatedly used or updated, and finally destroyed. In general, the creation of an object is invoked by some specific participant, who is then considered as the *owner* of the object.

Often, the owner is automatically granted a collection of privileges with respect to the new object at creation time. Such grants might be explicitly represented, or they might remain implicit when a representation of the `ownership` relationship is just inserted into the knowledge base, and such representations are used later on when access decisions are inferred.

Sometimes, the owner has exclusive privileges that cannot be shared with other participants. For example, one might wish that only the owner himself can grant privileges with respect to the object concerned, or that only the owner can determine further grantors. As another example, the privilege of destroying an object is often granted exclusively to the owner. Finally, one might provide a means whereby the present owner can transfer his ownership of an object to another participant.

9.1.2 Differentiating Controlled Objects

So far, we have treated controlled objects as mutually independent entities. In many applications, however, there are various *structural relationships* between objects and several *specializations* of the object class. Such relationships and specializations might demand consistent grants, or might be relevant to access decisions. Figure 9.5 shows some examples that stem from the field of database management systems.

Complex Objects with Subobject/Superobject Relationships and Aggregation. A controlled object might be *complex* (or *compound*), and its components might be complex again. Moreover, several objects can be *aggregated* into a higher-order object that in some context is treated like an atomic object.

More abstractly, an object might contain various *subobjects*, and it might itself be a subobject of another *superobject*, as described by `part_of` relationships. In all cases, when a privilege with respect to an object is granted, the precise *scope* has to be fixed, i.e., one has to specify the impact of the grant on the subobjects and superobjects.

Specialization/Generalization Hierarchy and Inclusion of Extensions. According to the paradigm of object-oriented programming, a single controlled object can be understood as an instance of a class. The class *declaration* is then a special object that states the available operations (methods), on which the operational modes are based in turn. And each class declaration has the *collection* of current class *instances* as its extension object. For class declarations, a *specialization/generalization hierarchy* might be given, inducing *inheritance* of declarations from a (more) general class to the more special classes.

Additionally, one can specify an *inclusion hierarchy* of extensions, in simple cases just inverse to the inheritances, i.e., the extension of a subclass is seen as a subset of the extension of the superclass. Again, given the hierarchies, the precise *scope* of granting a privilege has to be specified.

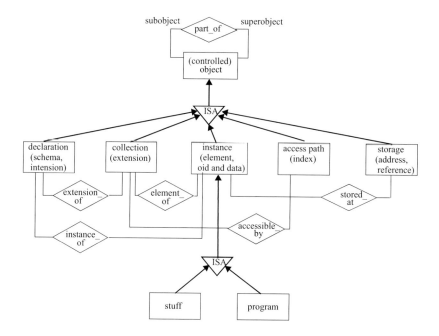

Fig. 9.5. ER model of some relevant structural relationship classes and specializations of the entity class *(controlled)* *object*

Semantic Relationships. Uniformly applying the paradigm of object-oriented programming, (class) *declarations* are also objects and thus are to be controlled like all other objects. Similarly, *access paths*, virtual or physical *storage*, and any other items can be treated and thus controlled as objects, too. The control then has to respect the various *semantic relationships* between objects. Some examples are shown in Figure 9.5: a *declaration* is `extension_of`-related to a *collection* as the extension; each *instance* is `instance_of`-related to its declaration, and `element_of`-related to the corresponding *collection*, and furthermore `stored_at`-related to its *storage*; finally, a *collection* might be `accessible_by`-related to an *access path* (e.g., a B*-tree for efficient key-based searching).

Again, given a privilege with respect to a specific object, the impact on the related objects must be specified. In particular, the following question must be settled: Does a privilege with respect to an object necessarily require additional privileges with respect to related objects, to be granted beforehand as a precondition, or granted by automatic follow-up grants? For example, in general, a read access to a collection object *ext* also demands a read access to the declaration object *class*, but not vice versa. How should we treat this dependence?

Programs. Executable *programs* are a distinguished specialization of *instance* objects: a program might be *executed* by a process, thereby establishing a further relationship of unique flavor, to be discussed next.

9.1.3 Programs, Processes and Masterships

The refinements presented so far refer basically to one abstraction layer dealing with participants as (more or less) abstract subjects. Considering how an abstract subject really acts within a computing system, we now introduce a second layer: roughly outlined, any action of a subject – expressed externally by some command – is *implemented* internally by generating a process that executes a program selected by the command. Accordingly, all specifications about permissions and prohibitions for the external layer of abstract subjects have to be appropriately *translated* into the internal layer of processes.

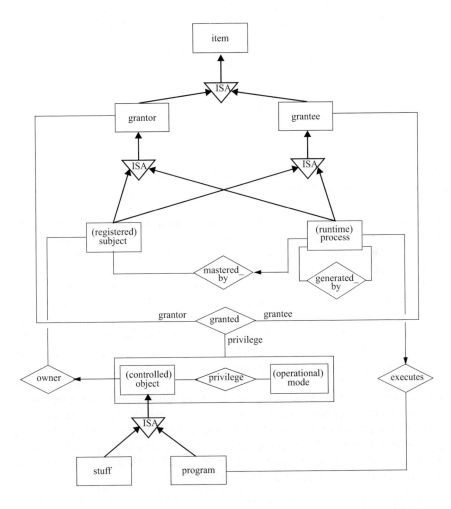

Fig. 9.6. ER model of the relationship class *granted* together with the relationship classes *executes* and *mastered_by* for processes and programs or subjects, respectively

Processes. A *process* is a dynamic *runtime object* that is involved in various relationships, as indicated in simplified form in Figure 9.6. Typically, a process is *generated* as a *child* by some already running process acting as the *father*. Therefore, each process has a chain of ancestors. This chain includes a process that has been generated for a *session* of a participant that is seen as a registered *subject* in the external layer. This subject is treated as the *master* of the session process, and by default this mastership is inherited by all recursively generated descendant processes. Furthermore, a process *executes* a *program*, which can be seen as a controlled *object*. In general, both the `mastered_by` relationship and the `executes` relationship of a process can dynamically be changed by special commands.

Given specified access rights in the external layer of subjects and controlled objects, these specifications now have to be translated into access rights of processes in the internal layer. Basically, the translation is implemented by exploiting the relationships mentioned above, which can be roughly outlined as follows:

- As a primary rule, the privileges granted to a subject are also made available to all processes mastered by that subject. In some sense, this rule is necessary in order that a subject can enjoy its privileges, since an external subject can only act by means of internal processes.
- As an additional rule, privileges granted to an ancestor process might be transferred to the generated child processes. This additional rule implies that the full ancestor chain can be relevant to access decisions.
- Sometimes, a process might require a privilege that is not conveniently acquired by the standard rules, since the privilege essentially depends on the currently executed program (rather than on the creation history of the process). However, usually – and accordingly also in our conceptual model – flat program files are not treated as active entities qualified to be a subject. In such cases, a program file can be assigned special access rights that are made available appropriately for an executing process.

The translation must also capture the revocation of access rights, and it must regulate the interactions between transfer and revocation of access rights on the one hand and modifications of the relationships of a process on the other hand.

9.1.4 Differentiating Operational Modes

Like objects, *operational modes* may be related or specialized, too, as indicated in Figure 9.7 and discussed below.

Functional Modes. The operations belonging to a controlled object o are classified into operational modes. In general, several operations might be classified into the same mode. As a special case, using the finest classification, each single operation op is also treated as a mode. Then, holding a privilege $[o, op]$ means a permission to perform the operation op on the object o.

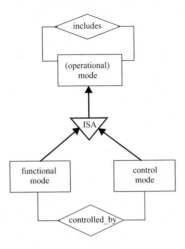

Fig. 9.7. ER model of the entity class (*operational*) *modes* and its relationship classes

The set of available operations, and accordingly of operational modes, depends on the kind of object. If the object is a generic text file, usually at least the operations *read* and *write* are defined. A more special object might offer additional operations such as *append*, or only specialized operations such as *pop* and *push* for a stack object. For an object of kind *program*, the operation *execute* is particularly important.

The available operations or operational modes are sometimes related such that a permission to perform an operation is declared to *include* also a permission to perform another operation. For example, it might be reasonable to declare such an includes relationship between the operation *write* and the more special operation *append*, but not, in general, vice versa.

In a pure object-oriented environment, operations are called by sending, receiving and interpreting *messages*. Accordingly, the following distinctions are often useful:

- An object o_{act}, acting as a subject, can be granted a permission to *invoke* an operation *op* on an object o_{exec}, i.e., o_{act} is permitted to *send* a message to o_{exec}, where the body of the message contains an identifier for the operation *op*. (Thus, in this context, from the point of view of the subject o_{act}, the *message* is the "controlled object" under the basic operation *send*.) The object o_{act} is then seen as the *activator* of an operation to be performed by the object o_{exec}.

- In turn, the object o_{exec}, also acting as a subject, can be granted a permission to *interpret* a message *received* from the object o_{act} such that the operation *op* denoted in the body of the message is actually executed. (Thus, again, now from the point of view of the subject o_{exec}, the *message* is the "controlled object" under the basic operation *receive and interpret*.) The object o_{exec} is then seen as the *executor* of an operation invoked by the object o_{act}.

In this framework, *two* permissions have to be *independently* granted, one for the activator and one for the executor, in order that a request for the operation *op* is actually performed.

This feature is particularly appropriate in *distributed systems* with autonomous component objects acting as activators and executors, respectively. In this case control and monitoring of the basic operations *send* and *receive and interpret* can be implanted into the channel between the activators and the executors. Basically, on the activator side, outgoing messages have to be controlled and, correspondingly, on the executor side, the incoming messages have to be inspected, as, for example, is actually implemented by *firewalls*.

Control Modes. So far, we have assumed that the privileges are *functional* in the sense that the objects and operational modes under consideration are immediately relevant to an application. Functional privileges can be treated as controlled objects in turn. In this context, the pertinent operations or operational modes refer to the control of the privileges themselves (rather than to the control of the operations denoted in privileges). For example, a subject can perform the following *control operations* on privileges:

- *granting* a privilege to a subject as a grantee;
- *transferring* a privilege to another subject;
- *taking* a privilege from another subject;
- *delegating* the usage of a privilege to another subject;
- *revoking* a privilege from a subject.

For controlling privileges, the following operation is also important:

- *generating* a new item, classified as potentially acting as a subject, a controlled object or both; thereby, the new item is often supplied with some initial privileges, and the creator often gets some privileges concerning the new item.

An operational mode signifying control operations is called a *control mode* and, accordingly, we speak about *control privileges*. Usually, the applicability of a control operation on privileges is restricted to a specific kind of functional privilege or even to a single functional privilege. Mainly in the latter case, the operand of the control operation is often not explicitly treated as a controlled object but rather as part of a specialized operation.

For example, instead of a generic *grant* operation, for each functional mode m, or even for each specific privilege $[o, m]$, there might be a special $grant_m$ operation, or even a more special $grant_{[o, m]}$ operation. In this case a functional mode m is controlled_by related to the corresponding control modes.

In principle, control operations on privileges have to be controlled in turn. Thus, in general, we obtain a *control hierarchy*, where control privileges of level $k+1$ permit operations on control privileges of level k. However, for practical reasons, this hierarchy is usually limited to one or two levels only.

9.1.5 Qualifications and Conditions

In the modeling presented so far, granting a privilege is treated as specifying a *permission*. Actually, an access decision for a request is inferred from the data in the knowledge base, where the data comprise explicitly granted privileges, as well as further relevant data on subjects, controlled objects and operational modes. If no positive access right can be inferred for a request, then, by default, the request is rejected. Rather than using only this default rule for *implicit* prohibitions, sometimes *explicit* prohibitions can also be specified. More generally, a `granted` relationship can be qualified as a *permission* or a *prohibition*, and constrained further in various ways, as roughly indicated in Figure 9.8.

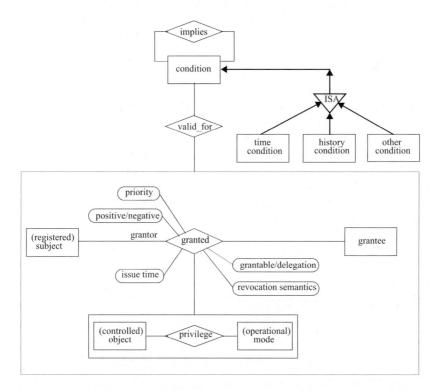

Fig. 9.8. ER model of the relationship class *granted* with qualifications and conditions

Negative Privileges (Prohibitions). An administrator might want to explicitly specify that a subject *s* is prohibited to perform an operation of mode *m* on a controlled object *o*. Therefore, the administrator must have expressive means to qualify a corresponding `granted` relationship as a *prohibition* or as a *permission*. This can be done, for example, by use of an additional attribute for indicating the *negative* or *positive* interpretation.

Once both explicit permissions and prohibitions have been introduced, *conflicts* might arise, in particular owing to additional data and rules that are exploited for inferring an access decision. To support *conflict resolution*, a qualified `granted` relationship can be annotated further with a *priority*.

Control Qualifications. `granted` relationships can also be qualified regarding control operations. In particular, a granted privilege can be declared to be *grantable* again, i.e., the grantee is permitted to grant the received privilege to other subjects in turn; similarly, a granted privilege can be declared to be *delegable*.

Moreover, several different *revocation semantics* can be specified. Each revocation semantics determines a specific option for how recursively granted privileges are treated when an original privilege is revoked. Basically, the options differ in whether deletions of permissions are cascading or not. For a revocation, the data about the *grantors* of a privilege and the pertinent *issue times* might be relevant.

Validity Conditions. Finally, a `granted` relationship can be regarded as *valid* only under particular constraints. In principle, any *condition* that is expressible by some constraint language can be used. Special examples are *time conditions* that restrict the usage of a privilege to certain periods of time, and *history conditions* that refer to *previous usages* of privileges, for example to limit the performance of an operation to three times only. Conditions might be evaluated individually, as well as under a logical `implies` relationship.

9.1.6 Managing Privileges with Collectives

Collectives serve to enhance the discretionary management of privileges. As indicated for *groups* and *roles* in Figure 9.9, collectives are typically employed as abstract *grantees* of privileges, though collectives are not able to act on their own. Rather, acting *individual* subjects are independently assigned to collectives, thereby implicitly acquiring the privileges of those collectives. Moreover, collectives can be organized into inheritance hierarchies.

Groups and Individuals. Roughly outlined, a *group* assembles together *individuals* who are supposed to be simultaneously equipped with the same set of privileges. Establishing a group is particularly useful if the members are entitled to cooperate on a specific task and therefore have to *share* some common resources. In this case, the required privileges are *granted* directly to the group as a *grantee*, and individuals are independently determined to be group *members*. Thereby, an administrator can guarantee that every group member has full access to the respective resources.

The administrator will have even set up provisions for consistently permitting resource sharing for individuals who join the group later on. Moreover, a group can be *contained* in another group. Thereby, members of a *subgroup* can share all resources permitted to a *supergroup*.

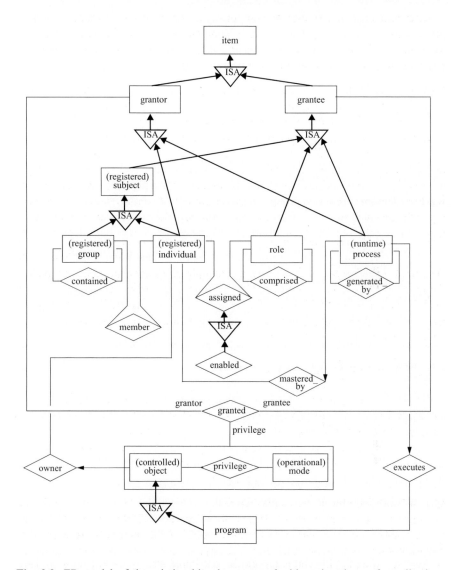

Fig. 9.9. ER model of the relationship class *granted* with entity classes for collectives, *groups* and *roles*, together with their relationship classes

Roles. Roughly outlined, a *role* assembles together *privileges* that are needed for a well-understood organizational task within an application. Establishing roles is particularly useful for applications that are run within a finely structured organization based on division of labor. In this case, an administrator might first aim at (mostly statically) mapping the *business model* and the *organizational structure* of *job descriptions* or related task documents, including also concepts of *social roles*, onto roles (used as collectives for access control).

Later on, the administrator can dynamically *assign* specific individuals to appropriate roles, thereby implicitly granting the roles' privileges to the respective individuals. Thereby, the administrator can ensure that a newly assigned individual will be given all privileges needed for his intended job function. Moreover, a role can be *comprised* by another role, whereby the *subrole's* privileges are inherited by the *superrole*.

In practice, an individual might act in distinct roles over time. Then, usually, following the administrative principle of *need-to-know* or *need-to-act*, when starting a session or at other appropriate points in time, an individual has to *enable* exactly one of his roles, thereby making temporarily available to him the privileges of just the selected role but not of the other roles.

Layered Design. Formally, groups and roles look quite similar, sharing the following independent features: on the one hand, both of these collectives can hold privileges, and on the other hand, individuals can be assigned to both collectives. The differences depend mostly on the point of view and the application (which can have various motivations), as discussed above.

Clearly, though this is not shown in Figure 9.9, the two kinds of concept can be combined by allowing a group to be assigned to a role, thereby implicitly granting all group members the role's privileges. Moreover, one might imagine a more general layered design, where an individual is implicitly related to a privilege by a chain of intermediate concepts; chains of the kind *individual–group–privilege*, *individual–role–privilege* and *individual–group–role–privilege* are widely used examples.

9.1.7 Role-Based Access Control (RBAC)

Above, we have presented roles as an optional feature of discretionary access rights. Some researchers, however, advocate *role-based access control*, *RBAC* for short, as a third alternative besides the *discretionary* or *participant-oriented* approach and the *mandatory* or *organization-oriented* approach. This view is supported by the rich body of insight and tools that have been provided for exploiting roles in practice, and by a comprehensive treatment of implementation and application aspects.

Anyway, as an intellectual compromise, one could also argue that roles are used *discretionarily* for *organizational* purposes. And, obviously, one could always clumsily simulate the achievements of role-based access control by privileges directly granted to individuals, essentially by expanding all implicit inferences due to roles. Furthermore, it has been demonstrated that the main effects of the mandatory approach can be simulated using either roles or explicit privileges, and vice versa. Finally, some features presented here for privileges can also be employed for roles. In particular, the distinction between functional and control modes can be converted into a distinction between *functional* and *control roles*, each having their own hierarchy, and roles can also be constrained by various *conditions*.

Though role-based access control has many widely acknowledged benefits, it also suffers from specific pitfalls. The difficulties arise mainly when organizational concepts identified in the application environment are not properly translated into computing concepts. We shall briefly discuss two examples.

In an application environment, an exposed individual might be charged with many obligations and tasks, which can be partly overlapping and partly quite separate. Simply defining one very powerful role for such an individual would often violate the administrative principle of *need-to-know* or *need-to-act* and the requirement of *separation of roles*, when single actions are considered. Then, a careful design of mutually exclusive elementary and restricted roles and combinations of them into gradually more powerful superroles is demanded, together with the feature of temporarily enabling a minimally powerful appropriate role for performing the task currently due.

Hierarchies in organizations are often interpreted concerning *operational power* or *authority*: an individual acting in a higher organizational or social role is supposed to be permitted to act like any individual in a lower organizational or social role. In particular, a *senior* might take the right to perform all actions that his *subordinates* are permitted to perform. Already doubtful in general, the naive translation of this idea into roles can turn out to be extremely dangerous: the computing system can have an omnipotent user who is possibly not even well trained to successfully operate the system. Then, at least potentially, a superior's slip can cause enormous damage.

9.2 Semantics for Access Decisions

Given an instance of a knowledge base on *permissions* and *prohibitions*, and possibly also on the usage history, the control and monitoring component has to take *access decisions* concerning incoming requests from subjects to perform operations on controlled objects. Conceptually, the decision is taken by calling a function decide that is declared as

function decide(subject, object, operation): Boolean.

In the simplest case, this function is implemented by a lookup of a tuple (subject, object, mode(operation)) in a table *Granted* that suitably represents the specified access rights.

In more sophisticated cases, complex inferences are necessary, based on various features managed by the knowledge base. As a foundation, precise semantics must be defined and ultimately implemented for each of the pertinent features, as well as for their mutual interactions. In the following, we exemplarily treat three issues, first informally and then by formal means:

- How to deal with *hierarchical relationships* between entities?
- How to resolve *conflicts* between permissions and prohibitions?
- How to always ensure a *defined decision*?

9.2.1 Informal Semantics

Concerning *hierarchical relationships*, *inheritance rules* that capture the intended meaning of the hierarchies are usually exploited. We present some (debatable) suggestions for important examples, summarized in Table 9.10, emphasizing that sometimes alternative approaches could be supported.

Regarding *roles*, it is often suggested that permissions should be inherited upwards from a *subrole* to a *superrole*, whereas prohibitions should be inherited downwards from a superrole to a subrole. These rules are motivated by considering a role (a collection of privileges) as some kind of real-world *job description*, and the role hierarchy as reflecting *operational power* or *authority*. The rules are then justified as follows: if a *subordinate* is permitted to do something, then his superior is equally permitted; and conversely, if a *superior* is prohibited to do something, so are his subordinates.

Regarding *objects*, it is often suggested that both permissions and prohibitions should be inherited downwards from a *superobject* to a *subobject*. These rules are motivated by seeing an object (a programming construct) as representing a possibly compound real-world entity. The rules are then justified as follows: any specification concerning a compound entity should extend to all its parts.

Regarding *operational modes*, it is often suggested that permissions should be inherited downwards from a more general mode to an *included* more specific mode, whereas prohibitions should be inherited upwards from a more specific mode to a more general mode. These rules are motivated by interpreting an operational mode (which signifies a collection of operations) as some kind of real-world action pattern. The rules are then justified as follows: if it is permitted to exploit a comprehensive pattern, it is necessarily permitted to exploit all included subpatterns as well; and conversely, the prohibition of a subpattern must be enforced by a prohibition of all comprehensive patterns.

Table 9.10. Examples of reasonable inheritance rules for permissions and prohibitions

Hierarchical relationship	Permission	Prohibition
subrole $\leq_R$ superrole	upwards	downwards
subobject $\leq_O$ superobject	downwards	downwards
more special mode $\leq_M$ more general mode	downwards	upwards

Conflicts between permissions and prohibitions typically result from explicit declarations made by several autonomously acting administrators on the one hand and implicit specifications due to inheritances on the other hand. Basically, *conflict resolution* can be achieved by annotating declarations (and even rule conclusions) with *priorities*, or by applying *priority rules* when inferring an access decision.

Explicit declarations of priorities for single permissions and prohibitions appear to be difficult to manage. In particular, all administrators would need a common understanding of priorities and of their impact on access decisions in order to achieve reliable results overall. Therefore, priority rules are usually preferred. In the following, we discuss some reasonable examples:

- *Prohibition prevails over permission.* This is a commonly accepted conservative rule, justified by preferring interests enforced by prohibitions, for example *confidentiality* and *integrity*, to interests enforced by permissions, mainly *availability*.
- *Specialization prevails over generalization*, i.e., the specification for a more special or "smaller" case beats the specification for a more general or "larger" case. This rule is motivated by considering a more special case as some kind of an *exception* to a larger case. Then, the majority of requests are expected to be uniformly captured by a more general "normal case", whereas presumably rare exceptional situations are treated differently by more special cases that overrule the normal case on the basis of specific considerations.

  In some sense, if only permissions (*positive access rights*) are explicitly declared, then this reasoning also underlies the commonly used *default rule* that every request is prohibited unless it is explicitly proven to be permitted. Thereby, most of the syntactically possible requests are gathered into a "normal case" for forbiddance, whereas permissions are "exceptionally" granted.
- *A higher-ranked grantor prevails over a lower-ranked grantor.* Whereas the former rules refer to an attribute or the privilege part of a `granted` relationship, this rule considers the grantor part. Grantors are seen to be ranked in a *command hierarchy*, where orders of higher-ranked individuals are supposed to invalidate conflicting orders of lower-ranked individuals.

Obviously, sometimes a collection of these or similar rules still cannot uniquely resolve all conflicts, since several rules might be equally applicable but deliver different results. A simple solution to this problem is to follow a *metarule* for priority rules: the selected priority rules of the collection are always considered in a fixed *predetermined sequence*, and the result of the first applicable priority rule is always taken as the final access decision. This solution, however, can turn out to be rather dangerous, since in general the impact of sequencing rules is difficult to understand and to manage.

While conflicts can be seen as a kind of *overspecification*, there might arise *underspecifications* as well, i.e., the knowledge base may not provide enough information for the decision function to define a result. In order to avoid this deficiency, some completion rules for undefined situations can be employed. For example:

- *Closed completion.* This rule states that an undefined situation results in a final *prohibition*, i.e., a request is finally permitted *only if* a permission can be derived from the information in the knowledge base.
- *Open completion.* This rule states that an undefined situation results in a final *permission*, i.e., a request is finally permitted not only if a permission can be derived but also if no prohibition can be derived.

9.2.2 Formal Semantics

When aiming at formal semantics for access decisions, we have to balance several possibly conflicting requirements. In particular, a formal language for expressing access rights specifications as a basis for access decisions should have the following properties:

- *expressiveness*: a rich variety of conceptual features is covered;
- *manageability*: administrators can easily declare their wishes;
- *completeness*: for any request, an access decision can be inferred;
- *soundness*: for any request, the access decision is unique;
- *computational efficiency*: access decisions and control operations can be implemented such that the storage overheads and runtimes are acceptable in practical applications.

In the following, we exemplarily outline two proposals. Both proposals formally express conceptual models by means of logic programming, thereby leaving substantial room for varying application-dependent details. Whereas the first proposal favors practicability, the second allows one to resolve conflicts in a highly sophisticated and dynamic way.

9.2.3 The Flexible Authorization Framework (FAF)

In the *Flexible Authorization Framework*, *FAF* for short, a computing system and basic (and possibly further) concepts of the *discretionary* approach to access rights management – as informally introduced in Section 9.1 – are formally modeled by the following components:

- A set *Inst* of *instance objects* and a set *Coll* of *collections* or similar concepts with a (for simplicity) common *hierarchy* $\leq_{IC}$, where instance objects are minimal elements, denoting `element_of` relationships or `part_of` relationships.
- A set *Ind* of *individual users* and a set *Gr* of *groups* with a (for simplicity) common *hierarchy* $\leq_{UG}$, where users are minimal elements, denoting *group memberships* or *group containments*.
- A set *Ro* of *roles* with a *hierarchy* $\leq_R$, denoting *role comprising*.
- A set *Mode* of operational *modes*.
- Possibly, for representing further relationship classes of interest, including for example *ownerships*, some relations $Rel_1, \ldots, Rel_n$ of appropriate arities, including the binary relation *Owner*.
- The set of (possible) *grantees*, composed of individual users, groups and roles,

  $Grantee = Ind \cup Gr \cup Ro$.

- The set of (possible) controlled *objects*, composed of instance objects, collections and roles,

  $Object = Inst \cup Coll \cup Ro$.

- A set of *qualifications*,

  Qual = {pos,neg}.

- A relation

  QGranted ⊆ *Grantee* × *Object* × *Mode* × *Qual*

  for representing *explicitly* declared granted relationships that are *qualified* as *positive* (for permissions) or *negative* (for prohibitions). A role r can occur in a tuple of *QGranted* in two different positions: in a tuple (r,o,m,q), the role r is a grantee that holds the privilege $[o,m]$ with qualification q; in a tuple (u,r,m,q) with $m \in$ {assign, enable}, the individual user u has the role r assigned or enabled, respectively, qualified by q.

- A relation

  Done ⊆ *Ind* × *Ro* × *Object* × *Mode* × *Time*

  for recording selected aspects (u,r,o,m,t) of the *usage history*, namely that an *individual user* u acting in a *role* r has operated on an *object* o in some *mode* m at a specific *time* t, where *Time* is an appropriate set of points in time. As usual, an individual user is assumed to have at most one role enabled.

Additionally, going beyond previous treatments, FAF introduces some additional concepts for inferring implicit qualified granted relationships from explicit declarations, for specifying the overall security policy, and for error handling:

- A relation

  QGranted* ⊆ *Grantee* × *Object* × *Mode* × *Qual*,

  derived by use of rules for extending the relation *QGranted* by further *explicit* *qualified* granted relationships, which might be conditional in terms of basic items and the usage history.

- A relation

  Derived ⊆ *Grantee* × *Object* × *Mode* × *Qual*,

  derived by use of rules for representing *implicit* qualified permissions and prohibitions, where an auxiliary relation *Override* together with appropriate rules is used to prepare for *resolving conflicts*.

- A relation

  Decide ⊆ *Grantee* × *Object* × *Mode* × *Qual*,

  derived by use of *decision* rules for representing the overall *security policy*, including final conflict resolution and enforcing completeness.

- A relation (Boolean predicate)

  Error ⊆ {∅},

  derived by use of *integrity* rules to detect erroneous specifications.

These components constitute the *knowledge bases* on permissions and prohibitions and, for the component *Done*, on the usage history.

Additionally, there is a functional component for taking actual *access decisions* for functional and control *requests*. Basically, *functional requests* are decided according to the intended meaning of the knowledge bases. In this context, this meaning is formally captured by a unique *fixpoint* of the facts and rules stored in the knowledge bases.

Control requests are handled in the same manner; for this purpose, the knowledge bases are extended to deal with control privileges too. Additionally, a control request is interpreted as a specification for an update *transaction* for the knowledge bases. Such a transaction has to maintain the invariant that the *integrity* rules are satisfied. In this text, we briefly treat the latter aspect of control requests but not the former one. The overall architecture of FAF is roughly displayed in Figure 9.11, and some selected more formal details are treated in the following.

Formally, the components belonging to the *knowledge bases* (for simplicity, for functional privileges only here) are instantiated by sets of facts or rules that are expressed in the *(Flexible) Authorization Specification Language (FASL)*. FASL is a logical language that allows an administrator to express a security policy as a locally stratified *logical program*, and the control component to insert history facts into the bottom stratum. The *syntax* of FASL is defined along the following lines:

- The vocabulary is given by sorted *constant symbols* for any item occurring in the computing system, by suitable sorted *variables* for such items and by a sorted *predicate symbol* for each of the components listed above.
- *Terms* are either constants or variables, and thus, besides constants, there are no further function symbols.
- *Atoms* are formed by a predicate symbol followed by an appropriate list of terms. A *literal* is either an atom or a negated atom, written as $\neg atom$.
- *Rules* are implicational formulas of the following form: the *conclusion* (head) is a single atom, and the *premise* (body) is a conjunction of atoms and, under some essential restrictions defined in Table 9.12, of negated atoms too. Such rules are denoted by

  $atom \leftarrow literal_1 \wedge \ldots \wedge literal_n.$

  Rules with an empty premise are *facts*, written as $atom \leftarrow$.
- Rules must be formed according to six *strata* that correspond to the dependency structure shown in Figure 9.11 and are defined in Table 9.12.
- A (logical) *program* (in FASL) is a finite set of such rules.

The *semantics* of a logical program in FASL is determined as the unique minimal *fixpoint* of the program, with respect to *stable/well-founded semantics* for *locally stratified* programs. Roughly outlined, a rule – under a suitable substitution of variables by constant symbols for items – is interpreted as generating a new head fact from previously available body facts. Thereby, the rules of each stratum are exhaustively treated before proceeding to the next stratum.

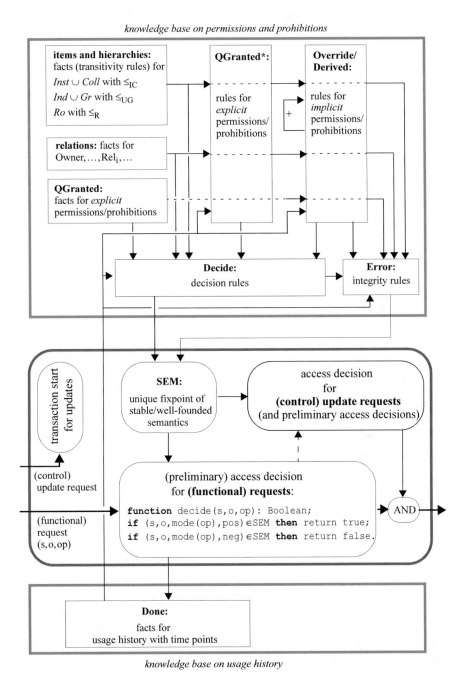

Fig. 9.11. Simplified architecture of the Flexible Authorization Framework as an example of a control and monitoring component (without identification and proof of authenticity)

Table 9.12. The strata of a logical program in the Flexible Authorization Specification Language

Stratum	Head	Body	Goal
1	$Inst(t)$, $Coll(t)$, $Ind(t)$, $Gr(t)$, $Ro(t)$	empty	facts for basic items
	$\leq_{IC}(t_1,t_2)$, $\leq_{UG}(t_1,t_2)$, $\leq_R(t_1,t_2)$	empty, or the respective relation symbols	facts and recursive closure rules for hierarchies
	$Owner(t_1,t_2)$, ...	empty	facts for relations
	$QGranted(t_1,t_2,t_3,t_4)$	empty	facts for explicit `granted` relationships
	$Done(t_1,t_2,t_3,t_4,t_5)$	empty	facts for usage history
2	$QGranted^*(t_1,t_2,t_3,t_4)$	literals for basic items, hierarchies, usage history	rules for explicit, `granted` relationships with conditions
3	$Override(t_1,t_2,t_3,t_4)$	(not treated in this text)	rules for preparing conflict resolution
4	$Derived(t_1,t_2,t_3,t_4)$	literals for basic items, hierarchies, usage history, explicit `granted` relationships, conflict resolution;	rules for implicit `granted` relationships
		atoms for implicit `granted` relationships	recursive rules for implicit `granted` relationships
5	$Decide(t_1,t_2,t_3,\text{pos})$	literals for basic items, hierarchies, usage history, explicit and implicit `granted` relationships;	decision rules for *final permissions*
	$Decide(x,y,z,\text{neg})$ as head of a *single* rule with *variables* x,y,z	the *single* literal $\neg Decide(x,y,z,\text{pos})$	one default decision rule for *final prohibitions*
6	$Error()$	literals for basic items, hierarchies, usage history, explicit and implicit `granted` relationships, decisions	integrity rules

Negative atoms from preceding strata are always treated according to *negation as failure*. Similarly, in stratum 5, the single negative atom ¬Decide(x, y, z, pos) from the same stratum is first determined by negation as failure and then the single rule for final prohibitions is used. Concerning negation, it is important to observe the difference between the "negation of a permission" (that is, a negated atom with qualification pos) and a "prohibition" (that is, an atom with qualification neg). Moreover, the requirements for the fifth stratum are designed to finally resolve conflicts that may have potentially occurred in preceding strata.

In the following, we present a very simple fragment of a security policy as an example of a *logical program* in FASL. This fragment deals with reading and writing a file *pub_f* of low sensitivity, an individual user *admin* acting as administrator, arbitrary *requestors* denoted by the variable *x*, and arbitrary operational modes denoted by the variable *m*:

- Concerning *explicit* permissions and prohibitions in stratum 1 and stratum 2, the administrator is granted a positive read privilege but a negative write privilege, while the owner of the file acquires both privileges:

```
QGranted(admin, pub_f, read, pos) ← .
QGranted(admin, pub_f, write, neg) ← .
QGranted*(x, pub_f, read, pos) ← Owner(x, pub_f).
QGranted*(x, pub_f, write, pos) ← Owner(x, pub_f).
```

- Concerning *implicit* permissions and prohibitions in stratum 4, the operational mode read is considered to be included in the more general mode write, whereby the corresponding inheritance rules are instantiated:

```
Derived(x, pub_f, read, pos) ← Derived(x, pub_f, write, pos).
Derived(x, pub_f, write, neg) ← Derived(x, pub_f, read, neg).
```

Furthermore, any explicit permission or prohibition is also converted into the corresponding implicit statement:

```
Derived(x, pub_f, m, pos) ← QGranted(x, pub_f, m, pos).
Derived(x, pub_f, m, pos) ← QGranted*(x, pub_f, m, pos).
Derived(x, pub_f, m, neg) ← QGranted(x, pub_f, m, neg).
Derived(x, pub_f, m, neg) ← QGranted*(x, pub_f, m, neg).
```

- Concerning *decisions* and *conflict resolution* in stratum 5, owing to the low sensitivity of the resource, read accesses should be finally permitted if some implicit permission can be derived or if an implicit prohibition cannot be derived, whereas write accesses should be finally permitted only in the former case (but not in the latter one). Thus, for both modes, a permission prevails over a prohibition, while an *open* policy is stated for reading (finally permitted if no prohibition can be derived), and a *closed* policy is preferred for writing (finally permitted only if a permission can be derived):

```
Decide(x, pub_f, read, pos) ← Derived(x, pub_f, read, pos).
Decide(x, pub_f, read, pos) ← ¬Derived(x, pub_f, read, neg).
Decide(x, pub_f, write, pos) ← Derived(x, pub_f, write, pos).
```

For *prohibitions*, as generally required for stratum 5 of any logical program in FASL, one generic default decision rule is specified:

```
Decide(x,y,z,neg) ← ¬Decide(x,y,z,pos).
```

- Concerning *integrity enforcement* in stratum 6, an implicit permission of a read or write access to the file *pub_f* together with the respective implicit prohibition should be treated as an error, i.e., any update request resulting in such a situation should be rejected:

```
Error() ← Derived(x,pub_f,read,pos) ∧ Derived(x,pub_f,read,neg).
Error() ← Derived(x,pub_f,write,pos) ∧ Derived(x,pub_f,write,neg).
```

The *control* and *monitoring* component takes *access decisions* as follows. Assume that the component receives a (*functional*) *request* (s,o,op), where s is supposed to denote the individual requestor u or, if applicable, his enabled role r, and op is the wanted operation on a controlled object o such that $m = mode(op)$ is the operational mode. The *knowledge bases* are then conceptually exploited roughly in three steps:

- The unique minimal *fixpoint SEM* of the logical program that is stored in the knowledge bases is computed.
- A preliminary *access decision* is taken using the following procedure:

```
function decide(s,o,op): Boolean;
if (s,o,mode(op),pos)∈SEM then return true  fi;      /permitted
if (s,o,mode(op),neg)∈SEM then return false fi.      /prohibited
```

- If the preliminary access decision returns `false`, then the request is immediately rejected; otherwise, if `true` is returned, then an appropriate tuple (u,r,o,m,t) is tentatively inserted into the *usage history Done*, and the fixpoint is recomputed and checked for integrity: if the integrity is preserved, the preliminary permission is finally confirmed and the tentative insertion is committed, otherwise the request is finally rejected and the tentative insertion is aborted.

If the control and monitoring component receives an *update request*, i.e., a *control operation* to modify the knowledge base on permissions and prohibitions is wanted, then, conceptually, the following actions are performed:

- An access decision is taken, similarly to what is done for a functional request.
- A transaction is started.
- The requested modifications are tentatively executed, allowing various *revoking* strategies to be implemented.
- The *Error* predicate for checking *integrity* is evaluated using the fixpoint *SEM*.
- Depending on the result of the integrity check, the transaction either commits or aborts.

Having outlined the formalism, we now comment on the properties achieved. Concerning *expressiveness*, the general design of the framework and of the specification language, together with the example, show that many features of access control can indeed be formally treated. Basically, the expressiveness is determined by

Table 9.13. A reasonable assignment of responsibilities for the strata

Stratum	Goal	Responsible agents
1	facts for basic items, hierarchies, relations	automatic extraction from declarations and runtime data
	facts for explicit granted relationships	system administrator and respective owners
	facts for usage history	monitoring component
2	rules for explicit granted relationships	respective owners and application administrator
3	rules for preparing conflict resolution	application administrator and security officer
4	(recursive) rules for implicit granted relationships	application administrator and security officer
5	decision rules for permissions and prohibitions	security officer
6	integrity rules	application administrator and security officer

the power of the chosen fragment of logic programming. Concerning *manageability*, we observe that the layered approach supports reliable administration of access rights, even if the administration is not centralized but partially distributed. For example, the responsibilities could be reasonably assigned to system components, several individual owners, a system administrator, an application administrator and a *security officer*, as outlined in Table 9.13.

Concerning *completeness* and *soundness*, the stratification and the restrictions shown in Table 9.12 ensure the following theorem.

Theorem 9.1   [FASL programs are complete and sound]

Let *AS* be a logical program according to the syntax of the Flexible Authorization Specification Language. The following properties then hold:

1. *AS* has a unique minimal fixpoint *SEM* as a stable/well-founded model.

2. For each (functional) request (s,o,op), exactly one of the literals

   $(s,o,mode(op),\text{pos})$ and $(s,o,mode(op),\text{neg})$

   is an element of *SEM*.

Sketch of Proof: The claimed properties are derived from known results of the discipline of logic programming. The existence of a unique minimal fixpoint is ensured by local stratification, i.e., the restrictions concerning negation. Completeness is enforced by the default decision rule for prohibitions together with negation as failure. Soundness is a consequence of having just one default decision rule for prohibitions. ❑

Concerning *efficiency*, the general design clearly allows tractable (polynomial-time computable) access decisions. If advanced techniques of logic programming are employed, including *materialization* of the fixpoint *SEM*, then decisions with an acceptable delay appear to be achievable.

9.2.4 The Dynamic Authorization Framework (DAF)

The expressiveness of the Flexible Authorization Framework is restricted in two related ways. Syntactically, a logical program in the Flexible Authorization Specification Language has to be locally stratified, with decision rules for final permissions and prohibitions obeying additional narrow requirements. Semantically, such a program has to be fully deterministic in such a way that its semantics is determined by a unique minimal, stable/well-founded model. In the *Dynamic Authorization Framework, DAF* for short, these restrictions are, essentially, relaxed, offering administrators even more options to *discretionarily* declare their security policies. In particular, by introducing *nondeterminism*, conflicts can be dynamically resolved on the basis of the computing history.

Basically, DAF varies the logical FAF approach and thereby drops restrictions on using negation. The basic components of DAF for dealing mainly with *functional requests* can be outlined as follows; further reasonable variations and additions for update requests (not fully treated in this text) are allowed as well:

- A set *Object* of (possible) controlled *objects* with an object *hierarchy* $\leq_O$, denoting `part_of` relationships or similar concepts (including those for collections not explicitly treated here), and having a generic largest element top_O.
- A set *Ind* of *individual users*.
- A set *Ro* of *roles* with a *hierarchy* $\leq_R$, denoting simultaneously *role comprising* (in the sense of job descriptions) and *ranking* concerning *commands*, and having a generic largest (most powerful) element top_R; concerning commands, for convenience of notation, $\leq_R$ is extended to *Ind* such that $u \leq_R top_R$ for all $u \in Ind$.
- A set *Gr* of *groups* with a *hierarchy* $\leq_G$, denoting *group containments*; the members of a group are individual users and (specifically to this approach) roles as well.
- A set *Mode* of operational *modes* with a *hierarchy* $\leq_M$, denoting *mode inclusions*.
- Two special *control modes* {own,admin}. In a control privilege [o,own], the mode own indicates *ownership* of an object o and signifies the control operations of *granting* and *revoking* privileges of the form [o,m], where m may be any applicable *functional mode* or the special mode admin. In a control privilege [o,admin], the mode admin indicates *administrative control* of an object o and signifies the control operations of granting and revoking privileges of the form [o,m], where m may be any applicable functional mode (but *not* the special mode admin).

- Possibly, to represent further relationship classes of interest, including *group memberships* or *role enabling* for example, some relations $Rel_1,\ldots,Rel_n$ of appropriate arities, including the binary relations *GrMember* and *RoEnabled*.
- The set of (possible) *grantors*, composed of individual users and roles,

  Grantor = *Ind* $\cup$ *Ro*.

  Thus, specifically to this approach and deviating from our conceptual modeling, roles are seen here as grantors too, on the basis of the following (debatable) reasoning. If an individual user acts in an enabled (unique) role, then the user's actions should be attributed to the role rather than to the individual.
- The set of (possible) *grantees* or *subjects*, composed of individual users, groups and roles,

  Subject = *Ind* $\cup$ *Gr* $\cup$ *Ro*.
- A set of *qualifications*,

  Qual = {pos,neg}.
- A relation

  Done $\subseteq$ *Subject* $\times$ *Object* $\times$ *Mode*

  for recording selected aspects (s,o,m) of the *usage history*, namely that a *subject s* has operated on an *object o* in some *mode m*.

A basic *permission* or *prohibition* is represented by a tuple of the relation

  Grantor_QGranted $\subseteq$ *Grantor* $\times$ *Subject* $\times$ *Object* $\times$ *Mode* $\times$ *Qual*.

Such a tuple denotes an extended granted relationship that also captures the *grantor* and a *qualification* as *positive* (for permissions) or *negative* (for prohibitions). More specifically, a tuple (g,s,o,m,q) formalizes the event that the grantor g has assigned the privilege $[o,m]$ with qualification q to the subject s as a grantee. Such permissions and prohibitions are specified explicitly as *facts* or implicitly by means of *rules*.

An administrator can express such facts and rules in the *Dynamic Authorization Specification Language, DASL* for short, as part of a *logical program*. The *syntax* of DASL is defined along the following lines:

- The vocabulary is given by sorted *constant symbols* for any item occurring in the computing system, by suitable sorted *variables* for such items and by a sorted *predicate symbol* for each of the components listed above. To denote partial relationships of the 5-ary predicate symbol *Grantor_QGranted*, a 4-ary predicate symbol *QAuth* is additionally provided. The corresponding component is the relation

  QAuth $\subseteq$ *Grantor* $\times$ *Subject* $\times$ *Mode* $\times$ *Qual*.
- As with *Grantor_QGranted* and *QAuth*, if required, the other predicate symbols can be used as well with an additional qualification (but, in this text, we shall not treat this feature further).

- *Terms* are either constants or variables, and thus, besides constants, there are no further function symbols.
- *Atoms* are formed by a predicate symbol followed by an appropriate list of terms. A *literal* is either an atom or a negated atom, written as $\neg atom$.
- *Rules* are implicational formulas of the following form: the *conclusion* (head) is a single atom, and the *premise* (body) is a conjunction of literals. Such rules are denoted by

  $atom \leftarrow literal_1 \wedge \ldots \wedge literal_n$.

  Thus, in DASL, negation is freely usable in a premise, but is still not allowed in a conclusion. If required, qualifications can be used to simulate some aspect of negation in conclusions. Rules with an empty premise are *facts*, written as $atom$ $\leftarrow$.
- A (logical) *program* (in DASL) is a finite set of such rules.

The *semantics* of a logical program P in DASL is given by a set *SEM** of stable models of P. In rough outline, any such model can be constructed as follows:

- The specified program P is fully *instantiated* by substituting variables by constants in all possible ways.
- The resulting ground (variable-free) program is *expanded* into a program $G(P)$ by using *hierarchical relationships* and *group memberships* for propagating permissions and prohibitions according to suitable *inheritance metarules* (which are *not* rules in the sense of DASL).
- A *consistent interpretation M* of the vocabulary is selected, i.e., an assignment of truth values to ground atoms. Thereby, two ground atoms that are identical except for *complementary* qualifications (pos and neg, respectively) are given *different* truth values. Formally, M is the set of ground atoms assigned to be true and relevant for the program P.
- The interpretation M is called a *model* of the expanded ground program $G(P)$ if each ground rule in $G(P)$ is either *true* in M or *defeated* by M. Here, "defeated" means that, with respect to appropriate metarules for conflict resolution, a *prevailing* rule is made applicable by M, i.e., the body of the prevailing rule is true in M.
- The *metarules for conflict resolution* employ the following built-in preferences, where priorities are determined by the predetermined sequence given below:

  – A higher-ranked grantor prevails over a lower-ranked grantor.
  – A more special object prevails over a more general object.
  – Prohibition prevails over permission.

  Clearly, if reasonable for a specific application, different preferences could be agreed to be built-in.
- If M is indeed a model, then M is used to *reduce* $G(P)$ by discarding defeated rules.
- Finally, the interpretation M qualifies as *stable model* if M is equal to the *fixpoint* of the reduction under *negation as failure*.

knowledge base on permissions and prohibitions

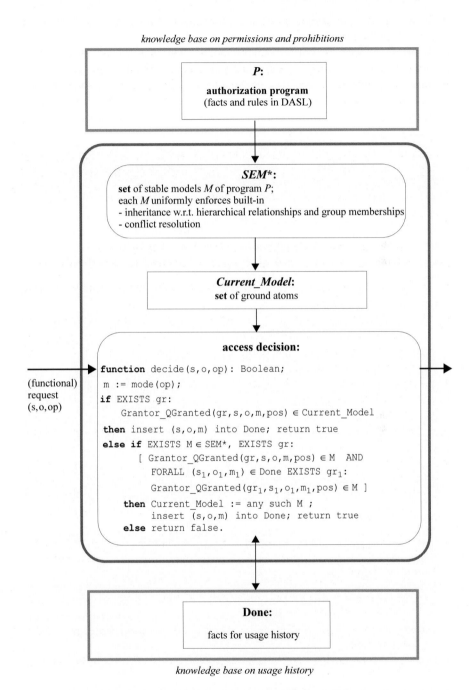

Fig. 9.14. Simplified architecture of the Dynamic Authorization Framework, as an example of a control and monitoring component (without identification and proof of authenticity)

To summarize, an interpretation M is an element of the semantics SEM^* of a program P if M represents a consistent instantiation of the specifications given by the program P, satisfying uniform conditions for inheritance concerning hierarchical relationships and group memberships and for conflict resolution. In general, a program P in DASL has several such instantiations, and in this sense the program P is *nondeterministic*.

The *control* and *monitoring* component essentially exploits this nondeterminism for taking *access decisions*, as illustrated in Figure 9.14 and explained in the following. In an *initial phase*, an administrator declares a logical program P in DASL, and this program is stored in the *knowledge base* on *permissions and prohibitions*. Then, conceptually, the semantics SEM^* is determined, and one of the models in SEM^* is selected as *Current_Model*. Clearly, it suffices to actually compute *Current_Model*.

For the *working phase*, assume that the component receives a (*functional*) *request* (s,o,op), where s is supposed to denote the individual requestor, and op is the wanted operation on a controlled object o such that $m = mode(op)$ is the operational mode.

Then, first, *Current_Model* is inspected to find out whether the request has been permitted by some grantor gr, i.e., whether the atom *Grantor_QGranted* (gr,s,o,m,pos) is true in *Current_Model*. If this is the case, the request is immediately permitted, and its success is logged in the *knowledge base* on *usage history*, i.e., the tuple (s,o,m) is inserted into the relation *Done*.

Otherwise, the control component searches for an *alternative* stable model M in SEM^* that could have been successfully used for the logged usage history and additionally for the current request too, i.e., under the alternative model M, all previous access requests would have been permitted and, additionally, the actual request is permitted as well. If the search is successful, *Current_Model* is redefined to be a suitably selected alternative model, and henceforth the selected alternative model is inspected. Otherwise, if the search fails, the current request is considered incompatible with the specified program P and the usage history *Done*, and thus the current request is prohibited. *Update requests* are treated similarly, with additional provisions for *transaction* management.

More formally, during the *working phase*, the control and monitoring component reacts to a (functional) request by calling the following procedure:

```
function decide(s,o,op): Boolean;
m := mode(op);                              / determine mode of operation
if   EXISTS gr: Grantor_QGranted(gr,s,o,m,pos) ∈Current_model
                          / inspect currently used model for a permission by some grantor
then insert (s,o,m) into Done;              / log permitted request
     return true                            / permitted
else                      / currently used model does not provide permission
     if   EXISTS M ∈ SEM*, EXISTS gr:
          [ Grantor_QGranted(gr,s,o,m,pos) ∈M  AND
            FORALL (s₁,o₁,m₁) ∈Done EXISTS gr₁:
            Grantor_QGranted(gr₁,s₁,o₁,m₁,pos) ∈M ]
```

                                    / *search for alternative model,*
                                    / *compatible with usage history and providing a permission*
    then `Current_Model := any such M;`   / *change currently used model*
        `insert (s,o,m) into Done;`   / *log permitted request*
        `return true`   / *permitted*
    else `return false.`   / *prohibited*

Having outlined the formalism, we now comment on the properties achieved. Concerning *expressiveness*, we observe a trade-off in comparison with FAF. On the one hand, DAF gives an administrator more options to specify an authorization program, since most of the restrictions of FAF on using negations are dropped. On the other hand, DAF has uniform built-in inheritance for hierarchical relationships and uniform built-in conflict resolution, whereas FAF allows more flexibility and finer granularity for inheritance and conflict resolution.

Concerning *management*, we expect that most administrators will be challenged by the sophisticated treatment of nondeterminism, and thus DAF is likely to be applied for special applications only. *Completeness* and *soundness* are achieved by design.

Concerning *efficiency*, in general the approach is computationally hard, since computing stable models is believed to require exponential time. Thus, for practical applications, some restrictions are required, either concerning the size of the program or concerning the actual usage of negation.

9.3 Policy Algebras

In the context of the discretionary approach to access rights management, access decisions are taken with respect to a security policy that, at least conceptually, is given by a subset of possibly qualified `granted` relationships. The *extension* of the policy can be represented by a relation of the form

$ExtPolicy \subseteq Subject \times Object \times Mode$ or
$ExtPolicy \subseteq Subject \times Object \times Mode \times Qual$.

In simple cases, this extension is directly defined. In more advanced cases, this extension is implicitly determined, for instance in the Flexible Authorization Framework as the unique fixpoint of an authorization program, or in the Dynamic Authorization Framework as the currently selected model of an authorization program.

In all cases, deliberately abstracting from details, an actual request (s,o,op) is *decided* by inspecting the extension and evaluating whether

$(s,o,mode(op)) \in ExtPolicy,$

or whether

$(s,o,mode(op),\texttt{pos}) \in ExtPolicy$ or $(s,o,mode(op),\texttt{neg}) \in ExtPolicy,$

respectively.

In Section 9.2, logic programming was employed to specify a policy extension *ExtPolicy*. In doing so, a layered approach was advocated for handling the pertinent issues, for example explicit declarations of permissions and prohibitions, inheritance for hierarchical relationships, rules for implicit permissions, and conflict resolution. While logic programming is clearly suitable for this task, in some situations a more abstract view might be preferable. In particular, specifications in logic programming might be perceived as "low level", since facts and rules are syntactically expressed in terms of atoms, i.e., speaking more informally, by referring to single "tuples being an element of relations". Semantically, however, by using variables as tuple entries, *sets* of ground atoms are implicitly generated by substituting variables by constant symbols. But the resulting sets are not automatically encapsulated.

These and related considerations suggest that complex policy extensions should be specified by applying algebraic operations on more simple extensions, letting the algebraic operations work homogeneously on the level of sets. As is well known in the discipline of knowledge bases, such an algebraic approach is possible in many cases. A prominent example of this experience is the equivalence of the relational calculus and the relational algebra, when considered with respect to expressiveness as query languages for relational databases.

Owing to the high abstraction level, the algebraic approach facilitates a modular design of specifications. Modularity and compositionality not only support the issues mentioned above but also are particularly useful for the following and related situations:

- administration of a distributed computing system with high local autonomy of components;
- integration of component systems into a more comprehensive federation;
- more generally, incremental system specification with knowledge about subsystems that is as yet incomplete;
- stepwise analysis of complex systems.

In the following, we present and discuss two examples of how the algebraic approach can be exploited for access rights management.

9.3.1 A Basic Policy Algebra

In the first example, a policy extension is seen as a subset of

$$Subject \times Object \times Mode,$$

where an element (s,o,m) of a policy extension is interpreted as a permission, saying that the policy extension permits a subject $s \in Subject$ to access a controlled object $o \in Object$ by means of an operation of mode $m \in Mode$. Policy specifications are expressed in the *Algebraic Authorization Specification Language, AASL* for short. The *syntax* of policy expressions in AASL is outlined by the following inductive definition:

- Each policy variable $P_1, P_2, P_3, \dots$ is a *policy expression*.
- If E, E_1 and E_2 are *policy expressions*, so are:
  - $E_1 \cup E_2$,   denoting the *union* of E_1 and E_2;
  - $E_1 \cap E_2$,   denoting the *intersection* of E_1 and E_2;
  - $E_1 \setminus E_2$,   denoting the *difference* of E_1 and E_2;
  - $E {\char`^} C$,   denoting the *restriction* of E with respect to a *condition C*,
    where the condition C, expressed in some suitable language,
    is identified with the satisfying set of tuples,
    i.e., C is treated as a subset of *Subject* $\times$ *Object* $\times$ *Mode*;
  - $E {*} R$,   denoting the *closure* of E with respect to a *rule* set R,
    where each rule has the form $atom \leftarrow atom_1 \wedge \dots \wedge atom_n$
    with suitable predicate symbols occurring in the atoms.

For the convenience of administrators, an additional algebraic operator is offered as well:

  - $\tau P_i.E_1(E_2)$,   denoting *substitution* of the policy variable P_i in E_1 by E_2.

The *semantics* of an expression E in AASL is fully determined by an interpreting environment *env* that assigns policy extensions to policy variables. Such an environment is inductively extended to arbitrary expressions, whereby the operation symbols of AASL, i.e., $\cup, \cap, \setminus, {\char`^}C, {*}R$ and τ, obtain the intended meaning:

- A function

  $env : \{P_1, P_2, P_3, \dots\} \rightarrow \wp(\text{Subject} \times \text{Object} \times \text{Mode})$

  is an interpreting *environment*.
- An environment *env* is inductively extended to arbitrary policy expressions according to the syntactic structure of expressions:
  - union: $env(E_1 \cup E_2)$ $= env(E_1) \cup env(E_2)$;
  - intersection: $env(E_1 \cap E_2)$ $= env(E_1) \cap env(E_2)$;
  - difference: $env(E_1 \setminus E_2)$ $= env(E_1) \setminus env(E_2)$;
  - restriction: $env(E{\char`^}C)$ $= env(E) \cap C$;
  - closure $env(E{*}R)$ $= fixpoint(env(E) \cup R) \cap$
                    $\text{Subject} \times \text{Object} \times \text{Mode}$,
                    where the fixpoint is computed by
                    exhaustive rule applications;
  - substitution: $env(\tau P_i.E_1(E_2)) = env(E_1[P_i/E_2])$,
                    where the policy expression $E_1[P_i/E_2]$
                    is obtained from E_1 by substituting each
                    occurrence of the policy variable P_i
                    in the policy expression E_1
                    by the policy expression E_2.

In the following, the properties of AASL concerning *expressiveness* and the potential for *management* are outlined by means of some application heuristics and an example. The application heuristics state how each concept of AASL is typically handled by administrators.

An interpreting *environment* of policy variables is defined by declarations of explicit *permissions* or, depending on the occurrences of a variable within an expression, of explicit *prohibitions*. More specifically, for each variable P_i, a responsible administrator enumerates the triples (s,o,m) that should belong to the pertinent extension. If the variable P_i is only "positively used", then the triples are interpreted as permissions. However, if the variable P_i is only "negatively used", i.e., roughly speaking, P_i is in the scope of the second argument of a difference operator, then the triples are interpreted as prohibitions for such a usage.

The syntax allows both usages to simultaneously appear in one policy expression, and then special care is needed. In general, different policy variables can be assigned different responsible administrators. The reasonable assignments depend on the application, but also on the occurrences of variables in the policy expressions, as will be clear from the application heuristics for the operators.

Inductively, using the *union* operator, an administrator typically accepts the permissions of a "positive usage" (or, depending on the usage context, the prohibitions of a "negative usage") that are specified by the administrators of the operands: if *any* of the two administrators has specified a permission (or prohibition, respectively), then this specification is held to be valid in the composing level as well.

Correspondingly, using the *intersection* operator inductively, an administrator typically accepts the permissions (or prohibitions) that are specified by the administrators of the operands. But now, these specifications are approved at the composing level only if *both* administrators have specified a permission (or prohibition, respectively).

The *difference* operator is used inductively in a similar way, but in this case the specification of the first operand is treated as permissions and that of the second operand as prohibitions (assuming an occurrence outside the scope of another difference).

Basically, using a *restriction* operator $\wedge C$ inductively corresponds to using the intersection operator, whereas the second argument is treated like a "constant policy". Using a *closure* operator $*R$ inductively means accepting the specification of the single argument and then discretionarily adding further consequences, as derivable by the rules R.

Finally, the inductive use of a *substitution* operator τP_i may be motivated by either of the following situations. An administrator may want to *refine* a previously unspecified part P_i of some expression E_1 by use of some more detailed policy expression E_2, or the administrator may want to *replace* a part P_i that was previously instantiated by declarations of explicit permissions (or prohibitions) by more implicit means, as expressed by E_2.

The following example explains further some of the application heuristics. We consider the policy expression

$$E = ((P_1 \cap P_2 {}^\wedge C)*R \cup (P_3 \setminus P_4)) \setminus P_5.$$

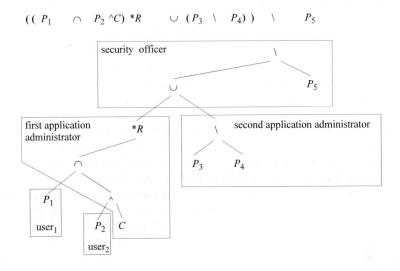

Fig. 9.15. A policy expression in AASL, annotated with assigned responsible agents

Figure 9.15 shows the syntax tree of the expression E and illustrates our explanation. We suppose that a *security officer* is responsible for the first and the second level of the expression, which has the syntactic structure

$$(E_{app\_1} \cup E_{app\_2}) \setminus P_5 .$$

On the one hand, the security officer "normally" accepts the permissions stated by two *application administrators*, who contribute the specifications of the operands E_{app_1} and E_{app_2}, respectively. On the other hand, as exceptions, the security officer enforces prevailing prohibitions that he explicitly declares himself by the interpretation of the policy variable P_5.

The first application administrator, in turn, "normally" accepts the permissions specified by two users, who are responsible for the extensions of the variables P_1 and P_2, respectively. However, this application administrator approves a permission only if that permission has been granted by both users. Additionally, concerning the second user, permissions are accepted only if they satisfy the condition C. Beyond just approving permissions stemming from lower levels, the first application administrator also adds further permissions by computing the closure $*R$, which, for example, captures inheritance rules.

The second application administrator maintains two explicitly declared subpolicies. The subpolicy denoted by the variable P_3 consists of permissions, and the subpolicy denoted by the variable P_4 consists of "local" prohibitions that, however, at the level of the security officer, can be overridden by permissions stated by the first application administrator.

9.3.2 An Algebra on Policy Transformations

Following good engineering practice, administrators should design a complex security policy in a layered way, dealing with well-understood subtasks in specific layers. In the Flexible Authorization Framework, using logic programming, this advice is supported by arranging the logic authorization program in strata. A similar level structure could be defined for the Dynamic Authorization Framework. Moreover, in the latter framework, an additional layer has been introduced for dynamically resolving nondeterminism. In an algebraic framework, layering is naturally supported by the level structure of policy expressions, where policy variables and operators correspond roughly to subtasks. An example of this view is presented above, using the basic operators of AASL.

For more advanced situations, there is a need for additional and more sophisticated operators. As in the logic programming approach, qualifications for distinguishing permissions and prohibitions are often useful in the algebraic approach as well. Moreover, rather than treating *individual* permissions and prohibitions, one might want to explicitly specify *sets* of them and, going one step further, *sets of such sets* as nondeterministic alternatives. These and other features are expressible in an algebraic specification language that we call the *Transformational Authorization Specification Language, TASL* for short. In the following, we briefly introduce selected key concepts of this language.

TASL deals with permissions and prohibitions in four stages. In the basis stage, qualified `granted` relationships are represented by elements of

$$Subject \times Object \times Mode \times Qual,$$

where the first component $s \in Subject$ is seen as a *grantee*, and an aggregation of the last three components, i.e., a tuple $(o,m,q) \in Object \times Mode \times Qual$, is regarded as a *qualified privilege*, assigned to the grantee.

In the first set stage, given a grantee $s \in Subject$, several qualified privileges are gathered into a *privilege set* (with qualifications)

$$qpriv \subseteq Object \times Mode \times Qual,$$

with the intention of expressing that all qualified privileges contained are *simultaneously* assigned to the grantee. Thus, in the first set stage, TASL deals with relationships of the form

$$(s,qpriv) \in Subject \times \wp(Object \times Mode \times Qual).$$

In the second set stage, again given a grantee $s \in Subject$, *nondeterminism* is introduced by assigning to the grantee an *alternative set*

$$QPriv \subseteq \wp(Object \times Mode \times Qual)$$

of privilege sets. Thus, in this stage we have relationships of the form

$$(s,QPriv) \in Subject \times \wp \wp(Object \times Mode \times Qual).$$

Finally, in the transformation stage, a *transformational policy extension* is seen as a transformation that maps each granted privilege set $(s,qpriv)$ occurring in the domain of the transformation onto a granted alternative set $(s, QPriv)$. Thus a transformational policy extension *TExtPolicy* has the following signature:

TExtPolicy :

$Subject \times \wp(Object \times Mode \times Qual) \rightarrow Subject \times \wp\wp(Object \times Mode \times Qual)$,

where the subject component is never changed, i.e., if $TExtPolicy(s_1, qpriv) = (s_2, QPriv)$, then $s_1 = s_2$.

The *transformational flavor* of policies is used in the specification process only. Later on, at run time, given a specified transformational policy extension, actual *access decisions* are taken by inspecting the *range* of the extension. More specifically, the decision set

$ExtPolicy \subseteq Subject \times Object \times Mode \times Qual$

that is needed for access decisions, as explained at the beginning of this section, is conceptually constructed by going back from the transformational stage to the basic stage:

- Let $Nonder\_ExtPolicy \subseteq Subject \times \wp\wp(Object \times Mode \times Qual)$ denote the "nondeterministic" range of a transformational policy extension *TExtPolicy*.
- Resolve the nondeterminism into an intermediate "deterministic set" $Der\_ExtPolicy \subseteq Subject \times \wp(Object \times Mode \times Qual)$ by selecting, for each granted alternative set $(s, QPriv) \in Nonder\_ExtPolicy$, exactly one privilege set $qpriv \in QPriv$.
- Unnest each $(s, qpriv) \in Der\_ExtPolicy$ by expanding the assigned privilege set $(s, qpriv)$ into the corresponding set of assigned privileges $\{(s, o, m, q) \mid (o, m, q) \in qpriv\}$.

The following simple example illustrates how the stages are employed. We consider only one subject, identified as `alice`. One administrator might want to simultaneously permit `alice` to read a file `appl` but not to write it. So he forms the privilege set

$\{(\texttt{appl}, \texttt{read}, \texttt{pos}), (\texttt{appl}, \texttt{write}, \texttt{neg})\}$.

Since he wants no other alternatives, he assigns the singleton alternative set $\{\{(\texttt{appl}, \texttt{read}, \texttt{pos}), (\texttt{appl}, \texttt{write}, \texttt{neg})\}\}$ to `alice`, resulting in the relationship

$(\texttt{alice}, \{\{(\texttt{appl}, \texttt{read}, \texttt{pos}), (\texttt{appl}, \texttt{write}, \texttt{neg})\}\})$

in the second set stage. Finally, in the transformational stage, the first administrator declares, for his transformational policy extension $TExtPolicy_1$, that

$TExtPolicy_1(\texttt{alice}, \emptyset) = (\texttt{alice}, \{\{(\texttt{appl}, \texttt{read}, \texttt{pos}), (\texttt{appl}, \texttt{write}, \texttt{neg})\}\})$.

Similarly, a second administrator might want the same subject to be given the complementary qualified privileges, resulting in the declaration of

$TExtPolicy_2(\texttt{alice}, \emptyset) = (\texttt{alice}, \{\{(\texttt{appl}, \texttt{read}, \texttt{neg}), (\texttt{appl}, \texttt{write}, \texttt{pos})\}\})$.

Given the policies $TExtPolicy_1$ and $TExtPolicy_2$, the security officer might then approve a situation where the subject might act according to either specification, leaving the actual selection open, resulting in a composed policy *TExtPolicy* with

TExtPolicy(alice,Ø) = (alice, {   {(appl,read,pos),(appl,write,neg)},
                                     {(appl,read,neg),(appl,write,pos)} }).

According to the algebraic approach, compositions of policies already defined can be systematically described by suitable *operators*. In the example above, the the composed policy is obtained by applying the external union.

- Roughly speaking, for any given subject, the *external union* collects the alternatives of the operands into a new, in general more comprehensive, alternative set that comprises exactly the privilege sets found in any of the operands, while leaving each privilege set involved unchanged.
- Similarly, further *external operators* can be defined, for example *external intersection* or *external difference*: the application of such an external operator manipulates the alternative sets of the operands (as indicated by the name of the operator) without changing the alternative privilege sets.

Besides the well-known Boolean operators, further *external operators* are offered. For example:

- *External scoping* of a policy T with a condition SC on granted *privilege sets* modifies T, seen as a function, such that all arguments $(s,qpriv)$ in the domain of T that do not satisfy the condition SC are mapped onto $(s,\{\emptyset\})$, i.e., previously granted permissions or prohibitions are totally invalidated.
- *External provisioning* of a policy T with a condition SC on granted *privilege sets* modifies T such that the alternative set of each function value is intersected with SC, i.e., previously granted alternative sets are approved only if they additionally satisfy the condition SC.
- *External sequencing* of a policy T_1 with a policy T_2 applies the policies, seen as functions, sequentially roughly as follows: for each assigned privilege set $(s,qpriv)$ in the domain of T_1, first T_1 is applied, yielding an alternative set $(s,QPriv)$, and then, for each privilege set $qpriv_1 \in QPriv$, the second policy T_2 is applied. When this is done, all resulting privilege sets are gathered into one alternative set for the final result.

In contrast to the external operators, the *internal operators* manipulate the privilege sets themselves. For example, if we take the internal union of the policies *TExtPolicy*₁ and *TExtPolicy*₂ considered above, then we obtain a different composed policy T such that

T(alice,Ø) = (alice, { { (appl,read,pos), (appl,write,neg),
                           (appl,read,neg), (appl,write,pos) } }).

More generally, the internal versions of the Boolean operators, i.e., the *internal union*, *internal intersection* and *internal difference*, consider all pairs of privilege sets where the first component stems from the first operand and the second component stems from the second operand, and then applies the set operation denoted to the two components. As the final outcome, all resulting privilege sets are gathered into a new alternative set.

Similarly, *internal scoping* and *internal provisioning* with a condition *PC* on qualified privileges eliminate those privileges from a privilege set that do not satisfy *PC.*

Policies can contain complementary privileges for a subject. In particular, the application of internal operators can easily result in such policies, even if the operands have not suffered from this deficiency, as in the example given above. Moreover, a policy may contain neither qualified privilege of a complementary pair for a subject. In the former case, the policy lacks soundness, and in the latter case completeness. In order to enforce *soundness* and *completeness*, if needed, additional internal operators are suggested:

- *Permission prevailing* resolves conflicts by eliminating the negative version of a complementary pair, if such a pair appears in a privilege set.
- *Prohibition prevailing* resolves conflicts the other way round.
- *Open completion* adds a permission to a privilege set whenever the complementary prohibition is not present.
- *Closed completion* adds a prohibition to a privilege set whenever the complementary permission is not present.

For example, if we apply the permission-prevailing operator *PermPrev* to the policy *T* that we obtain from the internal union, then the resulting policy yields

$PermPrev(T)(\texttt{alice},\varnothing) = (\texttt{alice},\, \{\, \{(\texttt{appl},\texttt{read},\texttt{pos}),(\texttt{appl},\texttt{write},\texttt{pos})\,\}\,\})$.

Assuming that docu is the only further object and that there are no further modes, subsequently applying the closed-completion operator *CloseCom* results in

$(CloseCom;PermPrev)(T)(\texttt{alice},\varnothing) =$
$$(\texttt{alice},\, \{\ \{\ (\texttt{appl},\texttt{read},\texttt{pos}),\ (\texttt{appl},\texttt{write},\texttt{pos}),$$
$$(\texttt{docu},\texttt{read},\texttt{neg}),\ (\texttt{docu},\texttt{write},\texttt{neg})\,\}\,\})\,.$$

9.4 Granting and Revoking

9.4.1 A Conceptual Model

As the basis of access decisions, the knowledge base on permissions and prohibitions has to be appropriately instantiated by *control operations*. Examples of control operations are granting, transferring, taking, delegating and revoking a privilege, and generating a new item. In this section, we concentrate on some versions of granting and revoking.

Granting means here that a current holder of a privilege, as a grantor, assigns this privilege to a subject as a further grantee. In doing so, the grantor can declare the privilege to be grantable again, i.e., that the grantee is permitted to grant the received privilege to other subjects in turn. More specifically, for example, the following options for the values of the *grantable* attribute can be meaningful:

- *no*: the receiver is not permitted to grant the received privilege further.
- *limited*: the receiver is permitted to grant the received privilege further, but only under the provision that the *grantable* attribute is then set to the value *no*, i.e., the further grantees are *not* permitted to grant the privilege in turn.
- *unlimited*: the receiver is permitted to grant the received privilege further, without any restrictions.

Under the last option, a privilege can ultimately be held by many grantees. Moreover, a single grantee might have repeatedly received a privilege in several ways, from different *grantors* and at different *issue times*.

Revoking means here that a grantor wants to invalidate a previous granting. Again, various options for precise *revocation semantics* are meaningful: should invalidation refer only to a specific granting or, alternatively, affect further grantings in a cascading way too?

We shall study such options under the following simplifying assumptions. Originally, a privilege is held only by the *owner* of the object concerned, and all grantings are recorded with the *issue time* and permit further *unlimited* grantings. Figure 9.16 shows the underlying ER model of the knowledge base for permissions (and prohibitions). This model can be implemented as a database relation *KB* with the following five attributes (columns):

(Issue) Time, Grantor, Grantee/Subject, (Controlled) Object, (Operational) Mode.

A tuple $(t, g, s, o, m) \in KB$ has the following meaning:

at the issue time *t*,
a grantor *g* has assigned
to the grantee/subject *s* a privilege with respect to
the controlled object *o*
for the operational mode *m*.

In this context, we employ the special mode own to indicate ownership.

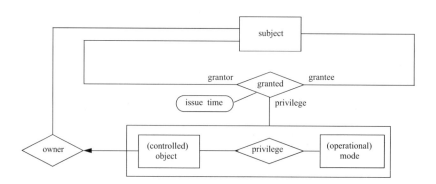

Fig. 9.16. ER model of the relationship class *granted*, enriched with further concepts needed for studying unlimited grantings and various options for revoking

Figure 9.17 shows an instance of the relational implementation. As an initialization by grantings of an administrator *admin*, at time 0 a subject *owner* has received the special privilege [*o*,*own*], indicating ownership of the object *o*, and at time 1 the privilege [*o*,*m*] for some operational mode *m*. Subsequently, at time 2, the owner has granted the privilege to a further subject *b*, who in turn has granted it to subject *c* at time 3. At times 4 to 7, additional grantings have occurred.

KB	Time	Grantor	Grantee/ Subject	Object	Mode
	0	admin	owner	o	own
	1	admin	owner	o	m
	2	owner	b	o	m
	3	b	c	o	m
	4	c	d	o	m
	5	owner	c	o	m
	6	d	e	o	m
	7	c	d	o	m

$H\_View_{owner,o,m}$ Granted   Grantor_Granted

Fig. 9.17. An instance of the relational implementation of the relationship class *granted* enriched with further concepts

Three subrelations of *KB*, denoted by *Granted*, *Grantor_Granted* and $H\_View_{owner,o,m}$, are marked in the figure. The subrelation *Granted* corresponds to a database relation that implements the basic relationship class *granted* without ownerships, as exemplified in Figure 9.2. This subrelation, shown again in the left part of Figure 9.18 without duplicates, captures only the pure actual *possession* of privileges. The subrelation *Grantor_Granted*, shown again without duplicates in the right part of Figure 9.18, adds the information about grantors but still does not distinguish several similar grantings that differ only in the issue time.

Granted	Subject	Object	Mode
	owner	o	m
	b	o	m
	c	o	m
	d	o	m
	e	o	m

Grantor_Granted	Grantor	Subject	Object	Mode
	admin	owner	o	m
	owner	b	o	m
	b	c	o	m
	c	d	o	m
	owner	c	o	m
	d	e	o	m

Fig. 9.18. The subrelations *Granted* and *Grantor_Granted* of the relation *KB* with duplicates removed

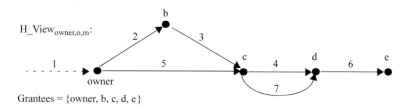

Grantees = {owner, b, c, d, e}

Fig. 9.19. A grant graph, indicating successive grant operations in time

The subrelation $H(istory)\_View_{owner,o,m}$ exhibits the full history of grantings for a single privilege $[o,m]$ that originate directly or indirectly from the subject *owner*. This subrelation is shown again in Figure 9.19 as a *grant graph*: each triple (*time, grantor, grantee*) $\in H\_View_{owner,o,m}$, i.e., each granting, is represented by a labeled, directed edge with origin *grantor*, target *grantee* and label *time*. The actual holders of the privilege $[o,m]$ are captured by the node set *Grantees*.

9.4.2 A Formalization of Granting

For the sake of simplicity, as in the example, we continue to deal only with one specific owner and a single privilege, and, accordingly, we shall sometimes suppress the parameters *owner* and $[o,m]$. Under the specified assumptions and simplifications, granting and revoking can now be formalized as operating on a grant graph of the form $G = (Grantees, H\_View)$. In this context, t_{max} denotes the maximal time label occurring in H_View, always implicitly supposed to be correctly evaluated. The following procedure exemplarily refines and formalizes the control operation *granting*.

```
procedure grant_owner,o,m (time,grantor,grantee);
{ precondition: owner ∈ Grantees;
  import:      Grantees, H_View, t_max}
if                                    / access decision:
  [ grantor = owner                   / owner is always permitted
    OR
    EXISTS t, EXISTS x ∈ Grantees: (t,x,grantor) ∈ H_View
                                      / a current holder is permitted
  ]
  AND t_max < time                    / issue times are monotone
  AND grantor ≠ grantee               / no self-granting
  AND grantee ≠ owner                 / no grantings for owner
then                                  / updating of grant graph:
  Grantees := Grantees ∪ {grantee};   / insert grantee
  H_View := H_View ∪ {(time,grantor,grantee)}
                                      / insert privilege with issue time
fi.
```

The instance $H\_View_{owner,o,m}$, shown in Figure 9.17 as a subrelation and in Figure 9.19 as a grant graph, was produced by the following calls, where all requested updates have been permitted:

```
grant_owner,o,m (2, owner,  b),
grant_owner,o,m (3, b,      c),
grant_owner,o,m (4, c,      d),
grant_owner,o,m (5, owner,  c),
grant_owner,o,m (6, d,      e),
grant_owner,o,m (7, c,      d).
```

9.4.3 Formalizations of Revoking

There are several options for *revocation semantics*, i.e., the meaning of a request by a revoker r to revoke a privilege [o,m] from a grantee s at a time t. We present five options by doing the following for each option:

- providing a short description of the motivation and a short discussion;
- indicating the part of the knowledge base on permissions that is exploited;
- specifying a precondition for a permission to perform a revocation, and an invariant for the knowledge base if applicable;
- stating a postcondition for the updated knowledge base; and
- indicating a possible implementation.

The options are briefly summarized in Table 9.20, and the last of these options is investigated in depth at the end of this section.

Simple Deletion. The first option considers only the actual possession of privileges, i.e., only the subrelation *Granted*, which also represents ownerships here. Accordingly, a permitted revocation request completely eliminates the possession of a privilege [o,m] by a grantee s. Since the knowledge base does not maintain data on grantors, access decisions have to be reasonably founded in some other way. Here we suggest the following: a special system administrator *admin* is always permitted, and, additionally, for each object o, also its unique owner r_{owner} that is characterized by $(r_{owner}, o, own) \in Granted$. More formally:

- Precondition for a permission to revoker r: $r = admin$ or $(r,o,own) \in Granted$.
- Postcondition for knowledge base: $(s,o,m) \notin Granted'$.
- Implementation: `Granted := Granted \ { (s,o,m) }.`

Grantor-Specific Deletion. The second option additionally takes the grantors of privileges into consideration, i.e., it exploits the extended subrelation *Grantor_Granted*. If a revoker r requests to revoke a privilege [o,m] held by a grantee s, then this request is interpreted to refer only to a previous granting by just the revoker as the grantor. Accordingly, only the respective grantor of a privilege is permitted to later revoke it.

Table 9.20. Summary of options for revocation semantics

Option	Knowledge base	Precondition for permission/invariant	Postcondition for knowledge base
simple deletion	*Granted*	revoker is administrator or owner	granting is completely deleted
grantor-specific deletion	*Grantor_ Granted*	revoker has been grantor	granting of revoker is deleted
deletion with renewed further grantings	*Grantor_ Granted*	revoker has been grantor invariant: unique grantor, and existence of unique granting chain from owner	granting is deleted, and further grantings are renewed
deletion with deleted further grantings	*Grantor_ Granted*	revoker has been grantor invariant: existence of granting chains from owner	granting is deleted, and invariant is satisfied
time-specific deletion with recursive revocation of further grantings	*KB* (all *H_View*'s)	revoker has been grantor invariant: existence of time-increasing granting chains from owner	*KB'* is the instance that would be produced if revoker had never granted the privilege to grantee

Furthermore, in contrast to simple deletion, grantings by different grantors are not affected, and thus a grantee might happen to still enjoy a privilege after a grantor-specific deletion. More formally:

- Precondition for a permission to revoker r: $(r,s,o,m) \in$ *Grantor_Granted*.
- Postcondition for knowledge base: $(r,s,o,m) \notin$ *Grantor_Granted'*.
- Implementation: `Grantor_Granted := Grantor_Granted \ {(r,s,o,m)}`.

Deletion with Renewed Further Grantings. The third option both specializes and extends the second one. The specialization requires, as an invariant, that a subject s can be the grantee of a privilege $[o,m]$ only as a result of exactly one granting. Accordingly, enforced by a suitable modification of the granting procedure, for each `granted` relationship (s,o,m) there exists at most one grantor g with $(g,s,o,m) \in$ *Grantor_Granted*.

The extension handles possible *further grantings* by a grantee s. If, after receipt from g, the grantee s has granted the privilege $[o,m]$ to another subject y, then such a granting is interpreted as being done "on behalf of peer g". If, later on, grantor g requests to revoke his granting to grantee s, then he is permitted to do so – and he is the only permitted subject – but the further grantings of s should remain effective. Their interpretation of "on behalf of peer g" is then captured by "*renewing*" the grantings, now with the peer g as the grantor.

As a side effect, the properties of the granting procedure and of this revocation option together guarantee the following invariant for the extended subrelation *Grantor_Granted*: for each occurring grantee y of a privilege $[o,m]$, there is a unique chain of grantings for the privilege $[o,m]$ originating from the unique owner of the object o. Thus the subrelation *Grantor_Granted* represents a forest, i.e., a collection of tree-like structures. More formally:

- Precondition for a permission to revoker r: $(r,s,o,m) \in$ *Grantor_Granted*.

- Invariant for knowledge base:
  existence of unique granting chains from owner to grantees, as described above.

- Postcondition for knowledge base:

  $(r,s,o,m) \notin$ *Grantor_Granted'* and

  for all $y \neq r$ with $(s,y,o,m) \in$ *Grantor_Granted*:
  $(s,y,o,m) \notin$ *Grantor_Granted'* and $(r,y,o,m) \in$ *Grantor_Granted'* .

- Implementation:
  ```
  Grantor_Granted := Grantor_Granted \ {(r,s,o,m)};
  forall y do
  if    (s,y,o,m) ∈ Grantor_Granted  AND  y ≠ r
  then
        Grantor_Granted := Grantor_Granted \ {(s,y,o,m)};
        Grantor_Granted := Grantor_Granted ∪ {(r,y,o,m)}
  fi.
  ```

Deletion with Deleted Further Grantings. The fourth option also extends the second one concerning further grantings, but in a different way. Instead of further grantings by the grantee s being simply renewed, these grantings are now examined for *ongoing justification* and if necessary are also deleted.

More specifically, further grantings of a privilege $[o,m]$ by a grantee s to a subject y are defined to be *justified* after a revocation if, in the subrelation *Grantor_Granted*, there still exists a granting chain for the privilege $[o,m]$ from the owner to the grantee s. If further grantings are no longer justified, then they are recursively revoked under the same semantics, now taking s as the revoker. More formally:

- Precondition for a permission to revoker r: $(r,s,o,m) \in$ *Grantor_Granted*.

- Invariant for knowledge base:
  existence of granting chains from owner to grantees, as described above.

- Postcondition for knowledge base:
  $(r,s,o,m) \notin$ *Grantor_Granted'* and the invariant.

- Sketch of implementation:

  Initially, the entry (r,s,o,m) is deleted in *Grantor_Granted.*
  Then we might apply a graph search algorithm
  to enforce the invariant by minimal further deletions.

Time-Specific Deletion with Recursive Revocation of Further Grantings. The fifth option varies the fourth one concerning further grantings in a very sophisticated way. After a revocation, the ongoing justification of further grantings is again examined, but now also taking the *issue times* into consideration. Accordingly, the full relation *KB* is exploited.

More specifically, the required granting chain for the privilege $[o,m]$ from the owner of the object o to the grantee s must now additionally respect correct issue times, i.e., a further granting of the privilege $[o,m]$ by the grantee s at a past issue time t_2 is considered to be *ongoing justified* only if, in retrospect, the grantee can still be seen as the holder at this time, owing to a granting still valid at a preceding time t_1. More formally:

- Precondition for a permission to revoker r: $(r,s,o,m) \in$ *Grantor_Granted*.

- Invariant for knowledge base:
  existence of issue time respecting granting chains from owner to grantees, as sketched above.

- Postcondition for knowledge base, informally expressed:
  KB' is the instance that would have been produced if the revoker r had never granted the privilege $[o,m]$ to the grantee s.

- Discussion of implementation:
  The sophisticated postcondition appears to be difficult to meet. In particular, the implementation has to maintain enough information to allow one to construct *fictitious* instances of the knowledge base that could have been produced *in the past*. We shall show, however, that the information represented in *KB* suffices. Easy further thoughts indicate that this information is also necessary. Below, we shall declare a revocation procedure and prove its correctness.
  As before, for simplicity we treat only one privilege $[o,m]$, with the object o uniquely belonging to the subject *owner*, the only one who initially possesses the privilege. Under this simplification, the relevant part of the relation *KB* is captured by the subrelation $H\_View_{owner,o,m}$ or, alternatively, by the corresponding grant graph. Furthermore, we assume that all grantings have occurred by calls of the granting procedure $\text{grant}_{owner,o,m}$, with strictly increasing issue times up to t_{max}. Basically, the revoking procedure $\text{revoke}_{owner,o,m}$ only calls an auxiliary recursive procedure $\text{revoke}*$ that performs the essential part of the task: at a fictitious time t, a revocation of the privilege by a recursively determined revoker x from a subject y.

9.4.4 Recursive Revocation

In this subsection, we present and investigate the option of time-specific deletion with recursive revocation of further grantings in more detail. Complementing the procedure for granting, the following procedure formalizes the control operation *revoking*:

procedure revoke$_{owner,o,m}$ (time, revoker, grantee) ;
{ **precondition:** owner ∈ Grantees;
   import: Grantees, H_View, t$_{max}$}

                                   / at *time* the *revoker* invalidates his grantings
                                   / of privilege [*o*,*m*] concerning object *o* of *owner*
                                   / to grantee
if   / *access decision*:
    t$_{max}$ < time   / issue times are monotone
then   / *updating of grant graph*:
    revoke* (time, revoker, grantee);   / first call of recursive auxiliary procedure
    delete isolated elements from Grantees except owner
fi.

procedure revoke* (t, x, y);   / recursive auxiliary procedure for *revoke$_{owner,o,m}$*
{ **precondition:** owner ∈ Grantees;
   import: Grantees, H_View, t$_{max}$}
if   / *access decision*:
    EXISTS t$_{early}$: t$_{early}$ < t AND (t$_{early}$, x, y) ∈ H_View
                                     / *x* has granted privilege to *y* **before** time *t*
then   / *updating of grant graph*:
    H_View := H_View \ { (t$_{early}$, x, y) | t$_{early}$ < t };
                                     / delete grantings from *x* to *y* **before** time *t*

    VALID := { t$_{other}$ | EXISTS x$_{other}$: (t$_{other}$, x$_{other}$, y) ∈ H_View };

    if VALID ≠ ∅ **then** t := minimum(VALID) **else** t := ∞ **fi**;
                             / compute earliest **different** granting time *t* for *y*;
                             / if there is none, define this time as greater than all "real times"

    forall w ∈ Grantees **do** revoke* (t, y, w)
                     / *y* recursively revokes all invalidated grantings, namely
                     / those before the earliest different granting time *t* for *y*
fi.

Figure 9.21 illustrates a run of the procedure call revoke$_{owner,o,m}$(8,b,c) applied to the grant graph *H_View$_{owner,o,m}$* of Figure 9.19. Most notably, the example illustrates our motivation for using multiple edges (with different time labels).

    We now prepare to prove that – under the assumptions of this section – the revocation procedure actually meets its specification, i.e., the wanted postcondition is always satisfied. As a first step, we formalize the postcondition as follows. Suppose that

$$\Gamma = (C_t(t, x_t, y_t))_{t=1,\ldots,n}$$

is an actual sequence of procedure calls, with C_t being either *grant* or *revoke*, and with time points assumed to range from 1 to *n*, just to simplify the notation.

Initial instance of grant graph *H_View* when the procedure

$$\text{revoke}_{\text{owner},o,m}(8,b,c)$$

is called.

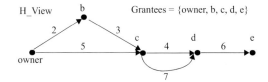

First call of auxiliary procedure, revoke* (8,b,c), delivers *H_View$_1$* with *VALID$_1$* = {5} and t_1 = 5.

Recursive calls for $w \neq d$ do not change the grant graph.

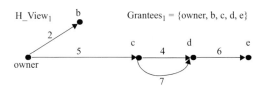

Recursive call for $w = d$, revoke* (5,c,d), delivers *H_View$_2$* with *VALID$_2$* = {7} and t_2 = 7.

Recursive calls for $w \neq e$ do not change the grant graph.

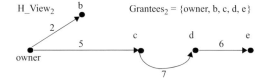

Recursive call for $w = e$, revoke* (7,d,e), delivers *H_View$_3$* with *VALID$_3$* = ∅ and t_3 = ∞.

All further recursive calls do not change the grant graph.

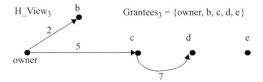

Finally, all isolated nodes are removed.

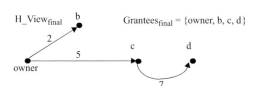

Fig. 9.21. Evaluation of a call of the revocation procedure

This sequence transforms an initial grant graph *H_View$_{init}$* = G_0 stepwise into a final grant graph G_n = *H_View$_\Gamma$*:

$$H\_View_{init} = G_0 \vdash C_1(1,x_1,y_1)\ G_1 \vdash \dots \vdash C_n(n,x_n,y_n)\ G_n = H\_View_\Gamma.$$

On the basis of Γ, we construct a fictitious *alternative* sequence Π that is intended to capture the idea that *revoked grantings have never occurred*. Intuitively, we obtain Π from Γ by "deleting"

- all occurrences of *grant* calls that are explicitly revoked later on, i.e., $grant(t,x_t,y_t)$ is "deleted" if for some $t' > t$ a *revoke* call of the form $revoke(t',x_{t'},y_{t'})$ with $(x_t,y_t) = (x_{t'},y_{t'})$ follows in Γ; and
- all occurrences of *revoke* calls.

Formally, we consider the "non-deleted" calls by identifying their time points:

$$NonDeleted_\Gamma = \{\, t \mid t \in \{1, \dots, n\},\ C_t \equiv grant, \text{ and}$$
$$\text{for all } t' > t: \text{if } C_{t'} \equiv revoke \text{ then } (x_t,y_t) \neq (x_{t'},y_{t'})\, \}.$$

"Deleting" is then formalized by replacing the original call by a call of a procedure *ident* that does not change the grant graph. Thus

$\Pi = (\, A_t(t,x_t,y_t)\,)_{t=1,\dots,n}$ is defined by

$$A_t \equiv C_t, \qquad \text{if } t \in NonDeleted_\Gamma, \text{ and}$$
$$A_t \equiv ident, \quad \text{otherwise (i.e., if } C_t \text{ is "deleted").}$$

The new sequence transforms the initial grant graph $H\_View_{init} = F_0$ stepwise into a final grant graph $F_n = H\_View_\Pi$:

$$H\_View_{init} = F_0 \ \longmapsto^{A_1(1,x_1,y_1)}\ F_1 \ \longmapsto \dots \longmapsto^{A_n(n,x_n,y_n)}\ F_n = H\_View_\Pi.$$

In Π, only *grant* calls appear. According to the permission clause in the body of the granting procedure, the entries in F_n are characterized as follows:

$(t,r,s) \in F_n$ iff   there exists a *justified* Π-*chain* $j_1 < \dots < j_l$ for (t,r,s)
such that for all i:

$$C_{j_i} \equiv grant,\ x_{j_i} \neq y_{j_i},\ y_{j_i} \neq owner,\ j_i \in NonDeleted_\Gamma, \text{ and}$$
$$x_{j_1} = owner,\ x_{j_{i+1}} = y_{j_i},\ (j_l, x_{j_l}, y_{j_l}) = (t,r,s).$$

In our example (using the earlier notation, and starting at time 2), the original sequence is given by

```
grant_owner,o,m(2, owner, b),
grant_owner,o,m(3, b,     c),
grant_owner,o,m(4, c,     d),
grant_owner,o,m(5, owner, c),
grant_owner,o,m(6, d,     e),
grant_owner,o,m(7, c,     d),
revoke_owner,o,m(8, b,    c).
```

In the fictitious alternative sequence, the calls at times 3 and 8 are "deleted", i.e., they are replaced by `ident(3,b,c)` and `ident(8,b,c)`, respectively. Note that in the new sequence, not only the *ident* calls at times 3 and 8 but also, owing to denied permissions, the grant calls at times 4 and 6 do not change the grant graph. The formalization of the postcondition then requires that $H\_View_\Gamma = H\_View_\Pi$.

Theorem 9.2   **[recursive revocation satisfies required postcondition]**

Under the assumptions of this section and using the notation introduced above, for all sequences Γ of procedure calls of *grant* or *revoke*, the original sequence Γ and the corresponding fictitious alternative sequence Π produce the same final grant graph when started with the same initial grant graph H_View_{init}, i.e.,

$$H\_View_\Gamma = H\_View_\Pi.$$

Sketch of Proof: To prove $H\_View_\Gamma \supseteq H\_View_\Pi$, we assume indirectly that some $(t,r,s) \in H\_View_\Pi \setminus H\_View_\Gamma$, with t chosen to be minimal. Let $(j_1 < \ldots < j_l)$ be a *justified* Π-*chain* for (t,r,s). We distinguish two cases:

- If $l \geq 2$, then

    $(j_{l-1}, x_{j_{l-1}}, y_{j_{l-1}}) \in H\_View_\Pi \cap H\_View_\Gamma,$

    since the prefix $(j_1 < \ldots < j_{l-1})$ is a *justified* Π-*chain* too, and since l is minimal. Thus $(j_{l-1}, x_{j_{l-1}}, x_{j_l})$ is never discarded by the original sequence Γ.
- Otherwise, if $l = 1$, then $x_{j_l} = owner$.

For both cases, we consider the possible reasons why $(t,r,s) = (j_l, x_{j_l}, y_{j_l})$ might have been discarded by the original sequence Γ:

- Either, in Γ, there has been a *direct* call $revoke(t', x_{j_{l}}, y_{j_{l}})$ with $j_l < t'$, but then $j_l \notin NonDeleted_\Gamma$, a contradiction to $(j_1 < \ldots < j_l)$ being justified;
- or Γ causes a *recursive* call $revoke^*(t', x_{j_{l}}, y_{j_{l}})$ with $j_l < t'$. Then, however $x_{j_{l}} \neq owner$, and thus the first case above applies. Accordingly, by the definition of t', when preparing the recursive call, we also have $j_l < t' \leq j_{l-1}$, since $(j_{l-1}, x_{j_{l-1}}, x_{j_l})$ is never discarded. This is a contradiction to time points being monotone.

The opposite inclusion $H\_View_\Gamma \subseteq H\_View_\Pi$ can be justified by an induction on the length n of the sequences.

For $n = 1$, we can immediately verify the claim, just by the definitions.

For the induction step, let Γ, of length $n+1$, be composed of a prefix Σ of length n followed by a call $C_{n+1}(n+1, x_{n+1}, y_{n+1})$, and let Δ denote the fictitious alternative sequence corresponding to Σ. By the induction hypothesis and the first part of the proof, we have $H\_View_\Sigma = H\_View_\Delta$.

For the case $C_{n+1} \equiv grant$, the definitions again easily support the claim.

For the case $C_{n+1} \equiv revoke$, we distinguish two cases: either the call of $revoke(n+1, x_{n+1}, y_{n+1})$ modifies the current grant graph, or the call does not.

In the latter case, we use the case assumption, then apply the induction hypothesis and, finally, verify that $NonDeleted_\Sigma = NonDeleted_\Gamma$ and $A_{n+1} \equiv ident$; in summary, we obtain $H\_View_\Gamma = H\_View_\Sigma = H\_View_\Delta = H\_View_\Pi$.

The former case needs more sophisticated considerations, which basically follow the line of reasoning used in the first part of the proof: we assume indirectly that the claim is violated at a minimal point in time, examine a pertinent justified Δ-chain of length l, and exclude first a length $l = 1$ and then lengths $l \geq 2$, by inspecting the declarations of the procedures.   ❑

9.5 Dynamic and State-Dependent Permissions

Usually, a specification of access rights has to balance conflicting security interests. In particular, a requested resource that is needed and is bound to an accepted purpose should actually be made *available*, whereas accesses that go beyond the intended usage of the computing system should be prevented in order to enforce *confidentiality*, *integrity* or related interests.

Basically, the concepts of control and monitoring that are described in the preceding sections ensure availability in two steps:

- First, some administrator grants the needed permissions, which are then *permanently* represented in the *knowledge base* on *permissions* and *prohibitions*.
- Second, a grantee can *repeatedly* employ his permissions whenever he *himself* wants to do so.

Possibly, but not always and not so often in practice, in a third step, the availability of a resource can be explicitly terminated by revoking the pertinent privileges.

However, these concepts also allow one to *further restrict* the availability of a resource by employing the *knowledge base* on the *usage history*: using this knowledge base, an administrator can express a policy that "statically" permits a requestor to access a resource, but additionally requires the validity of some "dynamic conditions" for any actual request. In particular, such conditions might refer to some suitably defined aspects of the *state* of the computing system, reflecting what actions the *requestor* or other participants have performed in the past.

Speaking more abstractly, the preceding considerations identify two important notions of control and monitoring, namely the *validity period* and the *state dependence* of permissions (and, correspondingly, of prohibitions):

- The *validity period* of a permission might range from being purely *static*, indefinitely allowing multiple use (until an explicit revocation), to *dynamic* versions that enable a wanted access for one specific usage at the request time only.
- The *state dependence* of a permission might range from being *unconditional* to sophisticated *state conditions*, which can refer to the *past behavior* of participants.

These two notions are closely related. On the one hand, *static permissions* allow memoryless administration, whereas *dynamic permissions* require stateful monitoring. On the other hand, state conditions often refer to timing aspects. In the following, we treat both notions jointly when we present various examples of state conditions for dynamic access rights.

Such conditions can be roughly classified into those that (primarily) refer to properties and actions of a *single individual subject* and those that (primarily) deal with the *relationships* of subjects and their *interactions*. The first class includes *role enabling*, *process mastership*, *context selection* and *information flow monitoring*. The second class includes *separation of privileges* and *workflow control*.

Most examples of these two classes can be described on the basis of a unifying design pattern that exploits finite or more powerful automatons. For simplicity, we concentrate mainly on *permissions*, assuming a *closed completion* as the default for *prohibitions*.

9.5.1 Control Automatons

Relational representation, logic programming and algebraic operations are powerful means for formally specifying security policies. For dealing with the *dynamic* aspects of *validity periods* and *state dependence*, control automatons are an additional, worthwhile tool, to be employed alternatively or complementarily. Generally speaking, we can use *control automatons* to abstractly represent relevant parts of the computing history, and thus to base access decisions on dynamically evolving *state conditions*. Clearly, we could see the knowledge base on permissions (and prohibitions) and the knowledge base on the usage history as a huge automaton as well, whose current instances reflect the previously performed control operations and functional operations, respectively. However, in this subsection, we shall concentrate on more goal-oriented usages of automatons.

Basically, these usages are modeled in two (or more) layers. In a *static* layer, the "principally permitted" options for using a computing system are declared in some way. In a *dynamic* layer, control automatons specify *security contexts* by their states. A security context represents the collection of those permissions (and prohibitions) that are actually exploitable by an individual or a community at a specific point in time. For example, compared with the "principally permitted" options, the security context might be aimed at one or several of the following purposes:

- *selecting* a narrow subset of the "principally permitted" options or *selecting* one alternative out of several mutually exclusive possibilities;
- monotonically *decreasing* the usability of "principally permitted" options, owing to previous information flows or other critical actions, and, if applicable, also *resetting* previously decreased usability;
- temporarily *amplifying* the "principally permitted" options for special tasks;
- partially *implementing* "principally permitted" options by means of runtime concepts of operating systems and programming languages;
- *enhancing* the runtime complexity of access decisions with respect to the "principally permitted" options, owing to appropriate precomputations;
- *sequencing* the actual employment of "principally permitted" options.

State *transitions* of control automatons, i.e., *switches* of security contexts, occur mainly in three forms:

- explicitly, owing to a *control operation*;
- implicitly (as a side effect), owing to a *functional operation*;
- "spontaneously", owing to an *error condition* or a detected *security violation*.

We distinguish between an automaton *schema* (or, in terms of object-oriented programming, an automaton *class*) and the corresponding automaton *instances*. A schema determines the general structure of states and transitions (of data and methods) needed for an application. The instances result from instantiating the schema by assigning actual *parameters* to formal parameters at creation time, and maintain actual state-dependent data during their lifespan. In particular, schema parameters might denote formal subjects or formal objects, and instance parameters then indicate the specific individuals whose permissions with respect to the specific objects are controlled.

9.5.2 Role Enabling and Disabling

As an instructive example of *selecting* an alternative subset of the "principally permitted" options, we review a simplified concept of *roles*, as introduced earlier. In a *static* layer, a *role* assembles privileges, which later on are implicitly and "in principle" granted to each individual that is *assigned* that role. In a *dynamic* layer, such an individual can *enable* at most one of the assigned roles, and only then enjoy the privileges of this role (and of no other role). Using a relational representation, this concept can be captured by three knowledge base relations, namely

- *Granted* $\subseteq$ *Role* $\times$ *Object* $\times$ *Mode*, for the privileges assembled into roles;
- *Role_Assignment* $\subseteq$ *Subject* $\times$ *Role*, for the assignments of subjects to roles; and
- *Role_Enabling* $\subseteq$ *Subject* $\times$ *Role*, for the dynamic enablings.

Additionally, the inclusion dependency *Role_Enabling* $\subseteq$ *Role_Assignment* and the functional dependency *Role_Enabling*: *Subject* $\rightarrow$ *Role* are enforced as semantic constraints. Figure 9.22 shows an example for a specific subject *s*.

The same figure also displays a corresponding automaton instance, called `role_monitor(s)`. The states of this finite automaton are the roles that are assigned to *s*, with one further initial state *lazy* that indicates that no role has been enabled. The transitions correspond to successfully completed control operations that permit the subject *s* to enable exactly one of the assigned roles or to disable it. More generally, whenever a subject *s* starts a session, such a monitoring automaton is constructed as an instance of a class `Role_Monitor`. This class might have a declaration sketched as follows:

```
class Role_Monitor;
    state: Role ∪ {lazy};              / returns the current state
    transition(role: Role ∪ {lazy}); / switches to new state role, if applicable
    Role_Monitor(subject: Subject, assigned: ℘Role).
                                   / constructs new monitoring automaton
                                   for subject with state set assigned ∪ {lazy}
```

At the start of a session, the constructor is called by the following control procedure, which first determines the applicable set of states from the relation *Role_Assignment*:

Granted	Role	Object	Mode
.	.	.	.
.	.	.	.
r_i	$o_{i,1}$	$m_{i,1}$
...	...	...
r_i	$o_{i,k}$	$m_{i,k}$
.	.	.	.
.	.	.	.

Role_Assignment	Subject	Role
	.	.
	.	.
	s	r_1
	...	...
	s	r_i
	...	...
	s	r_n
	.	.

Role_Enabling	Subject	Role
	.	.
	.	.
	s	r_i
	.	.

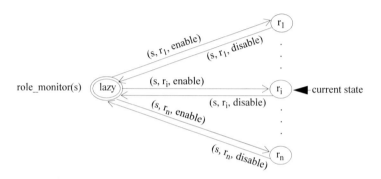

Fig. 9.22. Relational representations of an instance of the concept of a role, together with an instance of the corresponding control automaton

```
procedure role_initialize(subject);
  { export: role_monitor(subject) }
  assigned := { r | (subject,r) ∈ Role_Assignment };
  role_monitor(subject) := new Role_Monitor(subject, assigned).
```

Afterwards, the subject may call control procedures for role *enabling* or role *disabling* that are outlined as follows:

```
procedure role_enable(subject, role);
  { import: role_monitor(subject) }
  if      role_monitor(subject).state = lazy
  then    role_monitor(subject).transition(role) fi.

procedure role_disable(subject, role);
  { import: role_monitor(subject) }
  if      role_monitor(subject).state = role
  then    role_monitor(subject).transition(lazy) fi.
```

Then, access decisions can easily be taken by calling the following procedure, which basically inspects the currently enabled role for an appropriate privilege:

```
function decide(subject, object, operation): Boolean;
{ import: role_monitor(subject) }

  m := mode(operation);
  return (role_monitor(subject).state, object, m) ∈ Granted.
```

This two-layer approach – where one first "statically" converts role assignments into a monitoring automaton, and then "dynamically" exploits the automaton to control role enablings – has apparent advantages and disadvantages, which are shared with many similar approaches. As an advantage, role assignments are looked up *only once*, when the monitoring automaton is constructed. As a disadvantage, a revoked role assignment is *not immediately reflected* in an already existing automaton.

9.5.3 Information Flow Monitoring

We now review several examples where the usability of "principally permitted" options is *monotonically decreased* owing to previous information flows. The general approach balances *availability* of information in general and *hiding* information under specific conditions as follows:

- Initially, an individual subject is *statically* granted a permission to access some information sources "in principle".
- While the individual is enjoying his privileges, a monitoring automaton aims at *dynamically* preventing the individual from gathering "more information than intended", as declared by an administrator.
- Additionally, *cooperation* among several subjects to accidently or purposely combine the information gained might be taken into consideration. For the sake of simplicity, we only sketch this important issue in the following and thus do not present detailed justifications concerning writing.

Clearly, owing to the well-known difficulties of dealing algorithmically with the notion of *information*, specific instantiations of the general approach might turn out to be highly sophisticated or even beyond practical feasibility and then demand appropriate approximations. One elementary approximation is based on assuming that each operation is either a reading or a writing, as described by the operational modes read and write.

If a subject *reads* an object, then the object's information content is supposed to (*potentially*) *flow* to the subject. Correspondingly, if a subject *writes* into an object, then the information at the subject's disposal is supposed to (*potentially*) *flow* to the object. Accordingly, a monitoring automaton for a subject must keep track of previous readings, in order to (in general over)estimate the information available to the subject. On the basis of this estimate, the automaton might restrict further readings or writings, as described by some *information flow policy*.

Chinese Walls. This example is motivated by a special type of commercial application. In this example, a participant – acting as a *subject* in a computing system – might give professional advice to a *company*, thereby needing access to controlled *objects owned* by that company. In principle, a participant can advise several companies, and thus, "in principle", he should be permitted to access objects owned by different companies. However, if two companies are *competing*, then the consultant should not simultaneously obtain *information* from both companies.

Furthermore, any *information flow* from one company via a consultant to the other competing company must be strictly prevented. Accordingly, once the consultant has read an object owned by the former company, he is dynamically prohibited both to read any object of the latter company and to write into any object of the latter company. In fact, in order to avoid transitive information flows, writing must be restricted further, basically to objects of just one company.

A formalization of this information flow policy can be sketched as follows:

- *Subject* is the set of *consulting* participants.
- *Company* is the set of *companies* that are potential consulting clients.
- *public* denotes a further fictitious realm that always contains only *publicly available information*.
- *Compete* $\subseteq \wp$ *Company* is a *competition* partition of *Company* into mutually disjoint subsets of *Company*, covering all of *Company*, with the following intuitive meaning:
  for all blocks $X \in$ *Compete*, any two companies $c_1 \in X$ and $c_2 \in X$ are considered as competing. The function *compete* : *Company* $\to$ *Compete* assigns each company c its unique competition block X, with $c \in X$. Note that *compete*(*public*) is undefined.
- *Object* is the set of controlled *objects*.
- *Granted* $\subseteq$ *Subject* $\times$ *Object* $\times$ {read,write} represents statically permitted privileges that are "in principle" granted to subjects.
- *owner* : *Object* $\to$ *Company* $\cup$ { *public* } is a function that assigns each object either a unique company or the above fictitious realm as its *owner*.

For each subject s, a monitoring automaton for reading, read_monitor(s), and a monitoring automaton for writing, write_monitor(s), are maintained. The states of these automatons dynamically represent those companies that are *not excluded* from further operations on the basis of the computing history. Accordingly, after a subject has performed an operation, the automatons might switch to a new state that discards some previous options.

For *reading*, the monitoring automaton read_monitor(s) has the state set $\wp$ (*Company* $\cup$ { *public* }), with initial state $state^{read} :=$ *Company* $\cup$ { *public* }. On a permitted reading request $(s,o,operation)$, with $mode(operation)$=read (and $owner(o) \neq public$), the state transition discards those companies that are competing with the accessed object's owner:

$$state^{read} := state^{read}$$

$$\setminus \{ c \mid compete(c) = compete(owner(o)) \text{ and } c \neq owner(o) \}.$$

For *writing*, the monitoring automaton `write_monitor(s)` has the state set $\wp\,(Company \cup \{public\})$, with initial state $state^{write} := Company \cup \{public\}$. Over the full lifespan of an application, the state is changed only twice. The first switch is due on the *first permitted* reading request $(s,o,operation)$ with $mode(operation)=$ `read` and $owner(o) \neq public$: the state transition then discards all companies that are different from the accessed object's owner:

$$state^{write} := \{\ owner(o)\ \}.$$

Subsequently, a second switch is due on the *next permitted* reading request with $(s,o,operation)$, with $mode(operation) = $ `read`, $owner(o) \neq public$ and, additionally, $owner(o) \notin state^{write}$: the state transition then also discards the single remaining company in $state^{write}$:

$$state^{write} := \emptyset.$$

Afterwards, the state is *never* changed again. Assuming the stated preconditions, the effects of both switches and the subsequent tranquility can be uniformly described by $state^{write} := state^{write} \cap \{\ owner(o)\ \}$.

Finally, *access decisions* are taken by the following procedure:

```
function decide(s, o, operation): Boolean;
{ import: read_monitor(s), write_monitor(s) }
m := mode(operation);
```

if m = read   **then**
    return [(s,o,m) ∈ Granted   */ statically permitted **and***
        AND owner(o) ∈ read_monitor(s).state ^{read}] **fi** ; */ dynamic condition satisfied*

if m = write   **then**
    return [(s,o,m) ∈ Granted   */ statically permitted **and***
        AND owner(o) ∈ write_monitor(s).state ^{write}] **fi** ./ *dynamic condition satisfied*

The phrase "Chinese wall" suggests that this access decision procedure constructs a strong protection wall around competing companies, in order to strictly avoid the unwanted disclosure of confidential information by allowing external consulting. If correctly implemented, the protection is strong indeed, but the phrase is rather misleading concerning the dynamic aspects.

Dynamic Mandatory Access Control. As explained in Section 9.8, the approach of *mandatory access control* approximates *information flows* based on reading and writing by means of *security levels*. The set of security levels forms a finite partial order, or, even more strongly, a finite lattice, that is exploited to express the *relative sensitivity* of the information contained or flowing in objects or subjects. A monitoring finite automaton can dynamically keep track of the current relative sensitivity by determining the *least upper bound* of the relevant security levels.

More details of this example of the use of automatons are given in Section 9.8. Here, we note only that Chinese walls can be regarded as a special instantiation of dynamic mandatory access control.

Controlled Query Evaluation. In general, as can be seen from the discussion in Part Two of this monograph, finite automatons are too weak to precisely describe *information flows*. Therefore, more powerful automatons with less restricted or even unrestricted memory facilities are needed.

In fact, when dealing with a concept of information flow that is based on *logical implication*, we need the full power of Turing machines, and even then only *partial computability* can be achieved (since the relationship of logical implication is known to be recursively enumerable but not recursive). As an example, we shall sketch roughly a model of *controlled query evaluation* for information systems, as treated more extensively in Section 5.4.

In this model, a single subject is *statically* permitted to submit arbitrary sequences of queries to the information system. "In principle", the system is expected to return the pertinent answer to any query. However, as specified by some *information flow policy*, the system also tries to keep some specific information confidential. Accordingly, the system maintains a monitoring (Turing-machine-like) automaton that represents the information supposed to be at the disposal of the subject, gathered by *a priori knowledge* and *previous query answers*.

This automaton *dynamically restricts* the current options for obtaining correct answers to further queries. Basically, the automaton evaluates, for each requested query, whether the currently available information together with the correct answer would violate the information flow policy, i.e., whether the subject could infer any information that is to be kept confidential.

Controlled Statistical Query Evaluation. The control of *statistical queries* can be seen as a special instantiation of controlled query evaluation. In this instantiation, the information system manages data that relates "real-world entities" to real numbers, and queries ask for a *statistical numeric value* to be returned for some specified *sample*, such as an *average* or a *median*. On the one hand, "in principle" the system should return correct values, but on the other hand, the *information flow policy* requires data related to individual "real-world entities" to be kept confidential, for example owing to *privacy* concerns.

In this numerical context, information flow based on logical implication can be equivalently reformulated as the *solvability* of systems of equations that are constructed according to *a priori knowledge* and *previous query answers*. Thus, basically, a monitoring automaton has to *dynamically* evaluate the subject's options for constructing a solvable system of equations, the solution of which would reveal *individual* data.

Owing to basic undecidability results, as a feasible approximation, an automaton in practice only monitors the numbers of related queries and some appropriate properties of queries. These properties includes the *size* of samples and their *overlap*, both of which should not be "too small" or "too large". More specific details are presented in Section 5.5.

9.5.4 Process Masterships and Procedure Calls

The expressiveness of the control automatons inspected so far ranges from simple finite automatons to sophisticated universal computing devices. Well-known experience in computing suggests that an intermediate expressiveness is both functionally necessary and efficiently manageable. In particular, *pushdown automatons*, *stack mechanisms* or similar device models corresponding to *context-free grammars* and their variants are highly worthwhile, for example for dealing with unrestricted nestings in a structured way. This insight is used in an essential way in most programming environments, including operating systems and the runtime systems of universal programming languages. Considering three examples, we shall briefly discuss how the basic functional features are complemented by control mechanisms.

UNIX Operating System. As presented in more detail in Section 17.1, the UNIX *operating system* maintains a (dynamically growing and shrinking) *process tree* for process management. In rough, simplified terms, each process can repeatedly fork into a new *child process* and its own continuation as a *father process*, where each such pair has to eventually synchronize in order to end the child process. Each process is run on behalf of a *registered user* of the pertinent UNIX installation. This user is seen as the master of the process, where, usually, a *mastership* is inherited by child processes. Moreover, each *process* (dynamically) executes some program, which is (statically) stored in a file. During its lifespan, the process can exchange the program executed.

If a process, seen as a subject from the point of view of access control, requests to access some object according to some access mode, the current privileges of the process are determined by both the mastering user and the executed program, i.e., by the process history as represented by the current UNIX process tree and the recorded program exchanges. Accordingly, each access decision is based on the current state of the corresponding automaton that actually *implements* the runtime concepts of the operating system sketched above.

The basic design of the UNIX "control automaton" outlined here has been extended to deal with a specific kind of dynamic *right amplification*, i.e., to dynamically and temporarily increase the privileges of a process in a well-understood way. The fundamental goal is to enable a process (and thus the mastering user) to restrictedly access some object for a dedicated purpose even though this object is prohibited from being accessed by others in general. In other words, the owner of this object aims at both protecting it from foreign usages most of the time and sharing it for exceptional cases. Basically, this goal can be achieved in UNIX roughly as follows:

- The owner permits processes mastered by him to access the object considered.
- The owner encodes the dedicated purpose and the corresponding restrictions into a suitable program that comprises commands to access the object as desired. This program is stored in a file that is owned by the same user, and priv-

ileges are set such that the owner is permitted to execute the program. Accordingly, while it is mastered by the owner, a process executing this program is permitted to access the object.

- Additionally, the owner can discretionarily permit selected other users to execute (the program stored in) this file, and the owner can discretionarily set an *execution flag* (called a *suid*) for this file. The semantics of this flag results in the following: whenever a process executes this file, the *current mastership* of the process (known as its *effective uid*) is temporarily changed to the owner of the executed file, deviating from the usual rule. As a consequence, during the execution of this file, the process is permitted to access the object.

For each entry of the process tree, the UNIX system keeps an additional finite automaton whose state suitably represents the original mastership initialized at creation time, the current mastership triggered by execution flags, and some further related runtime data. More technical details are visualized in Figure 17.5.

HYDRA Operating System. The experimental operating system HYDRA comprises a related mechanism for *right amplification* as part of a uniform object-oriented approach to managing *procedure calls* and determining the privileges of the resulting procedure executions. As in similar approaches, the system maintains a *runtime stack* for procedure calls. Each procedure call triggers the dynamic creation of an object (corresponding to a stack frame) of the type *local name space*. This object contains or references all runtime data needed for executing the called procedure, including the privileges needed to access other objects. Usually, these privileges are dynamically *granted* in two ways, described roughly by the following rules:

- The (dynamic) local name space object of the calling procedure can copy any selection of its own privileges and pass the copies as actual parameters.
- The (static) program object of the called procedure transmits its own privileges.

According to these rules, the permitted operational options of a specific execution of a procedure are strictly bounded by the permissions held by the two source objects mentioned above. Moreover, once the execution is completed, the pertinent local name space object is removed from the runtime stack, and thereby the dynamically granted privileges are implicitly *revoked*.

A further rule deals with *right amplification*, offering the possibility to supply a created object of type "local name space" with a privilege that is neither held by the calling dynamic object nor possessed by the called static object. Hence a created local name space object can be made more powerful than both of the source objects together.

The underlying mechanism employs an *amplification template* instead of a "real" privilege, intended to be possessed by a static program object. Roughly outlined, such a template of the form $[am/cm]$ specifies that some (abstract) access mode *am* occurring in a privilege $[o, am]$ held by a caller should be replaced by a concrete access mode *cm*.

To intuitively exemplify the intended usage of a template, we assume the caller to hold a privilege $[o,am]$ to access some owned data object o by a specific method represented by the abstract access mode am; so far, however, this privilege is useless, since the caller can neither actually read nor actually write to the object o. Moreover, the caller is supposed to hold a privilege to call (or "enter") a procedure AM that implements the method considered; this privilege might be represented by $[AM, enter]$. Finally, let this procedure possess an amplification template $[am/read]$; so far, however, the procedure is not permitted to actually access any object. If the procedure is called, then the passed privilege $[o,am]$ is "merged" with the transmitted template $[am/read]$, resulting in the privilege $[o,read]$ for the created local name space object. Accordingly, this specific procedure execution can read the particular object o.

To simplify and summarize, the most recent local name space object (i.e., the top frame of the runtime stack) determines the currently permitted actions. The quite subtle details of the protection concepts of HYDRA are neatly intertwined with the overall design of a *kernel*-based multiprocessor operating system.

Java Stack Inspection. The programming language *Java* offers a comprehensive protection framework, including rules for deciding on access requests issued by the execution of either local or remote (program) code. While *local* code generated by an owner of a computing system might be assumed to be "trustworthy" and thus be seen as qualified to discretionarily receive privileges to access local resources, code stemming from *remote* systems is seen to be potentially "suspicious" and thus is treated with special care.

Accordingly, as an extreme option, such remote code can be executed within a nearly isolated environment, called a *sandbox*, that only permits restricted runtime activities. In particular, the following restrictions might be enforced: external communications are only permitted with the site from which the code originates; the dynamic creation of new (child) processes is prohibited; and privileges regarding local resources cannot be dynamically granted beyond some statically declared specifications.

However, for cooperation between participants by means of a distributed computing system, more flexible solutions are additionally provided. Basically, following the class-based approach of Java, *subjects* in the sense of access control are formed by a set of Java classes that are characterized by (the URL of) their origin, the acceptance of digital signatures generated for the code (to ensure its integrity), corresponding certificates and related items.

Such a subject is assigned a *protection domain* (which is similar to a role), which, in turn is granted concrete *privileges*. Later on, all runtime instance objects of the pertinent classes inherit these privileges from the protection domain, which thus determines the "principally permitted" options. However, these options are further dynamically restricted according to the preceding relevant computing history, as represented by the runtime stacks.

Roughly outlined, Java maintains a *runtime stack* for each thread to keep track of a chain of pending *method invocations* (*procedure calls*), i.e., nested calls to execute the code of the referenced methods, that have not been completed so far. As a fundamental rule, to strictly avoid undesired right amplifications, Java enforces the condition that a nested execution of a method may not be more powerful that any of its predecessors in the chain. Accordingly, whenever a running method execution requests to access a resource, not only the privileges of the current protection domain assigned to the relevant subject (in particular, the instantiated class declaration of the requesting method) are inspected, but also the privileges of all protection domains assigned to the predecessors.

The request is permitted only if all items in the chain possess appropriate privileges. Thus, in general, the Java control mechanism has to *inspect* the full runtime *stack*, in contrast to the basic approaches of UNIX and HYDRA, for example, which consider only the control data attached to the current process or procedure call, respectively, i.e., the top of the pertinent structure.

The fundamental rule, however, demands further refinements, optimizations and even exceptions, which are beyond the scope of this monograph. For example, the creation of a new thread and thus of an additional runtime stack must be handled appropriately; compilation of the dynamic stack inspection into more static concepts can decrease the control overhead at run time; and an option to temporarily grant a missing privilege (i.e., a concept of right amplification) might be devised.

9.5.5 Discretionary Context Selection

The dynamic *security contexts* of UNIX, HYDRA, Java and other programming systems described above are mainly selected *automatically* according to the specific runtime software mechanism. Following the same approach, a processor *state register*, which holds the current *protection state* or *mode* regarding privileged instructions, is handled according to the mechanisms employed in the hardware layer, as sketched in Subsection 6.2.2.

Alternatively or complementarily, we can design context selections to be *discretionarily* performed by some subject. The concept of role enabling and disabling, treated in Subsection 9.5.2, can be seen as an example. Further examples can be found in CORBA *middleware*, briefly sketched in Subsection 17.3.3, and in several other application-oriented systems as well. In the following, we list only three of the many variants.

OSKAR. In a somewhat mixed approach, the experimental OSKAR system maintains *security contexts* as *subsystems*. A subsystem can be seen as a collection of objects that are uniformly treated regarding access control. Roughly outlined, subjects are given extended privileges of a form such as

$$[\, subsystem \, , object \, , mode \, , p_1(PV_1) \, , \ldots , p_n(PV_n) \, , r_1(RV_1) \, , \ldots , r_m(RV_m) \,]$$

that explicitly refer to a subsystem, specify an operational mode of an object and, additionally, describe the set of *parameter values* that are permitted to be passed and the set of *result values* that are permitted to be returned.

Procedure calls from one subsystem to another are intercepted and controlled by a *kernel*. The kernel also mediates the delivery of the result values, and accordingly can inspect their compliance with the description in the extended privilege employed. Basically, modern middleware systems follow a closely related approach, except that the control is distributed between the components involved, i.e., between the site of the caller and the site of the callee.

DORIS. The *privacy-oriented* information system DORIS treats a proprietary concept of *roles* as a kind of *security context*. In this approach, a role defines privileges such that only one role (per group) can be used for executing a high-level *query* expression, in order to support a rudimentary form of *separation of roles*. Basically, in rough, simplified form, such an expression is executed in three stages:

- First, sets of all relevant objects to be accessed are determined by suitable set-oriented navigations, yielding the set of pertinent object identifiers (surrogates).
- Second, appropriate methods for extracting data from these objects are invoked.
- Third, the returned data is gathered and processed further by relational operations, as in a relational database.

The first stage, of navigation, is controlled according to privileges (called "acquaintances") to navigate to subsets of specified object sets (extensions of "groups"), employing mechanisms similar to *capability-based* addressing with additional protection features.

The second stage, of method invocations, requires privileges referring to roles that are statically declared for sets of objects (groups) and inherited by the member objects. However, for each specific execution of an expression, only one role may be employed for each group involved. For as long as possible, the selection of a suitable role and thus of a dynamic *security context* is supported by the runtime system: this system dynamically keeps a list of roles that still satisfy the ongoing invocation requests, cancelling those roles that fail to permit all requests inspected so far; however, as soon as no suitable role is left, the system refuses to return a result for the expression to be executed.

If applicable, the third stage is seen as the processing data that has already been permitted to be read, and thus there are no further controls.

Well-Formed Transactions. While OSKAR is a general-purpose system and DORIS is a dedicated information system, the concept of *well-formed transactions* is meant to be applicable for a wide range of business applications. Basically, this concept exploits some general insight regarding isolation and control, encapsulation, and (organizational) roles as follows. When acting in a specific role as an enduser regarding some high-level applications, a participant should have no direct access to the underlying objects regarding low-level operations. Rather, the two levels should first be clearly separated on the one hand and then mediated in a controlled way on the other hand.

More specifically, at the higher level, participants should only receive privileges to call well-formed transactions that capture the overall business activities. At the lower level, such well-formed transactions may be granted privileges to access and elementarily manipulate the underlying objects, as needed to finally implement the business activities captured. In a sense, by calling a well-formed transaction, a participant implicitly selects a *security context* and thereby indirectly acquires the low-level privileges needed for his current task in a disciplined form.

9.5.6 Workflow Control

Business applications, whether for administration or production, might span many individual activities, coordinating the cooperation of the participants involved in a well-structured and supervised way. Typically, an administrator statically declares a possible structure in a *workflow schema* and, later on, suitable participants dynamically execute one or more *workflow instances* as constrained by the schema. While a workflow instance is progressing, at any point in time during its lifespan, two opposing requirements regarding access decisions must be enforced:

- On the one hand, any participant scheduled to perform the next step should have available all needed resources and thus effectively hold the pertinent privileges.
- On the other hand, all other participants deemed to be waiting for a call should be temporarily prevented from actually employing "principally permitted" options.

Moreover, according to the progress of the workflow instance, another kind of access decision has to be taken:

- After the completion of a step, one or more succeeding steps must be enabled.

Thus, the workflow schema and the current state of progress of an instance jointly specify a *security context* that determines the operational options currently at the disposal of the various parties. Such a security context can be conveniently described by a *control automaton*, formed as a suitably enhanced finite automaton or, alternatively, as a Petri net, in particular if concurrent steps are considered. Neglecting concurrency for the sake of simplicity, in the following we sketch an approach using finite automatons.

Basically, a *workflow schema* is specified by two components: (1) a *head*, listing the *formal typed subject parameters* and the *formal typed object parameters*; and (2) a *body*, consisting of a (nondeterministic) labeled finite automaton, intended to be used for accepting a regular language over the alphabet of labels:

- a finite set of *states*, where an *initial state* and an *accepting state* are designated;
- a set of labeled *transitions*, where a *label* is a *formal permission* (s,o,m) composed of
  - a formal subject parameter s occurring in the head,
  - a formal object parameter o occurring in the head, and
  - a (control or functional) mode m applicable to the type of o.

Seen as a *template* of a control automaton, a schema permits the execution of any sequence of activities that corresponds to an accepted word over the alphabet of labels, provided the formal parameters are suitably bound to actual parameters of the correct type. Thus a schema can be interpreted as specifying "principally permitted" options.

Given a workflow schema, a *workflow instance* is created by binding the formal parameters, generating a copy of the body with correspondingly instantiated labels and starting the resulting *control automaton* in its initial state. Progressively, in any state, the control automaton enables one of the currently available transitions by temporarily granting the permission expressed by the instantiated label. After the permission has been exploited, the control automaton switches to the pertinent next state.

A workflow instance is completed when the control automaton reaches the accepting state, and then the instance together with the control automaton is removed, prohibiting any further activities within this scope. In this way, a control automaton of an instance can be interpreted as *sequencing* and temporarily *enabling* and *disabling* the actual employment of "principally permitted" options.

Many further conceptual details must be treated, in particular the privileges for *control operations* in the schema layer and in the instance layer, including:

- declaring a workflow schema;
- creating a new workflow instance, i.e., starting a sequence of activities;
- binding actual parameters, in particular, designating actual subjects;
- deciding on nondeterministic choices, i.e., selecting alternative next steps.

Moreover, a *distributed* implementation of the conceptual control automatons constitutes a major challenge, suggesting that the current state should be represented by a cryptographically protected *token*, to be passed, in turn, as a *capability* to the subject to act.

9.6 Analysis of Control States

9.6.1 Task and Abstract Model

Basically, the knowledge base on permissions and prohibitions is first appropriately *initialized*, and then, by interleaving, participants employ *control operations* to generate the actual instances, and the control and monitoring component uses the respective actual instance to take *access decisions* on requests. Control operations are subject to access decisions as well and, accordingly, the knowledge base also deals with *control privileges*. Thus, in principle, an actual instance determines not only the *current* access decisions but also the possible *future* instances and, accordingly, also the possible *future* access decisions.

The latter feature raises the problem of analyzing a current instance concerning the security achievements during its further dynamic development. This problem has two dual aspects, which deal with the opposing interests of (potential) *availability* on the one side and *confidentiality* and *integrity* on the other side:

- May a subject *s* ever acquire a privilege [*o,m*]? More specifically, given the current instance of the knowledge base, does there exist a sequence of permitted control operations such that, afterwards, a request from subject *s* to perform an operation of mode *m* on object *o* is *permitted*? And, in the positive case, which participants, using which control operations, can achieve such acquisition?
- Can a subject *s* never acquire a privilege [*o,m*]? More specifically, given the current instance of the knowledge base, will a request from subject *s* to perform an operation of mode *m* on object *o* be *always prohibited,* under all possible sequences of permitted control operations?

In general, an administrator of a control and monitoring component has to consider both aspects when setting up the *control operations* offered and initializing the *knowledge base* on permissions and prohibitions, including the initial assignment of control privileges. Ideally, the administrator should *specify* concrete requirements concerning the opposing interests, then *implement* the specification by a suitable setting and initialization and, finally, *analyze* the achievements by proving an invariant for the possible instances of the knowledge base that enforces the requirements. In the case of distributed control, the local administrators should basically follow the same paradigm when configuring their realm of responsibility.

In the following, we concentrate on the analysis part of this ambitious task for administrators, while exploring algorithmic solutions to the underlying problem within a simple abstract model. This model combines a relational representation of the elementary ternary relationship class *granted* with a generic template for control operations that are controlled in turn. The model allows three kinds of *generalized operational modes*: as before, *functional* modes that are suitable for the application investigated and *control* modes for the pertinent control operations, and, additionally, *relational* modes for modeling relationships between two items such as ownership. The model comprises time-independent declarations and time-dependent instances as follows.

The time-independent declarations are:

- an infinite set *I* of potential system *items*, each of which may act both as a subject and thus also as a grantee, and as a controlled object;
- an infinite set *Actor* $\subseteq I$ of *actors* that may request control operations such as granting and revoking;
- a finite set *Mode* of generalized control *modes*, where $FM \subseteq Mode$ is the set of *functional modes* and $KM \subseteq Mode$ is the set of *control* and *relational modes* such that $FM \cup KM = Mode$ and $FM \cap KM = \varnothing$;
- the set $Priv := \{ [x,m] \mid x \in I \text{ and } m \in Mode \}$ of (generalized) *privileges*.

The time-dependent features of the knowledge base are gathered together in a *control state* ($L_t, Granted_t, Cond_t$), defined as follows:

- the actual abstract *time t* taken from a discrete total order with a minimal element (without loss of generality, we always let *t* be a natural number and, where appropriate, we suppress the time parameter);
- a finite set $L_t \subseteq I$ of system items that are *alive* at time *t*, having been generated earlier and not yet discarded;
- a ternary database relation $Granted_t \subseteq L_t \times L_t \times Mode$ that represents the actual *permissions* or other *relationships* at time *t*;
- a possibly parameterized *further condition Cond_t* that is occasionally employed to capture additional requirements for access decisions.

As before, for a functional mode $m \in FM$, a tuple $(s,o,m) \in Granted_t$ represents a *permission* for subject *s* to access object *o* by an operation of mode *m*. As the default, $(s,o,m) \notin Granted_t$ means the corresponding *prohibition*. In the context of this model, we are interested only in the presence or absence of such tuples and not in actually performing functional operations.

For a control mode $m \in KM$, a tuple $(s,o,m) \in Granted_t$ represents the (potentially) *conditional permission* for a subject *s* to manipulate a privilege of the form $[o,.]$ concerning the controlled object *o* by a control operation of mode *m*. As the default, $(s,o,m) \notin Granted_t$ again means the corresponding *prohibition*. For the purpose of analyzing instances, we have to study the impact of (actually or virtually) performing permitted control operations.

Control states are manipulated by control operations. A control operation is performed as a call of a parameterized *control procedure*, commonly called a *control schema*, that has the following simple syntactic structure:

```
procedure control_schema_ident (formal_mode_list; formal_item_list);
{ import: Granted, L, Cond }
if      subrelation Required is contained in relation Granted
        AND condition Cond is satisfied
then    modify Granted and, if required, also L;
        if required, adapt Cond
fi.
```

More specifically, such a control schema must obey the following restrictions. The *formal parameters* are operational modes or items. The control state (here, for the sake of simplicity, without the time *t*) is assumed to be globally declared.

The *body* of the schema consists of just one guarded command, which refers only to the formal parameters and the globally declared control state. The guard simply checks for the presence of some entries, denoted by *Required*, in the relation *Granted*, and possibly additionally verifies the further condition *Cond*. In doing so, the guard also captures the *access decision* by inspecting the required *control privileges*. The command can only modify the relation *Granted* and possibly also the set *L* of alive items, and additionally adapt the further condition *Cond*.

A modification of *Granted* or *L* consists of a sequence of elementary actions that can have the following forms:

insert(*s*,*o*,*m*)	[into *Granted*], i.e.,	*Granted*	:= *Granted* $\cup$ { (*s*,*o*,*m*) },
delete(*s*,*o*,*m*)	[from *Granted*], i.e.,	*Granted*	:= *Granted* \ { (*s*,*o*,*m*) },
create(*y*)	[as *new* element of *L*], i.e.,	*L*	:= *L* $\cup$ { *y* } with *y* $\notin$ *L*,
destroy(*y*)	[and remove from *L*], i.e.,	*L*	:= *L* \ { *y* }.

It should be noted that the procedures grant$_{owner,o,m}$ and revoke$_{owner,o,m}$, defined in Section 9.4 for the purpose of studying granting and revoking, do not fully fit the restrictions of the model studied in this section, since both of these procedures employ issue times and data on grantors, and the latter procedure has a far more sophisticated body. Thus the present model constitutes an essential simplification of the features needed in practice.

Under the present restrictions, we declare an alternative control schema for *granting* as an example. This schema requires, for a positive access decision, that the requesting *grantor* holds two privileges: first, a *control privilege* of the form [*grantee*, grant] with a control mode grant that permits a granting operation favoring *grantee*; and second, the functional privilege [*object*, *mode*] that the requestor wants to grant. More formally:

```
procedure grant(mode;grantor,grantee,object);
{ import: Granted, Actor }

if                              / access decision:
[ (grantor,grantee,grant) ∈ Granted
                                / grantor has control privilege [grantee,grant]
  AND (grantor,object,mode) ∈ Granted
                                / grantor has functional privilege [object,mode]
  AND grantor ∈ Actor ]         / further condition: grantor is actor
then                            / modification of control state:
  insert(grantee,object,mode)   / insert new entry into relation Granted
                                / further condition remains unchanged
fi.
```

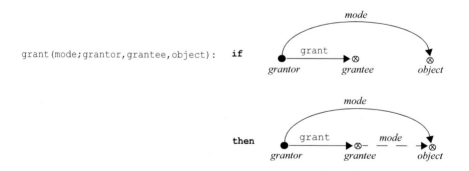

grant(mode;grantor,grantee,object):

Fig. 9.23. The control schema for granting, interpreted as a (sub)graph replacement rule

This control schema, like many others, can be interpreted as some kind of *(sub)graph replacement rule* that operates on access control graphs. For this purpose, full nodes denote actors, and empty nodes visualize items that are not actors; crossed nodes indicate that we do not care about the status of an item. With this convention, the control schema grant(mode;grantor,grantee, object) has the interpretation shown in Figure 9.23.

Using the model presented so far, we can now fully formalize the problem underlying the task of analyzing the achievements of an administrator, namely whether or not a subject s may ever acquire a privilege $[o,m]$:

- An application of the control schema $C(mode_1,\ldots,mode_k; item_1,\ldots,item_l)$ with actual parameters $(m_1,\ldots,m_k; x_1,\ldots,x_l)$ *transforms* a control state $S_1 = (L_1, Granted_1, Cond_1)$ into a control state $S_2 = (L_2, Granted_2, Cond_2)$,

  $$S_1 \vdash C(m_1,\ldots,m_k; x_1,\ldots,x_l) \; S_2 \,,$$

  iff for the actual parameters
  (i) the access decision (taken by the guard in the body of C) is positive, and
  (ii the command in the body of C modifies S_1 into S_2.

- A finite set *Control* of control schemes *can transform* a control state $S_1 = (L_1, Granted_1, Cond_1)$ into a control state $S_2 = (L_2, Granted_2, Cond_2)$,

  $$S_1 \vdash_{Control} S_2 \,,$$

  iff there exists a control schema $C(mode_1,\ldots,mode_k; item_1,\ldots,item_l)$ in *Control* and corresponding actual parameters $(m_1,\ldots,m_k; x_1,\ldots,x_l)$ such that

  $$S_1 \vdash C(m_1,\ldots,m_k; x_1,\ldots,x_l) \; S_2 \,.$$

- $\vdash^*_{Control}$ is the reflexive and transitive closure of the binary relation $\vdash_{Control}$ on the set of control states.

- The predicate $can\_acquire(Control, S_1, s, o, m)$, where

Control	is a finite set of control schemes,
$S_1 = (L_1, Granted_1, Cond_1)$	is a control state,
$s \in L_1$	is a (system) item,
$o \in L_1$	is a controlled object, and
m	is a (generalized) operational mode,

  holds iff there exists a control state $S_2 = (L_2, Granted_2, Cond_2)$ such that
  (i) $S_1 \vdash^*_{Control} S_2$, and
  (ii) $(s,o,m) \in Granted_2$.

Under this formalization, at the core of the *analysis task* we have to algorithmically decide meaningful instances, or classes of instances, of the predicate *can_acquire*. Though the set *Mode* of modes and the set *Control* of control schemes are supposed to be finite, the *decision problem* is nevertheless nontrivial, since the set I of potential system items is infinite. Thus, starting with a finite control state S_1, we can potentially generate infinitely many further control states. Accordingly, in general, the decision problem cannot be solved simply by a finite and exhaustive enumeration of all relevant possibilities.

9.6.2 Undecidability

In fact, we show first that the decision problem is not solvable in general.

Theorem 9.3   **[predicate *can_acquire* is undecidable]**

For the *unrestricted* class of control schemas, as specified above for the abstract model, the predicate $can\_acquire(Control, S_1, s, o, m)$ is undecidable.

Sketch of Proof: The assertion is proved by reducing the undecidable *halting problem* of Turing machines to the decision problem of the predicate *can_acquire*. Therefore, using a suitable formalization of Turing machines, a computable reduction *reduce* of a Turing machine *TM* to a parameter set $reduce(TM) = (Control, S_1, s, o, m)$ of *can_acquire* is constructed such that the following holds:

Turing machine *TM* halts if and only if $can\_acquire(Control, S_1, s, o, m)$.

Roughly outlined, a *Turing machine TM* is specified by the following items:

Σ is a finite tape *alphabet*,
     containing the special symbol ~ for indicating empty tape fields;

K is a finite set of (internal) *states*;

k_{init} is the *starting* state;

k_{halt} is the *halting* state;

$\delta: K \setminus \{k_{halt}\} \times \Sigma \rightarrow K \times \Sigma \times \{left, right\}$ is the *transition* function that, given

  – a *current* state $k \in K \setminus \{k_{halt}\}$ and
  – the symbol $m \in \Sigma$ just *read* from the currently inspected tape field,

determines

  – the *next* state $k' \in K$,
  – the symbol $m' \in \Sigma$ to be *written* on the inspected tape field and
  – the direction $d \in \{left, right\}$ for *moving* the read/write head.

For the purpose of the reduction, without affecting the undecidability of the halting problem, we assume that such a Turing machine *TM* is started in the state k_{init} with an "empty tape", and *TM* is said to *halt* if it reaches the halting state k_{halt} with the read/write head inspecting the tape field numbered 1.

A *configuration* of a Turing machine *TM* is given by the following items, as visualized in the upper half of Figure 9.24:

$m_1 m_2 ... m_e \in \Sigma^*$ is the *current content* of the actually used initial part of the tape, consisting of the fields numbered $1, ..., e$ (without empty fields at the right);

$i \in \{1, ..., e\}$ indicates the *position* of the read/write head, i.e., the currently inspected tape field;

$k \in K$ is the current *state*.

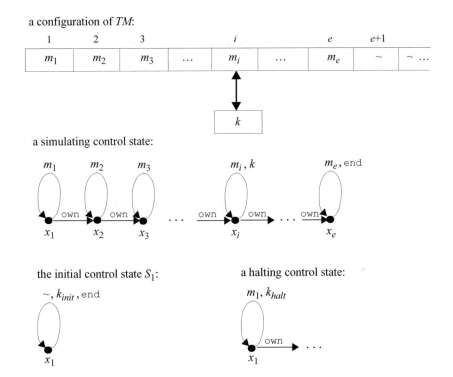

Fig. 9.24. Turing machine configurations and simulating control states

The reduction *reduce* maps the Turing machine *TM* to a parameter set that is defined as follows:

- *I* is used to represent the tape fields of TM, i.e., the *item* $x_i \in I$ represents the tape field numbered *i*.
- *Mode* is constructed as a set of "artificial" *operational modes*, which comprise the tape alphabet and the states of *TM*, and two special modes denoted by own and end, i.e., $Mode := \Sigma \cup K \cup \{\text{own}, \text{end}\}$.
- A configuration of the Turing machine *TM* can then be represented as a *control state*, as indicated in the lower half of Figure 9.24.
- *Control* simulates the transition function δ by providing for each argument $(k, m) \in K \setminus \{k_{halt}\} \times \Sigma$ one or two suitable *control schemas*, to be described below.
- S_1 is a *control state* that represents the *initial* configuration of *TM*, as visualized at the bottom of Figure 9.24.
- *s*, *o* and *m* are defined as x_1, x_1 and k_{halt}, respectively, in accordance with the convention on halting introduced above.

Finally, we sketch the simulating *control schemas*, denoted by $sim_{k,m}(x,y)$ and $sim\_tape\_ext_{k,m}(x,y)$. For this purpose, we distinguish whether the read/write head is moved left or right. Basically, the schemas proceed as follows:

- The item that represents the currently inspected tape field is identified by the unique alive item x_i that has a privilege with an operational mode taken from the state set K, i.e., such that $(x_i, x_i, k) \in Granted$ for some $k \in K$.
- Similarly, the symbol $m \in \Sigma$ just *read* from the currently inspected tape field is determined as the unique privilege with $(x_i, x_i, m) \in Granted$ for some $m \in \Sigma$. This privilege (x_i, x_i, m) is replaced by a new privilege (x_i, x_i, m') that represents the written symbol m'.
- Then the privilege (x_i, x_i, k) is deleted, and the neighboring item, on the left or on the right depending on the *transition* function δ, is granted an appropriate privilege that represents the *next* state k'.
- As a special case, some care is needed when the read/write head has reached the right end of the part of the tape actually used and a right move is demanded. The right end is detected if $(x_i, x_i, \text{end}) \in Granted$, and then a new item x_{i+1} is created, linked with x_i by inserting $(x_i, x_{i+1}, \text{own})$ into *Granted* and marked as the new right end, before the standard actions are performed.

More formally, the simulating control schemas are defined as follows and, additionally, are visualized as (sub)graph replacement rules in Figure 9.25:

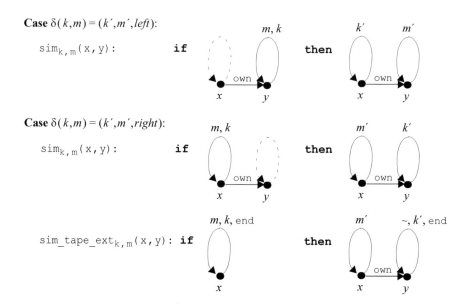

Fig. 9.25. The simulating control schemas, visualized as (sub)graph replacement rules

Case 1: For $\delta(k,m) = (k',m',left)$, define one control schema:

```
procedure sim_{k,m}(x,y);
{ import: Granted }
```

if	/ *access decision*:
(y,y,k) ∈ Granted	/ y represents the currently inspected tape field, with state k
AND (y,y,m) ∈ Granted	/ m has been read from this tape field
AND (x,y,own) ∈ Granted	/ x represents the tape field left of y
then	/ *modification of control state*:
delete(y,y,m); insert(y,y,m');	/ replace m by m' on the tape field y
delete(y,y,k); insert(x,x,k')	/ move head left to x, with new state k'
fi.	

Case 2: For $\delta(k,m) = (k',m',right)$, define two control schemas:

```
procedure sim_{k,m}(x,y);
{ import: Granted }
```

if	/ *access decision*:
(x,x,k) ∈ Granted	/ x represents the currently inspected tape field, with state k
AND (x,x,m) ∈ Granted	/ m has been read from this tape field
AND (x,y,own) ∈ Granted	/ y represents the tape field right of x: x is **not right end** of actually used tape part
then	/ *modification of control state*:
delete(x,x,m); insert(x,x,m');	/ replace m by m' on the tape field x
delete(x,x,k); insert(y,y,k')	/ move head right to y, with new state k'
fi.	

```
procedure sim_tape_ext_{k,m}(x,y);
{ import: Granted }
```

if	/ *access decision*:
(x,x,k) ∈ Granted	/ x represents the currently inspected tape field, with state k
AND (x,x,m) ∈ Granted	/ m has been read from this tape field
AND (x,x,end) ∈ Granted	/ x is **right end** of actually used tape part
then	/ *modification of control state*:
delete(x,x,m); insert(x,x,m');	/ replace m by m' on the tape field x
create(y); insert(x,y,own);	/ create y for representing the right neighbor of x
insert(y,y,~);	/ indicate y as empty
delete(x,x,end); insert(y,y,end);	/ mark y as new right end
delete(x,x,k); insert(y,y,k')	/ move head right to y, with new state k'
fi.	❏

The details of the simulating control schemas indicate the following crucial insights: though control schemas appear to be very simple, they are expressive enough to simulate the *local behavior* of a Turing machine. Together with the option to *create* new items, the full computational power of *universal* programming languages is the consequence. In contrast, if we suitably restrict the expressiveness of control schemas, then we can achieve the decidability of the predicate $can\_acquire(Control, S_1, s, o, m)$. We present three kinds of examples of such restrictions:

- On the basis of a formal analysis of the Turing machine simulation in the undecidability proof, the first kind merely aims at preventing this simulation (see Theorem 9.4 below).
- The second kind deals with a case study of the interaction of the control operations of granting and taking together with creating, and how to avoid the resulting shortcomings (see Subsection 9.6.3).
- The last kind attempts to employ typing in order to achieve decidability (see Subsection 9.6.4).

Concerning the first kind, we exemplarily consider two classes of control schemas. The first class simply forbids the elementary action of *creating* a new element of L. The second class forbids *sequences* of elementary actions, as used in the control schemas $sim_{k,m}(x,y)$ and $sim\_tape\_ext_{k,m}(x,y)$.

Theorem 9.4   [essentially restricted control schemas]

The predicate $can\_acquire(Control, S_1, s, o, m)$ is decidable for the following restricted classes of control schemas:

1. The command in the body of a control schema uses *only inserting* (and deleting) as elementary actions.

2. The command in the body of a control schema is *mono-operational*, i.e., it permits only a *single* elementary action of either inserting or creating (or deleting or destroying).

Sketch of Proof: For the first class, we have a *finite* problem that can be solved by an *exhaustive enumeration* of all relevant possibilities.

For the second class, the proof is based on the following observation: whenever a new item y has been created by a call of a control schema, it can *not* be characterized and later identified as *specifically different* from any previously alive item, since immediately after creation, y cannot be involved in any `granted` relationship, owing to the restriction of mono-operationality. Accordingly, any impact of a newly created item can be simulated by an already existing one. Thus, basically, we are led again to a finite problem.   ❑

9.6.3 Take–Grant and Send–Receive Control Schemas

In this subsection, we provide a case study of the interaction of the control operations of granting and taking together with creating, and of how to avoid the resulting shortcomings. For this study, the schema for *granting* is defined as in Section 9.6.1 and visualized in Figure 9.23. The schema for *taking* is specified rather similarly, as visualized as a (sub)graph replacement rule in the upper half of

Figure 9.26. Now the *grantee* (as the "active taker") is the requesting actor (rather than the "passive *grantor*") and, accordingly, the *grantee* needs a control privilege of the form [*grantor*,take] with the control mode take for a positive access decision:

```
procedure take(mode; grantor, grantee, object);
{ import: Granted, Actor }

if                              / access decision:
[ (grantee, grantor, take) ∈ Granted
                                / grantee has control privilege [grantor,take]
  AND (grantor, object, mode) ∈ Granted
                                / grantor has functional privilege [object,mode]
  AND grantee ∈ Actor ]         / further condition: grantee is actor
then                            / modification of control state:
    insert(grantee, object, mode)  / insert new entry into relation Granted
                                / further condition remains unchanged
fi.
```

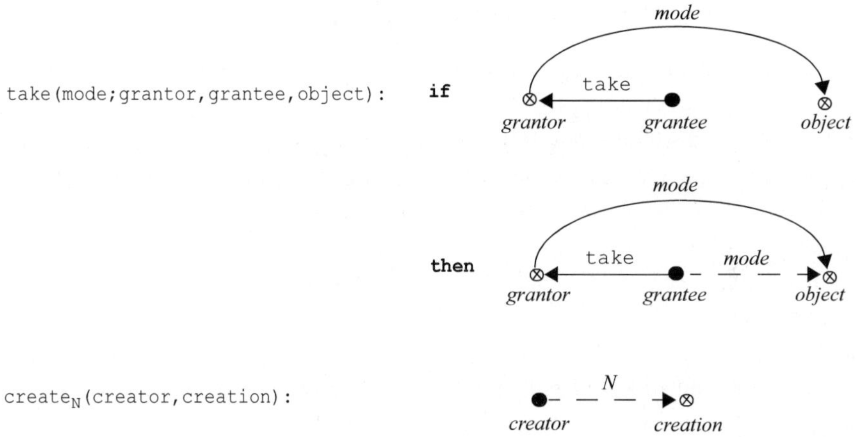

Fig. 9.26. The control schema for taking and creating, visualized as (sub)graph replacement rules

For *creating*, as shown in the lower half of Figure 9.26, there is a control schema $create_N(creator, creation)$ for each subset N of the pertinent set of control modes *Mode* with $\{take, grant\} \subseteq Mode$. Thereby, the *creator* obtains all privileges with respect to his *creation* according to N, and thus the control schemas are *not* monooperational:

```
procedure create_N(creator,creation);
{ import: Granted, Actor }
```

if	/ **access decision**:
creator ∈ Actor	/ further condition: *grantee* is actor
then	/ **modification of control state**:
create(creator,creation);	/ insert *creation* as alive item into set L
forall mode ∈ N **do**	/ according to N
insert(creator,creation,mode)	/ insert new privileges for *creator*
od	/ into relation *Granted*
fi.	

Theorem 9.5   **[predicate *can_acquire* is decidable for take/grant/create$_N$]**

For the *take/grant/create$_N$ class* of control schemas, as specified above and visualized in Figure 9.23 and Figure 9.26, and assuming that all items are actors, the predicate *can_acquire*$(Control,S_1,s,o,m)$ is decidable. More specifically:

The predicate *can_acquire*$(Control,S_1,s,o,m)$ holds iff

there exists an item $p \in L_1$ such that

(i) $(p,o,m) \in Granted_1$, i.e.,
      p already holds the examined privilege $[o,m]$ in the control state S_1, and

(ii) p and s are *take/grant-connected* in the control state S_1, i.e.,
      in the corresponding access control graph there is a path from p to s,
      such that, ignoring directions,
      each edge on the path is labeled with take or grant.

Sketch of Proof: For the if-part, we show that the examined privilege $[o,m]$ can be forwarded stepwise from p to s along the supposed *take/grant connection* as a *transmission path*. For each step, we inductively assume that actor s_i already holds the privilege $[o,m]$, and distinguish the four possible cases for the direct connection to the next actor s_{i+1}:

- If $(s_i,s_{i+1},\text{grant}) \in Granted_1$ or $(s_{i+1},s_i,\text{take}) \in Granted_1$, then the privilege $[o,m]$ can immediately be granted by s_i or taken by s_{i+1}, respectively.

- Otherwise, if only $(s_{i+1},s_i,\text{grant}) \in Granted_1$ or $(s_i,s_{i+1},\text{take}) \in Granted_1$, then the grant privilege or the take privilege occurs in S_1 only with an "inappropriate direction".

  However, in these cases the actors involved can "reverse the directions" by two suitable calls of control schemas, thereby reaching a new control state that immediately allows them to forward the privilege via a new "assisting actor" n. The suitable calls are

      $create_{\{\text{take,grant}\}}(s_{i+1},n)$, $grant(\text{grant}; s_{i+1},s_i,n)$ and
      $create_{\{\text{take,grant}\}}(s_{i+1},n)$, $take(\text{grant}; s_{i+1},s_i,n)$, respectively,

  and their effects are visualized in Figure 9.27.

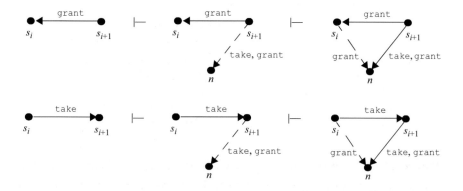

Fig. 9.27. "Reversing inappropriate directions" of grant and take privileges

The only-if part is more subtle. Roughly, the following two more general arguments are inductively justified. First, whenever an actor a acquires the privilege $[o,m]$ in a control state S_2 with $S_1 \mathbin{|\!\!-}^* Control\ S_2$, then a is take/grant-connected in S_2 with some original holder p_a. Second, a suitable take-grant connection between p_a and a then already exists in S_1. ❑

The preceding theorem has several refinements and extensions. The refinements analyze the contributions of the actors involved, in particular which actors play an *active* role, and which actors are only *passively* employed as some kind of *privilege box*.

For example, as can be seen from the proof, for establishing a "reversal of an inappropriate grant privilege", only the intended receiver has to submit requests for control operations, whereas for establishing a "reversal of an inappropriate take privilege", both the intended sender and the intended receiver have to be active. Once the deviation via the new actor is available, again both the intended sender and the intended receiver must submit requests for forwarding the pertinent privilege, while the new actor can remain passive.

The extensions consider the case where there are items that are *not actors*. Basically, these items can only be employed as "privilege boxes". In fact, they can form some kind of *contractible bridge* between connected *islands of actors*, as can be seen in the example shown in Figure 9.28. In this example, the bridge spans from the original holder s_1 of a privilege $[o,m]$ to the intended receiver s_6. Then, by suitable takings, the holder and the receiver independently contribute to establishing the non-actor item s_4 as a *privilege box*, which is then used to forward $[o,m]$ in two further steps.

Theorem 9.5 also shows some shortcomings of the take/grant/create$_N$ class of control schemas. More specifically, an administrator usually aims at achieving the following useful properties:

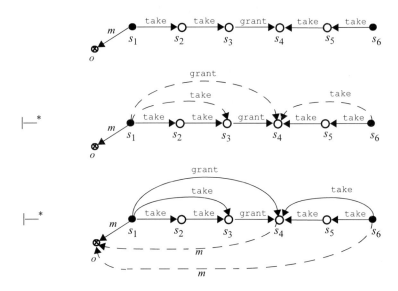

Fig. 9.28. Contracting a bridge formed by non-actor items and employing non-actor item s_4 as a "privilege box"

- A transmission path can be used *selectively* for specific privileges.
- A transmission path for privileges is *directed*.
- For each item, a *bound* for the maximal set of privileges that can be acquired is determined *solely* from the item's initial privileges, as given by the initial control state S_1 or when the item is dynamically created.

In general, the *take/grant/create$_N$ class* of control schemas does not possess any of these features: if there is a take/grant connection between two actors, then *any privilege* can be forwarded in *any direction*, and a grantee of a granting call can receive arbitrary privileges, *without* any precondition in terms of his *own initial* privileges. Hence, the analysis of the take/grant/create$_N$ class has revealed essential deficiencies that exclude the class from practical exploitation.

As a remedy, a *send/receive/create class* has been proposed. Basically, two additional features are introduced for this class:

- A requested transmission of a privilege from a *sender* to a *receiver* – whether by granting, taking or any similar control operation – is permitted only if *both items* involved *independently* possess an appropriate privilege, say send and receive, respectively.
- The further condition *Cond* defines, for each alive item, two predicates that specify fixed *bounds for the usability* of control privileges for sending and receiving privileges, respectively.

The second feature allows many variations. For example, a predicate might restrict the controlled objects and operational modes of transmitted privileges, the potential receivers or senders, and the concrete computing device used to request a transmission. Moreover, whenever an already existing item creates a new item, the predicates for the creation should be *at least as restrictive* as the predicates for the creator.

This proposal is particularly suitable for distributed systems where a sender and a receiver are seen as autonomous actors whose respective control operations of sending and receiving are independently controlled on each side of the transmission channel. Accordingly, *firewalls* for network security essentially follow this proposal.

9.6.4 Typed Control Schemas

The preceding discussions challenge a system designer to define and employ a model that combines the decidability of the pertinent variant of the predicate $can\_acquire(Control, S_1, s, o, m)$ with the desired expressiveness regarding *selectivity* and *directedness* of transmission paths, bounds for maximally obtainable privileges, and related properties, as demanded by practical considerations. The *Schematic Protection Model, SPM* for short, constitutes a suggestion for achieving these goals in a flexible way.

Basically, this model can be seen as a sophisticated elaboration of the *send/receive/create class*, additionally featuring the following components:

- a finite set of statically declared (protection) *types* for the (potentially) infinite set of items, each of which is strongly typed at creation time (without the possibility of changing the type afterwards);
- for any pair of suitable types, statically declared further *filter conditions* regarding the transmission options from one item to another item of the respective types;
- an acyclic *can-create relation* on types which restricts the potential for creating new items;
- regarding create actions, type-based *create conditions* to grant privileges only to the creator and the created item;
- special type-based *attenuation conditions* for creating a new actor of the same type as the creator.

Thus, the dynamic evolution of a system is *statically* constrained by the declared types together with the further type-based restrictions listed.

Taking all features together, whenever an actor a requests to grant (copy) a privilege $[o, m]$ to a grantee g, the guard of the pertinent control schema in SPM essentially verifies four independent conditions:

- Does the grantor a possess the privilege $[o,m]$?
- Does the grantor possess the corresponding specific *control privilege* to *copy* the privilege $[o,m]$? In the model, the copy privilege is denoted by adding the annotation :c to the original privilege, i.e., by writing $[o,m]{:}c$.
- Does a further system-dependent *link condition* in terms of additional control privileges such as send and receive hold, to be possessed by either the grantor a or the grantee g, or even both of them?
- Does the declared *filter condition* for the type of the grantor a and the type of the grantee g hold?

Without giving details, we can state that the statically declared constraints turn out to be sufficient to algorithmically analyze the dynamic behavior of a control system given its initial control state. The concept of typing has also been successfully adapted to the more elementary model presented in Subsection 9.6.1, and later carefully relaxed to allow the type of an item to change dynamically in a suitably restricted way.

9.7 Privileges and Information Flow

In the preceding section, the analysis of control states concentrates on the problem of determining which *privileges* an item can acquire. Clearly, in the end, an administrator also has to evaluate what *functionality* is enabled by the privileges acquired. In fact, in order to support security interests such as *confidentiality* or *integrity*, the functionality enabled is most important, whereas the privileges are merely a means to permit or prohibit accesses.

In this section, we exemplarily investigate the impact of privileges on the functionality of (potential) *information flows*, while dealing with the security interest of *confidentiality*. Thus we extend the analysis problem as follows:

- May a subject s ever be enabled to *learn the information* contained in some object o? More specifically, but still tentatively, given the current instance of the knowledge base on permissions and prohibitions, does there exist a sequence of permitted *control* operations and *functional* operations such that, afterwards, the subject s (potentially) *knows* some of the information initially contained in the object o? And, in the positive case, which participants, using which control or functional operations, can achieve this effect?
- Will a subject s never be enabled to *learn the information* contained in some object o? More specifically, but still tentatively, given the current instance of the knowledge base on permissions and prohibitions, will the subject s never *know* the information initially contained in the object o, under all possible sequences of permitted operations?

As tentatively stated, the problem is not tractable in general, without first selecting some simplifying notions of (potential) information flow, learning and knowledge.

Rather than proposing specific notions of this kind, whose appropriateness tends to be application-dependent, we shall use a simple, abstracting assumption that is based on the functional operations of *reading* and *writing*. We purposely ignore further options for information flows based on a priori knowledge and inferences or related features:

- For the purpose of this section, we postulate that an *information flow* from an item s to an item o occurs if and only if either s writes to o or o reads from s.
- Accordingly, simplifying further, we abstract from the commonly used functional modes `read` and `write`, and employ the functional mode `flow` instead. If $(s,o,\text{flow}) \in Granted$, then any operation causing an information flow from s to o is permitted; otherwise, it is prohibited by default.

The assumed notion of information flow is obviously *transitive*, and therefore administrators should be careful in granting `flow` privileges if they aim at preserving *confidentiality* interests. If, for example, an administrator specifies that $(x_0,x_1,\text{flow}) \in Granted$ and $(x_1,x_2,\text{flow}) \in Granted$, then an information flow from x_0 to x_2 might occur, independently of whether $(x_0,x_2,\text{flow}) \in Granted$ or not, just by performing two permitted flow-causing functional operations. Thus an often useful piece of advice is to maintain an access control graph whose set of edges marked with the functional mode `flow` is transitively closed.

However, if it is important to distinguish which participants *contribute* to an achieved information flow, it clearly makes a difference whether a single permitted operation suffices, i.e., a single direct flow from x_0 to x_2, or whether two permitted operations are required, i.e., sending the information from x_0 via x_1 to x_2.

More generally, to analyze an initial control state and the control operations concerning the potentially enabled *functionality* of an information flow from some item s to some item o, the interaction of two features must be examined:

- The *distribution of control privileges* by permitted *control operations*, in particular the transmission of one or several crucial control privileges along appropriately established *transmission paths for privileges*.
- The *flow of information* according to permitted *functional operations*, in particular the transmission of information-carrying data along previously established *transmission paths for data*.

Figure 9.29 shows a simple example, where the interaction of control operations and functional operations causes an information flow from a source item $s = x_0$ via an intermediate item x_1 to a destination item $x_2 = o$. In this example, the control operations alternatively enable a functional operation to transmit the data from one item to another. After a successfully completed data transmission, the pertinent control privilege is no longer needed, as indicated in the figure by a dotted line.

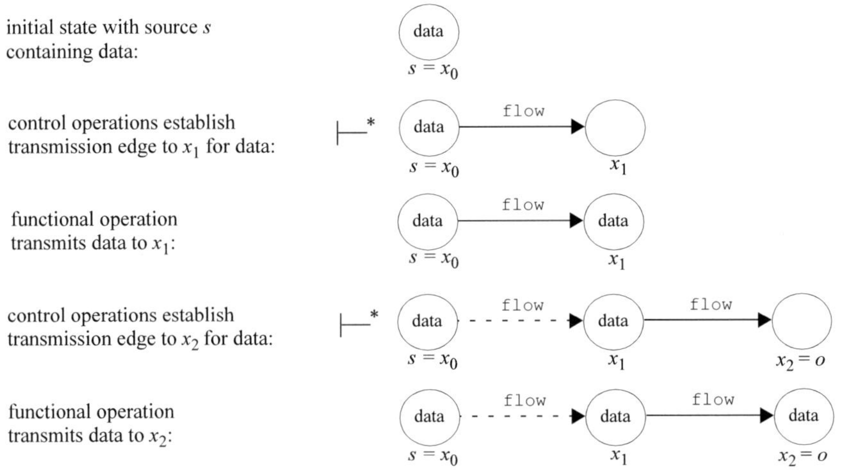

Fig. 9.29. Interaction of control operations and functional operations that cause an information flow from a source item $s = x_0$ via an intermediate item x_1 to a destination item $x_2 = o$

Generalizing the example, the formalization of the *analysis problem* can now be extended as follows, by considering the second feature as well:

- The predicate *can_flow(Control,S,s,o)*, where

Control	is a finite set of control schemes,
$S = (L, Granted, Cond)$	is a control state,
$s \in L$	is an item,
$o \in L$	is an item,

  holds iff there exist

  – a sequence of control states $S = S_0, \ldots, S_k$ with $S_i = (L_i, Granted_i, Cond_i)$ and
  – a sequence of items $s = x_0, \ldots, x_k = o$

  such that for $i = 1, \ldots, k$,

  (i) $x_i \in L_i$,
  (ii) $S_{i-1} \vdash^*_{Control} S_i$ and
  (iii) $(x_{i-1}, x_i, \texttt{flow}) \in Granted_i$.

These conditions imply that *can_acquire(Control,S_{i-1},x_{i-1},x_i,flow)* holds with witness S_i, provided that $x_i \in L_{i-1}$ already. Clearly, part (iii) of the above definition could be replaced by any more subtle consideration of (potential) information flows, thereby leading to even more challenging problems.

9.8 Conceptual Model of Mandatory Approaches

So far, we have presented *discretionary* or *participant-oriented* approaches to specifying permissions and prohibitions. These approaches are highly flexible and
therefore widely preferred. As a trade-off, however, individuals acting as administrators of access rights have to analyze all consequences, in particular the enabled
information flows, by themselves.

The alternative approaches, called *mandatory* or *organization-oriented*, attempt
to guarantee the coherence of granted access rights concerning enabled *information
flows* (or, alternatively, concerning *integrity preservation*) by design.

In the basic conceptual model, as shown in Figure 9.30, there are two relationship classes *cleared* and *classified* that assign a (*confidentiality*) *security level*
(sometimes also called a *label*) to each identifiable, registered *subject* and each
controlled *object*, respectively. A security level l is an abstract entity, taken from
the domain SL of a finite partial order $\leq_{SL}$. Security levels can have two different,
though closely connected meanings and are used to characterize subjects and
objects as follows:

- A security level assigned to a *subject* as a *clearance* roughly expresses a degree
  of *trustworthiness* (concerning confidentiality) of the subject.
- A security level assigned to an *object* as a *classification* roughly expresses a
  degree of *sensitivity* (concerning confidentiality) of the object.

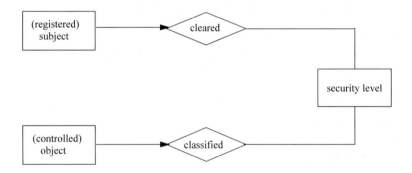

Fig. 9.30. ER model of the relationship classes *cleared* and *classified* for mandatory access
control

The definition of the security levels and the partial order on them should reflect the
organizational needs. On behalf of the organization under consideration, an administrator has to evaluate the trustworthiness of subjects (concerning their will and
capability to preserve confidentiality) and the sensitivity of objects (concerning the
need to preserve confidentiality), and then the administrator has to consistently
express his evaluations by appropriate clearances and classifications.

The partial order on security levels serves two purposes. On the one hand, orderings (of the form $l_1 \leq_{SL} l_2$) can express *relative trustworthiness* ("less trustworthy than") and *relative sensitivity* ("less sensitive than"). On the other hand, and more importantly, connecting the two meanings, the orderings determine the *access decisions* of a control component: a request is *permitted* only if the trustworthiness of the *requestor* suffices for the sensitivity of the object to be accessed, i.e., the postulated properties of the subject are expected to cover the protection requirements for the object; all other requests are *prohibited*. In this way, every single request is *mandatorily* controlled, without any exception.

More formally, access decisions should strictly enforce the *security policy* that information flows must respect the orderings between security levels, or, more precisely, that

information may flow from an item with level l_1 to an item with level l_2 only if $l_1 \leq_{SL} l_2$.

Apparently, in order to deal with this goal, for each possible operation we have to know exactly the direction of the potential information flows. The most elementary point is that *reading* causes an information flow from the accessed object to the requesting subject, whereas *writing* causes an information flow from the requesting subject to the accessed object. More generally, each possible operation must behave either like reading or like writing, and, accordingly, a function `mode` has to correctly assign either the operational mode `read` or the operational mode `write` to an operation. The following procedure then determines *access decisions*:

```
function decide(subject, object, operation): Boolean;
if     mode(operation) = read
then   return classification(object) ≤_SL clearance(subject) fi;
if     mode(operation) = write
then   return clearance(subject) ≤_SL classification(object) fi.
```

For this declaration, the function `decide` is implicitly assumed to be supported by a conceptual *knowledge base* on permissions and prohibitions that suitably materializes the pertinent `cleared` relationships of the form (*subject, clearance*) and `classified` relationships of the form (*object, classification*). The achievements of the function are often briefly referred to as the *read-down/write-up rule* for *upwards information flow*.

At first glance, the mandatory approach seems to be ideally designed for controlling information flows by means of controlling access rights. However, the achievements are debatable for at least three reasons:

• First, the achievements rely on strong suppositions concerning a common understanding of security levels by all administrators and on correct assignments of operational modes to all operations. For complex and distributed applications, these suppositions are hardly fully satisfiable.

- Second, often the achievements are far too restrictive, since they essentially allow only *unidirectional* information flows and thus, in general, prevent full back and forth communications between cooperating participants.
- Third and conversely, the achievements might turn out nevertheless to be too weak, since potential *inferences* about the results of permitted operations, i.e., reading or writings, are not captured in general. As an example, in Section 5.6 we treat an approach to *inference-proof* label assignments for items of an information system. This approach also comprises the concept of *polyinstantiation* to resolve conflicting requirements of confidentiality and integrity.

9.8.1 Dynamic Mandatory Access Control

The considerations in the preceding subsection assume that an object is *statically* assigned a fixed security level as its *sensitivity*. These considerations can be refined by capturing the *dynamic* evolution of the sensitivity during a sequence of operations. As an important example, dealing with such an evolution can be reasonable if the object is treated as a *container*, which initially might even be empty, and is subsequently "filled" with sensitive data. In that case, we could successively increase the classification for the object like a *high-water mark*, according to the most sensitive information that has ever flowed in.

Basically, such a treatment corresponds closely to the considerations of carriers, labels and expressions presented in Subsection 5.1.6 for programming languages and the application for dynamic monitoring exemplified in Subsection 5.1.7. As in those subsections, it is highly convenient to postulate that the partial order $\leq_{SL}$ on the domain SL of security levels even forms a finite lattice, in particular for guaranteeing the existence of *supremums* (*least upper bounds*).

In principle, for each container object, we would like to keep track of which items the current content of the container actually depends on. As an efficient approximation, however, for each container object co we can maintain only a *dynamic* (high-water mark) security level $sl_{co}(t)$, where t denotes the time parameter, according to the following rules for reading and writing:

- If some data is *read* from the container at some point in time t, that data inherits the container's current security level $sl_{co}(t)$ as its *dynamic classification*.
- If some data d, supposed to carry some security level sl_d, is *written* to the container at some point in time t, then the container's security level is updated to the least upper bound of the container's previous level and the data's level, i.e.,

$$sl_{co}(t) := sup_{SL}\{ sl_{co}(t-1), sl_d \}.$$

As a crucial issue, it remains to specify convincingly how the data d to be written obtains its dynamic classification sl_d.

The rule for reading already suggests a partial answer: if d is just read and then written without any further interactions, we can take the inherited dynamic classification. Similarly, if d results from performing some operation op on the arguments a and b, each of which has only been read before the operation, then we can take

the supremum of the inherited dynamic classifications. The latter procedure gener-
alizes to arbitrary expressions, yielding the supremum of all the inherited dynamic
classifications involved.

A full answer has to deal with the situation where some subject actively participates in forming the data to be written. If the participation is supposed to be
restricted to just persistently storing previously read data over time, every subject
could be treated like a container. Each subject su then obtains a dynamic security
level $sl_{su}(t)$ as well, governed by the same rules as for container objects. Otherwise, if a subject is supposed to dynamically "generate" new data, we can argue
that the data inherits either the subject's static clearance or some lower label.

Combining the static approach to mandatory access control with the dynamic
features outlined above, we can model the overall situation roughly as follows:

- Each subject su obtains a static security level $clearance(su)$ expressing its *trust-worthiness*.
- Each container object co obtains a static security level $classification(co)$ expressing its *initial sensitivity*.
- All operations are monitored by a *control automaton* whose internal *states* are composed of the dynamic security levels $sl_{co}(t)$ and $sl_{su}(t)$ for each container object co and each subject su, respectively.
- For $t=0$, the starting state is formed by initializing the dynamic security levels such that the following holds:

$$sl_{co}(0) \quad := \quad classification(co), \quad \text{for each container object } co, \text{ and}$$

$$sl_{su}(0) \quad \leq_{SL} clearance(su), \quad \text{for each subject } su.$$

- An access request issued at time $t>0$ is decided according to the current state resulting from time $t-1$, similarly to what is done in the static approach, and a state transition reflecting the decision is performed, as sketched for the dynamic features. More specifically, the following rules are enforced.
- If a subject su requests to *read* from a container object co, then

the access is permitted   iff $sl_{co}(t-1) \leq_{SL} clearance(su)$,

and in the case of a permission, we set

$$sl_{su}(t) := sup_{SL} \{ sl_{su}(t-1), sl_{co}(t-1) \},$$

leaving all other components of the state unchanged.
- If a subject su requests to *write* to a container object co, then

the access is permitted,

and we set

$$sl_{co}(t) := sup_{SL} \{ sl_{su}(t-1), sl_{co}(t-1), l \}, \text{ where } l \leq_{SL} clearance(su),$$

leaving all other components of the state unchanged.

Evidently, such a model satisfies a *security invariant (for confidentiality)* of the
following kind:

$$sl_{su}(t) \quad \leq_{SL} \quad clearance(su), \quad \text{for each subject } su, \text{ at any point in time } t.$$

This invariant ensures that each subject sees only data which results from operating on arguments whose sensitivities have been classified as lower than or equal to the clearance of the subject.

Models of this style can be attributed to Bell and LaPadula, who carefully elaborated a sophisticated version in a seminal study. In this study, these authors explored the fundamental concepts of a "secure state", basically characterized by satisfying a security invariant as set out above, and a "secure action", essentially characterized by preserving the invariant as outlined above. In particular, a *(star)-security property* was enforced, requiring the following:

Reading an object and subsequently writing to another object   (9.1)
is permitted only if
the label of the former object is lower than or equal to the label of the latter object.

The *Basic Security Theorem* then affirms that starting a system in a secure state and employing only secure actions guarantee that the system is "secure", i.e., the system always satisfies the invariant.

9.8.2 Downgrading and Sanitation

A pure mandatory approach enforces unidirectional information flows only, namely in the direction from lower-labeled items to equally or higher-labeled items. Many applications, however, require exceptions from the strict principle to be allowed.

For example, a controlled object might contain data representing some critical information to be kept top secret for some time. But, over the years, the information ages and thus becomes less critical, or even is supposed to be made public. In that case, some *downgrading* of the object is due, i.e., the original classification label "top secret" is substituted by "unclassified". The downgrading may possibly be preceded by *sanitation*, i.e., the data is inspected for parts that are still critical, which are then individually removed or suitably replaced by harmless variants.

Another example of downgrading refers to a subject that acts in highly critical missions for some time but subsequently is given a less critical task. Accordingly, the subject first needs a "top secret" clearance, but later on this clearance is downgraded to "confidential" only.

More generally, both subjects and objects can be *downgraded*, i.e., have a lower security level assigned, possibly after being suitably *sanitized*, i.e., being somehow modified. Usually, downgrading and sanitation are performed by special subjects that are considered as *trusted*. In this context, the technical meaning of "trusted" is that the respective subject is *exempted* from obeying the pure rules of mandatory access control.

Clearly, downgrading may violate the basic security property that ensures information flows from low to high only. Accordingly, in the presence of downgrading, only suitably relaxed formal security properties are still valid; in the extreme case, there are no formal guarantees of confidentiality anymore. However, from a practical point of view, a "trusted" subject is supposed to act consciously in order to preserve the "practically needed" confidentiality nevertheless.

9.8.3 A Dual Approach to Enforcing Integrity

Using *confidentiality* security levels, the mandatory approaches preserve *confidentiality* in the following sense: some data – and, neglecting inferences, the information represented therein – contained in or accessed by an item can be forwarded only to those other items that have been assigned the same or a higher security level, and, accordingly, the data is inaccessible to all other items (which have a strictly lower or an incomparable security level). In other words, such data can potentially be distributed to exactly the equally or higher-labeled items.

In particular, such data can be written into these items. Consequently, in principle, all these items can be modified as the effect of such writings, and thus are subject to concerns about their *integrity*. In fact, in general, integrity will evidently not be preserved. This obvious observation is closely related to the theoretical results about the close relationship between the notion of "(no) information flow" and the notion of "(non)interference", as presented in Section 5.7. Roughly summarized, these two notions are dual in the sense that there might be an information flow from some item a to another item b if and only if item a might interfere with item b (i.e., a might have an impact on the behavior of b).

Hence, for preserving *integrity*, we have to fully *dualize* the mandatory approaches, including the procedure for access decisions. Accordingly, for enforcing integrity, *reading* is allowed upwards, i.e., from equally or higher-labeled items, and *writing* is allowed downwards, i.e., to equally or lower-labeled items. Thus, for integrity, a *read-up/write-down rule* for *downwards interference* is employed.

If the interests *both* of confidentiality and of integrity are essential for an application, then the respective "read-down/write-up rule" and "read-up/write-down rule" have to be jointly applied. As a result, only accesses within the set of equally labeled items are allowed, and all others are prohibited, independently of whether the operational mode is read or write. Clearly, this result can be rather restrictive, thereby possibly impeding the wanted application functionality.

As a partial remedy, the use of a separate set SL_{int} of *integrity security levels* has been proposed. The meanings of such levels are defined similarly to those of (*confidentiality*) *security levels*, but with an emphasis on the interest of *integrity*:

- An integrity security level assigned to a *subject* as a *clearance* roughly expresses a degree of *trustworthiness* of the subject concerning preserving the *integrity* of items.
- An integrity security level assigned to an *object* as a *classification* roughly expresses a degree of *sensitivity* of the object concerning the need for its *integrity* to be preserved.

In general, trustworthiness and sensitivity concerning confidentiality and the corresponding concepts concerning integrity might differ essentially, and, accordingly, both kinds of security levels should be applied in parallel, simultaneously following the rules for *upwards information flow* and *downwards interference*, respectively.

9.9 Bibliographic Hints

Basically all textbooks on security in computing systems contain introductory sections on access rights; see Section 1.7. General surveys of access rights are provided by Sandhu/Samarati [429] and Samarati/De Capitani di Vimercati [423]. De Capitani di Vimercati/Samarati/Jajodia [158] give a concise introduction. Numerous contributions deal with a large variety of specific proposals for access rights and investigate their diverse properties. The aspects presented in this section are based mainly on selected references as follows.

The concept of roles goes back to early work on application-oriented discretionary access rights; for example, Biskup/Brüggemann [59, 60] describe a personal model of data that allows one to capture social roles, and Ting [482] and Lochovsky/Woo [326] deal with roles in database management as well.

The current approach to role-based access role (RBAC) has been advocated by Sandhu [430]; it is firstly summarized by Sandhu/Coyne/Feinstein/Feinstein [431], it is proposed for standardization by Ferraiolo/Sandhu/Gavrila/Kuhn [204] and it has been elaborated by many other researchers. The work of Sandhu/Bhamidipati [432], Osborne/Sandhu/Munawar [382], Ahn/Sandhu [10], Saunders/Hitchens/Varadharajan [434], Park/Sandhu/Gail [383], Koch/Mancini/Parisi-Presicce [297] and Sejong/Seog [439] is just a selection.

The Flexible Authorization Framework has been introduced by Jajodia/Samarati/Sapino/Subrahmanian/Bertino [274, 275] and investigated further by, for example, Wijesekera/Jajodia/Parisi-Presicce/Hagström [500]. The Dynamic Authorization Framework stems from the work of Bertino/Buccafurri/Ferrari/Rullo [44, 45].

There are several further logic-oriented approaches. For example, Barker/Stuckey [30] use constraint logic programming, dealing with roles and temporal authorizations; Siewe/Cau/Zedan [446] study composition of policies with temporal aspects; Bertino/Catania/Ferrari/Perlasca [49] employ a logic-oriented model based on C-Datalog, an object-oriented extension of Datalog, to represent and compare discretionary, mandatory and role-based approaches within a unifying framework; and Bonatti/Samarati [96] give a general introduction.

The policy algebra presented has been introduced by Bonatti/De Capitani di Vimercati/Samarati [94]. Biskup/Wortmann [76] sketch a credential-based partial implementation of this algebra. Wijesekera/Jajodia [499] propose the algebra on policy transformations.

Granting and revoking has been studied from various points of view. For example, Griffiths/Wade [241] invent recursive revocation for the early relational database management system System/R; Fagin [197] provides a correction and thorough verification of this invention; Bertino/Samarati/Jajodia [43] study non-cascading revocation in an extended relational framework; and Wijesekera/Jajodia/Parisi-Presicce/Hagström [500] investigate revocation in the Flexible Authorization Framework.

Dynamic and state-dependent permissions arise in many different forms. Some approaches deal explicitly with temporal aspects; for example, Bertino/Bonatti/Ferrari [48] suggest a temporal role-based access control model, and Joshi/Bertino/Shafiq/Ghafoor [286] elaborate various temporal constraints for access control, including several kinds for role enabling/disabling. Bacon/Moody/Yao [29] deal with task appointments in OASIS.

Other approaches monitor information flows; for example, Brewer/Nash suggest Chinese walls [102] for this purpose; Biskup/Bonatti [75] employ controlled query evaluation; and many of the results about controlled statistical query evaluation are surveyed by Leiss [313]; see also Chapter 5.

Various examples of the dynamic aspects of access rights related to processes and procedures can be found in the field of operating and programming systems, for example the following. Ritchie/Thompson [407] introduce UNIX, whose security features are described by Garfinkel/Spafford [216] and many others; see also Section 17.1. Wulf/Levin/Harbison/et al. [502, 503] design and implement HYDRA. McGraw/Felton [339] summarize security in Java, while Gong [236] describes the specific design of stack inspection in Java, Wallach/Felton [493] use a simplified model based on pushdown automatons and Pottier/Skalka/Smith [398] treat a static type-based variant.

Variants of discretionary context selections have been proposed by, among others, Dittrich/et al. [172] for OSKAR, Biskup/Brüggemann [59] for the personal model of data underlying DORIS, and Clark/Wilson [135] for specific commercial applications. Bertino/Ferrari/Atluri [46] exploit a logical language for authorization constraints concerning workflows, whereas Knorr [292] deals with workflows as Petri nets. Biskup/Eckert/Leineweber/Parthe [63, 70, 71, 77] base the enforcement of permissions and prohibitions on a distributed implementation of appropriate finite automatons.

Concerning the analysis of control states, Harrison/Ruzzo/Ullman [250, 251] prove the undecidability in general and exhibit some restricted decidable classes. For the specific take/grant model, Lipton/Snyder/et al. [324, 325, 452, 453] investigate all important aspects. Lockman/Minsky [327, 356] propose the send/receive model. D. Denning [163] provides an early detailed exposition. Biskup [58] observes that some crucial effects of the create operation can be simulated by reflexive privileges. Sandhu [424, 425, 426] investigates the impact of typing. Soshi/Maekawa/Okamoto [456, 457] introduce dynamic typing. Koch/Mancini/Parisi-Presicce [296, 297] study graph-based decision procedures. Jaeger/Tidswell [272] and Solworth/Sloan [455] emphasize the design of manageable systems.

The impact of information flow considerations on access rights management and vice versa is well-known but not always made explicit. Examples of explicit studies are provided by Bishop/Snyder [55, 56] for a flow predicate in the take/grant model; by Biskup [61], comparing several approaches for databases; and by Solworth/Sloan [455], introducing dynamic approvals of mayFlow relationships.

The mandatory approaches are founded on the pioneering formal study of Bell/LaPadula [36, 37]. McLean [342, 343] reconsiders the Basic Security Theorem of that study. Lindgreen/Herschberg [322] present a critical view of the achievements of the study. Sandhu [428] gives a concise summary of the many variants and applications that evolved. The mandatory approach constitutes a challenge for various application systems. As an example, we mention database transaction management, for example studied by, among others, Ray/Ammann/Jajodia [404], Jajodia/Atluri/Keefe/et al. [276] and Bertino/Catania/Ferrari [47].

Olivier/von Solms [377] and Cuppens/Gabillon [147] describe consistent assignment of labels for an object model, taking care of inference control. Lunt/Denning/et al. [166, 329] employ polyinstantiation in SeaView. Winslett/Smith/Qian [501] propose semantics for polyinstantiation based on believing and seeing. See Chapter 5 for further references.

Biba [53] studies the impact of integrity considerations and suggests the dualization of the confidentiality features; again, see also Chapter 5.

10 Elements of a Security Architecture

In this chapter, several lines of reasoning are brought together in order to outline and justify the elements of an exemplary *security architecture* that is based on the techniques of *control* and *monitoring*. In fact, this architecture also includes two other techniques sketched in Chapter 7, namely (the basic usage of) *cryptography* and the amalgam called *certificates* and *credentials*. The relevant reasonings consider mainly

- the abstract design of the three techniques;
- basic technical enforcement mechanisms for achieving *isolation* and, to a minor extent, *redundancy* and *indistinguishability*;
- the basic *vulnerabilities* of computing systems; and
- the need for establishing *trust*.

As a starting point, we first summarize the essentials of control and monitoring and the impact of the other techniques.

The fundamental part of the generic model for the techniques of local control and monitoring, as introduced in Subsection 7.2.2 and visualized in Figure 7.8, is the *control and monitoring component*. This fundamental part is composed of several subcomponents that serve the following purposes:

- *identification* and *proof of authenticity*;
- *knowledge base* on *permissions* and *prohibitions*;
- *knowledge base* on the *usage history*;
- *access decision* and *monitoring*; and
- *result inspection* and *monitoring*.

Besides the fundamental component, the model comprises further important concepts:

- a *trusted* (*message*) *channel* between subjects and the fundamental component;
- a *trusted* (*message*) *channel* between the fundamental component and the controlled objects;
- *tamper-resistant protection* of the fundamental component; and
- the *isolation* of subjects from controlled objects, by means of the fundamental component, which cannot be bypassed.

The techniques of *certificates* and *credentials*, introduced in Subsection 7.2.2 and visualized in Figure 7.10, can be seen as a variant. The two techniques differ mainly in how subjects are represented: in the former techniques, *identities* are used, and in the latter techniques, cryptographic *surrogates* are employed. A cryptographic surrogate is formed by a matching pair of a *secret* or *private* (*signature*) *key* and a *public* (*verification*) *key*, where the public key denotes the pertinent subject in certificates and credentials. The main difference causes further differences; namely, a proof of *authenticity* must refer to surrogates rather than to identities, and the conceptual knowledge base on permissions (and prohibitions) is constituted by the set of granted certificates and credentials and thus is distributed among grantees and the control component.

The main motivation for the differences between the two techniques stems from a variation in the intended applications: the techniques of local control and monitoring evolved for *centralized* computing systems with *registered* and thus known subjects, and the techniques of certificates and credentials was designed for *distributed* computing systems with subjects that are possibly unknown and appear as *strangers*. Clearly, for each single site of a distributed system, the former techniques are still relevant for *local* requests. But in order to deal with *remote* requests from strangers, the individual sites must also contribute to the latter techniques.

Centralized and distributed systems also differ in their requirements and options regarding message *channels*. Whereas in centralized systems the channels can be *physically* protected, at least partially, for enforcing *authenticity*, *integrity* and *confidentiality*, the channels in distributed systems strongly demand *cryptographic* protection. Moreover, the interaction of strangers in distributed systems might make the interests of *anonymity* and *non-observability* important, thereby adding further requirements for the channels. Having these summarized essentials of the techniques in mind, in the rest of the chapter we exemplify the exploitation of some basic technical enforcement mechanisms as countermeasures to the vulnerabilities of unprotected computing systems, and we outline how the participants involved can gain *informationally assured* trust in the final achievements.

In doing so, we first sketch a *layered design*, covering the whole range from a hardware basis to an application system. This design is fictitious in the sense that we have tentatively integrated some essential proposals for the individual layers into a larger framework. Notably, this framework does *not* reflect an actually implemented and approved architecture, but only models the author's understanding of how the various security mechanisms could fit together. Clearly, other researchers and practitioners might have differing opinions, and only a fully implemented and carefully evaluated system could finally solve any disputes. This task, however, is far beyond the scope of this monograph, and even beyond what we can expect from the community as a whole, unfortunately.

Second, we reconsider some selected topics in more detail, with an emphasis on *distributed systems*. More specifically, after briefly reviewing centralized access rights management and access control, we summarize and discuss the security services in middleware, the usage of certificates and credentials with the delegation of control privileges, and the design of firewalls. The issues of monitoring are treated in a separate chapter. As before, we concentrate on concepts and mostly refrain from describing implemented systems, examples of which are presented in Chapter 17, covering UNIX, Oracle/SQL, CORBA, Kerberos, SPKI and PGP.

10.1 Establishing Trust in Computing Systems

The concept of *trust* is fundamental to *social relationships* between *human individuals*. The concept also extends to relationships between an individual and a *community* of individuals, and between communities. Usually, trust is a directed concept, such that one part trusts another one but not necessarily vice versa. Concerning the trusted part, the concept also applies to entities that are neither individuals nor communities but instead are real-world *things* or human *artefacts* such as components of a *computing system*. In such cases, trust in an individual or community is often transferred to trust in an entity under the control of that individual or community. Or, seen conversely, trust in an entity really means trust that the controlling individual or community assures the properties of the entity that are expected in the trust relationship.

As already revealed by common language, trust has many facets. For example, we say that an individual "trusts in a friend", that a society "trusts in God" or that a community "trusts that" it will achieve a goal. Language also indicates the modality of a personal decision, for example when we say that an individual "has put his trust" in a helpful companion. This modality is also revealed when speakers distinguish between *trustworthiness* and trust. Trustworthiness is then often seen as a useful, more objective and fact-oriented precondition for the more subjective concept of trust. But we all also know examples of "blind trust".

Over the centuries, traditional disciplines such as theology, philosophy, sociology and linguistics have gathered enormous insight into the concept of trust. So have all other forms of socially traded experience, for example fairy tales, literature and religious sermons. Moreover, the concept has variations in legislation and law enforcement, and in many other fields as well. Though all this insight and experience is highly useful in the computing context too, in the following we shall concentrate on roughly sketching four selected aspects of trust in a computing system or a component of it.

Trust is *directed toward* a specific entity. This entity might range from being conceptual, such as a security policy seen as security requirements or a specification of *wanted* behavior, to being implementational, such as a concretely installed system with its *actual* behavior. Notably, any such entity, and suitable combinations as well, can be treated as a *target of evaluation* according to *security evaluation criteria* such as ITSEC or CC.

Trust can be partially *based on* various other concepts, including knowledge, experience, and social and legal rules. Preferably, the other concepts should introduce more objective and fact-oriented foundations, and thus they should meet suitable qualifications. For example, *knowledge* should be evaluated, verifiable and public; *experience*, whether personal or reported, should be controlled or reproducible; and *social* and *legal rules* should be normative and widely accepted. Again, we note that such bases for trust are required to be provided for the purpose of an *evaluation* procedure according to ITSEC or CC.

Trust can be *assured* by parties that are not directly involved in the relationship. Such assurances might include established forums of *public discourse* as provided within a civil society, *liability rules* as declared by civil law, or *law enforcement* on the basis of criminal law. *Security agencies* that are responsible for security evaluation criteria such as ITSEC and CC contribute as well.

Trust is *assigned by* principally free and (hopefully) informed decisions from among several alternatives. When assigning trust, an individual often acts by personally adopting a social agreement or a recommendation of a third party. An example of a specific foundation of a decision is the *assurance level* determined by a security agency as the result of a security evaluation.

Given the aspects sketched, we can tentatively summarize an *informational concept* of *trust* in a technical target such as a component of a computing system as follows, and as visualized in Figure 10.1:

- The following items can serve as a foundation for *trustworthiness* of a target of interest:
  - a security policy that meets explicitly claimed interests;
  - an appropriately designed and reliably implemented functionality;
  - verified knowledge;
  - justified experience;
  - compliance with social and legal rules; and
  - effective assurances.

- On the basis of the trustworthiness of a target, an individual or a community may *decide to put trust* in that target, roughly meaning the following: the decider's own behavior is firmly grounded on the expectation that the target's current or future actual behavior – which is often fully or at least partly hidden and thus only partially observable – will match the specified or promised behavior.

- Trust in the technical target is inseparably combined with trust in the agents controlling that target.

While trust is preferably based on trustworthiness, trust itself constitutes the basis of further consequences, which might be behavioral or intellectual. *Behavioral* consequences are shown in the way the trusting entity acts in an environment that is affected by the target of trust.

Intellectual consequences appear in formal or informal reasonings that take the expectations of assigned trust for granted and exploit them as suppositions for further inferences. Typically, in such reasonings we aim to distinguish at least three categories:

- suppositions that are somehow *known* to be valid;
- suppositions that are *assumed* to hold by assigned trust; and
- *logically derived* consequences of the first two kinds of supposition.

As a result, we obtain assertions of the form: "If the assigned trust is indeed justified, then some properties expressed by the consequences are always enforced".

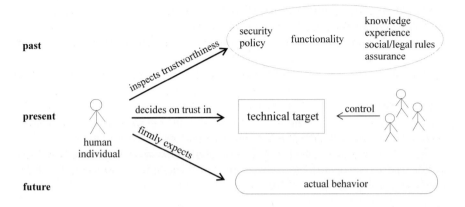

Fig. 10.1. Some aspects of an informational concept of trust

Clearly, such assertions are more useful the less restrictive the trust assumptions and the more powerful the consequences are. Speaking more practically, we would like to *minimize* the trust needed while simultaneously *maximizing* the properties achieved concerning the functionality and security of our computing system. In the extreme case, we might even prefer to get rid of trust altogether and base all our achievements on firm knowledge. However, common sense indicates that this goal is impossible to achieve in general. Moreover, when reasoning about security, this extreme wish is even substantially inappropriate: we want to ensure security properties of computing systems that might include potentially *threatening* and actually *attacking* opponents; clearly, we *explicitly* do *not* trust these opponents.

Being aware of threats and attacks in a potentially hostile computing environment, we nevertheless still want to cooperate with others, and thus we need at least some well-selected trust, which should be both *minimized* and *justified*. A common approach aims at establishing reasonable *trust reductions*: an individual or community

- identifies small parts of a computing system, if possible preferably under their direct control, as indispensable targets of trust,
- and then argues that the wanted behavior of the whole system is a consequence of justified trust in only these small components.

Later on in this chapter, we shall fully describe two of the main streams of reduction of the whole system to small parts. Here, we shall only outline these streams.

First, for *control* and *monitoring*, the starting point might be an overall computing system consisting of clients, servers, networks and many other components. The reduction chain might then span, stepwise, a distributed application subsystem, the underlying operating system installations, the operating system kernels and. finally, the "reference monitors" that implement access control within a kernel. Furthermore, the reduction might be extended to hardware support for the monitoring functionality, to "trusted platform modules" for enforcing the authenticity and integrity of the running installation, and to personal computing devices for storing and processing cryptographic secret keys. Along the chain, usually, various individuals and communities are responsibly involved in designing, implementing and maintaining the above items.

Second, for *cryptography*, we might take the same starting point, and then consider the reduction chain spanned by cryptographic mechanisms, cryptographic key generation and distribution, and storing and processing secret keys. Again, various individuals and communities are responsible for the various items. Moreover, there is an obvious link between the first chain and the second at the roots.

An additional third stream of reduction arises in relation to the techniques of *certificates* and *credentials* when licensing and delegation for issuing digital documents are exploited. Then we see "trusted superauthorities" and trusted third parties, but also instantiations of "self" at the roots.

Nearly any attempt to reason along reduction chains is faced with the *transitivity problem* of trust: stated abstractly, given that A trusts B and B trusts C, we are challenged with the problem of drawing a conclusion about the trust relationship between A and C. Usually, transitivity is urgently needed but unfortunately not always justified.

Moreover, we are faced with the *well-foundedness problem* of trust: stated abstractly, given an iterative and transitive descending chain of trust, we have to cut the chain somewhere, select the current item as a candidate for a root of trust and then decide to actually put our trust in that selected root.

10.2 Layered Design

Our exemplary, fictitious architecture spans from a hardware basis to some application software. Regarding distributed computing, the design conforms to a variant of the ISO/OSI model. Figure 10.2 presents a rough overview, indicating selected tasks of the layers, which are outlined as follows in a top-down view.

We suppose that the overall security requirements of an *application* are expressed by an *application security policy*, abstractly specifying the pertinent *permissions* and *prohibitions*. In general, to enforce its policy, the application relies on the lower layers in two ways, implicitly and explicitly. It relies implicitly, so far as the application aims to handle security on its own (not shown in Figure 10.2). The responsible mechanisms must then be appropriately protected in lower layers; in particular, the corresponding processes must be strictly isolated. Furthermore, if cryptography is employed, the key management must be protected. The application relies explicitly on the lower layers, so far as the application only provides the parameters for the security mechanisms in the lower layers. The application security policy must then be correctly translated into the options offered for the pertinent parameters.

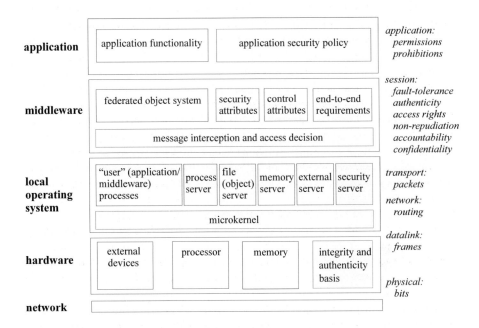

Fig. 10.2. A layered component of a distributed computing system, where the layers are annotated (in italics) with related ISO/OSI terms and selected tasks

In the supporting *middleware*, this policy is expressed in two ways: first, in terms of access rights, i.e., by the security attributes of principals that can be authenticated and by the control attributes of objects with their methods; and second, by the properties of the dynamically established end-to-end connections between principals for exchanging messages, regarding, besides authenticity, also integrity, non-repudiation, accountability and confidentiality. Moreover, fault-tolerant protocols might also support the interests of availability and integrity. Regarding access rights, the basic enforcement mechanism employs message interception and subsequent access decisions. Regarding secure end-to-end connections, cryptographic mechanisms such as encryption and digital signatures are used. Again, the middleware relies on the lower layers.

The *local operating system* provides a virtual platform for executing the (programs of the) application and the middleware as processes which access files or more general objects. Processes and files (objects) are managed regarding a virtual memory, to be mapped onto hardware memory, and external devices are driven so as to offer basic input/output operations. Accordingly, the security server deals mainly with access rights of processes to perform operations on files (methods on objects) and external devices, and it controls and monitors the actual access requests both for the operations on files and for the control operations on access rights. Still, like all other processes, the "user" processes as well as the server processes, the processes of the security server cannot directly enforce their rules on the hardware but need to employ the microkernel. Horizontally, this microkernel mediates all messages between processes, and vertically, it completely wraps the actual hardware.

Finally, the *hardware* physically performs all actions specified by the virtual software layers. It also provides the tamper-resistant foundation of all security mechanisms. In particular, the control operations and the final enforcement of access decisions are grounded on physical memory protection and privileged instructions. Moreover, an *integrity and authenticity basis* assists in ensuring basically the following: the upper software layers are configured as expected; the needed cryptographic keys are appropriately generated, stored and employed; and the computing system is both globally identifiable and bound to its (human) owner.

10.2.1 Integrity and Authenticity Basis

The *integrity and authenticity basis* should supply the wanted assistance in a physically *tamper-resistant* or at least *tamper-evident* way. Accordingly, its services must be provided in specially protected hardware, comprising its own dedicated processor and shielded storage, firmly attached to the traditional hardware parts. In order to be *interoperable*, the hardware of the integrity and authenticity basis must be standardized, to be employed by both the respective *owner* and all potentially *cooperating participants*.

In some sense, an instance of it physically supports the *security interests* of its owner and, at the same time, the possibly *conflicting interests* of the owner's cooperation partners. In other terms, an owner uses the integrity and authenticity basis for his own purposes but also accepts that others might exploit this basis for *observing* or even *controlling* the owner's behavior. Which aspects prevail depends finally on two main factors: is the actual hardware basis generic enough to ground more dedicated security mechanisms in software for both sides, and will the *information society* agree on fair *informational assurances* for *multilateral security*?

In this monograph, we introduce the term "integrity and authenticity basis", *IAB* for short, as an abstraction of the ongoing and to some extent controversial development of a *trusted platform module*, *TPM*, which is being undertaken by a strong group of IT companies. Our abstraction concentrates on viewing an IAB as a tool for physically founding the classical notions of *identification* or *classification* and *proof of authenticity*, as presented in Section 7.1, and for considerably extending these notions.

Classically, *identifiers*, assigned *properties* (*attributes*) and *cryptographic keys* have been the fundamental concepts. As an extension, an IAB exploits the actual *configuration state* of the attached computing system, including substantial parts of the operating system or even higher-layer software components, as a further fundamental concept. Accordingly, a system can be distinguished not only by externally attributed identifiers or properties but also by its *actual being as it is*.

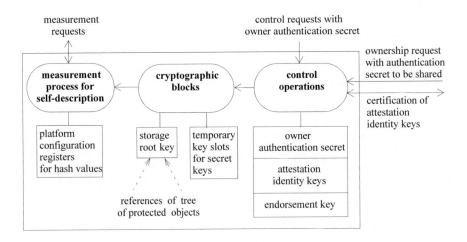

Fig. 10.3. The main functions and the corresponding protected registers of an integrity and authenticity basis (an abstraction of a "trusted platform module")

Furthermore, on the one side an IAB explicitly demands worldwide *global identification* of an instance of the basis, and on the other side it requires a *personalization* by binding a (human) individual to an instance as its owner. These extensions raise controversies; in particular, the exclusion of systems (and their owners) from services owing to discriminations is suspected, for example because a "commercially correct state" is missing; and breaches of *privacy* or even personal surveillance may occur.

In our abstraction, an IAB has three main functions, which are visualized in Figure 10.3 and can be roughly outlined as follows.

First, an instance of the basis enables the attached system to generate and store a tamper-resistant *self-description* regarding its actual *configuration state* at a specific point in time, typically after booting or reconfiguration. Technically, the configuration state is represented by a sequence of chained hash values that are iteratively computed from suitably defined software components by a *measurement process*. These hash values are stored in protected registers, called *platform configuration registers*.

Afterwards, both the owner and any other suitably authorized participants can compare the stored self-description with another description: either a normative one for checking the system's *integrity* in the sense of *correct content*, or a current, regenerated one for checking the system's *integrity* in the sense of *detection of modification*. In the former case, some appropriate "norm" is needed. For example, the owner might consider a description of the expected software components, which the owner selected for his system owing to a certified security evaluation according to the Common Criteria. Cooperating participants might be interested in the same norm, in order to convince themselves of the uncorrupted state of their partner, or they might prefer some "proprietary norm", in order to restrict the cooperation at their discretion.

Second, an instance of the basis encapsulates and protects implementations of basic *cryptographic blocks*, including the key generation, storage and employment that is applicable. These blocks are used in a dedicated way for specific purposes, which include the following:

- symmetric encryption and decryption for internal data,
- asymmetric decryption for external messages,
- asymmetric authentication (digital signatures) for external messages,
- anonymization by using public (authentication) keys as pseudonyms,
- random sequences for key generation and nonces,
- one-way hash functions for generating the self-descriptions as hash values, and
- inspection of timestamps by a built-in timer.

This cryptographic functionality corresponds closely to the needs of a *personal computing device* that enables its holder to autonomously enforce his security interests while cooperating in the presence of threats.

In order to store cryptographic keys and other data to be kept secret, an instance of the basis maintains a tree structure for *protected objects* that is rooted in an asymmetric key pair, called a *storage root key*. Whenever a new child object is generated, its secret part is encrypted with the encryption key stored in the parent object. The main secret at the root node of the tree, i.e., the storage root key, is securely held in the basis, whereas all other nodes (where the secret parts are encrypted) are stored outside the basis, and thus the tree structure might grow arbitrarily. To employ a secret key stored as part of a protected object, the corresponding ciphertext is loaded into the basis, decrypted there using the decryption key stored in the parent object and then passed as a parameter to the pertinent cryptographic algorithm. To conveniently keep secret keys temporarily accessible, the basis maintains several protected registers, called *key slots*.

Third, on the one hand, an instance of the basis is globally identified by a physically implanted, in general unchangeable, and worldwide unique asymmetric key pair for encryption and decryption, called the instance's *endorsement key*. Accordingly, the *public* (encryption) part of the endorsement key can serve as a persistent *global identifier* of the instance, and the instance is uniquely *distinguished* as the holder of the *secret* (decryption) part of the endorsement key, and thus as the sole receiver of messages exclusively devoted to that instance.

On the other hand, after the delivery of an instance and before its deployment, that instance has to be taken over by a participant, who is subsequently considered as the unique *owner*. Taking ownership is accomplished by inserting some (preferably random) data into the instance, which then persistently stores this data as an *authentication secret* shared with the owner. The instance recognizes its owner by using the shared secret as *verification data* in a *proof of authenticity*. The owner is exclusively permitted to perform *control operations* on the instance, such as enabling or disabling the instance.

In principle, the binding between an instance and its owner transforms the global identifiability of the instance, a piece of hardware, into the global identifiability of its owner, which might be any participant, and a human individual in particular. Thus all activities of the owner explicitly or implicitly referring to the endorsement key are *linkable*, and finally *accountable* to the owning participant; this is feared to provide the potential for personal surveillance. As a countermeasure, while acting, the owner should be able to involve the endorsement key to only the minimum extent. Basically, this goal is accomplished as follows.

Only the owner is permitted to generate *attestation identity keys*. An attestation identity key is an asymmetric key pair for authentication whose public part serves as a *pseudonym* of the instance and thus of the owner as well. For the purpose of actually employing such a pseudonym, i.e., for digitally signing a message on behalf of the instance, the endorsement key is used exclusively to acquire the needed evidence that the public part of the attestation identity key belongs to an instance satisfying the requirements of the IAB. Hence, when cooperating with other participants in normal mode, the instance (and the owner) appear under pseudonyms while still being able to convince their partners of IAB compliance, and still being able to provide the corresponding functionality, in particular by signing a communicated self-description.

10.2.2 Establishing the Trustworthiness of an Instance

Basically, an instance of an *integrity and authenticity basis* is employed by its owner in three intertwined ways:

- as a *personal assistant*, supporting cryptographic mechanisms at the owner's discretion, including rudimentary identity management for using pseudonyms;
- as an *integrity-checking* mechanism, enabling the owner to compare the actual system configuration with a "normal" one or the configuration after booting or reconfiguration;
- as an *IAB compliance* and *integrity-confirming* mechanism, for convincing cooperating participants of its own trustworthiness without revealing its identification.

In particular, the third way is *multilateral* in the sense that the cooperating participants can be seen as exploiting a strange instance too. In the following, we concentrate on the aspect of multilaterality, i.e., on the one hand, how an instance pseudonymously provides evidence for being in a "trustworthy configuration", and, on the other hand, how a remote cooperating participant inspects the claimed "trustworthiness".

As a prerequisite, both sides should agree on a common understanding of "trustworthiness". In this context, such an agreement basically refers to two features:

- an *accepted standard* for an IAB (more concretely, to the standard for "trusted platform modules", for example), and
- an *accepted configuration state* of a system.

On the basis of this prerequisite, the owner has to present evidence that the features referred to *actually hold* for the specific instance and the current configuration, respectively, such that the inspecting partner is convinced of the evidence (and then either is ready to put his trust in the owner's system or is not). Since his own (system's) properties are involved, the owner cannot provide the needed evidence without external assistance by (*trusted*) *third parties*.

For efficiency, this assistance should be provided *beforehand*, for multiple usage. For interoperability in a distributed environment, the third parties should deliver the assistance in the form of *certificates*, i.e., digitally signed digital documents asserting suitable *static* aspects of the features to be proven. For example, the certified static aspects could include the following tree (and preferably even more), visualized in Figure 10.4:

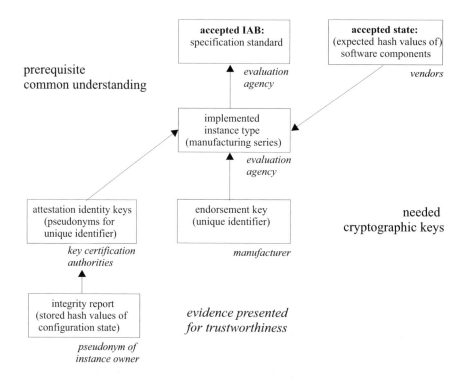

Fig. 10.4. Evidence presented for trustworthiness, and a tree of supported static aspects, as asserted in certificates issued by third parties; the arrows indicate references

- A certificate for the accepted IAB *specification standard* asserting the achievable security properties: this is issued by some public *evaluation* agency.
- A certificate for the conformance of the *implemented instance type* (manufacturing series) with the accepted IAB specification standard: this is issued by some *evaluation* agency, also known as a *Conformance Entity* (and is preferably further supported by certificates regarding the licenses and the performance of the Conformance Entity).
- A certificate for the unique *endorsement key* asserting that this key has been correctly implanted in an instance of the type considered: this is issued by the manufacturer, also known as the *Trusted Platform Module Entity/Platform Entity* (and is preferably further supported by certificates regarding the manufacturer's actual performance with respect to the instance type). If a basis is split into a kernel "module" and a surrounding "platform" delivered by different vendors, two certificates are provided accordingly.
- A certificate for an *attestation identity key* asserting that this key has been generated within an instance of the type considered: this is issued by some key certification agency selected at the owner's discretion, also known as a *Privacy Certification Authority* (and is preferably further supported by certificates regarding the licenses and performance of the certification agency).
- One or more certificates for the *software components* that are captured by the *self-description* asserting the expected hash values of the accepted configuration state, as generated by an instance of the type considered: these are issued by the vendors of those components, also known as *Validation Entities* (and are preferably further supported by certificates regarding evaluations of these components and the performance of the vendors).

On the basis of this assistance of third parties regarding the static aspects, the owner can autonomously provide the remaining *dynamic* aspect in two steps:

- While booting or reconfiguring, the owner's instance generates the hash values of the *self-description* and stores them in the protected platform configuration registers.
- When challenged by a cooperating participant sending a *measurement request* with a nonce for assuring freshness, the owner's instance
  - retrieves the hash values;
  - concatenates them with the received nonce;
  - digitally signs the result with an *attestation identity key*;
  - adds the supporting certificates, except the certificate for the endorsement key for the sake of privacy; and
  - returns all these documents to the challenger as a reply.

In turn, the challenging participant verifies the signatures of the received documents and inspects their assertions. If these assertions conform to the common understanding, the challenger will be convinced regarding the agreed notion of trustworthiness. However, even in the case of conformance, the challenger might still reject the evidence, just by deviating from the supposed agreement. In fact, the *challenge–response* protocol sketched does not require such a prerequisite techni-cally, but only for convenience and fairness.

For achieving multilateral security – respecting the privacy concerns of the owner *and* ensuring that the hash values originate from an instance of the type (manufacturing series) considered – it is crucial that the endorsement key and the corresponding certificate are used only indirectly, namely for acquiring a certifi-cate for an *attestation identity key* from a key certification authority. An initial pro-posal for an acquisition protocol proceeds roughly as follows:

- The *owner's instance* generates an asymmetric key pair for authentication. Then the instance sends a certification request to a key certification authority, com-prising the following items: the public test key of the generated pair; an arbi-trary, owner-selected identifier (as the "real pseudonym"); and the full certificate path from the certificate for the (public encryption part of the) endorsement key, through the certificate for the implemented instance type, to the certificate for the specification standard.

- After successfully inspecting the received items, the *key certification authority* issues a certificate for the public test key, which binds this key to the selected identifier and references the submitted certificates for the implemented instance type and for the specification standard (but *not* the certificate for the endorse-ment key). Intuitively, the issued certificate confirms the required assertion, basically saying that the public test key originates from an IAB-compliant instance.

  In order to securely pass the issued certificate to the requestor, the authority selects a session key, encrypts the issued certificate using this session key, encrypts the session key with the public encryption part of the endorsement key (extracted from the received endorsement certificate) and, finally, returns the two encrypted items.

- The *owner's instance* first decrypts the session key, and then decrypts the certif-icate; *only* this instance, as the *designated* holder of the secret decryption part of the endorsement key, is able to do so.

Whereas this initial proposal employs the endorsement key for encryption and decryption, a variant exploits that key for authentication. Basically, in the first step, the owner's instance signs the request using the secret authentication part of the endorsement key.

In the overall process of establishing trustworthiness, both sides essentially rely on the key certification authority. In particular, the owner expects that the authority will keep their interaction strictly confidential, and the owner's partner expects that the certificate's assertion will actually hold. Reconsidering Figure 10.4, one might wonder whether the gap between an integrity report and the certificate for an instance type could be closed by other means that do *not* require the assistance of a third party, or at least reduce the dependence on the third party. In other words, the challenging question is the following:

How can an owner directly employ his endorsement key, or a suitable variant, to produce a convincing assertion, basically saying that a generated integrity report originates from an IAB-compliant instance, without repeatedly showing the certificate for the endorsement key (and thereby making all his interactions linkable)?

Astonishingly enough, cryptography suggests a positive answer, known as *direct anonymous attestation*, and thus an alternative to the proposal sketched above. Basically, the answer combines two extremes suitably:

- Each IAB uses a *different* key for obtaining a certificate for an attestation identity key, as sketched above for the endorsement key. Linkability and its negative consequences regarding privacy are the apparent drawback, whereas revealing a single key affects only the pertinent IAB.
- All IABs use the *same* key for obtaining a certificate for an attestation identity key, where this key would be uniformly implanted into the IABs by the manufacturer. An individual IAB would then be *indistinguishable* among all complying instances, and thus the actions of an individual IAB would not be linkable. In the case of a malicious or accidental revealing of that single key, a global failure would be the apparent drawback.

The combination dynamically forms *groups* of sufficiently many IABs that share something like a cryptographic *group key*. Then, on the one hand, the activities stemming from a particular group might still be linkable, as in the first extreme (of groups having just one member), but each individual member IAB can hide within its group, as in the second extreme (of one group comprising all IABs). On the other hand, the revealing of a group key would result only in a bounded failure. Moreover, an additional mechanism for *frequency counts* of key usages could be used, aimed at detecting a supposedly suspicious behavior defined by a threshold of an acceptable number of key usages.

The subtle cryptographic details are beyond the scope of this sketch, and even beyond our expositions of authentication and anonymity in Chapter 14 and Chapter 15, respectively.

10.2.3 Personal Computing Devices

An integrity and authenticity basis is just one proposal for adding a further tamper-resistant device to the traditional hardware parts. Other proposals can be summarized by and abstracted to the vision of a *personal computing device*. In fact, these and similar proposals open up a whole range of options. In this monograph, we discuss and compare the abstractions of an IAB and of a personal computing device as two remarkable instantiations of a more general approach. A summary is provided in Table 10.6 at the end of this subsection.

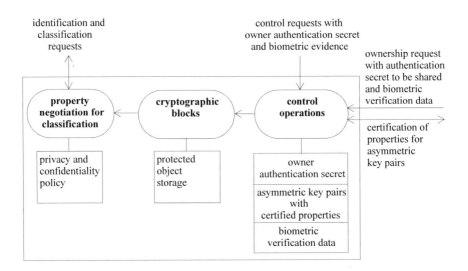

Fig. 10.5. The main functions of a personal computing device

Basically, a personal computing device (*PCD*) assists in ensuring the following. An owning human individual manages his *appearances* regarding *identifiers*, *pseudonyms* and *properties* for the purpose of cooperating with other participants; the needed cryptographic keys are appropriately generated, stored and employed; and since it is only temporarily connected to a larger computing system, the activities of a PCD within the computing system are bound to the controlling human owner of the PCD; this should preferably be based on biometrics. Figure 10.5 visualizes three main functions of our abstraction of a PCD, already indicating some similarities to and differences from an IAB. The main functions can be roughly outlined as follows.

First, a PCD enables an owning human individual to manage and negotiate his appearance contacting a remote participant. Basically, this *identity management* comprises the following:

- accessing the owner's *identifiers*, *pseudonyms* and other *properties*, each of which is bound to (the public part of) an *asymmetric key pair*, where the binding is expressed by a suitable *certificate*;
- managing a *privacy and confidentiality policy*, specifying in which communication contexts which items are permitted or prohibited to be revealed;
- *negotiating properties*, i.e., dynamically deciding on actually showing an item to a potentially cooperating participant.

Declaratively, *property negotiation* for classification aims at either finding an *appearance* in terms of certified properties that satisfy both the owner's policy and the contacted participant's *identification* and *classification* requests, or concluding that such an appearance does not exist. For showing a property, the owner's policy might require conditions that the contacted participant has previously fulfilled some specific identification and classification requests. Additionally, that participant might follow his own policy. In total, each side autonomously expresses *constraints* regarding that side's own and the opponent's properties, the timely coordination of revealing them, and possibly other aspects, and both sides together then want to find a constraint-satisfying solution. The policies might even include a requirement to find a minimal solution, where minimality refers to some measurement of information content. Algorithmically, the negotiation is typically performed as some kind of strategic game in which each side makes a move in turn, while being involved in a rule-based search process.

Second, like an instance of an IAB, a PCD encapsulates and protects implementations of basic *cryptographic blocks*, including the key generation, storage and employment that is applicable. These blocks are used in an owner-determined way; in particular, they enable the owner to autonomously enforce his security interests while cooperating in the presence of threats. Among other things, the cryptographic blocks assist in generating *asymmetric key pairs* to be bound to *properties*, and in establishing *end-to-end encryption* and *authentication* with a suitably prepared remote partner, independently of the services of the intermediate network.

Third, after the delivery of a device and before a deployment, that device has to be *personalized*, i.e., taken over by a participant who is subsequently considered as the unique *owner*. Taking ownership is accomplished in the following ways:

- by inserting some (preferably random) data into the instance, which then persistently stores this data as an *authentication secret* shared with the owner;
- by providing *biometric verification data* regarding the owner, assuming that the device has the necessary sensor and mechanism to generate and process biometric evidence.

The personalized device recognizes its owner by using the shared secret or the provided biometric verification data, or both, in a *proof of authenticity*, depending on the application. Applications requiring the personal and physical presence of the owner strongly suggest a *biometric binding* of the device to the owner. Moreover, a PCD is typically designed for applications where the owner is the only and exclusive user, and thus a purely biometric binding would be possible. However, there are also concerns about biometrics, mainly regarding the quality of the matching procedure presented in Subsection 7.1.5 and the more general vulnerabilities mentioned in Subsection 3.1.1. In particular, biometrics might unintentionally reintroduce a global identifiability and thereby endanger attempts to act anonymously.

In principle, a PCD enables some kind of *anonymity*, since the owner can bind his properties to diverse asymmetric key pairs whose public parts serve as his *pseudonyms*. The privacy and confidentiality policy should then also specify which pseudonyms are permitted to be used under which circumstances. In the end, all activities employing the same key pair are *linkable* by the pertinent cooperating participants, whereas two activities that use different key pairs might remain unlinkable.

Table 10.6. Selected aspects of a tamper-resistant foundation of security mechanisms in personalized hardware devices, and abstracted example choices for an integrity and authenticity basis and a personal computing device, respectively

	Integrity and authenticity basis (as trusted platform module)	**Personal computing device (as vision)**
Focus	(device) instance-centric	(human) individual-centric
Mobility	firmly attached to the hardware of a specific computing system	occasionally connected to various computing systems
Connectivity	normally fully connected	normally physically isolated
Identification	uniquely identifiable device (by endorsement key)	indistinguishable among all devices
Personalization	personalized: individual often holds several ownerships	personalized: individual preferably holds one ownership
Sharing	shared by owner and further users	only employed by owner, as single user
Proof of ownership	personalization by shared owner authentication secret	personalization by shared owner authentication secret and biometric verification data
Pseudonyms	pseudonyms bound to asymmetric key pairs certified as attestation identity keys for device instance	pseudonyms bound to asymmetric key pairs certified at the owner's discretion for owner's properties
Support of interests	balances interests of owner and cooperation partners	favors interests of owner
Observers	general built-in observing facility for partners	only dedicated observer on demand
Appearance	standardized measurement of system's configuration state	policy-driven negotiation of owner's properties
Cryptography	basic cryptographic blocks, with key generation, storage and employment	basic cryptographic blocks, with key generation, storage and employment
Universality	uniformly restricted, mainly by dedicated hardware	discretionarily restricted, mainly by dedicated software

10.2.4 Hardware and Operating System with Microkernel

The enormous computational power but also some basic *vulnerabilities* of traditional hardware arise from *program-storing* and the resulting *universality*; in particular, it enables the *sharing* of computational resources by different participants. In some sense, *operating systems* are invented to manage and discipline the great expressiveness of the *hardware* while preserving it in principle.

Accordingly, an operating system can be designed as a countermeasure to the vulnerabilities, in particular by first *isolating* computational activities and then *controlling* their interactions. In fact, these goals demand careful coordination of the physical hardware basis with the first virtual layer of the operating system. Most importantly, the operating system or, more precisely, a dedicated part of it, should completely shield the hardware. In this subsection we outline the basic approach, using a coarse abstraction, deliberately mixing an idealized vision and the actual, highly sophisticated details found in real systems.

First, we survey some fundamental features of traditional *hardware* and the physical primitives for protecting against the basic vulnerabilities:

- The *central processor* executes a stored program by repeatedly running through the *instruction cycle*: this consists of fetching the next instruction; analyzing and interpreting it by loading some data, performing some basic logical or arithmetic operation, or storing some data; and determining the next instruction.

  As a protection primitive, the processor can be physically set to different *states* (*modes*), such that for each state only a specific subset of the instructions is permitted to be interpreted. There might be only two states, one for "system administration", permitting all instructions including *privileged* instructions, and another for "user activities", prohibiting the privileged instructions. More advanced approaches might employ a refined classification of instructions and their arguments and, accordingly, a larger number of processor states.

- The *main memory* stores all kinds of data, including programs and their runtime information, according to a machine word structure, enabling random read or write access based on specified addresses. As an extension for distributed computing, the facilities of the *physical layer* according to the *ISO/OSI model* are included as well.

  As a protection primitive, memory access can be physically restricted, typically by constraining the currently permitted address range by a *basis register* and a *bound register*, or by constraining the usage of individual memory cells by *memory tags*. A suitable adaptation of this idea applies to access to physical telecommunication lines.

- The *external devices* serve to input or output data to or from the main memory, basically either to communicate with the environment or to persistently save the data, in particular for large amounts that do not fit into the main memory. The processor, the main memory and the external devices are connected by an *internal channel* (a *bus*) that transfers data back and forth.

  As a protection primitive, this channel is physically protected in order to prevent deviation from the channel or other attacks and failures. In particular, the channel between the dedicated external device (typically the keyboard) employed by participants to provide evidence for their authenticity is shielded from both passive and active interception.

- The *initialization* mechanism loads a *bootstrapping* program into the main memory and prepares the processor for running through the instruction cycle, starting with the first instruction of the bootstrapping program.

As a protection primitive, the built-in bootstrapping program is stored in dedicated, physically tamper-resistant or at least tamper-evident *read-only memory*, and the initialization mechanism physically behaves as an *atomic action*, i.e., it is performed completely without any outside interference (or fails totally).

- The *interrupt* mechanism breaks the repetition of the processor's instruction cycle; it is triggered by the external devices for the coordination of internal executions and external events, or it is raised by hardware-detectable error conditions, or it is caused by a special instruction of the currently executed program. More specifically, on an interrupt signal, this mechanism first saves the current configuration of the processor and then prepares the processor for switching to another program.

    As a protection primitive, there is physical support for keeping saved configurations uncorrupted, and for reliably restarting the processor with interrupt routines, including switching the processor from the current state (or mode) into a suitable successor state.

Second, we review the fundamental virtual concepts of an *operating system* and state the respective security requirements:

- A *process* is the activity of executing some possibly changing program, which includes the full lifespan, from being generated, through possibly repeatedly running on the processor and being suspended, waiting and rescheduled, to finally being terminated. A process employs its own process space, i.e., (virtual) memory, basically holding the static program (considered as text) being executed and additional dynamic runtime data. Mainly for the purpose of enhancing efficiency, there are also collections of *lightweight processes*, called *threads*, which have an independent control flow for execution while sharing a program and some dynamic items.

    As a security requirement, process spaces should be strictly *separated*, and processes should *communicate explicitly*, preferably by interceptable messages.

- A *file* or, more generally, an *object*, is the kind of entity a process can access. In elementary cases this is for executing, reading or writing; in more advanced cases, for performing a method declared in the pertinent class. As a special case, *encapsulated external devices* are treated like dedicated objects.

    As a security requirement, access requests should be *controlled* and subject to explicit *access decisions* that are based on declared permissions and prohibitions.

- The *virtual memory* is given by an abstract address space, which is much larger than the physical address space of the main memory but fits into external storage, and is structured into appropriate units, for example using *pages* swapped between the main memory and an external magnetic disk. As an extension for *distributed computing*, the access to *remote services* and *data* is enabled by facilities described by the *transport*, *network* and *datalink* layers according to the ISO/OSI model.

As a security requirement, the mapping of the virtual memory onto the physical memory must respect the necessary *isolation* regarding the process spaces, the communication data of processes, the files and other relevant items, including the separation of "crucial" management and control tasks from "normal" activities. A suitable adaptation of this idea applies to access to the *packets* and their *frames* transported and routed within a connected computer network.

- The special activity of *booting* aims at reproducing a wanted runtime *configuration* of the computing system, including the full operating system after restarting the hardware, i.e., this activity converts the static programs (more specifically, program texts) of the operating system and possibly further software systems, accessed from an external device such as a disk or over a network, into a suitable collection of dynamically generated processes and their process spaces. The booting facility relies on a *self-description* of the operating system and makes it self-reproducing concerning its dynamic appearance. The self-description might extend to the expected external devices, and accordingly the *self-reproduction* then also comprises the recognition and reproduction of the configurations of these devices.

  As a security requirement, the reproduced configuration should be *authentic* and possess *integrity* (be uncorrupted), i.e., the participant pushing the start button should obtain precisely the configuration that he himself, or some administrator acting on behalf of him, has determined previously – without any additions, deletions or substitutions – and in exactly the anticipated form – without any modifications.

Third, we outline how the virtual concepts of an operating system and their security requirements could be implemented using the protection primitives of the fundamental hardware features. As already emphasized before, we are presenting a vision rather than an actual product. This vision complies with a common agreement on concentrating crucial functionality into small, (more) easily manageable subparts of the overall system, often called *kernels*. Whereas in more traditional approaches this agreement typically leads to a *security kernel* (an implemented *reference monitor*) as part of the *operating system kernel*, our vision favors an apparently more promising way, employing an operating system organized as a *microkernel* with a series of dedicated servers on top of it, including a *security server*.

More specifically, this organization partitions the operating system horizontally into two layers. The lower layer, a ("really") small *microkernel*, provides only the most basic services needed to use the hardware, and conversely, any usage of the hardware must be mediated by the microkernel. The microkernel is executed in a *processor state* (*mode*) that permits one to employ all instructions, including the *privileged* ones. In doing so, the microkernel can achieve basically the following: setting processor registers, in particular for switching the processor between processes; capturing hardware interrupts; mediating and controlling messages for interprocess communication; and mapping page references into physical addresses.

The upper layer consists of several mutually separated *servers* that supply the classical operating system functionality, such as the management of processes, files, memory and external input/output devices. These servers send requests for actually accessing the hardware to the microkernel, and they communicate with each other by passing messages via the microkernel. The processes of these components are executed in a processor state that enables only the instructions permitted for user processes.

In some sense, one classical component of an operating system is split into a small, indispensable, hardware-oriented fraction that contributes to the microkernel, and a larger remainder gathered into one of the servers. This splitting applies to the security mechanisms, too. Inspecting the security requirements postulated above, we see that the division of labor between the microkernel and the various servers (hopefully) accomplishes the following properties:

- All kinds of *processes* in the upper layer, the "user" (application/middleware) processes as well as the server processes, are mutually isolated by the microkernel, which fully controls the interprocess communication.
- An *access request* leads to an interprocess communication and is thus controlled by the microkernel, which delegates access decisions and the underlying maintenance of a knowledge base for declared permissions and prohibitions to the security server.
- The needed *isolations* come as a consequence of the specific organization. "Normal" activities are mutually isolated, since their explicit communications must be mediated by the microkernel, and implicit communications are totally prevented by the microkernel's careful address mapping and appropriate interrupt handling. The "crucial" tasks are concentrated in the microkernel, which is suitably separated from the rest of the overall system, in particular by exploiting processor states and careful address mapping.
- Finally, booting into a configuration state that is *authentic* and possesses *integrity* (is uncorrupted) is facilitated by the strict modularization of the whole operating system, which, in particular, offers the ability to load largely independent components, namely the microkernel and the additional servers.

Whatever organization of the operating system is employed, the *granularity* of the controlled *access requests* impacts on the overall achievements too, in particular regarding the support supplied for the upper layers. While traditional operating systems tend to rely on a simple notion of a file and the basic operations of executing, reading and writing, more advanced approaches are based on the principles of *object-oriented programming*, handling objects as dynamically created instances of statically declared classes that define the applicable methods. Moreover, in this case an access request is basically perceived as a *message* sent from (a process or thread executing a method of) one object to another object aimed at invoking a method at the receiving object and possibly getting some data returned. This perception neatly fits both the needs of access control and monitoring, and the actual mechanisms of a microkernel-based operating system with a generic object server.

10.2.5 Booting and Add-On Loading

Booting into a *configuration* that has *authenticity* and *integrity* is a crucial task, and so is the later add-on *loading* of additional software. Basically, booting and loading should result in precisely the configuration the owner (or user) of the system expects on the basis of previous approvals and decisions. And afterwards, on a *measurement request*, the system should be able to produce convincing *evidence* about its actual configuration. In the following, we present an abstract version of several proposals for achieving these goals.

Our abstraction is based on various assumptions, to be ensured by the system designer, the owner and diverse further participants concerned:

- The overall system, seen as a set of programs, is organized into a hierarchical component structure without loops.
- There is one initial component that has *authenticity* and *integrity*, a *bootstrapping* program, evaluated at manufacturing time to be trustworthy, and securely implanted into the hardware, employing a tamper-resistant read-only memory.
- Each noninitial component (program) originates from a responsible source, which can be verified in a *proof of authenticity*. Such a proof is enabled by a certificate referring to the component and digitally signed by the pertinent source.
- Each noninitial component has a well-documented state that can be measured. Such a state is represented as a *hash value*. The expected state, as specified by the source, is documented in the *certificate* for the component.
- Each component, or some dedicated mechanism acting on behalf of it, can perform an *authenticity and integrity check* of another component, by measuring the actual state of the other component and comparing the measured value with the expected value.
- The *hardware* parts involved are authentic and possess integrity, too, which is ensured by additional mechanisms or supposed by assigning trust.
- The *certificates* for the components are authentic and possess integrity.

The basic booting and loading procedure inductively follows the hierarchical component structure. Roughly outlined, after an initialization by the bootstrapping program, the whole system is reproduced componentwise under the invariant that all components loaded so far are authentic and possess integrity, until either the overall goal has been achieved or some failure has been detected. In more algorithmic terms, the initialization and the repetition can be sketched as follows.

1. load initial component;

2. `repeat` [invariant: all components loaded so far are authentic and possess integrity]: after having been completely loaded, a component

   - first checks a successor component for authenticity and integrity, and
   - then, depending on the returned result,
     either   lets the whole procedure fail
     or   loads the checked successor component,

   `until` all components are loaded.

Obviously, the basic procedure allows many extensions and variants, which then require appropriately adapted assumptions. We mention some examples here:

- [Recovery from failures] Instead of exiting on a failure, the procedure might automatically search for an uncorrupted copy of the expected component, if suitable and possible, perhaps even by contacting remote sites via the Internet.
- [Chaining] The hash values, both expected and recomputed, can be chained, superimposing the next value on the previous value, for producing a hash value of a sequence of components, or even of the overall configuration.
- [Data with "integrity semantics"] Besides considering the pure programs (texts) only, the procedure might also inspect further data that is relevant to the overall integrity of the system, such as separately stored installation parameters.
- [Integrity measurement] After loading a component, the procedure might recompute the hash value of the component actually loaded and store this value into dedicated storage for reporting on the components actually loaded.
- [Reporting] The recomputed and stored hash values might be reported to external participants as the current self-description.

The aspects of integrity measurement and reporting are exemplified in more detail for the *IAB* in Subsection 10.2.2. In terms of the industrial proposal leading to the IAB abstraction, reporting responds to a challenging measurement request: starting with the *CRTM* (*Core Root of Trust for Measurement*), each component in a chain measures its successor, securely stores the resulting integrity metric into the *platform configuration registers* of the *TPM*, and then passes control to the successor until all components in the chain are captured.

10.2.6 Network and Middleware

Disregarding many details and variations, we see the *middleware* as a *federated object system* that enable users of the participating local sites to *share* objects in a unified, interoperable manner. We first outline the rough static and dynamic aspects, then consider the impact of distribution and, finally, discuss the resulting features of control and monitoring. The static and dynamic aspects are given roughly as follows:

- The *static* aspects comprise the programs (texts) of the system, including the pertinent class declarations, and the persistently stored (instance) objects.
- The *dynamic* aspects comprise the collection of processes and threads that execute methods of the existing objects, as invoked by passing messages, and the activated (main memory) workspace copies of objects.

These aspects are federated within a distributed environment, providing a homogeneous virtual view of the actual local implementations, which may be spread over potentially many remote sites. Basically, at each site we find the following local situation:

- local hardware (processor, memory, and external devices),
- possibly supported by an IAB or PCD,
- extended by local hardware equipment for *wired* or *wireless connection* to the next *router*, which performs local *bit transmission* and *frame handling* (the *physical* and *datalink layers* according to the ISO/OSI model);
- a loaded operating system,
- extended by loaded software for *local frame handling*, *routing* and *packet services* (the *datalink*, *network* and *transport layers* according to the ISO/OSI model);
- an installed middleware system.

On the basis of the local underlying layers, the middleware offers several services:

- managing the local fractions of the static and dynamic aspects of the system, including *local control and monitoring*;
- enabling interoperability across the participating sites, and also contributing to *global control and monitoring* by regarding incoming and outgoing messages as *access requests*;
- establishing virtual *end-to-end connections* to remote sites, dealing in particular with *fault tolerance*, *authenticity*, *access rights*, *non-repudiation*, *accountability* and *confidentiality* (the *session layer* according to the ISO/OSI model).

All sites together rely on an appropriate informational *infrastructure* of a *network* and the needed *organizational environment*: there are *network servers*, suitably connected by the overall network structure, where, for each site, the site's next *router* has access to one of these servers. Among other things, the infrastructure assists in performing the following tasks:

- with regard to sites (i.e., their extended operating systems), enabling *mutual authentication* using *certificates* for the public parts of *asymmetric key pairs*, and generating and distributing symmetric *session keys*;
- with regard to "user processes", autonomous *tunneling*, i.e., *wrapping* data by encryption and authentication under the mastership of the *endusers* (as proposed for *Virtual Private Networks*, *VPNs*);
- enabling *anonymity*, by employing (the public parts of) asymmetric key pairs as *pseudonyms*, and by dedicated *MIX servers* with *onion routing*.

To summarize, the middleware is essentially supported by both the local instantiations of the underlying layers and the global infrastructure, as displayed in Figure 10.7 in some more detail. As indicated in the figure, the support of the infrastructure is also crucial for the local activities aimed at control and monitoring.

The middleware instantiates the generic model of *control and monitoring*, while taking care of the peculiarities of *distributed computing systems*. First, the *isolation* of participating subjects on the one side and controlled objects on the other side is split into two parts:

- at a subject's site, a *subject*, acting as a *client*, is confined concerning *sending* (messages containing) *access requests*, and

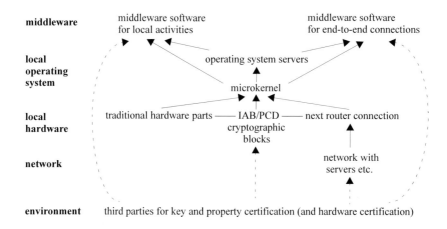

Fig. 10.7. Support relationships for middleware, local sites and global infrastructure

- at an object's site, a target *object*, acting as a *server*, is shielded concerning *receiving* such (messages containing) access requests and then actually interpreting them.

While in principle and following the practice of security enforcement in many other areas, *subject confinement* (*client control*) and *object shielding* (*server control*) can always be implemented by two components, in a centralized system there is usually no advantage to doing so, and, accordingly, confinement and shielding are commonly integrated into a single control component. In a distributed system, however, the two components can operate largely independently and autonomously, hopefully resulting in a double protection.

Second, as a prerequisite for splitting control into two parts, the fundamental relationships between subjects and objects regarding *permissions* (and *prohibitions*) are suitably represented for the purposes of the two complementary views in the distributed approach. As a simple example, a ternary *discretionary* granted relationship (s,o,m) is split into a *privilege* (or *capability*) $[o,m]$ for the subject s and an entry $[s,m]$ for the *access control list* of the object o.

More generally, a subject can be assigned *security attributes*, for example a privilege of the form $[o,m]$, and an object can be assigned *control attributes*, for example an entry of the form $[s,m]$. A similar observation applies to the *clearances* of subjects and *classifications* of objects in the *mandatory* approach. Figure 10.8 visualizes both the centralized and the distributed view. Obviously, in the distributed case, keeping both views *interoperable* becomes even more demanding and challenging than in the centralized case. In particular, both sides must have a common understanding of the concepts and denotations employed, in order that the meaning of a subject's shown properties, as expressed by security attributes, can be related to the meaning of control attributes assigned to an object.

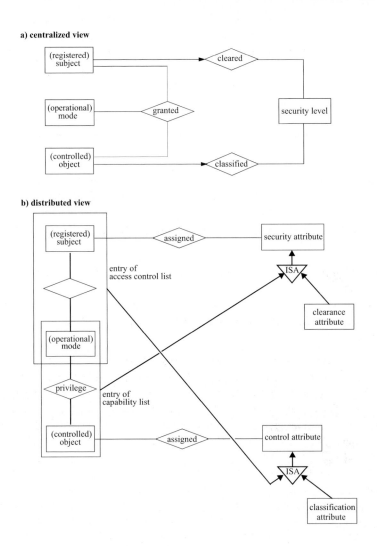

Fig. 10.8. Summarized ER models of fundamental relationship classes for permissions (and prohibitions) in the discretionary and the mandatory approach, reconsidered in a centralized and a distributed view

A split control component still has to inspect an intercepted message for *authenticity*, including the communicated *access request* and the requestor's *security attributes*, among which there might be an *identifier*. This task, the question of interoperability and some further issues are discussed in more depth in Section 10.3, dealing with *certificates* and *credentials* in a more general framework, and they are exemplified for the CORBA middleware in Section 17.3.

Third, once object-oriented *method calling* has been divided into *method invoking* by an *activator* object at the client site and *method executing* by a *target object* at the server site, and the conceptual control component has been split into two parts accordingly, the messages forwarded by the client part can be *intercepted* and inspected further at additional intermediate checkpoints, before eventually reaching the final server part. In fact, *firewalls* can be seen as such intermediate checkpoints, as discussed further in Section 10.4.

Such additional more global control options can only enforce additional *prohibitions*, restricting the autonomy of the sites directly involved. These options also introduce new *vulnerabilities*, since the intermediate checkpoints might turn out to be threatening themselves, or could be corrupted by any other malicious participant. However, decoupling message sending and message receiving could also be exploited to produce *indistinguishability* for the sake of *anonymity*, for example by using *MIX servers*, described in Section 15.4.

Finally, the observations regarding control basically apply for *monitoring* as well, which leads to the concepts of *cooperative intrusion detection* and *reaction*, treated in Section 11.4.

10.2.7 Programming Languages and Programming

Using a layered design, as outlined at the beginning of this section and sketched in Figure 10.2, we might employ numerous instantiations of the upper *application layer*. For example, we might run an information system, a workflow management system or any other system supporting the *informational activities* of the respective participants. More generally, the application layer might evolve from *any program* whatsoever. Furthermore, in the end, the lower layers result from exploiting programs as well. Accordingly, in this subsection we shall refrain from dealing with specific applications, but shall consider the basic tools and generic procedures for engineering programs from the point of view of security instead.

More specifically, we collect together selected aspects of programming languages and their usage in software engineering. Regarding a *programming language*, basically the following features are relevant:

- the *syntax*, i.e., the formal expressions for the constructs of the language;
- the *abstract semantics*, i.e., the constructs ideally offered, assigned to formal expressions as their formal meaning;
- the *implemented semantics*, i.e., the constructs actually usable in an algorithmically available form, for example as provided by a compiler, an interpreter, a runtime system, an execution environment or even some facilities for mobile code;
- the *pragmatics*, i.e., the guidelines for converting an idea of a wanted program behavior into appropriate formal expressions.

Regarding *software engineering*, including "programming", the full design and life cycle of a "programmed system" is important, as introduced in Section 1.5 and Section 1.6, dealing with the following features, among others:

- *compositionality*, *refinement* and related notions;
- *construction principles*;
- *risk assessment*;
- *specification*, *implementation*, *verification* and *maintenance*.

Obviously, "security-aware" engineering should be encouraged and facilitated by "security-supporting" languages and tools. When we aim to produce secure systems by the techniques of control and monitoring, as modeled in Figure 7.8, we first of all have to achieve appropriate explicit *isolation* of acting subjects from controlled objects, complemented by provisional countermeasures against unwanted circumvention of the intended isolation, and explicit *access decisions* about suitably granulated requests.

In a more general perspective, as discussed in Section 1.4, such security mechanisms should lead to a "secure system" that ensures *reliable correctness* (satisfaction of a functional specification even in adverse environments) and *confinement* (absence of harmful computations by modulation, unexpected usage, malicious exploitation of vulnerabilities or related misbehavior). In the following we list useful approaches towards these goals, selectively presenting recommendations regarding the syntax and the abstract semantics, the runtime system and the execution environment of a programming language, and regarding software engineering.

Regarding the *syntax* and the *abstract semantics*, the most general advice is to *discipline* the powerful constructs of a programming language while preserving its *universality*. Though "practitioners" sometimes claim to need highly flexible constructs without any restrictions for the sake of productivity, they rarely master all the intrinsic pitfalls of "tricky programming". Accordingly, the following examples mainly impose well-defined, conveniently manageable structures on a program, thereby prohibiting (or at least discouraging) a hacking style of programming. Most of the features mentioned can be controlled at *compile time*.

- *Object-orientation* contributes a specific kind of *encapsulation*, ensuring that (the data of) an instance object is accessible only by the *methods* declared in the pertinent class.
- Explicit commands for the *lifespan* of instance objects assist in keeping track of the current object population, for example by *generating* (`new`) an instance object with explicit parameters and *releasing* (`delete`) it after finishing its usage, possibly together with *erasing* the previously allocated memory.
- *Modularization* of programs, together with strong *visibility* (*scope*) rules for declarations, crucially supports confinement. Visibility might be classified regarding a class specialization hierarchy. For example, a declaration might be private, public or protected. Roughly outlined, a *private* declaration can only be employed from methods declared in the same class; in principle, a *public* decla-

ration can be employed from outside as well; and a *protected* declaration can be employed from methods declared in the same class or its specializations.

- Strong *typing* of objects and designators, including typed references (disabling "pointer arithmetic") together with disciplined *type embeddings* (*coercions*), prevent unintended usage too.
- *Explicit interfaces* of modules, procedures and other fragments, requiring full parameter passing and prohibiting global variables, shared memory or a related implicit supply of resources, avoid unexpected *side effects*.
- Explicit *exception handling* forces all relevant cases to be handled appropriately.
- For *parallel computing*, (full) *interleaving* semantics and explicit *synchronization* help to make parallel executions understandable and verifiable.
- For supporting *inference control*, whether by static verification or by dynamic monitoring, built-in declarations of *permitted information flows* are helpful.
- If *self-modification* of programs is offered at all, it should be used only carefully, where favorable for strong reasons.

Regarding the *runtime system*, the most general strategy is to cover the crucial *dynamic* aspects that are not statically resolved at compile time, whether such resolution is impossible or not done for other reasons. Additionally, memory management should obey the key idea of isolation. These issues are treated as illustrated by the following examples:

- runtime checks for *array bounds*;
- runtime checks for *types*, in particular for the proper *actual parameters* of procedure calls;
- actual enforcement of *atomicity* (no intervening operations), if supplied by the programming language;
- *dynamic monitoring* of compliance with permitted information flows;
- space allocation in *virtual memory* only, i.e., physical-memory accesses must be mediated by the (micro)kernel of the operating system;
- allocation of carefully *separated memory spaces* (with dedicated *granting* of access rights) for the program (only *execute* rights), its own static own data (if possible, only *read* rights), the *runtime stack* and the *heap*.

Regarding the *execution environment*, we list some further useful features, mainly devoted to protecting against unwanted effects of interacting procedures, modules or programs, in particular if these items originate from resources outside the direct control of the executing site.

Ideally, any executable code should be *digitally signed* by a responsible authority, and preferably also *verified* with respect to its crucial properties and *certified* accordingly. Before loading and executing a piece of code, a local control component should appropriately test the signatures and inspect the certificates. For example, this general advice is followed by the basic *booting* and *loading* procedure sketched in Subsection 10.2.5, and by an IAB's *measurement process* introduced in Subsection 10.2.1 and discussed further in Subsection 10.2.2.

Other proposals apply to *mobile code* that a site has received for execution from a remote source. As far as possible, the control component could also autonomously employ a plausibility evaluation of the received code. This option includes, for example, checking for implanted *computer viruses* or similar *malware*, but also for static features such as proper *typing*.

Once some code has been loaded, the control component should explicitly grant *access rights* (*privileges*) to the executing *processes* with regard to the objects residing in the execution environment, in particular the local assets. For example, each piece of mobile code can be seen as belonging to some known class that in turn is assigned to a locally declared protection domain.

Like a role, a *protection domain* is associated with a set of privileges. Then the executing processes of the mobile code inherit the privileges of the protection domain. An environment might also provide for a special protection domain with an empty or (in some sense) minimally needed set of privileges, called a *sandbox*, assigned to received mobile code as a default. In this case, the execution of the mobile code is (nearly) completely isolated from the hosting environment and thus is maximally confined, guaranteed to leave no (essential) effects in the environment.

Another useful mechanism is *wrapping* of entities evaluated as critical concerning the security requirements considered. Wrapping functions similarly to *encapsulation*, but can be employed with any entity at the discretion of the current execution environment. Basically, and in rough terms, the wrapped entity obtains a new, shielding interface that controls any interaction of the entity with the environment, for example by intercepting and possibly manipulating all messages sent by the entity or entitled to be received by it. In this way, the entity can be confined to executing only activities that are explicitly permitted by the controlling interface, and to requesting accesses accordingly.

Obviously, a *sandbox* can be seen as equivalent to a wrapper that, basically, catches any incoming or outgoing messages.

We should also mention that some instantiations of *dynamic* and *state-dependent permissions,* as presented in Section 9.5, can be interpreted as a feature of the execution environment or the runtime system, depending on one's point of view. In particular, this interpretation is appropriate for dealing with process masterships and procedure calls, discretionary context selection, and workflow control. In each case, the pertinent execution environment keeps track of some part of the entities' *usage history*, and the control component bases its access decisions on the recorded history. As a prominent example, Java *stack inspection* demands that a requested access must be permitted not only for the requesting stack frame but also for all its predecessors on the stack.

Finally, regarding general *software engineering*, the most general advice is to closely follow the spirit of the syntactic and semantic features listed, even if they are not fully enforced or have to be simulated in a suitable form. For example, the following recommendations are helpful:

- explicitly *guarding* external input values and output values;
- explicitly *guarding* values passed for the expected range, well-definedness (e.g. no division by zero and no null pointer references) or related properties;
- elaborating a complete *case distinction* for guarded commands;
- carefully considering *visibility* and naming conventions, in order to avoid unexpected equalities or inequalities;
- handling *error conditions* wherever appropriate;
- restoring a safe execution state and immediately terminating after a security-critical failure has been detected;
- explicitly stating *preconditions*, *invariants* and *postconditions*, in particular for the sake of compositionality;
- *verifying* the implementation with respect to a specification;
- inspecting *executable code* as well, in particular, capturing all interleavings for parallel constructs;
- *certifying* and *digitally signing* executable code, possibly providing a hash value for *measurements*;
- *statically verifying* the compliance with declarations of *permitted information flows*, if applicable.

10.3 Certificates and Credentials

In a distributed system, a specific entity cannot directly see the other entities. In some sense, the (*real*) *world* of the other entities is hidden behind the interface to the communication lines. But the entity can certainly send and receive messages to and from this hidden (real) world. On the basis of these messages, the entity can produce a *virtual view* which is actually visible to that entity. As a consequence, security policies and permission decisions are grounded solely on the locally available visible view of the global (real) world. This outline exposition is visualized in Figure 10.9 and is described in more detail as follows.

An identifiable *entity* in the (real) world might be an *individual*, a *computer* or something similar that can act in the distributed system. An entity may *possess* various *properties* which might be relevant to security policies and permission decisions. In most cases, such properties are *assigned* to an entity by another entity.

In general, neither the entities themselves nor their properties are visible to other entities. Thus we need a notifiable representation of such circumstances. In a *public key infrastructure*, entities are represented by one or more *keys* for *asymmetric cryptography*. More precisely, an entity is uniquely represented and distinguishable from other entities by one or more pairs of *private* and *public keys*: while the entity must keep the private key strictly hidden, that entity uses the matching public key as a *visible surrogate* for itself.

From the perspective of the visible virtual views, these surrogates are called *principals*. In general, an entity may possess several key pairs. For the sake of conciseness, in this section we assume that each entity has exactly one key pair for *dig-*

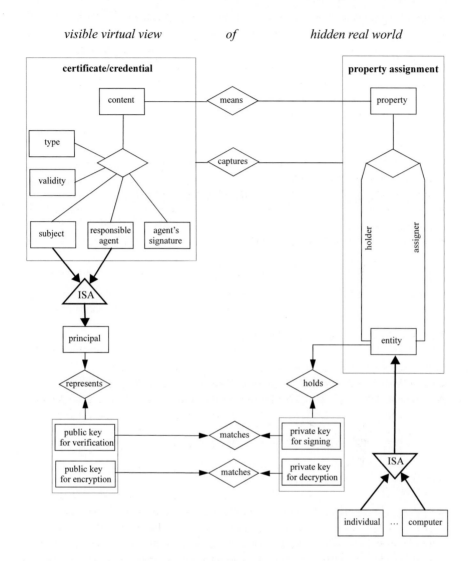

Fig. 10.9. Two faces of a property assignment process: the hidden (real) world and a visible virtual view

ital signatures and one key pair for *encryption*. Hence, a principal is specified here by a *public key for verification*, which is good for proving the integrity and authenticity of messages *from* the entity represented, and by a *public key for encryption*, which is good for sending confidential messages *to* the entity represented.

Then, a property assignment to an entity in the (real) world is *presumably captured by* a *digital document* in the visible virtual world. Such a document is called a *certificate* or a *credential*, depending on the details explained below. In all cases, the document has at least the following fields:

- a *subject* field, which contains the principal that visibly represents the entity under consideration;
- a *content* field, which textually describes the assigned property (where, depending on the concrete format, we can also allow compound properties);
- a field for a *responsible agent*: this field contains the principal that visibly represents the entity that is responsible for the property assignment and has generated and digitally signed the document;
- a *signature* field, which contains a digital signature for the document: the signature is valid iff it can be verified with the responsible agent's public key for verification, i.e., if it has been generated with the matching private key for signing.

Depending on the specific format for digital documents, additional fields are usually needed, for example

- a *type* field, which indicates the meaning of the document and provides further technical hints on how to process the document;
- a *validity* field, which might indicate that the responsible entity limits the property assignment to a certain time period or that the responsible entity otherwise restricts the usability of the document.

In the following subsections, we classify the properties of entities and thus the contents of certificates and credentials according to two aspects. The first aspect deals with properties which characterize entities with security policies in mind. The second aspect touches upon the administration of characterizing properties.

10.3.1 Characterizing and Administrative Properties

We distinguish two kinds of such *characterizing properties*, which are illustrated in Figure 10.10:

- A *free property* is intended to express some feature of an entity by itself (e.g., personal data, a technical detail, a skill or an ability). Other entities may possibly base their security policies and permission decisions on shown free properties, but in general they will not have expressed any obligation as to whether to or how to do so. In particular, possessing a free property usually does not entail a guarantee that a permission for a specific service will be obtained.
- A *bound property* is intended to express some relationship between a client entity and another entity which might act as a server (e.g., a ticket, a capability or a role). Typically, such a server has declared in advance that it will recognize a shown bound property as a permission to use some of its services. In particular, possessing a bound property entails a promise that a specific service will be obtained as expressed in the relationship.

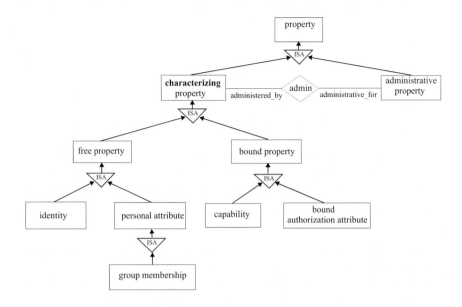

Fig. 10.10. A coarse classification of characterizing properties

   Though in most situations the distinctions between the two kinds of characterizing properties are more or less obvious, they are difficult to fully describe generically. Rather than trying to do so, we shall merely emphasize that an entity can exploit its free properties in order to acquire bound properties, i.e., to convince a server entity to grant it a permission to use some services.

   The assignment of characterizing properties to entities is regulated by corresponding *administrative properties*, which must be held by the entity that is responsible for such an assignment. We distinguish two kinds of administrative properties, which are illustrated in Figure 10.11:

- The *administration status* expresses whether an entity can make assignments in its own right or only on behalf of another entity. In the former case, the assigning entity has the status of an *origin* (for the characterizing property administered), and in the latter case, it is considered as a *dependant* (for the characterizing property administered). The relationship between an origin and its direct or indirect dependants must be suitably expressed, again by appropriate administrative properties.
- The *administration function* expresses the following roles. In the role of a *distributor*, an entity can responsibly assign the corresponding characterizing property to a qualifying entity. In the role of an intermediate, an entity can establish new dependants.

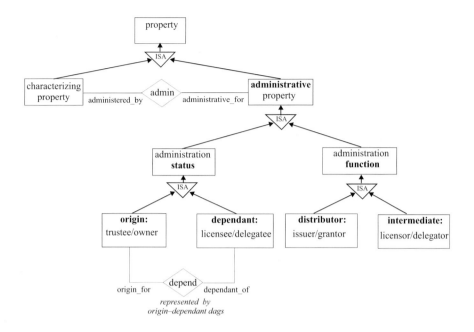

Fig. 10.11. A coarse classification of administrative properties

Though administrative properties look quite similar for free properties and bound properties, there are also some differences, explained in Subsections 10.3.3 and 10.3.4 below. Moreover, different terms are usually used:

- for free properties, an origin is called a *trusted authority*, or *trustee* for short, and a dependant is called a *licensee*;
- for bound properties, an origin is seen as an *owner* (of a service) and a dependant is seen as a *delegatee*. Accordingly, a distributor is an *issuer* or a *grantor*, respectively, and an intermediate is a *licensor* or a *delegator*, respectively.

We emphasize that all (potentially hidden) properties of entities, whether characterizing or administrative properties, have to be represented in the visible virtual world of certificates and credentials. The specialization hierarchy for properties is mirrored in corresponding specialization hierarchies for certificates and credentials. As an important example, a (potentially hidden) relationship between an origin (which is administrative for a specific characterizing property) and its dependants is visibly reflected by an appropriate *chain* (or, more generally, an appropriate directed acyclic graph, *dag* for short) of certificates or credentials.

10.3.2 Evaluating Trust Recursively

The relationships of *presumably captured by* are *ideal claims* that do not necessarily hold. A specific entity has to evaluate its individual *trust* about such an ideal claim. More specifically, and among other things, the specific entity seeing a document must evaluate its trust with respect to the following issues:

- Did the supposed assigning entity follow good practice in generating and signing the document?
- Do the principals (keys) appearing in the document represent the supposed entities?

The very purpose of the administrative properties – and the corresponding certificates and credentials and the gathering of them into appropriate chains or dags – is just to provide a reliable foundation for such *trust evaluations*, as explained in the following.

Conceptually, *permission decisions* are intended to be based on *characterizing properties* of entities appearing as clients. However, since property assignments occur in the hidden (real) world, the permission decisions must actually be based on available, visible digital documents, the contents of which *mean* the respective characterizing properties.

Consider any such document as a *main document* from the point of view of an entity entitled to take a permission decision. Then, the question arises of whether the literal meaning of the content is indeed valid in the hidden (real) world, i.e., whether the digital document *captures* a "real" property assignment. This question is answered using further *supporting documents*, the contents of which mean appropriate administrative properties. However, for each of these supporting documents, the same question arises: is the literal meaning of the content indeed valid in the hidden (real) world? Thus, we are running into a recursion:

- The "main document" concerning a characterizing property needed for a permission decision is supported by a first level of "supporting documents" concerning administrative properties for that characterizing property.
- For each "supporting document" at the i-th level, one of the following cases holds. Either it is supported by further "supporting documents" at the next level, thereby expressing that the responsible agent of the former document (which must be identical to the subject of the latter documents) represents a *dependant* of the responsible agents of the latter documents, or it expresses that its responsible agent represents an *origin* for the characterizing property administered, expressed by the content of the "main document".

In order to be helpful, the "main document" and its "supporting documents" should form a *directed acyclic graph* with respect to their relationships concerning *support*. As a special case, we may obtain just a *chain*. For example, Figure 10.16 in Subsection 10.3.5 shows two chains, one for a free-property certificate as the "main document", and another for a bound-property credential as the "main document".

In any case, the ultimate trust about all ideal claims pertinent to the documents relies on the *non-supported* documents referring to *origins* as responsible agents. Rather than using explicit documents for origins, the evaluating entity often just decides at its own discretion that it wants to treat the responsible agent of a "supporting document" as denoting an origin. This situation is shown in Figure 10.16, where no explicit documents occur for origins, i.e., the trustee and the owner. A major difference between administrative properties for free properties and for bound properties stems from the different treatments of and assumptions about origins and how origins determine their dependants.

Furthermore, the (dynamic) *recursive* procedure for *evaluating trust* has to be justified by (static) *transitivity* properties of *trust relationships*. As an example, such a property might express roughly the following: if an intermediate trusts a distributor and that distributor trusts an issuer, then the intermediate trusts that issuer as well.

10.3.3 Model of Trusted Authorities and Licensing

Following and extending the basic approach of X.509, free properties and the corresponding certificates are handled by *trusted authorities* using *licensing*. Figure 10.12 visualizes an instance of the general situation. In the simplest case, an entity *acts* and may *be considered* as a "trusted authority" for a free property.

In *acting*, such an entity assigns a free property to another entity and, accordingly, *issues* a suitable certificate (called a *free-property certificate*) about this assignment. In the certificate, the content expresses the free property, the subject is the principal (public key(s)) representing the entity possessing the property (the holder), and the responsible agent is the principal (public key(s)) representing the trustee (the issuer). The integrity and authenticity of the certificate are assured by a digital signature that the issuer generates with his private key for signing.

In *being considered* as a "trusted authority", such an entity is afterwards evaluated by a further entity acting as a *verifier*. This verifier, seeing the issued certificate, may decide to treat the issuing entity as an origin for the free property. Thus, after having verified the signature of the certificate, the verifier concludes his trust evaluation of whether or not the certificate captures the corresponding property assignment. The crucial point of the model of trusted authorities and licensing is that, in general, the issuer and the holder of a certificate are different from the verifier who inspects that certificate afterwards.

In more advanced cases, additionally *licensing* is used. Then, basically, an entity engaged in licensing does not assign free properties in its own right. Rather, it has to be *explicitly licensed* to do so. More specifically, some other entity, acting as a *licensor* and trusting the *licensee*, has expressed by a *license certificate* that the licensee should be entitled to assign a specific free property, i.e., to issue corresponding certificates.

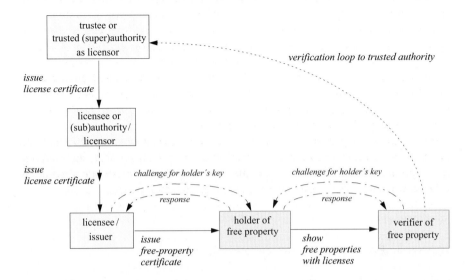

Fig. 10.12. Outline of an instance of the model of trusted authorities and licensing

In the license certificate, the content means trustworthiness to assign the specific free property, the subject is the principal (public key(s)) representing the licensee, and the responsible agent is the principal (public key(s)) representing the licensor.

Additionally, licensing can be organized *recursively*: a licensor can express his trust in a licensee to act as a licensor in turn, again by a suitable license certificate. Here, suitability depends on the application context: generally speaking, the precise scope of the license must be described somehow. For instance, the license to act as a licensor can be restricted to a fixed predetermined free property, or it can include defining new free properties of a certain kind. It might also be the case that a licensee needs to be trusted by several licensors.

Table 10.13. Certificate types in the model of trusted authorities and licensing

Certificate type	Content
identity certificate (X.509 term)	identifying name
attribute certificate (X.509 term)	personal attribute
accreditation certificate (mediation term)	personal attribute
private certificate (Brands' term)	personal attribute
trustee self-certificate (X.509 term: root certificate)	*administration status*: trustee
license certificate (X.509 term: certification authority certificate)	*administration function*: licensor

A free-property certificate and its license certificates form a directed acyclic graph. As a special case, we may obtain just a *certificate chain*. *Chain evaluation* (the X.509 term is *certification path validation*) is done as described in Subsection 10.3.2.

Whenever an issuer certifies a free property for a subject, i.e., a public key, on the basis of real-world circumstances, the issuer must follow good practice in order to authenticate the public key. Also, when the verifier of a free property wants to gain assurance as to whether the holder of a shown, asserted free property is also the holder of the matching private key, in most cases the verifier must follow good practice in order to authenticate the subject, i.e., a public key. In both cases, the issuer or verifier has to *challenge* the claiming entity to prove that they hold the matching private key. Usually, the proof is accomplished by an appropriate *response*, which is generated with the matching private key.

In this model of trusted authorities and licensing, certificates of a special kind occur, namely *identity certificates* (the X.509 term is *public key certificate*), which deal with free properties that can be used to identify an entity. Typically, such a free property is a name or some number (hopefully) uniquely used within a domain. Identity certificates are needed whenever, on seeing a public key, there is an interest in identifying the entity that possesses the key.

We emphasize, however, that in many cases the identity of an entity is not important at all. Rather, the interest is directed toward other free properties and the licenses of the issuers of these free properties. Again, the direct issuer's identity might also not be important; rather, one might prefer to look at the issuer's licensors instead. Avoiding identification is also a necessary condition for supporting the feature of *anonymity* and enables the use of dedicated anonymity techniques. Nevertheless, in most cases, by following the dag of supporting license certificates, the origins should be identifiable. Thus, normally such origins suitably publish identity certificates that enable an evaluating entity to take discretionary trust decisions.

Table 10.13 summarizes some terms for certificates. A characterizing certificate might be a *free-property certificate*, whose content means a *free property*. A free-property certificate might be an *identity certificate* or a (personal) *attribute certificate*, which in some contexts is also called an *accreditation certificate* or a *private certificate*. An administrative certificate might be a *trustee self-certificate* or a *license certificate*. A trusted authority, acting as a trustee, signs its own certificate. The resulting certificate is called a *trustee self-certificate*. A trusted authority, acting as a licensee, is certified by another trusted authority, acting as a licensor. In this case, the resulting certificate is called a *license certificate*.

10.3.4 Model of Owners and Delegation

In the model of trusted authorities and licensing, it is only possible for some trusted authorities to assign properties and to issue corresponding certificates to entities that possess the assigned properties. Naturally, it should be possible for any entity, as the *owner* of his resources, to define his own vocabulary for properties, to grant corresponding digital documents and to even express his trust in delegatees, each of which is entitled to assign a specific property (i.e., one defined in the owner's vocabulary for properties) to other entities. These requirements are fulfilled by the model of *owners* and *delegation*.

Following and extending the basic approach of *SPKI* (*Simple Public Key Infrastructure*), *bound properties* and the corresponding *credentials* (the SPKI term is *authorization certificates*) are handled by owners of services using delegation. Figure 10.14 visualizes an instance of the general situation. In the simplest case, an entity *acts* as an owner of its services (resources) offered to other entities and *is explicitly addressed* by these other entities.

In *acting*, such an entity assigns a bound property to another entity and, accordingly, *grants* a suitable credential (a *bound-property credential*) about this assignment. Similarly to a certificate, in a credential, the content means a bound property, the subject is the principal (public key(s)) representing the entity that possesses the property (the grantee), and the responsible agent is the principal (public key(s)) representing the owner (the grantor). Again, the integrity and authenticity of the credential is assured by a digital signature that the grantor generates with his private key for signing.

In *being addressed* as an owner, such an entity is afterwards contacted by some further entity which requests the service offered. The request is accompanied by showing a credential in order to obtain the permission to access the service. The addressed owner inspects the credential for whether he himself has granted it, i.e., he checks the signature with his public key for verification. In the positive case, the owner interprets the bound property expressed by the content of the credential according to his security policy:

- If the bound property is interpreted as a traditional *capability*, then the owner immediately allows access to the requested service, provided that the capability is good for the service. Thus, for a capability, the essential *permission decision* has been taken previously at the time of granting the credential.
- If the bound property is interpreted as a more general *bound authorization attribute*, then the owner might base his final permission decision not only on the shown bound authorization attribute granted some time before, but also on additional factors which are not directly encoded in the credential.

It is important to observe the difference from the model of trusted authorities and licensing: the owner needs no *trust evaluation*, except for whether he is willing to accept his own signatures. The crucial point of the basic model of owners is that the grantor of a credential is identical to the entity that afterwards inspects that credential. These observations are somewhat simplified, however, in that they neglect the potential misuse of stolen credentials, and the options for delegation to be described next.

In more advanced cases, *delegation* is additionally used. In this case, an entity engaged in delegation does not assign bound properties in its own right and for its

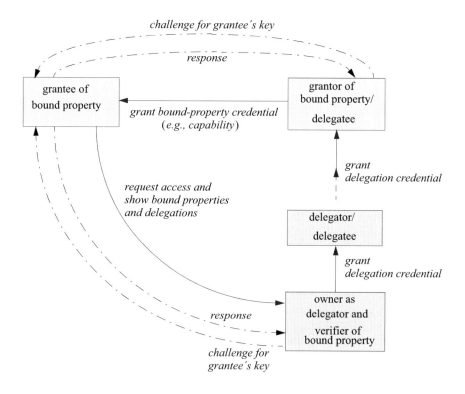

Fig. 10.14. Outline of an instance of the model of owners and delegation

own services. Rather, it acts on behalf of, and in explicit delegation of, a different owner. More specifically, some other entity, acting as a *delegator* and trusting the *delegatee*, has expressed by a *delegation credential* that the delegatee should be entitled to assign a specific bound property, i.e., to grant corresponding credentials.

In the delegation credential, the content means trustworthiness to assign a specific bound property, the subject is the principal (public key(s)) representing the delegatee, and the responsible agent is the principal (public key(s)) representing the delegator.

Additionally, delegation can be organized *recursively*: a delegator can express his trust in a delegatee to act as a delegator in turn, again by a suitable delegation credential. It might also be that a delegatee needs to be trusted by several delegators. A bound-property credential and its delegation credentials form a directed acyclic graph; in most cases we obtain a *credential chain*. *Chain evaluation* (the SPKI term is *certificate reduction*) is done as described in Subsection 10.3.2.

In this model of owners and delegation, if any bound-property credential is used as a "main document", then it is shown to the owner of the services to which the bound property refers. Moreover, any dag of supporting delegation credentials contains just one origin, namely the owner himself.

Table 10.15. Credential types in the model of owners and delegation

Credential type	Content
capability credential (SPKI term: authorization certificate)	capability
bound-authorization-attribute credential	bound-authorization attribute
delegation credential (SPKI implementation: true delegation bit)	*administration status*: delegatee

Whenever the grantor of a bound property grants a bound property for a subject, i.e., a public key, the grantor must follow good practice in order to authenticate the public key. Also, when a resource owner decides on a permission for a service on the basis of a shown credential, in most cases the owner must follow good practice in order to authenticate the subject, i.e., a public key. In both cases, the grantor or resource owner has to *challenge* the claiming entity to prove that it holds the matching private key. Usually, the proof is accomplished by an appropriate *response*, which is generated with the matching private key.

Table 10.15 summarizes some terms for credentials. A characterizing credential might be a *bound-property credential*, whose content means a *bound property*. A bound-property credential might be a *capability credential* or a *bound-authorization-attribute credential*. An administrative credential is a *delegation credential*.

In the specific SPKI approach, the assignments of a characterizing property and the corresponding administrative property are captured in the same digital document. The value of a *delegation bit* determines whether or not a bound-property credential is also interpreted as a *delegation credential*. In this approach, a delegatee can always use the bound property to access the services associated with that property for himself.

In cases where a delegatee is intended to be authorized only to grant characterizing properties to other eligible entities, it might be necessary to bind a delegatee to certain obligations with respect to granting bound-property credentials. In any subsequent dispute, a delegator can use these obligations to blame a delegatee for detected misuse. In such cases, distinguishing between administrative credentials and characterizing credentials is useful, since such obligations could be encoded in corresponding delegation credentials.

10.3.5 Converting Free Properties into Bound Properties

Many applications require the use and linkage of both kinds of PKI approach into a *hybrid PKI model*. Basically, the linkage deals with the following problem: Why is a grantor, whether the owner of a service himself or any of the owner's delegatees, willing to assign a bound property to an entity and to grant a corresponding credential, i.e., to express a possibly conditional permission to access a service? The general answer is that the grantor follows a *property conversion policy* that maps free properties to bound properties, where the property conversion policy is a part of the grantor's whole security policy. More precisely, the property conversion policy specifies

> which set of free properties an entity has to possess in order to obtain a bound property assignment.

Rephrased more technically in terms of the visible world of digital documents, this means the following: the property conversion policy specifies

> which free-property certificates, as the "main documents", together with which "supporting license certificates", are accepted in order to obtain the granting of which bound-property credential.

The middle part of Figure 10.16 visualizes the situation. The entity on the right is a grantor following a property conversion policy. The entity in the center requests a promise for a permission, i.e., a bound property. The grantor:

- *verifies* the submitted free-property certificates with the supporting licenses;
- *extracts* the contents of the free-property certificates and interprets them as free properties;
- *applies* its conversion policy to the extracted free properties; and
- finally, if all checks have been successfully completed, *grants* a bound-property credential where the subject (grantee) is the same as in the submitted free-property certificates.

Accordingly, an instance of a full hybrid PKI model consists of overlapping components of three kinds:

- trusted authorities (also called trustees) and licensees for a free property, and a holder of that property (see Subsection 10.3.3), together with a verifier of the free property;
- an owner and delegatees for, and a grantee of, a bound property (see Subsection 10.3.4); and
- a holder of free properties and a grantor of a bound property.

Components of the first two kind can form *loops*. Figure 10.16 shows a simple example, in which two loops for chains are linked. A verifier for a free property in a component of the first kind has to *close* the verification loops to the trusted authorities in order to found his trust. More precisely, *closing the loop* means here that the verifier *decides* which entities he wants to trust and to accept as origins. A grantee of a bound property *automatically closes* a loop when addressing the pertinent owner.

A component of the third kind is used as a link between a component of the first kind and a component of the second kind. The link identifies the verifier of the former component with the grantor of the latter component, and the holder of the first component with the grantee of the latter component. In some special cases, a linked component may appear to be degenerate.

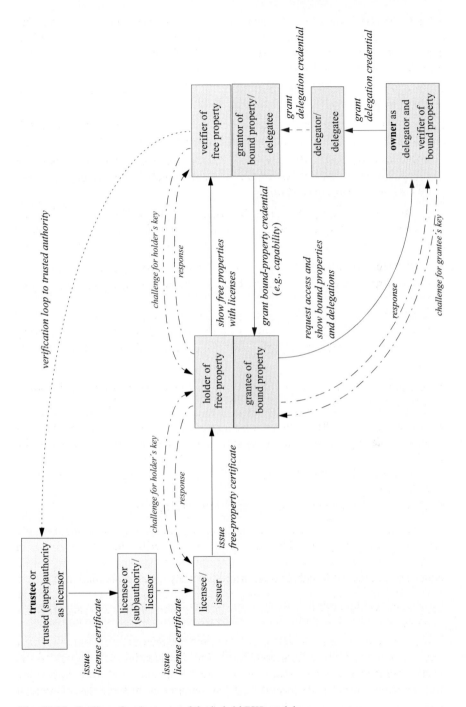

Fig. 10.16. Outline of an instance of the hybrid PKI model

10.4 Firewalls

Considering computing systems in the large, as depicted for example in Figure 6.1, we can see partly federated and partly nested structures built from individual subjects, shared client computers and servers, local area networks, and wide area networks. Basically, the techniques of control and monitoring are applicable at the borderline of any substructure; in particular, they should be aimed at the following goals:

- *confining* the inner side with respect to sending messages to the outside, thereby restricting the transfer of information to the outside and the requests to foreign entities;
- *shielding* the inner side with respect to receiving messages, thereby restricting interference by foreign entities and incoming requests.

10.4.1 Placement and Tasks

In each case, we have to adapt the specific security mechanisms to the main functionality provided at the borderline, i.e., to the pertinent layers within the overall layered design as sketched in Figure 10.2. In this subsection we treat *firewalls* as the protection employed in *wide area networks* (*WANs*); this protection is needed, for example, for the Internet or a middleware system seen as a federated object system:

- each *local area network* (*LAN*) autonomously protects its borderline by a firewall, serving as the exclusive checkpoint for outgoing and incoming messages;
- additionally, each intermediate *server* might protect both itself and the message traffic on behalf of its customers by a firewall, serving as a further checkpoint.

The general situation is sketched in Figure 10.17. The checkpoints handle messages in the form of single *packets* and sequences of packets, mainly according to well-established standards conforming to the *ISO/OSI model* for computer networks. Accordingly, roughly outlined, a firewall intercepts the packets passing the checkpoint and examines the following layers, where increasingly complex data can be inspected:

- ranging from the network layer to the transport layer, only the packet *headers* are considered;
- ranging from the transport layer to the session layer, *sequences* of packet headers are considered, in particular regarding compliance with session protocols;
- ranging from the session layer to the application layer, additionally, the packet *contents* are evaluated, in particular, the intended semantics of encoded messages is captured.

The practically available firewalls can be roughly classified by how they treat the basic aspects of *control and monitoring*. Depending on the layer placement and

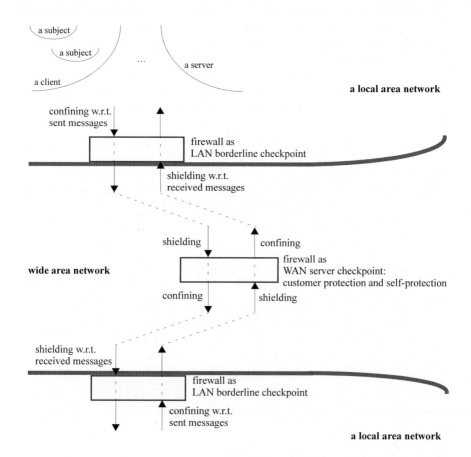

Fig. 10.17. Firewalls serving as LAN borderline and WAN server checkpoints, which provide confinement with respect to outgoing messages and shielding with respect to incoming messages in the form of packets

the data accordingly available, the actual achievements might vary considerably, from simple syntactic plausibility checks to more sophisticated semantic evaluations. Most importantly, however, a firewall must always realize its achievements in real time, without causing a substantial delay in the message traffic controlled, and therefore its effectiveness is limited in principle.

A first aspect of control and monitoring is the *proof of authenticity* of intercepted messages. The achievements of a firewall might range from none, in the case of considering only single packets, to verifying authentication data provided in the packet sequences according to known protocols for virtually establishing *secure connections*.

A second aspect is the abstraction level of the captured *semantics* underlying the intercepted messages, in particular regarding the *granularity* of the subjects and the controlled objects and the operations on them. Basically, the achievements of a firewall vary with the parts of the packet exploited, ranging from using only the *headers* to fully interpreting the *contents*. The latter option might be completely prevented if the participants hide the meaning of the content fields by employing *end-to-end encryption* at their discretion. Even otherwise, in general, interpreting the contents presupposes some a priori *domain knowledge* underlying the messages. A general- purpose firewall can rarely acquire sufficient domain knowledge about all potential communication partners, and thus its interpretation results are necessarily only fragmentary. More dedicated firewalls, however, might be aware of the details of specific domains, and accordingly might perform much better.

A third and a fourth aspect are the degree of *result inspection* and the impact of the *usage history*. For a firewall, these aspects are closely intertwined, since the available options vary together with its mode of working. If the firewall works *statelessly*, considering only single packets, result inspection and employment of the usage history are impossible. If the firewall works *statefully*, considering sequences of packets, its achievements depend strongly on the ability to recognize which packets within the streams belong together in the sense that they represent the full communication between some remote participants. Again, in general, some *domain knowledge* is necessary, or at least an awareness of sufficient details of the permitted protocol standards.

A final aspect is the employment of intercepted messages for the sake of *auditing* and *intrusion detection*, or even immediate *reaction*. Notably, some kind of reaction is always due, since after inspecting an intercepted packet, the firewall must either forward it to the next destination or treat it differently.

10.4.2 Components and their Combination

In general, a firewall consists of several components. In the following, we first characterize packet filters and proxies as two standard components, and then outline proposals for their combination.

A (simple) *packet filter* is placed in a layer corresponding to the *network* and *transport* layers. Neglecting authentication, a packet filter inspects only the header of each single intercepted packet and, accordingly, works statelessly. It is implemented as a linear list of *event–action rules* of the form

if *event* then *action*,

where the *event* is expressed in terms of values of header fields, and the *action* might demand, for example a *forwarding*, a *blocking* or some other simple option. For each packet considered, the linear list is scanned from the beginning until the first satisfied event is found; then this rule "fires" by performing the indicated action.

The filter's working as a linear *first-fit search* requires a careful arrangement of the rule ordering. In particular, a security administrator should pay attention to the following points. For the sake of efficiency, he should set the most frequently occurring events towards the beginning of the list. For the sake of *completeness*, he should close the list with a final *default rule* for blocking the remaining cases not already captured.

More generally, any *case distinction* regarding some feature should be completed by a *default rule* with the wanted action. Moreover, the only means to *resolve* potential *conflicts* between the actions of overlapping events, for example between a *forwarding*, considered as a *permission*, and a *blocking*, considered as a *prohibition*, is a proper arrangement in the list, setting the rule with the preferred action in front of the other rule.

A *proxy* simulates the complete services of a specific higher-layer communication *protocol*, for example FTP, by two strictly separated parts, each of which deals with the functionality of one side of the borderline. For a firewall used as a LAN borderline checkpoint, the inner part first inspects the outgoing packet stream from inside in order to confine the subjects inside. As far as they have been evaluated as permitted, and possibly modified, the packets are then forwarded to the outer part. In turn, the outer part can inspect the received stream, in order to support some security interests of the outside communication partners.

Conversely, the outer part first inspects the incoming packet stream from outside to shield the subjects inside, and only forwards a permitted and possibly modified stream to the inner part. In principle, both parts could perform any evaluations before taking an access decision. In practice, however, the actual achievements are limited by the data provided by the simulated protocol and the timing constraints.

Typically, a *proxy* is placed in a layer corresponding to the *session* and *application* layers. Depending on the simulated protocol, a proxy must deal with both the headers and the contents of sequences of packets and, accordingly, works statefully.

Packet filters and proxies should run on *dedicated hardware* where a minimum of supporting software is installed. In particular, only the *executable code* needed for the components should be loaded, and only the administrator should be given minimal *access rights*.

Placed in different layers, packet filters and proxies complement each other. Basically, the proposed combinations of packet filters and proxies result in a rudimentary *auxiliary network* between the networks on both sides being configured. This auxiliary network, also known as a *demilitarized zone*, might contain further servers that an administrator wants to locate on neither side, for example a WWW server where inside users can post data for outside partners. Typically, though with many variations, this auxiliary network is separated from each neighboring network by a packet filter. These two packet filters serve not only to confine and shield one side but also to protect the further servers located in the auxiliary network.

Moreover, when forwarding a packet, the packet filters redirect the packet either to a pertinent proxy, to some further server in the auxiliary network, or directly to the dual packet filter. Figure 10.18 shows a generic example of a LAN borderline firewall.

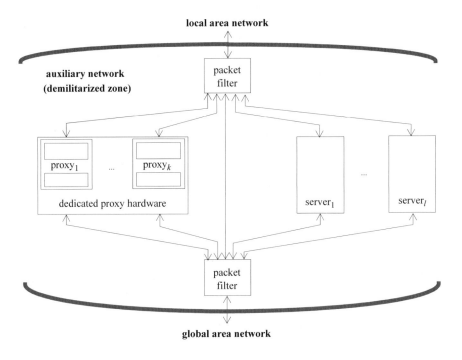

Fig. 10.18. A LAN borderline firewall considered as an auxiliary network with surrounding packet filters, several proxies and further servers (arrows indicate the flow of packets)

10.5 Bibliographic Hints

In some sense, any advanced text on security in computing systems must treat the overall security architecture in some way. In particular, most textbooks have chapters on topics such as operating system security, network security, application security or database security, thereby implicitly or explicitly following the layered design of a computing system. However, apparently for good reasons, in general, the authors of these textbooks refrain from advocating a specific detailed architecture, and so do we in this monograph: the overall task is just too complex to give a generally valid solution. Accordingly, the following references reflect the background knowledge from which we have tentatively extracted the fictitious design discussed in this chapter.

The notion of trust has many facets, dealt with in some way by nearly every work on security, ranging from the early governmental Trusted Computer Systems

Evaluation Criteria (TCSEC, also known as the "Orange Book") [167] to the ongoing industrial activities of the Trusted Computing Group [484, 485, 486, 487]. Besides many more organizational and sociological studies, several authors have elaborated the controversial proposal to map trust onto real numbers or related formal constructs. For a few examples out of many more pieces of work, Maurer [336] calculates trust values in a probabilistic model of a public key infrastructure using the exclusion–inclusion principle; Josang [284] suggests that one should employ an "opinion space" spanned by normalized real values for belief, disbelief and uncertainty; Coetzee/Eloff [138] consider trust issues for Web services; Ray/Chakraborty [405] combine several aspects into a "trust vector"; and Josang/Ismail/Boyd [285] provide a recent survey.

Other authors have aimed at founding the notion of trust by looking for an appropriate formal logic. For example, Abadi/Burrows/Lampson/Plotkin/Wobber [1, 309] pioneer the logic-oriented investigation of the transitivity of trust when control privileges are delegated in a distributed system, and Abadi [4] and Howell/Kotz [259] adapt this approach for SPKI/SDSI. Yu/Winslett/Seamons [508], Hess/Holt/Jacobson/Seamons [255] and Bertino/Ferrari/Squicciarini [50] study how strangers can establish trust stepwise by exchanging certificates and credentials.

The Trusted Computing Platform Alliance (TCPA) [488], formed by leading IT companies, first propose a "trusted platform module" as a hardware basis of "trusted computing". Pearson/et al. [386] provide a broad introduction to the TCPA specification. The Trusted Computing Group (TCG) [484, 485, 486, 487] develops the specification further. Pfitzmann/Pfitzmann/Schunter/Waidner [390] discuss the security issues related to personal computing devices.

Security of operating systems was one of the main concerns of early work on security, and is still waiting for a widely employed solution. The following references select a sample of important contributions. Organick [381] examines the design and the implementation of Multics, which, among many other features, uses several "protection rings" and supports mandatory access control, as elaborated by Bell/LaPadula [36, 37]. Among many other reports on Multics, Saltzer [420] summarizes and discusses the basic security design. Karger/Schell [288] reexamine the great achievements of Multics, complaining that the lessons have been largely ignored up to now. Fabry [196] studies capability-based addressing.

As some kind of response to Multics, Ritchie/Thompson [407] engineer UNIX, favoring discretionary access control regarding file accesses. A comprehensive treatments of today's UNIX security is provided, for example, by Garfinkel/Spafford [216].

Early work on security kernels and their formal assessment is reported by Popek/Farber [397] and Millen [352]. Wulf/Levin/Harbison/et al. [502, 503] build the Hydra prototype as a fully object-oriented operating system with dedicated hardware support, in particular for employing capabilities efficiently. Härtig/et al. [252, 253, 300, 243] develop the BirliX prototype, which is also fully object-oriented. Tanenbaum/Mullender/van Renesse/et al. [476, 477, 478] propose Amoeba as an operating system for distributed systems, using protected capabilities.

Härtig/et al. [252, 300, 243] introduce secure booting for BirliX. Arbaugh/Farber/Smith [18] resume this topic in a more general framework. The Trusted Computing Platform Alliance/Trusted Computing Group [484, 485, 486, 487, 488] makes TPM-based integrity measurement and reporting a crucial issue of their design. Sailer/Jaeger/Zhang/van Doorn [417, 418] extend integrity measurement to the software up to the application layer, in a Linux environment. Brickell/Camenisch/Chen [114, 105] invent direct anonymous attestation.

Network security has been extensively treated as well. Stallings [462, 463] and Davis/Price [153] provide broad introductions. We shall mention only two examples of more specific contributions. Saltzer/Reed/Clark [422] discuss end-to-end security. Steiner/Neuman/Schiller/et al. [464, 353, 298, 369] invent Kerberos as an authentication framework for distributed systems.

Application security has been studied from many points of view. For example, Castano/Fugini/Martella/Samarati [118] collect together early material on database security; Bertino/Sandhu [51] present a recent perspective on database security; Bertino/Ferrari/Atluri [46] treat workflow management systems; Minsky/Ungureanu [357] propose security-law-governed interactions; and Adam/Atluri/Bertino/Capuozzo/Ferrari [7, 205] consider a digital library authorization system.

Jones/Liskov [282, 283] pioneer the integration of access control into programming languages. Myers/Liskov [360] resume and extend this issue for the programming language Java. Viega/McGraw [490] give an introduction to the building of secure software in general, and McGraw/Felton [339] treat software written in Java and mobile code in particular. Bishop [57] summarizes programming guidelines covering in particular implementation and management.

The usage of credentials and certificates is pioneered by Chaum [122, 123]. The specific model of trusted authorities and licensing is standardized in the X.509 framework [8]. The specific model of owners with delegation is based on the work of Clarke/Ellison/Lampson/Rivest/et al. [184, 185, 136] on SPKI/SDSI.

Some examples of further work are the following: Blaze/Feigenbaum/Keromytis/et al. [88, 89] propose PolicyMaker and KeyNote; Biskup/Karabulut [72, 73] suggest the hybrid model based on the experience with a system for secure mediation [11]; Li/Mitchell/Winsborough [316, 317] combine credentials with role-based access control, and Li/Grosof/Feigenbaum [318] study a delegation logic for credentials; Ellison/Dohrmann [187] deal with group collaboration; Bonatti/Samarati [95] use a generic model for expressing access and disclosure policies for Web services. Brands [101] elaborates a comprehensive system for using credentials and certificates, emphasizing the support of privacy. Ellison/Schneier [186] critically review public key infrastructures

Firewalls are often treated as part of network security. For example, Chapman/Zwickey [121] and Cheswick/Bellovin [131] provide dedicated introductions.

In Chapter 17, we give further references related to our presentation of selected examples of actually implemented (sub)systems: the operating system UNIX, the database system Oracle/SQL, the middleware specification CORBA, and the support systems for distributed computing Kerberos, SPKI and PGP.

11 Monitoring and Intrusion Detection

Ideally, an application of the techniques of *control and monitoring* is perfectly established: a security policy specifies exactly the wanted permissions and prohibitions; administrators correctly and completely declare the policy, which subsequently is fully represented within the computing system; and the control and monitoring component can never be bypassed, and it enforces the policy without any exception. As a result, all participants are expected to be confined to employing the computing system precisely as intended. Unfortunately, reality often differs from the ideal; for instance, the following shortcomings might arise:

- The security policy is left imprecise or incomplete.
- The declaration language is not expressive enough.
- The internal representation contains flaws.
- The enforcement does not cover all access requests.
- Administrators or users disable some control facilities for efficiency reasons.
- Intruders find a way to circumvent the control and monitoring component.

Some shortcomings might stem from careless or even malicious behavior of various persons involved in the overall process of building a secure computing system. However, we cannot blame only the responsible participants, but should recognize the inherent difficulties in fully meeting the ideals. Moreover, there are further, intricate difficulties. For example:

- In general, as indicated by undecidability results, control privileges and information flow requirements are computationally difficult to manage.
- For the sake of efficiency, information flow requirements can only be roughly approximated by access rights.
- A user might need some set of specific permissions for his legitimate obligations, but not all possible combinations of the permissions are seen to be acceptable.
- A user might exercise his permissions excessively and thereby exhaust the resources of the computing system.
- A user might exploit hidden operational options that have never been considered for acceptable usage.

Summarizing, we have to face the above shortcomings and difficulties and related ones, and, admitting an imperfect reality, have to prepare for them with additional protection mechanisms. Fortunately, the generic model of local control and monitoring, suitably extended, already provides a useful basis:

- Access requests are intercepted and thus can be documented persistently in the *knowledge base* on the *usage history*. This feature can be extended to *logging* further *useful data* about computing activities, including data that is only indirectly related to a malicious user's requests and thus is not subject to circumvention.
- In addition to deciding on each individual access request, the control and monitoring component can *audit* and *analyze* the data on request sequences and other recorded activities available. These actions are aimed at searching for *intrusions*, i.e., patterns of unexpected or unwanted behavior, and reacting as far as is possible or convenient.

Clearly, such additional secondary mechanisms cannot achieve perfection either, since otherwise we could construct perfect primary control mechanisms right from the beginning. Thus these secondary mechanisms should be designed to work *complementarily*, aiming at narrowing the gap left by the primary mechanisms.

11.1 Intrusion Detection and Reaction

11.1.1 Tasks and Problems

A *control and monitoring component* primarily permits or prohibits requests for controlled objects, aiming at enabling the needed usages of objects and at preventing undesirable accesses to system resources by all kinds of participating subjects. At least conceptually, the "needed usages" and "undesirable accesses" are precisely specified by a normative *security policy*, leading to *formal semantics* for *access decisions*.

Secondarily, and mainly complementarily, a control and monitoring component can be extended to provide *intrusion detection* and *reaction*. This functionality aims at the following:

- *identifying*, on-the-fly, activities of potentially *malicious users* who might try to employ system resources in an *undesirable way*, or *recognizing*, after the fact, that such an unfortunate event has already occurred;
- *responding* appropriately, as far as possible, once an intrusion has been detected.

Again, we need a notion of "undesirable accesses" or of "employment in an undesirable way". It could also be useful to have a notion of the positive counterpart, namely "acceptable usages" or "tolerable usages". Unfortunately, however, such notions are now much more difficult to define than in the context of access control:

- On the one hand, in order to achieve our eventual aim of automating intrusion detection, we have to come up with an algorithmic version of these notions.

- But, on the other hand, we somehow have to anticipate situations in which the precise security policy, which is used normatively for access decisions, is already on the way toward failing to fully serve its purpose.

In the following, we shall refer to such notions as an *intrusion defense policy*. There are various suggestions for determining such an intrusion defense policy as a reasonable compromise between the seemingly incompatible requirements – to be both purely algorithmic, and sufficiently flexible and adaptable to various circumstances. Below, we tentatively outline some common features of these suggestions.

For this outline, the computing system under consideration is assumed to be abstractly defined by its possible *states* and its possible *state transitions*. A *behavior* of the collection of all users, or, if identifiable, of a single user, can then be represented by a *trace*, i.e., a sequence of state transitions. For simplicity, we present our exposition mainly in terms of such traces. Alternatively, or for some variations complementarily or even necessarily, we can express anything more statically oriented in terms of system states or, better, in terms of suitably extended states that also capture at least a part of the preceding *usage history*. Thus most of the following considerations about sets of behaviors (or traces) can be translated into considerations about states as well.

As a base set, we postulate the set of "possible" behaviors. This set is intended to capture all operational options that can be exercised by a fictitious version of the computing system considered, whereby no restrictions are enforced by security mechanisms. A subset of possible behaviors is seen as *acceptable*, and another subset as *violating*. While the participating subjects continue to engage in their behaviors, i.e., request and activate state transitions, the control and monitoring component continuously checks whether the transitions are remaining within the "acceptable behaviors" or whether they are going to approach a "violating behavior". Figure 11.1 displays a rough visualization of the sets involved and their supposed inclusion relationships.

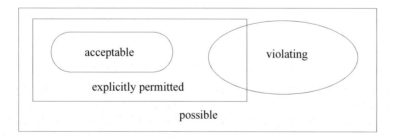

Fig. 11.1. Inclusion relationships of the relevant sets of behaviors (or of states)

Obviously, we want to be able to *separate* "acceptable" behaviors from "violating" ones. In particular, no behavior should be classified both as acceptable and as violating. Furthermore, "acceptable behaviors" should definitely be permitted according to the security policy for access control. However, at least in general, access control will allow more behaviors than just the "acceptable" ones: access control can be understood as enforcing a syntactic specification of what might happen, but only a minor fraction of the syntactically permitted behaviors can be considered *semantically acceptable*.

One of the main reasons for this troublesome discrepancy stems from the fact that access control traditionally deals mostly with *one-step* transitions only, whereas "acceptability" is assigned to *sequences* of transitions. Moreover, beyond keeping track of histories, the notion of "acceptability" typically exploits further information that is not used for access control, for example information that is related to the "semantics" of requests or "contents" of messages. Consequently, in general, the set of "semantically acceptable" behaviors is strictly included in the set of behaviors syntactically permitted by access control.

Under the precondition of a user or a collection of users having behaved "acceptably" and not in a "violating" way so far, access control features are aimed at checking a *request* for a state transition for whether it would *immediately* result in a "violating behavior", as implicitly declared by the precise security policy. And, if applicable, these features directly *prohibit* the crucial transition. As a result, the property of behaving "acceptably" and not in a "violating" way is hoped to be maintained as an invariant.

In contrast, there are two features of intrusion detection that work on different issues. The first feature explores whether an inspected state transition could possibly be a *dangerous step towards* reaching a "violating behavior". In this framework, it may well happen that a sequence of permitted requests, each of which appears to be harmless according to the precise security policy, nevertheless may end in a "violating behavior" according to the intrusion defense policy. The second feature investigates whether a "violating behavior" has *already been reached*. In both cases, appropriate *reactions* are due. Apparently, for these features, we need a notion of something like a *distance* from the already observed behavior or an anticipated behavior to the set of "violating behaviors".

Among other features, this distance should also provide indications that can be used to estimate the number and kind of permitted requests required to leave the "acceptable behaviors" or to reach a "violating behavior" from the present one. Such an estimation could be based on two kinds of presumably available knowledge:

- first, the mismatch between the design of the granting of permissions and prohibitions and the specification of "acceptable behaviors" and "violating behaviors"; and
- second, some patterns of "most likely" behaviors of friendly and malicious users. Both kinds of knowledge should be dynamically updated on the basis of past experience.

The features sketched can also be viewed as moves in a strategic game. One player is the control and monitoring component, and the adversary player is the collection of all users or some single user, as far as single users are identifiable. The goal of the control and monitoring component is to confine transitions to "acceptable behaviors" and not to reach a "violating behavior" or, even more strongly, to keep the already shown behavior "far away" from being extendable to a "violating behavior", whereas the adversary player (potentially or actually) tries the opposite, namely to complete a "violating behavior".

11.1.2 Simple Model

Figure 11.2 shows a simple model of intrusion detection and reaction. The main components form a feedback loop as follows:

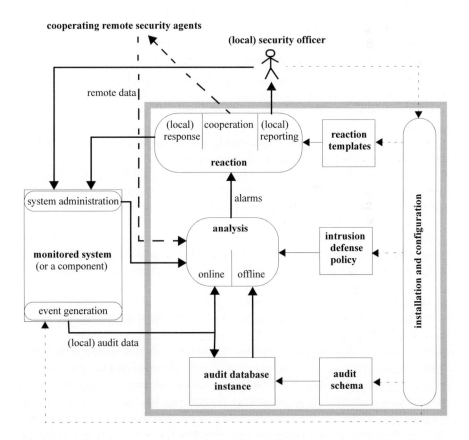

Fig. 11.2. A simple model of intrusion detection and reaction

- The *event generation*, appropriately implanted in the *monitored computing system*, delivers local *audit data* to the monitoring system, to be immediately processed online, or later offline.
- The *audit database instance* constitutes the intermediately stored audit data gathered for offline analysis.
- The *analysis* component directly inspects the currently delivered audit data in an *online* mode, or examines a larger amount of audit data *offline*. Besides the local audit data, the analysis component usually needs some basic *configuration data* about the monitored system, and, if applicable, the analysis is enhanced by *remote data* stemming from cooperating *remote security agents*. If the analysis component detects suspicious behaviors or states, it raises *alarms*.
- The *reaction* component deals with alarms in basically three ways. The reaction can be a purely algorithmically generated *local response* that intervenes in the monitored system, say by modifying some administration parameters or, in the extreme case, by totally closing down the system. Alternatively or additionally, *local reporting* to a human *security officer* is performed. The security officer, in turn, can then intervene in the monitored system, if this is considered necessary or convenient. If intrusion detection is done in *cooperation* with *remote security agents*, appropriate messages are sent out.

At initialization time or when an update is due, these main components have to be installed and configured appropriately. Therefore the local security officer provides the needed information: an *audit schema* for storing audit data, an *intrusion defense policy* for guiding the analysis efforts, and *reaction templates* for dealing with alarms. Additionally, the security officer has to implant one or several suitably configured *event generators* into the monitored system.

The *intrusion defense policy* appears to constitute the most crucial information, although it might be equally important to closely coordinate all information provided. Basically, the intrusion defense policy formally describes the intuitive notions of "acceptable" and "violating", and in this way it defines a specific *classification task* for the analysis component: on the basis of available data, the analysis component has to algorithmically decide whether – or in more sophisticated cases, to what extent – the actually observed behavior within a monitored system or the actually observed sequence of states is *evaluated* to be "acceptable" or "violating" (with respect to the given security defense policy).

Typically, the *security officer* determines the intrusion defense policy on the basis of previous experience. Thus, before the first installation or before a reconfiguration, some *learning* of the notions of "acceptable" and "violating" is required. This learning either can be done purely manually, or can be at least partially supported by algorithmic tools. In the latter case, such a *learning tool* is given *training data*, which might stem from two sources: the training data can be gained from logging suitable aspects of the specific system to be monitored, or it may be taken from publicly available or proprietary repositories of examples of "acceptable" or "violating" behavior.

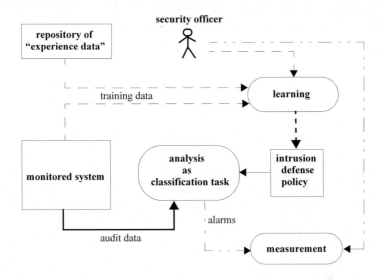

Fig. 11.3. Learning, operation and measurement for an intrusion defense policy

Additionally, the notions learnt have to be suitably formally represented in a compressed way such that the classification task of the analysis component is best supported, from the point of view, mainly, of *effectiveness* and *efficiency*. Furthermore, at an appropriate time, the actual achievements have to be measured. The *learning phase*, the *operation phase* and the *measurement phase* of an intrusion defense policy are schematically outlined in Figure 11.3.

The *effectiveness* of an analysis component guided by an intrusion defense policy is usually measured in terms adapted from the field of *information retrieval*. Basically, the measurement relates experimental items to (more or less fictitious) ideal items. The *experimental items* are taken from controlled experiments that observe the outputs of the analysis component for a given monitored system, i.e., the *alarms* raised that denote supposedly "violating" behaviors. The *ideal items* constitute a priori (more or less fictitious) knowledge about the "real status" of the behaviors underlying the experiments. For each such behavior, there are four possibilities in principle:

- The analysis component raises no alarm (it classifies the behavior as "acceptable"), and the "real status" of the behavior is indeed acceptable.
- The analysis component raises an alarm (it classifies the behavior as "violating"), and the "real status" of the behavior is indeed violating.
- The analysis component raises an alarm (it classifies the behavior as "violating"), but the "real status" of the behavior is actually acceptable. In this case, the analysis component raises a *false* alarm and, accordingly, the classification result is said to be a *false positive*.

- The analysis component raises no alarm (it classifies the behavior as "acceptable"), but the "real status" of the behavior is actually violating. In this case, the analysis component fails to generate a *correct* alarm and, accordingly, the classification result is said to be a *false negative*.

Clearly, one would like to prevent both of the last possibilities, where the analysis fails. In practice, however, there is usually a trade-off. Roughly speaking, in order to avoid false positives, the analysis has to justify alarms by very strong reasons, thereby potentially allowing more false negatives. Conversely, in order to avoid false negatives, the analysis has to raise alarms not only for strong reasons but also in questionable cases, thereby potentially allowing more false positives.

Efficiency is mandatory for online analysis. In this case, basically, the analysis component has to perform the classification task in linear real time. This requirement suggests that one should internally represent an intrusion defense policy as a pair of suitably enhanced finite automatons or by means of closely related computing abstractions, to be used as *recognizers* for "violating" and "non-acceptable" inputs.

11.2 Signature-Based Approach

The signature-based approach contributes to representing *violating behaviors* and constructing a corresponding recognizer. More specifically, long-term observation and evaluation of violating behaviors have led to a large collection of samples of known attacks on a computing system. Intuitively, a *signature* is a formal representation of a known *attack pattern*, preferably including its already seen or merely anticipated variations, in terms of generic *events*, instances of which can be generated by the *event generation* and reported in the form of *audit data*.

More formally, in the simplest case, a *signature* σ is given as a finite time-ordered sequence of abstract events taken from a finite event space Σ; accordingly, we can consider a signature as a word over the event space seen as an alphabet, i.e., $\sigma \in \Sigma^*$. The *event space* is determined by the layer where the event generation is located. Typically, the event generation is coupled to an internal interface of the monitored system where requests or more general messages are easily interceptable and can be inspected in some way. For example, in the layer of an operating system, events might be *system calls* to the kernel; in the layer of a network system, events might be *packet moves*; and in the layer of some application, events might be *method invocations*. Depending on the actual location, intrusion detection systems are sometimes classified as *host-based* or *network-based*.

Still considering the simplest case for the sake of conciseness, the *analysis component* has two inputs:

- a fully known signature $\sigma \in \Sigma^*$, as the intrusion defense policy;
- an eventwise supplied behavior $\beta \in \Sigma^\infty$, as the (ongoing) recorded activities within the system, given as a (possibly) infinite word of audited events.

The basic *classification task* is then to determine whether and where "the signature σ *compactly occurs* in the behavior β", i.e., to find *all* position sequences for β that give the signature σ such that each prefix cannot be completed earlier (or some similar property holds). Accordingly, the analysis component must provide a corresponding recognizer, which should raise an alarm for *each* such compact occurrence of σ in β. An abstract example is shown in Figure 11.4.

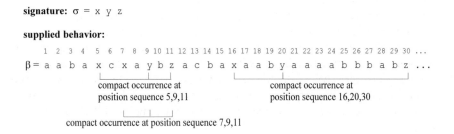

Fig. 11.4. The compact occurrences of a signature in a supplied behavior

Clearly, an actual analysis component should be much more sophisticated, dealing at least with the features sketched in the following.

In principle, a compact occurrence of the signature σ can be spread widely. Accordingly, while checking whether "σ compactly occurs in β", the recognizer must memorize and handle each detected occurrence of a prefix of σ in β until the prefix has been completed. In practice, in particular for the sake of efficiency, one would like to "forget" non-completed prefixes after a while.

A basic concept for doing so is to declare explicit *escape conditions* for terminating an initialized occurrence. As a simple implementation, one can employ a *sliding window* of some appropriate length *l* for the behavior β, and to search only for occurrences of the signature that fit into one window position. As a trade-off, all more widely spread occurrences are missed in the hope that they do not reflect an "actual attack". For the example shown in Figure 11.4, if we restricted the window to a length of 10, then the occurrence at position sequence 16,20,30 would be ignored.

Depending on the intercepting interface, in most cases events appear to be structured and composed of several items. As a typical example, a *parameterized event* $e[\dots, A_i : v_i, \dots]$ might consist of an event type e and a list of specific attribute–value pairs $A_i : v_i$. In the case of system calls, e would be an operator, and the $A_i : v_i$ would denote the arguments. Correspondingly, a *parameterized signature* would be a sequence of parameterized events, where some or all values might be replaced by variables.

When one is searching for the compact or otherwise suitably restricted occurrences of the signature in the supplied behavior, the values in the signature have to *match* the audited values, whereas the variables in the signature are *bound* to the pertinent audited values. Thus each detected occurrence of a prefix of the parameterized signature is linked to a *binding list* for variables, and once a variable is bound for a detected prefix, the binding also applies to the tail of the signature, i.e., audited values there have to match the bound values. Notably, the recognizer must maintain a partially instantiated signature instance for each detected occurrence of a prefix. Figure 11.5 shows a simple abstract example.

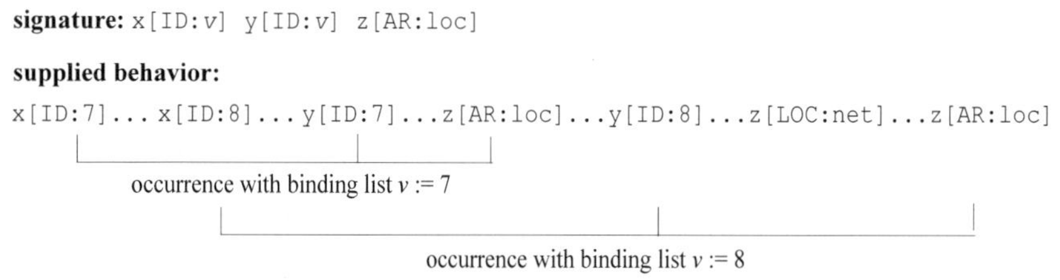

signature: x[ID:v] y[ID:v] z[AR:loc]

supplied behavior:

x[ID:7]... x[ID:8]... y[ID:7]...z[AR:loc]...y[ID:8]...z[LOC:net]...z[AR:loc]

occurrence with binding list *v* := 7

occurrence with binding list *v* := 8

Fig. 11.5. Detected occurrences with binding lists

In order to capture variations of an attack, several closely related event sequences might be represented concisely as a directed acyclic graph (dag) built from events. Given a signature in this form, the recognizer has to search for a compact occurrence for any path from some start event to some end event within the supplied behavior.

Finally, in general, "violating" behavior is described by hundreds of known attacks, and thus by a large number of signatures that the analysis component has to handle in parallel.

Summarizing, and subject to many variations, the signature-based approach consists of the following steps:

- In the *learning phase*, an administrator – possibly assisted by a tool – models the known attacks by an intrusion defense policy, specified as a set of parameterized dag-like signatures using some appropriate formal language. Then a suitable tool transforms the specified policy into an integrated collection of recognizers that become a part of the analysis component.
- In the *operation phase*, the recognizers instantiate the given signatures according to the prefixes and their bindings for variables, as detected in the supplied behavior within a sliding window, and raise an alarm whenever an instantiation has been completed.
- In the *measurement phase*, the effectiveness might be improved by revising or refining the policy or by enlarging the length of the sliding window, and the efficiency might be improved by optimizing the collection of recognizers and by diminishing the length of the sliding window. To deal with the apparent trade-off regarding the sliding window, its length might also be adapted dynamically.

11.3 Anomaly-Based Approach

The anomaly-based approach contributes to representing *acceptable behaviors* and constructing a corresponding recognizer for non-acceptable behaviors. More specifically, with some precautions, a large collection $N \subset \Sigma^*$ of actual behaviors, i.e., sufficiently long event sequences generated by the event generator as audit data in the past, is supposed to constitute a representative sample of "acceptable" behaviors. Clearly, in particular, the precautions have to ensure that there are no hidden attacks, and that the sample covers the full range of the real users' activities.

Roughly speaking, a recognizer is then constructed that is trained to let each collected behavior $\sigma \in N$ pass, and sufficiently similar behaviors as well, but raises an alarm for all other behaviors. Intuitively, the former behaviors are seen as supposedly *normal* and thus "acceptable", whereas the latter behaviors are seen as deviating from the norm and thus *anomalous*, giving rise to an alarm.

Briefly outlined, and subject to many variations, the anomaly-based approach thus consists of the following steps:

- In the *learning phase*, an administrator gathers a sample set N of supposedly normal behaviors, and selects a length l of a *sliding window* on the behaviors. Then, a suitable tool for *machine learning*, for example a neural network, is employed to construct an efficient finite-automaton-like recognizer for anomalous parts of behaviors.
- In the *operation phase*, the recognizer searches for anomalous parts in the supplied behavior within the sliding window, raising an alarm whenever such a part has been detected.
- In the *measurement phase*, the effectiveness might be improved by adapting the sample set N or by enlarging the length of the sliding window, and then reconstructing the recognizer. The efficiency might be improved by optimizing or even smoothing the recognizer, for example by letting some additional behaviors pass or by diminishing the length of the sliding window, again facing a trade-off with effectiveness.

11.4 Cooperation

In a distributed system, each site might apply intrusion detection and reaction for its own purposes. Additionally, the administrators of the various sites might agree to cooperate in order to more effectively protect against attacks spanning more than one site. A *distributed denial-of-service* (*DDoS*) *attack* is an example, where some malicious participants try to flood some sites with too many requests such that these sites' expected services degrade or even are no longer available.

Any *cooperation* requires making some of the local information available to the remote partners. Figure 11.2 indicates a natural approach: some of the local alarms are forwarded to the cooperating agents and, vice versa, the communicated remote alarms are treated as further input data for the analysis component. Basically, the analysis component then has to perform the additional subtask of correlating its own (more) *elementary alarms* with the received (more) *elementary alarms* in order to produce a (more) *complex alarm*. A complex alarm should inform the reaction component about the overall situation regarding a suspected attack, and thereby facilitate an effective response.

Evidently, although producing useful local elementary alarms is already a tedious and often only unsatisfactorily accomplished task, correlating them into informative complex alarms is even more challenging. Nevertheless, standardization has laid a foundation, and recent work has outlined a heuristic method for achieving this ambitious goal. In the following, we briefly sketch what the steps of such a method are intended to achieve:

- *Normalization* maps local alarms to a common format with common semantics and mandatory features, for example the attack's start time, end time, source and target.
- *Fusion* discards obvious duplicate alarms generated by different sites observing the same activity.
- *Verification* identifies irrelevant alarms and false positive alarms, for example by judging a current alarm regarding a knowledge base of "known harmless situations".
- *Thread reconstruction* gathers together subsequent alarms describing attacks that originate from an attacker residing at the same source, on the same target.
- *Session reconstruction* correlates alarms that describe events on the network and in a host, for example by exploiting knowledge about how network transport protocol port numbers are mapped to the identifiers of the processes on the host listening on the respective ports, and knowledge about the parent–child relationships of the processes on the host.
- *Focus recognition* integrates alarms describing attacks where a given attacker attacks many targets or where a given target is attacked by many sources, for example distributed denial-of-service attacks.
- *Multistep correlation* combines alarms suspected to constitute a complex attack, for example on the basis of a suitable collection of complex signatures.
- *Impact analysis* and *alarm prioritization* determine the suspected effect of an attack in order to prioritize the respective alarm accordingly, for example on the basis of an asset database, which measures the importance of the services offered and models their dependencies.

11.5 Bibliographic Hints

Amoroso [15], Bace [24] and Marchette [333] have authored recent books about intrusion detection. Current work on cooperation is summarized and extended by Ning/Jajodia/Wang [374], emphasizing the communication needs of an "abstraction-based approach", and by Kruegel/Valeur/Vigna [301], elaborating the heuristic correlation method outlined above. Taxonomies that survey the various approaches have been proposed by Debar/Dacier/Wespi [157] and Axelsson [22].

Examples of the signature-based approach are presented by Mounji/et al. [359], Ilgun/Kemmerer/Porras [264, 265], Lindquist/Porras [323], Eckmann/Vigna/Kemmerer [181, 491], Lee/Stolfo [312] and others. Castano/Fugini/Martella/Samarati [118] give an introduction to some early approaches to anomaly detection. More specific work is reported by Forrest/Hofmeyr/Longstaff [214], D.Denning [165], Javitz/Valdes [278], Ko/Ruschitzka/Levitt [294], Lane/Brodley [310], Wespi/Dacier/Debar [498], Michael/Ghosh [351] and others. Cooperation is considered by Huang/Jasper/Wicks [261], Bass [31], Ning/Xu/et al. [372, 373] and others.

Axelsson [23] argues that the false-alarm rate limits the effectiveness of intrusion detection in principle. McHugh [340] critically examines the actual achievement of intrusion detection systems. Iheagwara/Blyth/Singhal [263] report on a more recent performance study for high-speed networks.

Monitoring raises many more specific problems. As an example, Julisch [287] treats the problem of identifying the root causes underlying the bulk of reported alarms. As another example, Fischer-Hübner/Sobirey/et al. [454], Büschges/Kesdogan [112], Lundin/Jonsson [328], Biskup/Flegel [67, 68, 208, 209, 210], Xu/Ning [504] and others investigate the problem that individuals might have conflicting security interests, for example, on the one side, accountability for the sake of pursuing attackers, and on the other side, non-observability or anonymity for the sake of privacy.

12 Techniques of Cryptography: Essentials

12.1 Requirements, Mechanisms and their Quality

In order to meet security requirements, at design time the participants or the *security officers* acting on behalf of the participants have to specify security policies, which express which agents are permitted or prohibited to perform which operations on which objects. Within the computing system, the *permissions* actually declared and, if applicable, the *prohibitions* are persistently represented and managed by a *knowledge base*.

This knowledge base might exist only conceptually, as is the case for *cryptography*. For cryptography, as sketched in Section 7.2 and visualized in Figure 7.9, a permission is determined by a *secret*, commonly called a cryptographic *key*, that is available to an agent. A subject's request is performed as intended only if the subject can exhibit a key that is specific to that request. Otherwise, the request might still somehow access the pertinent object but the result will in general not be "meaningful", though possibly "harmful". With this usage of keys, the conceptual knowledge base can be seen as realizing some kind of implicit *access decisions*.

Besides the interpretation suggested in preceding chapters and that we have repeated above, cryptography has other flavors as well. In fact, cryptography has evolved as a discipline in its own right and, only recently, cryptography has been identified and widely recognized as what it is treated as in this monograph:

- Cryptography provides crucially needed combined *techniques of security* in computing systems, usually closely intertwined with the techniques of control and monitoring. To achieve its specific goals, cryptography binds a successful and meaningful execution of an operation or interaction to providing a suitable *secret key* as input.

We should mention two further flavors of cryptography, which are discussed in more detail below:

- Cryptography achieves *virtual isolation* between participants: participants that share a cryptographic key are virtually isolated from those that do not.
- Cryptography enables *cooperation in the presence of threats* based on limited trust: participants that autonomously generate and secretly keep appropriate cryptographic keys can enforce their security *interests* by themselves while interacting with other participants, even if these are remote, appear as strangers and are potentially hostile.

Roughly summarized, cryptography meets the requirements of autonomous participants to support their basic interests in *confidentiality, integrity, authenticity, non-repudiation*, and *anonymity*, and some other interests (but excluding availability), by virtually *isolating* key holders from other participants and thereby providing countermeasures against *threats* from potentially malicious cooperation partners.

Cryptography usually serves its purposes by more or less complicated *protocols* that have to be appropriately executed by the partners involved in a cooperation in order to be successful. In most cases, a cryptographic protocol extends over several *rounds*. Since cooperation typically takes place in a *distributed computing system*, a round normally consists of both local computations and message exchanges. Since it faces *threats* and thus potentially occurring actual *attacks* by some of the partners, the local part of a round is often structured as a guarded action, where the guard checks for the correct execution of the expected behavior of the other partners.

The *security requirements* for a protocol typically demand that either all partners of an execution behave well and then the wanted properties are actually achieved, or some partner is cheating and then this fact is at least discovered or is not harmful at all.

Most protocols are composed of appropriate instantiations of a few *basic cryptographic blocks*. When a protocol is being designed and implemented, the actual *compositionality* of the *security properties* of the building blocks is crucial, i.e., the *verification* has to investigate whether the presumably known security properties of an instance of a building block are preserved under the specific composition, and whether the properties of the components contribute to the final security properties of the overall protocol as anticipated.

This kind of verification is far beyond the scope of this monograph, and in fact in several cases it is beyond even the current state of our knowledge, though in principle it is highly important for applying cryptography in a provably secure way. In this monograph, we restrict ourselves mainly to *informally outlining* the *hopefully* (!) achieved properties, mostly leaving open the question of exact, mathematically expressed statements and thorough proofs of them.

Exactly determining the quality of a basic cryptographic block or a protocol usually requires one to employ strong mathematical skills applied to various concepts. The needed concepts include those of number theory, finite algebras, classical probability theory and computing, in particular those for protocol design and verification, the general theory of computational complexity, with an emphasis on lower bounds for specific problems, and complexity analysis of concrete algorithms for operations in number theory and finite algebras.

For example, an assertion about quality might be as follows: "Provided that a key of length l has been appropriately generated and kept secret by the pertinent participant, any cheating partner that employs a polynomially time-bounded probabilistic Turing machine for his attack has an expected success rate that is less than $1/2^l$, while the computations of honest participants require at most $O(f(l,n))$ time, where f is a polynomial of low degree, for example quadratic, and n denotes the size of the input data". Intuitively, the upper bound on the expected success rate of attacks often expresses that a malicious partner can succeed essentially only if he *guesses by chance* some binary-encoded item of length l. Clearly, if l is small enough, an attacker might try to substitute "guessing by chance" by an *exhaustive search* for a suitable item, and thus l is always required to be large enough to resist such vulnerabilities.

Assertions of this or a similar kind have a *security parameter l* that is usually determined by the length of the cryptographic *key* used. This parameterization allows one to balance computational effort and the security achievements, which are often subject to a trade-off: a longer key might require a higher computational cost but ensures improved security. Seen from the point of view of the expected degree of security to be met, the trade-off determines the required key length and thus the computational effort to be expended. The most important example is making *exhaustive-search* attacks highly expected to fail, given the presumably available resources of potential attackers.

The example quality assertion sketched above indicates that (important parts of) cryptography relies on two crucial, closely related suppositions, the exact status of which is an open problem of computer science, unfortunately:

- It is possible to algorithmically provide *sufficient randomness*.
- It is possible to construct *one-way functions* that differentiate a computationally easy problem from a computationally hard one.

These suppositions can be expressed a little more precisely but still intuitively, as follows.

The "sufficient randomness" supposition postulates that there are efficient (algorithmic) *pseudorandom generators* that achieve the following property: from short *truly random* inputs, they generate long bit sequences that are *computationally indistinguishable* from "truly random" bit sequences of the corresponding length.

The "one-way function" supposition postulates that there are functional algorithms that do not allow feasible algorithms for the *inverse function*, except for "rare exceptional values".

Basically, pseudorandomness avoids "easy algorithmic guessing", and (suitably customized) "one-way functions" allow an honest participant to efficiently prepare against "threatening partners", who are faced with an intractable problem.

12.2 Cryptographic Isolation and Indistinguishability

Many challenges to security interests result from the fact that participants *share* computing resources, i.e., the computing system as a whole or some specific components are jointly used by several individuals, either sequentially or (at least virtually) in parallel. While some kinds of sharing are purposely required for cooperation, other kinds arise from the need to save costs or from related considerations. For example, in order that two partners A and B can exchange messages, they need a physical communication line. In most cases, however, there will not be a private, physically isolated line exclusively available to A and B. Instead, in preparing for sending or receiving a message, each of A and B connects to a shared *network* with switching nodes that establish a (possibly virtual) connection on demand. While A and B might have the illusion that they are using that connection exclusively, in reality they are not. Rather, they share all the resources and services of the network with many others, who are using (virtually) established connections as well.

Isolation, one of the three identified key ideas for enforcing security, then aims at avoiding the possibly harmful effects of sharing by deliberately reintroducing some kind of *exclusive usage* of specific components, in many cases under some administrative control and monitoring. While some foundation in *physical isolation* is advisable, most forms of isolation are only *virtual*. Moreover, a participant taking advantage of isolation might be forced to share the administrative facilities with others.

Cryptography offers another form of *virtual isolation* that is particularly suitable for situations with the following characteristics:

- A virtual isolation of the form sketched above is in danger of occasionally failing, for instance owing to unexpected behavior of an actual implementation in a lower layer.
- A virtual isolation of the form sketched above appears to be not achievable at all.
- Administrative intervention by third parties is unavoidable, but not acceptable to the individuals concerned.

Such situations typically occur in *distributed computing systems* that are based on *networks*. In these systems, messages are ultimately seen as *bit strings* and physically handled as electromagnetic signals, using copper cables, glass fibers or wireless means such as radio or infrared. Unfortunately, all these means are in one way or another subject to passive eavesdropping or active interference, depending on their specific properties. Moreover, the messages are forwarded along the selected transport route from one node to another, and each of these nodes somehow processes the transported bit string, and thus at least *reads* it, and potentially also *manipulates* it.

Cryptographic virtual isolation can deal with such situations, on the basis of the advisable *physical isolation* of the secret cryptographic keys involved. For example, as discussed in more detail in subsequent sections, *encryption* and cryptographic *authentication* can achieve the following.

Suppose a (potentially malicious) participant is not entitled to read a bit string to be transmitted to a designated receiver, but we want to be prepared for the possibility that nevertheless the participant somehow manages to learn the bit string. In that case, the preparation consists of *encrypting* the bit string. Encryption is designed to ensure that learning the encrypted bit string does not imply an increase in any meaningful information, seen from the perspective of that participant. On the other hand, the designated receiver of the bit string, being equipped with the secret *decryption key*, can recover the original bit string, and thus presumably can derive the encoded meaningful information as well. In this example, the secret decryption key serves to *virtually isolate* the designated receiver, the key holder, from any other participant, thereby enforcing the designated receiver's interest in *confidentiality*, while *sharing* a public network. Note that encryption cannot prevent unauthorized reading but only makes such an action useless.

Suppose, additionally, that the same potentially malicious participant may succeed in modifying a bit string during the transmission. In general, without additional preparation, the receiver cannot detect such a modification. In that case, the preparation consists of cryptographically *authenticating* the bit string. Cryptographic authentication is designed to ensure that a receiver can effectively *test* whether the received message originates from the indicated sender and has not been modified afterwards. In order to achieve this goal, the indicated sender employs a secret cryptographic *authentication key*. Accordingly, this key serves to *virtually isolate* the sender, the key holder, from any other participant, thereby supporting the interests of *integrity* as *unmodified state*, *authenticity* or even *non-repudiation*, while the sender is *sharing* a public network. Note that cryptographic authentication cannot avoid attempts at unauthorized modification but only makes such an action detectable.

In the discussion above, cryptographic virtual isolation has been described as the effect of employing a secret key: the key holder is *virtually isolated* (with respect to the functionality considered) from all other participants, and thus the key holder is also *distinguished* (with respect to the functionality considered) among all other participants.

The effect on all the other participants can often be described alternatively in terms of *indistinguishability*, a further key idea for enforcing security: for the other participants, the potential or actual actions of the key holder appear to be *indistinguishable* from *random behavior*. Very roughly outlined, whatever the other participants observe or attempt to do, from their point of view they do not have enough computational or other resources to make their observations or actions meaningful (with respect to the functionality considered). In this context, "meaningful" is meant to refer to some external social or intellectual expectation and to be the opposite of "arbitrary", where "arbitrary" is like the result of (supposedly meaningless) repeated coin flipping.

More technically, but still intuitively, cryptography exploits the key idea of indistinguishability by carefully relaxing the notion of "equality": items that are *computationally indistinguishable* are treated as if they were identical. For example, the "sufficient randomness" supposition considers bit sequences that are "computationally indistinguishable" from "truly random" bit sequences as if they were random. The way in which the relaxation is taken care of is hidden in the precise technical definition of "computationally indistinguishable", which refers to an assumed available amount of computing resources for an attempt to tell (collections of) two items apart, and in the amount of computing resources assumed to be available for attackers: both amounts are supposed to be bounded by polynomially time-bounded probabilistic Turing machines, finite compositions of which are polynomially time-bounded and probabilistic too.

12.3 Cooperation in the Presence of Threats

Modern computing systems are often embedded, distributed and federated. Accordingly, there might be numerous, different direct participants, and many more individuals will usually have contributed to the design, implementation and management of such a system. Moreover, possibly many others are indirectly affected.

Typically, in such a diverse environment, any individual participant can assign direct *trust* only to selected parts of the system, preferably to those that he himself is able to acquire and then to control. The rest of the system, in particular remote components, might then be considered as potentially *threatening*. Correspondingly, an individual participant might immediately *trust* only a few selected persons involved, while all the others might be seen as potentially malicious *threats*. In fact, for example in traditional commerce and so in *electronic commerce*, not only mediators but direct communication partners as well might turn out to be cheating.

Nevertheless, individuals are willing or obliged to cooperate by using a computing system. In this situation, the power of cryptography stems from aiming at and partially achieving the following goal:

- An individual participant acting in a cooperation in the presence of threats is supported in enforcing his *security interests* by himself, using *technical security mechanisms* that are under his direct control or selected in *self-determination*.
- The support applies even if only the directly controlled or *autonomously selected* components operate as expected and any of the others might be misbehaving.

12.4 Basic Cryptographic Blocks

In this section, we roughly outline six *basic cryptographic blocks*, instantiations of which contribute to most of cryptographic security mechanisms:

- encryption,
- authentication,
- anonymization,
- randomness and pseudorandomness,
- one-way hash functions, and
- timestamps.

The definition of the blocks is motivated by the intended *application* purposes and the *threats* they are designed to resist, rather than by an analysis of their dependencies and their contributions to engineering actual implementations. The applications and threats are treated mostly in terms of *message transmissions*, where a *sender S* transmits a meaningful *message m* to a designated *receiver R*, as discussed in Chapter 2. In the following, we mostly identify a message with its representing *bit string*. In this context, message transmission is exploited as a fundamental abstraction of computing, in particular for distributed forms of computing in *networks*.

12.4.1 Encryption

In order to enforce the interest in *confidentiality*, i.e., to ensure the correctness of the receiver of a message as visualized in Figure 2.8, the sender can employ *encryption*. Encryption refines the situation of Figure 2.2 into those shown in Figure 12.1 and Figure 12.2. Moreover, the counterpart of encryption, decryption, can be seen as drawing *inferences*, as discussed in Subsection 2.1.2 and sketched in Figure 2.4.

Using *encryption*, the sender S transforms the original bit string m to be transmitted into another bit string m° such that only the designated receiver R (and possibly the sender) is enabled to recover the original bit string. The transformation is performed by a (possibly probabilistic) *encryption* algorithm *Enc* that requires (at least) two parameters:

- an *encryption key ek_R* that, in particular, distinguishes the designated receiver R;
- an original message m, which is called the *plaintext*.

For any application of the encryption algorithm, the transformed bit string, called the *ciphertext*, is denoted by

$$m^\circ = Enc(ek_R, m). \tag{12.1}$$

The ability of the designated receiver R to recover an original message is materialized by a *decryption key dk_R* that only the *distinguished* receiver (and possibly the sender) is supposed to know. The inverse transformation is performed by a (possibly probabilistic) *decryption* algorithm *Dec* that requires two parameters too:

- a *decryption key dk_R* that, in particular, distinguishes the designated receiver R;
- an observed bit string m°, i.e., a *ciphertext*.

The encryption algorithm *Enc* and the decryption algorithm *Dec* should be inverse whenever a *matching key pair* has been employed, i.e., the following *correctness property* is required:

$$\text{For all plaintexts } m, \quad Dec(dk_R, Enc(ek_R, m)) = m. \tag{12.2}$$

Additionally, a specific *secrecy property* must hold. *Naively*, and taken literally not appropriately expressed, such a secrecy property requires the following:

> For all plaintexts m, without a knowledge of the decryption key dk_R,   (12.3)
> m cannot be "determined" from the ciphertext m°.

Better versions of the needed secrecy property are more sophisticated and readily include the naive version. The *semantic* version of the secrecy property can be interpreted as requiring that an unauthorized observer of a ciphertext cannot infer anything new about the corresponding plaintext. A little more precisely, such an observer can infer only those properties that he has already "known in principle" before learning the ciphertext:

> For all plaintexts m, without a knowledge of the decryption key dk_R,   (12.4)
> any *property* of m that can be "determined" from the ciphertext m°
> could also be "determined" without knowing m° at all.

An *operational* version of the secrecy property requires that an unauthorized observer of ciphertexts cannot separate apart any pair of ciphertexts, and thus cannot solve the problem of assigning a specific plaintext to a ciphertext. To be a little more precise, we need, essentially, a setting where encryption is *probabilistic* and, furthermore, sequences of plaintexts and of matching key pairs of increasing length are considered (instead of simply fixing the length), where the length is taken as a *security parameter*. The *indistinguishability of ciphertexts* can then be expressed roughly as follows:

> For any pair of plaintext sequences   (12.5)
> $(m_1', m_1'', m_1''', \ldots)$ and $(m_2', m_2'', m_2''', \ldots)$,
> without a knowledge of the sequence of decryption keys employed,
> the resulting sequences of ciphertexts are "computationally indistinguishable".

For whatever version of the secrecy property, the algorithms *Dec* and *Enc* are always supposed to be publicly known, while the decryption keys are required to be kept strictly secret. Thus, given approved algorithms and seen from the perspective of the endusers, enforcing the *confidentiality* of messages by encryption basically relies only on selecting appropriate keys and on actually hiding the decryption keys.

The encryption mechanisms commonly used can be classified according to the relationship between the encryption key and the decryption key:

- For a *symmetric* (or *secret-key*) mechanism, the encryption key is (basically) equal to the decryption key, and thus both keys are often referred to as the *secret key*. Accordingly, the sender is *distinguished* too, and thus is responsible for protecting the key as well. Furthermore, any designated pair of a sender and a receiver have to secretly exchange a secret key before messages can be confidentially transmitted. In some situations, this key exchange is supported by a mediating *third party* that must be *trusted* by the sender and the receiver, since the third party then knows the secret key and thus is *distinguished* as well.

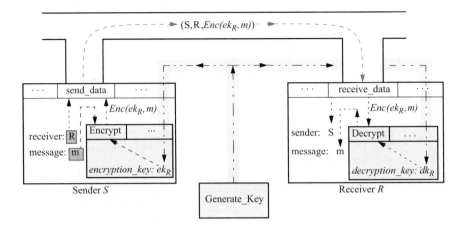

Fig. 12.1. Key generation and subsequent encryption, transmission and decryption of a message, using a *symmetric* cryptographic mechanism (the light gray area must be hidden from other participants; the key generation can be performed by either the sender, the receiver or a trusted third party)

- For an *asymmetric* (or *public-key*) mechanism, the encryption key is essentially different from the decryption key. Moreover, an additional *secrecy property* is required, a *naive* version of which can be described as follows:

$$\text{The decryption key } dk_R \qquad (12.6)$$
$$\text{cannot be "determined" from the encryption key } ek_R.$$

Accordingly, only the receiver is *distinguished*, and the sender is *not*, and there is no need to keep the encryption key secret; in fact, it can be made public and used by many senders.

On the basis of these observations, the encryption key and the decryption key are called the *public* and the *private key*, respectively (the private key is also often called the *secret key*). In principle, a participant, acting as a receiver, secretly generates a matching key pair by himself, stores the private (decryption) key under strict protection, and openly communicates the matching public (encryption) key to any potential sender.

In general, however, the communication of the public key has to be assisted by a mediating *trusted third party*. This party is needed to *certify* that the public key indeed belongs to the indicated receiver, i.e., that the matching private key is actually held by the indicated receiver (and not by somebody else).

The two kinds of mechanism differ essentially, and most crucially, in the procedures for *generating* and *distributing* keys: whereas for asymmetric mechanisms the designated receiver has a *distinguished* role, for symmetric mechanisms both partners are equally involved. The differences are visualized in Figure 12.1 and

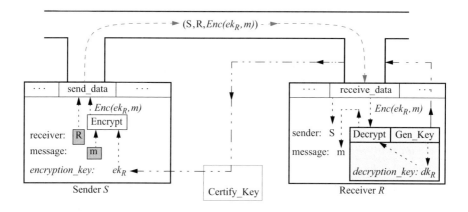

Fig. 12.2. Key generation, key certification and subsequent encryption, transmission and decryption of a message, using an *asymmetric* cryptographic mechanism (the light gray area must be hidden from other participants and from the sender as well)

Figure 12.2 by the components to be kept hidden. For asymmetric mechanisms, the key generation and the storage of the private key must be protected on the side of the receiver only, without further secrecy obligations for the sender or the communication of the public key. For symmetric mechanisms, the key generation, the actual communication of the secret key and the storage of the secret key on both sides must be protected. Moreover, if applicable, the contributions of the trusted third parties are different: for asymmetric mechanisms, they certify public keys, whereas for symmetric mechanisms, they generate and distribute secret keys.

12.4.2 Authentication

In order to support an interest in *integrity, authenticity* or *non-repudiation*, i.e., to ensure the unmodified state of a message as visualized in Figure 2.6 or the correctness of the sender of a message as visualized in Figure 2.7, the basic cryptographic block of *authentication* or, more specially, of (cryptographic) *perpetuation of evidence* can be employed. More precisely, integrity and authenticity are enforced as *detection of modification* and of *impersonation*, respectively. Authentication refines the situation of Figure 2.2 into those shown in Figure 12.3 and Figure 12.4. Moreover, authentication is part of the more general framework for inspection and exception handling, as discussed in Subsection 2.1.3 and sketched in Figure 2.5.

Using *authentication*, when preparing for transmitting a bit string m as a message, the designated sender S computes another bit string $red_{S,m}$ as a *cryptographic piece of evidence* (*cryptographic exhibit* or *cryptographic check redundancy*). The designated sender then forwards the compound $(S,m,red_{S,m})$ of the sender identification and both the original and the computed bit string to the receiver. After receiving such a compound of the form $(S°, m°, red_{S,m}°)$, the receiver can check whether the message part originates from the claimed sender without modification. For this purpose, the included cryptographic exhibit must, essentially, depend on some property of the designated sender and on the message.

More specifically, the computation of a cryptographic exhibit is performed by a (possibly probabilistic) *authentication* algorithm *Aut* that requires (at least) two parameters:

- an *authentication key* ak_S that, in particular, *distinguishes* the designated sender S, and which is supposed to be known only by the designated sender (and possibly the receiver);
- a message m.

For any application of the authentication algorithm, the computed bit string, called the *cryptographic exhibit*, is denoted by

$$red_{S,m} = Aut(ak_S, m). \tag{12.7}$$

The ability of the receiver R to inspect the cryptographic exhibits computed by S is materialized by a *test key* tk_S that matches the authentication key ak_S. The inspection is performed by a (possibly probabilistic) Boolean-valued *authenticity verification* algorithm *Test* that requires (at least) three parameters:

- a *test key* tk_S that, in particular, distinguishes the designated sender S;
- a received message m;
- a cryptographic exhibit *red*.

The authentication algorithm *Aut* and the authenticity verification algorithm *Test* should be complementary whenever a *matching key pair* has been employed, i.e., the following (weak) *correctness property* is required:

$$\text{For all messages } m, \ Test(tk_S, m, Aut(ak_S, m)) = true. \tag{12.8}$$

Additionally, a specific *unforgeability property* must hold. Naively expressed, such an unforgeability property requires the following:

For all messages m, without a knowledge of the authentication key ak_S, (12.9)
one cannot "determine" a bit string *red* such that $Test(tk_S, m, red) = true$.

Formal versions of the unforgeability property are more sophisticated. If achievable for a specific setting, the weak correctness property and the unforgeability property can be combined into a *strong correctness property* that is complemented by a *weak unforgeability property*:

For all messages m and for all bit strings *red*, (12.10)
$Test(tk_S, m, red) = true$ iff $red = Aut(ak_S, m)$;
and without a knowledge of the authentication key ak_S,
one cannot "determine" that *red*.

The algorithms *Aut* and *Test* are always supposed to be publicly known, while the authentication keys are required to be kept strictly secret. Thus, given approved algorithms and seen from the perspective of the endusers, enforcing the *integrity* and *authenticity* of messages (in the sense of detection of violations) by authentication basically relies only on selecting appropriate keys, and on actually hiding the authentication keys.

The authentication mechanisms commonly used can be classified according to the relationship between the authentication key and the test key:

- For a *symmetric* (or *secret-key*) mechanism, the authentication key is (basically) equal to the test key, and thus both keys are often referred to as the *secret key*. The authenticity verification algorithm simply recomputes the cryptographic exhibit for the received message and compares the result with the received exhibit: the verification is seen as successful iff both exhibits are equal. Accordingly, the receiver is *distinguished* too, leading to the following consequences. First, in a *dispute* where a third party is involved as an *arbitrator*, the receiver cannot use a received cryptographic exhibit to blame the sender for being responsible for the corresponding message; for the receiver could have produced the cryptographic exhibit by himself. Second, the receiver is responsible for protecting the key as well. Furthermore, any designated pair of a sender and a receiver have to secretly exchange a secret key before messages can be authentically transmitted. In some situations, this key exchange is supported by a mediating *third party* that must be *trusted* by the sender and the receiver, since the third party then knows the secret key and thus is distinguished as well.

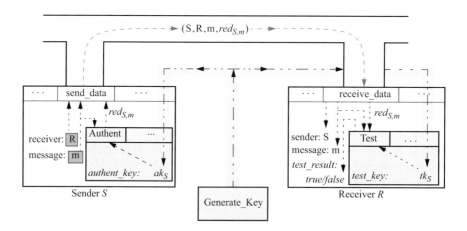

Fig. 12.3. Key generation and subsequent authentication, transmission and verification of a message, using a *symmetric* cryptographic mechanism (the light gray area must be hidden from other participants; the key generation can be performed by either the sender, the receiver or a trusted third party)

- For an *asymmetric* (or *public-key*) mechanism, the authentication key is essentially different from the test key. Moreover, an additional *secrecy property* is required, a *naive* version of which can be described as follows:

$$\text{The authentication key } ak_S \qquad (12.11)$$
$$\text{cannot be "determined" from the test key } tk_S.$$

Accordingly, only the sender is *distinguished*, and the receiver is *not*, leading to the following consequences. First, in a *dispute* where a third party is involved as an *arbitrator*, the receiver can use a received cryptographic exhibit to blame the sender for being responsible for the corresponding message. Thus cryptographic exhibits can be employed in a similar way to traditional *handwritten signatures* on paper documents. Therefore, cryptographic exhibits are often called *digital signatures*. Second, there is no need to keep the test key secret; in fact, it can be made public and used by many receivers.

On the basis of these observations, the authentication key and the test key are called the *private* and the *public key*, respectively (the private key is also often called the *secret key*). The private (authentication) key is often also called a *signature key*, and the public (test) key is often also called a *verification key*. In principle, a participant, acting as a sender, secretly generates a matching key pair by himself, stores the private (authentication or signature) key under strict protection, and openly communicates the matching public (test) key to any potential receiver.

In general, however, the communication of the public key has to be assisted by a mediating *trusted third party*. This party is needed to *certify* that the public key indeed belongs to the indicated sender, i.e., that the matching private key is actually held by the indicated sender (and not by somebody else).

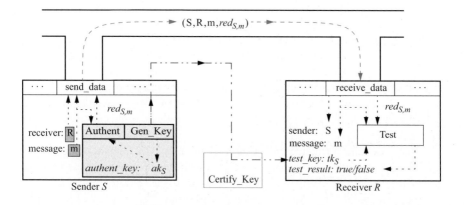

Fig. 12.4. Key generation, key certification, and subsequent authentication (digital signing), transmission and verification of a message, using an *asymmetric* cryptographic mechanism (the light gray area must be hidden from other participants and from the receiver as well)

The two kinds of mechanism differ essentially, and most crucially, in the procedures for *generating* and *distributing* keys: whereas for asymmetric mechanisms
the designated sender has a *distinguished* role, for symmetric mechanisms both
partners are equally involved. The differences are visualized in Figure 12.3 and
Figure 12.4 by the components to be kept hidden. For asymmetric mechanisms, the
key generation and the storage of the private key must be protected on the side of
the sender only, without further secrecy obligations for the receiver or the communication of the public key. For symmetric mechanisms, the key generation, the
actual communication of the secret key and the storage of the secret key on both
sides must be protected. Moreover, if applicable, the contributions of the trusted
third parties are different: for asymmetric mechanisms, they certify public keys,
whereas for symmetric mechanisms, they generate and distribute secret keys.

12.4.3 Anonymization

In order to support the interest in *anonymity* or, more generally, in *non-observability*, various mechanisms of *anonymization* can be employed as a basic cryptographic block. These interests can be seen as strengthened forms of (message)
confidentiality, as enforced by encryption: now, not only the message itself should
be kept secret, but also the full *activity* of a message transmission or some aspect of
it, as set out in Subsection 2.2.8 and Subsection 2.2.9.

Interpreted in terms of *indistinguishability*, which is advocated in Section 6.3 as
a key idea for enforcing security, the confidentiality goal of encryption can be
roughly rephrased as follows: from the point of view of a non-designated observer
who does not know the decryption key, the actual plaintext is *indistinguishable*
from any other element of a preferably large text domain from which the plaintext
has been chosen.

Generalizing this interpretation, we can roughly rephrase the anonymity or non-
observability goal of anonymization as follows: from the point of view of an
observer who is not designated to learn about (some aspect of) an activity or a
sequence of activities, (the pertinent aspect of) any actually occurring activity is
indistinguishable from (the pertinent aspect of) any other activity in a preferably
large activity domain from which the actually occurring activity has been selected.
In other words, the actual plaintext or activity, respectively, is indistinguishably
hidden in a preferably large domain of other possibilities, often called an *anonymity class*.

In the following we sketch three examples of an activity domain regarding message transmission with an aspect of interest, together with an appropriate version of
an *indistinguishability property*. The examples are visualized in Figure 12.5.

First, consider the activity domain of a fixed group $\{S_1, \dots, S_n\}$ of participants
S_j sending and receiving messages. We are interested in the aspect of who is the
sender of an actual message m, i.e., we wish to hide the origin of messages and thus
to enable anonymous sending. This interest should be enforced for any participant

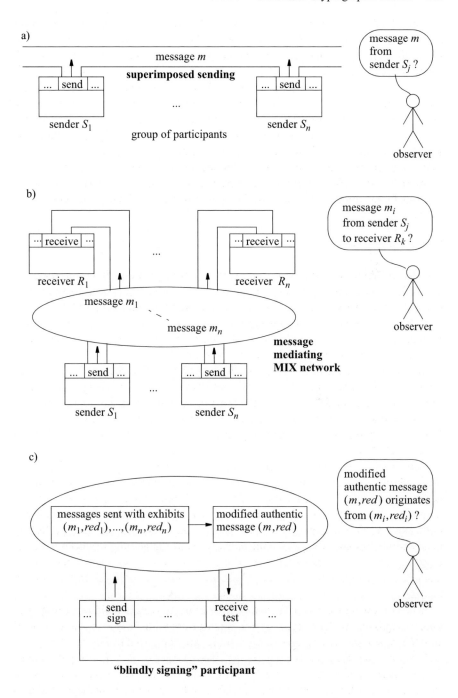

Fig. 12.5. Visualization of anonymization by (a) superimposed sending, (b) MIX networks and (c) blind signing: the observer cannot determine the relationships

in the group, clearly except for the actual sender, but including the actual receivers. Accordingly, an *anonymity property* of the following rough form is required:

$$\text{By observing an actual message } m, \tag{12.12}$$
$$\text{a non-designated observer cannot "determine" the actual sender } S_j.$$

This property can be rephrased in two ways: first, a non-designated observer cannot determine the relationship between an observed message and its sender; second, for this observer, all group members appear *equally likely* to be the actual sender or, equivalently, the actual sender appears as if it has been *randomly* selected from the group. The required property is achieved by the anonymization mechanism of *superimposed sending* presented in Section 15.3.

Second, consider the activity domain of a set of senders S_j and a set of receivers R_k employing some mediating network for message transmissions. We are interested in the aspect of which pair of a sender and a receiver belongs to an actual message m, i.e., we wish to hide the connection between the origin and the destination of messages and thus to enable anonymous communications. This interest should be enforced for any participant who has access to the mediating network, except for the actual sender and the actual receiver of a pertinent pair, but including the participants mediating messages within the network. Accordingly, an *anonymity property* of the following rough form is required:

$$\text{By observing an actual message } m, \tag{12.13}$$
$$\text{a non-designated observer cannot "determine"}$$
$$\text{the pair of the actual sender } S_j \text{ and the actual receiver } R_k.$$

This property can be rephrased in two ways: first, a non-designated observer cannot determine the relationship between an observed message and its sender/receiver pair; second, for this observer, all possible pairs appear *equally likely* or, equivalently, the actual pair appears as if it has been *randomly* selected from the activity domain. Under some appropriate restrictions, the required property is achieved by the anonymization mechanism of *MIX networks* presented in Section 15.4.

Third, consider the activity domain of one distinguished participant sending digitally signed messages of the form (m_i, red_i) to some receivers. Each such signed message is understood as a *digital document* expressing some *obligation* of the sender to whoever presents this document later on; from the point of view of a receiver, or holder, such a signed message is seen as a *credential* (a *digital legitimation*) to be redeemed by the sender, as confirmed by the sender's digital signature. In one prominent instantiation, the distinguished participant acts as a *bank* issuing *digital coins* (as obligations to reimburse some amount of "real money") to *clients*, who might transfer such coins to some *dealers*; whoever presents such a coin to the bank later on expects to receive the promised amount of "real money".

More abstractly, the activity domain consists of two kinds of activities:

- the distinguished participant *issues* (sends) digital documents of an agreed form to receivers;
- the receivers or holders *present* digital documents of that form to the distinguished participant.

Obviously, on being faced with a presented digital document as a credential, the distinguished participant will first verify the signature before regarding the digital document as authentic and accepting the obligation expressed. We are interested in the aspect of which issued digital document corresponds to which presented digital document, i.e., we wish to hide the *links* between issuing obligations and presenting them and thus to enable anonymous redeeming. This interest should be enforced for any observer who has access to the activities mentioned, except for the receiver and holder involved, but in particular for the distinguished participant.

Regarding the instantiation sketched above, this interest means that the bank's clients can *spend* their *digital coins* anonymously, i.e., the bank cannot trace back the usage of presented coins. Clearly, this interest can only be enforced if receivers or holders are able to modify issued documents while maintaining their authenticity, i.e., for a modified document (m, red), the exhibit *red* must still successfully pass the pertinent authenticity verification, even though the distinguished participant has *not* been involved in the modification. Summarizing, besides the standard properties for authentication, an additional *unlinkability property* of the following rough form is required:

Knowing the issued documents $\{(m_1, red_1), \dots, (m_n, red_n)\}$ and   (12.14)
seeing a presented modified document (m, red) with a verified signature *red*,
a non-designated observer cannot "determine" the link
from the presented document to the corresponding issued document.

This property can be rephrased in two ways: first, a non-designated observer cannot determine the relationship between a modified document and its originally issued version; second, for this observer, all original documents appear *equally likely* or, equivalently, the actual original document appears as if it has been *randomly* selected from the set of all issued documents. Astonishingly enough, the required property can be achieved by the anonymization mechanism of *blind signatures* presented in Section 15.2.

For these and many other examples of anonymization, it might be crucial to define a precise notion of a "participant" and, if applicable, to differentiate between several possible meanings. Two natural meanings are straightforward:

- On the one hand, a participant may denote a *human individual* (identified by name, given name, place of birth and date of birth).
- On the other hand, a participant may denote a *computing device* (identified, for instance, by an IP number) or even a *process* (identified, for instance, by an internal process number) running on such a device, usually employed on behalf of one or more human individuals.

An additional artificially introduced meaning might be important as well:

- A participant may denote a *pseudonym* that is used as a substitute for a human individual, a computing device or any other *subject* of interest.

Such pseudonyms can be coarsely classified as follows:

- Regarding the *dissemination of knowledge* about the relationship between the pseudonym and the substituted subject, at some specific point in time, a pseudonym can be seen as *public* (e.g., a phone number of an employee), *confidential* (e.g., a bank account of a citizen) or *secret*. A secret pseudonym is also called an *anonym*, and is often discretionarily selected by a substituted human individual, and, accordingly, only this individual (and possibly some confidant) knows the relationship between him and the anonym.
- Regarding the intended *potentials for multiple use* and the resulting linkability, there are *subject pseudonyms* for a broad range of activities, *role pseudonyms* for specific activities, *relationship pseudonyms* for activities addressing specific partners, combined *role–relationship pseudonyms* for specific activities addressing specific partners, and *transaction pseudonyms* (*event pseudonyms*) for *single use* only.

Figure 12.6 visualizes a typical situation, where these meanings occur in three layers, and also depicts the relationships. Obviously, when enforcing an indistinguishability property that refers to "participants" with a specific meaning, we must take care not only to design a sufficiently large participant domain (anonymity class) but also to prevent *inferences* from known relationships between the layers. For example, within a large organization, a phone number, selected from a range of some hundreds or even thousands, might reveal important details about the assigned employee, thus substantially narrowing the set of potentially assigned employees (e.g., restricting them to a small department).

The techniques of *certificates* and *credentials*, as introduced in Chapter 7 and elaborated further in Section 10.3, rely on a special kind of pseudonym, namely the *public keys* employed for asymmetric cryptographic mechanisms as verification keys for digital signatures or as encryption keys. In general, a *trusted third party* should *certify* a relationship between a public key (considered as a pseudonym) and the human individual or the computing device (e.g., an integrity and authenticity basis or trusted platform module) holding the matching private key.

This certification need not necessarily refer to an identifier of the individual or the device; in distributed computing systems, referring to *characterizing properties* of the holder often suffices and might then be much more worthwhile. In particular, a public key can be used as an *anonym* if only the certifying trusted third party, treated as a confidant, knows the actual relationship to the identifiable subject. Moreover, on a legitimate demand, for example in the case of a suspected *misuse* of the anonym, the confidant may be willing or obliged to reveal the related identity.

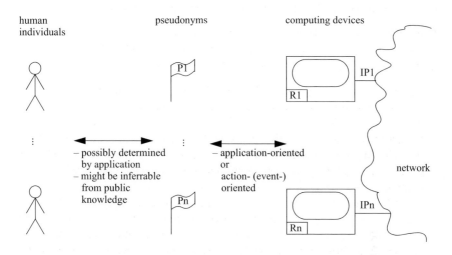

Fig. 12.6. Some meanings of the notion of "participant" and their relationships

12.4.4 Randomness and Pseudorandomness

In order to achieve the indistinguishability goals of encryption, authentication, ano-nymization and other *cryptographic mechanisms, sufficient randomness* is needed. As set out Subsection 6.3.1, a cryptographic mechanism *superimposes* the random-ness of a secretly selected key, and possibly further inputs, on the returned items of interest in such a way that the output items (ciphertexts, exhibits, …) again appear to be randomly taken from the respective domain.

As already indicated in the introduction to this chapter, making "sufficient ran-domness" algorithmically available is an outstanding open problem in computer science. In fact, precisely defining the notion of "sufficient randomness" has already turned out to be a great challenge that has raised various proposals for an answer. For the purpose of cryptography, the following ambitious guidelines for generating and employing *pseudorandom sequences* are very promising:

- As a starting point for providing "sufficient randomness", some *physical source* for supplying (supposedly) "truly random" *seeds* of short length is used.
- Then, a *pseudorandom generator* is used; this is a deterministic polynomial-time algorithm that stretches a short and supposedly random input into a much larger sequence such that the output appears again to be "sufficiently random".
- "Appearing sufficiently random" means here that the outputs of the pseudoran-dom generator are *computationally indistinguishable* from a family of (ideal) uniformly distributed sequences of the respective length, i.e., roughly described, there is no probabilistic polynomial-time algorithm that can distinguish the algorithmic outputs from the abstract ideal sequences with a non-negligible probability without knowing the seeds.

- A further cryptographic mechanism (for encryption, authentication, etc.) is *designed* to take a "truly random" input and to superimpose the randomness of this input on the returned items, i.e., these items must be proven to comply with a pertinent property of indistinguishability as well.
- An actual *implementation* of this mechanism, however, replaces the (ideal) "truly random" input by an actually available pseudorandom sequence returned by the pseudorandom generator.
- The design of the mechanism and a verified compositionality property of the two *indistinguishability properties* involved then ensure that this replacement does not affect the quality of the returned items.

A formal, mathematically precise elaboration of these guidelines and their underlying concepts is beyond the scope of this monograph. But even an intuitive understanding should recognize the crucial role of randomness within cryptography.

While nearly any cryptographic mechanism relies on at least one random input, there are many variations of the intended goals of these inputs. In the following, we list five examples:

- to *generate* a *secret key* for some cryptographic mechanism, in order to designate its holder(s) as distinguished from all other participants and thus to virtually isolate those holder(s) from the others;
- to employ the random input as a *nonce*, in order to mark a message within some cryptographic protocol as unique and personal;
- to *pad* a value from some (too small) domain of interest with a random input, in order to define a modified domain that is sufficiently large to prevent successful guessing;
- to *blind* some other data of interest with a random input using a reversible algebraic operation, in order to present the data of interest to somebody else without revealing the actual value;
- most generally, to *randomize* some algorithm of a cryptographic mechanism, in order to achieve a wanted indistinguishability property.

12.4.5 One-Way Hash Functions

In order to achieve the goals of a cryptographic mechanism, some item of interest is often represented in a concise, disguised and unforgeable form, called a *fingerprint*, a *digest* or a *hash value*. *Conciseness* here means roughly that a representation consists of a suitably short bit string of an agreed format; *disguise* demands that a represented item cannot be "determined" from its representation; and *unforgeability* requires, intuitively, that nobody can "determine" a representation of an item without knowing that item. Moreover, since by this conciseness a (usually) large domain of items is mapped onto a (suitably) small domain of representations, there must be collisions, i.e., several items will share a common representation. Accordingly, *collision resistance* is required, in the sense that nobody can "determine" pairs of items that share a representation.

Such representations are typically applied within a cryptographic protocol in the following situations. First, the protocol demands an argument complying with a fixed short format for further processing, but the items of interest might vary or even be of arbitrary length. As an example, some authentication protocols digitally sign the representations instead of the represented items. Second, the protocol needs to enforce the *integrity* (as *detection of modification*) of some item, as described in the following, and partially visualized in Figure 12.7:

- At some point in time, the item considered is mapped onto its representation, and then the item and its representation are stored in different locations.
- At a later point in time, the item is inspected to determine whether it has been (accidently or maliciously) modified. The representation (of the current version of the item) is recomputed and compared with the stored representation (of the original version); if both values are equal, then the item is supposed to have remained intact over the period of time, otherwise some modification has occurred.

Owing to the collision resistance, the inspection is particularly supposed to detect a fraud where the holder of an item intentionally attempts to replace the original version with a different one.

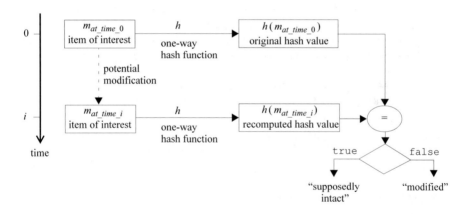

Fig. 12.7. Applying a hash function for enforcing integrity as detection of modification

Representations of the kind described are computed by means of a *one-way hash function*. The construction of such a function is closely intertwined with the mechanisms of encryption and authentication and the generation of randomness. A more detailed exposition is beyond the scope of this monograph. In the following, we outline only the basic definitions and requirements for a specific variant.

A one-way hash function h maps any element of a domain D, which might even be infinite, onto a bit string of a fixed length l, i.e., onto an element of $\{0,1\}^l$. Given an argument $m \in D$, the assigned value $h(m)$ is called the *hash value* of m.

The function h must be efficiently computable, i.e., there is an efficient algorithm H that computes $h(m)$ on input of m, but the *inversion* of h must be computationally infeasible, i.e., the following roughly circumscribed *one-way property* is required:

$$\text{For all values } z \in \{0,1\}^l, \qquad\qquad (12.15)$$
$$\text{one cannot "determine" a domain element } m \in D \text{ such that } h(m) = z.$$

Additionally, two further properties regarding the inevitable collisions are required. The *weak collision-resistance property* should protect against a fraud where a given message m is exchanged for another one:

$$\text{For all domain elements } m \in D, \qquad\qquad (12.16)$$
$$\text{one cannot "determine" a different domain element } m' \in D$$
$$\text{such that } h(m) = h(m').$$

The *strong collision-resistance property* should totally block any attempt at a fraudulent exchange:

$$\text{One cannot "determine" two different domain elements } m \in D \text{ and } m' \in D \quad (12.17)$$
$$\text{such that } h(m) = h(m').$$

The two versions are closely related: the strong version is equivalent to requiring that one cannot "determine" an element $m \in D$ that violates the weak version.

12.4.6 Timestamps

In order to support the interest in *integrity* as *detection of modification* and *authenticity* as *detection of impersonation* or even *non-repudiation*, the cryptographic mechanisms for *authentication* can be employed, as introduced in Subsection 12.4.2. In some applications based on message sending, the interest in *integrity* as *temporal correctness* should be supported as well: in this case, in a proof of authenticity, the receiver should be able to evaluate not only *who* has formed and sent a message but also *when* these two events happened. Note that, in principle, forming a message and sending it are two separate activities, between which some time might pass.

This difference could be exploited by an attacking participant for a *replay attack* of the following kind, or some variation thereof. The designated sender forms a message, digitally signs it and then forwards it to an intended receiver. The attacker intercepts the transmission of the message and keeps it for his own purposes, such that neither the intended receiver nor any further participant involved realizes even the existence of the intercepted message. Some time later, maliciously claiming to be the former of the message, the attacker attempts to *impersonate* the designated sender by replaying the message and delivering it to some receiver of his choice. Finally, this receiver would be able to verify the signature and thus to confirm the claimed *former* of the message. But, additionally, he could be tempted to falsely believe to have received the message *directly* from that former and thus to cur-

rently communicate with him, since without any further exhibits, the receiver cannot determine the *freshness* of the message.

To prevent such replay attacks or to achieve related goals, before authenticating a message, the designated sender can include a current *timestamp*. Then, considering the time span between when the message was *formed* and when it was *received*, the receiver can decide whether he is willing to accept the message as authentic or not. Clearly, for this purpose, all participants involved must share *synchronized clocks*, and the receiver should take tolerable discrepancies in local times into account. Roughly summarized, the following combined *temporal correctness and unforgeability property* is desired:

For all messages *m* with an included timestamp *ts*   (12.18)
and suitably authenticated by the sender,
from the perspective of a receiver,
the actual *forming time* of the message coincides with the included *timestamp*.

Obviously, in general, this property is difficult both to fully formalize and to effectively enforce. Accordingly, whenever appropriate and possible, participants might prefer to employ weaker but more readily manageable means than timestamps reflecting *real time*. For example, if for a family of messages only their *relative* forming times are important, the sender might include *serial numbers* instead of timestamps. As another important example, a receiver not willing to rely on synchronized clocks might ask a sender to follow a *challenge–response procedure* in order to obtain evidence for the freshness of a received message, as described in Subsection 7.1.5.

12.5 Quality in Terms of Attacks

Cryptography aims at enabling participants in a computing system to autonomously enforce their security interests even in the presence of threats. A *threat* is instantiated by somebody or something performing a specific *attack*. In many theoretical investigations, an attack is modeled by an execution of a polynomially time-bounded probabilistic Turing machine. More practically oriented investigations consider concrete attacking strategies. In any case, a cryptographic mechanism has to be examined to determine whether it resists the anticipated attacks. More generally, in the field of cryptography, *security requirements* are already specified in terms of attacks, and thus *evaluating* a cryptographic security mechanism for whether or to what extent it satisfies the specification already includes an analysis of the mechanism's robustness against attacks.

In this section, we outline a rough *classification framework* for attacks on encryption mechanisms. Suitably adapted, this framework is also useful for other cryptographic mechanisms. In this framework, the mechanism under consideration is inspected from the point of view of attackers, and in each case the attacker's options for success are described. Clearly, the viewpoints of attackers and those of participants defending security interests are dual: a lack of success for an attacker corresponds to an actually achieved protection for the participant.

First, an attack on an encryption mechanism can result in two *kinds* of success:

- The success can be *exact* in the sense that the attacker acquires exact new knowledge about the information hidden from him, in particular about the meaningful information represented by a ciphertext or even about the decryption key of the designated receiver.
- The success can be *probability-theoretic* in the sense that the attacker acquires an improved probability distribution for the information hidden from him. The improvement relative to an *a priori probability distribution* means roughly that the *a posteriori distribution* differs, in a way that is better, from the equal distribution that represents *complete uncertainty*.

Second, an attack can be successful to the following *extents*:

- The attacker can be *universally* successful, by finding an algorithm that is *functionally equivalent* to the algorithm used by the designated receiver when the receiver inputs the secret decryption key. In this case, the attacker has acquired the functional power of the designated receiver, though possibly at higher computational cost.
- The attacker can be *completely* successful, by determining the secret *decryption key* of the designated receiver. In this case, the attacker becomes as powerful as the designated receiver with respect to computational cost as well.
- The attacker can be *selectively* successful, by determining the plaintexts corresponding to one or several *ciphertexts* that he himself has *selected at his discretion*. Depending on the number of ciphertexts decrypted and the value of the information represented therein, the resulting damage can be as harmful as for functional equivalence.
- The attacker might be *existentially* successful, when there *exists at least one* ciphertext for which the attacker can determine the corresponding plaintext. The actual damage depends on the concrete content of the potentially revealed plaintext(s), but even identifying the pure existence of successful attacks can raise serious concerns.

Third, an attack can address different *targets*:

- The attacker might try to affect selected *human individuals* who contribute to the design, implementation or administration of the message transmission process or the whole computing system and its security mechanisms, or might even try to subvert a *group* of them. Some reports say that addressing such targets is not uncommon in practice, in particular in connection with love affairs, friendships, dependencies or extortion. Clearly, technical mechanisms cannot prevent human interactions outside the computing system. However, careful design of technical mechanisms should aim at minimizing the needed *trust* in individuals and the components under their control.
- The attacker might concentrate on the *computing system* as such.

- The attacker might follow a *combined strategy*, affecting individuals and exploiting the computing system *in coordination*.

Fourth, an attack can take place at different points in *time* and, accordingly, it can address different *parts* of the overall activity of protected message transmission and the necessary preparations. For example:

- The attack "subverts" the *overall activity*; for example, a manufacturer of an encryption mechanism or a few members of its personnel manage to convince endusers about security properties that the product purposely does not satisfy.
- The attack "subverts" the *key generation*; for example by maliciously replacing the correct key generation component by a faked one.
- The attack "subverts" the *key distribution*; for example, by enabling eavesdropping on the communication line used to communicate a secret key.
- The attack refers to the actual *message transmissions*.

Fifth, the attack can exploit different *methods*. For the "subverting attacks" exemplified above, it is rarely possible to provide a complete list of possibilities. For attacks on the actual transmissions, assuming the general setting of an *open design* of the mechanism and correct and secret key generation and storage, the following distinctions are useful:

- The attack may be *passive* in the sense that an unauthorized observer sees only messages that designated senders transmit to designated receivers. In the simplest case (of *known-ciphertext attacks*), examples of *ciphertexts* can be obtained. In more crucial cases (of *known-ciphertext/plaintext attacks*), examples of pairs that comprise a *ciphertext and the corresponding plaintext* become known to the observer.
- The attack may be *active* in the sense that the attacker *chooses* one component of a matching ciphertext–plaintext pair at his discretion, and then succeeds in obtaining the other component as well.

For active attacks, another distinction can be made concerning *planning*:

- The attacker *statically* determines his choices right at the beginning.
- The attacker *dynamically* and *adaptively* makes his choices, depending on the the current state of his attack.

Finally, the attack might be seen in terms of different *expectations* of success:

- The success of a single attack can occur with a specific *probability*. For an attack pattern, the success probability of any given attack might be *bounded from above* (by a hopefully *small* value, seen from the perspective of the defender).
- The success of a single attack can be achieved only if a certain amount of *computational resources* is available, in particular enough time and space, i.e., the expectation is expressed in terms of *computational complexity*. For an attack pattern, the needed computational resources might be *bounded from below* (by a hopefully *large* term, seen from the perspective of the defender). Note that, in

general, such complexity bounds allow finitely many exceptions and that attacks might be probabilistic, and thus statements about needed computational resources often have a probabilistic flavor too.

• More generally, success expectations are expressed in terms of *both* needed computational resources *and* probabilities. Then, at the best, an upper bound for the probability of success under the assumption of an attack using bounded resources can be achieved.

The framework outlined is summarized in Table 12.8. Clearly, when we face the full range of real-life attacks and artefacts of maliciousness, this framework does not at all constitute an orthogonal, complete coverage of all possibilities: some options might be missing, the classifying properties might be chosen differently, some distinctions overlap, and some combinations of the properties discussed might be meaningless. Nevertheless, the framework can give useful hints for practical evaluations and their understanding, and it presents important parts of the terminology used in the literature.

Table 12.8. A classification framework for attacks against encryption mechanisms, and their success

Property	Options
kind of success	*exact*: exact new knowledge *probability-theoretic*: improved probability distribution
extent of success	*universal*: functional equivalence with decryption algorithm *complete*: gain of secret key *message-selective*: plaintexts of selected ciphertexts *message-existential*: plaintext of some ciphertext
target of attack	affect *human individuals* exploit *computing system* affect individuals and the system in *coordination*
time of attack/ attacked *part*	subvert *overall system* subvert *key generation* subvert *key distribution* exploit *message transmissions*
method of attack (against message transmissions)	*passive*: observe messages [ciphertext/plaintext pairs] *active*: observe plaintexts [ciphertexts] of chosen ciphertexts [plaintexts]
planning of active attack	*non-adaptive*: choose statically at the beginning *adaptive*: choose dynamically depending on progress
expectation of success	*probability-theoretic*: upper bound for success probability *complexity-theoretic*: lower bound for needed resources *combined*: upper bound for success probability with limited resources

12.6 Probability-Theoretic Security for Encryption

In this section, we present an example of a precise mathematical model for a special class of encryption mechanisms. The basic mathematical approach employs *probability theory* for describing the *knowledge* of an *attacker* (or, more neutrally expressed, an *observer*) about the items under consideration, i.e., a *secret key*, a *hidden plaintext* and an *observed ciphertext*. In doing so, we restrict ourselves to *single instances* of a specific *symmetric, deterministic* mechanism that is designed to use a key only *one time*, to guarantee the confidentiality of *just a single message*. Though this is a very special situation, the insight gained can be employed more widely in more advanced protocols, for example by using the special situation as a subcomponent or by adapting the basic ideas into another setting. The wanted *secrecy property*, as sketched in (12.3), (12.4) and (12.5), is precisely captured and characterized in terms of probability theory. The characterization obtained immediately provides hints about how to construct concrete instances. The characterization also states that these constructions are the *best possible* for the special situation considered.

In the probabilistic view, (the knowledge of an attacker about) each of the items considered is treated as a *random variable* that is specified by the potential values and a probability distribution of these values. In particular, before the message is sent, the hidden plaintext is assumed to have an *a priori probability distribution* known to the attacker. Correspondingly, on the basis of an observation of the ciphertext, the attacker can infer an *a posteriori probability distribution*. In a *semantic* version, the *secrecy property* then requires that nothing new has been learnt by the attacker, i.e., that both distributions are the same.

The mathematical model is based on the general setting outlined in Subsection 12.4.1. For simplicity of the presentation, we assume that the encryption key and the matching decryption key are always identical; they are referred to as the *secret key*. As usual, the secret key is generated independently of the plaintext to be communicated. With some further simplifications, the attacker then knows the following, at best:

- the finite set K of the possible *secret keys*, as a random variable with an a priori probability distribution $Prob_K : K \rightarrow [0,1]$, where each secret key $k \in K$ occurs with a positive probability $Prob_K(k) > 0$;
- the finite domain set D of the possible *plaintexts*, as a random variable with an a priori probability distribution $Prob_D : D \rightarrow [0,1]$, where each plaintext $x \in D$ occurs with a positive probability $Prob_D(x) > 0$;
- the (deterministic) *encryption* algorithm $Enc : K \times D \rightarrow R$ and the (deterministic) *decryption* algorithm $Dec : K \times R \rightarrow D$, satisfying the *correctness property* $Dec(k,Enc(k,x)) = x$, where Enc is a surjective function, i.e., each $y \in R$ is a possible ciphertext;
- the finite range set R of the possible *ciphertexts*, as a random variable with a derived probability distribution $Prob_R : R \rightarrow [0,1]$ that can be calculated from

$$Prob_R(y) = \sum_{\substack{k \in K, x \in D \\ Enc(k,x) = y}} Prob_K(k) \cdot Prob_D(x) > 0 \ , \tag{12.19}$$

where the positiveness is implied by the assumptions about $Prob_K$, $Prob_D$ and *Enc*.

Additionally, by determining *conditional probabilities*, the attacker can describe the relationships between the possible (hidden) plaintexts $x \in D$ and the observable ciphertexts $y \in R$: the conditional probability $Prob_{R|D}(y|x)$ is assigned to the event "ciphertext $y \in R$ observed under the condition plaintext $x \in D$ sent", and the conditional probability $Prob_{D|R}(x|y)$ is assigned to the event "plaintext $x \in D$ sent under the condition $y \in R$ observed". The conditional probabilities of the former relationships are calculated elementarily:

$$Prob_{R|D}(y|x) = \sum_{\substack{k \in K \\ Enc(k,x) = y}} Prob_K(k) . \tag{12.20}$$

The conditional probabilities of the latter relationships can be derived by use of *Bayes' Theorem*, which allows us to express one relationship in terms of the other:

$$Prob_{D|R}(x|y) = \frac{Prob_{R|D}(y|x) \cdot Prob_D(x)}{Prob_R(y)} \tag{12.21}$$

$$= \frac{\left(\sum_{\substack{k \in K \\ Enc(k,x) = y}} Prob_K(k) \right) \cdot Prob_D(x)}{\sum_{\substack{k \in K, z \in D \\ Enc(k, z) = y}} Prob_K(k) \cdot Prob_D(z)} .$$

Having observed a specific ciphertext $y \in R$, in principle the attacker also has an updated knowledge about the hidden plaintext $x \in D$. This updated knowledge is represented by the a posteriori probability distribution $Prob_{D|y}$, where $Prob_{D|y}(x) = Prob_{D|R}(x|y)$. A potential *information gain* concerning the plaintext is given if the a posteriori distribution $Prob_{D|y}$ "improves" the a priori distribution $Prob_D$. However, if the two distributions are the same, then the attacker has gained nothing, and the defender has achieved the best possible result.

Accordingly, (an instance of) an *encryption mechanism* (within the setting considered in this subsection) is defined to be *probability-theoretic secure* or *perfect* if the following *secrecy property* is achieved:

For all a priori probability distributions $Prob_D$,   (12.22)
and for all ciphertexts $y \in R$,
$$Prob_D = Prob_{D|y}.$$

Alternatively, a perfect mechanism can be seen as solving the following *optimization problem*:

- As sketched above, an attacker is supposed to aim at improving his a priori knowledge. The best possible improvement for a specific observation is described by

$$\text{MAX}_{y \in R} \ \text{MAX}_{x \in D} \ \left| Prob_D(x) - Prob_{D|y}(x) \right| . \tag{12.23}$$

- Thus the defender might try to minimize the attacker's maximum, i.e., to select an encryption algorithm and a key generation algorithm such that the following minimum is achieved by the selection:

$$\text{MIN}_{Enc, Prob_K} \ [\text{MAX}_{y \in R} \ \text{MAX}_{x \in D} \ \left| Prob_D(x) - Prob_{D|y}(x) \right|] . \tag{12.24}$$

At the best, this minimum is equal to 0, and a minimum of 0 is achieved iff the selections are perfect in the sense of (12.22). For the special setting of this subsection, the following theorems state that perfect encryption mechanisms are indeed achievable, and show how to construct them.

Theorem 12.1   [perfect encryption mechanisms]

Let an encryption mechanism be given by a (deterministic) encryption algorithm *Enc* and a key generation algorithm with probability distribution $Prob_K$, and let $Prob_D$ be an a priori probability distribution of the plaintexts. The following properties are then pairwise equivalent:

1. For all $x \in D, y \in R$: $Prob_D(x) = Prob_{D|R}(x|y)$.
2. For all $x \in D, y \in R$: $Prob_R(y) = Prob_{R|D}(y|x)$.
3. For all $x_1 \in D, x_2 \in D, y \in R$: $Prob_{R|D}(y|x_1) = Prob_{R|D}(y|x_2)$.

If, additionally, the keys are equally distributed, i.e., $Prob_K(k) = 1 / \text{card } K$ for all $k \in K$, then the following property is equivalent too:

4. For all $x_1 \in D, x_2 \in D, y \in R$:
   card $\{ k \mid Enc(k,x_1) = y \}$ = card $\{ k \mid Enc(k,x_2) = y \}$.

Sketch of Proof: The equivalence "1⇔2" immediately follows from Bayes' Theorem, which, under the conditions considered, can be written as

$$\frac{Prob_{D|R}(x|y)}{Prob_D(x)} = \frac{Prob_{R|D}(y|x)}{Prob_R(y)} . \tag{12.25}$$

Concerning the equivalence "2⇔3", consider any $y \in R$. Assuming property 2, all conditional probabilities $Prob_{R|D}(y|x)$ are the same, and thus any pair of them as well. Conversely, assume property 3. Then $Prob_R(y)$ can be shown to be equal to $Prob_{R|D}(y|z)$, where z is an arbitrarily selected plaintext, by suitably applying the definitions and some elementary reformulations.

The equivalence "3⇔4" for $Prob_K(k) = 1/\text{card } K$ is shown by applying the definitions, and then observing that probabilities for an equal distribution are basically given by cardinalities. ❑

Note that the conversion of probabilities, as given in properties 1–3, into cardinalities, as specified in property 4, provides the essential hint needed for an actual construction. This insight is summarized in the following corollary to the implication "4⇒1", which basically restates a *sufficient* condition for perfect encryption mechanisms (within the given setting):

Theorem 12.2   [sufficient condition for perfectness]

An encryption mechanism of the form discussed above is *perfect* if the following properties hold:

1. The keys are *equally distributed*, i.e., for all keys $k \in K$,
   $Prob_K(k) = 1/\text{card } K$.

2. For all plaintexts $x \in D$, and for all ciphertexts $y \in R$,
   card $\{ k \mid Enc(k,x) = y \} = 1$.

Basically, the next theorem claims that constructions according to Theorem 12.2 are the only ones that achieve perfectness, i.e., that under a reasonable restriction, the conditions of Theorem 12.2 are also *necessary*.

Theorem 12.3   [necessary condition for perfectness]

If an encryption mechanism of the form discussed above is *perfect*, where, additionally, the basic sets involved have the same cardinality, i.e., in particular $1/\text{card } K = 1/\text{card } D = 1/\text{card } R$, then the properties of Theorem 12.2 hold.

Sketch of Proof: According to "1⇒2" of Theorem 12.1, the supposed perfectness ensures that $0 < Prob_R(y) = Prob_{R|D}(y|x)$ for all $x \in D$, $y \in R$. This means that for each plaintext $x \in D$ and each ciphertext $y \in R$, there exists *at least one* key $k \in K$ with $Enc(k,x) = y$. The assumed equalities of the cardinalities then imply that there is *exactly one* such key, as claimed in property 2.

To show property 1, from "1⇒2" of Theorem 12.1 and the definitions, we derive the probability of any ciphertext $y \in R$ as follows:

$$Prob_R(y) = Prob_{R|D}(y|x) = \sum_{\substack{k \in K \\ Enc(k,x) = y}} Prob_K(k) = Prob_K(k_{x,y}), \quad (12.26)$$

where $x \in D$ is any plaintext, and $k_{x,y}$ is the unique key that maps x on y. Since each key occurs exactly once, (12.26) implies that $Prob_K(k) = Prob_R(y)$ for all keys $k \in K$, and thus the keys are equally distributed. ❑

The situation of Theorem 12.2 and Theorem 12.3 is visualized in Figure 12.9. In this figure, the functional algorithm *Enc* is represented as a complete bipartite graph. The plaintexts form the first class of nodes, and the ciphertexts the second class. Each pair of nodes x_i and y_j, taken from the first and the second class, respectively, is connected by an edge that is marked with the unique key $k_{i,j}$ where

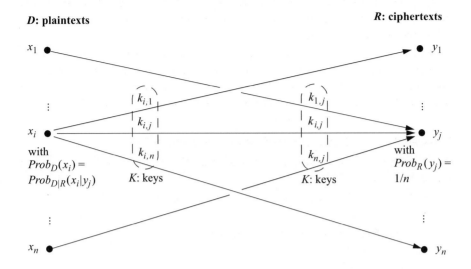

Fig. 12.9. Visualization of a perfect encryption mechanism

$Enc(k_{i,j}, x_i) = y_j$. For each plaintext node x_i, the outgoing edges comprise exactly the set of all keys, and so do the ingoing edges for each ciphertext node y_j.

The general situation visualized can easily be instantiated by employing the mathematical structures of *groups* as follows. Given a group $(G, \bullet, e)$, where G is the underlying set of group elements, $\bullet$ is the binary *group operation*, assumed to be efficiently computable, and e is the neutral element, we uniformly take keys k, plaintexts x and ciphertexts y as group elements. The group properties then ensure in particular the *solvability of equations*: each equation of the form $k \bullet x = y$, where two of the items are given, has a unique solution for the third item. Accordingly, we specify

- the *encryption algorithm* by $Enc(k, x) = k \bullet x$, and
- the *decryption algorithm* by $Dec(k, y) = k^{inverse} \bullet y$, where the inversion is uniquely determined by the equation $k^{inverse} \bullet k = e$.

The *correctness property* is implied by the definitions and the group properties:

$$Dec(k, Enc(k, x)) = k^{inverse} \bullet (k \bullet x) = (k^{inverse} \bullet k) \bullet x = e \bullet x = x. \qquad (12.27)$$

Interestingly, this group-based construction raises a problem concerning the computational complexity of the *inversion*. If $k^{inverse}$, used as a decryption key, can be easily computed from k, used as an encryption key, then we obtain a *symmetric mechanism* indeed. There are many examples of this case, including, for each number n, the *additive group* of *residues* modulo n, and, for each *prime* number p, the *multiplicative group* of residues modulo p.

However, if for some group it turns out that it is "computationally infeasible to determine" the inverse, then one could try to exploit this fact to construct an *asymmetric mechanism*, where a pair (k, k^{inverse}) constitutes a matching pair of a public encryption key and the corresponding private decryption key. Unfortunately, this idea does not work directly, but its further exploration has led to actual asymmetric mechanisms, as discussed further in Section 12.9.

Figure 12.9 also shows the probabilities for each node:

- For a *plaintext* node x_i, the defining property of *perfectness* is specified, namely the probability $Prob_D(x_i) = Prob_{D|R}(x_i\,|y_j)$, which is independent of the actual ciphertext node y_j.
- For a *ciphertext* node y_j, the probability $Prob_D(y_j) = 1/n$ is specified, which can be derived as follows:

$$Prob_R(y_j) = \sum_{}^{x_i \in D} Prob_K(k_{i,j}) \cdot Prob_D(x_i) \qquad (12.28)$$

$$= \sum_{}^{x_i \in D} \frac{1}{n} \cdot Prob_D(x_i) = \frac{1}{n}\ .$$

Accordingly, a perfect encryption mechanism always generates an *equal distribution* of the ciphertexts, *independently* of the a priori probability distribution of the plaintexts. More intuitively expressed, a ciphertext looks "as if it is random".

However, the a priori probability distribution of the plaintexts does influence the *a posteriori probability distribution* of the *keys*:

$$Prob_{K|R}(k_{i,j}|y_j) = \sum_{Enc(k_{i,j},x)\,=\,y_j}^{x \in D} Prob_D(x) = Prob_D(x_i)\,. \qquad (12.29)$$

Thus an attacker might learn new information about the secret key from observing a ciphertext. This fact emphasizes that, in general, perfectness can be achieved only if a secret key is employed *one time* only, i.e., it is never reused. In Section 12.8, we present a probability-theoretic model for studying how dangerous the multiple usage of keys might be.

12.7 Probability-Theoretic Security for Authentication

In Section 12.5 we classify the quality of a cryptographic mechanism in terms of attacks against encryption. Basically, from the point of view of the designated participants, the quality expresses the circumstances in which an attacker can be prevented from gaining information about secret data, and the extent to which this is done. For encryption, the secret data is given by a generated key pair and a plaintext. In Section 12.6, we exhibit and analyze an example of a precise probability-theoretic model of a specific kind of encryption mechanism. In the context of this model, the design of the best possible encryption mechanism is understood as an optimization problem: the mechanism should minimize the maximally achievable information gain with respect to a single item. This problem is shown to be solved by a perfect encryption mechanism, which makes the optimization term equal to 0.

In this section, we present similar considerations for a related *probability-theoretic* model of a specific kind of *authentication* mechanism. We again restrict ourselves to *single instances* of a specific *symmetric*, *deterministic* mechanism designed to use a key only *one time*, to guarantee the integrity and authenticity of just a *single* message. In this setting, the secret data consists only of the generated key pair, since the message and the corresponding cryptographic exhibit are not further protected.

An attacker might aim at achieving the effects that the designated sender is enabled to achieve by means of the secret authentication key. Basically, the attacking effect would be to discretionarily select a message z and to compute a bit string *red* that is accepted by the receiver's authenticity verification algorithm, thereby violating the required *unforgeability property*, as sketched in (12.9) and (12.10). More specifically, attacks might appear as impersonation or substitution:

- An *impersonation* attack is performed *before* the designated sender employs his authentication key. If successfully executed, the attack fakes the following facts: the designated sender has actually sent a message (although the designated sender has not yet done so), and that message is the one (maliciously) selected by the attacker.
- A *substitution* attack is performed *after* the designated sender has employed his authentication key and then has sent out the original message and the correct cryptographic exhibit. While these items are being transmitted, the attacker *intercepts* the transmission, substitutes the original message by another one at his (malicious) discretion, and replaces the original cryptographic exhibit by another bit string that he hopes will be accepted as the cryptographic exhibit. If successfully executed, the attack fakes just the content of the message.

In both cases, the attacker's success depends on his ability to acquire appropriate knowledge about a specific cryptographic exhibit delivered by the authentication algorithm *Aut*, without knowing the authentication key of the designated sender. In the probabilistic view, for each message x, the corresponding cryptographic exhibit is treated as a *random variable* that is specified by the potential values and a probability distribution of these values. In turn, this probability distribution is fully determined by the pertinent probability distribution of the authentication key:

- For the *impersonation* attack, the *a priori probability distribution* of the authentication key is pertinent, and assumed to be known to the attacker.
- For the *substitution* attack, however, a slightly improved distribution is pertinent, namely the *a posteriori probability distribution* of the authentication key under the condition that the actual authentication key has produced the value observed in the interception.

A rational attacker is then modeled as performing his attack with a most likely value of a cryptographic exhibit for the fake message, and thus the attacker's probability-theoretic *expectation of success* is bounded by the maximum of the respective probabilities.

The precise mathematical model is based on the general setting outlined in Subsection 12.4.2. For simplicity of the presentation, we again assume that the authentication key and the matching test key are always identical; they are referred to as the *secret key*. As usual, the secret key is generated independently of the message to be communicated. With some further simplifications, the attacker then knows the following, at best:

- the finite set K of the possible *secret keys*, as a random variable with an a priori probability distribution $Prob_K : K \to [0,1]$, where each secret key $k \in K$ occurs with a positive probability $Prob_K(k) > 0$;
- the finite domain set D of the possible *messages*;
- the (deterministic) *authentication* algorithm $Aut : K \times D \to R$ and the (deterministic) *authenticity verification* algorithm $Test : K \times D \times R \to \{true, false\}$, satisfying the following *strong correctness property*: $Test(k,x,y)$ iff $Aut(k,x) = y$, where Aut is a surjective function, i.e., each $y \in R$ is a possible cryptographic exhibit;
- the finite range set R of the possible *cryptographic exhibits*, where, for each message $x \in D$, the random variable $R|x$ has the derived *a priori* probability distribution $Prob_{R|x} : R \to [0,1]$ such that

$$Prob_{R|x}(y) = \sum_{\substack{k \in K \\ Aut(k,x) = y}} Prob_K(k). \tag{12.30}$$

Additionally, for each *intercepted* observation (z, red) with $z \in D$ and $red \in R$, the attacker can calculate the conditional *a posteriori* probability distribution $Prob_{K|z, red} : K \to [0,1]$ for the events "key $k \in K$ selected under the condition $Aut(k,z) = red$ observed":

$$Prob_{K|z, red}(k) = Prob_{K|D,R}(k|z, red) \tag{12.31}$$

$$= \frac{Prob_{K,D,R}(k, z, red)}{Prob_{D,R}(z, red)} \qquad \text{by the definition (A.3) in Appendix A.3.1,}$$

$$= \frac{Prob_{K,D}(k, z) \cdot Prob_{R|K,D}(red|k, z)}{Prob_D(z) \cdot Prob_{R|D}(red|z)} \qquad \text{again by the definition (A.3),}$$

$$= \frac{Prob_K(k) \cdot Prob_D(z) \cdot \chi_{Aut(k,z) = red}}{Prob_D(z) \cdot Prob_{R|z}(red)} \qquad \text{by the independence of } K \text{ and } D,$$

$$= \frac{Prob_K(k) \cdot \chi_{Aut(k,z)\,=\,red}}{Prob_{R|z}(red)} \tag{12.32}$$

$$= \left[\begin{array}{ll} \dfrac{Prob_K(k)}{Prob_{R|z}(red)} & \text{if } Aut(k,z) = red, \\[3mm] 0 & \text{otherwise,} \end{array} \right. \tag{12.33}$$

where $\chi_{Aut(k,z)\,=\,red}$ denotes the characteristic function of the specified property of k.

On the basis of this probability distribution for keys, for each intercepted observation (z, red) with $z \in D$ and $red \in R$, the attacker can also calculate the conditional a posteriori probability distribution $Prob_{R|x}^{cept(z,\,red)} : R \to [0,1]$ for the events "cryptographic exhibit $y = Aut(k,x)$ computed under the condition $Aut(k,z) = red$ intercepted":

$$Prob_{R|x}^{cept(z,\,red)}(y) = \sum_{\substack{k \in K \\ Aut(k,x)\,=\,y}} Prob_{K|z,\,red}(k) \tag{12.34}$$

$$= \sum_{\substack{k \in K \\ Aut(k,x)\,=\,y}} \frac{Prob_K(k) \cdot \chi_{Aut(k,z)\,=\,red}}{Prob_{R|z}(red)} \qquad \text{according to (12.32),}$$

$$= \frac{\displaystyle\sum_{\substack{k \in K \\ Aut(k,x)\,=\,y \,\wedge\, Aut(k,z)\,=\,red}} Prob_K(k)}{\displaystyle\sum_{\substack{k \in K \\ Aut(k,z)\,=\,red}} Prob_K(k)} \qquad \text{according to (12.33) and (12.30).}$$

Accordingly, (an instance of) an *authentication mechanism* (within the setting considered in this subsection) is defined to be *probability-theoretic secure* or *perfect* if it solves the following *optimization problem*:

- The attacker is supposed to aim at choosing a most likely cryptographic redundancy for a faked message. For an *impersonation* attack, on the basis of (12.30), a best possible choice for a specific faked message is described by

$$MaxProb_{imp} = \underset{x \in D}{MAX} \ \underset{y \in R}{MAX} \ Prob_{R|x}(y) \geq \frac{1}{card\ R}, \tag{12.35}$$

where the inequality is implied by the probability distributions being normalized to add up to 1. For a *substitution* attack, on the basis of (12.34), first we similarly obtain

$$MaxProb_{subst}^{cept(z,\,red)} \qquad\qquad (12.36)$$

$$= MAX_{x\,\in\,D}\ MAX_{y\,\in\,R}\ Prob_{R|x}^{cept(z,\,red)}(y) \ge \frac{1}{card\ R}.$$

Then the dependence on the interception is eliminated by considering the probability-weighted mean value of (12.36), namely

$$MeanProb_{subst} = \overset{(z,\,red)\,\in\,D\,\times\,R}{\sum}\ Prob_{D,\,R}(z,red) \cdot MaxProb_{subst}^{cept(z,\,red)} \quad (12.37)$$

$$\ge \overset{(z,\,red)\,\in\,D\,\times\,R}{\sum}\ Prob_{D,\,R}(z,red) \cdot \frac{1}{card\ R} = \frac{1}{card\ R}.$$

- Then the defender might try to minimize what the attacker is maximizing, i.e., select an authentication algorithm and a key generation algorithm such the following minima for the impersonation attack and the substitution attack, respectively, are achieved by his selection:

$$MIN_{Aut,\,Prob_K}\ [MAX_{x\,\in\,D}\ MAX_{y\,\in\,R}\ Prob_{R|x}(y)] \qquad (12.38)$$

and

$$MIN_{Aut,\,Prob_K} \qquad\qquad (12.39)$$

$$\left[\overset{(z,\,red)\,\in\,D\,\times\,R}{\sum}\ Prob_{D,\,R}(z,red) \cdot MAX_{x\,\in\,D}\ MAX_{y\,\in\,R}\ Prob_{R|x}^{cept(z,\,red)}(y) \right].$$

At the best, these minima are equal to $1\,/card\ R$. For the special setting of this subsection, the following theorem summarizes the preceding exposition and states that perfect authentication mechanisms are indeed achievable, and shows how to construct them.

Theorem 12.4   [perfect authentication mechanism]

Let an authentication mechanism be given by a (deterministic) authentication function *Aut* and a key generation algorithm with probability distribution $Prob_K$. Then, using the notation introduced above, the following properties hold:

1. The maximal expectation for success of an *impersonation* attack, $MaxProb_{imp}$, is at least $1\,/card\ R$.

2. This bound is achieved, i.e., $MaxProb_{imp} = 1\,/card\ R$, iff the a priori probability distributions for cryptographic exhibits $Prob_{R|x}$ are equal distributions, i.e., for all messages $x \in D$, and for all cryptographic exhibits $y \in R$,

$$\sum_{\substack{k \in K \\ Aut(k,x)=y}} Prob_K(k) = \frac{1}{card\ R} \ .$$

3. The mean value of the expectation for success of a *substitution* attack, *Mean-Prob*$_{subst}$, is at least $1/card\ R$.

4. This bound is achieved, i.e., *MeanProb*$_{subst}$ = $1/card\ R$, iff for $x \neq z$ the conditional a posteriori probability distributions for cryptographic exhibits $Prob_{R|x}^{cept(z,red)}$ are equal distributions, i.e., for all messages $x \in D$, $z \in D$ with $x \neq z$, and for all cryptographic exhibits $y \in R$, $red \in R$,

$$\frac{\displaystyle\sum_{\substack{k \in K \\ Aut(k,x)=y \wedge Aut(k,z)=red}} Prob_K(k)}{\displaystyle\sum_{\substack{k \in K \\ Aut(k,z)=red}} Prob_K(k)} = \frac{1}{card\ R} \ .$$

5. The bounds for the impersonation attack and the substitution attack are *simultaneously* achieved, i.e., *MaxProb*$_{imp}$ = *MeanProb*$_{subst}$ = $1/card\ R$, iff for all messages $x \in D$, $z \in D$ with $x \neq z$, and for all cryptographic exhibits $y \in R$, $red \in R$,

$$\sum_{\substack{k \in K \\ Aut(k,x)=y \wedge Aut(k,z)=red}} Prob_K(k) = \frac{1}{(card\ R)^2} \ .$$

If, additionally, the keys are equally distributed, i.e., $Prob_K(k) = 1/card\ K$ for all $k \in K$, the last equation is equivalent to

$$card\ \{\ k\ |\ Aut(k,x)=y \wedge Aut(k,z)=red\ \} = \frac{card\ K}{(card\ R)^2} \ .$$

6. If *MaxProb*$_{imp}$ = *MeanProb*$_{subst}$ = $1/card\ R$, then card $K \geq (card\ R)^2$.

Sketch of Proof: The first assertion is justified by (12.35). The second assertion is an immediate consequence of the first assertion. The third assertion is justified by (12.37). The fourth assertion results from substituting (12.34) into (12.37).

The fifth assertion is an immediate consequence of the fourth assertion, by substituting the expression in the denominator of the left-hand side according to the second assertion.

Finally, the sixth assertion is easily derived from the fifth assertion, by considering any fixed selection of messages $x \in D$, $z \in D$ with $x \neq z$: for each of the $(card\ R)^2$ pairs $y \in R$, $red \in R$, there exists at least one corresponding key $k \in K$, and all these keys are different.   ❑

D: messages   **R: cryptographic exhibits**

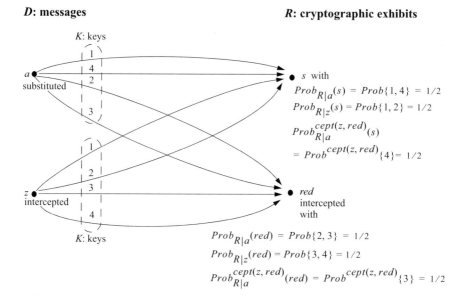

Fig. 12.10. Visualization of a best possible authentication mechanism for given cardinalities of the set of messages and of the set of cryptographic exhibits

The situation of Theorem 12.4 is visualized in Figure 12.10, which shows the simplest example. In this figure, the *authentication* algorithm *Aut* is represented as a graph. The messages form the first class of nodes, and the cryptographic exhibits the second class. In the example, both classes have only two elements, denoted by a, z and s, *red*, respectively.

In order to satisfy the inequality in the sixth assertion of Theorem 12.4, we need at least four keys; in the example, we denote the keys by 1, 2, 3 and 4. In order to comply with the equation of the fifth assertion of Theorem 12.4, the keys are employed as follows: whatever interception is assumed (thereby determining a set of still possible keys), any substituted message can still be mapped onto any of the cryptographic exhibits (under the still possible keys), i.e., for each pair of a substituted message and a cryptographic exhibit, there exists exactly one still possible key that is appropriate for the mapping.

In the figure, all a priori probabilities $Prob_{R|x}(v)$ are displayed, where an expression of the form $Prob\{i,j\}$ denotes the a priori probability for the pertinent still possible set of keys $\{i,j\}$. However, for the sake of clarity, the conditional a posteriori probabilities for the substitution attack are shown only for the case where the interception is (z, red) and a is the substituted message; all remaining cases are treated completely symmetrically:

- A priori, all four keys are possible, each with an a priori probability $1/4$.

- After (z, red) has been intercepted, only the keys 3 and 4 remain still possible, each with an a posteriori probability $1/2$.
- The substituted message a is mapped onto the exhibit s by the still possible key 4, and onto the exhibit red by the still possible key 3, where each of the mappings occurs with a probability $1/2$.
- Accordingly, an attacker cannot take advantage of having intercepted (z, red), since for the substituted message a, the a priori probabilities and the a posteriori probabilities for the possible cryptographic exhibits are equal, namely $1/2$. Hence, the attacker cannot perform better than by just guessing the cryptographic exhibit that the designated sender would compute.

12.8 Information Gain about a Secret Encryption Key

In general, communication partners might want to *multiply* reuse a key in order to save the overhead of repeated key generation and distribution. However, as already suggested by the results of Section 12.6 about perfect encryption mechanisms, every usage of a key can potentially reveal some information about that key. Therefore we have to take care that an attacker's expectation of success in deriving essential information about a multiply employed key remains sufficiently bounded. Briefly rephrased, an *attacker* should *not* be *completely successful*.

In this section, we exemplarily study the danger of multiple usage of an encryption key by extending the *probability-theoretic* model for *symmetric*, deterministic *encryption* mechanisms that we introduced in Section 12.6. Seen from the perspective of an attacker, all crucial items are formally treated in this model as *random variables*. In particular, a secret (encryption) key $k \in K$, a plaintext $x \in D$ and an observed ciphertext $y \in R$ are associated with respective probabilities. In order to describe the impact of an attacker observing a ciphertext, concerning keys and plaintexts we distinguish between the a priori probabilities and the a posteriori probabilities, where the latter are given in the form of *conditional probabilities*.

As a basic prerequisite for further investigations, we first present a general theorem about the impact of observing a ciphertext on the attacker's information about the key employed. This impact is characterized in terms of the *entropy* (*information content*; see Appendix A.3.2) of the *random variables* involved, where the entropy of the plaintexts will play a crucial role later.

Theorem 12.5   **[conditional entropy of keys under ciphertext observation]**

Let an encryption mechanism be given by a deterministic *encryption algorithm* $Enc : K \times D \to R$ and a *key generation algorithm* with an a priori probability distribution $Prob_K : K \to [0,1]$, and let $Prob_D : D \to [0,1]$ be an a priori probability distribution of the plaintexts. Then $H(K|R)$, i.e., the *a posteriori conditional entropy* of the random variable K under the condition of the random variable R, is related to the entropies of the random variables K, D and R as follows:

$$H(K|R) = H(K) + H(D) - H(R). \tag{12.40}$$

Sketch of Proof: We consider the product random variable K,D,R. The key component and the plaintext component of this product are stochastically independent, and thus, according to (A.10), we have $H(K,D) = H(K) + H(D)$. Moreover, the key component and the plaintext component together functionally determine the ciphertext component and, additionally, by the correctness property, the key component and the ciphertext component together functionally determine the plaintext component. Thus, according to (A.8), we derive $H(R|K,D) = 0$ and $H(D|K,R) = 0$ as well. On the basis of these observations and using (A.12), we can express the entropy of the full product K,D,R in the following two ways:

$$H(K,D,R) = H(K,D) + H(R|K,D) = H(K) + H(D) \text{ and} \tag{12.41}$$

$$H(K,D,R) = H(K,R) + H(D|K,R) = H(K,R). \tag{12.42}$$

Finally, first using (A.12) once again and then appropriately applying (12.42) and (12.41), the conditional entropy $H(K|R)$ is calculated as claimed in the theorem:

$$H(K|R) = H(K,R) - H(R) = H(K,D,R) - H(R) = H(K) + H(D) - H(R). \quad \square$$

We now complement the basic prerequisite of the general theorem about the entropies involved by another prerequisite that considers the specific *entropy of plaintexts* for a special, (overly) simplified application (which is not at all recommended for practical purposes).

The application is special in that the plaintexts are supposed to be syntactically correct and meaningful sentences in some *natural language*, for example English. For such an application, an attacker can approximate the *a priori probability distribution* of the plaintexts by the *relative frequencies* of occurrence of short letter strings within a sufficiently rich and representative sample of documents. The application is simplified in that a plaintext in the natural language is encrypted letterwise, by reusing a secret key to encrypt each letter individually.

More specifically, given the underlying *alphabet A* of the natural language considered, the attacker can perform a *statistical analysis* and thereby determine the relative frequencies of occurrence of a single letter in A, of pairs of letters in A, of triads of letters in A and so on. In general, the relative frequencies of the elements of A^l, i.e., of *strings* over the alphabet A of length l, must be calculated empirically and cannot be derived from those of a shorter length, in particular because letters, and longer strings as well, do not occur independently within sentences of a natural language.

For the sake of a simplified formal investigation, in the following we treat the "natural language" L under consideration as a set of *infinite* strings over the alphabet A, i.e., we assume that $L \in \wp A^\infty$. In order to estimate the *entropy* of L, for increasing l, we employ the relative frequencies determined for A^l, calculate the corresponding entropy $H(A^l)$ and determine the normalized information content per letter by dividing $H(A^l)$ by l.

Summarizing and abstracting, we study the *empirical entropy* of the "natural language" $L \in \wp A^\infty$, which is defined as

$$eH(L) = \lim_{l \to \infty} \frac{H(A^l)}{l}. \tag{12.43}$$

In general, the empirical entropy is much less than the best possible entropy among all random variables that have the letters of the alphabet A as events. According to (A.6) and (A.7), the optimum is achieved for the equal distribution $Prob_A(x) = 1/$ card A and has the value $H(A) = $ ld card A. The difference between the optimum and the empirical entropy is considered to be the *absolute redundancy* (per letter) of the natural language. Finally, the *(relative) redundancy* (per letter) of $L \in \wp A^\infty$ is defined as

$$Red(L) = \frac{H(A) - eH(L)}{H(A)} = \frac{\text{ld card } A - eH(L)}{\text{ld card } A} = 1 - \frac{eH(L)}{\text{ld card } A}. \tag{12.44}$$

This formal notion of redundancy reflects the common observation that a natural language is "redundant" in the intuitive sense that we often do not need all letters of a sentence in order to distinguish it from other sentences or to grasp its meaning.

We now exploit the two prerequisites above to estimate the expectation of an attacker of being *completely successful* in the special, simplified application: the attacker attempts to determine the secret key from observing a ciphertext where the plaintext, in some natural language, has been encrypted letterwise by *multiply* employing the same secret key for each letter. This exploitation is based on the following refinement and extension of the probability-theoretic model used earlier:

- The encryption mechanism treats *plaintexts* that are strings over some alphabet A where only the elements of some natural language $L \in \wp A^\infty$ actually occur. For practical purposes, we consider prefixes in $L|^n$ for a fixed length n, and approximate $L|^n$ by a random variable A^n with an a priori probability distribution that is supposed to satisfy the following property:

$$Prob_{A^n}(x_1 x_2 \ldots x_n) > 0 \quad \text{iff} \quad x_1 x_2 \ldots x_n \in L|^n. \tag{12.45}$$

- For encryption, a secret key $k \in K$ is multiply used by mapping each letter $x_i \in A$ onto some element $y_i \in B$, where B is an alphabet for forming *ciphertexts*. Thus the (deterministic) *encryption algorithm* $Enc^n: K \times A^n \to B^n$ for plaintexts is the *canonical extension* of an encryption algorithm $Enc: K \times A \to B$ for single letters, i.e.,

$$Enc^n(k, x_1 x_2 \ldots x_n) = Enc(k, x_1)\, Enc(k, x_2) \ldots Enc(k, x_n). \tag{12.46}$$

- For decryption, the secret key is used elementwise and multiply in a corresponding way. Thus the decryption algorithm Dec^n for ciphertexts is related to the corresponding *decryption algorithm Dec* for single elements of B as follows:

$$Dec^n(k, y_1 y_2 \ldots y_n) = Dec(k, y_1)\, Dec(k, y_2) \ldots Dec(k, y_n). \tag{12.47}$$

- For each ciphertext $y_1 y_2 \ldots y_n$, we consider the set

$$goodkeys_n(y_1y_2 \ldots y_n) := \{ k \mid k \in K, \ Prob_{A^n}(Dec^n(k, y_1y_2 \ldots y_n)) > 0 \} \quad (12.48)$$

of those keys that appear possible or "good", since they map the ciphertext to a prefix of the language L.

In this model, if the attacker observes a ciphertext $y_1y_2 \ldots y_n$, then he knows the following: there is *exactly one* key in $goodkeys_n(y_1y_2 \ldots y_n)$ that the sender has actually employed, whereas the remaining keys only guarantee that the corresponding plaintext could occur as an element of $L|^n$. Accordingly, the attacker can obtain a potential partial *information gain* about the key actually used whenever $goodkeys_n(y_1y_2 \ldots y_n) \neq K$. The attacker might even be *completely successful* iff card $goodkeys_n(y_1y_2 \ldots y_n) = 1$, provided he can then actually determine the unique element of $goodkeys_n(y_1y_2 \ldots y_n)$. With some appropriate additional *a priori knowledge* about the attacked communication, the attacker might also succeed if $goodkeys_n(y_1y_2 \ldots y_n)$ contains only sufficiently few elements, just by discarding the nonpertinent keys on the basis of additional reasoning.

In general, the crucial cardinality of $goodkeys_n(y_1y_2 \ldots y_n)$ depends on the specifically observed ciphertext $y_1y_2 \ldots y_n$. The following theorem estimates the expected value of this cardinality on the basis of the derived probability distribution of ciphertexts.

Theorem 12.6   [expected value of the number of good keys]

Suppose the probability-theoretic model introduced above, comprising (1) a key generation algorithm with an equal distribution $Prob_K(k) = 1/card\ K$, (2) an encryption algorithm with multiple usage of a secret key for the letterwise encryption of prefixes of plaintexts stemming from a natural language $L \in \wp A^\infty$ with redundancy $Red(L)$, and (3) the corresponding decryption algorithm, where card A = card B. Furthermore, define $goodkeys_n$ as the expected value of the cardinality of $goodkeys_n(y_1y_2 \ldots y_n)$, i.e.,

$$goodkeys_n = \sum^{y_1y_2 \ldots y_n \in B^n} Prob_{B^n}(y_1y_2 \ldots y_n) \cdot card\ goodkeys_n(y_1y_2 \ldots y_n). \ (12.49)$$

The following inequality then holds for sufficiently large n:

$$goodkeys_n \geq \frac{card\ K}{(card\ A)^{n \cdot Red(L)}}. \quad (12.50)$$

Sketch of Proof: Our first prerequisite, Theorem 12.5, yields the equation

$$H(K|B^n) = H(K) + H(A^n) - H(B^n). \quad (12.51)$$

The left-hand side of this equation, the conditional entropy of keys under ciphertexts, can be estimated and related to $goodkeys_n$ as follows, using the definition (A.11) of a conditional entropy, the upper bound (A.6) for entropies, Jensen's inequality and the definition (12.49):

$$H(K|B^n) \;=\; \sum_{y_1 y_2 \dots y_n \in B^n} Prob_{B^n}(y_1 y_2 \dots y_n) \cdot H(K|y_1 y_2 \dots y_n)$$

$$\leq \sum_{y_1 y_2 \dots y_n \in B^n} Prob_{B^n}(y_1 y_2 \dots y_n) \cdot \text{ld card } goodkeys_n(y_1 y_2 \dots y_n)$$

$$\leq \text{ld} \left[\sum_{y_1 y_2 \dots y_n \in B^n} Prob_{B^n}(y_1 y_2 \dots y_n) \cdot \text{card } goodkeys_n(y_1 y_2 \dots y_n) \right]$$

$$= \text{ld } goodkeys_n.$$

Concerning the terms on the right-hand side of (12.51), we observe the following. First, by assumption (1) of the theorem, the entropy of keys yields $H(K)$ = ld card K. Second, for sufficiently large n, the entropy of the approximated plaintext prefixes can be estimated as n times the empirical entropy $eH(L)$ of the natural language L, which then yields an approximation in terms of the redundancy $Red(L)$ of L by (12.44):

$$H(A^n) \approx n \cdot eH(L) = n \cdot \text{ld card } A - n \cdot Red(L) \cdot \text{ld card } A .$$

Third, by the upper bound (A.6) for entropies, the entropy of ciphertexts is bounded by

$$H(B^n) \leq n \cdot \text{ld card } B = n \cdot \text{ld card } A .$$

Combining all results and simplifying, we finally obtain

ld $goodkeys_n$

$\geq H(K|B^n)$

$\geq$ ld card $K + (n \cdot \text{ld card } A - n \cdot Red(L) \cdot \text{ld card } A) - n \cdot \text{ld card } A$

$=$ ld card $K - n \cdot Red(L) \cdot \text{ld card } A$

$= \text{ld } \dfrac{\text{card } K}{(\text{card } A)^{n \cdot Red(L)}} .$ ❑

Theorem 12.6 supports a heuristic reasoning about the *minimum* number of repeated usages of a key such that the attacker is expected to be completely successful, i.e., the *unicity distance* $unicity(L) = \text{Min } \{ n \mid goodkeys_n = 1 \}$ of the language L. In order to reason about the unicity distance, we interpret the asserted inequality (12.50) as an equation, set its left-hand side to 1 and solve the equation for the repetition number n:

$$1 = \dfrac{\text{card } K}{(\text{card } A)^{n \cdot Red(L)}} \quad \text{iff} \quad (\text{card } A)^{n \cdot Red(L)} = \text{card } K$$

$$\text{iff} \quad n = \dfrac{\text{ld card } K}{Red(L) \cdot \text{ld card } A} .$$

12.9 Complexity-Theoretic Security for Encryption

For probability-theoretic security, basically, the *knowledge* of an attacker is modeled by probability distributions of the items under consideration. Using this model, the attacker is assumed to be rational and omnipotent, i.e., he is both willing and able to actually infer the a posteriori probability distributions that are enabled by his observations. In particular, the attacker is seen as having unlimited resources for computation. Roughly summarized, such an attacker is modeled as *actually knowing* all reasonable inferences from his a priori knowledge and his observations, or, equivalently, his knowledge is always taken to be *closed* under all reasonable inferences. In more intuitive terms, his *actual knowledge* is identified with his *potential knowledge*.

In practice, however, any computing agent is subject to limitations that are described by the theory of *computability* and *computational complexity*. In particular, an agent might not be able to fully materialize his potential knowledge owing to a lack of the time or space inevitably needed to algorithmically explore the inferential closure of his immediately accessible knowledge. Though in many situations these limitations are unpleasant, cryptography purposely takes advantage of them. Cryptography then aims at constructing a setting with the following two-sided *complexity-theoretic* properties:

- Pieces of information to be hidden from a potential attacker, for example a ciphertext or a private key, are deliberately taken from the inferential closure of public knowledge and potentially malicious observations or actions. But the general computational problem of actually determining such pieces is proven (or at least strongly suggested) to be infeasible. This is formalized in terms of computational complexity by requiring that any polynomially time-bounded probabilistic Turing machine can solve the general problem only with a negligible probability.
- On the other hand, a designated participant should be able to efficiently solve the corresponding problem when equipped with an appropriate secret, i.e., a suitable private key.

12.9.1 One-Way Functions with Trapdoors

At the core of many such settings, there are families of *one-way functions f_k with trapdoors*, where k serves as a private key to open the "trapdoor". Pieces of information to be hidden are taken as elements of the domains of those functions, whereas function values are treated as public or at least potentially observable. Intuitively, *hiding* an element x of a domain is accomplished by computing the function value $f_k(x)$. In order to meet this purpose, each of the functions should have three basic properties.

First, as a *technical enforcement mechanism* of security, such "hiding" computations should be *efficient*.

Second, the "hiding" must be *effective* in terms of the theory of computational complexity. Clearly, for a well-defined function f_k, the function value y is associated with all the domain elements x such that $f_k(x)=y$, and thus an observer of y "knows" this *pre-image*. More specifically, in principle, the observer can infer, from a knowledge of the function definition and his observation, that the hidden piece of information x is an element of the pre-image. In the following, we restrict the discussion mainly to functions publicly known to be injective: then, in principle, the observer even "knows" the hidden x exactly. However, effective hiding is achieved by ensuring that this knowledge remains *potential*, i.e., the computational problem of actually determining the hidden item x from the observation of $y = f_k(x)$ is required to be computationally infeasible.

Third, any agent that is *designated* by knowing the private key k can efficiently compute an element x of the pre-image under f_k given an observed function value y.

More abstractly, a family of functions f_k is called a family of *injective one-way functions with trapdoors* if the following properties hold for each k:

1. The function $f_k : D_k \to R_k$ is injective and computable in polynomial time.
2. The inverse function $f_k^{-1} : R_k \to D_k$ is computationally infeasible without a knowledge of k: roughly, there is no probabilistic polynomially time-bounded algorithm for computing f_k^{-1} without a knowledge of k.
3. The inverse function $f_k^{-1} : R_k \to D_k$ is computable in polynomial time if k (the private key) is used as an additional input.

It is an outstanding *open problem* of computer science whether such families actually exist. This unfortunate situation holds even if we drop the "trapdoor property". In fact, the existence of one-way functions is closely related to the famous open problem of whether $P \neq NP$. This relationship is roughly indicated by the following reasoning.

First, we observe that the inverse of any computable function $f : D \to R$ is computable as well, as can be seen from the following straightforward *inversion algorithm*:

On input $y \in R$, start enumerating all elements $x \in D$:
   for each $x \in D$ considered, compute $f(x)$ and compare with y;
   if equality is found, then exit with output x.

Second, suppose additionally that the elements of the domain and the range are finite bit strings, i.e., $D = R = \{0,1\}^*$, and that the function f is length-preserving, i.e., x and $f(x)$ are always of equal length. The inversion algorithm can then be refined to examine only those arguments x that have the same length as the input y. Since there are $2^{\text{length}(y)}$ such x, the refined inversion algorithm for f^{-1}, in general, needs exponential time in the length of its input.

Third, under the same assumptions, f^{-1} is computable in *nondeterministic* polynomial time by just guessing the pertinent x and then approving the required equality. Summarizing, if f is indeed a one-way function, then the inverse function f^{-1} is computable in *nondeterministic* polynomial time but not in *deterministic* polyno-mial time, i.e., we would have found a witness that nondeterministic polynomially bounded computations are more powerful than deterministic polynomially bounded computations, as suggested by the conjecture that $P \neq NP$.

Though we do not have a proof of the existence of one-way functions, there are nevertheless *candidates* for families of injective one-way functions with trapdoors, as needed by cryptography for constructing *asymmetric mechanisms* with *complex-ity-theoretic security*. In the following, we shall present two well-examined exam-ples that are commonly strongly believed to meet the requirements. For the sake of simplicity, the examples are treated in the framework of *encryption*. Similar con-siderations are possible for other cryptographic mechanisms.

The ideas leading to the candidates presented are quite ingenious. Their com-mon starting point is the group-based construction of perfect one-time encryption mechanisms, as already sketched at the end of Section 12.6. This construction pro-duces a *symmetric mechanism* whenever group elements can be efficiently con-verted. However, if the process of inverting group elements were known or supposed to be computationally infeasible, then one could try to base an *asymmet-ric mechanism* on that fact. Unfortunately, since this simple approach does not work directly, a more sophisticated indirect way has ben explored, as roughly out-lined in the following.

The exploration has been performed in the framework of *number theory*, by con-sidering the additive structure and the multiplicative structure of *residues modulo* some appropriate integer n. More specifically, one considers the ring $(\mathbf{Z}_n, +, \cdot, 0, 1)$, where $\mathbf{Z}_n$ is represented as $\{0, 1, \ldots, n-1\}$ and all calculations are done modulo n, i.e., all operations deliver the residue after the normal arithmetic result is divided by the modulus n. While the *additive structure* is always a *group*, the *multiplicative structure* forms a group only if the modulus is a *prime number*; it then yields a finite field. More generally, concerning multiplication modulo n, only those x where $0 < x < n$ that are relatively prime to n have a multiplicative inverse.

Two kinds of functions that are based on multiplication have crucial properties concerning their inversion. First, considering positive integers, given a set of prime numbers, we can calculate their *multiplicative product*, and conversely, given a positive integer, we can determine its prime factors. While multiplication can be computed efficiently, no probabilistic polynomial-time algorithm for *factorization* is known, despite all the efforts that have been made for more than two millennia (!). Factorization is also believed to be computationally infeasible if we restrict ourselves to positive integers that are the product of two prime numbers only.

Second, now considering residues modulo n, *exponentiation* can be defined as *repeated multiplication*, i.e., for a nonzero base element b, $0 < b < n$, the result of multiplying b by itself exactly e times is denoted as b^e, where e is any non-negative integer. While exponentiation can be efficiently implemented, this is believed not to be the case for some special versions of an inverse operation:

- One version appropriately fixes the exponent e, making the computation of the base for a given y infeasible, i.e., on input of y, it is infeasible to determine b with $b^e = y$. In turn, the construction of the exponent e is related to the *factorization problem* in the integers. This version is treated below in the framework of *RSA functions*.
- Another version selects the modulus as a prime number p, and additionally fixes a *primitive* element g as a base, where primitivity here means that g is a generator of the multiplicative group, i.e., $\{g^0, g^1, g^2, \ldots,\ g^{p-2}\}$ equals $\mathbf{Z}_p^* = \{1, \ldots, p-1\}$. Then, given an element y, it is infeasible to compute the exponent, i.e., it is infeasible to determine the *discrete logarithm* e such that $g^e = y$. This version is treated below in the framework of *ElGamal functions*.

The latter version suggests a rich class of generalizations, known as *elliptic-curve* cryptography, such that participants can autonomously select their favorite (presumable) injective one-way function. In any of these generalizations, the multiplicative group of $\mathbf{Z}_p^*$ is replaced by another suitable cyclic group, while the rest of the construction is reused.

12.9.2 RSA Functions

An *RSA function* $RSA_{p, q, d}^{n, e}$ is a number-theoretic function that can be exploited for *asymmetric cryptography*, where the triple (p, q, d) is used as the *private key* and the pair (n, e) as the *public key*, as explained in the following.

The parameters p and q are two different, sufficiently large *prime numbers* of approximately the same length (in binary encoding). In applications, a designated *secret holder* generates such prime numbers *randomly* and *confidentially*. The multiplicative product of the prime numbers, $n := p \cdot q$, is published as the modulus of the ring $(\mathbf{Z}_n, +, \cdot, 0, 1)$, where all computations are performed.

The multiplicative group of this ring is formed by those elements that are relatively prime to the modulus n, i.e., $\mathbf{Z}_n^* = \{x \mid 0 < x < n \text{ with } gcd(x, n) = 1\}$. This group has a cardinality $\phi(n) = (p - 1) \cdot (q - 1)$. The function ϕ, generally known as the *Euler phi function*, is used for investigating properties of exponents for exponentiations: such properties then refer to computations modulo $\phi(n)$ as follows.

Besides the first component n, the designated secret holder *randomly* selects the second component e of the *public key* such that $1 < e < \phi(n)$ and $gcd(e, \phi(n)) = 1$. Additionally, besides the first and the second component p and q, the designated secret holder *confidentially* computes the third component d of the *private key* as the multiplicative inverse of e modulo $\phi(n)$, i.e., such that $1 < d < \phi(n)$ and $e \cdot d \equiv 1 \bmod \phi(n)$.

Though, in principle, multiplicative inverses can be efficiently computed, in this specific situation a knowledge of $\phi(n)$ is needed, which, in turn, requires one to know the secretly kept prime numbers p and q, as will be indicated below.

Now, the *RSA function* for the selected parameters is defined by

$$RSA^{n, e}_{p, q, d} : \mathbf{Z}_n \to \mathbf{Z}_n \text{ with } RSA^{n, e}_{p, q, d}(x) = x^e \bmod n. \tag{12.52}$$

As can be seen from the definition, this function can be computed by whoever knows the public key (n,e). More specifically, we shall reason that the required properties of *injective one-way functions with trapdoors* (are conjectured to) hold. The first and the third property, injectivity and efficiency of both the function and the keyed inverse, are immediate consequences of the following theorem, since the exponentiation by e can be reversed by an exponentiation by d (and vice versa), and exponentiation in $\mathbf{Z}_n$ can be implemented efficiently (see Appendix A.4.3). Moreover, a designated secret holder can efficiently generate the large prime numbers needed (see Appendix A.4.4).

Theorem 12.7   [injectivity and trapdoor]

In the setting of the *RSA function* $RSA^{n, e}_{p, q, d}$, for all $x \in \mathbf{Z}_n$, $(x^e)^d \equiv x \bmod n$.

Sketch of Proof: The following congruences modulo n are valid for all $x \in \mathbf{Z}_n$:

$$(x^e)^d \equiv x^{e \cdot d} \qquad \text{according to the exponentiation rules,}$$
$$\equiv x^{k \cdot \phi(n) + 1} \quad \text{with } e \cdot d = k \cdot \phi(n) + 1 \text{ , by the definition of } d,$$
$$\equiv x \cdot (x^{\phi(n)})^k \text{ according to the exponentiation rules.}$$

Case 1: $x \in \mathbf{Z}_n{}^*$. Since the multiplicative group $\mathbf{Z}_n{}^*$ has order $\phi(n)$, we conclude that $(x^{\phi(n)})^k \equiv 1^k \equiv 1 \bmod n$, and thus $(x^e)^d \equiv x \bmod n$.

Case 2: $x \notin \mathbf{Z}_n{}^*$. In this case $gcd(x,n) \neq 1$ and, thus, since n is the product of the prime numbers p and q, $gcd(x,p) \neq 1$ or $gcd(x,q) \neq 1$. Below, we infer for each subcase that both $(x^e)^d \equiv x \bmod p$ and $(x^e)^d \equiv x \bmod q$. Then, by the definitions of n, p and q, $(x^e)^d \equiv x \bmod n$ holds as well, as a consequence of the *Chinese remainder theorem*.

Subcase 2a: $gcd(x,p) \neq 1$. In this case, since p is prime, p divides x and thus any multiple of x as well. Hence $(x^e)^d \equiv x \bmod p$. Similarly, $gcd(x,q) \neq 1$ implies $(x^e)^d \equiv x \bmod q$.

Subcase 2b: $gcd(x,p) = 1$. In this case $x \in \mathbf{Z}_p{}^*$ and, accordingly, the following congruences modulo p are valid:

$$x^{\phi(n)} \equiv x^{(p - 1) \cdot (q - 1)} \qquad \text{by the definition of } \phi(n),$$
$$\equiv (x^{p - 1})^{q - 1} \qquad \text{according to the exponentiation rules,}$$
$$\equiv 1^{q - 1} \equiv 1 \qquad \text{since } x \in \mathbf{Z}_p{}^* \text{ has order } \phi(p) = p - 1 \text{ .}$$

As in Case 1, we then obtain the following congruences modulo p:

$$(x^e)^d \equiv x^{e \cdot d} \equiv x^{k \cdot \phi(n) + 1} \equiv x \cdot (x^{\phi(n)})^k \equiv x \cdot 1 \equiv x.$$

Similarly, $gcd(x,q) = 1$ implies $(x^e)^d \equiv x \bmod q$.   ❑

Concerning the second property, computational infeasibility of the non-keyed inverse of an RSA function, a precise treatment would demand thorough a background in computational *number theory* and the theory of computational complexity. Accordingly, we shall only outline the basic reasoning. We also emphasize that for some parameter choices, the basic reasoning does not fully apply.

As before, supposing an intuitive understanding of the notion that a problem is computationally infeasible, we explore the *relative complexity* of the *non-keyed inversion problem*, i.e., the problem of inverting an RSA function while knowing the public key but *not* the private key, relative to some other problems, including *factorization*. Regarding full formalizations of the intuitive notions, we note only that they are essentially based on the expected success of probabilistic polynomially time-bounded algorithms to achieve the problem considered.

The exploitation of RSA functions for cryptography relies fundamentally on several conjectures that are widely believed to be true but, unfortunately, so far have resisted all attempts to formally prove them, despite many efforts. The starting point is the *factorization conjecture* of computational number theory:

> The factorization problem   (12.53)
> restricted to products of two prime numbers,

i.e., given a number n of known form $n = p \cdot q$ where p and q are prime numbers, to determine the actual factors p and q, is computationally infeasible.

The seminal proposal to exploit RSA functions relates the non-keyed inversion problem to the factorization problem by suggesting the *RSA conjecture*:

> If the non-keyed inversion problem for RSA functions   (12.54)
> was computationally feasible,

then the factorization problem would be computationally feasible as well.

In terms of "attacks", as introduced in Section 12.5, these conjectures basically say the following: we are encouraged to hope that a *universal success* of "unauthorized inversion" will not happen, since otherwise we would have to believe that some "attacker" will eventually invent an efficient solution to the open factorization problem.

The RSA conjecture has been specialized in various ways, considering specific "attacks" to achieve the inversion. For example, a "known-ciphertext/plaintext attack" aiming at a *complete success* is conjectured to fail as well, as claimed by the following *specialized RSA conjecture*:

> If the non-keyed inversion problem for RSA functions   (12.55)
> by means of determining the private exponent d from an argument–value pair
> was computationally feasible,

then the factorization problem would be computationally feasible as well.

The RSA conjectures can be briefly summarized by saying that "factorization" is *feasibly reducible* to "RSA inversion". Obviously, the converse claim, namely that "RSA inversion" is feasibly reducible to "factorization", provably holds. In fact, if an "attacker" was able to feasibly factor the public modulus n into the prime numbers actually employed, then he could feasibly determine the full private key by just repeating the computations of the designated secret holder to find the private exponent d, and thus he would be completely successful. Several similar claims can be proven as well, for example that "factorization" is feasibly reducible to any of the following problems, and vice versa:

- the *Euler problem*, i.e., given a number n of known form $n = p \cdot q$ where p and q are prime numbers, to determine the value $\phi(n)$; and
- the *public-key-to-private-exponent problem*, i.e., given the public key (n,e), to determine the private exponent d.

The above conjectures and proven claims about the problems considered and their relations regarding feasible reducibility are summarized in Figure 12.11.

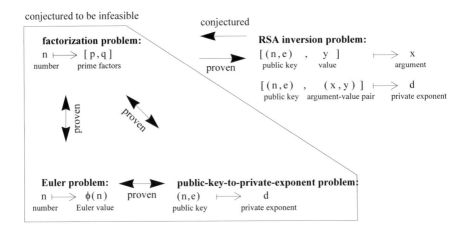

Fig. 12.11. The RSA conjecture and related proven claims regarding feasible reducibility

12.9.3 ElGamal Functions

An *ElGamal function* $EG_a^{p,\,g,\,A}$ is another number-theoretic function that can be exploited for *asymmetric cryptography*, where the parameter a is used as the *private key* and the triple (p,g,A) as the *public key*, as explained in the following.

The parameter p is a sufficiently large *prime number* to be used as a modulus, and the parameter g is a primitive element of the cyclic multiplicative group of the finite field $(\mathbf{Z}_p,+,\cdot,0,1)$, i.e., g generates $\mathbf{Z}_p^{*}$ such $\mathbf{Z}_p^{*} = \{1,2,\ldots,p-1\} = \{g^1,g^2,\ldots,g^{p-1}\}$, where $g^{p-1} \equiv 1 \equiv g^0$. Accordingly, exponents for generating $\mathbf{Z}_p^{*}$ can be taken from $\mathbf{Z}_{p-1} = \{0,1,\ldots,p-2\}$. The parameter $a \in \{0,1,\ldots,p-2\}$ is used as an exponent to determine the last parameter $A = g^a \bmod p$.

   In applications, a designated *secret holder* first appropriately selects the modulus p and the generator g as part of the *public key*. Then, the secret holder *randomly* and *confidentially* selects an exponent $a \in \{0, 1, \ldots, p-2\}$ as his *private key*. Additionally, he "hides" his secret a by computing the number $A = g^a \bmod p$, which becomes a further part of the *public key*. Though, in principle, the *discrete logarithm* of A with respect to the base g, i.e., the secret a, is uniquely determined, it nevertheless cannot be efficiently computed from the public key, as will be indicated below.

   Now, the *ElGamal function* for the selected parameters is defined by

$$EG_a^{p, g, A} : \mathbf{Z}_p^* \times \mathbf{Z}_{p-1} \to \mathbf{Z}_p^* \times \mathbf{Z}_p^* \text{ with } EG_a^{p, g, A}(x, k) = (y_1, y_2) \quad (12.56)$$

$$\text{such that } y_1 = g^k \bmod p \text{ and } y_2 = x \cdot A^k \bmod p.$$

When this function is exploited for encryption, the sender takes the first argument x as the plaintext, and he *randomly and confidentially* selects the second argument k for two purposes. First, the second argument introduces *randomization* such that, for an attacker, it is much more difficult to successfully apply a straightforward *inversion algorithm*. Second, the additional argument k enables the sender to share a *common secret* with the designated receiver, namely the value

$$A^k = (g^a)^k = g^{a \cdot k} = (g^k)^a = y_1^a. \quad (12.57)$$

The sender computes the common secret on the basis of the public value A, whereas the designated receiver computes the common secret from the first part y_1 of the communicated function value and his private exponent a. This common secret is then used as a kind of one-time key for transforming the plaintext x by a multiplication in $\mathbf{Z}_p^*$, as employed for group-based constructions of perfect encryption mechanisms.

   As can be seen from the definition, an ElGamal function can be computed by whoever knows the public key (p, g, A). More specifically, we shall reason that the required properties of *injective one-way functions with trapdoors* (are conjectured to) hold. The first and the third property, injectivity with respect to the first argument (the plaintext) and efficiency of both the function and the keyed inverse, are immediate consequences of the following theorem, since the "blinding" multiplication of the plaintext can be reversed by using the multiplicative inverse of the common secret, and multiplication, (multiplicative) inversion and exponentiation in $\mathbf{Z}_p^*$ can be implemented efficiently (see Appendix A.4.3). Moreover, the large prime number needed can be generated efficiently (see Appendix A.4.4), and a primitive element to be used as a generator can be found efficiently as well.

Theorem 12.8   [injectivity and trapdoor]

In the setting of the *ElGamal function* $EG_a^{p, g, A}$, for all $x \in \mathbf{Z}_p^*$ and $k \in \mathbf{Z}_{p-1}$,

$$y_2 \cdot (y_1^a)^{-1} \equiv x \bmod p.$$

Sketch of Proof: The following congruences modulo p are valid for all $x \in \mathbf{Z}_p^{\,*}$ and $k \in \mathbf{Z}_{p-1}$:

$$y_2 \cdot (y_1^{\,a})^{-1} \equiv (x \cdot A^k) \cdot ((g^k)^a)^{-1} \qquad \text{by the definitions of } y_1 \text{ and } y_2,$$

$$\equiv (x \cdot (g^a)^k) \cdot ((g^k)^a)^{-1} \qquad \text{by the definition of } A,$$

$$\equiv x \cdot g^{a \cdot k} \cdot (g^{a \cdot k})^{-1} \qquad \text{according to the exponentiation rules,}$$

$$\equiv x \qquad\qquad \text{exploiting the inverse occurrences of the common secret.} \qquad \Box$$

Concerning the second property, computational infeasibility of the non-keyed inverse of an ElGamal function, a precise treatment would again demand a thorough background in computational *number theory* and the theory of computational complexity. We shall only outline the fundamental conjectures and claims, which have been investigated extensively and formally, similarly to the RSA functions. We also emphasize that for some parameter choices, the reasoning sketched does not fully apply.

For ElGamal functions, the starting point is the *discrete logarithm conjecture* of computational number theory:

> The discrete logarithm problem   (12.58)
> for a prime number p and a generator g,
> i.e., given an exponentiation result y, to determine the exponent e such that $g^e = y$,
> is computationally infeasible.

The ingenious proposal to exploit ElGamal functions relates the *non-keyed inversion problem* to the discrete logarithm problem by suggesting the *ElGamal conjecture*:

> If the non-keyed inversion problem for ElGamal functions   (12.59)
> was computationally feasible,
> then the discrete logarithm problem would be computationally feasible as well.

In terms of "attacks", as introduced in Section 12.5, these conjectures basically say the following: we are encouraged to hope that a *universal success* of "unauthorized inversion" will not happen, since otherwise we would have to believe that some "attacker" will eventually invent an efficient solution to the open discrete logarithm problem. Again, the converse claim of the conjecture, i.e., the feasible reducibility of "ElGamal inversion" to "discrete logarithms", can be proven.

Interestingly, "ElGamal inversion" can be proven to be mutually feasibly reducible with the *Diffie–Hellman problem* regarding the common secret A^k shared by the sender and the designated receiver: given the modulus p and the generator g and, additionally, two "blinded exponents", i.e., for two randomly selected numbers a and k, the values $A = g^a$ and $B = g^k$, the problem is to determine the *common secret $A^k = g^{ak}$*. The interest in this problem stems from the fact that the given values are known to an attacking eavesdropper if an ElGamal function is used for encryption.

The above conjectures and proven claims about the problems considered and their relations regarding feasible reducibility are summarized in Figure 12.12.

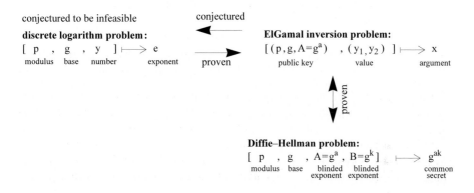

Fig. 12.12. The ElGamal conjecture and related proven claims regarding feasible reducibility

12.9.4 Elliptic-Curve Functions

The construction of ElGamal functions has the potential to be transferable to a broad class of closely related settings. Essentially, all we need is the following:

- A finite *cyclic group* $(\mathbf{G}, \bullet, u)$ with the following two-sided computational properties.
- On the one hand, the binary group operation $\bullet$ and the related unary inversion operation $^{-1}$ (written in a *multiplicative* style, for solving an equation $a \bullet x = u$ with respect to x) are *efficiently* implementable.
- On the other hand, the *exponentiation* g^e of a generator g (written in a multiplicative style, for the iterated application of the group operation to that *generator*, defined by $g^0 = u$ and $g^{e+1} = g^e \bullet g$) has a computationally *infeasible* discrete logarithm problem.

The special ElGamal setting exploits the cyclic multiplicative group $(\mathbf{Z}_p^*, \cdot, 1)$ of *residues* modulo a *prime number* with an arbitrary generator g; anything else can be defined in terms of the group and the generator.

Thus, the main challenge is to identify further appropriate cyclic groups. This is a great challenge, since obviously not all cyclic groups fit the requirements, even if they are (algebraically) isomorphic.

An immediate counterexample is the additive group $(\mathbf{Z}_{p-1}, +, 0)$, which is cyclic and has $p-1$ elements too. But, in this group, "exponentiation" means iterated addition modulo $p-1$ and thus basically coincides with multiplication modulo $p-1$.

Accordingly, in this context, the "discrete logarithm" basically coincides with inverting a multiplication modulo $p-1$, and thus the "discrete logarithm" is related to computing a multiplicative inverse modulo $p-1$, which, in turn, can be efficiently determined by the extended Euclidean algorithm.

A closer inspection of the challenge suggests the following computational view of (*algebraic*) *isomorphisms* between two cyclic groups of the same cardinality: if one group has an efficient "discrete logarithm problem", such as $(\mathbf{Z}_{p-1},+,0)$, and the other group has a computationally infeasible "discrete logarithm problem", such as $(\mathbf{Z}_p^*,\cdot,1)$, then any isomorphism (which maps a generator of the former group to a generator of the latter group and then is suitably extended for the other elements) is computationally infeasible as well. For otherwise, we could exploit an efficiently computable isomorphism to obtain a computational reduction of the infeasible problem to the efficient one, yielding a contradiction to the supposed infeasibility.

This reasoning about isomorphisms leads to a restatement of the main challenge: we have to identify classes of (algebraically) isomorphic cyclic groups that contain a representative member with efficient group operations but an infeasible "discrete logarithm problem", and to explicitly construct such a *group representation*. There have been various attempts to solve the challenge. In the following, we briefly introduce a specific approach, known as a part of *elliptic-curve cryptography*, that has been successfully explored over the last two decades. This approach offers a whole world of practically available alternatives to the commercially still predominant RSA and ElGamal functions, thereby also relaxing our dependence on the latter functions.

Roughly sketched, and in a somewhat specialized sense, an *elliptic curve* is the finite set of solutions to an equation in two variables x and y of the form

$$y^2 \equiv x^3 + a \cdot x + b \mod p ,\qquad(12.60)$$

where the modulus $p > 3$ is a prime number, any element is taken from and any operation is performed in the underlying finite field $(\mathbf{Z}_p,+,\cdot,0,1)$, and the coefficients a and b satisfy the further condition that $\neg(4 \cdot a^2 + 27 \cdot b^2 \equiv 0 \mod p)$.

Thus an elliptic curve $E^{p,a,b}$ contains all pairs $(x,y) \in \mathbf{Z}_p \times \mathbf{Z}_p$ that solve the equation (12.60) for a specific selection of p, a, and b satisfying the stated conditions; additionally, one further element ∞, called the *point at infinity*, is put into $E^{p,a,b}$. On any such set $E^{p,a,b}$, we can uniformly define a binary operation $+_{ec}$ (written in additive style, by convention and for convenience) that can be geometrically interpreted by a *chord-and-tangent rule*, as exemplarily visualized in Figure 12.13. This operation can be verified to satisfy the group properties with the point at infinity as the neutral element.

More specifically, we define the binary (group) operation $+_{ec}$ together with the unary (group) inversion operation $-_{ec}$ by distinguishing the following four cases:

1. [neutrality]   For all $P \in E^{p,a,b}$: $P +_{ec} \infty = \infty +_{ec} P = P$,
   in particular $-_{ec} \infty = \infty$.

2. [inversion]   For all $P = (x,y) \in E^{p,a,b}$: $(x,y) +_{ec} (x,-y) = \infty$,
   and accordingly $-_{ec}(x,y) = (x,-y)$.

3. [chord rule]   For all $P = (x_1,y_1) \in E^{p,a,b}$ and $Q = (x_2,y_2) \in E^{p,a,b}$ such that
   $P \neq Q$ and $P \neq -_{ec}Q$:
   $P +_{ec} Q = (x_3,y_3)$, where

   $$x_3 = \left(\frac{y_2 - y_1}{x_2 - x_1}\right)^2 - x_1 - x_2 \text{ and } y_3 = \frac{y_2 - y_1}{x_2 - x_1} \cdot (x_1 - x_3) - y_1.$$

4. [tangent rule] For all $P = (x_1,y_1) \in E^{p,a,b}$ such that $P \neq -_{ec}P$:
   $P +_{ec} P = (x_3,y_3)$, where

   $$x_3 = \left(\frac{3 \cdot x_1^2 + a}{2 \cdot y_1}\right)^2 - 2 \cdot x_1 \text{ and } y_3 = \frac{3 \cdot x_1^2 + a}{2 \cdot y_1} \cdot (x_1 - x_3) - y_1.$$

Strictly speaking, the geometric interpretations of the chord rule and the tangent rule apply only for a variant of the elliptic curves where the infinitely many and continuous real numbers are taken as the underlying field, rather than the finitely many and discrete residue classes. Nevertheless, the geometric interpretation provides a visualization that may be helpful (for the non-expert reader):

- For adding P and Q with $P \neq Q$ and $P \neq -_{ec}Q$, the chord rule suggests the following geometric construction in a plane: draw a line through P and Q, determine the intersection of this line with the graph of $E^{p,a,b}$, and mirror the intersection point in the x-axis.
- In particular, for doubling P with $P \neq -_{ec}P$, the tangent rule suggests the following geometric construction in a plane: draw a tangent to the graph of $E^{p,a,b}$ through P, determine the intersection of this line with the graph of $E^{p,a,b}$, and mirror the intersection point in the x-axis.

Figure 12.13 visualizes an example of the chord rule for the solutions of the equation $y^2 = x^3 - x$, taking the real numbers as the underlying field.

In the first step of the overall construction, an elliptic curve $E^{p,a,b}$ and a group operation $+_{ec}$ on its points are defined. The second step is to determine a point G that generates an appropriate cyclic subgroup. In particular, it should be computationally infeasible to solve the corresponding *discrete logarithm problem*:

> Given the generator G, whose order is denoted by n,   (12.61)
> and an element Y of the generated subgroup,
> determine the "exponent" $e \in \{0,1,\ldots,n-1\}$ such that $Y = G +_{ec} \ldots +_{ec} G$,
> where the group operation is applied as often as is indicated by e.

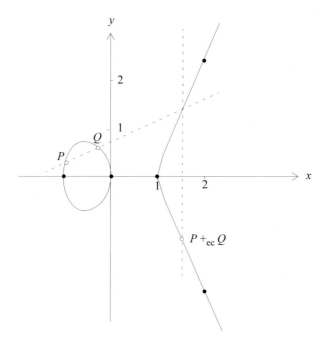

Fig. 12.13. The solution graph of the equation $y^2 = x^3 - x$ over the real numbers, and a geometric interpretation of the group operation

The second step is based on the following fundamental characterization of elliptic curves. Let $E^{p,a,b}$ be an *elliptic curve* with group operation $+_{ec}$. There are then cardinals k and l such that

- the group $(E^{p,a,b}, +_{ec}, \infty)$ is (algebraically) isomorphic to the product group built from the groups $(\mathbf{Z}_k, +, 0)$ and $(\mathbf{Z}_l, +, 0)$, and
- $l \mid k$ and $l \mid p-1$.

Thus, basically, the second step consists of determining the claimed cardinals k and l and exploiting their properties. In particular, the fundamental characterization implies that $E^{p,a,b}$ has a subgroup that is (algebraically) isomorphic to the cyclic group $\mathbf{Z}_k$ and, accordingly, that subgroup is cyclic as well. In the special case where $l = 1$, the elliptic curve $E^{p,a,b}$ itself is isomorphic to $\mathbf{Z}_k$ and thus is cyclic.

If the constructions and the generalization of the ElGamal functions sketched above are carefully performed, in particular by selecting and investigating appropriate parameters, then the required properties of *injective one-way functions with trapdoors* (are conjectured to) hold. The first and the third property, injectivity and efficiency of both the functions and the keyed inverses, are proven along the same lines as for ElGamal functions. Concerning the second property, infeasibility of the non-keyed inverses, we again rely on the pertinent conjectures.

12.10 Cryptographic Security

Cryptography is aimed at supporting secure cooperation in the presence of threats. Threats might be instantiated in many ways as specific attacks against the design, implementation, installation or administration of a cryptographic mechanism. The overall quality of such a mechanism depends crucially on appropriate security requirements being sufficiently satisfied during the whole *development phase* and the whole *life cycle*. If all pertinent requirements are indeed met, then we speak about achieving *cryptographic security*. In the following, we summarize some general aspects that are important for many specific mechanisms.

- When cryptography is employed, a participant is designated by holding some secret or private keys and, accordingly, he must be able to secretly generate, store and use these keys. To achieve this goal, it is best if the participant possesses and controls a *personal tamper-resistant computing device*, or any virtual equivalent thereof.
- Secret and private keys and possibly further items have to appear as random, and, accordingly, some *source of randomness* should be available, the best possibility being a *truly random* physical source.
- The items to appear as random must have *sufficient length* in order to resist attacks based on *exhaustive search and trials*, often even if these attacks are performed many years in the future, running innovative computing equipment.
- Depending on the kind of keys used, some assistance of a *trusted third party* is normally required, and this party must indeed comply with the expectations of it. Typically, for a symmetric mechanism such a third party *distributes a secret key* between the partners involved, and for an asymmetric mechanism such a third party *certifies that a public key* belongs to the claimed holder of the matching private key.
- In addition to trusted third parties, in most cases various further *external participants* will have contributed to an application of a cryptographic mechanism by delivering ideas or an implemented component. Assigning trust to such external participants should be based on their compliance with the construction principle of *open design* and, where applicable, on appropriate *informational assurances*.

12.11 Bibliographic Hints

Basically all textbooks on security in computing systems contain introductory sections on cryptography; see Section 1.7.

The dedicated, comprehensive presentations of cryptography include the work of Stinson [470], Menezes/van Oorschot/Vanstone [347], Schneier [437] and Salomaa [419], as well as the very fundamental treatments of Goldreich [226, 228, 229], which are concisely set out and summarized in [227]. Further introductions are given, for example, by Buchmann [108], Tilborg [480] and Delfs/Knebl [159]. Tilborg/et al. [481] provide an encyclopedia. Bauer [32] describes cryptology, which includes the attacker's view of analyzing ciphertexts. There are many further highly specialized monographs; for example, B. Pfitzmann [392] investigates digital signatures, Daemen/Rijmen [156] describe their design of AES, the Advanced Encryption Standard, and Hankerson/Menezes/Vanstone [248] treat elliptic-curve cryptography. The EU-funded Network of Excellence in Cryptology ECRYPT [182] evaluates implemented cryptographic mechanisms regarding many aspects including security analysis, recommended key sizes and efficiency.

Numerous original contributions deal with a great variety of aspects of cryptography. Specific references to selected aspects are provided in the respective further chapters on cryptography. The aspects presented in this chapter are based mainly on the general expositions mentioned above and on further selected references as follows.

Probability-theoretic security for encryption and the use of entropies have been pioneered by Shannon [443, 444]. Our discussion of the cryptanalysis of a multiply used encryption key is inspired by the work of Beauchemin/Brassard [34] and the exposition given by Stinson [470]. Probability-theoretic security for authentication has been pioneered by Gilbert/MacWilliams/Sloane [219] and further elaborated by Simmons [448, 450] and Stinson [465, 466, 467, 470].

Complexity-theoretic security for encryption and the exploitation of one-way functions have been pioneered by Diffie/Hellman [171] and Rivest/Shamir/Adleman [409], and later supplemented by Merkle [349], ElGamal [183], Koblitz [295] and Miller [354], and many others as well.

Whereas encryption and authentication have been traditional topics of cryptography, anonymization has been introduced later by the pioneering work of Chaum [122, 123, 124]. Subsequently, A. Pfitzmann [389] and many others elaborate the approach; for example, more recently, Brickell/Camenisch/Chen [114, 105] invent "direct anonymous attestation", usable for trusted platform modules. Diaz/Claessens/Preneel/et al. [168, 169] investigate how to combine building blocks to achieve anonymity, and A. Pfitzmann/Hansen [391] propose a consolidated terminology for the field.

Randomness and pseudorandomness have attracted many researchers from various fields. For example, Knuth [293] analyzes the art of programming for generating pseudorandom sequences; Kolmogorov [299], Chaitin [119], Martin-Löf [334], Schnorr [435], Levin [314] and others aim at the conceptual foundations; and Blum/Micali [91], Goldwasser/Micali/[231], Goldreich/Goldwasser/Micali [221], Goldreich/Krawcyzk/Luby [224] and Yao [505] emphasize the application to cryptography. Our summary is extracted from the broad exposition given by Goldreich [228].

Damgard [149], Merkle [350] and Goldwasser/Micali/Rivest [232] explore basic constructions for hash functions. Rivest [410, 411] proposes the practically applied hash functions MD4 and MD5; the U.S. National Institute of Standards and Technology (NIST) [366] publishes the Secure Hash Standard (SHA). Though widely used, there are known collisions for these specifications, as reported by Dobbertin [173] and Wang/Feng/Lai/Yu [495]. Backes/B. Pfitzmann/Waidner [28] investigate a specific difficulty in analyzing the achievements of hash functions within protocols.

Distributed computing systems require synchronization of the participant's activities, whether based on real time, logical time, a virtual global state or some related concept. Tanenbaum/van Steen [478] give a general introduction to this widely studied topic. In addition, for example, Ramanathan/Shin/Butler [402] and Mills [355] treat clock synchronization, Lamport [306, 307] suggests logical clocks, Massias/Serret Avila/Quisquater review the main issues [335], and Adams/Chain/Pinkas/Zuccherato [9] propose a protocol for using timestamps in X.509 certificates.

Finally, we point to the recent development of quantum cryptography, surveyed, for example, by Bruss/et al. [107], which will potentially require us to totally revise the traditional view of cryptography.

13 Encryption

13.1 Survey and Classification

13.1.1 Definition and Application Scenario

An *encryption* mechanism aims at keeping information *confidential* while it is being transmitted or stored on a medium that is potentially subject to unauthorized accesses. Basically, this goal is achieved by transforming the data underlying the crucial information such that the transformed data looks as if it is *random*. Accordingly, an unauthorized eavesdropper should not be able to infer any meaningful information from the transformed data. However, the designated receiver of the information is equipped with a *secret* that is used as a decryption key for inverting the transformation and thus for reconstructing the original data.

A more detailed introduction to encryption is presented in Subsection 12.4.1, where the basic ideas are visualized in Figure 12.1 and Figure 12.2. Quality aspects are sketched in Section 12.5. Afterwards, some selected quality aspects are studied in more technical terms: Section 12.6 investigates *perfect encryptions* within a *probability-theoretic* approach, leading to effective constructions based on *groups*. Section 12.9 discusses an alternative *complexity-theoretic* approach, leading to effective constructions based on *one-way functions* with *trapdoors*. Section 12.8 deals with the potential danger of *multiply* employing a secret key; more precisely, it deals with an estimate of the information revealed by using a secret key.

In this section, we survey the main concepts and results in the field of encryption and their impact on security in a more systematic way and in more technical depth, without fully repeating the introductory discussion already given in Chapter 12.

Basically, and with some variations, the target of interest in this section is an *encryption mechanism*, or a family of such mechanisms, that is given by three algorithms operating on three underlying sets:

- A domain set D of (possible) *plaintexts*.
- A range set R of (possible) *ciphertexts*.
- A set K of (possible) *keys*, each of which comprises an *encryption key ek* and a *decryption key dk*. If there is a need to distinguish the components, or whenever it appears to be convenient to do so, we use a suitable notation such as $K = EK \times DK$, with $ek \in EK$ and $dk \in DK$.

- A *key generation* algorithm *Gen*: → *K*, which might take a natural number *l* as a *security parameter*, typically for specifying the size of the generated key components.

- An *encryption* algorithm *Enc*: *EK* × *D* → *R* that transforms a plaintext *x* ∈ *D* into a ciphertext *y* = *Enc*(*ek*, *x*) ∈ *R* using an encryption key *ek* ∈ *EK*.

- A *decryption* algorithm *Dec*: *DK* × *R* → *D* that transforms a ciphertext *y* ∈ *R* into a plaintext *x* = *Dec*(*dk*, *y*) ∈ *D* using a decryption key *dk* ∈ *DK*.

The algorithms should satisfy (suitable variants of) the following properties:

- *Correctness*. Using a generated key pair, any encryption can be reversed by the corresponding decryption, i.e., for all keys (*ek*, *dk*) ∈ *EK* × *DK* generated by *Gen*, and for all plaintexts *x* ∈ *D*,

$$Dec(dk, Enc(ek, x)) = x.$$

- *Secrecy*. Without knowing the pertinent decryption key *dk*, an (unauthorized) observer of a ciphertext *y* = *Enc*(*ek*, *x*) cannot "determine" the corresponding plaintext *x*. This *naive* version should be strengthened to a *semantic* version requiring that such an observer can "determine" only those properties of the corresponding plaintext *x* that he could "determine" without knowing the ciphertext *y* at all.

- *Efficiency*. The algorithms *Gen*, *Enc* and *Dec* are efficiently computable.

In a typical application scenario, there are at least two designated participants, Alice and Bob. Bob, or, if applicable, some other participant acting on behalf of Bob, who might be Alice, prepares for a confidential *message transmission* from Alice to Bob by invoking the key generation algorithm *Gen*. Then the components of the generated key are distributed: the designated *sender* Alice gets the encryption key *ek*, and the designated *receiver* Bob keeps the decryption key *dk*.

Later on, wanting to send a confidential message to Bob, Alice calls the encryption algorithm *Enc* in order to conceal the pertinent plaintext *x* with the help of the encryption key *ek*.

Having received the corresponding ciphertext *y*, Bob calls the decryption algorithm *Dec* to recover the original plaintext from the received ciphertext *y* with the help of the decryption key *dk*. Clearly, as far as is actually required for the specific mechanism, only the designated participants should know the respective key components; in any case, the designated receiver Bob must strictly protect his decryption key *dk*.

Besides the designated participants, another participant, Malory, might observe the ciphertext *y* as well. Even worse, Malory might purposely eavesdrop on the communication and take some further actions in order to "attack" the intended *confidentiality* of the message, i.e., to learn the concealed plaintext *x*. However, under all anticipated circumstances, the *secrecy property* should guarantee that the *attacker* Malory never achieves his goal.

13.1.2 Classification

For our exposition, we employ a rough classification of encryption mechanisms by identifying three particularly important aspects and their respective alternatives:

- *Mode of operation*: *blockwise* or *streamwise*.
- *Relationship between keys*: *symmetric* or *asymmetric*.
- *Justification of a secrecy property*: *one-time key* or *one-way function* or *chaos*.

We emphasize, however, that in general these aspects are not independent of each other, nor are the alternatives sharp.

Regarding the *mode of operation*, the plaintexts are considered as strings over some alphabet of letters. A *blockwise* working mechanism, often called a *block cipher*, takes a sequence of letters that has a fixed, usually relatively small length as an input "block" that is transformed as a whole. For example, a *block* may be built from 16 letters, each of which is represented by 1 byte, resulting in a block of 128 bits. A *streamwise* working mechanism, often called a *stream cipher*, treats each letter individually, but possibly in a suitably connected way. The distinction is not sharp, in particular for two reasons. First, the notion of a "letter" is somewhat arbitrary. In our example, rather than seeing a single byte as a "letter", we could alternatively consider 16 bytes as a "letter". Second, applications often require large messages to be sent that contain data with a size in the range of several kilobytes up to even many gigabytes. In this case, the data has to be partitioned into small units anyhow, into "blocks" or single "letters", and, accordingly, the overall encryption procedure has in the end to transform a stream of blocks or letters, respectively.

Regarding the *relationship between the keys*, i.e., between an encryption key and the matching decryption key, there are two options. For a *symmetric* mechanism, the two components of a matching key pair are basically the same. For an *asymmetric* mechanism, however, the two components have to be essentially different, allowing one to make the encryption key *public* whereas the decryption key has to remain *private* for the designated receiver of ciphertexts. For asymmetric mechanisms, the *secrecy property* must include the condition that an (unauthorized) observer cannot determine the private decryption key from the public encryption key.

Regarding *the justification of a secrecy property*, there are basically three approaches, called succinctly in this monograph the *one-time key*, *one-way function* and *chaos*.

The *one-time key* approach exploits *probability-theoretic perfect encryption* in the sense of Section 12.6. This approach can be roughly summarized as follows. A key is randomly generated as a string of letters, each of which is interpreted as an element of some suitable *group*. Such a key is valid to be used only one time, to encrypt a single plaintext of the same kind and length. Encryption is done *streamwise* by applying the group operation to each corresponding pair of a plaintext letter and a key letter. Decryption is done by reversing the group operation, taking the inverted key, and thus this approach is used as a *symmetric* mechanism. In the sim-

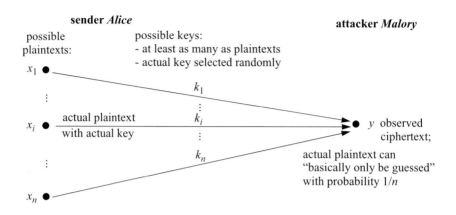

Fig. 13.1. A probability-theoretic secrecy property for the one-time key approach

plest and most often used case, the letters are simply either 0 or 1, the group operation is XOR and inverting the key is trivial.

Figure 13.1 visualizes the justification of the probability-theoretic secrecy property from the perspective of an attacker Malory who has observed a ciphertext y.
Since for every possible plaintext there is a possible key leading to the observation
of y, Malory can, basically, only guess the actual plaintext x_i. If no further a priori
knowledge about plaintexts is available, then the randomness of the key selection
makes all possible plaintexts equiprobable. This justification is valid only for
exactly one usage of the selected key k_i.

The *one-way function* approach exploits *complexity-theoretic* reasoning, as
introduced in Section 12.9. This approach can be roughly summarized as follows.
A key is randomly selected as a parameter set that determines a specific member of
some suitable family of functions. The key is used in an *asymmetric* way. Anybody
can use the public key as an encryption key, but the private key is held only by the
designated receiver, as a decryption key. Encryption is done by applying the determined member function to an appropriate *block*, considered as the plaintext.
Decryption is done by inverting the determined member function for the received
ciphertext. This inversion is computationally feasible if the private decryption key
is available as a "trapdoor", but otherwise the inversion is computationally infeasible.

Figure 13.2 visualizes the justification of the complexity-theoretic secrecy property from the perspective of an attacker Malory who has observed a ciphertext y.
Though, in principle, Malory could find the unique plaintext x_i by exploiting the
publicly known encryption key, he will not actually succeed, since the computational effort required will be too high. This justification is valid even for (suitably
limited) multiple usage of the selected key.

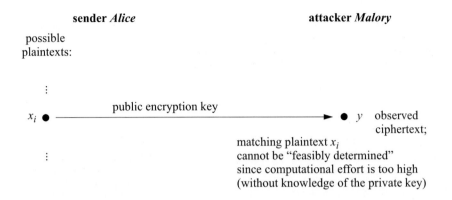

Fig. 13.2. A complexity-theoretic secrecy property for the one-way function approach

Finally, instances of the *chaos* approach ingeniously combine the basic ideas underlying the other approaches. The chaos approach can be roughly sketched as follows, and is exemplified in more detail in Sections 13.7 to 13.9 below. A key is randomly generated as a bit string of appropriate length. Encryption is done by repeatedly applying a *round*, consisting of a short sequence of rather elementary functions. These functions operate on a suitable representation of a *block* structure, which is initialized with the plaintext as an input block. The elementary functions are tailored to achieve "confusion" and "diffusion", thereby ultimately transforming the plaintext in a "chaotic way".

In this context, *confusion* is aimed at blurring the relationship between an input value and an output value of a function application. Non-linear *substitution* functions that replace a short bit string by another one are often employed for producing confusion. *Diffusion* is aimed at making each output bit essentially dependent on each input bit. For this purpose, *permutation* functions on bit positions are often used.

Additionally, some of the elementary functions inject *randomness* into the whole process by taking a suitable "round" version of the encryption key as a second input. The XOR function, where block instances and key versions are seen as bit strings, is often used for this purpose. The key is used in a *symmetric* way: each single elementary function, or a short composition of them, is designed to be invertible, where, if applicable, a suitable key version is again provided.

Figure 13.3 visualizes the justification of the *empirical* secrecy property obtained from the perspective of an attacker Malory who has observed a ciphertext y. On the basis of the supposedly known construction of the mechanism, Malory can try to reason in terms of the *pre-image* set of y under all possible keys, i.e., by investigating the set of plaintexts that can be mapped on y under some possible key. In general, on the one hand this pre-image set is not the full set of all plaintexts, unlike in the one-time key approach, and on the other hand it is not a singleton, unlike in the one-way function approach. In fact, the construction aims basically at

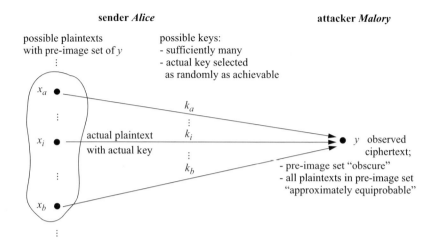

Fig. 13.3. An empirical secrecy property for the chaos approach

the following two features. For Malory, the pre-image set remains "obscure" in the sense that Malory cannot efficiently determine its actual extension, similarly to the case in the one-way function approach. Moreover, the pre-image is sufficiently large, and its elements appear to be "approximately equiprobable" to be the actual plaintext x_i, similarly to the case in the one-time key approach. This justification should be valid even for (suitably limited) multiple usage of the selected key.

Unfortunately, in contrast to the other approaches, we lack a clear, simple, mathematically elaborated theory for the chaos approach. Thus, for each instance of the chaos approach, the justification sketched above must be *empirically* elaborated case by case by exploiting *theory-based experience*. In fact, in this field, many proposals had looked promising at first glance but later on turned out to fail.

13.1.3 A Tabular Summary

Table 13.4 summarizes the material about encryption presented. We take the *justification of a secrecy property* as the primary feature, and briefly indicate the pertinent further features for each of the three alternatives. Some more details can be found in the respective sections of this and other relevant chapters. However, in general, we only sketch the mechanisms and only discuss selected aspects. For more refined expositions, thorough justifications of the secrecy property, extensive analyses of known weaknesses, recommended key lengths, standards, available implementations, experience in various application fields and many further aspects, the reader should consult the rich literature. Moreover, in addition to the few examples presented, there are many further encryption systems, whose comprehensive treatment is beyond the scope of this monograph.

Table 13.4. Basic approaches to encryption, and their features

	One-time key	**One-way function**	**Chaos**
Key length	as long as plaintext	short, but too long for exhaustive search	short, but too long for exhaustive search
Key usage	single	multiple	multiple
Key kind	random string over elements of some group	derived from random elements of some algebraic structure; with a public and a private component	random bit string
Key relationship	symmetric	asymmetric	symmetric
Secret holder	sender and receiver	receiver	sender and receiver
Key distribution	secret communication from generator to sender and receiver	certification and open dissemination of public key	secret communication from generator to sender and receiver
Mode of operation	streamwise	blockwise	blockwise
Encryption algorithm	simple group operation with each corresponding plaintext element and key element	algebraic operation used as one-way function with trapdoor, as selected by the public key	repeated rounds of elementary functions, including group operations, non-linear substitutions, permutations of positions or similar operations, while using round keys
Decryption algorithm	as for encryption, but with inverted key elements	inverted algebraic operation, as enabled by the private key (as trapdoor)	essentially like reverse encryption, but taking suitably modified round keys and/or inverted elementary functions
Secrecy	probability-theoretic	complexity-theoretic	empirical (theory-based experience)
Justification of secrecy	all possible plaintexts of same length are equiprobable, since sufficiently many keys are possible	inversion of one-way function without knowing the private key (trapdoor) is computationally infeasible	confusion and diffusion

Table 13.4. Basic approaches to encryption, and their features (cont.)

	One-time key	**One-way function**	**Chaos**
Trust requirements	randomness and secrecy of the key	randomness and correctness of the key; secrecy of the private key; validity of complexity-theoretic assumption	randomness and secrecy of the key; effectiveness of confusion and diffusion
Efficiency of special hardware	transmission speed of streams	about 100 to 1 000 kilobyte/s (rough estimate only)	about 100 to 1 000 megabyte/s (rough estimate only)
Software efficiency	transmission speed of streams	about 10 to 100 kilobyte/s (rough estimate only)	about 1 to 10 megabyte/s (rough estimate only)
Variants	long operational key as pseudorandom sequence generated from short user key (Vigenère)	streamwise treatment of blocks with asymmetrically applicable block modes	streamwise treatment of blocks with block modes
Application fields	primarily of theoretical interest; practical applications as elementary function in chaos approach, as variant with pseudorandom sequence, or as basis of block modes CFB and OFB	primarily for short messages and a need for full control of key handling by designated receiver; in hybrid systems, for encrypting symmetric keys	primarily for long messages with bulk data and tolerance of control of key handling by trusted environment; in hybrid systems, for encrypting the application data
Examples	Vernam	RSA, ElGamal, EC	DES, IDEA, AES

13.2 One-Time Keys and Perfect Ciphers (Vernam)

The *one-time key* encryption mechanism in the special form of *Vernam* is based on Theorem 12.2 about a sufficient condition for *perfectness* and the resulting group-based construction, as presented in Section 12.6. The mechanism is *symmetric*; in fact, the encryption key and the decryption key are identical, and restricted to a *single* key usage. It operates *streamwise* by considering a plaintext as a sequence of bits, each of which is treated separately. It achieves *perfect* or *probability-theoretic security*, provided the key is *truly randomly* selected and used only once.

More specifically, for treating a single bit, the *plaintext* domain, the *ciphertext* range and the *key* set are chosen as $\{0,1\}$. This set is seen as the carrier of the *group* $(\mathbf{Z}_2,+,0)$ of *residue classes* modulo 2, where the residue classes are identified with their representatives 0 and 1. The *group operation* of addition modulo 2 is identical to the Boolean operation XOR (exclusive or, denoted by the operator $\oplus$) and thus efficiently implementable, even on standard hardware. Figure 13.5 shows the effects of the two possible key bits 0 and 1 on the two possible plaintext bits 0 and 1.

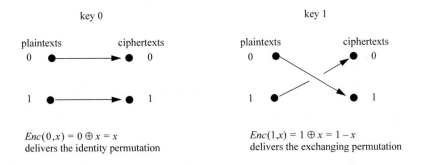

$$Enc(0,x) = 0 \oplus x = x$$
delivers the identity permutation

$$Enc(1,x) = 1 \oplus x = 1 - x$$
delivers the exchanging permutation

Fig. 13.5. A perfect encryption mechanism with a two-element set of plaintexts

For handling *bit strings* of length n, the corresponding *product group* resulting from taking the group $(\mathbf{Z}_2,+,0)$ n times and defining the *group operation* componentwise is employed. Thus, under suitable identifications, the algorithms of the mechanism operate on the following sets:

- plaintexts: bit strings of length n, i.e., "streams" $(x_1,\ldots,x_n)$ of length n over the set $\{0,1\}$;
- ciphertexts: bit strings of the same length n, i.e., "streams" $(y_1,\ldots,y_n)$ of length n over the set $\{0,1\}$;
- keys: bit strings of the same length n, i.e., "streams" $(k_1,\ldots,k_n)$ of length n over the set $\{0,1\}$.

The three algorithms of the mechanism can be outlined as follows:

- The *key generation* algorithm *Gen(erate_Cipher_Key)* selects a "truly random" cipher key $(k_1,\ldots,k_n)$.
- The *encryption* algorithm *Enc* handles the plaintext $(x_1,\ldots,x_n)$ and the cipher key $(k_1,\ldots,k_n)$ as streams, and treats each corresponding pair of a plaintext bit x_i and a cipher key bit k_i as input for a XOR operation, yielding a ciphertext bit $y_i = k_i \oplus x_i$, as shown in Figure 13.6, on the sender's side.
- The *decryption* algorithm *Dec* handles the ciphertext $(y_1,\ldots,y_n)$ and the cipher key $(k_1,\ldots,k_n)$ as streams accordingly, and treats each corresponding pair of a ciphertext bit y_i and a cipher key bit k_i as input for a XOR operation, as shown in Figure 13.6, on the receiver's side. This XOR operation yields the original plaintext bit x_i *correctly*, since we have

$$k_i \oplus y_i = k_i \oplus (k_i \oplus x_i) = (k_i \oplus k_i) \oplus x_i = 0 \oplus x_i = x_i.$$

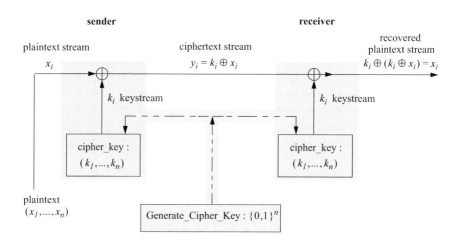

Fig. 13.6. A perfect symmetric stream cipher with a long one-time key (the light gray area must be hidden from other participants)

The restriction to using a key only once is crucial: an attacker Malory, observing a ciphertext/plaintext pair, can achieve complete success just by solving, for each position i, the equation $y_i = k_i \oplus x_i$, regarding the secret key bit as $k_i = y_i \oplus x_i$.

Considering the transmission of a *single* message, the one-time key encryption mechanism is qualified to the best possible extent regarding the *secrecy property* and the *efficiency property* of the encryption and decryption algorithms. However, as a trade-off for the best secrecy – proved to be inevitable by the results of Section 12.6 – the secret cipher key can be used only once, and it must be as long as the anticipated plaintext. Hence, as a stand-alone mechanism, pure one-time key encryption is practically employed only in dedicated applications with extremely high secrecy requirements.

However, the basic approach is widely exploited in variants and subparts of other mechanisms. Examples are the *Vigenère* encryption mechanism, which replaces the "truly random" key by a pseudorandom one (see Section 13.3); the stream ciphers using *block modes* CFB (cipher feedback) and OFB (output feedback) (see Section 13.10); the block ciphers DES, IDEA and AES (see Sections 13.7, 13.8 and 13.9); the generic construction for encryption mechanisms aimed at *semantic secrecy* (see Section 13.11); and *anonymous sending* (see Section 15.3).

13.3 Stream Ciphers with Pseudorandom Sequences (Vigenère)

The *Vigenère* encryption mechanism is a variant of the *one-time key* encryption mechanism. As shown in Figure 13.7, the former is obtained from the latter by replacing the "truly random" *cipher key* by a *pseudorandom* one that, in turn, is determined by a short(er) *pseudo-key*. Accordingly, the Vigenère mechanism is *symmetric*, and it operates *streamwise* by considering a plaintext as a sequence of bits, each of which is treated separately. In practice, the pseudo-key is often substantially shorter than the generated cipher key, and then the Vigenère mechanism cannot be *perfect* or *probability-theoretically secure*, as stated by Theorem 12.3.

With suitable simplifications, the algorithms of the mechanism operate on the following sets:

- plaintexts: bit strings of arbitrary length, i.e., "streams" $(x_1,\ldots,x_n)$ of some length n over the set $\{0,1\}$;
- ciphertexts: bit strings of the corresponding length, i.e., "streams" $(y_1,\ldots,y_n)$ of the length n of the corresponding plaintext over the set $\{0,1\}$;
- pseudo-keys: bit strings of a fixed short length s, used to pseudorandomly produce cipher keys, i.e., for a plaintext of length n, a "stream" $(k_1,\ldots,k_n)$ of length n over the set $\{0,1\}$.

The three algorithms of the mechanism can be outlined as follows:

- The *key generation* algorithm *Gen(erate_Pseudo_Key)* selects a "truly random" pseudo-key $(p_1,\ldots,p_s)$.
- The *encryption* algorithm *Enc* takes the pseudo-key $(p_1,\ldots,p_s)$ as input for a *pseudorandom generator*, whose output is used as a cipher key. The algorithm handles the plaintext $(x_1,\ldots,x_n)$ and the cipher key $(k_1,\ldots,k_n)$ as streams, and treats each corresponding pair of a plaintext bit x_i and a cipher key bit k_i as input for a XOR operation, yielding a ciphertext bit $y_i = k_i \oplus x_i$, as shown in Figure 13.7, on the sender's side.
- The *decryption* algorithm *Dec* proceeds correspondingly. It takes the pseudo-key $(p_1,\ldots,p_s)$ as input for an identical *pseudorandom generator*, whose output is used as a cipher key, which equals the cipher key produced by the encryption algorithm. The decryption algorithm handles the ciphertext $(y_1,\ldots,y_n)$ and the cipher key $(k_1,\ldots,k_n)$ as streams, and treats each corresponding pair of a ciphertext bit y_i and a cipher key bit k_i as input for a XOR operation, as shown in Figure 13.7, on the receiver's side. This XOR operation yields the original plaintext bit x_i *correctly*, since we have

$$k_i \oplus y_i = k_i \oplus (k_i \oplus x_i) = (k_i \oplus k_i) \oplus x_i = 0 \oplus x_i = x_i.$$

In some practical variations, the pseudo-key is split into two components: the first component configures the pseudorandom generator persistently, and the second component initializes the pseudorandom generator with a *seed* for producing a fresh pseudorandom cipher key. Accordingly, the first component is for multiple usage and can be distributed separately in advance (and thus we could also see it as a part of the pseudorandom generator), whereas the second component is for a *single usage* and thus must be appropriately provided before each individual transmission of a plaintext.

Compared with the one-time key encryption mechanism, the Vigenère encryption mechanism still shares the efficiency property of the encryption and decryption algorithms, provided the pseudorandom generator works (nearly) as fast as bit

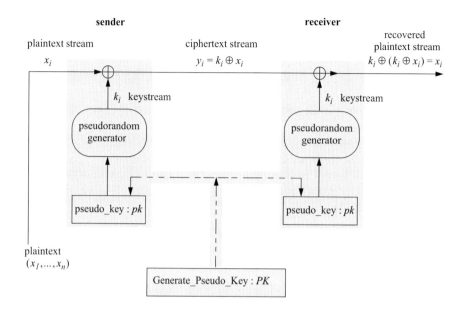

Fig. 13.7. Symmetric stream cipher with a short pseudo-key that generates a long pseudorandom keystream (the light gray area must be hidden from other participants)

strings can be transmitted. However, for the sake of a short pseudo-key, the Vigenère encryption mechanism loses perfectness. The pseudo-key can still be used only once, since otherwise two plaintexts would be treated with the same cipher key, leading to the known *ciphertext/plaintext vulnerability* discussed earlier in the context of the one-time key encryption mechanism.

The advantage of the Vigenère encryption mechanism depends crucially on the *pseudorandom generator* employed: it must be fast, permitting small pseudo-keys, while approximating "true randomness" and thus ensuring "sufficient secrecy". There have been many attempts to find good compromises for the obviously conflicting requirements. In the following, we briefly sketch and discuss a simple approach that actually mostly fails regarding the security property but can be taken as a basis for more advanced solutions.

Abstractly, the pseudorandom generator is designed to be a *finite state automaton* with the following properties:

- The *internal states* are represented by an m-bit register, and thus the automaton has 2^m internal states.
- The automaton is *initialized* in some state, i.e., by loading the register with a bit string $(k_0, \ldots, k_{m-1})$, and then iteratively performs a *state transition*, basically determined by some switching network.
- In each iteration, one (or more) new cipher key bit(s) are derived from the current state by another switching network.

More concretely, a specialized case of the pseudorandom generator can be constructed as a *linear feedback shift register* (LFSR), as shown in Figure 13.8, where the following properties hold:

- The register is a (left) *shift register*.
- A state transition just shifts all bits to the left and fills the rightmost bit with the result of a simple switching network that computes a weighted *XOR operation* on the bits of the current state, with the *weights* c_i being either 0 (not relevant/ not used) or 1 (relevant/fed back), for $i = 1,\ldots,m-1$, and a weight $c_0 = 1$ (relevant/fed back).
- In each transition, the leftmost bit fed out during shifting is delivered as the next cipher key bit (without employing a second switching network). In particular, the first m bits k_i of the cipher key, $i = 1,\ldots,m$, are just given by the initialization $(k_0,\ldots,k_{m-1})$ of the shift register.

Formally summarizing, given the overall design, an LFSR is statically specified by the selected weights $c_0,\ldots,c_{m-1}$, and its dynamic behavior is described by the initializing register values $k_0,\ldots,k_{m-1}$ according to the following linear induction:

$$k_{i+m} := c_0\, k_{i+0} \oplus c_1\, k_{i+1} \oplus \ldots \oplus c_{m-1}\, k_{i+(m-1)}. \tag{13.1}$$

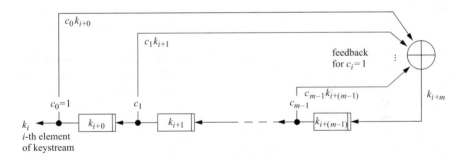

Fig. 13.8. A linear feedback shift register (LFSR)

Obviously, the best achievement of an LFSR is to guarantee that for *each* non-zero initial state, the full cycle of all 2^m-1 internal nonzero states is produced. Clearly, the actual achievement of an LFSR depends on the choice of the feedback weights c_i; moreover, given the overall design, nothing else can be selected. It can be shown that the best achievement is accomplished by feedback weights that – taken suitably as coefficients of a polynomial of degree $m-1$ over $\mathbf{Z}_2$ – lead to a *primitive* polynomial, i.e., the resulting polynomial "generates" all polynomials of degree $m-1$ over $\mathbf{Z}_2$.

The LFSR approach suffers from a serious *ciphertext/plaintext vulnerability*. Suppose an attacker Malory knows some subsequence $y_1,y_2,\ldots,y_n$ of the ciphertext stream together with the matching subsequence $x_1,x_2,\ldots,x_n$ of the plaintext stream. Then Malory can determine the corresponding subsequence $k_1, k_2, \ldots, k_n$ of the keystream by solving the equations $y_i := k_i \oplus x_i$. If the subsequence is sufficiently long, namely if $n \geq 2m$, then Malory can find the weights $c_0, c_1, \ldots, c_{m-1}$ of the LFSR considered by solving the following system of linear equations derived from the linear induction (13.1):

$$k_{m+1} := k_1 c_0 \quad \oplus \quad k_2 c_1 \quad \oplus \ldots \oplus \quad k_m c_{m-1}$$
$$k_{m+2} := k_2 c_0 \quad \oplus \quad k_3 c_1 \quad \oplus \ldots \oplus \quad k_{m+1} c_{m-1}$$
$$\ldots$$

$$k_{2m} := k_m c_0 \quad \oplus \quad k_{m+1} c_1 \oplus \ldots \oplus \quad k_{2m-1} c_{m-1}$$

Clearly, once Malory knows the weights and m subsequent bits of the keystream, he can compute all succeeding bits by the linear induction (13.1).

13.4 The RSA Asymmetric Block Cipher

The *RSA encryption* mechanism is an example of the *one-way function* approach, originally pioneering but now in widespread use. It is based on RSA functions and their properties, as presented in Subsection 12.9.2. The mechanism is *asymmetric*, admitting *multiple* key usage, and it operates *blockwise*, where the block length is determined by the parameters of the underlying RSA function. It achieves *complexity-theoretic security*, provided the *factorization conjecture* and the *RSA conjecture* hold, the key is properly generated and sufficiently long, and some additional care is taken.

More specifically, given a suitable *RSA function* $RSA_{p,q,d}^{n,e}$ with a *private key* (p,q,d) and a *public key* (n,e), we obtain an encryption mechanism that operates essentially as follows, at least similarly regarding the preprocessing and postprocessing:

- A message m is preprocessed by adding a nonce *non*, for the sake of *probabilistic encryption*, and a hash value $h(m,non)$, for the sake of *authenticated encryption*, using an agreed protocol for the *hash function* and the needed separators.
- If the resulting object $x = (m,non,h(m,non))$ can be interpreted as a positive number less than n, this object is encrypted by computing $y = x^e \bmod n$.
- The decryption is performed by computing $y^d \bmod n$.
- The three components of the decryption result are then extracted, and the hash value of the first two components is recomputed and compared with the third component, the received hash value. If the received hash value is verified, the first component of the decryption result is returned as the (presumably) correct message.

Accordingly, for each fixed setting of an RSA function $RSA_{p,q,d}^{n,e}$, the RSA encryption mechanism operates on the following sets:

- plaintexts: bit strings over the set $\{0,1\}$ of some fixed length $l_{mes} \leq \mathrm{ld}\, n$;
- ciphertexts: bit strings over the set $\{0,1\}$, basically of length $\mathrm{ld}\, n$, seen as positive numbers less than n (residues modulo n);

- keys: given the public key (n,e), in principle there is a unique residue modulo n that can be used as the private decryption exponent d, whose binary representation is a bit string, basically of length ld n or less; however, from the point of view of the nondistinguished participants, this decryption exponent cannot be "determined".

The three algorithms of the mechanism can be outlined as follows:

- The *key generation* algorithm *Gen* selects the parameters of an RSA function, depending on a given *security parameter* that basically determines the length of the key. Briefly summarized, the algorithm proceeds as follows: generate randomly two large prime numbers p and q of the length required by the security parameter; compute the modulus $n := p \cdot q$; select randomly an encryption exponent e that is relatively prime to $\phi(n) = (p-1) \cdot (q-1)$; and compute the decryption exponent d as the solution of $e \cdot d \equiv 1 \bmod \phi(n)$.

- The *encryption* algorithm *Enc* takes a possibly padded message m of length l_{mes} as a plaintext, generates a random bit string *non* as a nonce of length l_{non}, computes a hash value $h(m,non)$ of length l_{hash} and concatenates these values with appropriate separators. The resulting bit string x must, basically, have length ld n; in particular, we have $l_{mes} + l_{non} + l_{hash} \le$ ld n, such that it can be seen as a binary representation of a positive number less than n (a residue modulo n). Finally, taking the public key (n,e), the ciphertext $y = x^e \bmod n$ is computed and returned.

- The *decryption* algorithm *Dec*, taking the first component of the public key (n,e) and the third component of the private key (p,q,d), inverts the given ciphertext y by computing $x' = y^d \bmod n$ and then decomposes the result into the message part m', the nonce part non' and the hash value part *hash*, according to the separators employed. If the received hash value is verified, i.e., if $h(m',non') = hash$, then m' is returned as the (supposedly) correct message; otherwise, an error is reported.

The fundamental properties of *correctness*, *secrecy* and *efficiency* are discussed in Subsection 12.9.2, Appendix A.4.3, and Appendix A.4.4. From today's perspective, the security parameter should enforce the condition that the *modulus n* has a length of at least 1024; to comply with unforeseeable future progress in computing and mathematics, even a larger length might be worthwhile to resist dedicated attacks. Clearly, there is a trade-off between secrecy and efficiency: roughly estimated, the key generation consumes time $O((\text{ld } n)^4)$, and the operations of modular arithmetic needed for encryption and decryption consume time at most $O((\text{ld } n)^3)$. There exists substantial insight that can be used to achieve high performance in practice by employing specialized algorithms for both software and hardware.

More advanced considerations are due regarding some known weaknesses of specific choices of the parameters of the RSA function. The preprocessing and postprocessing of the message suggested above, or something similar, are required for the reasons sketched in the following.

Probabilistic encryption is mandatory for achieving sophisticated forms of the secrecy property, as investigated in Section 13.11. Intuitively, the added nonce is needed for two purposes:

- For an application with an a priori known and possibly small domain of meaningful plaintexts, to enlarge the search space for the straightforward *inversion algorithm* that an attacker could use given a ciphertext and the public key; see Subsection 12.9.1.
- To prevent a possible known *ciphertext/plaintext* vulnerability, by ensuring that a given plaintext m will produce different ciphertexts when being sent multiple times.

Authenticated encryption is needed to prevent active attacks that are enabled by the following *multiplicativity property* (a *homomorphism property*) of the exponentiation function, namely

$$\text{for all } x, y \text{ and } w: \ (x \cdot y)^w = x^w \cdot y^w. \tag{13.2}$$

Since this property is inherited by any RSA function, a pure application of such a function would allow an attacker to decrypt an observed ciphertext y as follows, for instance. The attacker selects a multiplicatively invertible element $u \in \mathbf{Z}_n^*$ and then, employing the public key (n,e), computes $t := y \cdot u^e \bmod n$. Suppose that the attacker somehow succeeds in presenting t as a (harmless-looking) ciphertext to the holder of the private key and obtaining the corresponding plaintext t^d. For this plaintext, the following properties hold:

$$t^d \equiv (y \cdot u^e)^d \equiv y^d \cdot u^{e \cdot d} \equiv y^d \cdot u \bmod n.$$

The attacker can solve the congruence for the wanted value y^d by computing

$$y^d = t^d \cdot u^{-1} \bmod n.$$

In general, this attack and similar ones will not succeed with the suggested employment of a hash function, provided this hash function does not suffer from the same multiplicativity property. For, presumably, the attacker would fail to manipulate the ciphertext in such a way that the decryption algorithm would accept the extracted third component as a correct hash value.

13.5 The ElGamal Asymmetric Block Cipher

The *ElGamal encryption* mechanism is another well-known example of the *one-way function* approach. It is based on ElGamal functions and their properties, as presented in Subsection 12.9.3. The mechanism is *asymmetric*, admitting *multiple key usage*, and it operates *blockwise*, where the block length is determined by the parameters of the underlying ElGamal function. It achieves *complexity-theoretic security*, provided the *discrete logarithm conjecture* and the *ElGamal conjecture* hold, the key is properly generated and sufficiently long, and some additional care is taken.

More specifically, given a suitable *ElGamal function* $EG_a^{p,\,g,\,A}$ with a *private key a* and a *public key* (p,g,A), we obtain an encryption mechanism that directly employs the ElGamal function for encryption and the pertinent inverse function for decryption. Accordingly, for each fixed setting of an ElGamal function $EG_a^{p,\,g,\,A}$, the ElGamal encryption mechanism operates on the following sets:

- plaintexts: bit strings over the set $\{0,1\}$, basically of length ld p, seen as positive numbers less than p (residues modulo p);
- ciphertexts: pairs of bit strings over the set $\{0,1\}$, basically of length ld p, seen as positive numbers less than p (residues modulo p);
- keys: given the public key (p,g,A), in principle there is a unique positive number less than $p-1$ used as the private exponent a, whose binary representation is a bit string, basically of length ld $p-1$; however, from the point of view of the nondistinguished participants, this private exponent cannot be "determined".

The three algorithms of the mechanism can be outlined as follows:

- The *key generation* algorithm *Gen* selects the parameters of an ElGamal function, depending on a given *security parameter* that basically determines the length of the key. Briefly summarized, the algorithm proceeds as follows: generate a large prime number p of the length required by the security parameter; select a primitive element g of $\mathbf{Z}_p^*$; select randomly a private exponent a; and compute the public "blinded exponent" $A = g^a \bmod p$.
- The *encryption* algorithm *Enc* takes a possibly padded message x, basically of length ld p, as a plaintext, generates a random bit string k seen as a positive number less than $p-1$ and, employing the public key (p,g,A), computes and returns $EG_a^{p,\,g,\,A}(x,k) = (y_1, y_2)$ such that

$$y_1 = g^k \bmod p \text{ and } y_2 = x \cdot A^k \bmod p \,.$$

- The *decryption* algorithm *Dec*, taking the public key (p,g,A) and the private key a, inverts the given ciphertext (y_1, y_2) by computing

$$y_2 \cdot (y_1^{\,a})^{-1} \bmod p,$$

which is then returned.

The fundamental properties of *correctness*, *secrecy* and *efficiency* are discussed in Subsection 12.9.3, Appendix A.4.3, and Appendix A.4.4. From today's perspective, the security parameter should enforce the condition that the *modulus p* has a length of at least 512; to comply with unforeseeable future progress in computing and mathematics, even a larger length might be worthwhile to resist dedicated attacks. Clearly, there is a trade-off between secrecy and efficiency: roughly estimated, the key generation consumes time at most $O((\mathrm{ld}\,p)^4)$, and the operations of modular arithmetic needed for encryption and decryption consume time at most $O((\mathrm{ld}\,p)^3)$. As with the RSA encryption mechanism, there exists substantial insight that can be used to achieve high performance in practice by employing specialized algorithms for both software and hardware.

More advanced considerations are due regarding some known weaknesses of specific choices of the parameters of the ElGamal function. *Probabilistic encryption*, which is mandatory for achieving sophisticated forms of the secrecy property, as investigated in Section 13.11, is a built-in feature of the ElGamal approach, and thus there is no need for additional randomization. As with the RSA encryption mechanism, *authenticated encryption* is advisable for the ElGamal encryption mechanism and its derivatives based on elliptic curves as well.

13.6 Asymmetric Block Ciphers Based on Elliptic Curves

The *elliptic-curve* encryption mechanism is a generalization of the ElGamal encryption. In recent years, the elliptic-curve approach has become an increasingly important example of the *one-way function* approach. It is based on generalized ElGamal functions that are defined over appropriately constructed finite cyclic groups derived from elliptic curves based on a finite field. The basic approach and its properties are presented in Subsection 12.9.4. The resulting mechanism is *asymmetric*, admitting *multiple* key usage, and it operates *blockwise*, where the block length is determined by the parameters of the underlying elliptic curve. It achieves *complexity-theoretic security*, provided the pertinent *discrete logarithm conjecture* and related conjectures hold, the key is properly generated and sufficiently long, and some additional care is taken.

Without presenting further technical details, we emphasize that the elliptic-curve approach offers a large variety of alternatives to the still predominant RSA approach, and will hopefully diminish the dependence of secure computing on the special unproven conjectures regarding the RSA approach. Moreover, the elliptic-curve approach promises to achieve the wanted degree of secrecy with improved efficiency in comparison with the RSA approach. It should also be noted that further families of alternatives have been proposed and are currently under research.

13.7 The DES Symmetric Block Cipher

The *DES* (*Data Encryption Standard*) *encryption* mechanism has been a most influential example, used worldwide, of the *chaos* approach. Designed by IBM and the National Security Agency (NSA) of the USA, it was standardized by the National Bureau of Standards (NBS) in 1976/77 for "unclassified government communication", and adopted by the American National Standards Institute (ANSI) in 1981 for commercial and private applications. The mechanism is *symmetric*, admitting *multiple* key usage, and it operates *blockwise*, where the block length is 64 bits. The key has a length of 56 bits. Today, the pure form of this mechanism is considered to be outdated, as it suffers from a too short key length that permits successful attacks by exhaustive key searching and it lacks an open, well-understood design.

Basically, the algorithms of the mechanism operate on the following sets:

- plaintexts: bit strings (blocks over the set $\{0,1\}$) of length 64;
- ciphertexts: bit strings (blocks) of the same length, 64;
- keys: bit strings of length 56, where each substring of seven bits is supplemented by a parity bit for the sake of error detection.

The three algorithms of the mechanism can be outlined as follows:

- The *key generation* algorithm selects a "truly random" bit string of length 56, and computes a parity bit for each substring of 7 bits, to be inserted directly after the substring.
- The *encryption* algorithm $DES(k,x)$ takes a key k and a plaintext x as input. In addition to some preprocessing and corresponding postprocessing, the algorithm basically performs 16 uniform *rounds*, where each round consists of applying a *Feistel network* with a plugged-in *DES function* f_{DES}. The DES function processes the right half r_i of the current block and the current round key k_i. Some more details are described below.
- The *decryption* algorithm is basically the same as the encryption algorithm, except that the round keys k_i are used in reverse order. The justification for this feature is given below.

Figure 13.9 shows the overall structure of the encryption algorithm: *preprocessing* the plaintext block, performing the 16 *rounds* on the current block using the Feistel network with the plugged-in DES function, *postprocessing* of the resulting block and, in parallel, computing the *round keys*. In the following, we outline each of these components, show how they achieve the *correctness* property, and roughly indicate how they contribute to the *secrecy* property by producing *chaos* in the form of *confusion* and *diffusion*.

The plaintext block x of 64 bits is preprocessed by first applying an initial *permutation IP* (of positions) and then splitting the resulting block into two half-blocks of 32 bits each, yielding a left half l_0 and a right half r_0 as follows:

$l_0 := left\_half(IP(x))$ and
$r_0 := right\_half(IP(x))$.

Subsequently, the algorithm performs 16 uniform rounds $i=1,\ldots,16$ that iteratively take the current left half-block l_{i-1} and the current right half-block r_{i-1} together with a round key k_i as inputs and yield the new half-blocks l_i and r_i as outputs.

In each round, a *Feistel network* is used to compute the outputs as follows:

$l_i := r_{i-1}$ and
$r_i := l_{i-1} \oplus f_{DES}(r_{i-1},k_i)$,

i.e., the previous right half-block is simply forwarded to be used as new left half-block, whereas the previous left half-block and the result of applying the DES function to the current inputs are superimposed by computing the *XOR operation* bitwise.

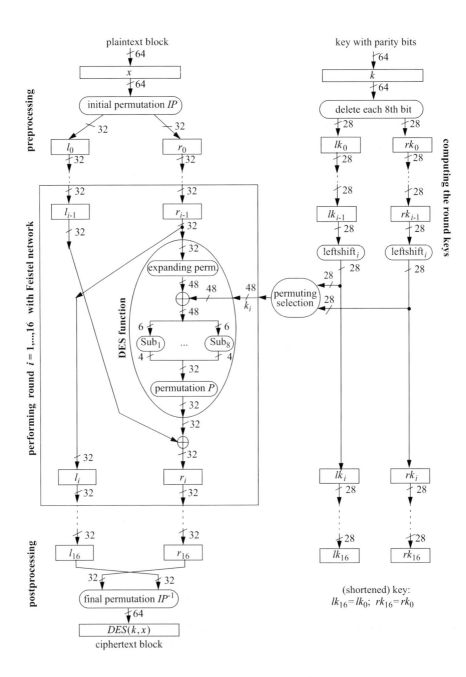

Fig. 13.9. Structure of the DES symmetric block cipher

The plugged-in DES function f_{DES} is the core operation, which, in particular, directly employs the secret key and introduces *non-linearity* by appropriate *substitutions*. More specifically, the input r_{i-1} of 32 bits is first enlarged to 48 bits by an *expanding permutation* that duplicates some original positions and then diffuses all positions. The resulting bit string is then *superimposed* with the *randomness* of the current round key k_i by computing the *XOR operation* bitwise. The result is partitioned into eight parts of length 6. For each part, there is an appropriately tailored *substitution box Sub$_j$* that maps any six input bits into four output bits. In total, the eight substitution boxes yield an output of length 32. This output is further diffused by a permutation P that returns the final result of the DES function.

Finally, the postprocessing exchanges the two half-blocks l_{16} and r_{16}, recombines them into a full block and then applies the inverse IP^{-1} of the initial permutation as a final *permutation*, whose output is returned as the ciphertext

$$DES(k,x) := IP^{-1}(r_{16}, l_{16}).$$

In parallel to the treatment of the current half-blocks, the *round keys* k_i are computed. As a preprocessing step, the parity bits are deleted and the remaining 56 bits are split into a left half-key lk_0 and a right half-key rk_0. Subsequently, round i iteratively takes the current left half-key lk_{i-1} and the current right half-key rk_{i-1} as inputs and yields the new half-keys lk_i and rk_i and the new round key k_i as outputs. The new half-keys are obtained by cyclic left-shift operations *leftshift$_i$*, where for $i = 1,2,9,16$ the bits are moved one position to the left, and for all other rounds they are moved two positions. The new round key k_i is computed from the new half-keys by applying a *permuting selection* function that permutes the total input bit string of 56 bits and then selects 48 positions.

All further details of the components sketched are publicly known; in particular, the exact definitions of the various permutations and the eight substitution boxes are well documented and can be inspected in any appropriate source, for example in most textbooks on cryptography.

Regarding the *correctness* property, recall that the decryption algorithm performs exactly the same operations as the encryption algorithm but uses the round keys in reverse order. Basically, the inductive justification is grounded only on the special structure of the *Feistel network*, whose definitions can be rewritten as

$r_{i-1} := l_i$ and
$l_{i-1} := r_i \oplus f_{DES}(r_{i-1}, k_i) = r_i \oplus f_{DES}(l_i, k_i)$.

Regarding the *secrecy* property, the wanted *chaos* effect results basically from repeatedly applying *permutations* (of positions) for achieving *diffusion*, performing *non-linear substitutions* for producing *confusion*, and *superimposing* the *randomness* of the key by means of the *XOR operation*. A detailed analysis is beyond the scope of this monograph. Unfortunately, however, the design criteria for the DES function, in particular for the permutation boxes, were published only belatedly. Even then, these criteria listed only some apparently useful properties, whose general flavor is exemplified by the following instances:

- No output position of a substitution box can be approximated as a linear or affine function of the input positions.
- For any fixed values of the leftmost input position and the rightmost input position of a substitution box, the four remaining input positions produce all possible outputs.
- If two inputs to a substitution box differ in exactly one position, then the corresponding outputs differ in at least two positions.
- If two inputs to a substitution box differ in exactly the two middle positions, then the corresponding outputs differ in at least two positions.

Historically, the uncertainty about the original design criteria and the secrecy properties actually achieved motivated not only criticism but also numerous thorough investigations. On the one hand, these investigations led to the public development of sophisticated attack methods, for example those known as *linear cryptanalysis* and *differential cryptanalysis*, and on the other hand, they promoted many alternative block ciphers and, even more importantly, a culture of *open design* and *public verification*.

Regarding the *efficiency* property, the DES encryption permits transmission rates high enough to treat even *multimedia objects*. If implemented in special hardware and extended to a stream cipher by some block mode (see Section 13.10) rates up to hundreds of megabytes/s are achievable.

To exploit such high rates if the drawbacks of symmetric encryption are not tolerable, DES encryption and, similarly, other efficient symmetric block ciphers are often used as part of a *hybrid encryption method*:

- In a first *key distribution* phase, a sender uses a (relatively slow) *asymmetric* encryption method to confidentially communicate a (relatively small) secret symmetric key to the intended receiver.
- In a second *message transmission* phase, the sender employs a (high-speed) *symmetric* encryption method to confidentially transmit the (in general relatively large) message of interest to the receiver.

Although the pure form of the DES encryption mechanism employs a key that is too short to successfully prevent exhaustive search attacks, the variant of *Triple-DES* is still useful. In principle, the basic approach of this variant is applicable to other symmetric block ciphers with an encryption algorithm *Enc* and a decryption algorithm *Dec* as well. Given a plaintext x and three different keys k_1, k_2, and k_3, the *triple-encryption* method successively performs an encryption, a decryption and another encryption, yielding the ciphertext y as

$$Enc(k_3, Dec(k_2, Enc(k_1, x))),$$

which is decrypted correspondingly as

$$Dec(k_1, Enc(k_2, Dec(k_3, y))).$$

At first glance, seemingly a *double encryption* with two different keys would be helpful as well, since by doubling the overall key length, one would expect an infeasible explosion of the *key search space*. However, this expectation might not be true. In the following we present two obstacles, to be understood as a warning against delusive countermeasures of too simple-minded a design.

First, given an encryption algorithm $Enc(.,.)$, consider the set of all functions of the form $Enc(k,.)$, where the first parameter is fixed by a possible key k. It might happen that this set is *closed* under functional composition, i.e., for all keys k_1 and k_2 there exists a key k_3 such that for all plaintexts x we have $Enc(k_3,x) = Enc(k_2,Enc(k_1,x))$. In that case, the key search space under double encryption would be the same as under single encryption. Fortunately, however, for most keys DES encryption does not suffer from compositionality.

Second, in principle, the key search space can be substantially reduced by a known *ciphertext/plaintext vulnerability*. Suppose the attacker Malory knows two plaintext–ciphertext pairs (a,b) and (c,d) under double encryption such that for some keys k' and k'',

$$Enc(k'',Enc(k',a)) = b \text{ and}$$
$$Enc(k'',Enc(k',c)) = d.$$

Malory then aims at determining the key pair (k',k''). Let us assume further that there are 2^m plaintexts and 2^n keys, with $m > n$. Rather than exhaustively searching over all 2^{2n} key pairs, Malory could perform the following *meet-in-the-middle attack*, which has two phases, the first of which is visualized in Figure 13.10.

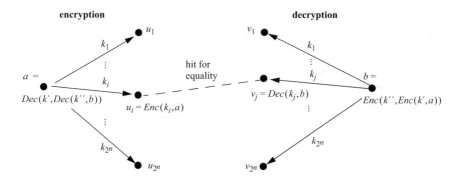

Fig. 13.10. Hit for the meet-in-the-middle attack

In the first phase, on the one hand, starting from the plaintext a, all possible intermediate encryption values $Enc(k_i,a) = u_i$ are determined; on the other hand, starting from the overall ciphertext b, all possible intermediate decryption values $Dec(k_j,b) = v_j$ are determined. Malory can expect to find $2^{n+(n-m)}$ "hits", i.e., events where $u_i = v_j$. For, assuming an equal probability distribution, each of the 2^n values u_i will find a "hit" with some value v_j with probability 2^{n-m}. For example, in the DES setting with $n = 56$ and $m = 64$, Malory can expect $2^{56+(56-64)} = 2^{48}$ hits.

In the second phase, Malory then checks, for each found hit $u_i = v_j$, whether the keys k_i and k_j involved match the second plaintext–ciphertext pair as well, i.e., whether $Enc(k_j, Enc(k_i, c)) = d$. A key pair (k_i, k_j) satisfying this property equals the wanted key pair (k', k'') Malory is looking for with high probability. For, still assuming equiprobability, a wrong key pair is expected to match the second plaintext–ciphertext pair, i.e., to map c on d, only with probability 2^{-m}; thus, among the $2^{n+(n-m)}$ checks in the second phase, the event where any of the $2^{n+(n-m)} - 1$ wrong key pairs produces a match only occurs with an overall probability

$$2^{-m} \cdot (2^{n+(n-m)} - 1) \approx 2^{2(n-m)}.$$

For example, in the DES setting, Malory suffers from an "erroneously" verified key pair with a probability of only about 2^{-16}.

The meet-in-the-middle attack sketched here needs 2^{n+1} encryptions and decryptions in the first phase, and a further $2^{(n+(n-m))+1}$ encryptions in the second phase. Hence, the attack consumes time for approximately 2^{n+1} cryptographic operations, rather than 2^{n+n} as required for an exhaustive key search. However, the attack unrealistically demands space for storing 2^n intermediate values of either kind.

13.8 The IDEA Symmetric Block Cipher

The *IDEA* (*International Data Encryption Algorithm*) *encryption* mechanism was developed as an alternative to the DES encryption, and is a further example of the *chaos* approach. IDEA attracted reasonable scientific interest, in particular owing to its innovative combination of a DES-like round structure operating on block parts and round keys on the one hand, and algebraic group operations on the other hand. For example, IDEA was adopted for the system Pretty Good Privacy (PGP) (see Section 17.6), but never reached common acceptance. The mechanism is *symmetric*, admitting *multiple* key usage, and it operates *blockwise*, where the block length is 64 bits. The key has a length of 128 bits, which is still sufficient from today's perspective.

Basically, the algorithms of the mechanism operate on the following sets:

- plaintexts: bit strings (blocks over the set $\{0,1\}$) of length 64;
- ciphertexts: bit strings (blocks) of the same length, 64;
- keys: bit strings of length 128.

The three algorithms of the mechanism can be outlined as follows:

- The *key generation* algorithm selects a "truly random" bit string of length 128.
- The *encryption* algorithm $IDEA(k, x)$ takes a key k and a plaintext x as input. Besides some preprocessing and postprocessing, which, in particular, splits a block into four quarter-blocks of 16 bits each and finally recombines them, the algorithm basically performs eight uniform *rounds*. Each round starts by applying a first layer of two 16-bit additions and two 16-bit multiplications to the

quarter-blocks and appropriate parts of the round key. Afterwards, a *self-inverse structure* made by combining two keyed 16-bit *additions*, two keyed 16-bit *multiplications* and six 16-bit *XOR operations* is performed. Some more details are described below.

- The *decryption* algorithm is basically the same as the encryption algorithm, except that the round keys are used in reverse order and the parts for the starts of the rounds and the postprocessing are algebraically inverted. The justification for this feature is sketched below.

Figure 13.11 shows the overall structure of the encryption algorithm: *preprocessing* the plaintext block; performing the eight *rounds* on the current block, starting with a first layer of keyed algebraic operations and followed by performing the self-inverse structure; and *postprocessing* of the resulting block. In parallel, not shown in the figure, the parts of the *round keys* are computed. In the following, we outline each of these components, show how they achieve the *correctness* property, and indicate roughly how they contribute to the *secrecy* property by producing *chaos* in the form of *confusion* and *diffusion*.

The plaintext block x of 64 bits is preprocessed by splitting it into four quarter-blocks x_1, x_2, x_3 and x_4 of 16 bits each.

Subsequently, the algorithm performs eight uniform rounds $i = 1, \ldots, 8$ that iteratively take the current quarter-blocks and yield new quarter-blocks as outputs.

In each round i, in the first layer, using four 16-bit parts $k_1^{(i)}$, $k_2^{(i)}$, $k_3^{(i)}$ and $k_4^{(i)}$ of the round key, the current quarter-blocks are transformed by applying arithmetic group operations that are supposed to be available in standard hardware, namely *16-bit additions* and *16-bit multiplications*. More precisely, the operations are addition modulo 2^{16} and a modified multiplication modulo $2^{16} + 1$, where the all-zero bit string $0 \ldots 0$ represents the residue $2^{16} \equiv -1 \bmod 2^{16} + 1$. Afterwards, using six 16-bit *XOR operations*, a *self-inverse structure* basically diffuses and superimposes the current four quarter-blocks and two additional, intermediately computed quarter-blocks. These are obtained by applying two further 16-bit additions, as well as two further 16-bit multiplications keyed with the 16-bit parts $k_5^{(i)}$ and $k_6^{(i)}$ of the round key.

Finally, the postprocessing first exchanges the inner quarter-blocks, then applies a last layer of arithmetic group operations to the current quarter-blocks and 16-bit parts $k_1^{(9)}$, $k_2^{(9)}$, $k_3^{(9)}$ and $k_4^{(9)}$ of the ninth round key, and recombines the current quarter-blocks into the final result $IDEA(k, x)$.

In parallel, the round keys are computed and the six respective 16-bit parts for the rounds and the four 16-bit parts for the postprocessing are determined. Basically, the current key, consisting of 128 bits, is split into eight 16-bit parts. Round 1 uses the first six parts of the original key; round 2 uses the remaining two parts and four further parts from the next round key, which is obtained by a cyclic left shift of 25 positions; and so on.

Regarding the *correctness* property, recall that the decryption algorithm performs exactly the same operations as the encryption algorithm but uses the pertinent parts of the round keys in reverse order and, except within the self-inverse

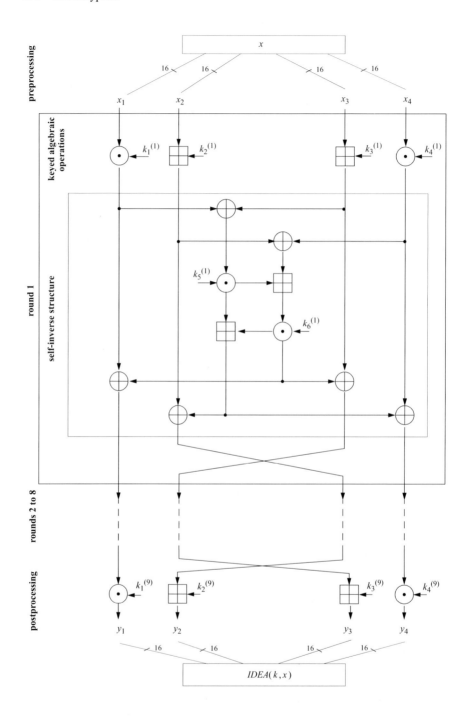

Fig. 13.11. Structure of the IDEA symmetric block cipher (without round key computation)

structure, algebraically inverted. Clearly, under the conditions sketched, any algebraic operation outside the self-inverse structure will be undone by applying it a second time with the respective inverted key part.

The claim of self-inverseness of the inner structure of a round is justified as follows. Denote the inputs and the outputs of this structure by in_1, in_2, in_3, in_4 and out_1, out_2, out_3, out_4, respectively. Furthermore, denote the outputs of the introductory XOR operations and the subsequent multiplications and additions by $xor_{1,3}$, $xor_{2,4}$, $mult_{1,3}$, $add_{2,4}$, $add_{1,3}$, $mult_{2,4}$, respectively. The first run of the structure yields the following results:

$$
\begin{aligned}
out_1 &:= in_1 \oplus mult_{2,4}, \\
out_2 &:= in_2 \oplus add_{1,3}, \\
out_3 &:= in_3 \oplus mult_{2,4}, \\
out_4 &:= in_4 \oplus add_{1,3}.
\end{aligned}
$$

Using these results as inputs in_1', in_2', in_3', in_4' for a second run, the introductory XOR operations produce the same results as in the first run:

$$
\begin{aligned}
xor_{1,3}' &:= in_1' \oplus in_3' = (in_1 \oplus mult_{2,4}) \oplus (in_3 \oplus mult_{2,4}) = in_1 \oplus in_3, \\
xor_{2,4}' &:= in_2' \oplus in_4' = (in_2 \oplus add_{1,3}) \oplus (in_4 \oplus add_{1,3}) = in_2 \oplus in_4.
\end{aligned}
$$

Thus, using the same key parts as in the first run, the subsequent multiplications and additions return the same results too, namely $add_{1,3}$ and $mult_{2,4}$. Accordingly, the outputs of the second run are computed as follows:

$$
\begin{aligned}
out_1' &:= in_1' \oplus mult_{2,4} = (in_1 \oplus mult_{2,4}) \oplus mult_{2,4} = in_1, \\
out_2' &:= in_2' \oplus add_{1,3} = (in_2 \oplus add_{1,3}) \oplus add_{1,3} = in_2, \\
out_3' &:= in_3' \oplus mult_{2,4} = (in_3 \oplus mult_{2,4}) \oplus mult_{2,4} = in_3, \\
out_4' &:= in_4' \oplus add_{1,3} = (in_4 \oplus add_{1,3}) \oplus add_{1,3} = in_4.
\end{aligned}
$$

Regarding the *secrecy* property, the wanted *chaos* effect results basically from repeatedly applying keyed *group operations*, which can also be interpreted as generalized *substitutions*, to produce *confusion*, and mixing distant quarter-blocks to achieve *diffusion*, while mixing by use of the *XOR operation* introduces further confusion and indirectly *superimposes* the *randomness* of the key. A detailed analysis is beyond the scope of this monograph.

Regarding the *efficiency* property, the IDEA encryption permits transmission rates high enough to treat even *multimedia objects*. At design time, IDEA appeared well-tailored to be implemented in software on standard 16-bit hardware by exploiting the built-in arithmetic. To exploit such high rates if the drawbacks of symmetric encryption are not tolerable, IDEA, like other efficient symmetric block ciphers, is often used as part of a *hybrid encryption method*.

13.9 The AES–Rijndael Symmetric Block Cipher

The *AES–Rijndael encryption* mechanism (where "AES" stands for *Advanced Encryption Standard*) was designed and selected to become the successor of *DES*, which is seen to be outdated, and, accordingly, AES will presumably evolve as the most commonly used example of the *chaos* approach. Designed by the Belgian researchers J. Daemen and V. Rijmen under the name *Rijndael*, AES was the winner of a public competition and evaluation organized by the U.S. National Institute of Standards and Technology (NIST) between 1997 and 2000. The competition and evaluation process indicated a great shift toward achieving *cryptographic security* in the sense of Section 12.10 for the welfare of the *information society* and its needed *informational assurances*, as discussed in Section 1.3: from administratively releasing a secretly invented product to a worldwide *open* discussion of the *security requirements*, the *design* and the *properties* actually *satisfied*.

The mechanism is *symmetric*, admitting *multiple* key usage, and it operates *blockwise*, where, in principle, the block length might vary from 128 bits to any larger multiple of 32 bits. The key length might in principle vary as well, from 128 bits to any larger multiple of 32. For standardization, however, the block length is fixed at 128 bits, and the key length is restricted to be 128, 192 or 256 bits, which is regarded as sufficient to resist *exhaustive search* and *trial attacks*, both today and in the predictable future.

AES–Rijndael successfully combines several long-approved techniques – such as operating *roundwise* on block parts and round keys, *superimposing* the randomness of the key on the blocks by use of the *XOR operation*, and *permuting* the positions of a block or a key, as used in DES, IDEA and many other examples – with the employment of advanced algebraic operations showing *one-way behavior*. For these combinations, a theoretical justification of the claimed chaos can be provided which is much better founded as before.

Basically, the algorithms of the mechanism operate on the following sets:

- plaintexts: bit strings (blocks over the set $\{0,1\}$) of length 128 (or a larger multiple of 32), represented as a byte matrix of four rows and four columns, thus having 16 entries of eight bits each (or an appropriate adaptation of the column number for larger blocks);
- ciphertexts: bit strings (blocks) of the same length as the plaintext blocks;
- keys: bit strings of length 128 (or a larger multiple of 32), again represented as a byte matrix like the plaintexts.

The three algorithms of the mechanism can be outlined as follows:

- The *key generation* algorithm selects a "truly random" bit string of length 128.
- The *encryption* algorithm $AES(k,x)$ takes a key k and a plaintext x as input and first represents them as byte matrices. Besides some preprocessing and postprocessing, the algorithm basically performs 10 (or more for larger block or key lengths) uniform *rounds*, each of which operates on the current (*state* of the) byte matrix in four steps: (1) bytewise substitutions, (2) permutations that shift positions within a row, (3) transformations on columns and (4) bitwise XOR operations with the round key. Some more details are described below.
- The (straightforward) *decryption* algorithm performs the inverses of all of the byte matrix transformations in reverse order, employing the round keys accordingly.

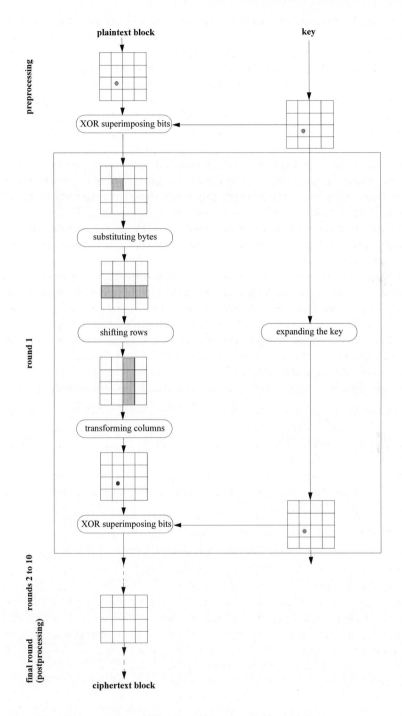

Fig. 13.12. Structure of the AES–Rijndael symmetric block cipher

Figure 13.12 shows the overall structure of the encryption algorithm: *preprocessing* the plaintext block, performing the 10 *rounds* on the current block using the four steps already mentioned, *postprocessing* of the resulting block by a final round where the third step is skipped and, in parallel, computing the *round keys*. In the following, we outline each of these components, indicate how they achieve the *correctness* property, and sketch how they contribute to the *secrecy* property by producing *chaos* in the form of *confusion* and *diffusion*.

The plaintext block x of 128 bits is preprocessed by first representing it as a 4×4 byte matrix and then computing the *XOR operation bit*wise with the original key k, which is represented as a 4×4 byte matrix as well. As in all similar applications of the XOR operation, the *randomness* of the key is *superimposed* on the plaintext, and to *correctly* recover the plaintext, the decryption algorithm merely has to apply the operation once again.

Step (1) of a round, *bytewise substitutions*, is defined by a *non-linear*, invertible function S_{RD} on bytes, i.e., each byte of the current matrix is independently substituted by applying S_{RD}. Invertibility ensures that a *correct* decryption is possible just by applying the inverse function S_{RD}^{-1}. The non-linearity is aimed at achieving *confusion*, in terms of both algebraic complexity and small statistical correlations between argument and value bytes.

The substitution function S_{RD} has two convenient representations. The tabular representation is organized as a lookup table of size 16×16: an argument byte a is seen as composed of two hexadecimal symbols li and co, and the value byte v for a is given by the table entry for line li and column co, as depicted in Table 13.13.

The algebraic representation is based on considering a byte as an element of the finite field $GF(2^8)$, where the eight bits of a byte are the coefficients of a polynomial with degree at most 7. The multiplicative structure is defined by the usual multiplication of polynomials, followed by a reduction modulo the irreducible polynomial $x^8 + x^4 + x^3 + x + 1$ to obtain again a result that is a polynomial of degree at most 7. On the basis of this algebraic structure, the function S_{RD} has a representation of the form $S_{RD}(a) = f(a^{-1}))$, where the inversion operation refers to the multiplicative structure of $GF(2^8)$, and f is an affine function in $GF(2^8)$, basically described by a suitable 8×8 bit matrix F and a suitable constant byte c such that $f(a) = (F \times a) \oplus c$.

Step (2) of a round, *permutations* that shift the positions within a *row*, has a simple definition in terms of the offsets to be used for each of the rows: the offsets are 0, 1, 2 and 3 byte positions, meaning that the first row remains invariant, and the second, third and fourth rows are shifted by 8, 16 and 24 bit positions, respectively, to the left. The shiftings are aimed at achieving good *diffusion*, and can be easily redone for a *correct* decryption.

Step (3) of a round, transformations on *columns*, is defined by a linear, invertible function MC_{RD} on "columns", i.e., each column of the current matrix is considered as an element of $\{0,1\}^{32}$ and independently substituted by applying MC_{RD}. Invertibility again ensures that a *correct* decryption is possible. The specific selection of MC_{RD} is aimed mainly at achieving *diffusion*, now regarding the rows of the byte

Table 13.13. The lookup table for the substitution function S_{RD} of AES–Rijndael

	0	1	2	3	4	5	6	7	8	9	A	B	C	D	E	F
0	63	7C	77	7B	F2	6B	6F	C5	30	01	67	2B	FE	D7	AB	76
1	CA	82	C9	7D	FA	59	47	F0	AD	D4	A2	AF	9C	A4	72	C0
2	B7	FD	93	26	36	3F	F7	CC	34	A5	E5	F1	71	D8	31	15
3	04	C7	23	C3	18	96	05	9A	07	12	80	E2	EB	27	B2	75
4	09	83	2C	1A	1B	6E	5A	A0	52	3B	D6	B3	29	E3	2F	84
5	53	D1	00	ED	20	FC	B1	5B	6A	CB	BE	39	4A	4C	58	CF
6	D0	EF	AA	FB	43	4D	33	85	45	F9	02	7F	50	3C	9F	A8
7	51	A3	40	8F	92	9D	38	F5	BC	B6	DA	21	10	FF	F3	D2
8	CD	0C	13	EC	5F	97	44	17	C4	A7	7E	3D	64	5D	19	73
9	60	81	4F	DC	22	2A	90	88	46	EE	B8	14	DE	5E	0B	DB
A	E0	32	3A	0A	49	06	24	5C	C2	D3	AC	62	91	95	E4	79
B	E7	C8	37	6D	8D	D5	4E	A9	6C	56	F4	EA	65	7A	AE	08
C	BA	78	25	2E	1C	A6	B4	C6	E8	DD	74	1F	4B	BD	8B	8A
D	70	3E	B5	66	48	03	F6	0E	61	35	57	B9	86	C1	1D	9E
E	E1	F8	98	11	69	D9	8E	94	9B	1E	87	E9	CE	55	28	DF
F	8C	A1	89	0D	BF	E6	42	68	41	99	2D	0F	B0	54	BB	16

matrices, and complementing the confusion regarding the columns produced by the shiftings in step (2). Additionally, the selection was influenced by efficiency reasons.

The function MC_{RD} admits an algebraic definition in terms of polynomial multiplication which results in the following representation by a 4×4 byte matrix, where all entries are bytes given as two hexadecimal symbols:

$$MC_{RD}\left(\begin{bmatrix} a_0 \\ a_1 \\ a_2 \\ a_3 \end{bmatrix}\right) = \begin{bmatrix} 02 & 03 & 01 & 01 \\ 01 & 02 & 03 & 01 \\ 01 & 01 & 02 & 03 \\ 03 & 01 & 01 & 02 \end{bmatrix} \times \begin{bmatrix} a_0 \\ a_1 \\ a_2 \\ a_3 \end{bmatrix}.$$

Step (4) of a round, *bit*wise *XOR operations* with the *round key*, again *superimposes* the *randomness* of the sophisticatedly manipulated key on the intermediate state of the byte matrix. The effects of the superimposition can be *correctly* undone by applying these XOR operations with the same key arguments.

Unlike the case for DES or IDEA, each of which uses a simple shifting scheme for generating the round keys, AES–Rijndael computes the round keys inductively by employing complex algebraic operations, while at the same time achieving an acceptable efficiency. More specifically, for the given block length and key length of 128 bits each (or suitably adapted for other possible lengths), the initial 4×4 byte matrix for the key k given as input is *expanded* into a $4×(1+10)·4$ byte matrix, i.e., for each of the 10 rounds, four new columns are generated and taken as the *round key*.

The *key expansion* scheme distinguishes between the first column of a new round key and the remaining columns, but each column i is defined in terms of the corresponding column $i-4$ of the preceding round key and the immediately preceding column $i-1$. In the latter case, the column i is computed by directly applying the bitwise *XOR operation*, whereas in the former case the preceding column is first transformed by a non-linear function that is a suitable composition of the bytewise application of the substitution function S_{RD}, a permutation that shifts the positions in a column and the addition of a round constant.

On the basis of the invertibility of each individual step, there is a *straightforward decryption algorithm* that basically performs the inverses of all byte matrix transformation in reverse order, employing the round keys accordingly. However, the design also includes an equivalent decryption algorithm which maintains the sequence of steps within a round, replacing the steps by their respective inverses.

Regarding the *efficiency* property, the NIST requirements demanded, in particular, that the successor of DES could be efficiently implemented on *smartcards*, which could, for example, be used as *personal computing devices*. As a winner of the competition, the Rijndael proposal convinced the community not only regarding high chaos-based secrecy but also regarding efficiency for implementations in both hardware and software; in fact, besides the details mentioned above, the construction as a whole enables high efficiency even though it operates on structures consisting of 128 bits (or even more). One can expect that AES–Rijndael in combination with some block mode (see Section 13.10) will be able to achieve transmission rates that are suitable for large multimedia objects. Clearly, like any other symmetric block cipher, AES–Rijndael can be used as part of a *hybrid encryption method* to combine high efficiency with the advantages of asymmetric key generation and distribution.

13.10 Stream Ciphers Using Block Modes

A *block cipher* encrypts plaintext blocks and decrypts ciphertext blocks of a fixed length l_B. If a message to be transmitted is longer, it can be divided into appropriate *fragments*. Then the resulting stream of fragments can be treated by using the block cipher in what is known as a *block mode* (*mode of operation*). There are two basic approaches to designing the resulting *stream cipher*:

- The original message is divided into fragments of length equal to exactly the block length l_B of the underlying block cipher. Then the block cipher treats the fragments either separately (electronic codebook mode) or in a suitably chained way (cipher block chaining mode).
- The original message is divided into fragments of length $l \le l_B$. Typically, we have $l = 1$ or $l = 8$ such that a plaintext stream of bits or bytes results. Then the underlying block cipher is used to generate a corresponding (apparently pseudo-random) cipher key stream that is superimposed on the plaintext stream by using the *XOR operation* (in the cipher feedback mode, output feedback mode and counter-with-cipher-block-chaining mode). Accordingly, this approach can be seen as a variant of the *one-time key* encryption mechanism, where *perfectness* is abandoned for the sake of a reusable, short key as demanded by the underlying block cipher.

13.10.1 Electronic Codebook (ECB) Mode

The *electronic codebook (ECB) mode* follows the first basic approach: each plaintext block x_i resulting from the fragmentation is separately encrypted by the underlying algorithm *Block_Enc(ryption)* and, accordingly, the transmitted ciphertext block y_i is decrypted by the underlying algorithm *Block_Dec(ryption)*. The last fragment of the message is suitably padded to obtain the full block size. Figure 13.14 shows the overall design for a symmetric block cipher.

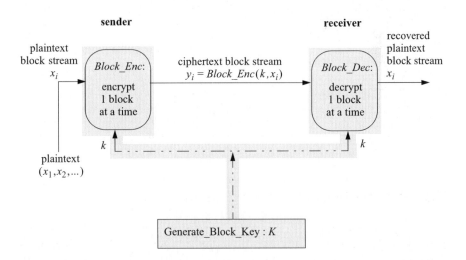

Fig. 13.14. The electronic codebook (ECB) mode (the light gray area must be hidden from other participants)

The characteristic feature of the electronic codebook mode is that all blocks are treated completely independently; in principle, all blocks could even be considered in parallel, as visualized in Figure 13.15. While it is worthwhile for efficiency, this feature causes a *ciphertext-block/plaintext-block vulnerability*, and exposes the ciphertext stream to *substitution attacks*.

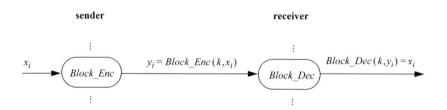

Fig. 13.15. The electronic codebook mode treats all blocks independently

13.10.2 Cipher Block Chaining (CBC) Mode

The *cipher block chaining (CBC) mode* follows the first basic approach too, but in a chained way: each plaintext block x_i resulting from the fragmentation is first superimposed on the preceding ciphertext block y_{i-1} using the *XOR operation* and only then encrypted by the underlying algorithm *Block_Enc(ryption)*. Accordingly, a ciphertext block y_i is first decrypted by the underlying algorithm *Block_Dec(ryption)* and then the decryption output is superimposed on the preceding ciphertext block y_{i-1} using the *XOR operation*, thereby cancelling the effect of the superimposition before the encryption.

Again, the last fragment is suitably padded to obtain the full block size. Moreover, for the first superimposition, an *initialization vector init* is needed, which should be used only once but can be communicated to the receiver without protection. Figure 13.16 shows the overall design for a symmetric block cipher.

The *correctness property* of this mode is justified as follows. The resulting encryption algorithm *Enc* yields, for the first block x_1,

$$Enc(k, x_1) := Block\_Enc(k, x_1 \oplus init),$$

and for all further blocks x_i with $i > 1$,

$$Enc(k, x_i) := Block\_Enc(k, x_i \oplus Enc(k, x_{i-1})).$$

The corresponding decryption algorithm *Dec* then satisfies the following equations:

$$
\begin{aligned}
Dec(k, y_1) &:= Block\_Dec(k, y_1) \oplus init \\
&= Block\_Dec(k, Block\_Enc(k, x_1 \oplus init)) \oplus init \\
&= (x_1 \oplus init) \oplus init = x_1
\end{aligned}
$$

and, for $i > 1$,

$$
\begin{aligned}
Dec(k, y_i) :&= Block\_Dec(k, y_i) \oplus y_{i-1} \\
&= Block\_Dec(k, Enc(k, x_i)) \oplus Enc(k, x_{i-1}) \\
&= Block\_Dec(k, Block\_Enc(k, x_i \oplus Enc(k, x_{i-1}))) \oplus Enc(k, x_{i-1}) \\
&= (x_i \oplus Enc(k, x_{i-1})) \oplus Enc(k, x_{i-1}) = x_i.
\end{aligned}
$$

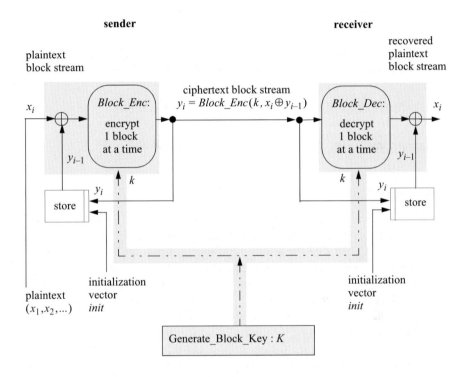

Fig. 13.16. The cipher block chaining (CBC) mode (the light gray area must be hidden from other participants)

The characteristic feature of the cipher block chaining mode is that all blocks are treated in a connected way requiring strict serialization, as visualized in Figure 13.17. Accordingly, the last resulting ciphertext block can be seen as a *message digest* and can thus be employed as a piece of *cryptographic evidence* (a *cryptographic exhibit*) for an *authenticity verification* algorithm.

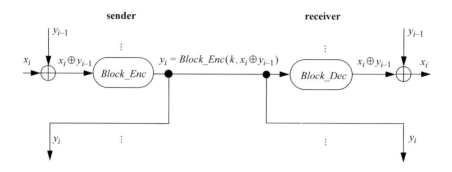

Fig. 13.17. The cipher block chaining mode treats all blocks in a chain

13.10.3 Cipher Feedback (CFB) Mode

The *cipher feedback* (*CFB*) *mode* follows the second basic approach, namely it achieves a variant of the one-time key encryption mechanism. The required pseudorandom *cipher key* stream is generated by means of the encryption algorithm *Block_Enc*(*ryption*) of the underlying block cipher, notably without employing the corresponding decryption algorithm. Hence, this mode cannot be used for an asymmetric block cipher.

Basically, the cipher key stream is extracted from the outputs of the block cipher encryption, whose inputs are taken as a feedback from the ciphertext stream. At the beginning, before the feedback is available, an *initialization vector init* is used as a *seed*, which must be used only once but can be communicated to the receiver without protection. Figure 13.18 shows the overall design, where the fragment length is defined as $l = 8$ and the block size of the underlying block cipher is assumed to be $l_B = 64$.

The *correctness property* of this mode is justified as follows. The resulting encryption algorithm *Enc* yields, for each plaintext byte x_i,

$$Enc(k, x_i) := x_i \oplus Left(Block\_Enc(k, shift\_sender_i)).$$

The corresponding decryption algorithm *Dec* yields, for each ciphertext byte y_i,

$$
\begin{aligned}
Dec(k, y_i) &:= y_i \oplus Left(Block\_Enc(k, shift\_receiver_i)) \\
&= (x_i \oplus Left(Block\_Enc(k, shift\_sender_i))) \\
&\quad \oplus Left(Block\_Enc(k, shift\_receiver_i)) \\
&= x_i, \text{ provided } shift\_sender_i = shift\_receiver_i.
\end{aligned}
$$

The required equality of the *shift_i* inputs on both sides is achieved by using the same initialization vector *init* and then, inductively, by employing the same operations and inputs to generate them.

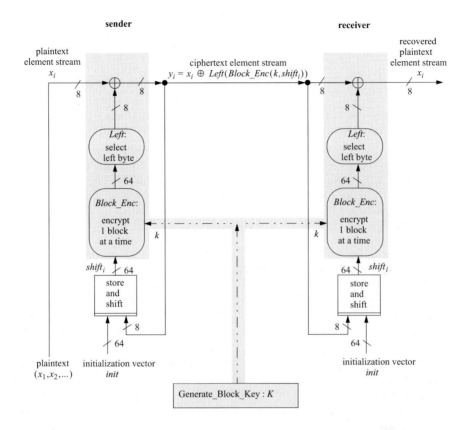

Fig. 13.18. The cipher feedback (CFB) mode (the light gray area must be hidden from other participants)

An important feature of the cipher feedback mode is that the last resulting ciphertext block depends potentially on the full plaintext stream. Accordingly, this block can be seen as a *message digest* and can thus be employed as a *cryptographic exhibit* for an *authenticity verification* algorithm.

13.10.4 Output Feedback (OFB) Mode

The *output feedback* (*OFB*) *mode* follows the second basic approach too. The required pseudorandom *cipher key* stream is generated as for the cipher feedback mode, except that the block cipher encryption takes the feedback directly from its own outputs. As before, since only the encryption algorithm of the underlying block cipher is involved, this mode cannot be used for an asymmetric block cipher. Figure 13.19 shows the overall design, where again the fragment length is defined as $l = 8$ and the block size of the underlying block cipher is assumed to be $l_B = 64$.

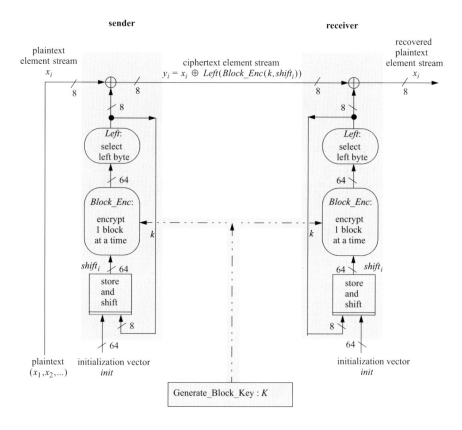

Fig. 13.19. The output feedback (OFB) mode (the light gray area must be hidden from other participants)

13.10.5 Counter-with-Cipher-Block-Chaining Mode (CCM)

The *counter mode* is another variant of the second basic approach. The required pseudorandom *cipher key* stream is generated by encrypting a sequence of *counters* $count_i$ using the underlying block encryption. Assuming a block size l_B of the block cipher and taking an *initialization vector init* of that size, the counters are defined by

$$count_i := init + i \bmod 2^{l_B}.$$

As before, since only the encryption algorithm of the underlying block cipher is involved, this mode cannot be used for an asymmetric block cipher. The characteristic feature of counters is that for each $i = 1, 2, \ldots$, the following properties hold: the pair of the counter $count_i$ and the corresponding plaintext block x_i is treated independently of all other pairs, as for ECB, and the counter $count_i$ is independent of the ciphertext stream (and thus of the plaintext stream), as for OFB.

In order to achieve *authenticated encryption*, the sender additionally performs CBC encryption without transmitting the resulting ciphertext blocks. Instead, the last resulting CBC ciphertext block y_{fin} is superimposed on the counter $count_0 = init$ and the resulting block $y_{fin} \oplus count_0$ is appended as a *message digest*.

13.10.6 A Comparison of Block Modes

Primarily, an encryption mechanism should enforce technically the interest of *confidentiality*. In many applications, additional interests such as *availability*, *authenticity* and *integrity* are important as well. Moreover, *efficiency* is often a major concern. Table 13.20 summarizes some technical properties that may be used to assess the suitability of a block mode regarding these goals.

Table 13.20. A rudimentary comparison of block modes

	ECB	CBC	CFB	OFB	CCM
Initialization vector/ parameterization	no	yes	yes	yes	yes
Propagation of error in plain-text fragment	limited to block	unlimited up to end of stream	unlimited up to end of stream	limited to error position	limited to error position, except for superimposed last CBC cipher block
Suitable for producing a message digest	no	by last cipher block	by last cipher block	no	by superimposed last CBC cipher block
Propagation of error in cipher-text fragment	limited to block	limited to block and succeeding block	limited to block and succeeding block	limited to error position	limited to error position

The first technical property is related to the need for and the impact of an *initialization vector*. If required, on the one hand some computational overhead is necessary, and on the other hand a *parameterization* of the encryption is achieved, if the initialization vector is varied for identical messages. If the initialization vector is kept secret, the encryption could even be seen as *probabilistic*.

A further property is related to *fault tolerance* and thus the interest of *availability*. More specifically, the propagation of a *modification error* is considered, which might occur in the plaintext stream or, during transmission, in the ciphertext stream. It is easy to see that all modes recover shortly after a modification error in the ciphertext stream; OFB and CCM even behave optimally, since only the error position is affected, as in the perfect one-time key encryption mechanism.

However, there is an essential difference regarding a modification error in the plaintext stream: whereas ECB, OFB and the main part of CCM recover shortly after the error position or totally prevent propagation, for CBC, CFB and the digest production part of CCM, an error might "diffuse" through the full succeeding cipher stream. Accordingly, the resulting final cipher block can be seen as a *message digest* and can thus be employed as a piece of *cryptographic evidence* (a *cryptographic exhibit*) for an *authenticity verification* algorithm, supporting the interests of *authenticity* and *integrity* as *detection of modification*.

Moreover, but not mentioned in Table 13.20, *synchronization errors* might occur owing to *lost fragments*. For all modes, additional measures must be employed to ensure resynchronization, for example by suitably inserting separators at agreed fragment borders.

On the basis of these and related considerations, a security administrator can select the block mode that is assessed as the most suitable for the application considered. For example:

- The electronic codebook mode is suitable for short, randomly selected messages such as nonces or cryptographic keys of another mechanism.
- The cipher block chaining mode might be employed for long files with any non-predictable content.
- The cipher feedback mode, output feedback mode and counter mode support the transmission of a few bits or bytes, for example as needed for connections between a central processing unit and external devices such as a keyboard and monitor.
- The output feedback mode and counter mode might be preferred for highly failure-sensitive applications, since modification errors are not propagated at all (except for the added message digest).

13.11 Introduction to a Theory of Encryption

In the introductory Section 12.1, we announced that, throughout our treatment of cryptography, we would only informally outline the hopefully (!) achieved security properties. Accordingly, nearly all proposed assertions about the appropriateness of the encryption mechanisms presented need further formal justification. As an exception, we have precisely stated and mathematically proved the classical theorems about perfect encryption mechanisms.

In this section, we attempt to give an introduction to a thorough theoretical treatment of *encryption*, which has been developed only recently. In doing so, we concentrate on a specific formalization approach for two versions of the secrecy property: *semantic secrecy*, already informally introduced in (12.4), and *operational secrecy* considered as *indistinguishability of ciphertexts*, intuitively expressed in (12.5). These versions are studied within four settings that result from independently varying two aspects. First, we distinguish the two alternatives for the key relationship: *symmetric* or *asymmetric*. Second, we distinguish the two alternatives for the key usage: *single* or *multiple*. Once again, we emphasize that our introduction remains sketchy and leaves many subtle details and various possible variants open.

For simplicity, in the following all objects such as security parameters, keys, plaintexts and ciphertexts are considered to be encoded over the alphabet $\{0,1\}$, i.e., we deal uniformly only with bit strings in $\{0,1\}^*$. Rather than speaking about a specific encryption mechanism or a family of such mechanisms as before, in this section we adopt a notion of an encryption scheme that is intended to be more flexible.

More specifically, an *encryption scheme* consists of three algorithms:

- A *key generation* algorithm *Gen*: on input of a security parameter 1^n, the algorithm *Gen* returns a pair (ek, dk) of an encryption key ek and a decryption key dk. The algorithm Gen_{EK} returns only the encryption key ek generated by *Gen*.
- An *encryption* algorithm *Enc*: on input of an encryption key ek and a plaintext x, the algorithm *Enc* returns a ciphertext y.
- A *decryption* algorithm *Dec*: on input of a decryption key dk and a ciphertext y, the algorithm *Dec* returns a plaintext x.

These algorithms should satisfy the following properties:

- *Correctness*. For all plaintexts x, and for all key pairs (ek, dk) generated by *Gen*,
  $Prob[\,Dec(dk, Enc(ek, x)) = x\,] = 1$.

  We could also use a suitable relaxation that tolerates a "small" decryption error or some "rare" exceptions. Moreover, the length of the plaintexts considered could be bounded polynomially in the security parameter.
- *Secrecy*. We shall study two versions within four settings, as announced above. Further variations are treated in the literature.
- *Efficiency*. *Gen*, *Enc* and *Dec* are *probabilistic polynomial-time* algorithms.

13.11.1 The Symmetric/Single-Usage Setting

In this subsection, we exemplarily present detailed formal definitions of *semantic secrecy* and *operational secrecy* for a setting where a *symmetric* key is used *only once*, and where attacks are *passive* carried out by observing ciphertexts. These definitions can be modified and adapted for other settings. In the subsequent subsections, we sketch such modifications for settings where keys are used in an asymmetric way and for multiple usage of keys. Further modifications are possible for various active attacks but are not treated in this monograph.

The formal definition of *semantic secrecy* comprehensively captures all the intuitions about secrecy that we have discussed before:

- The anticipated threats are modeled by a *passive* attacker who *observes a ciphertext* and attempts to derive the corresponding plaintext, or at least some properties of the plaintext.
- Such an *attacker* is not at all confined in his actions, except by the restrictions of limited computational resources. More precisely, the secrecy should be protected against *any* probabilistic polynomial-time algorithm acting as an attacker.
- From the perspective of an attacker, the *plaintext* sent is treated as a *random variable*.
- In his attempts, the attacker might exploit some *a priori auxiliary knowledge* about the hidden plaintext.
- The secrecy requirement applies not only to the full plaintext but also to *any property* which might be *of interest* to the attacker.
- The *probability-theoretic* view and the *complexity-theoretic* view are *combined* for the purpose of expressing the *expectation of success* of an attack, namely for bounding the success probability under the condition of limited computational resources.
- In the complexity-theoretic view, the secrecy property is expressed in terms of a *security parameter* whose values determine a bound for the success probabilities, except for a finite number of exceptions.
- Finally, given that an attacker might have a priori knowledge, in general he clearly cannot be hindered in his efforts to compute some properties of the plaintext. Hence, the observation of the ciphertext should not enable the attacker to derive *anything new* about the plaintext.

Concisely summarized, the following definition requires that whatever can be efficiently computed from observing a ciphertext can already be efficiently computed given some data about the encryption protocol.

Definition 13.1   [semantic secrecy]

In the setting of a *symmetric* key relationship and a *single* key usage, an encryption scheme (Gen, Enc, Dec) satisfies the *semantic secrecy* property iff:

For any probabilistic polynomial-time algorithm *Att* [an *attacker*] that inputs

- a security parameter 1^n,
- a ciphertext $Enc(Gen_{EK}(1^n), X_n)$,
  which is produced with an encryption key $Gen_{EK}(1^n)$,
- the plaintext length $1^{|X_n|}$, and
- the a priori auxiliary knowledge $h(1^n, X_n)$

there exists a probabilistic polynomial-time algorithm *Att'*
[an *alternative investigator*] that inputs only
the security parameter, the plaintext length and the a priori auxiliary knowledge
(but not the ciphertext) such that:

for every probability ensemble $\{X_n\}_{n \in \mathbb{N}}$
[of plaintext domains considered as *random variables*] such that
the lengths of elements in X_n are polynomially bounded in n, i.e., $|X_n| \le \text{poly}(n)$,

for every function $f: \{0,1\}^* \to \{0,1\}^*$ with
polynomially length-bounded values [*property of interest* regarding plaintexts],

for every function $h: \{0,1\}^* \to \{0,1\}^*$ with
polynomially length-bounded values
[*a priori auxiliary knowledge* regarding plaintexts],

for every positive polynomial p, for all sufficiently large n:

$$Prob[Att(1^n, Enc(Gen_{EK}(1^n), X_n), 1^{|X_n|}, h(1^n, X_n)) = f(1^n, X_n)] \qquad (13.3)$$

$$< Prob[Att'(1^n, 1^{|X_n|}, h(1^n, X_n)) = f(1^n, X_n)] + \frac{1}{p(n)} .$$

Thus semantic secrecy ensures that an attacker can gain only a *negligible advantage* from having observed the ciphertext, in comparison with another investigator that has the same generic protocol data and a priori knowledge but not the specific ciphertext.

The formal definition of *operational secrecy* provides a link to the theory of *pseudorandomness* by requiring the computational *indistinguishability of single ciphertexts*. In this context, indistinguishability is expressed in terms of *circuits* that are used as acceptors. Roughly sketched, a circuit performs Boolean operations on inputs of fixed size, and it accepts those inputs for which the value 1 is returned. A circuit can be used to simulate the operations of an *algorithm* (a *Turing machine*) when inputs are restricted to a fixed size. A *time bound* for the algorithm can then be translated into a corresponding *size bound* for the simulating circuit. For each algorithm, we can derive a simulating family of circuits, where each member deals with a specific input size. For the converse, however, some assumptions about the uniformness of the circuits are required, or the notion of an algorithm must be extended in order to provide the information that is necessary to resolve the problems arising from non-uniformness.

Definition 13.2   [indistinguishability of ciphertexts as operational secrecy]

In the setting of a *symmetric* key relationship and a *single* key usage, the *indistinguishability of ciphertexts* holds for an encryption scheme (Gen, Enc, Dec) as the *operational secrecy* property iff:

For any polynomial-size circuit family $\{C_n\}_{n \in \mathbb{N}}$
[*attacking distinguisher* including *a priori auxiliary knowledge*],
for every positive polynomial p, for all sufficiently large n,
for every pair [of plaintexts] x, y of equal length $\text{poly}(n)$:

$$\left| Prob[C_n(Enc(Gen_{EK}(1^n), x)) = 1] \right. \qquad (13.4)$$

$$\left. - Prob[C_n(Enc(Gen_{EK}(1^n), y)) = 1] \right| < \frac{1}{p(n)} .$$

The following theorem relates the two versions of the secrecy property by stating their equivalence. In applying this theorem, indistinguishability of single ciphertexts is seen as an operational property that can be verified for actual constructions. The statement that indistinguishability of single ciphertexts implies semantic secrecy for a single key usage can then be interpreted as a result about the *semantic correctness* of verified constructions. Vice versa, the statement that semantic secrecy for a single key usage implies indistinguishability of single ciphertexts indicates the *completeness* of the class of all verified constructions.

Theorem 13.3   [equivalence of semantic and operational secrecy]

In the setting of a *symmetric* key relationship and a *single* key usage, an encryption scheme satisfies the *semantic secrecy* property (for a single key usage) if and only if the *indistinguishability of* (single) *ciphertexts* holds.

Sketch of Proof: "⇐" Let $\{X_n\}_{n \in \mathbb{N}}$, f and h be any probability ensemble, property function and auxiliary knowledge, respectively. Given an attacker algorithm *Att*, we first uniformly construct the alternative-investigator algorithm *Att'* as an oracle machine that uses *Att* as an oracle. Then, on the basis of the supposed indistinguishability of ciphertexts, we show that *Att'* guesses the property of interest $f(1^n, X_n)$ as well as *Att*, except for a negligible difference in the probabilities, as required by the relation (13.3).

The algorithm *Att'* inputs $(1^n, 1^{|x|}, h(1^n, x))$ and then performs the following steps:

1. Invoke *Gen* with the security parameter 1^n and obtain an encryption key:
   $ek \leftarrow Gen_{EK}(1^n)$.

2. Invoke *Enc* with *ek* and the dummy plaintext $1^{|x|}$ and obtain the resulting ciphertext:
   $z \leftarrow Enc(ek, 1^{|x|})$.

3. Invoke the oracle *Att* with $(1^n, z, 1^{|x|}, h(1^n, x))$ and output the returned result:
   $Att' \leftarrow Att(1^n, Enc(Gen_{EK}(1^n), 1^{|x|}), 1^{|x|}, h(1^n, x))$.

For the purpose of verifying the relation (13.3), we abbreviate the notation by dropping the security parameter 1^n and the plaintext length $1^{|X_n|}$, by conveniently simplifying the expressions accordingly and by indicating the encryption key just by "…". Moreover, we rewrite (13.3) by substituting the expression for the alternative investigator *Att'* by the result output according to step 3. With these conventions, we still have to verify the following relation:

$$Prob[Att(Enc(\dots, X_n), h_n(X_n)) = f_n(X_n)] \qquad (13.5)$$
$$< Prob[Att(Enc(\dots, 1^{|X_n|}), h_n(X_n)) = f_n(X_n)] + \frac{1}{p(n)}.$$

Assume indirectly that there exist a polynomial p and infinitely many n violating the claimed relation (13.5). Then, by applying some arguments of probability theory, for each violating n there exists a plaintext $x_n \in \{0, 1\}^{\text{poly}(n)}$ that witnesses a non-negligible difference in the success probabilities as follows:

$$\left| Prob[Att(Enc(\ldots, x_n), h_n(x_n)) = f_n(x_n)] \right. \tag{13.6}$$
$$\left. - Prob[Att(Enc(\ldots, 1^{|x_n|}), h_n(x_n)) = f_n(x_n)] \right| \geq \frac{1}{p(n)} .$$

Now, taking the sequence of items $x_n, h_n(x_n), f_n(x_n)$ for the infinitely many violating n, we construct polynomial-size circuits C_n that are then shown to distinguish the specific encryptions of x_n and $1^{|x_n|}$, contrary to the supposed indistinguishability of ciphertexts. Basically, C_n simulates the attacker Att for an input x of a suitable length and the auxiliary a priori knowledge $h_n(x_n)$, and finally decides whether Att would return the property of interest $f_n(x_n)$: on input $Enc(\ldots, x)$, C_n returns 1 iff the simulated invocation of $Att(Enc(\ldots, x), h_n(x_n))$ returns $f_n(x_n)$; otherwise C_n returns 0. This definition of C_n immediately implies that for all suitable x,

$$Prob[C_n(Enc(\ldots, x)) = 1] = Prob[Att(Enc(\ldots, x), h_n(x_n)) = f_n(x_n)]. \tag{13.7}$$

Finally, by substituting the probability expressions in (13.6) according to equation (13.7), we obtain the anticipated contradiction:

$$\left| Prob[C_n(Enc(\ldots, x_n)) = 1] - Prob[C_n(Enc(\ldots, 1^{|x_n|})) = 1] \right| \geq \frac{1}{p(n)} . \tag{13.8}$$

"$\Rightarrow$ (in contraposition)" Suppose that indistinguishability of ciphertexts does not hold, i.e., for suitably selected witnesses against this property, namely a polynomial-size circuit family $\{C_n\}_{n \in \mathbf{N}}$, a positive polynomial p, infinitely many n, and pairs of different plaintexts $x_n, y_n \in \{0, 1\}^{\text{poly}(n)}$,

$$\left| Prob[C_n(Enc(Gen_{EK}(1^n), x_n)) = 1] \right. \tag{13.9}$$
$$\left. - Prob[C_n(Enc(Gen_{EK}(1^n), y_n)) = 1] \right| \geq \frac{1}{p(n)} .$$

Taking these items, we construct a situation that can be shown to violate semantic secrecy. For each of the witnessing n, we define X_n as an equally distributed random variable over the two-element set $\{x_n, y_n\}$, the property of interest by $f(1^n, x_n) = 1$ and $f(1^n, y_n) = 0$, and the a priori auxiliary knowledge by $h(1^n, x) = C_n$, i.e., for each n, the auxiliary knowledge is given in the form of the fixed circuit C_n, independently of the plaintext input.

For this situation, we consider an attacker algorithm Att that, on input of $(1^n, Enc(Gen_{EK}(1^n), x), 1^{|x|}, h(1^n, x))$, performs the following steps:

1. Simulate the circuit $C_n = h(1^n, x)$ for the input $Enc(\dots, x)$, where we have reuse the abbreviated notation.
2. Output 1 iff the circuit C_n has returned 1 in the first step; otherwise output 0.

Using the definitions and some of the notational abbreviations above, we derive the attacker's success probability for the situation as follows, where the final inequality is implied by the relation (13.9) when the plaintexts involved are appropriately denoted:

$$Prob[Att(1^n, Enc(\dots, X_n), 1^{|X_n|}, h_n(X_n)) = f_n(X_n)]$$

$$= \frac{1}{2} \cdot Prob[Att(1^n, Enc(\dots, X_n), 1^{|X_n|}, h_n(X_n)) = f_n(X_n) | X_n = x_n]$$

$$+ \frac{1}{2} \cdot Prob[Att(1^n, Enc(\dots, X_n), 1^{|X_n|}, h_n(X_n)) = f_n(X_n) | X_n = y_n]$$

$$= \frac{1}{2} \cdot Prob[Att(1^n, Enc(\dots, x_n), 1^{|x_n|}, C_n) = 1]$$

$$+ \frac{1}{2} \cdot Prob[Att(1^n, Enc(\dots, y_n), 1^{|y_n|}, C_n) = 0]$$

$$= \frac{1}{2} \cdot Prob[C_n(Enc(\dots, x_n)) = 1] + \frac{1}{2} \cdot (1 - Prob[C_n(Enc(\dots, y_n)) = 1])$$

$$\geq \frac{1}{2} + \frac{1}{2 \cdot p(n)} .$$

On the other hand, for the situation defined, any alternative investigator Att' inputs values that are stochastically independent of the equally distributed property function, and thus we obtain the estimate

$$Prob[Att'(1^n, 1^{|X_n|}, h_n(X_n)) = f_n(X_n)] \leq \frac{1}{2} .$$

Hence, the derived success probability of the constructed attacker differs non-negligibly from the success probability of any alternative investigator, and thus the encryption scheme does not satisfy the semantic secrecy property.   ❏

13.11.2 The Asymmetric/Single-Usage Setting

Basically, for a setting where an *asymmetric* key is used *only once*, the *semantic secrecy* property is the same as for the corresponding symmetric setting, except that the attacker has the encryption key $Gen_{EK}(1^n)$ as an additional input. This additional input is not relevant to an alternative investigator who does not explicitly deal with a ciphertext. Clearly, the computational power of the alternative investigator would allow him to autonomously run the algorithm *Gen* and produce *some* encryption keys. Formally, in the definition of *semantic secrecy* given previously for a single key usage, the formula for the relationship between the success probabilities is replaced as follows:

$$Prob[Att(1^n, Gen_{EK}(1^n), Enc(Gen_{EK}(1^n), X_n), 1^{|X_n|}, h(1^n, X_n)) = f(1^n, X_n)]$$

$$< Prob[Att'(1^n, 1^{|X_n|}, h(1^n, X_n)) = f(1^n, X_n)] + \frac{1}{p(n)} .$$

Similarly, the *operational secrecy* property expressed as *indistinguishability of single ciphertexts* is the same as for the corresponding symmetric version, except that the attacking distinguisher has the encryption key $Gen_{EK}(1^n)$ as an additional input. Formally, in the definition of *operational secrecy* as *indistinguishability of single ciphertexts* given previously, the formula for the relationship between the success probabilities is replaced as follows:

$$\left| Prob[C_n(Gen_{EK}(1^n), Enc(Gen_{EK}(1^n), x)) = 1] \right.$$

$$\left. - Prob[C_n(Gen_{EK}(1^n), Enc(Gen_{EK}(1^n), y)) = 1] \right| < \frac{1}{p(n)} .$$

As in their original forms, the modified definitions are again equivalent, which can be proved by the same kind of reasoning:

Theorem 13.4   [equivalence of semantic and operational secrecy]

In the setting of an *asymmetric* key relationship and a *single* key usage, an encryption scheme satisfies the *semantic secrecy* property (for a single key usage) if and only if the *indistinguishability of* (single) *ciphertexts* holds.

13.11.3 The Settings for Multiple Key Usage

In order to save the overhead of key generation and distribution, in many applications the communication partners want to use an agreed key not only once but multiply. For these situations, we need appropriately adapted definitions of the secrecy properties. Basically, we only have to replace occurrences of a subexpression of the form $Enc(ek,term)$ by an expression of the form $\overline{Enc}(ek, term)$. In the latter expression, *term* denotes a sequence of plaintexts, to be encrypted using the same key ek, and, accordingly, $\overline{Enc}$ signifies the canonical extension of Enc, i.e.,

$$\overline{Enc}(ek, (x^1, \ldots, x^t)) = (Enc(ek, x^1), \ldots, Enc(ek, x^t)) .$$

Furthermore, in the definitions of the secrecy properties, the length t of the plaintext sequences considered must be bounded polynomially in the security parameter, and all plaintexts occurring in a sequence are assumed to be of equal length.

With a suitable elaboration of the adaptations sketched above, the equivalence of semantic secrecy and operational secrecy is valid for the symmetric case and for the asymmetric case as well, and the corresponding proofs are essentially the same as before.

Theorem 13.5   [equivalence of semantic and operational secrecy]

In the setting of a *symmetric* key relationship and *multiple* key usage, an encryption scheme satisfies the *semantic secrecy* property (for multiple key usage) if and only if the *indistinguishability of* (sequences of) *ciphertexts* holds.

Theorem 13.6   [equivalence of semantic and operational secrecy]

In the setting of an *asymmetric* key relationship and *multiple* key usage, an encryption scheme satisfies the *semantic secrecy* property (for multiple key usage) if and only if the *indistinguishability of* (sequences of) *ciphertexts* holds.

The multiple usage of a key raises the practically important question of whether an encryption scheme that has been proved to satisfy the secrecy property for *a single usage* necessarily does so for *multiple usage*. Surprisingly enough, there is a difference between the asymmetric and the symmetric setting. In the former case, the following theorem states a positive answer, the proof of which exploits substantially the availability of a public key.

Theorem 13.7   [in asymmetric setting: single usage iff multiple usage]

In the setting of an *asymmetric* key relationship, the indistinguishability of *single* ciphertexts holds for an encryption scheme if and only if the indistinguishability of *sequences* of ciphertexts holds.

Idea of Proof: In order to prove "⇒" in contraposition, a *hybrid argument* indicates that witnesses of a violation of the indistinguishability of *sequences* of ciphertexts can be used to construct a witness of a violation of the indistinguishability of *single* ciphertexts.   ❑

13.11.4 Constructions

The property of *semantic secrecy* is highly ambitious, and so one might wonder whether it can be satisfied at all. Basically, for both a symmetric setting and an asymmetric setting, the answers are affirmative provided a suitable assumption about *pseudorandomness* or *one-way functions with trapdoors*, respectively, holds. Thus semantic secrecy can be achieved, or at least approximated, according to one's success in producing pseudorandomness or in constructing one-way functions with trapdoors. Without giving formal details, in the following we shall only emphasize a general important lesson, and outline a generic construction method which has many variations.

The general important lesson is that secrecy-preserving encryptions must be *probabilistic*! Otherwise, if we used a deterministic encryption algorithm, then we could exhibit distinguishable ciphertexts. For an asymmetric setting, given a public key ek, the ciphertext of one plaintext x is easily distinguishable from the ciphertext of a different plaintext y. For a symmetric setting, a sequence of two ciphertexts stemming from the *same* plaintext x is easily distinguishable from a sequence of two ciphertexts belonging to two *different* plaintexts x_1 and x_2.

Regarding practical *asymmetric* mechanisms, *probabilistic encryption* is a built-in feature of ciphers that are based on *ElGamal functions* or *elliptic curves*. For ciphers based on *RSA functions*, some fresh *randomness* has to be suitably added for each usage of a public key.

Regarding practical *symmetric* mechanisms, the situation is more complicated and beyond the scope of this monograph. Roughly, whereas a single application of a block cipher such as DES, IDEA or AES works purely deterministically, a repeated application in the framework of *stream ciphers* offers options for introducing some kind of randomness.

For the *symmetric* setting, the generic construction method employs a simple but quite effective approach with four steps. On input of a plaintext string x and an encryption key ek, the *encryption algorithm* proceeds as follows:

1. Select a random bit string r.
2. Using ek, transform r by means of a suitable *keyed mechanism* and obtain some bit string k, to be used as a *one-time key* in the next step.
3. Compute $y = x \oplus k$, where the *XOR operation* is performed bitwise.
4. Send (r,y) as the ciphertext.

The corresponding *decryption algorithm* first recomputes the one-time key k from the received r by means of a decryption key dk matching ek, and then recovers the plaintext x from the received y by performing a bitwise *XOR operation* with the recomputed one-time key k.

Clearly, the second step of the encryption algorithm is most crucial, since it is responsible for producing something like a (pseudo)random *one-time key* for the *perfect encryption* in the third step.

A generic construction method for the *asymmetric* setting follows a similar approach, but employs a more sophisticated way to compute the one-time key needed for both encryption and decryption.

13.12 Bibliographic Hints

All textbooks on cryptography treat encryption as a main topic, and basically all textbooks on security in computing systems give at least an introduction to encryption; see Section 1.7 and Section 12.11. In particular, we acknowledge that the exposition by Stinson [470] was very helpful for our own presentation. The EU-funded Network of Excellence in Cryptology ECRYPT [182] is monitoring the recent achievements in efficiency, and many further aspects such as recommended key sizes as well. In addition to the general background, selected dedicated literature to the material presented in this chapter can be found as follows.

Shannon [443, 444] lays the foundation for analyzing the one-time key approach and for constructing perfect ciphers, which, however, has been known before. Stream ciphers with pseudorandom sequences are surveyed by Rueppel [414] and Schneier [437]. Goldreich [229] comments on such constructions, pointing to the foundational work of Blum/Micali [91] and Goldreich/Goldwasser/Micali [220].

The RSA encryption is based on the pioneering work of Rivest/Shamir/Adleman [409]. The ElGamal encryption is proposed by ElGamal [183], and Hankerson/Menezes/Vanstone [248] survey the elliptic-curve variants.

The standard documents for DES are published by the NBS [363] and ANSI [13]. Coppersmith [142] discusses some of the DES design criteria. Feistel [201] treats the Feistel network underlying DES. Smid/Branstad [451] examine the evolution of DES. Lai/Massey [304, 305] design and analyze IDEA, which is further investigated by, for example, Meier [348]. AES is fully described and investigated in depth by its inventors Daemen/Rijmen [156], who won the public NIST competition to design a successor to DES. The corresponding standard is published by NIST [365].

Block modes are published as standards by the NBS [364] and as a recommendation by Dworkin [178] for NIST.

Goldreich [229] provides a detailed exposition of a theory of encryption, from which we extracted our introduction, and where a rich bibliography with historical notes and suggestions for further reading can be found.

14 Authentication

14.1 Survey and Classification

An *authentication* mechanism aims primarily at enabling a receiver and, if applicable, further observers of a message to verify whether that message originates from the claimed sender and has not been substituted or modified since being sent. Thus, while messages might be generated and transmitted or stored in an environment that potentially facilitates manipulations against the interests of *integrity, authenticity* and *non-repudiation*, the receivers and possibly further participants have means to *detect* such manipulations.

Conversely and secondarily, given the possibility of manipulation, such a mechanism should prevent a sender from being successfully blamed for a message that he has *not* sent, either not at all or not in the version examined.

Basically, these two goals are achieved by equipping the sender with a *secret* that is used as an authentication key for adding a *cryptographic piece of evidence* (a *cryptographic exhibit*) to any of his messages. A particular cryptographic exhibit must be specific to the (exploited secret of the) actual sender and the message, in order to support verifications that are fair with respect to both the receiver's and the sender's concerns.

A more detailed introduction to authentication is presented in Subsection 12.4.2, where the basic ideas are visualized in Figure 12.3 and Figure 12.4. Most of the quality aspects presented in Section 12.5 for encryption can be adapted to authentication, though for authentication *active* attacks such as *impersonation* and *message substitution* are the primary concern. In Section 12.7, one selected quality aspect is studied in more technical terms, investigating *perfect authentication* within a *probability-theoretic* approach and leading to effective constructions that can be based on *combinatorial designs*. Like the approach discussed in Section 12.9 for encryption, an alternative *complexity-theoretic* approach based on *one-way functions* is available as well.

In this section, we survey the main concepts of and results on authentication and their impact on security in a more systematic way and in more technical depth, without fully repeating the introductory discussion already given in Chapter 12.

Basically, and with some variations, in this section the target of interest is an *authentication mechanism*, or a family of such mechanisms, that is given by three algorithms operating on three underlying sets. These sets and algorithms are as follows:

- A domain set D of (possible) *messages*.
- A range set R of (possible) *cryptographic exhibits*.
- A set K of (possible) *keys*, each of which comprises an *authentication key ak* and a *test key tk*. If there is a need to distinguish the components, or whenever it appears to be convenient to do so, we use a suitable notation such as $K = AK \times TK$, with $ak \in AK$ and $tk \in TK$.
- A *key generation* algorithm $Gen: \rightarrow K$, which might take a natural number l as a *security parameter*, typically for specifying the size of the generated key components.
- An *authentication* algorithm $Aut: AK \times D \rightarrow R$ that returns a cryptographic exhibit $red = Aut(ak,x) \in R$ for a message $x \in D$, using an authentication key $ak \in AK$.
- A *verification* algorithm $Test: TK \times D \times R \rightarrow \{true, false\}$ that, on input of (at least) a test key $tk \in TK$, a message $x \in D$ and a cryptographic exhibit $red \in R$, returns a Boolean value $Test(tk,x,red)$ that indicates *acceptance* (of the message as authentic and unmodified) or *rejection*.

The algorithms should satisfy (suitable variants of) the following properties:

- *Weak correctness*. Using a generated key pair, any authenticated message is accepted by the verification, i.e., for all keys $(ak,tk) \in AK \times TK$ generated by *Gen*, and for all messages $x \in D$,

  $Test(tk,x,Aut(ak,x)) = true$.

- *Unforgeability*. For all messages $x \in D$, without knowing the pertinent authentication key ak, an attacker cannot "determine" an element $red \in R$ such that $Test(tk,x,red) = true$. This *naive* version should be elaborated according to the peculiarities of the intended application and the mechanism applied.
- *Efficiency*. The algorithms *Gen*, *Aut* and *Test* are efficiently computable.

In some situations, the properties of weak correctness and unforgeability may be (naively) combined and strengthened as follows:

- *Strong correctness and weak unforgeability*. Regarding a generated key pair, *exactly* the authenticated messages are accepted by the verification, and without knowing the pertinent authentication key, an attacker cannot determine any authenticated message; i.e., for all keys $(ak,tk) \in AK \times TK$ generated by *Gen*, for all messages $x \in D$ and for all elements $red \in R$,

  $Test(tk,x,red) = true$ iff $red = Aut(ak,x)$,

  and without knowing the authentication key ak, an attacker cannot "determine" that red.

  In a typical application scenario, there are at least two designated participants Alice and Bob. Alice, or, if applicable, some other participant acting on behalf of Alice, who might be Bob, prepares for an authenticated *message transmission* from Alice to Bob by invoking the key generation algorithm *Gen*. Then the components of the generated key are distributed: the designated *sender* Alice keeps the authentication key *ak*, and the designated *receiver* Bob gets the test key *tk*. Later on, wanting to send an authenticated message to Bob, Alice calls the authentication algorithm *Aut* in order to compute the pertinent cryptographic exhibit with the help of the authentication key *ak*, and then she appends that cryptographic exhibit to the message. Having received the authenticated message, and while calling the verification algorithm *Test*, Bob exploits the test key *tk* in order to obtain a confirmation that the received object is authentic and unmodified. Some special authentication mechanisms use *interactive* verification algorithms that demand additional inputs from both the receiver and the sender, as *challenges* and *responses*, respectively. Clearly, as far as is actually required for the specific mechanism, only the designated participants should know the respective key components; in any case, the designated sender Alice must strictly protect her authentication key *ak*.

This description of the application scenario, however, ignores the possibility that another participant, Malory, might try to actively *forge* messages, possibly after passively observing (honestly) authenticated messages, and the description implicitly assumes that both the sender Alice and the receiver Bob are *honest*. However, under all anticipated circumstances, and to the specific extent of the mechanism under consideration, the required versions of the *correctness* property and the *unforgeability* property should guarantee that neither forgeries by Malory nor dishonest behavior by Alice or Bob will achieve their respective goal. Roughly outlined:

- An *attacker* Malory should not be able to successfully forge a message such that the message is accepted by Bob and thereby attributed to Alice.
- A *dishonest sender* Alice should not be able to successfully deny a message actually authenticated and sent by her.
- A dishonest (or misled) *receiver* Bob should not be able to successfully blame Alice for a message she has not actually sent.

14.1.1 Classification

For our exposition, we employ a rough classification of authentication mechanisms by identifying three particularly important aspects and their respective alternatives:

- *Relationship between keys*: *symmetric* or *asymmetric*.
- *Qualification of cryptographic exhibits in disputes*: only for *internal* usage, or for *external* presentation to any third party as an arbitrator.
- *Justification of the security properties*: *one-time key*, *one-way function* or *chaos*.

We emphasize that these aspects are dependent on each other, and that in general the alternatives are not sharply separated.

Regarding the *relationship between the keys*, i.e., between an authentication key and the matching test key, there are two options. For a *symmetric* mechanism, the two components of a matching key pair are basically the same. For an *asymmetric* mechanism, however, the two components have to be essentially different, allowing one to make the test key *public* whereas the authentication key has to remain *private* for the designated sender of authenticated messages. For asymmetric mechanisms, the security properties must include a *secrecy property*, requiring that one cannot determine the private authentication key from the public test key.

Regarding the *qualification of cryptographic exhibits in disputes*, the alternatives are strongly dependent on the alternative selected with respect to the relationship between the keys.

For a *symmetric* authentication mechanism, all key holders are equally *distinguished* and, accordingly, they can exploit authentication only for their *internal* usage. Typically, the sender and the receiver mutually trust each other (and, if applicable, both of them trust the third party that has generated the secret key), and their joint interest is to detect malicious impersonation and substitution or modification potentially performed by somebody else.

For an *asymmetric* authentication mechanism, only the sender is *distinguished*, by exclusively knowing the authentication key, and, additionally, with the provision of *certification*, the matching test key is (potentially) available to any third party that is applied to as an *arbitrator*. Accordingly, all participants involved can exploit authentication for *external* presentation to anybody, which clearly includes internal usage too. Typically, the sender and the receiver, as well as any third party, do not fully trust each other, and thus each of them might be seen not only as a cooperation partner but also as a dishonest attacker as well, in addition to further malicious participants aiming at impersonation and substitution or modification. As important examples, this situation occurs in informational activities such as Internet communication between strangers, and in electronic commerce and administration based on such communication. For such applications, the asymmetric cryptographic exhibits, which are also called *digital signatures*, are intended to be employed in a similar way to traditional *handwritten signatures*.

Regarding *the justification of the security properties*, there are basically three approaches, called succinctly in this monograph the *one-time key, one-way function* and *chaos*, as for encryption. For the sake of brevity, we shall not provide summaries of these approaches; instead, we refer to the corresponding expositions for encryption mechanisms in Subsection 13.1.2 (where some changes are necessary because of the differences with respect to distinction and trust relationships), the tabular summary presented in the following subsection, and the more detailed treatments throughout this and other sections.

14.1.2 A Tabular Summary

Table 14.1 summarizes the material about authentication presented. We take the *justification of a secrecy property* as the primary feature, and briefly indicate the pertinent further features for each of the three alternatives. Some more details can be found in the respective sections of this and other relevant chapters. However, in general, we only sketch the mechanisms and only discuss selected aspects. For more refined expositions, thorough justifications of the unforgeability property, extensive analyses of known weaknesses, recommended key lengths, standards, available implementations, experience in various application fields and many further aspects, the reader should consult the rich literature. Moreover, in addition to the few examples presented, there are several further authentication systems, whose comprehensive treatment is beyond the scope of this monograph.

Table 14.1. Basic approaches to authentication, and their features

	One-time key	**One-way function**	**Chaos**
Key length	longer than message	short, but too long for exhaustive search	short, but too long for exhaustive search
Key usage	single	multiple	multiple
Key kind	random row index of a suitable orthogonal array, implemented, e.g., as a pair of elements of some field	derived from random elements of some algebraic structure; with a public and a private component	random bit string
Key relationship	symmetric	asymmetric	symmetric
Secret holder	sender and receiver	sender	sender and receiver
Key distribution	secret communication from generator to sender and receiver	certification and open dissemination of public key	secret communication from generator to sender and receiver
Qualification for disputes	only internal usage	external presentation as digital signature	only internal usage
Authentication algorithm	determine entry in suitable orthogonal array, e.g., algebraic operations in some field	algebraic operations used as one-way functions, as selected by the private key	hash of blockwise encryption with suitably chained block modes
Verification algorithm	recomputation of exhibit and comparison with received exhibit	verification of an equation on algebraic terms, as enabled by the public key	recomputation of exhibit and comparison with received exhibit
Security	probability-theoretic	complexity-theoretic	empirical (theory-based experience)

Table 14.1. Basic approaches to authentication, and their features (cont.)

	One-time key	One-way function	Chaos
Justification of security	even after interception of an authenticated message, all possible exhibits are equiprobable, since sufficiently many keys are still possible	inversion of one-way function without knowing the private key (trapdoor) computationally infeasible	confusion and diffusion
Trust requirements	randomness and secrecy of the key	randomness and correctness of the key; secrecy of the private key; validity of complexity-theoretic assumption	randomness and secrecy of the key; effectiveness of confusion and diffusion
Application fields	primarily of theoretical interest	primarily when full control of key handling by designated sender is needed; for electronic commerce and administration	primarily when control of key handling by trusted environment is tolerated; for internal message protection
Examples	Authentication Code	RSA, ElGamal, DSA, EC	MACs produced by CBC, CFB, CCM

14.2 One-Time Keys and Perfect Authentication (Orthogonal Arrays)

The *one-time key* authentication mechanism in the special form derived from *orthogonal arrays* is based on Theorem 12.4 about a condition for *perfectness*, as presented in Section 12.7. The mechanism is *symmetric*; in fact, the authentication key and the test key are identical, and the verification algorithm merely checks whether the received cryptographic exhibit equals the recomputed one. The mechanism is restricted to a *single* key usage. If, additionally, the key is *truly randomly* selected, the mechanism achieves *perfect* or *probability-theoretic security*.

Before presenting the technical details of the mechanism, we shall rephrase the formal considerations of Section 12.7 in more intuitive terms, regarding first impersonation attacks and then substitution attacks.

An *impersonation* attack aims at faking the fact that the designated sender Alice has sent a message even though she actually has not. This attack is relevant even if the message set D contains only one element x_A. To prevent this attack, we need at least two different *cryptographic exhibits*. So let us assume that the set of actually occurring exhibits is $R = \{y_0, \ldots, y_{m-1}\}$ with $m \geq 2$. Accordingly, the needed authentication algorithm *Aut* partitions the set K of keys into m pairwise disjoint and nonempty pre-images $K_0, \ldots, K_{m-1}$ such that, for $i = 0, \ldots, m-1$,

$$Aut(k, x_A) = y_i \text{ for all } k \in K_i.$$

Assume that the designated sender Alice randomly selects a secret key $k_A \in K = K_0 \cup \ldots \cup K_{m-1}$ without having actually employed it so far. To impersonate the sender, the attacker Malory has to determine the exhibit $y_A = Aut(k_A, x_A)$ that the sender would use, i.e., to guess the pertinent pre-image K_A with $k_A \in K_A$. If all events "secret key k is element of pre-image K_i" are assumed to be equiprobable, Malory will succeed with probability $1/\text{card } R$. Thus, to keep Malory's success probability small, Alice should reserve a large number of possible exhibits and, accordingly, a large number of keys as well, as visualized in Figure 14.2.

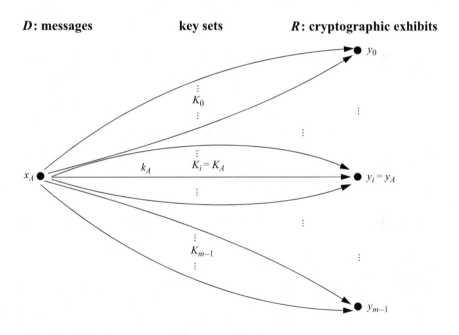

Fig. 14.2. Success probability $1/m$ for an impersonation attack under the assumption that the events "secret key k is element of pre-image K_i" are equiprobable

Extending the situation sketched so far to the case where there are two or more possible messages in D, assume now that Alice has used her secret key k_A for the message x_A and Malory has observed the authenticated message x_A with exhibit y_A. Malory can then potentially gain the information that the key involved is an element of the pertinent pre-image set K_A of keys mapping x_A on y_A, thereby substantially reducing the search space for the hidden key from the full set K to the $1/m$ fraction K_A. To avoid the resulting threat, Alice should never reuse the key.

Moreover, Alice must prepare for a *substitution attack* which aims at intercepting Alice's original message x_A, substituting it by another message x_M and replacing the exhibit accordingly. Exploiting his potential knowledge about Alice's secret key, Malory has to guess the exhibit that Alice would produce for the substituted message, i.e., Malory must select the pertinent key from within the search space K_A. To prevent this attack, Alice should ensure that K_A is still rich enough to map the substituted message x_M to *any* of the possible exhibits. Hence, the already reduced set K_A must contain at least as many keys as there are possible exhibits.

Generalizing the recommendations derived in the examples above, Alice should look for an authentication mechanism that uses equiprobable keys and satisfies the following *combinatorial design* property:

> For all pairs of an intercepted message $x_i \in D$ (14.1)
> and a substituted message $x_j \in D$ with $x_i \neq x_j$,
> and for all pairs of the correct, intercepted exhibit $y_i \in R$
> and a possible (potentially faked) exhibit y_j,
> there exists a key $k \in K$ such that both $Aut(k,x_i) = y_i$ and $Aut(k,x_j) = y_j$.

For the simple example of a message set $D = \{0,1\}$ and an exhibit set $R = \{0,1\}$, this property demands a key set with (at least) four elements, say $K = \{00, 01, 10, 11\}$. Figure 14.3 shows three forms of an implementation, as a graph, a function table and an algebraic expression. Except for notation, this implementation is identical to the example visualized in Figure 12.10 and, accordingly, it is *perfect* provided the keys are equally distributed.

The construction shown in Figure 14.3 can be generalized by interpreting the function table as an orthogonal array with parameters $(2,2,1)$. More specifically, an *orthogonal array* with parameters (m,n,λ) is given as a matrix

$$A = \left[y_{k,x} \right]_{1 \leq k \leq \lambda m^2, \, 1 \leq x \leq n}$$

of size $\lambda m^2 \times n$, over an underlying set R with card $R = m$, satisfying the following *combinatorial design* property:

> for each pair of different columns $x_i \neq x_j$ and   (14.2)
> for each pair $(y_i, y_j) \in R \times R$,
> there exist exactly λ rows k with $y_{k,x_i} = y_i$ and $y_{k,x_j} = y_j$.

Given any such orthogonal array, we can construct an *one-time key authentication mechanism* with the following sets:

- messages: (bit strings representing) positive integers in the set $D = \{1, 2, ..., n\}$ according to the columns of the orthogonal array;
- cryptographic exhibits: (bit strings representing) positive integers in the set $R = \{1, 2, ..., m\}$ according to the underlying set of the orthogonal array;
- keys: (bit strings representing) positive integers in the set $K = \{1, 2, ..., \lambda m^2\}$ according to the rows of the orthogonal array.

a)   **D: messages   K: keys**   **R: cryptographic exhibits**

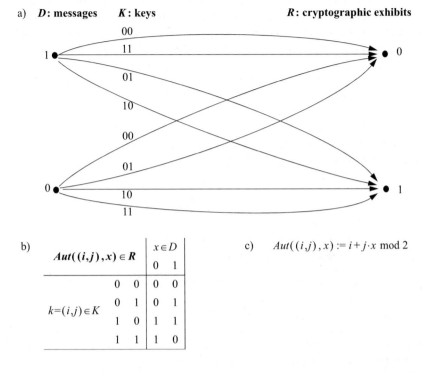

b)

$Aut((i,j),x) \in R$		$x \in D$	
		0	1
$k=(i,j) \in K$	0 0	0	0
	0 1	0	1
	1 0	1	1
	1 1	1	0

c) $Aut((i,j),x) := i + j \cdot x \bmod 2$

Fig. 14.3. A (best possible) authentication mechanism, specified as (a) graph, (b) a function table and (c) an algebraic expression

The three algorithms of the mechanism can be outlined as follows:

- The *key generation* algorithm *Gen* selects a "truly random" element k of the key set $\{1,2,...,\lambda m^2\}$.
- The *authentication* algorithm *Aut* returns $Aut(k,x) = y_{k,x}$.
- The *verification* algorithm *Test* merely checks whether the received cryptographic exhibit *red* equals the recomputed exhibit $Aut(k,x)$ for the received message x, i.e., $Test(k,x,red)$ returns *true* iff $red = Aut(k,x)$.

The one-time key authentication mechanism is obviously (strongly) *correct* by the definition of the verification algorithm. Considering the transmission of a *single* message, the mechanism achieves a best possible *unforgeability property* according to Property 5 stated in Theorem 12.4, since by the combinatorial design property (14.2) and the definitions of the mechanism, we have, for $x_i \neq x_j$ and all y_i and y_j,

$$\text{card } \{ k \mid Aut(k,x_i) = y_i \ \wedge \ Aut(k,x_j) = y_j \} = \lambda = \frac{\lambda m^2}{m^2} = \frac{\text{card } K}{(\text{card } R)^2} . \quad (14.3)$$

Notably, for $\lambda = 1$ and each prime number p, there actually exists a suitable *orthogonal array* with parameters $(p,p,1)$, which can be obtained by further generalizing the construction shown in Figure 14.3. We simply consider the algebraic expression for the set $\{0,1\}$ as a special case of an expression for the set $\{0,1,\ldots,p-1\}$, seen as the underlying set of the *finite field* $(\mathbf{Z}_p,+,\cdot,0,1)$. More precisely, we select the column set (for messages) and the underlying set (for exhibits) as $\mathbf{Z}_p$, and the row set (for keys) as $\mathbf{Z}_p \times \mathbf{Z}_p$, and define

$$y_{(i,j),x} = i + j \cdot x \bmod p. \tag{14.4}$$

This definition satisfies the required design property for $\lambda = 1$. For, with respect to the above finite field, the two equations

$$i + j \cdot x_1 = y_1 \bmod p \text{ and}$$

$$i + j \cdot x_2 = y_2 \bmod p$$

have a unique solution for the unknown i and j (representing a row), for all given (columns) $x_1 \neq x_2$ and all (elements of the underlying set) y_1 and y_2.

To apply this construction in an arbitrary context, we can proceed as follows. Given a message set D and a required quality $MaxProb_{imp} \leq \varepsilon$ and $MeanProb_{subst} \leq \varepsilon$ of the wanted authentication algorithm in the sense of Section 12.7, we determine a sufficiently large prime number p such that $1/p \leq \varepsilon$ and card $D \leq p$, and consider a suitable orthogonal array with parameters $(p,p,1)$; out of the p columns of this array, we select card D of them for the representation of the messages in D.

Considering the transmission of a *single* message, the one-time key authentication mechanism is qualified to the best extent possible regarding the *unforgeability property* under both impersonation and substitution attacks. However, as a trade-off for best unforgeability – proved to be inevitable by the results of Section 12.7 – the secret (authentication and test) key can be used *only once*, and it must be *substantially longer* than the anticipated message. Hence, this perfect approach can be employed in practice only for dedicated applications with extremely high unforgeability requirements.

14.3 RSA Asymmetric Digital Signatures

The *RSA authentication* mechanism is an example of the *one-way function* approach, originally pioneering but now in widespread use, and leads to *digital signatures*. It is based on RSA functions and their properties, as presented in Subsection 12.9.2. The mechanism is *asymmetric*, admitting *multiple* key usage. It achieves *complexity-theoretic security*, provided the *factorization conjecture* and the *RSA conjecture* hold, the key is properly generated and sufficiently long, and some additional care is taken.

More specifically, given a suitable *RSA function* $RSA_{p,q,d}^{n,e}$ with a *private key* (p,q,d) and a *public key* (n,e), we obtain an authentication (digital signature) mechanism that essentially exchanges the roles of encryption and decryption, operating as follows, at least similarly regarding the preprocessing and postprocessing:

- A message m is preprocessed by computing a hash value $h(m)$ using an agreed protocol for a *one-way hash function*.
- The authentication treats the hash value like a ciphertext by computing the "RSA decryption" $red = h(m)^d \bmod n$, to serve as the cryptographic exhibit for the message m sent by the distinguished holder of the private key.
- The verification recovers the presumable hash value by computing the "RSA-encryption" $red^e \bmod n$ and compares the result with the freshly recomputed hash value of the received message m.

Accordingly, for each fixed setting of an RSA function $RSA_{p,q,d}^{n,e}$, the RSA authentication (signature) mechanism operates on the following sets:

- messages: bit strings over the set $\{0,1\}$ that can be mapped by the agreed one-way hash function h to bit strings basically of length ld n, seen as positive numbers less than n (residues modulo n);
- cryptographic exhibits: bit strings over the set $\{0,1\}$, basically of length ld n, seen as positive numbers less than n (residues modulo n);
- keys: given the public key (n,e), in principle there is a unique residue modulo n that can be used as the private decryption exponent d, whose binary representation is a bit string, basically of length ld n or less; however, from the point of view of the nondistinguished participants, this decryption exponent cannot be "determined".

The three algorithms of the mechanism can be outlined as follows:

- The *key generation* algorithm *Gen* selects the parameters of an RSA function, depending on a given *security parameter* that basically determines the length of the key. Briefly summarized, the algorithm proceeds as follows: generate randomly two large prime numbers p and q of the length required by the security parameter; compute the modulus $n := p \cdot q$; select randomly an encryption exponent e that is relatively prime to $\phi(n) = (p-1) \cdot (q-1)$; and compute the decryption exponent d as the solution of $e \cdot d \equiv 1 \bmod \phi(n)$.
- The *authentication* (*signature*) algorithm *Aut* takes a message m of an appropriate length and returns $red = h(m)^d \bmod n$, where h is an agreed *one-way hash function*.
- The *verification* algorithm *Test* takes the received cryptographic exhibit *red* and computes $hash := red^e \bmod n$. Furthermore, the algorithm takes the received message m, determines its hash value $h(m)$ and then checks whether this (correct) hash value equals the (received) value *hash*, i.e.,

$Test((n,e),m,red)$ returns *true* iff $h(m) = red^e \bmod n$.

To investigate the fundamental properties of *correctness*, *unforgeability* and *efficiency*, we first ignore the application of the one-way hash function. The basic aspects of these properties can then easily be derived from the discussions in Subsection 12.9.2, Appendix A.4.3, Appendix A.4.4, and Section 13.4. In fact, regarding *correctness*, for example, the commutativity of multiplication and exponentiation, i.e.,

$$\text{for all } b, e_1, e_2: b^{e_1} \cdot b^{e_2} = b^{e_1 \cdot e_2} = b^{e_2 \cdot e_1} = b^{e_2} \cdot b^{e_1}, \tag{14.5}$$

is inherited by the encryption function $x^e \bmod n$ and the decryption function $y^d \bmod n$. Accordingly, Theorem 12.7 actually implies that these functions are mutually inverse, independent of the application order.

More generally, not only the RSA encryption mechanism, but also any *commutative* (asymmetric) *encryption* mechanism with encryption algorithms *Enc* and *Dec* that satisfy, for all plaintexts or ciphertexts x and for all keys (ek, dk), the equation

$$Dec(dk, Enc(ek, x)) = Enc(ek, Dec(dk, x)) \tag{14.6}$$

can be converted into an *authentication (signature) mechanism* with algorithms

$Aut(dk, x) = Dec(dk, x)$ and
$Test(ek, x, red) = true$ iff $x = Enc(ek, red)$,

using the private decryption key dk as the authentication key and the public encryption key ek as the test key.

The *correctness* of the authentication is then implied by the encryption correctness, since we have

$$Enc(ek, Aut(dk, x)) = Enc(ek, Dec(dk, x)) = Dec(dk, Enc(ek, x)) = x.$$

Similarly, the *unforgeability* is implied by the secrecy of the encryption. To show this, assume indirectly that an attacker, without knowing the private key dk, could "determine" an exhibit red_0 for a message x_0 such that $Test(ek, x_0, red_0) = true$, i.e., $x_0 = Enc(ek, red_0)$ and thus $Dec(dk, x_0) = Dec(dk, Enc(ek, red_0)) = red_0$. This attacker would then be able to "determine" the "plaintext" red_0 corresponding to the "ciphertext" x_0, thereby violating the property of encryption secrecy.

For the RSA authentication, as for many other authentication methods, the application of the *one-way hash function* is both convenient and necessary, but not harmful. It is convenient because (nearly arbitrarily) long messages can be treated in this way by replacing a message by a suitably short *fingerprint* that fits the size restrictions resulting from the key parameters.

The application of the one-way hash function is necessary in order to prevent some *existential forgeries*, i.e., attacks that succeed in some special situations. For example, without the one-way hash function, the *multiplicativity property* (*homomorphism property*) (13.2) of the exponentiation function enables one to compute the correct RSA signature of some composite messages from the already known signatures of factors without employing the private signature exponent d.

The simplest examples arise from the following congruences mod n, where the full authentication key is abbreviated by its private component d:

$$Aut(d, x_1 \cdot x_2) \equiv (x_1 \cdot x_2)^d \equiv x_1^d \cdot x_2^d \equiv Aut(d, x_1) \cdot Aut(d, x_2). \qquad (14.7)$$

More sophisticated examples need to exploit only one known signature and an appropriate invertibility condition, and are based on the following congruences mod n:

$$Aut(d, x_1 \cdot x_2^e) \equiv (x_1 \cdot x_2^e)^d \equiv x_1^d \cdot x_2^{e \cdot d} \equiv Aut(d, x_1) \cdot x_2. \qquad (14.8)$$

If the one-way hash function is applied, then these and similar attacks are still possible for some *hash values* (rather than the messages themselves). However, supposing the properties of one-way hash functions introduced in Subsection 12.4.5, an attacker would not be able to "determine" the messages that have the critical hash values, and thus such attacks would be useless.

Though, in principle, the application of the one-way hash function weakens the strength of the correctness and unforgeability of the overall mechanism, the properties of one-way hash functions referred to above also enforce the condition that the correctness and unforgeability are sufficiently well approximated.

14.4 ElGamal Asymmetric Digital Signatures

The *ElGamal authentication* mechanism is another well-known example of the *one-way function* approach, leading to *digital signatures*. It is based on the setting of ElGamal functions and their properties, as presented in Subsection 12.9.3. The mechanism is *asymmetric*, admitting *multiple* key usage. It achieves *complexity-theoretic security*, provided the *discrete logarithm conjecture* and appropriate variants of the *ElGamal conjecture* hold, the key is properly generated and sufficiently long, and some additional care is taken.

Roughly, given the setting of a suitable *ElGamal function* $EG_a^{p, g, A}$ with a *private key a* and a *public key* (p, g, A), we obtain an authentication (digital signature) mechanism that essentially blinds a randomly selected argument k, as the ElGamal function itself does, and additionally determines a suitable "verification exponent" for calculations with exponents of the public generator g. This verification exponent depends on the blinded k, the hash value of the message m, and the private exponent a.

More specifically, for each fixed setting of an ElGamal function $EG_a^{p, g, A}$, the ElGamal authentication mechanism operates on the following sets:

- messages: bit strings over the set $\{0,1\}$ that can be mapped by an agreed *one-way hash function h* to bit strings basically of length ld $(p-1)$, seen as positive numbers less than $p-1$ (residues modulo $p-1$);

- cryptographic exhibits: pairs (red_1, red_2) of bit strings over the set $\{0,1\}$, basically of length ld p and ld ($p-1$), respectively, where the first component is seen as a positive number less than p (a residue modulo p) and the second component is seen as a positive number less than $p-1$ (a residue modulo $p-1$);
- keys: given the public key (p,g,A), in principle there is a unique positive number less than $p-1$ that can be used as the private exponent a, whose binary representation is a bit string, basically of length ld ($p-1$); however, from the point of view of the nondistinguished participants, this private exponent cannot be "determined".

The three algorithms of the mechanism can be outlined as follows:

- The *key generation* algorithm *Gen* selects the parameters of an ElGamal function, depending on a given *security parameter* that basically determines the length of the key. Briefly summarized, the algorithm proceeds as follows: generate a large prime number p of the length required by the security parameter; select a primitive element g of $\mathbf{Z}_p^*$; select randomly a private exponent a; and compute the public "blinded exponent" $A = g^a \bmod p$.
- The *authentication (signature)* algorithm *Aut* takes a message m of an appropriate length and first computes the hash value $h(m) \in \mathbf{Z}_{p-1}$ with $h(m) \neq 0$, where h is an agreed *one-way hash function*. Then the algorithm generates a random bit string k, seen as a positive number less than $p-1$ that is multiplicatively invertible modulo $p-1$, i.e., under this interpretation, $k \in \mathbf{Z}_{p-1}^*$, and the algorithm returns

$$red_1 = g^k \bmod p \quad \text{and} \quad red_2 = k^{-1} \cdot (h(m) - a \cdot red_1) \bmod p - 1. \quad (14.9)$$

- The *verification* algorithm *Test* takes the received message m, determines its hash value $h(m)$, and then basically checks whether this (correct) hash value and the received cryptographic exhibit (red_1, red_2) match with respect to the public key (p,g,A) by verifying the following conditions:

$$1 \leq red_1 \leq p - 1, \quad (14.10)$$

$$A^{red_1} \cdot red_1^{red_2} \equiv g^{h(m)} \bmod p. \quad (14.11)$$

Test$((p,g,A),m,(red_1,red_2))$ returns *true* iff both conditions hold.

Regarding the properties of *correctness* and *unforgeability*, to simplify, we first ignore the application of the one-way hash function and consider the achievements of the mechanism for $x := h(m)$. A signature (red_1, red_2) produced by the authentication algorithm *Aut* satisfies the condition (14.10) by the first part of the definition (14.9). Furthermore, we have the following congruences modulo p according to the exponentiation rules:

$$A^{red_1} \cdot red_1^{red_2}$$

$$\equiv g^{a \cdot red_1} \cdot g^{k \cdot k^{-1} \cdot (x - a \cdot red_1)} \qquad \text{by the definition of } A, red_1 \text{ and } red_2$$

$$\equiv g^{x} \qquad\qquad\qquad\qquad \text{by exponent calculations modulo } p-1.$$

Thus the condition (14.11) is satisfied as well. Hence the mechanism is weakly correct.

Conversely, suppose that some (red_1, red_2) matches some x, in particular, that the simplified condition (14.11) holds. Considering the discrete logarithm of red_1, i.e., the uniquely determined k with $g^k \equiv red_1 \bmod p$, substituting the second occurrence of red_1 in condition (14.11) accordingly, and replacing A by its definition, we derive the following congruences modulo p according to the exponentiation rules:

$$g^{a \cdot red_1} \cdot g^{k \cdot red_2} \equiv g^{a \cdot red_1 + k \cdot red_2} \equiv g^{x}. \qquad (14.12)$$

Since g is a primitive element and thus a generator of the multiplicative group, the second congruence modulo p of (14.12) is equivalent to the corresponding congruence modulo $p-1$ for the exponents, i.e., we obtain the property

$$a \cdot red_1 + k \cdot red_2 \equiv x \bmod p - 1. \qquad (14.13)$$

Supposing that k is multiplicatively invertible modulo $p-1$, the congruence (14.13) has a unique solution for red_2, namely just the value that the authentication algorithm computes according to (14.9) for the second component of the exhibit. Thus, under the above simplification, the mechanism is also strongly correct and, under appropriate conjectures regarding the infeasibility of determining the blinded private exponent a and the blinded random element k, the mechanism achieves unforgeability.

It is important to note that the above reasoning requires that the random bit string k is kept secret and never used twice. Otherwise, if an attacker knows a k that has been employed, he can determine the private exponent a from the defining equations (14.9) and thus achieve *complete success* regarding *forgeries*. Similarly, if an attacker knows that a random bit string k has been used for two different messages, he can inspect the solutions regarding k for the two instances of the verification congruence (14.11) and, finally, determine the value actually used, which then again enables complete success.

On the one hand, in principle the application of a one-way hash function weakens the strength of the correctness and unforgeability. But, supposing the properties introduced in Subsection 12.4.5, strong correctness is still sufficiently well approximated in practice, as is unforgeability. On the other hand, as with many other authentication methods, the one-way hash function is needed to prevent some *existential forgeries*, and it conveniently enables the treatment of (nearly arbitrarily) long messages.

Further aspects of the properties of *unforgeability* and *efficiency* are discussed in Subsection 12.9.3, Appendix A.4.3, Appendix A.4.4, and 13.5, and will not be repeated here.

14.5 DSA, the Digital Signature Algorithm

The *Digital Signature Algorithm* (*DSA*) is an *authentication* mechanism that has been standardized by NIST (the U.S. National Institute of Standards and Technology). DSA follows the *one-way function* approach, leading to *digital signatures*. It is closely related to the ElGamal authentication method:

- DSA employs a variant of the setting of *ElGamal functions* by replacing the multiplicative group $\mathbf{Z}_p^*$, which has a non-prime cardinality $p-1$, by a suitably selected subgroup G_q whose cardinality is a prime number q. Basically, the properties presented in Subsection 12.9.3 also apply for this variant, but the prime cardinality of G_q offers additional advantages.
- For the sake of efficiency, DSA slightly changes the second component of a cryptographic exhibit and adapts the verification condition accordingly.
- DSA suggests a set of standardized variations regarding the key parameters.

The mechanism is *asymmetric*, admitting *multiple* key usage. It achieves *complexity-theoretic security*, provided the pertinent *discrete logarithm conjecture* and the appropriate variant of the *ElGamal conjecture* hold and the key is properly generated.

We shall only outline and briefly annotate the three algorithms of the mechanism:

- The *key generation* algorithm *Gen* first selects a prime number q satisfying the size condition $2^{159} < q < 2^{160}$, whose binary representation thus has a standard length of 160. Then the algorithm determines another prime number p such that the factorization condition $q \mid p-1$ and the size condition $2^{511+64t} < p < 2^{512+64t}$ for some $t \in \{0,1,\ldots,8\}$ hold; accordingly, the binary representation of p has a standardized length that is a multiple of 64 and might vary between 512 and 1024. By the factorization condition, the multiplicative group $\mathbf{Z}_p^*$ has a subgroup G_q with exactly q elements, i.e., about 2^{160} elements. The algorithm selects any non-unit element g of this subgroup as a generator. Finally, the algorithm randomly selects a private exponent a and derives the public "blinded exponent" $A = g^a \bmod p$. As a result, (p, q, g, A) and a are returned as the *public key* and the *private key*, respectively.
- The *authentication* (*signature*) algorithm *Aut* takes a message m of any length and first computes the hash value $h(m) \in \{1,2,\ldots,q-1\} = \mathbf{Z}_q^*$, where h is a standardized *one-way hash function*. Then the algorithm generates a random bit string $k \in \{1,2,\ldots,q-1\} = \mathbf{Z}_q^*$. Thus both $h(m)$ and k are suitable exponents for the generator g to produce elements of the selected subgroup G_q. Finally, the algorithm returns the cryptographic exhibit

$$red_1 \;=\; (g^k \bmod p) \bmod q \quad \text{and} \tag{14.14}$$

$$red_2 \;=\; k^{-1} \cdot (h(m) + a \cdot red_1) \bmod q , \tag{14.15}$$

provided these components are nonzero; otherwise, another selection of k is tried. Accordingly, both components are suitable to be used as exponents for the generator g as well.

- The *verification* algorithm *Test* takes the received message m, determines its hash value $h(m)$ and then, basically, checks whether this (correct) hash value and the received cryptographic exhibit (red_1, red_2) match with respect to the public key (p, q, g, A), by verifying the following conditions:

$$1 \leq red_1 \leq q - 1 \text{ and } 1 \leq red_2 \leq q - 1, \tag{14.16}$$

$$red_1 \equiv \left(\left(g^{red_2^{-1} \cdot h(m) \bmod q} \cdot A^{red_1 \cdot red_2^{-1} \bmod q} \right) \bmod p \right) \bmod q. \tag{14.17}$$

$Test((p, q, g, A), m, (red_1, red_2))$ returns *true* iff both conditions hold.

We conclude this outline by justifying the property of (*weak*) *correctness*, for simplicity ignoring the impact of the one-way hash function. A cryptographic exhibit (red_1, red_2) for the hash value $h(m)$ produced by the authentication algorithm *Aut* satisfies the condition (14.16) by the definitions (14.14) and (14.15) and the additional nonzero test. Furthermore, according to the exponentiation rules, we have the following congruences modulo p, where all calculations for the exponents are modulo q:

$$g^{red_2^{-1} \cdot h(m) \bmod q} \cdot A^{red_1 \cdot red_2^{-1} \bmod q}$$

$$\equiv g^{red_2^{-1} \cdot h(m) \bmod q} \cdot g^{a \cdot red_1 \cdot red_2^{-1} \bmod q} \qquad \text{by the definition of } A$$

$$\equiv g^{red_2^{-1} \cdot (h(m) + a \cdot red_1) \cdot k^{-1} \cdot k \bmod q}$$

$$\equiv g^{k} \qquad \text{by the definition of } red_2.$$

This congruence modulo p implies the corresponding congruence modulo q, and thus the condition (14.17) is satisfied as well.

14.6 Digital Signatures Based on Elliptic Curves

As already discussed in Subsection 12.9.4 in general and briefly exemplified in Section 13.6 for encryption, cryptographic mechanisms that are based on ElGamal functions or related functions and exploit the conjectured intractability of computing the discrete logarithm can be generalized and adapted to *elliptic curves*. Basically, the elliptic-curve approach follows the *one-way function* approach, and exploits the properties of appropriately constructed finite cyclic groups derived from elliptic curves based on a finite field.

The resulting *authentication* mechanisms are *asymmetric*, leading to *digital signatures*, and admit *multiple* key usage. They achieve *complexity-theoretic security*, provided the pertinent *discrete logarithm conjecture* and related conjectures hold, the key is properly generated and sufficiently long, and some additional care is taken. In particular, the Digital Signature Algorithm has been transferred to the elliptic-curve approach, resulting in the *Elliptic Curve Digital Signature Algorithm* (*ECDSA*), which has been standardized as well.

Without presenting further technical details, we emphasize that the elliptic-curve approach offers a large variety of alternatives to the still predominant RSA approach; hopefully, this will diminish the dependence of secure computing on the special unproven conjectures regarding the RSA approach. Moreover, the elliptic-curve approach promises to achieve the wanted degree of secrecy with an improved efficiency in comparison with the RSA approach. It should also be noted that further families of alternatives have been proposed and are currently under research.

14.7 Undeniable Signatures

The use of *undeniable signatures* provides a further example of an *authentication* mechanism that follows the *one-way function* approach. As with the DSA, a variant of the setting of *ElGamal functions* is used, where the multiplicative group $\mathbf{Z}_p^*$ is replaced by a suitably selected subgroup G_q with a prime cardinality. The mechanism is *asymmetric*, admitting *multiple* key usage. It achieves *complexity-theoretic security*, provided the pertinent *discrete logarithm conjecture* holds and the key is properly generated.

Undeniable signatures exhibit the following innovative features:

- The *verification algorithm* implements an *interactive challenge–response protocol*, where both the supposed signer and the tester are involved. Accordingly, even a valid signature can be successfully tested only if the supposed signer cooperates, and thus a legitimate signer cannot be held responsible for a message without being informed about the respective evaluation. Most notably, this property does not usually hold for traditional *handwritten* signatures on paper documents (except when the signer must appear in person and produce another signature to be compared with the one inspected).
- The verification algorithm ensures plain *unforgeability* with only a small, adaptable *error probability*, which basically reflects the provably unlikely event that a forger can determine an acceptable response to a challenge referring to a forged (invalid) signature.
- Given the indispensable need for a signer's cooperation in verifying a signature, the tester has to protect against a fraudulent signer who purposely deviates from the specified verification algorithm in order to deny a *valid* signature. The protection against this kind of attacking behavior is achieved by structuring the verification algorithm as follows: in two independent challenge–response rounds, the algorithm attempts to satisfy an *acceptance condition*; if both attempts fail, the evaluation of a *disavowal condition* leads to a final decision. The disavowal condition first of all enables the tester to detect a denial fraud of the kind mentioned, again with only a small, adaptable *error probability*. Clearly, the overall

algorithm must also respect the conflicting interest of the *distinguished* holder of the pertinent private signature key in not being blamed for an *invalid* signature.

- The remaining possibility of "attacking behavior" by a supposed signer, namely to totally refuse to participate in the interactive execution of the verification algorithm, must be treated outside the technical system, for example by uniformly blaming any refusing participant for a signature that is inspected. In practice, every participant who agrees to use undeniable signatures has to explicitly submit to such a *social rule*.

Neglecting the employment of a one-way hash function to replace a message by a fingerprint of it, we shall only outline and briefly annotate the three algorithms of the mechanism, together with a fourth acceptance algorithm *Acc* used as a subalgorithm for the verification algorithm *Test*.

- The *key generation* algorithm *Gen* selects a prime number q such that $p = 2 \cdot q + 1$ is prime as well. This condition implies the factorization condition $q \mid p-1$ and thus the existence of a subgroup G_q of the multiplicative group $\mathbf{Z}_p^*$ with the following properties: the subgroup has exactly q elements, and each of them except the neutral element is a generator. Basically, all further computations of this and the remaining algorithms remain within G_q. The algorithm selects an element $g \in G_q$ to serve as a public generator. Finally, the algorithm randomly selects a private exponent a and derives the public "blinded exponent" $A = g^a \bmod p$. As a result, (p, q, g, A) and a are returned as the *public key* and the *private key*, respectively.

- The *authentication (signature)* algorithm *Aut* takes a message $m \in G_q$ and returns the cryptographic exhibit

$$red = m^a \bmod p. \tag{14.18}$$

- The *acceptance* subalgorithm *Acc* is interactive with a *tester* and a *supposed signer* performing one round of communications:

The tester starts the subalgorithm by randomly selecting two exponents e_1 and e_2 from $\{1, 2, \ldots, q-1\} = \mathbf{Z}_q^*$, and then sends the challenge

$$cha = red^{e_1} \cdot A^{e_2} \bmod p. \tag{14.19}$$

The supposed signer has to answer with a response *res* taken from G_q; aiming at acceptance, the distinguished holder of the private key a determines his response *res* by computing

$$a_{inv} = a^{-1} \bmod q \text{ and} \tag{14.20}$$

$$res = cha^{a_{inv}} \bmod p. \tag{14.21}$$

The tester accepts the signature *red* for the message *m* with the computed challenge–response pair represented by (e_1, e_2) and *res* if the following *acceptance* condition holds:

$$res \equiv m^{e_1} \cdot g^{e_2} \bmod p. \tag{14.22}$$

- The full *verification* algorithm *Test* is again interactive, with the tester and the supposed signer basically performing two rounds of communication, jointly executing the acceptance subalgorithm *Acc* twice, and then the tester inspecting a final test equation:

  1. Started by the tester, who selects the exponents e_1 and e_2, the acceptance subalgorithm *Acc* is executed a first time.
     If the returned response *res* is accepted,
     i.e., $res \equiv m^{e_1} \cdot g^{e_2} \bmod p$ holds, then the signature is accepted and the algorithm exits.

  2. Started again by the tester, who selects new exponents $newe_1$ and $newe_2$, the acceptance subalgorithm *Acc* is executed a second time.
     If the returned response *newres* is now accepted,
     i.e., $newres \equiv m^{newe_1} \cdot g^{newe_2} \bmod p$ holds,
     then the signature is accepted and the algorithm exits.

  3. The *tester* finally disavows the signature *red* for the message *m*, under the condition of the two computed challenge–response pairs represented by e_1, e_2, *res* and $newe_1$, $newe_2$, *newres*, respectively, if the following *disavowal* condition holds:

     $$(res \cdot g^{-e_2})^{newe_1} \equiv (newres \cdot g^{-newe_2})^{e_1} \bmod p, \tag{14.23}$$

     where the inversions for the exponents involved
     are taken additively modulo *q*;
     if the disavowal condition does *not* hold, the signature is accepted.

Regarding the properties of *correctness* and *unforgeability*, we consider the tester always to interact "honestly", but distinguish several different behaviors of the participant acting as the supposed signer.

First, to prove the *weak correctness* property, we assume that the supposed signer is the distinguished holder of the private signature key, who "honestly" signs the message and later aims at acceptance. The acceptance condition (14.22) is then satisfied in the first round, as justified by the following congruences modulo *p*, where all calculations in the exponents are modulo *q*:

$$\begin{aligned}
res &\equiv (red^{e_1} \cdot A^{e_2})^{a^{-1}} && \text{by (14.19), (14.20), and (14.21)} \\
&\equiv red^{e_1 \cdot a^{-1}} \cdot A^{e_2 \cdot a^{-1}}
\end{aligned}$$

$$\equiv (m^a)^{e_1 \cdot a^{-1}} \cdot (g^a)^{e_2 \cdot a^{-1}} \qquad \text{by (14.18) and the definition of } A$$

$$\equiv m^{e_1 \cdot a^{-1} \cdot a} \cdot g^{e_2 \cdot a^{-1} \cdot a}$$

$$\equiv m^{e_1} \cdot g^{e_2}.$$

Second, to start reasoning about the *unforgeability* property, we now consider a forger who does not know the private key a. As suggested by the pertinent *discrete logarithm conjecture*, the forger cannot "determine" the private key from the public key or from previous interactions, and thus he can only guess the uniquely determined valid signature m^a with probability $1/q$, and even then he presumably would not be able to compute an acceptable response.

So we consider the case where the tester inspects a "forged signature" *for* with $for \neq m^a$. Then, as in the case of signing, basically, the forger can only guess a response leading to acceptance with probability $1/q$, as roughly justified in the following.

From the point of view of the forger, a received challenge *cha* has exactly q factorizations in G_q satisfying $cha \equiv f_1 \cdot f_2 \bmod p$, since for each selection of f_1 there is a unique matching f_2. Since each non-unit element of G_q is a generator, each potential factor f_1 is representable as for^{e_1} and, correspondingly, each potential factor f_2 is representable as A^{e_2}. Hence, the challenge *cha* can result from exactly q possibilities for the selections of the exponents e_1 and e_2 secretly made by the tester, and all these possibilities are equally likely. It remains to show that any response *res* taken from G_q is accepted under the condition of exactly one of these selections.

In fact, an accepted selection is a solution of the following equations:

$$cha \equiv for^{e_1} \cdot A^{e_2} \bmod p \qquad \text{by the definition (14.19),}$$

$$res \equiv m^{e_1} \cdot g^{e_2} \bmod p \qquad \text{by the acceptance condition (14.22).}$$

Expressing each of the occurring elements of G_q in terms of the public generator g, these equations can be rewritten as follows for suitable exponents i, j, l and k:

$$g^i \equiv g^{l \cdot e_1} \cdot g^{a \cdot e_2} \bmod p ,$$

$$g^j \equiv g^{k \cdot e_1} \cdot g^{e_2} \bmod p .$$

Equivalently, we obtain the corresponding equations for the exponents:

$$i \equiv l \cdot e_1 + a \cdot e_2 \bmod q ,$$

$$j \equiv k \cdot e_1 + e_2 \bmod q .$$

Since the assumption $for \neq m^a$ expressed in terms of elements of G_q implies the corresponding inequality $l \neq k \cdot a$ for the exponents, the equations for the exponents are linearly independent and thus admit only a unique solution for e_1 and e_2, as claimed.

Third, we note that for a "forged signature" with $for \neq m^a$, even the distinguished holder of the private key cannot perform better. Accordingly, that participant's cooperation in the verification will lead to an acceptance with only a (small) probability $1/q$ as well.

Fourth, if the distinguished holder "honestly" cooperates in both runs of the acceptance subalgorithm for a "forged signature" with $for \neq m^a$ and the unlikely event of acceptance does not happen, then the tester will disavow the forgery as expected, since the disavowal condition (14.23) is satisfied. In fact, the evaluation of the right-hand and left-hand sides of (14.23) results in congruent terms, where again all congruences are modulo p and all calculations in the exponents are modulo q:

$$(res \cdot g^{-e_2})^{newe_1}$$

$$\equiv \left((for^{e_1} \cdot A^{e_2})^{a^{-1}} \cdot g^{-e_2}\right)^{newe_1} \qquad \text{by (14.21), (14.20) and (14.19)}$$

$$\equiv for^{e_1 \cdot a^{-1} \cdot newe_1} \cdot g^{a \cdot e_2 \cdot a^{-1} \cdot newe_1} \cdot g^{-e_2 \cdot newe_1}$$

$$\equiv for^{e_1 \cdot a^{-1} \cdot newe_1} \cdot g^{(e_2 - e_2) \cdot newe_1} \equiv for^{e_1 \cdot a^{-1} \cdot newe_1}$$

and, correspondingly,

$$(newres \cdot g^{-newe_2})^{e_1} \equiv for^{newe_1 \cdot a^{-1} \cdot e_1}.$$

Fifth, and finally, we consider the case where the distinguished holder seemingly cooperates but actually attempts to cheat: the signature inspected is m^a and thus is valid, but as an interacting supposed signer, the distinguished holder aims at determining two responses res and $newres$ such that neither of them satisfies the acceptance condition (14.22), whereas the disavowal condition (14.23) is satisfied nevertheless. We shall sketch an argument that the distinguished holder will succeed in the latter goal only with probability $1/q$.

Suppose that the distinguished holder succeeds, and define

$$hres \equiv res^{e_1^{-1}} \cdot g^{-e_2 \cdot e_1^{-1}}.$$

Applying elementary calculations, one can show that the disavowal condition (14.23) is equivalent to the satisfaction of the congruence

$$newres \equiv hres^{newe_1} \cdot g^{newe_2} \bmod p,$$

which is just the acceptance condition (14.22) for $hres$, seen as a fictitious message, under the condition of the signature red and the exponents $newe_1$ and $newe_2$. On the other side, since the tester is considered to interact honestly and the acceptance condition (14.22) for res under the condition of the exponents e_1 and e_2 does not hold, one can conclude that $m \neq hres$. In conclusion, the holder's success probability is just the probability that a forged signature will pass the acceptance test, which is the event examined in the second case above.

14.8 Symmetric Message Authentication Codes Based on CBC Mode

Message authentication codes (*MACs*) are *authentication mechanisms* that follow the *chaos* approach and employ an underlying symmetric, chaos-based *block cipher* in a suitable *block mode*, as presented in Section 13.10. A widely applied example uses the *cipher block chaining* (CBC) *mode*, outlined in Subsection 13.10.2. The mechanism is *symmetric*, admitting *multiple* key usage. The verification algorithm merely checks whether the received cryptographic exhibit equals the recomputed one.

We shall only outline and briefly annotate the three algorithms of the mechanism:

- The *key generation* algorithm *Gen* randomly selects a secret key k for the underlying symmetric block cipher with the encryption algorithm *Block_Enc*.
- The *authentication* algorithm *Aut* takes a message x of any length and, basically, treats it with the stream cipher *Enc* that is derived from the underlying block cipher using the cipher block chaining mode. The algorithm feeds back each intermediate ciphertext block and immediately discards it afterwards, and then returns the last resulting ciphertext block as the cryptographic exhibit $Aut(k,x)$ of the message x for the selected key k. More specifically, the algorithm proceeds as follows:
  - possibly pad and fragment the message x into (plaintext) blocks x_i whose size fits the encryption algorithm *Block_Enc* such that $x = x_1 \ldots x_{fin}$;
  - define $y_0 = init$, where *init* is an *initialization vector* agreed or communicated beforehand;
  - iteratively, using the *XOR operation*, superimpose each "plaintext block" x_i on the preceding "ciphertext block" (or initialization vector) y_{i-1}, and then encrypt the superimposition, i.e., for $i = 1, \ldots, fin$, compute

    $y_i = Block\_Enc(k, x_i \oplus y_{i-1})$;
  - return y_{fin} as the cryptographic exhibit $Aut(k,x)$.
- The *verification* algorithm *Test* checks whether the received cryptographic exhibit *red* equals the recomputed one $Aut(k,x)$ for the received message x, i.e.,

  $Test(k,x,red)$ returns *true* iff $red = Aut(k,x)$.

The CBC-based message authentication codes are obviously (*strongly*) *correct* by the definition of the verification algorithm. A sufficiently strong *unforgeability property* could be proved if the underlying block cipher satisfied suitably strong *secrecy* properties considering active attacks. However, such secrecy properties are not known to be achievable, and thus must be assumed to hold. By the results of Section 12.7, the mechanisms are *not* perfect, and some *existential forgery* attacks are known.

CBC-based message authentication codes are roughly as *efficient* as the corresponding stream ciphers, and thus meet practical efficiency requirements smoothly.

Moreover, the stream cipher and the message authentication code can be used simultaneously, resulting in *authenticated encryption*.

Finally, we should mention that message authentication codes as described above are often called *keyed (one-way) hash functions*. In fact, the *unforgeability* property of authentication mechanisms and the properties of *one-way hash functions* – the *one-way property* (12.15), the *collision-resistance property* (12.16) and the *strong collision-resistance property* (12.17) – are closely related. Moreover, the verification algorithm for message authentication codes corresponds exactly to the application of one-way hash functions visualized in Figure 12.7. Whereas hash functions provide means to enforce *integrity* as *detection of modification*, message authentication codes additionally assist in enforcing *authenticity*, owing to the employment of a *secret key*.

14.9 Introduction to a Theory of Authentication

In the introductory Section 12.1 we announced that, throughout our treatment of cryptography, we would only informally outline the hopefully (!) achieved security properties. Accordingly, nearly all proposed assertions about the appropriateness of the authentication mechanisms presented need further formal justification. As an exception, we have precisely stated and mathematically proved the theorems about perfect authentication mechanisms.

In this section, we attempt to give an introduction to a thorough theoretical treatment of *authentication*, which has been developed only recently. In doing so, we concentrate on a specific formalization approach for the *unforgeability* property, already informally introduced in two versions in (12.9) and (12.10). We study primarily the former version, in terms of two aspects. First, we distinguish the alternatives for the key relationship: symmetric or asymmetric. Second, we outline the impact of size restrictions on the messages considered. Once again, we emphasize that our introduction remains sketchy and leaves many subtle details and various possible variants open.

For simplicity, in the following all objects such as security parameters, keys, messages and cryptographic exhibits are considered to be encoded over the alphabet $\{0,1\}$, i.e., we deal uniformly only with bit strings in $\{0,1\}^*$. Rather than speaking about a specific authentication mechanism or a family of such mechanisms as before, in this section we adopt a notion of an authentication scheme that is intended to be more flexible.

More specifically, an *authentication scheme* consists of three algorithms:

- A *key generation* algorithm *Gen*: on input of a security parameter 1^n, the algorithm *Gen* returns a pair (ak, tk) of an authentication key ak and a test key tk. The algorithm Gen_{TK} returns only the test key tk generated by *Gen*.
- An *authentication* algorithm *Aut*: on input of an authentication key ak and a message x, the algorithm *Aut* returns a cryptographic exhibit *red*.

- A *verification* algorithm *Test*: on input of a test key *tk*, a message *x* and a crypto-graphic exhibit *red*, the algorithm *Test* returns a Boolean value, indicating either *acceptance* (of the message as authentic and unmodified) or *rejection*.

These algorithms should satisfy the following properties:

- *Correctness*. For all key pairs (ak, tk) generated by *Gen*, and for all messages x,
$Prob[\ Test(tk,x,Aut(ak,x))=true\ ] = 1$.

  We could also use a suitable relaxation that tolerates a "small" error or some "rare" exceptions.
- *Unforgeability*. We shall consider a very strong version in terms of the aspects mentioned above. Further variations are treated in the literature.
- *Efficiency*. *Gen*, *Aut* and *Test* are *probabilistic polynomial-time* algorithms.

14.9.1 Definition of Unforgeability

In this subsection, we exemplarily present a detailed formal definition of *unforge-ability*. The definition is given first for a setting with a *symmetric* key without any size restrictions. The adaptation of this definition to the case of an *asymmetric* key pair is straightforward. The attacker obtains the public key, instead of a security parameter that merely provides some protocol information. In both cases, the defi-nition can be weakened by introducing some size restrictions on the messages con-sidered.

The formal definition of *unforgeability* captures several of the intuitions about attacking behavior that we have mentioned before:

- The anticipated threats are modeled by an *active* attacker who attempts to *forge* a message, i.e., to derive a cryptographic exhibit for a message *chosen* at his dis-cretion.
- Additionally, such an attacker can *passively* observe (correctly) authenticated messages at his discretion, except for the message to be forged, but without fur-ther restrictions. Thus the attacker's observations might result from *actively* made *choices*. The permitted choices and the observations are formally treated as queries to and corresponding answers from an *oracle* that is available to the attacker (with constant computational cost for one query).
- Such an *attacker* is not at all confined in his actions, except by the restrictions of limited computational resources. More precisely, the unforgeability should be protected against *any* probabilistic polynomial-time oracle algorithm acting as an attacker.
- From the perspective of an attacker, the output of the verification algorithms (about acceptance or rejection) is treated as a *random variable*. This random variable is derived from considering the following items as random variables too: the output of the key generation process, and the output and the oracle query set of the attacker.

- The *probability-theoretic* view and the *complexity-theoretic* view are *combined* for the purpose of expressing the *expectation of success* of an attack, namely for bounding the success probability under the condition of limited computational resources.
- In the complexity-theoretic view, the unforgeability property is expressed in terms of a *security parameter* whose values determine a bound for the success probabilities, except for a finite number of exceptions.

Concisely summarized, the following definition requires that, for any matching key pair, whatever information about correctly authenticated messages an attacker can access, he cannot efficiently forge any further message.

Definition 14.1   [unforgeability (for symmetric setting)]

In the setting of a *symmetric* key relationship, an authentication scheme $(Gen, Aut, Test)$ satisfies the *unforgeability* property iff:

For any probabilistic polynomial-time oracle algorithm $Att^{Aut(ak,.)}$ [an *attacker*] that

- inputs a security parameter 1^n,
- queries the elements of *oracle_in* at a (probabilistic) oracle $Aut(ak, .)$ for the authentication algorithm, and
- returns a "forged message" consisting of a message x [a *chosen* message] and a cryptographic exhibit *red* [a *forged* exhibit],

for every positive polynomial p, and for all sufficiently large n,

$$Prob[\ Test(tk,x,red)=true \ \ \text{and} \ \ x \notin oracle\_in \ \ | \qquad (14.24)$$
$$(ak,tk) \leftarrow Gen(1^n); (x,red,oracle\_in) \leftarrow Att^{Aut(ak,.)}(1^n) \ ] < \frac{1}{p(n)} \ .$$

Thus unforgeability ensures that an attacker has only a negligible expectation of success with respect to the following *probabilistic* event:

After input of a security parameter 1^n generating a key (ak,tk), and subsequently running the attacking algorithm $Att^{Aut(ak,.)}$ on the same input, with the oracle instantiated by the generated authentication key ak, the attacker obtains a chosen message x and a cryptographic exhibit *red* that are accepted by the verification algorithm on input of the generated test key tk, where, additionally, the chosen message x has not been submitted to the oracle.

In a setting where an *asymmetric* key is used, the *unforgeability* property remains the same, except that the attacking algorithm $Att^{Aut(ak,.)}$ is given the test key $tk = Gen_{TK}(1^n)$ instead of the security parameter 1^n as input. Thus the inequality (14.24) is changed into

$$Prob[\ Test(tk,x,red)=true \ \ \text{and} \ \ x \notin oracle\_in \ \ | \qquad (14.25)$$
$$(ak,tk) \leftarrow Gen(1^n); (x,red,oracle\_in) \leftarrow Att^{Aut(ak,.)}(tk) \ ] < \frac{1}{p(n)} \ .$$

For both variations of the first aspect concerning the key relationship, namely a symmetric or an asymmetric setting, we shall also treat the second aspect, concerning variations in restrictions on the size of the messages mentioned in the definitions. The definitions given so far only implicitly imply size restrictions, which result from the fact that all of the algorithms are probabilistic polynomial-time bounded and thus cannot produce arbitrarily large messages. In contrast, we want to consider schemes that are explicitly restricted to dealing with messages of a specified length that is fixed in a manner dependent on the security parameter. Such schemes are less powerful because they only ensure the correctness property for messages of the specified length and, more importantly, only prevent forgeries of messages of the specified length, where, additionally, the attacker can only query the oracle about messages of that length.

Definition 14.2   [length-restricted authentication schemes]

Let *fix* be a function on natural numbers. (*Gen*,*Aut*,*Test*) is a *fix*-(*length-*)*restricted authentication scheme* (with either symmetric or asymmetric keys) iff

1. The algorithms *Gen*, *Aut* and *Test* satisfy the general specifications for inputs and outputs for authentication schemes.
2. [*fix-restricted correctness*] For all keys (ak, tk) generated by $Gen(1^n)$, and for all messages x of length $fix(n)$,

   $Prob[\ Test(tk,x,Aut(ak,x))=true\ ] = 1.$

3. [*fix-restricted unforgeability*] The property given in Definition 14.1 holds with the following weakening: an attacking oracle algorithm $Att^{Aut(ak,.)}$ submits only messages of length $fix(n)$ as queries to the oracle, and outputs a message of length $fix(n)$.

14.9.2 Impact of Length-Restricted Schemes

Whether in the symmetric or the asymmetric setting, a *length-restricted authentication scheme* can serve as the basic component of a general authentication scheme. There are two approaches to such constructions, denoted as *fragment-and-authenticate* and *hash-and-authenticate*, respectively. Both approaches can be proved to guarantee unforgeability in general, provided the underlying length-restricted scheme enforces unforgeability in the restricted form and the length-restricting function $fix(n)$ grows faster than the logarithm function $log(n)$. The latter condition is needed to disable feasible attacks based on exhaustive probing: in fact, given the security parameter 1^n, restricting the procedure to items of size up to $log(n)$ and considering a resulting search space of essentially exponential growth relative to the restriction would require only polynomial-time bounded computations.

The *fragment-and-authenticate* approach first fragments the message into blocks of a size fitting the length restriction of the underlying length-restricted scheme, and appropriately annotates the blocks as ordered parts of the specific message. Then the underlying length-restricted scheme is *repeatedly* employed to authenticate each of the annotated blocks individually. Notably, the effectiveness of this approach depends essentially on a carefully designed annotation scheme that prevents forgeries by recombining known authenticated blocks. Roughly outlined, the *authentication algorithm* constructed has to proceed as follows for a given message x:

- identify the message x by generating a randomly selected (and thus supposedly unique) identifier *id*;
- determine the blocks $x_1, \ldots, x_n$ of the fragmentation and the respective number n of blocks;
- for each block x_i, form an annotation saying "this is the i-th block of the message identified by *id*, having n blocks in total";
- for each block x_i, authenticate the block together with the pertinent annotation, employing the underlying length-restricted scheme, yielding the exhibit red_i;
- return the tuple consisting of the identifier *id*, the block count n and the sequence of exhibits $red_1, \ldots, red_n$ as the overall *cryptographic exhibit* for the message x and the authentication key employed for the underlying scheme.

Accordingly, the *verification algorithm* constructed basically proceeds as follows, given a message x and an exhibit *red* of the form described above:

- reconstruct the fragmentation of x;
- reconstruct the annotations by using the communicated identifier *id*;
- check each individual exhibit for a reconstructed block, together with the pertinent reconstructed annotation;
- check the validity of the assertions expressed by the reconstructed annotations.

The *hash-and-authenticate* approach first computes a *fingerprint* of the message as the hash value of the message under an agreed *one-way hash function*, supposed to satisfy appropriate versions of the properties introduced in Subsection 12.4.5 – the *one-way property* (12.15), the *collision-resistance property* (12.16) and the *strong collision-resistance property* (12.17) – and which delivers hash values fitting the size restriction of the underlying length-restricted scheme. This scheme is employed only *once* to authenticate the hash value.

Notably, the existence of suitable one-way hash functions is an open problem of computer science that is closely related to the possibility of providing sufficient *randomness*, as intuitively discussed in our introduction to cryptography in Section 12.1. Accordingly, it is better to see the practical applications of the hash-and-authenticate approach – for instance in the *RSA, ElGamal, DSA* and *elliptic-curve authentication* mechanisms presented in Sections 14.3–6 – as suitable approximations of unforgeability at best.

14.9.3 Constructions

The property of *unforgeability* is highly ambitious, and so one might wonder whether it can be satisfied at all. Basically, for both a symmetric setting and an asymmetric setting, the answers are affirmative provided suitable assumptions about *pseudorandomness* and *one-way functions* hold. Thus unforgeability can be achieved, or at least approximated, according to one's success in producing pseudorandomness and in constructing one-way functions. A detailed presentation of effective constructions is beyond the scope of this monograph. Thus we shall only sketch some rough ideas indicating the motivation behind these constructions.

Regarding the *symmetric* setting, one fundamental idea is to take the message x, or a keyed fingerprint $hash(k_1,x)$ of it to satisfy size restrictions, and to apply a keyed, parameterized pseudorandom generator $rand(k_2, .)$ to the respective item. The resulting "random-appearing" value $rand(k_2, hash(k_1,x))$ is considered as the cryptographic exhibit *red* for the message x and the symmetric key (k_1,k_2). Basically, the second step aims at *hiding* the result of the first step to prevent an attacker from gaining useful information from observed exhibits. Hiding is clearly the task of encryption, and thus appropriate techniques used for encryption mechanisms can be adapted for this purpose. However, in contrast to encryption, in this context there is no need for decryption, i.e., for recovering the original item from the derived pseudorandom value, since in the symmetric setting for authentication, the verifier always recomputes an exhibit from the received message and compares the recomputed exhibit with the received one.

This fundamental idea leads to a variety of instantiations and modifications: some of them achieve full unforgeability under suitable assumptions; others achieve only approximations. For the purpose of hiding, a prominent class of examples employ the *XOR operation* on one or several items x_i produced in the first step and some suitably generated pseudorandom arguments $rand_i$ of the same size, i.e., the respective parts red_i of the cryptographic exhibit are computed as $red_i = x_i \oplus rand_i$. By the properties of the XOR operation, each part inherits the "random appearance" of the respective pseudorandom argument. Some care is needed to ensure that the pseudorandom arguments $rand_i$ are different and are discarded after their usage, for example by taking them as parts of an isolated keystream produced by a state-based generator as exemplified by the linear shift register in Section 13.3, or, better, by a non-linear improvement of the linear shift register. The *CBC*-based *message authentication codes* presented in Section 14.8 can be seen as another variant.

Regarding the *asymmetric* setting, one fundamental idea adds a combination of two further techniques to the reduction techniques to get rid of length restrictions:

- the construction of instances of an asymmetric *one-time length-restricted signature scheme*, each of which is used for *bitwise* signing of just one message;
- the *refreshment* of a given instance of such a scheme by producing two new linked instances, and building an *authentication tree* by such refreshments.

In this context, an instance means the result of a specific execution of the key generation algorithm. In the following, we shall outline and visualize these techniques. Figure 14.4 shows the basic features of an asymmetric *one-time signature scheme* where a message x consists of just *one bit*.

To sign the bit, the sender randomly generates a private *authentication key* $ak = ak^0 \, ak^1$, where the first component ak^0 is used if the bit is 0, and the second component ak^1 if the bit is 1. Thus the cryptographic exhibit (signature) for x is computed as ak^x and communicated to the receiver. Furthermore, the sender blinds the private authentication key by applying an agreed length-preserving "one-way function" *hide* to produce a public *test key* $tk = tk^0 \, tk^1 := hide(ak^0) \, hide(ak^1)$, and publishes the public blinded version.

The receiver, or any other verifier, takes a received bit y and applies the blinded (test) key similarly to the way the sender (presumably) did with the original (authentication) key, i.e., the receiver determines tk^y and compares this bit computed by himself with the received exhibit (signature) bit *red*.

More precisely, the receiver first applies the blinding "one-way function" *hide* to the received bit and obtains $hide(red)$, and then checks for equality with the bit tk^y computed using the blinded key, i.e., the receiver inspects the validity of the test equation $hide(red) = tk^y$.

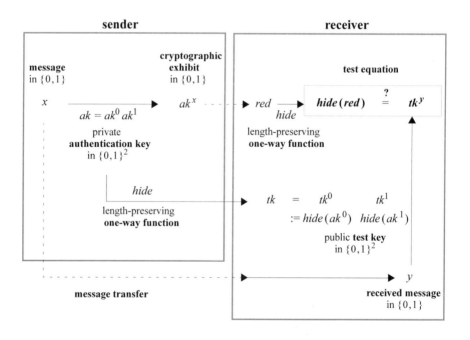

Fig. 14.4. Application of an asymmetric one-time signature scheme for a one-bit message

Obviously, such a signature scheme possesses the *correctness property*. For, supposing $red = ak^x$ and $y = x$, the test equation can be verified as follows:

$$hide(red) = hide(ak^x) = tk^x = tk^y.$$

The *unforgeability property*, however, depends crucially on the effectiveness of the attempt at blinding, i.e., in general, whether the blinding function is *one-way* indeed and thus prevents efficient unblinding. Clearly, the one-way property becomes effective only for longer arguments, as controlled by the *security parameter* input to the key generation algorithm. Moreover, only the following variant of the unforgeability property is achieved: referring to Definition 14.1, in accordance with the intended *one-time usage* of the scheme, the attacking oracle algorithm may query the oracle *at most once*.

The basic features are illustrated further in Figure 14.5, which also reveals similarities to *perfect symmetric authentication* mechanisms, as shown in Figure 12.10 and Figure 14.3, in all cases for messages of length 1. For both the asymmetric and the symmetric construction, we need "long keys" to prevent both impersonation and substitution attacks: an *impersonation attack* corresponds to an attacking algorithm that does not access the oracle, whereas a *substitution attack* is captured by an attacking algorithm that submits just one query to the oracle.

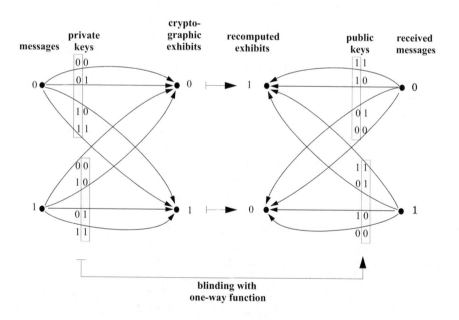

Fig. 14.5. An asymmetric one-time signature mechanism for one-bit messages with a blinding function $hide(x) = 1 \oplus x$

Given a function *fix* for expressing length restrictions and a length-preserving one-way function *hide* for blinding, a general construction of asymmetric *one-time fix-length-restricted signature schemes* may be outlined as follows:

- The *key generation* algorithm *Gen* takes the security parameter 1^n as input, randomly selects $fix(n)$ pairs of "bit keys" $ak_i = ak_i^0\ ak_i^1$, where each ak_i^b is a bit string of length n – one pair for each bit of a message of length $fix(n)$ – and then forms the private *authentication key*

$$ak = [ak_1^0\ ak_1^1,...,ak_i^0\ ak_i^1,...,ak_{fix(n)}^0\ ak_{fix(n)}^1].\qquad(14.26)$$

Then the algorithm blinds each of the selected ak_i^b, yielding $tk_i^b = hide(ak_i^b)$, and forms the public *test key*

$$tk = [tk_1^0\ tk_1^1,...,tk_i^0\ tk_i^1,...,tk_{fix(n)}^0\ tk_{fix(n)}^1].\qquad(14.27)$$

- The *authentication* (*signature*) algorithm *Aut* signs a selected message $x = x_1...x_i...x_{fix(n)}$ bitwise by determining $red_i = ak_i^{x_i}$ and returns

$$red = red_1...red_i...red_{fix(n)}.\qquad(14.28)$$

- The *verification* algorithm *Test* inspects a message $y = y_1...y_i...y_{fix(n)}$ with a claimed signature $red = red_1...red_i...red_{fix(n)}$ by employing the test key *tk* and accepts the message iff, for all $i = 1,..., fix(n)$, the test equation

$$hide(red_i) = tk_i^{x_i}\qquad(14.29)$$

holds.

In order to overcome the limitations of one-time signature schemes, the second construction idea of producing *refreshments* and building an *authentication tree* is exploited. More specifically, given an already established instance of a one-time signature scheme with a key pair (ak,tk), the distinguished key holder of the private component can proceed basically as follows:

- generate two new instances with key pairs (ak_0,tk_0) and (ak_1,tk_1);
- keep the private components ak_0 and ak_1 secret;
- form *one* key publication message $tk_0 \mid tk_1$, containing the public components according to an agreed protocol;
- sign this message $tk_0 \mid tk_1$ using the given private authentication key ak;
- publish the signed message containing the two public test keys;
- use the two new authentication keys for signing *two* discretionarily selected messages, in each case informing the recipient which one of the new test keys is to be used for the verification.

By repeatedly applying this refreshment procedure, the key holder of the original key pair (ak,tk) can build a binary *authentication tree* to prepare for signing a discretionarily selected number of messages to be sent to communication partners.

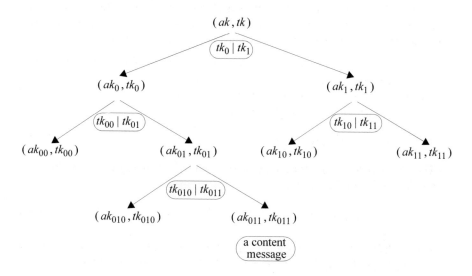

Fig. 14.6. Construction and usage of an authentication tree. A circled (key publication or content) message is signed and verified with the key pair depicted above the message

A *node* of this tree represents a key pair. An *edge* from a parent node to a child node indicates that the key pair at the parent has been used to authenticate the key pair at the child, which belongs to one of the new instances produced by a refreshment. Accordingly, as visualized in Figure 14.6, the authentication tree is formed and used as follows:

- The root λ represents the original key pair (ak,tk). This key pair is used for a refreshment generating two new key pairs (ak_0,tk_0) and (ak_1,tk_1), which are represented by the left child, with path name 0, and the right child, with path name 1, respectively.
- A node of depth $d>0$ with path name $i_1 \ldots i_d$ represents a key pair $(ak_{i_1 \ldots i_d}, tk_{i_1 \ldots i_d})$ that has been generated using the refreshment procedure given the key pair at the parent node, and thus has been authenticated accordingly.
- A node with path name $i_1 \ldots i_d$ is an *inner node* if the key pair represented is used for a refreshment that produces two new key pairs that are represented by the two children of the node, which are given the path names $i_1 \ldots i_d 0$ and $i_1 \ldots i_d 1$, respectively.
- A node with path name $i_1 \ldots i_d$ becomes a *leaf node*, if the key pair represented is used for signing a message containing some discretionarily selected content to be communicated to some partner.

If the distinguished holder of the original key pair (ak,tk) has employed a node as a leaf for signing a message, he has to communicate not only the signature for the message but also the path name of the node, together with all signed key publication messages along the path. Starting with the public key *tk*, the receiver then successively verifies the key publication messages and selects the pertinent public keys according to the path name communicated.

There are many options for organizing and maintaining such an authentication tree. For example, the distinguished key holder might generate a sufficiently deep full binary tree in advance before sending any message, and then in some way select a fresh leaf node for each message to be signed. If the number of leaf nodes is much larger than the expected number of messages, each leaf node can even be randomly selected, thereby avoiding the need to memorize the set of leaf nodes already used. Other examples might construct the authentication tree more dynamically and employ a less balanced tree structure to enable short path names for some messages, with a need to keep track of the current state of the tree.

14.10 Bibliographic Hints

All textbooks on cryptography treat authentication as a main topic, and basically all textbooks on security in computing systems give at least an introduction to authentication; see Section 1.7 and Section 12.11. In particular, we acknowledge that the exposition by Stinson [470] was very helpful for our own presentation. In addition to the general background, selected dedicated literature to the material presented in this chapter can be found as follows.

Probability-theoretic security for authentication and the usage of one-time keys for achieving perfectness have been pioneered by Gilbert/MacWilliams/Sloane [219] and elaborated further by Simmons [448, 450] and Stinson [465, 466, 467, 470].

The RSA authentication mechanism is based on the pioneering work of Rivest/ Shamir/Adleman [409]. The ElGamal authentication mechanism is proposed by ElGamal [183]. Johnson/Menezes/Vanstone [280] describe the Elliptic Curve Digital Signature Algorithm, and Hankerson/Menezes/Vanstone [248] survey further elliptic-curve variants. The standard document for the Digital Signature Algorithm is published by NIST [367].

Undeniable signatures are invented by Chaum/van Antwerpen [125] and investigated later by Chaum/van Heijst/B.Pfitzmann [126, 127] and others. Examples of other important variants of digital signatures not treated in this chapter include the following: group signatures with the option of deanonymization are studied by Chaum/Chen/van Heijst/Pedersen [128, 130] and Cramer/Damgard/Schoenmakers [144], and fail-stop signatures offering advanced signer security are investigated by Damgard/Pedersen/B.Pfitzmann [388, 150, 392].

ISO [268, 269] issues standards for symmetric message authentication codes based on CBC and on hash functions. Bellare/Kilian/Rogaway [40] and Preneel/ van Oorschot [399] study security properties of message authentication codes.

Goldreich [229] provides a detailed exposition of a theory of authentication, from which we extracted our introduction, and where a rich bibliography with historical notes and suggestions for further reading can be found.

15 Anonymization

15.1 Survey

An *anonymization* mechanism aims primarily at keeping the *activities* of participants *non-observable* to other participants, more precisely, the aim is to make an observed activity *unlinkable* to a specific person or computing device. Basically, this goal is achieved by hiding each individual activity within a class of preferably many other activities, called an *anonymity class*, where an individual activity is *indistinguishable* from any other possible activity. Accordingly, an unauthorized observer should not be able to infer useful information about the relationships between observed aspects of an activity and the participants actually acting. Some applications, however, might demand that one or more designated observers are nevertheless able to break the anonymity usually achieved, for example for the sake of a conflicting interest such as *accountability*.

A more extensive introduction to anonymization is presented in Subsection 12.4.3, where among other things, some examples are visualized in Figure 12.5. Moreover, Figure 12.6 exemplifies some meanings of the notion of a *participant*, which is crucial in the context of anonymity. The key idea of *indistinguishability* is illustrated for anonymization in Subsection 6.3.2 by introducing the concept of hiding among *standardized behavior*. Besides standardizing behavior, anonymization employs and combines a wide variety of other elementary mechanisms, such as encryption, authentication and one-way hash functions, which might follow a *probability-theoretic* approach or a *complexity-theoretic* approach. Many of the cryptographic quality aspects presented in Section 12.5 for encryption can be adapted to anonymization as well, but for anonymization, often both *passive* and *active* attacks are a concern.

Unlike encryption or authentication, anonymization appears as a collection of somewhat related mechanisms still lacking a unifying theory. Accordingly, without fully repeating the introductory discussion given earlier, in this section we only briefly gather together some important common aspects, and then present some technical details for the example mechanisms already sketched in Subsection 12.4.3, namely blind signatures, superimposed sending and MIX networks.

As indicated above, we concentrate on enforcing anonymity concerning *activities* rather than dealing with anonymity concerning collected *data*, which is an important topic in its own right. However, in many cases there are subtle connections between activities and data: an activity might be materialized and thus documented by an observable *message* that is a piece of data and, for example, stored in a database for later analysis; and a piece of data might represent a trace of some activity performed by some participant, and, accordingly, a database can then be seen as a documentation of the activity history of all participants under consideration.

Regarding the common aspects of the various anonymity mechanisms, we identify the following features, which, however, are not comprehensively treated in the examples presented below:

- application-specific *anonymity properties*, which define a specific version of *indistinguishability*;
- protection against *inferences*, which considers the *a priori knowledge* of attackers and their potential to *gain* new *information* from observable parts of behavior;
- formation of *anonymity classes*, which enforces a specific kind of *uniformity* shared by many similar activities;
- employment of more elementary mechanisms for *hiding*, which *standardizes behavior* and uses cryptographic *blinding*;
- *misuse detection* and *reidentification*, which employs *control and monitoring* and *keyed cryptographic mechanisms*.

As can be seen from this feature list, in general, an overall effective anonymization mechanism is neither a purely cryptographic technique nor an elementary block but a sophisticated combination of several appropriately adapted procedures.

15.2 Blind Signatures and Unlinkable Obligations

As sketched as the third example in Subsection 12.4.3, the anonymization mechanism of *blind signatures* is aimed at supporting the following *anonymity property*: a pair of participants can hide within an *anonymity class* of clients of an obligation system as the receiver of an obligation and the presenter of that obligation, i.e., the (receiver of the) issued version of the obligation cannot be *linked* to the (presenter of the) version presented later. Thus, from the perspective of an observer of issuing actions and presenting actions, the pertinent version of *indistinguishability* requires that for any specific observed presenting action, the following *unlinkability property* holds, even under *inferences* gained from all observable activities: all previously issued obligations are equally likely to be the origin of the obligation presented.

The anonymity property stated above refers to a system of digital documents that are employed as *obligations*. Figure 15.1 shows a prominent instantiation. A bank issues an obligation as a *digital coin* to a client, charging him in terms of "real" money outside the technical system. As compensation for some commercial goods or services, the client later transfers the coin to some *dealer*, who in turn finally presents the digital coin to the bank in order to convert it back into "real" money. There are many variations of such a scenario and, accordingly, the obligations are accompanied by many different denotations, for instance *credentials* and *digital legitimations*. A rough classification distinguishes the following features:

- the obligation is *transferable* either *only once* or *repeatedly*, an unlimited or at least a large number of times;
- either the obligation is *personalized* in the sense that only the "legitimate owner" can successfully present it, or any "copy holder" can achieve acceptance;
- the obligation is either *one-time presentable* or *reusable*.

Each particular application might require a dedicated specification of these and related features together with the desired kind of anonymity, and, then, appropriate enforcement methods are necessary for the features and kinds selected. In the following, we shall exemplarily examine the situation sketched in Figure 15.1 in a somewhat restricted form: the digital coin should be transferable only once (the dotted lines indicate alternatives that allow further transfers); it is not personalized; it should be only one-time presentable; and the action of the issuing is unlinkable to the action of presenting.

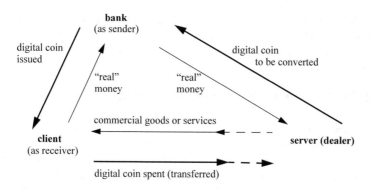

Fig. 15.1. Flow of a digital coin (obligation) and reverse flow of conventional "real" money and commercial goods or services

As an enforcement method, we outline a simple form of *blind signatures*, which must be either suitably refined or appropriately complemented by further mechanisms. The simple form outlined captures only the following properties: *correctness* and *unforgeability* (in particular, supporting the interest of *non-repudiation* of the bank's obligation to convert the digital coin into "real" money), and a single *transferability*, together with *unlinkability* of issued and presented versions.

Basically, the blind signatures presented here purposely exploit what is otherwise seen as a vulnerability of the asymmetric authentication mechanism of RSA signatures, namely the possibility of *existential forgeries* based on the algebraic properties of the underlying functions. A similar adaptation is known for *ElGamal signatures*, and there are further related proposals.

More specifically, *blind RSA signatures* exploit the congruences given in (14.8) roughly as follows, for handling unlinkably presentable digital coins:

- The bank generates an RSA key pair consisting of a private signature key (p,q,d) and a public test key (n,e).
- The bank publishes (a certificate for) the public key, promising to reimburse a specific amount of "real" money to the first presenter of any suitably formatted document with an attached digital signature verified by the test key (n,e).
- A client generates a random bit string *nonce* and forms a structured identifier *id* of the form $id = [nonce, hash(nonce)]$, where *hash* is an agreed hash function according to some format specification of the bank, such that *id* can be seen as a residue modulo n. In the following, *id* is used as an *identification* of a digital coin.
- Then the client *blinds* the identification *id* by randomly selecting a multiplicatively invertible element b and computing

  $c = id \cdot b^e \bmod n$;

  this can be paraphrased as putting the identification into a covering *envelope*.
- Afterwards, the client sends the covered identification c to the bank, requesting that it issues a digital coin as a promise of the kind published, i.e., the client requests the bank to digitally sign c with the private key matching the published test key (n,e). This request might be suitably authenticated, in order that the bank can charge the client a specific amount of "real" money.
- Following the request and the client being charged accordingly, the bank computes a valid digital signature for the covered identification c as

$$red = c^d \bmod n; \tag{15.1}$$

this signature is "blindly computed" regarding the identification *id*, and thus can be paraphrased as being given on the envelope without one needing to know the contents of the envelop.

- The bank returns an obligation in the form of a digitally signed digital document (c, red) consisting of c and the digital signature *red*.
- The client computes the value

$$red \cdot b^{-1} \bmod n \tag{15.2}$$

and employs it as the digital signature for the original identification *id*, i.e., considers the digitally signed digital document $(id, red \cdot b^{-1} \bmod n)$ as an obligation of the bank. The client's computation can be paraphrased as stripping away the envelope and obtaining a signature for the contents. In fact, the computed value equals the RSA signature id^d according to the following congruences mod n:

$$red \cdot b^{-1} \equiv c^d \cdot b^{-1} \equiv (id \cdot b^e)^d \cdot b^{-1} \equiv id^d \cdot (b^e)^d \cdot b^{-1} \equiv id^d. \tag{15.3}$$

- Anyone who presents the document (id, $red \cdot b^{-1} \mod n$) later to the bank, whether the client himself or any dealer to whom the document has been transferred, will succeed when the RSA verification algorithm is applied to the public key (n,e) and this document. Moreover, the verifier can check whether the identification id possesses the structured form agreed, and thus the verifier can detect a fraud that has generated a faked digital coin from a genuine one, by exploiting the possibility of existential forgeries.
- Accordingly, provided the action of presenting the document has not occurred earlier, the bank will redeem the accepted obligation.

The properties stated explicitly above hold for the following reasons. *Non-repudiation* is a consequence of (15.3), together with the structured form of the identification. *Single transferability* is partially achieved by determining the signature for id from the signature for c, notably without using the private signature key, but must be supported further by an additional protection against the double spending of a digital coin. *Unlinkability* within the *anonymity class* of all issued digital coins results from the randomness of the selected identification id and of the blinding factor b, together with the algebraic properties of the multiplicative structure underlying the RSA function.

Regarding protection against the *double-spending* problem, basically three approaches are known as a countermeasure to the inevitable *vulnerability* to copying a *bit string* without producing an observable difference between the original and the copy:

- A straightforward pessimistic online solution based on control and monitoring, which maintains a central repository of all (identifications of) digital coins already redeemed: this repository must be queried whenever a digital coin is presented to detect a repeated presentation, and updated after the first successful presentation of each digital coin.
- A cryptographically highly sophisticated, optimistic offline solution, which basically encodes *shares* of the client's identity into the digital coin and reveals a share during each execution of the protocol for the action of presenting: two shares are sufficient to identify a fraudulent presenter after two actions of presenting and then to pursue the presenter outside the technical system, whereas a single share still keeps the identity confidential.
- A dedicated hardware solution of *wallets with observers*, where a component called the bank's *observer* is embedded into a special-purpose computing device, a *wallet*, to handle the client's actions: this observer must mediate any action of presenting and thus can detect and prevent a repeated presentation of a digital coin.

15.3 Superimposed Sending

As already sketched in the first example in Subsection 12.4.3, the anonymization mechanism of *superimposed sending* is aimed at supporting the following *anonym-*

ity property: a participant can hide within a fixed *anonymity class* of communication partners as the actual sender of a message distributed to all class members. Thus, from the perspective of any class member except the actual sender, the pertinent version of *indistinguishability* requires that the behavior of the sender appears the same as the behaviors of all non-senders, even under *inferences* gained from observable messages.

We first exemplify this mechanism for a class of three participants A, B and C, and then outline some generalizations. Each of the three participants has to follow a *standardized behavior* that is organized in rounds. Each round consists of the following steps:

- Each pair of two participants agrees on a common symmetric one-time encryption key of a fixed length l for a perfect Vernam cipher, as presented in Section 13.2. The agreed keys are denoted by $k_{A,B}$, $k_{A,C}$ and $k_{B,C}$.
- At most one of the three participants selects a meaningful message with content of length l to be communicated to all class members, whereas all other members select the "empty" bit string of length l, consisting of 0's only. Without giving details, here we suppose that, later on, a collision can be detected without violating the wanted anonymity. The selected messages are denoted by m_A, m_B and m_C.
- Each participant encrypts his selected message with both of the agreed keys, i.e.,
  - A computes the XOR operation bitwise for the arguments m_A, $k_{A,B}$ and $k_{A,C}$;
  - B computes the XOR operation bitwise for the arguments m_B, $k_{A,B}$ and $k_{B,C}$;
  - C computes the XOR operation bitwise for the arguments m_C, $k_{A,C}$ and $k_{B,C}$.
- Each participant broadcasts his computed ciphertext without further protection.
- As the final result of the round, taking the broadcast ciphertexts as arguments, the XOR operation is computed bitwise, either by each of the participants individually or with the assistance of some further agent.

Obviously, the final result *correctly* equals the sole message with content. In fact, considering a single bit and misusing notation, suppose the participant X has selected the content message m_X and the two remaining participants have selected the "empty" message 0. Then, by the properties of the *XOR operation*, as exploited in the decryption algorithm for perfect ciphers, the final result r is computed as

$$r = (m_X \oplus 0 \oplus 0) \oplus (k_{A,B} \oplus k_{A,C}) \oplus (k_{A,B} \oplus k_{B,C}) \oplus (k_{A,C} \oplus k_{B,C}) = m_X.$$

Regarding the *anonymity property*, the properties of the XOR operation used for achieving *secrecy* are exploited as outlined intuitively as follows, again deliberately misusing the notation. Consider a participant Y that has selected the empty message. Y can observe both the broadcasting of the actual sender X, $m_X \oplus k_{X,Z} \oplus k_{X,Y}$, and the broadcasting of the remaining participant Z, $m_Z \oplus k_{X,Z} \oplus k_{Z,Y}$. By decrypting with the shared keys $k_{X,Y}$ and $k_{Z,Y}$, respectively, Y can determine $m_X \oplus k_{X,Z}$ and $m_Z \oplus k_{X,Z}$. However, these bit strings are indistinguishable ciphertexts for Y, who does not know the key $k_{X,Z}$ employed. Accordingly, Y cannot determine which of these *indistinguishable ciphertexts* stems from the sole message with content, i.e., the final result r, and thus whether X or Z was the sender of the content.

The mechanism exemplified can be generalized to any number of participants. Each participant generates two symmetric one-time encryption keys and shares each of them with a discretionarily chosen different class member; accordingly, using the XOR operation, each participant superimposes his selected message on his own two keys and all received keys. After all broadcastings have finally been superimposed, every key has been employed twice and thus its effects are cancelled, and the effects of the "empty" messages are neutral as well, delivering the sole message with content as the final result. Further generalizations might be obtained by replacing the XOR operation by another commutative, idempotent group operation.

15.4 MIX Networks

As already sketched in the second example in Subsection 12.4.3, the anonymization mechanism of *MIX networks* is aimed at supporting the following *anonymity property*: a pair of participants can hide within an *anonymity class* of network users as the source and destination that belong together for a specific message forwarded by the network servers.

Thus, from the perspective of any suitably *localized* observer of the network except the actual sender and the actual receiver, the pertinent version of *indistinguishability* requires that for any specific observed message, the following holds, even under *inferences* gained from all observable messages: if the sender is known, then all participants in the class are equally likely to be the intended receiver; if the actual receiver is known, then all participants in the class are equally likely to be the actual sender; if neither the actual sender nor the actual receiver is known, then all pairs of participants in the class are equally likely to be the actual pair of the sender and the receiver. Clearly, in general, the desired kind of indistinguishability cannot be achieved with respect to a *global* observer that has access to all servers and communication lines of the network.

The anonymity property stated above refers to a *horizontally distributed, networked* computing system consisting of clients as *endusers*, and *servers* as mediating agents for routing and forwarding *messages* in the form of *packets*, as described by the *ISO/OSI model*. Figure 3.1 visualizes some basic vulnerabilities of such a system; Figure 7.2 depicts the fiction of an *end-to-end connection* between two clients that actually can only send and receive appropriately treated messages; and Figure 10.7 shows some relationships between the network facilities and other components.

Assuming a general understanding of networked systems, we shall first summarize how clients can establish "end-to-end security" by *end-to-end encryption* for autonomously enforcing their interests in *confidentiality* and by *end-to-end authentication* for autonomously enforcing their interests in *integrity* and *authenticity*, and how servers can additionally establish "connection security" by use of local encryptions and authentications for each pair of mediating servers that directly exchange messages. We shall then outline how clients can additionally enforce their interest in *anonymity* by autonomously enveloping their messages in an onion-like way to direct them stepwise through a cascade of *MIX servers*, each of which is supposed to blur the relationships between incoming and outgoing messages.

The following summary of end-to-end and connection security is visualized in Figure 15.2. If an enduser S acting as a *sender* and an enduser R acting as a *receiver* want to securely send and receive a message, they can proceed conceptually as follows. In the preparation phase, they somehow agree on an encryption mechanism and an authentication mechanism, generate the needed keys, and distribute these keys appropriately. In the communication phase, the sender S

- selects the message m;
- computes a cryptographic exhibit $Aut(ak_S, m)$ for the selected message, using an authentication key ak_S that is private to S or secretly shared by S and R, depending on the key relationship;
- computes a ciphertext $Enc(ek_R, [m, Aut(ak_S, m)])$ of the authenticated message, using an encryption key ek_R that is public to R or secretly shared by S and R, depending on the key relationship;
- forms a packet $m^* = (S, R, Enc(ek_R, [m, Aut(ak_S, m)]))$ by adding a head containing the overall routing data;
- sends the packet m^* to his local network server Mf with a command to transport the packet over the network with the goal of delivering it as specified.

The local network server Mf acts as the *first* server in a *successively* determined chain of mediating network servers. On the basis of the *open* routing data in the head, the packet m^* eventually reaches the *last* server Ml, which is local to the intended receiver R. This server then delivers the packet. On the basis of the agreements made in the preparation phase, the receiver R decrypts the body $Enc(ek_R, [m, Aut(ak_S, m)])$ of the packet m^* using the matching decryption key dk_R, thereby recovering the authenticated message $[m, Aut(ak_S, m)]$, and then verifies the cryptographic exhibit using the matching test key tk_S.

Moreover, each neighboring pair of agents, i.e., the sender R and the first mediating server Mf, an intermediate server Mi and its direct successor Mj in the chain, or the final server Ml and the receiver R, can treat m^* as a content message and protect it by an additional authentication and an additional encryption that are based on local preparation of the pertinent direct connection. More specifically, for instance, the intermediate server Mi

- computes a cryptographic exhibit $Aut(ak_{Mi}, m^*)$, using an authentication key ak_{Mi} that is private to Mi or secretly shared by Mi and Mj, depending on the key relationship;
- computes a ciphertext $m_{Mi, Mj} = Enc(ek_{Mj}, [m^*, Aut(ak_{Mi}, m^*)])$, using an encryption key ek_{Mj} that is public to Mj or secretly shared by Mi and Mj, depending on the key relationship;

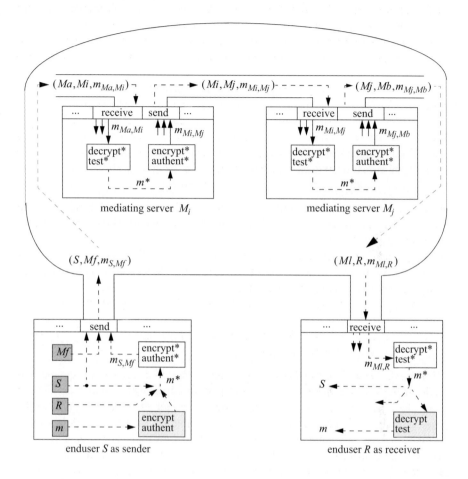

Fig. 15.2. End-to-end encryption and authentication (authent and encrypt, and decrypt and test, respectively) between endusers, complemented by additional connection encryption and authentication (authent* and encrypt*, and decrypt* and test*, respectively) between mediating servers and between an enduser and a mediating server, respectively

- forms a packet $m_{Mi,Mj} = (Mi, Mj, m_{Mi,Mj})$ by adding a head containing the routing data for the next step;
- delivers that packet directly to the next mediating server Mj.

This server Mj decrypts and verifies the received packet using the matching keys that are specific to the connection with Mi, inspects the recovered packet m^* to determine the next mediating server, and then proceeds accordingly for the next step in the chain by authenticating and encrypting m^* for the connection determined.

Even the combination of the end-to-end mechanism and the connection mechanisms does not fully enforce the wanted anonymity property, however: although any eavesdropper intercepting a protected packet at a local connection cannot determine the overall routing data contained in the head of $m*$, each mediating server still sees that routing data and thus learns the pertinent pair of the sender and the receiver. Moreover, an eavesdropper observing both the incoming and the outgoing messages might be able to link corresponding pairs, basing such an inference on the observation of further aspects of the traffic, for example the lengths of messages.

MIX servers and the corresponding protocols for MIX networks are designed to prevent the remaining vulnerabilities, basically aiming at achieving appropriate variants of the following refined anonymity properties:

- A single mediating server or even a collusion of all but one of the servers along a pertinent transmission path (i.e., there remains only one "honest server") should not be able to determine the overall routing data.
- An observer of the incoming and outgoing network traffic on the connections of a mediating server, or even of several of the servers involved, should not be able to link the packets that belong together and thereby infer the overall routing data.

Basically, for a *MIX network*, the preparation phases and communication phases of a network with end-to-end and connection security are conceptually modified as outlined in the following, where we neglect authentication for the sake of a concise description. The outline is exemplified in Figure 15.3, where the minimum number of two MIX servers is employed for three transmission requests.

In a MIX preparation phase, all participants involved, endusers as well as mediating MIX servers, agree on a common asymmetric encryption mechanism (which, in general, is complemented by an authentication mechanism, which we have neglected). Each participant P generates a matching pair of a public encryption key ek_P and a private decryption key dk_P and publishes the suitably certified public component.

In a MIX communication phase, the sender S

- selects the message m;
- *statically* determines not only the intended final receiver R but also the complete transmission path for the message, i.e., discretionarily chooses a path of connected MIX servers $M1, \ldots, Ml$, *trusted* by the sender;
- cryptographically *envelops* the message in an *onion-like* way as follows:

$m_R := Enc(ek_R, [R, m])$

is the innermost envelope, destined for the receiver R;

$m_{Ml} := Enc(ek_{Ml}, [R, Enc(ek_R, [R, m])])$

is destined for the last mediating MIX server Ml;

accordingly, for $i = l, \ldots, 2$,

$$m_{M(i-1)} := Enc(ek_{M(i-1)}, [Mi, m_{Mi}]),$$

the envelope destined for the MIX server $M(i-1)$, is composed of the (address of the) next server Mi in the path and the envelope to be forwarded to that server;

- suitably *pads* the outermost envelope

$$Enc(ek_{M1}, [M2, Enc(ek_{M2}, [\ldots Enc(ek_R, [R, m]) \ldots])]),$$

prepares the padded version for sending it over a secure connection to the first chosen MIX server $M1$, and then actually sends the prepared version with a command to forward it as specified.

Accordingly, each MIX server $M(i-1)$ in the chosen path

- cryptographically opens the received envelope $m_{M(i-1)}$ by decrypting it with the private decryption key $dk_{M(i-1)}$, and obtains $[Mi, m_{Mi}]$;
- extracts the (address of the) next MIX server Mi and the envelope m_{Mi};
- forwards the extracted envelope m_{Mi} to the next MIX server Mi.

Additionally, when doing the above for each individual request for message forwarding, every MIX server follows a strictly *standardized behavior*, uniformly treating a predetermined number of homogeneously formatted messages in each round. More specifically, in each round, a MIX server

- buffers the anticipated number of incoming envelopes;
- removes duplicates;
- opens the envelopes, suitably pads them and prepares them for forwarding over a secure connection to the pertinent next MIX servers;
- if necessary, adds suitable dummy envelopes;
- selects a random ordering of the received envelopes and the dummy envelopes;
- using the selected random ordering, forwards each of the extracted envelopes to the pertinent next MIX server over the prepared secure connection, and treats the dummy envelopes in an indistinguishable way.

Basically, the first refined anonymity property is achieved by the onion-like envelopes and the corresponding routing technique, since a single MIX server can only see the direct predecessor and the direct successor in a transmission path. Accordingly, one "honest server" suffices to hide a link in the chain from the sender to the receiver, and thus to conceal the full routing data.

To satisfy the second refined anonymity property as well, which does not make any trust assumption, the standardized behavior is additionally needed. In particular, *padding, removing duplicates* and *reordering* should prevent inferences about links between incoming and outgoing messages based on any secondary properties of encrypted messages that are still observable. An exact definition of the standardized behavior and a detailed analysis of a probability-based, formal notion of *indistinguishability* is beyond the scope of this monograph.

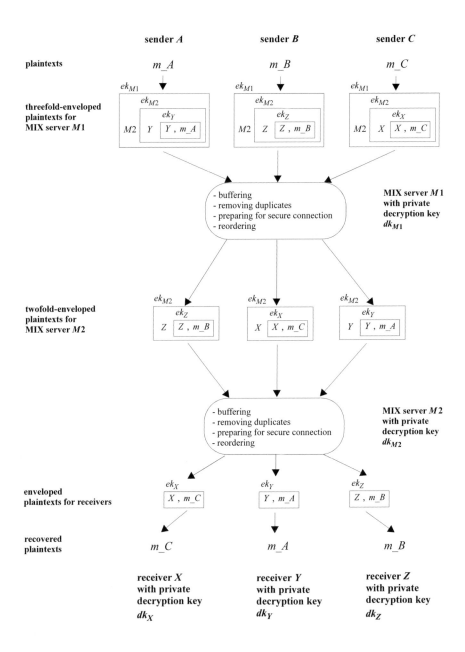

Fig. 15.3. An example MIX network with two MIX servers M1 and M2, employed for transmitting message *m_A* from sender *A* to receiver *Y*, message *m_B* from sender *B* to receiver *Z*, and message *m_C* from sender *C* to receiver *X*

15.5 Bibliographic Hints

Anonymization has been pioneered by Chaum [122, 123, 124]. Subsequently, A.Pfitzmann [389] and many others elaborate the approach; for example, more recently, Brickell/Camenisch/Chen [114, 105] invent "direct anonymous attestation", usable for trusted platform modules. Diaz/Claessens/Preneel/et al. [168, 169] investigate how to combine building blocks to achieve anonymity, and A.Pfitzmann/Hansen [391] propose a consolidated terminology for the field.

More specifically, blind signatures and their employment for achieving anonymity in terms of unlinkability regarding obligations, credentials and digital legitimations originate from the work of Chaum [120, 123], elaborated within the framework of RSA functions. Chaum/Pedersen [129] consider multilateral security for digital coins. Further work, exploiting ElGamal functions also, are contributed by, for example, Brands [100, 101], Stadler/Piveteau/Camenisch [458], Ferguson [203] and B.Pfitzmann/Sadeghi [393].

The concept of superimposed sending is proposed by Chaum [124] and since then is known as the DC network technique (after "dining cryptographers" or "David Chaum"). Further studies are contributed by, for example, Waidner [492] and Dolev/Ostrovsky [175].

Chaum [122] invent MIX networks. Goldschlag/Reed/Syverson [230] describe a variant known as onion routing. Serjantov/Dingledine/Syverson [441] provide a comparative analysis of various kinds of MIX network. Reiter/Rubin [406] introduce a related but more dynamic mechanism called Crowds, to be used for Web transactions.

16 Some Further Cryptographic Protocols

16.1 Survey

As set out in Section 12.1, cryptography enables *cooperation in the presence of threats*, based on limited trust between the participants involved, acting in a *distributed computing system*. In many cases, the participants follow a *cryptographic protocol*, executing several rounds of *local computations* and *message transmissions*. Such protocols are often composed of appropriate instantiations of more elementary cryptographic mechanisms, such as the basic blocks surveyed in Section 12.4 and treated more extensively in the preceding chapters. Moreover, even a particular "basic block" might be seen or might even have been designed as a protocol.

For instance, the ElGamal encryption mechanism (see Section 13.5) can be seen as being composed of a first round for key generation, involving among other things the (pseudo)random selection of the private exponent, a second round of key certification and key distribution, a third round of selecting a random string for enabling probabilistic encryption, encrypting a plaintext and communicating the resulting ciphertext, and a fourth round of decryption. The overall achievement of the properties of correctness and secrecy requires crucially that all rounds perform as expected, in a well-coordinated way.

Stream ciphers using block modes (see Section 13.10), undeniable signatures (see Section 14.7) and MIX networks (see Section 15.4) are examples of mechanisms that are designed as cryptographic protocols. Again, the overall success of these mechanisms depends on the coordinated properties of each of the respective components.

In all cases, first of all, each of the components of a protocol must satisfy the pertinent security properties. Additionally, the properties of the components must compose suitably to provide the required properties of the whole protocol. As outlined in Subsection 1.5.1, *compositionality* constitutes a great (and largely unsolved) challenge for computer engineering in general, and for cryptography in particular. Accordingly, we emphasize again that in this monograph we restrict ourselves to informal outlines of the arguments, leaving the needed thorough mathematical analysis to more specialized presentations.

More specifically, in this chapter we first present *covert commitments* and *secret sharing* as two frequently employed cryptographic protocols, taking them as examples of a rich variety of many protocols. In fact, over the last few decades, cryptographers have proposed an amazing world of often astonishing solutions to cooperation problems that seem to be unmanageable at first glance. Then we introduce two kinds of protocol that can be seen as major topics of recent research in cryptography.

The first kind deals with *zero-knowledge proofs*. In a nutshell, these protocols address a problem of the following sort. In cryptography, a specific participant is *distinguished* (from other participants) by knowing a *secret*, for example a cryptographic key or some random parameter. How can the specific participant convince a partner that he is indeed distinguished without revealing the secret? Protocols for zero-knowledge proofs are designed to enable an actual secret holder to provide enough evidence of the mere fact that he knows the secret, without giving his partner the opportunity to learn any more details about the secret; on the other hand, a cheating participant only maliciously claiming to know the secret should fail to convince his partner. Clearly, exact formalizations of the problem and the properties of their solutions have to be expressed in terms of computational complexity and probability theory, as exemplarily outlined for encryption and authentication in Section 13.11 and Section 14.9, respectively.

The second kind deals with *multiparty computations*. In a nutshell, these protocols deal with a core problem of cooperation in the presence of threats, namely how two or more participants ("parties") can reach a common conclusion about the value of some function (the result of a "computation") where each of the partners secretly provides one of the arguments while hiding that argument from the other partners. One example is known as the "millionaires' problem", where each of two partners has a certain amount of wealth to be kept secret, and the two want to conclude who is richer. More abstractly, they want to jointly compute a function that has two arguments x and y and returns a Boolean value that states whether $x < y$ or not, without revealing any further knowledge about the actual input figures. Again, notions of computational complexity and probability are essential.

For each cryptographic protocol presented, we sketch an application scenario, outline and discuss some reasonably required *security properties*. We indicate which party's security *interest*, in protecting against which *threats*, the properties are enforced for, following the paradigm of *multilateral security*. For each case, one or two actual *mechanisms* are exemplarily described and briefly evaluated.

Finally, in the last section, reinspecting some aspects of the specific protocols treated, we briefly consider how to design cryptographic protocols and how to analyze their properties in general. Basically, we sketch how the software engineering methods of *compositionality* and *refinement*, as introduced in Subsection 1.5.1, can potentially be instantiated for dealing with complex cryptographic protocols. In the *specification* layer, an imagined *trusted host* and (ideally secure) *private channels* are postulated, and security properties are expressed using an equational term framework often referred to as the *Dolev–Yao model*. In the *implementation* layer, the trusted host is refined into a protocol of local computations and message transmissions of the parties involved, and each single abstract component is refined (substituted) by a single concrete mechanism. As mentioned before, *compositionality* (of refinement and compositions) is the main challenge, which, unfortunately, admits only partial solutions.

16.2 Covert Commitments

16.2.1 Application Scenario and Security Requirements

Some cooperations give rise to a need for a participant to commit to a non-repudiable obligation regarding another participant without showing the actual content of the obligation in the first place. For example, in electronic commerce, a participant might submit a covert tender, to be opened only at a later point in time. In another example, to act anonymously, a participant might deposit a cover, with the details of his identity to be opened only later in the case of some agreed condition.

More abstractly, a two-party protocol for *covert commitments* comprises two phases:

- *Committing*. The committer discretionarily selects some value v_{com} and commits to this value, in a covert form regarding the receiver.
- *Revealing*. The committer reveals a value v_{show} to the receiver, who in turn either accepts or rejects it as the committed value.

These phases should be governed by the following complementary security requirements.

On the one hand, the committer should be actually bound to the selected value, i.e., the following (partial) *binding property* (a combined *correctness* and *unforgeability* property) is required:

$$\text{For all values } v_{com}: \text{if the committer enters the revealing phase at all,} \quad (16.1)$$
$$\text{then the receiver accepts the revealed value } v_{show}$$
$$\text{if and only if it is the committed value } v_{com}.$$

This property is "partial", since it applies only for the case where the committer actually enters the revealing phase. If an application demands that the revealing phase should be enabled without the committer's cooperation, then additional mechanisms are needed. For example, the committed value could be suitably deposited with several trustees, employing a *secret-sharing* protocol as presented in the next section.

On the other hand, after the committing and before the revealing, the following *secrecy property* is required:

$$\text{For all values } v_{com}, \text{ the receiver cannot "determine"} \quad (16.2)$$
$$\text{the committed value } v_{com} \text{ from the covert form.}$$

Usually, the (unforgeability part of the) binding property is mainly in the *interest* of the receiver, to protect against the *threat* of a (malicious) alteration of an obligation denoted by a committed value. The secrecy property is mainly in the *interest* of the committer, to protect against the *threat* of an unwanted information gain by the receiver.

Such a cryptographic protocol for covert commitments and its security properties can be illustrated by a "mechanical counterpart":

- When committing, the committer deposits the selected value or a suitable exhibit of that value, in a movable, locked strongbox that is handed over to the receiver afterwards, whereas the key is retained by the committer.
- When revealing, the committer transfers the key to the receiver, who can then open the box and see the value, or verify the exhibit with regard to the additionally communicated value.

The actual cryptographic algorithms simulate the mechanical analogue in a suitable way, roughly outlined as follows. The initial locking of the selected value or the exhibit of it in the strongbox is crafted as an encryption or an application of a one-way hash function, respectively. The later unlocking is captured by the corresponding decryption, or the later verification is performed by recomputing the hash value of the communicated value and comparing it with the previously received hash value, respectively. We shall describe two variants of this approach in more detail.

16.2.2 A Mechanism Based on Symmetric Encryption

This mechanism directly simulates a strongbox by *symmetric encryption*, given by an encryption algorithm *Enc* with a corresponding decryption algorithm *Dec*; in using this mechanism, the receiver connects the two phases by generating a random value r, used as a *nonce* to uniformly identify a protocol execution:

Round	Committer	Message	Receiver
1. Initializing:	select value v; generate secret key k;		randomly generate nonce r as execution identifier; send r to committer.
		$r \leftarrow$	
2. Committing:	concatenate v with r; encrypt concatenation using key k, i.e., *commit* := $Enc(k, v|r)$; send *commit* to receiver.		
		$\rightarrow commit$	
3. Requesting:			send r to committer as request for revealing.
		$r \leftarrow$	
4. Revealing:	send key k to receiver.		
		$\rightarrow k$	
5. Verifying:			decrypt *commit* using key k; verify identification, and either accept or reject the shown value.

Though at first glance this mechanism appears to be well designed, a thorough evaluation regarding the required properties of binding and secrecy is nontrivial. In particular, regarding (the *unforgeability* part of) *binding*, besides the usual properties, the symmetric encryption mechanism employed must additionally satisfy an appropriate *collision-resistance property*:

$$\text{For any communicated nonce } r, \qquad\qquad (16.3)$$
$$\text{the committer cannot "determine" two different values } v_1 \text{ and } v_2$$
$$\text{and corresponding keys } k_1 \text{ and } k_2$$
$$\text{such that } commit = Enc(k_1, v_1 | r) = Enc(k_2, v_2 | r)$$
$$[\text{and thus } Dec(k_1, commit) = v_1 | r \neq v_2 | r = Dec(k_2, commit)].$$

For, otherwise, the committer could first send *commit* and only later decide whether he shows the value v_1 or the value v_2, just by communicating the key k_1 or the key k_2. Besides its use for identifying a protocol execution, the nonce r also serves to impede such a fraud by enlarging the search space for a collision, if collisions cannot be totally avoided. Regarding the *secrecy property*, the underlying symmetric encryption mechanism must hide the plaintext even if the (concatenation) structure and some part (the second part of the concatenation) are already known.

16.2.3 A Mechanism Based on a One-Way Hash Function

This mechanism only indirectly simulates the usage of a strongbox for locking an exhibit, by using a *one-way hash function h*, exploiting features of computing beyond the possibilities of the mechanical world. When this mechanism is used, the committer connects the two phases by generating a *nonce* r_1 to uniformly identify a protocol execution, and additionally employs another random value r_2 to enlarge the domain of possible arguments of the hash function:

Round	**Committer**	Message	**Receiver**
1. Initializing:	select value v; randomly generate nonce r_1 as execution identifier; randomly generate r_2; concatenate v with r_1 and r_2.		
2. Committing:	compute hash value of concatenation, i.e., $commit := h(v \| r_1 \| r_2)$; send *commit* and r_1 to receiver.		
		$\rightarrow commit, r_1$	
3. Revealing:	send v with r_1 and r_2 to receiver.		
		$\rightarrow v, r_1, r_2$	
5. Verifying:			verify identification; recompute hash value; compare *commit* with recomputed hash value, and either accept or reject the shown value.

Again, a thorough analysis is nontrivial. The required *binding property* must be based on an appropriate *collision-resistance property* of the underlying hash function, and the required *secrecy property* must be implied by an appropriate *one-way property* of the underlying hash function.

16.3 Secret Sharing

16.3.1 Application Scenario and Security Requirements

Cooperation in the presence of threats might give rise to situation where a participant anticipates that some of his partners could act maliciously, but not all of them. Accordingly, he might be willing to trust sufficiently large groups of his partners while still distrusting individuals. Following the guideline of *separation of privileges*, the participant might then want to assign a permission for some activity to specific groups of partners such that the permission is effective only if all members of a permitted group cooperate honestly. For example, in a bank's strongroom, a safe deposit box can be opened only if two (supposedly independent) key holders, usually the box owner and a distinguished employee of the bank, use their respective (mechanical) keys in a coordinated way.

As a special case, a participant holding a secret might want to *share his secret* with specific groups of partners, i.e., only the cooperating members of a specified group should be able to jointly "recover" the secret. For example, a participant might see a need to *escrow* one of his *cryptographic keys* for emergencies such that specific groups of individuals can act as distinguishedly as the key holder himself. In another example, an anonymously acting participant might treat the details of his identity as a secret, to be recovered only by the cooperation of the members of a group of trustees in the case of some misbehavior.

For such and similar applications, several cryptographic protocols for *secret sharing* have been invented. Restricting ourselves to a subclass of such multi-party protocols, known as *threshold secret sharing*, there are essentially two phases:

- *Distributing*. The owner of the secret v computes *shares* $s_1,\ldots,s_n$ and distributes them to appropriate receivers.
- *Combining*. For some threshold $t \leq n$, t (or more) receivers collect their shares $s_{i_1},\ldots,s_{i_t}$ and use them to recover the secret.

These phases should be governed by the following complementary security requirements. On the one hand, any privileged group, consisting of t or more receivers, should be able to actually recover the original secret, i.e., the following *correctness property* is required:

> For all values v: the receivers succeed in determining the secret value v (16.4)
> from any set of t distinct shares $s_{i_1},\ldots,s_{i_t}$.

On the other hand, any non-privileged group, consisting of fewer than t receivers, should always fail to learn the secret, i.e., the following *secrecy property* is required:

> For all values v: the receivers cannot "determine" the secret value v (16.5)
> from any set of $t-1$ shares.

Usually, the secrecy property is mainly in the *interest* of the owner, to protect against the *threat* of a misuse of the shares. Sometimes, the secrecy property is strengthened to require *perfect secrecy* in the rough sense that under the given conditions, all possible values are equally likely to be the secret. Depending on the application, the *interest* in the correctness property might either be common to all parties or apply only to one of the sides. *Threats* might be caused by any party aiming at hindering the reconstruction of the original secret. Moreover, if the correctness is in the interest of only the receivers and not of the owner, for example if the secret is an identity to be recovered in the case of the owner's misbehavior, the receivers might require a strengthened form, ensuring that they can recognize the "validity" of a single share immediately on receipt. Unfortunately, known mechanisms for *verifiable secret sharing* that enforces the latter interest tend to suffer from a larger computational complexity.

16.3.2 A Mechanism Based on Distributing Linear Equations

This mechanism is based on a simple but very ingeniously elaborated idea, which also permits many variations. The initially *explicitly* available secret v is transformed into an *implicit* representation in the form of a *system of linear equations* that uniquely determines the secret. More specifically, using an appropriate algebraic structure, one determines a set of n linear equations for the secret v such that each subset of t equations has v as the unique solution but each set of $t-1$ equations admits any possible value as a solution.

The algebraic structure is given by addition and multiplication of residues modulo some prime number p, i.e., by a *finite field* $(\mathbf{Z}_p, +, \cdot, 0, 1)$, where p should be sufficiently large. The linear equations are constructed by use of a polynomial over $\mathbf{Z}_p$ in the variable x of degree $t-1$,

$$p(x) = a_0 + a_1 x^1 + \ldots + a_{t-1} x^{t-1},$$ (16.6)

where the *owner* defines the coefficients in the *distributing phase* as follows:

- The constant term a_0 is the secret, i.e., $a_0 = v$.
- The remaining terms $a_1, \ldots, a_{t-1}$ are randomly generated from $\mathbf{Z}_p$.

From the point of view of the *receivers*, all these coefficients, including the secret, are seen as unknowns, to be determined by solving equations that are suitably derived from the shares communicated in the *combining phase*.

The needed equations result from evaluating the polynomial p for n distinct arguments $x_i \neq 0$, delivering the evaluation results $y_i = p(x_i)$, and taking the pairs (x_i, y_i) as the shares. In fact, each such share (x_i, y_i) yields an equation

$$a_0 + a_1 x_i^1 + \ldots + a_{t-1} x_i^{t-1} = y_i \tag{16.7}$$

in the unknowns $a_0, a_1, \ldots, a_{t-1}$. Thus, as announced above, the *explicit* representation of the polynomial by its coefficients, which include the secret, can be transformed into an *implicit* representation by a set of shares.

These considerations suggest the following mechanism for secret sharing:

Round	**Owner**	Message	**... Receiver$_i$** ...

1. Initializing: select secret v;
   define $a_0 := v$;
   randomly generate $a_1, \ldots, a_{t-1}$;
   form polynomial p according to (16.6).

2. Distributing: define n distinct arguments $x_i \neq 0$;
   for $i = 1, \ldots, n$:
   compute $y_i := p(x_i)$;
   send share (x_i, y_i) to receiver$_i$.

$$\rightarrow (x_i, y_i)$$

3. Combining: collect (at least) t shares;

$$\leftrightarrow$$

solve resulting equations;
return solution for a_0.

Regarding the required *correctness property*, any t distributed shares enable the receivers involved to set up the following system of linear equations in the unknowns $a_0, a_1, \ldots, a_{t-1}$:

$$a_0 + a_1 x_{i_1}^1 + \ldots + a_{t-1} x_{i_1}^{t-1} = y_{i_1}$$

$$a_0 + a_1 x_{i_2}^1 + \ldots + a_{t-1} x_{i_2}^{t-1} = y_{i_2}$$

$$\ldots$$

$$a_0 + a_1 x_{i_t}^1 + \ldots + a_{t-1} x_{i_t}^{t-1} = y_{i_t}$$

This system of equations has a unique solution, since the coefficients of the system form a Vandermonde matrix

$$\begin{bmatrix} 1 & x_{i_1}^1 & x_{i_1}^2 & \ldots & x_{i_1}^{t-1} \\ 1 & x_{i_2}^1 & x_{i_2}^2 & \ldots & x_{i_2}^{t-1} \\ \cdot & \cdot & \cdot & \cdot & \cdot \\ 1 & x_{i_t}^1 & x_{i_t}^2 & \ldots & x_{i_t}^{t-1} \end{bmatrix} ;$$

its determinant is given by

$$\det X = \prod_{1 \le l < k \le t} (x_{i_k} - x_{i_l}) \bmod p$$

and evaluates in the finite field to a nonzero value, since the arguments x_i are pairwise distinct.

Regarding the required *secrecy property*, any $t - 1$ equations still admit any element z of $\mathbf{Z}_p$ as a solution for a_0. For we could add a further share $(0, z)$ and would obtain a uniquely solvable system of t linear equations whose solution comprises $a_0 = z$.

16.4 Zero-Knowledge Proofs

16.4.1 Application Scenario

Some cooperations give rise to the problem that a participant wants to convince another participant that some *assertion* is valid while ensuring that any further information beyond this validity is hidden. For example, the participant might hold a *secret* that, when used as a cryptographic key, *distinguishes* him to perform some operation. How can this participant convince somebody else that he is a key holder and thus distinguished, without revealing anything else about the key? In the following, we first inspect some basic features of the process of convincing in general, and then consider the additional secrecy requirement.

The process of *convincing* can be seen as a protocol execution performed by two (or more) parties. There are a *prover* (convincer) and a *verifier*. In a very simple example, in the first round the prover *presents* a text claimed to be a mathematical proof of some formalized assertion, and in the second round the verifier *evaluates* whether the presented reasoning proceeds from specified assumptions step by step to valid conclusions using agreed inference rules, finally reaching the claimed assertion. In many situations, however, more rounds are needed: typically, the verifier doubts some steps in the arguments and then challenges the prover to provide further or more detailed justifications, and such *challenges* and the corresponding *responses* might extend over several rounds. In fact, for example, legal proceedings largely follow this pattern: some prover, for example the prosecutor, aims to convince the verifier, the judge, step by step of his accusation by adequately responding to any challenging objections such as doubts, counterarguments or the testimony of a witness for the defense. If the prosecutor succeeds, the judge finally accepts the records of the challenges and responses as a *proof* of the assertion expressed by the accusation.

At first glance, it appears that any additional secrecy requirement would be only rarely enforceable: how does one react convincingly to the challenges without revealing more potentially "useful information"? In other words, how does one restrict the increase of the verifier's "knowledge" to the validity of the assertion under consideration? In yet other words, how does one let the verifier finally "know" that the assertion considered is valid without enabling him to "learn" anything else meaningful, and, in particular, without providing the verifier with the means to convince a further party of the assertion himself? A second thought indicates that it is very difficult even to precisely specify such a kind of secrecy property: for example, what do we exactly mean when we speak about "useful information", "knowledge" or "learning"?

Astonishingly enough, as answers to these questions, modern cryptography has developed sophisticated specifications, which are based in particular on advanced notions of classical *probability theory* and the theory of *computational complexity*; it has also developed ingenious mechanisms to meet these specifications, exploiting, for instance, the complexity analysis of *NP-complete problems, factorization* of numbers or *discrete logarithms*. In the following, we only outline a basic approach, with the strong disclaimer that the presentation is only an informal sketch, in need of many subtle and precisely defined formal concepts of mathematics and computing. The approach is presented in terms of formal mathematical proofs, i.e., inferences in some system of algorithmic theorem proving, and in terms of recursively enumerable, recursive, and NP-complete formal languages, supposed to be known to the reader or self-explanatory.

Given an application, we postulate a formal language over some alphabet Σ as the *universe of discourse*, to express *assertions*. For the sake of simplicity, we assume that this language is the full set Σ^*, i.e., each word over Σ is seen as a well-formed and meaningful assertion. Additionally, we postulate a precise definition of which assertions are *valid*; such a word is also called a *theorem*, and we designate the set of theorems by $T \subset \Sigma^*$. Finally, we represent *formal proofs* (*inferences, pieces of evidence, exhibits* or *witnesses*) of theorems as words over the same alphabet Σ, postulating a precise definition of a word w constituting a formal proof of a theorem t. On the basis of these postulates and some further assumptions, the set

$$R := \{ (t,w) \mid t \in T, w \in \Sigma^* \text{ is a formal proof for } t \} \subset \Sigma^* \times \Sigma^* \qquad (16.8)$$

of "theorems with an attached proof" is well defined.

Generalizing the notions introduced above, conversely, we can interpret any binary relation $R \subset \Sigma^* \times \Sigma^*$ as a set of "theorems with an attached proof", considering its projection onto the first component

$$T_R := \{ t \mid \text{exists } w \in \Sigma^* : (t,w) \in R \} \subset \Sigma^* \qquad (16.9)$$

as the corresponding set of "theorems". Then T_R contains the "provable assertions" without providing a "concrete formal proof".

Assigning these abstract concepts the meaning commonly used in *first-order logic*, we can summarize the classical results about its *completeness* and *undecidability* as follows:

- The set R of "theorems with an attached proof" is *recursive* (*algorithmically decidable*).
- The set T of "theorems" is *recursively enumerable* (*algorithmically semi-decidable*) but *not recursive* (*algorithmically undecidable*).

Accordingly, in terms of the theory of computation, in general the *verification* of a presented proof is easier than finding such a proof (more precisely, it is easier than confirming the *existence* of a yet unknown proof).

Assigning the abstract concepts a closely related meaning that has been explored for *propositional logic*, and now seeing a *satisfiable* propositional assertion as a "theorem" and a satisfying truth-value definition as a "proof", we can summarize a famous insight about computational *tractability* and *intractability* as follows:

- The set R of "satisfiable assertions with an attached satisfying truth-value definition" is *polynomial-time decidable*.
- The set T of "satisfiable assertions" is *NP-complete*. Thus T is *recognizable in nondeterministic polynomial time*, but it is widely believed to be only *exponential-time decidable*.

Hence again, in terms of the theory of computational complexity, in general the *verification* of a presented truth-value definition as satisfying is easier than *finding* such a satisfying truth-value definition (more precisely, it is easier than confirming the *existence* of a yet unknown satisfying truth-value definition).

Finally, we consider a specific graph-theoretical interpretation of the abstract concepts. In this context, a "theorem" is a *3-colorable graph*, i.e., an assertion that the graph admits a color assignment to its nodes such that any two edge-connected nodes are given different colors, and such a *3-coloring* is seen as a "proof". We can summarize the known results about computational *tractability* and *intractability* as follows:

- The set R of "3-colorable graphs with an attached 3-coloring" is *polynomial-time decidable*.
- The set T of "3-colorable graphs" is *NP-complete*. Thus T is *recognizable in nondeterministic polynomial time*, but it is widely believed to be only *exponential-time decidable*.

Accordingly, this example, like many others as well, confirms that in general the *verification* of a presented proof is computationally easier than finding such a proof (more precisely, it is easier than confirming the *existence* of a yet unknown proof).

However, this case exhibits a particularity of proofs: a 3-coloring can be easily verified by inspecting each edge of the graph one by one, totally independently, to determine whether the two connected nodes are differently colored. This feature suggests that one can *probabilistically* check a claimed 3-colorability by verifying random samples of edges, roughly outlined as follows.

Once the prover has committed to a coloring claimed to be a 3-coloring for the graph under consideration, the verifier repeatedly creates a *challenge* by selecting any edge, and the prover then shows the committed colors of the connected edges as a *response*. If the prover has indeed committed to a 3-coloring, he can convince the verifier of the claimed 3-colorability; otherwise, with an increasing number of challenges, the probability increases that the verifier will hit an edge that violates the property of 3-colorability, leading him to reject the claim. We reconsider this approach in Subsection 16.4.3 in more detail.

16.4.2 Security Requirements

Interactive proof protocols, here deliberately called *conviction protocols*, for two parties who are interactively proving a theorem, or, more precisely, for a *prover convincing* a *verifier* about a claimed *theorem*, should be

- governed by appropriate *security properties*
- that comprise suitable *computational complexity* requirements,
- capturing the possibility that one party might be a *threat* for the other party.

Below, we informally sketch four related security properties, intended to basically express the requirement that convincing should be successful if and only if the assertion considered is a theorem indeed, and that a verifier cannot learn anything else thereby. In doing so, we outline the pertinent complexity requirements separately.

We capture possible threats by constraining the worst-case effectiveness of an imagined *replacement* of an honest party by an attacking variant: essentially, an honest *prover* is imagined to be replaced by an attacking one that attempts to convince the verifier about a non-theorem; an honest *verifier* is imagined to be replaced by an attacking one that misuses the challenge–response procedure to gain additional knowledge. In preparing for *all* potential threats without knowing their details in advance, we essentially imagine replacement by *any probabilistic polynomial-time* algorithm.

Usually, a threatened party could easily recognize an open deviation from the message structure of the agreed protocol. Thus the main problem for the threatened party is to protect against the effects of a replaced party's covert misbehavior that is undetectable either in principal or for reasons of complexity.

First, a conviction protocol should satisfy a *completeness property*, requiring roughly the following:

$$\text{If the input assertion is indeed a theorem,} \qquad (16.10)$$
$$\text{then the prover can always convince the verifier.}$$

Concerning computational complexity, for abstracting from the difficulty in principle of finding a proof as discussed above, the *prover* might access a "formal proof" without counting the computational effort, for example just by asking a "private oracle". Besides this, however, the *verifier* alone, as well as the *cooperation* between the prover and the verifier, should be efficient, i.e., computable by probabilistic polynomial-time algorithms. Thus the easier task in principle of evaluating a given proof could be enabled, though the verifier should not see such a proof.

Second, a conviction protocol should satisfy a *correctness property*, requiring roughly the following:

$$\text{If the input assertion is } not \text{ a theorem,} \qquad (16.11)$$
then each attacking replacement of the prover
can convince the verifier, i.e., mislead him to acceptance,
with at most a small (error) probability.

Of course, we would prefer that the verifier would *never* be deceived into being convinced of a non-theorem. However, in general, this goal will not be achievable, for the following reasons. On the one hand, being restricted to probabilistic polynomial-time computations, the verifier alone cannot decide on theorems in general. On the other hand, even though the verifier could check a given proof, the prover will not exhibit such a proof, owing to the secrecy requirement.

Both the completeness and the correctness property are expressed in terms of an honest verifier, even though we can imagine two "silly replacements", each of which trivially satisfies one of these properties: a "silly yes-verifier" always accepts, and a "silly no-verifier" always rejects. However, no single verifier can show both silly behaviors, and thus these silly replacements are implicitly excluded by considering both properties simultaneously.

Third, we consider threats to an honest prover, presented by attacking replacements of the *verifier*. These threats consist of attempting to gain additional information from the challenge–response procedure. Clearly, in the given context, where only two parties are involved, the honest prover must help himself: if the input assertion is a theorem, the prover has to confine *his own part* in the cooperation such that he reveals essentially only "provability" and nothing else, whatever replacement of the verifier is involved. Owing to the intended applications, where theorems are interpreted as secrets, this confinement is considered to be irrelevant for non-theorems.

Similar to Definition 13.1, of semantic secrecy of an encryption scheme, the wanted prover's confinement is described in terms of *alternative investigators* that work in isolation. Roughly sketched, the results of any threatening behavior of a replaced verifier interacting with the prover should be *computationally indistinguishable* from the results obtained by a corresponding alternative investigator without any interaction. Thus, as far as one can computationally recognize, whatever a cheating verifier can learn on the basis of the prover's responses could also be learned without seeing those responses.

Slightly more precisely, but still informally stated, the following *zero-knowledge property* is required as a *secrecy property*:

$$\text{For each attacking replacement } V\hat{} \text{ of the verifier,} \qquad (16.12)$$
given as a probabilistic polynomial-time algorithm,
there exists a probabilistic polynomial-time algorithm
acting as an alternative investigator
such that, for each input assertion that is a theorem, the following holds:
the results produced by the (replaced) verifier $V\hat{}$ cooperating with the prover P
are computationally indistinguishable from
the results produced by the alternative investigator working in isolation.

Fourth, we consider an example of a further security property that has been proposed to complement the fundamental properties of completeness, correctness and zero knowledge. This example emphasizes a distinction made before:

- A prover might convince a verifier about "the existence of a formal proof".
- A prover might convince a verifier that he himself "knows" a formal proof.

The first alternative matches the definition (16.9) of a theorem but does not explain what "knowledge" enables the prover to be successful. For instance, we could imagine a non-constructive possibility that allows one to infer the pure existence of a proof from the "structure" of the assertion considered; for example, we could argue that a graph that is a tree admits a 3-coloring (even a 2-coloring) simply on the basis of the tree properties, without exhibiting a concrete coloring. However, in this example we also could derive a coloring procedure readily by constructing a concrete coloring.

Obviously, assuming "true knowledge" only, the second alternative comprises the first one but might be strictly stronger: it not only speaks about a state of an assertion, that it is a theorem, but also expresses a state of the prover, that he possesses a proof.

This distinction might be worthwhile in a situation where the verifier is already convinced about the provability but is still wondering whether a specific cooperation partner, the pertinent prover, "knows" a concrete proof. In fact, the verifier might want to get a hint of whether his remote partner, which could happen to be a malicious replacement, has correctly guessed the provability and successful responses just by chance, which is not excluded by the security properties presented so far.

Basically, the doubting verifier can only exploit the *communication data* that can arise as *messages* during a protocol execution, since nothing other than this data represents the actual prover at a remote site, whether that prover is the honest prover or any (malicious) replacement.

More specifically, the verifier's attempt to get the wanted hint is modeled as an imaginary and, in principle, computationally unrestricted *knowledge extractor* that works roughly as follows:

- It takes a theorem $t \in T_R$ as input.
- It might ask an additional *oracle* to provide the communication data resulting from one or more fictitious cooperations between the verifier V and (the possibly replaced) prover $P\hat{\ }$.
- It aims at probabilistically computing a concrete formal proof w for the theorem t by itself.

We can reasonably require that the following items are *inversely proportional*:

- $Prob(P\hat{\ }, t)$, defined as the probability that the replacement $P\hat{\ }$ of the prover succeeds in convincing the verifier V;
- $ExpectedTime(P\hat{\ }, t)$, defined as the expected time needed by the knowledge extractor to successfully compute a formal proof w with $(t, w) \in R$.

Such a requirement can be justified as follows. On the one hand, assuming that a "highly" convincingly operating (replaced) prover actually "knows" a formal proof, we suggest that such a (replaced) prover can deliver sufficient hints about its knowledge such that the knowledge extractor can construct its own proof with only a "small" computational effort. On the other hand, assuming conversely that a "slightly" convincingly operating (replaced) prover essentially only guesses, without possessing the corresponding "knowledge", we suggest that such a (replaced) prover cannot deliver helpful hints to the knowledge extractor, which thus has to expend "high" computational effort to construct its own proof. Summarizing and putting the preceding considerations slightly more precisely, the following *proof-of-knowledge property* can be additionally required:

> There exists a knowledge extractor for the verifier V that,   (16.13)
> for every replacement $P\hat{\ }$ of the prover, and for every theorem $t \in T_R$ as input,
> by exploiting oracle answers regarding the communication data between $P\hat{\ }$ and V,
> returns a formal proof w with $(t, w) \in R$ such that

$$ExpectedTime(P^{\wedge}, t) \leq \frac{p(length(t))}{Prob(P^{\wedge}, t)},$$

where p is some suitable polynomial, and *length* yields the size of the input t.

16.4.3 A Mechanism Based on an NP-Complete Problem

This mechanism elaborates the probabilistic checking of the *3-colorability* of a graph, introduced at the end of Subsection 16.4.1; it depends crucially on an underlying mechanism for *covert commitments*, as discussed in Section 16.2:

Round/Step	**Prover**	Message	**Verifier**

0. Initializing:

common input: a graph G
with n nodes and m edges

[the following steps (1) to (4) are repeated m^2 times]

1 to m^2. Challenging and Responding:

(1) asserting:
  randomly select a coloring of G,
  which is a 3-coloring if possible;

  randomly select a permutation of colors;

  for each node x:
    compute permuted color c_x of node x;
    commit covertly on c_x, and
    send commitment to verifier.

$\rightarrow$ commitment
for coloring

(2) challenging:

randomly select an edge (x, y),
and send it as challenge.

$(x, y) \leftarrow$

(3) responding:
  reveal committed colors c_x and c_y
  for connected nodes x and y, and
  send revelations as response to verifier;

$\rightarrow (c_x, c_y)$

(4) verifying:

verify revealed values, and
check inequality of c_x and c_y.

m^2+1. Accepting or rejecting:

accept (3-colorability) iff
all claimed inequalities hold.

Assuming appropriate complexity-theoretic conjectures, in particular that an NP-complete problem does not admit a polynomial-time decision function and that there exist collision-resistant one-way hash functions that can be employed for the commitments, one can demonstrate that the mechanism presented satisfies the four required properties. Some of the arguments are sketched in the following.

Regarding the required *completeness property*, whenever the common input graph is 3-colorable, in step (1) of every repetition round the prover can select a 3-coloring, and thus he will later succeed, in step (3), in sending a convincing response to any challenge received in step (2), finally leading to a certain *overall acceptance*.

Regarding the *correctness property*, whenever the input is *not* 3-colorable, in step (1) of every repetition round the prover necessarily selects a coloring that violates 3-colorability for at least one edge, and thus the verifier will hit one of these edges as the challenge in step (2) with probability at least $1/m > 0$. Assuming that the underlying commitment scheme possesses the pertinent correctness property, by his response in step (3) the prover has to reveal the violation, which the verifier easily detects in step (4), leading to an immediate overall *rejection*. Thus, in each *single* repetition round, the fact that the graph is not 3-colorable remains undetected by the verifier with probability at most $1 - 1/m$. Accordingly, after m^2 repetitions, the non-3-colorability still remains undetected only with probability at most

$$\left(1 - \frac{1}{m}\right)^{m^2} = \left(\left(1 - \frac{1}{m}\right)^m\right)^m \approx \left(\frac{1}{e}\right)^m, \tag{16.14}$$

indicating, in general, a small probability of an erroneous acceptance, which could be further diminished by additional repetitions. Thus the mechanism achieves the expected *overall rejection* with a high probability.

Regarding the *zero-knowledge property*, the mechanism depends strongly on the secrecy property of the underlying mechanism for covert commitments, together with the randomness of the selected colorings and permutations, in order to prevent inferences regarding the information revealed in different repetition rounds. Basically, a detailed analysis argues roughly as follows. In an accepting execution, for each challenge, the response shows two different colors that appear "as if they were randomly selected" and thus are computationally indistinguishable from the results that an isolated third party would produce. Moreover, this feature is preserved under the m^2-fold sequential *composition* of the commitment mechanism.

Regarding the *proof-of-knowledge property*, a detailed analysis also justifies the claim, by dealing with an appropriate "error function".

Finally, we should mention that this specific mechanism based on the NP-complete problem of 3-colorability of graphs delivers a rich class of further mechanisms. In fact, any other *NP-complete* problem can serve as a basis as well. We can describe this roughly as follows. Consider any NP-complete set T of "theorems". There then exists a polynomial-time computable reduction function f mapping potential theorems to graphs such that

$$t \in T \quad \text{if and only if} \quad f(t) \text{ is 3-colorable.} \tag{16.15}$$

This reduction function can be complemented by a corresponding reduction function for the respective "proofs". Exploiting the two reduction functions, one can construct a mechanism based on the given NP problem that essentially reduces all challenges regarding a proof of an element of T to a problem regarding the 3-colorability of a graph. For the effectiveness of the construction, we have to carefully demonstrate that the reductions preserve not only the *completeness property* and the *correctness property*, as indicated by the equivalence (16.15), but also the *zero-knowledge property* and the *proof-of-knowledge property*. Clearly, again these properties are known to be satisfied only under the pertinent complexity-theoretic assumptions.

16.5 Multiparty Computations

16.5.1 Application Scenario and Security Requirements

Multiparty computations address a very general situation of *cooperation in the presence of threats* between n participants, in this context commonly called parties. In principle, the parties aim at jointly computing the value y of some agreed n-ary function f, where each of the parties P_i secretly provides an argument x_i and, at the end of the execution of the protocol, each of them knows the computed value $y = f(x_1, \dots, x_n)$ without having learnt anything new about the other parties' arguments. However, anticipating that some parties involved might not be honest but *threatening* the remaining ones, this goal should be essentially achieved even if some parties turn out to have been replaced by attacking variants. As exemplified for encryption in Section 12.5, an *attacker* might deviate from the protocol in various ways. For example, an arbitrary "feasible but worst-case" attacker can be modeled by a *probabilistic polynomial-time* algorithm that possibly attacks both *actively*, by sending unexpected messages, and *adaptively*, by choosing its actions according to the state of the protocol execution.

In the introductory section of this chapter, we mention the Boolean-valued "less-than function" on natural numbers as a simple example, known as the "millionaires' problem". Another example is "addition with inputs restricted to elements of $\{0, 1\}$", which can be applied to *electronic voting* in the form of counting the positive votes, i.e., the number of 1's input by the parties.

Clearly, we cannot expect that a multiparty computation will return the wanted function value if all parties are attacking. Thus, making no initial distinctions between the parties, we have to lay down a *threshold* t for the number of attacking parties that are tolerated by the protocol: as long as there are at most t attacking parties forming an *adversary* to the remaining honest parties, the overall effectiveness of the computation should be guaranteed. Conjecturing (rightly) that, in general, only adversaries formed by a strict minority can be tolerated, if at all, we have a special situation for $n = 2$ (which is not treated in the remainder of this section).

Summarizing, a multiparty computation should be governed by security requirements of the following form, expressed tentatively, and not expressed appropriately if taken literally. First, for the sake of availability and integrity, a *correctness property* with respect to a threshold t is required:

For all inputs $x_1, \dots, x_n$ of the parties $P_1, \dots, P_n$, respectively, with $n > 2$, (16.16)
    if the adversary is formed by at most t attacking parties (a strict minority),
        then each of the honest parties obtains $f(x_1, \dots, x_n)$ as the final result.

Second, a *secrecy property* with respect to a threshold t is required:

For all inputs $x_1, \dots, x_n$ of the parties $P_1, \dots, P_n$, respectively, with $n > 2$, (16.17)
    an adversary formed by at most t attacking parties (a strict minority)
        cannot "determine" any of the secret inputs of the honest parties.

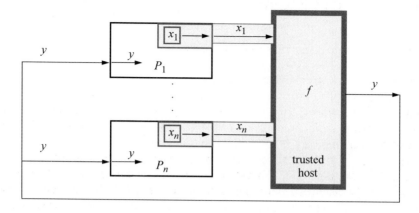

Fig. 16.1. A trusted host with private input channels (gray areas must be hidden)

To improve these requirements and to explore the options for actual mechanisms, we are going to consider three increasingly more complex models.

In the first model, visualized in Figure 16.1, a fictitious mechanism for a multi-party computation of the function f is built from an imagined *trusted host* together with (ideally secure) *private channels* between each of the parties and the trusted host:

- Initially, party P_i inputs its argument x_i, sending a corresponding message to the trusted host over the private channel (enforcing confidentiality and further security properties such as availability, authenticity and integrity).
- Then, without any interaction with its environment and completely protected against any observations from outside, the trusted host computes the requested function value $y = f(x_1, \ldots, x_n)$.
- Finally, the trusted host broadcasts the computed value, sending a corresponding message to each of the parties P_i.

Clearly, to achieve multiparty computations in practice, we do not want to rely on an external *third party* to be completely *trusted*, in particular trusted to functionally operate as expected, to hide secret information and to refrain from misusing secret information in any other way. We could improve the model by modifying it as sketched in the following.

In the second model, visualized in Figure 16.2, the postulated private input channels are implemented by a suitable encryption mechanism (and additional mechanisms for further security properties), and the host – still acting as a third party – now *operates on ciphertexts* and, finally, yields the encryption of the wanted result. Accordingly, the third party has to compute a function $f\_encrypt$ associated with the original function f such that the encryption of the f value $y = f(x_1, \ldots, x_n)$ for the arguments $x_1, \ldots, x_n$ equals the $f\_encrypt$ value for the encrypted arguments.

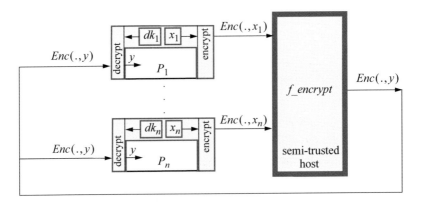

Fig. 16.2. A semi-trusted host operating on ciphertexts with open input channels (gray areas must be hidden)

Hence, given the original function f, we need an encryption mechanism and an *associated* function $f\_encrypt$ such that the encryption is *homomorphic* regarding the original function f by way of the third-party function $f\_encrypt$. Provided the encryption mechanism ensures a suitable *secrecy property* in this context, we now have to impose less trust on the third party than before: we still have to trust in the correct evaluation of the associated function, but the third party's compliance with the secrecy requirements is *technically enforced* by the cryptographic construction, and thus the host needs only to be *semi-trusted*. Expressed more carefully, some secrecy-related part of the needed trust is *reduced* to the underlying encryption mechanism and thereby substantially diminished.

In the third model, visualized in Figure 16.3, we attempt to go even further, getting totally rid of the third party and using only a suitable *network* for *exchanging messages* between the parties. In this case, each party has to enforce its *interests* by itself, without delegating crucial parts of the functionality to any kind of third party. Basically, as always in cryptography, such an enforcement would be based on local *secrets* (keys, nonces, ...) to be carefully hidden from any other party, complemented by *tamper-resistant* protection of each party's own computing equipment where secrets are processed. Regarding the specific semi-trusted host imagined before, the parties essentially have to jointly simulate first the *computation on ciphertexts*, i.e., of the *associated* function $f\_encrypt$, and then the final *decryption* of the encrypted result. More generally, given suitably encrypted inputs, the parties have to simulate the function that assigns the normal function value of f to the encrypted arguments, i.e., the composition of $f\_encrypt$ and decryption, in whatever form.

Resuming our attempt to appropriately express the security requirements, we make two observations. The first model of a trusted host indicates some inevitable events that (at least so far) cannot be treated at all. An attacking participant might

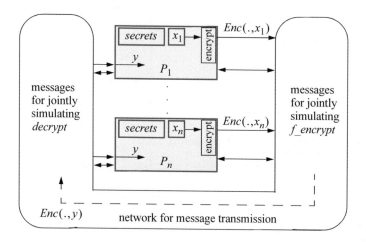

Fig. 16.3. Parties cooperating by use of protected local operations and message transmissions for a joint computation under limited trust (gray areas must be hidden)

use a "wrong" input; for example, a millionaire might use an input that does not reflect his wealth in the "real world". Since the input is kept secret, even in the trusted-host model nobody can prevent or detect such misbehavior (without any knowledge about the "real world"). Furthermore, an attacking party might refuse to contribute at all to the protocol execution. Again, nobody can force an unwilling party to be active. Clearly, the first observation applies to the other models as well, as does the second observation. For the third model, the second observation must in fact be extended, since an attacking party might now leave the computation at any point of time.

On the basis of these observations, taking the trusted-host model as a standard for the best achievable result, and intending to constrain the mechanisms complying with the third model, we can outline how to define the security requirements for multiparty computations more precisely, though leaving them still in need of further clarification. Without attempting to achieve precision, we shall sketch a combined *correctness and secrecy property* with respect to a threshold t, roughly expressing the following:

> Whatever violations of correctness and secrecy   (16.18)
> can be achieved in the model of
> parties cooperating by protected local operations and message transmissions
> can also (inevitably) happen in the trusted-host model, and thus, in particular,
> without observing messages of the honest parties at all.

Expanding in more technical terms, a combined *correctness and secrecy property* of the following kind is required:

Considering inputs $x_1, \ldots, x_n$ of parties $P_1, \ldots, P_n$, respectively, with $n > 2$, if the adversary is formed by replacing at most t parties $P_{i_1}, \ldots, P_{i_t}$ (a strict minority) with probabilistic polynomial-time attacking variants, then,

- regarding *correctness*, the adversary's impact on the outputs for the honest parties, and
- regarding *secrecy*, the final adversary's view (knowledge) about the inputs of the honest parties

are computationally *indistinguishable* from the respective effects of a corresponding adversary formed for the trusted-host model.

For constructing an actual mechanism that complies with the third model and satisfies the stated security requirements, many challenging subproblems must be solved in a *compositional* way, ensuring that a solution to one subproblem remains valid in the overall context. We mention only some of these subproblems and indicate some directions for managing them:

- When introducing a secret into a protocol execution, a party should be committed to the selected value of the secret, i.e., it should not be able to change the value without detection by other parties. Thus some kinds of *covert commitments* are helpful.
- If some operation is to be successfully performable only by the cooperation of all members of some group, each individual member is not completely *distinguished* but only partially so, and, accordingly, it shares its distinctiveness with its partners. Thus some kinds of *secret sharing* are needed.
- A participant claiming to hold a secret or distributing some item derived from a secret, for example a commitment or a share, should be able to convince a partner of being the holder of such a secret. Thus some kinds of *zero-knowledge proofs of knowledge* are needed.

These examples show that the protocols treated in the preceding sections of this chapter are not only interesting in their own right but also important as crucial parts of more general multiparty computations.

16.5.2 Employing Homomorphic Threshold Encryption

One specific approach to constructing mechanisms for a multiparty computation performed by n parties $P_1, \ldots, P_n$ in a finite field $(\mathbf{Z}_p, +, \cdot, 0, 1)$ of residues modulo some prime number p is based on an asymmetric *encryption* mechanism that possesses some special properties besides the usual ones. More specifically, such an encryption mechanism has

- a locally executable *encryption* algorithm *Enc*,
- a *decryption* algorithm *Dec* that is only jointly executable, and
- a jointly executable *key generation* algorithm *Gen*,

and additionally satisfies the following properties for every key pair with a public encryption key *ek*:

- The encryption mechanism has a *homomorphism property* regarding addition by multiplication, i.e., for all plaintexts x and y,

$$Enc(ek, x + y) = Enc(ek, x) \cdot Enc(ek, y). \qquad (16.19)$$

Thus, for every plaintext x and every plaintext y, any party that already possesses the ciphertexts of x and y can compute the ciphertext of $x + y$ without actually knowing the plaintext $x + y$. This feature potentially offers the possibility to operate on an intermediate value v arising in a normal computation using only the encrypted form $Enc(ek, v)$.

- The encryption mechanism has a *threshold property* regarding n parties, i.e., the key generation algorithm delivers only *shares* of the private decryption key to the parties such that the following holds:

> The n parties can correctly decrypt a ciphertext $Enc(ek, z)$ to z $\qquad$ (16.20)
> if and only if
> a strict *majority* of the parties *cooperate honestly*.

Thus, in particular, considering any ciphertext with an unknown plaintext, no adversary consisting of a strict minority of parties will succeed in gaining the plaintext.

Without describing a concrete mechanism, we observe only that it is reasonable to attempt the construction of such an encryption mechanism: a fundamental operation of asymmetric cryptography, namely *exponentiation* seen as a function of the exponent for a fixed basis b, is *homomorphic* regarding addition, i.e., $b^{x+y} = b^x \cdot b^y$, and *secret sharing* with a threshold t taken as $n/2$ has a related threshold property.

Basically, the full multiparty computation mechanism exploits these additional properties roughly as follows, By the *homomorphism property* (16.19), once the inputs have been locally encrypted, all further intermediate computations are performed on ciphertexts only. All intermediate ciphertexts may be observed by any party. However, by the *secrecy* ensured by the *only-if part* of the *threshold property* (16.20), the corresponding intermediate plaintext values are kept hidden from all unauthorized parties provided only a strict minority colludes. But, at the end of the process, by the *correctness* ensured by the *if-part* of the *threshold property* (16.20), a majority can decrypt the final result of the computation on ciphertexts, and thus determine the correct plaintext value of the overall computation.

Restricting ourselves to a function f expressible by an algebraic expression $Exp(x_1, \ldots, x_n)$ containing only (binary) additions and (binary) multiplications, by means of a tree walk we can transform the expression into a sequence of operations op_k, whose arguments $a_{k,1}$ and $a_{k,2}$ are either a global input x_i or the output o_l from a preceding operation. Aiming at *operating on ciphertexts* only rather than on plaintexts, we then replace each (normal) operation by the associated operation on ciphertexts, to be specified in detail below. An easy induction then justifies the assertion that the replacements return the encryptions of the normal values. Figure 16.4 shows the overall approach.

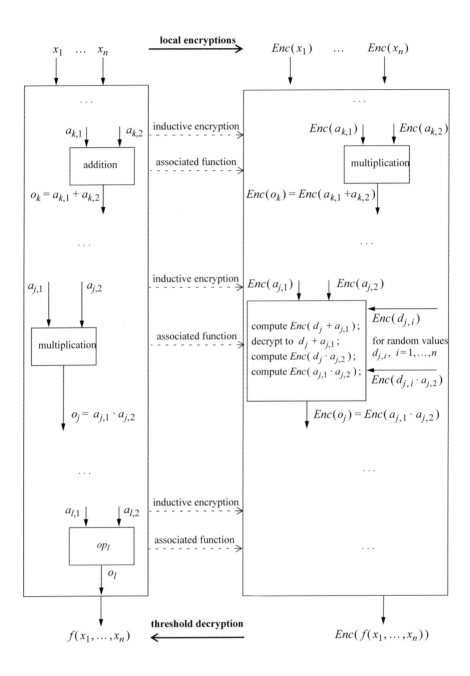

Fig. 16.4. Normal computation and a homomorphically simulating multiparty computation for evaluating an expression over addition and multiplication

Regarding a single *addition* $x + y$, the associated operation is simply a multiplication, as directly postulated by the homomorphism property (16.19).

Regarding a single *multiplication* $x \cdot y$, considerably more effort is needed. Basically, we can exploit the following features, where, for the sake of a concise presentation, we always drop the first encryption parameter ek.

1. By the design of asymmetric encryption, by holding the public key ek a party can locally encrypt any value z, i.e., determine $Enc(z)$.

2. By the homomorphism property (16.19), given any plaintext c and any ciphertext $Enc(z)$, a party can compute the ciphertext

$$Enc(c \cdot z) = Enc\left(\sum_{i = 1, \ldots, c} z \right) = \prod_{i = 1, \ldots, c} Enc(z).$$

3. By applying feature 2, given a ciphertext $Enc(z)$, and selecting a random value c for (fictitiously) blinding the (unknown) plaintext z as $c \cdot z$, each party can compute the ciphertext $Enc(c \cdot z)$ of the (unknown) blinding result.

4. If each party P_i secretly and independently selects a random value d_i, all parties together can (fictitiously) employ the value

$$d = \sum_{i = 1, \ldots, n} d_i,$$

which again appears random, without any single party actually knowing it, for additively blinding the first argument x as $d + x$ and for multiplicatively blinding the second argument y as $d \cdot y$, as explained further in the features 5, 6 and 7 below.

5. The ciphertext of the (unknown) blinding result $d \cdot y$ can be computed from locally determined ciphertexts of the blinding results $d_i \cdot y$, by the homomorphism property (16.19), using

$$Enc(d \cdot y) = Enc\left(\sum_{i = 1, \ldots, n} d_i \cdot y \right) = \prod_{i = 1, \ldots, n} Enc(d_i \cdot y).$$

6. The ciphertext of the (so far unknown) blinding result $d + x$ can be computed from the locally determined ciphertexts of the random values d_i, by the homomorphism property (16.19), using

$$Enc(d + x) = Enc(d) \cdot Enc(x) = Enc\left(\sum_{i = 1, \ldots, n} d_i \right) \cdot Enc(x)$$

$$= \left(\prod_{i = 1, \ldots, n} Enc(d_i) \right) \cdot Enc(x).$$

7. All parties together, and an honest strict majority of them by the threshold property (16.20) as well, can decrypt $Enc(d + x)$ and thus determine even the plaintext of the blinded first argument $d + x$.

8. Finally, given the ciphertexts $Enc(x)$ and $Enc(y)$, the ciphertext of $x \cdot y$ can be computed as follows, using besides elementary algebra, the homomorphism property (16.19), feature 7 to determine the blinded first argument $d + x$, feature 2 to then determine $Enc((d + x) \cdot y)$, and feature 5 to determine the ciphertext of the blinded second argument $Enc(d \cdot y)$:

$$Enc(x \cdot y) = \frac{Enc(d \cdot y) \cdot Enc(x \cdot y)}{Enc(d \cdot y)} = \frac{Enc(d \cdot y + x \cdot y)}{Enc(d \cdot y)} = \frac{Enc((d + x) \cdot y)}{Enc(d \cdot y)} .$$

Summarizing and exploiting these features, we sketch below the subprotocol for the n parties to jointly compute the function associated with a single multiplication, without presenting the additional mechanisms for taking appropriate care of further issues such as commitments and proofs of knowledge. Most notably, the sketch shows that, except for the final result, the only plaintext communicated during the execution is the blinding result $d + x$, which does not provide any information about x, since d is randomly selected such that only all parties together can determine this value. Of course, within the inductive framework, the initializing input is already available to all parties, as is the final result.

Round	**Party P_i**	Message
0. Initializing:		common input: ciphertexts $Enc(x)$, $Enc(y)$
1. Local blinding:	randomly select local blinding value d_i [feature 2]; encrypt d_i to $Enc(d_i)$ [feature 1]; compute $Enc(d_i \cdot y)$ [feature 2, 3]; broadcast $Enc(d_i)$ and $Enc(d_i \cdot y)$.	$\rightarrow Enc(d_i), Enc(d_i \cdot y)$
2. Global blinding:	compute $Enc(d + x)$ [feature 6].	
3. Decrypting:	contribute to determining $d + x$ by the threshold decryption of $Enc(d + x)$ [feature 7].	$d + x \leftarrow$
4. Evaluating:	compute $Enc(d \cdot y)$ [feature 5]; compute $Enc(x \cdot y)$ [feature 8].	$\rightarrow Enc(x \cdot y)$

16.5.3 Employing Boolean Circuits

A related approach to constructing mechanisms for multiparty computations applies to circuits performing *Boolean operations* on inputs of fixed size. Thus, under a suitable restriction regarding uniformness, *any* algorithm (or Turing machine) can be simulated.

Similarly to the procedure discussed in Subsection 16.5.2, the approach again proceeds inductively, by simulating each Boolean gate occurring in the circuit considered. Fortunately, without loss of generality, it suffices to *simulate* the gates of a complete set of Boolean functions. Rather than just employing (binary) conjunction and negation, we take (binary) *conjunction*, AND, and (binary) *exclusive disjunction*, XOR, denoted by the operator $\oplus$, which coincide with *multiplication* and *addition*, respectively, in the finite field $(\mathbf{Z}_2,+,\cdot,0,1)$ of residues modulo 2.

We shall only outline some selected, simplified features of these simulations.

1. By the results of Section 12.6 and Section 13.2, the additive structure $(\mathbf{Z}_2,+,0)$ is a group, and thus the XOR operation qualifies for *perfect encryption*. Any plaintext v can be encrypted by a key k to the ciphertext $v \oplus k$. By symmetry, we could exchange the roles of the plaintext and the key, seeing $v \oplus k$ as the ciphertext of the plaintext k using the key v. Alternatively, we can interpret $v \oplus k$ as a *secret*, and v and k as two *shares*: assuming equal distributions, each share does not reveal any information about the secret, but both shares together uniquely determine the secret.

2. Restricting ourselves to two parties P_1 and P_2 and following the *secret-sharing* interpretation, we treat the normal inputs of a gate as a *secret*, for which each party P_i only holds a *share*. Accordingly, from the point of view of party P_i, the gate is similar to *operating on ciphertexts*.

3. However, neither the gate nor the normal inputs are directly materialized. Instead, each party is enabled to obtain again a share of the normal output, treated as a secret in turn.

4. For a single *exclusive disjunction* (*addition*) with a first input $x = x_1 \oplus x_2$, such that party P_1 holds the share x_1 and party P_2 holds the share x_2, and, correspondingly, a second input $y = y_1 \oplus y_2$, each party can determine its share of the output completely by itself as $x_1 \oplus y_1$ and $x_2 \oplus y_2$, respectively. In particular, we have

$$x \oplus y = (x_1 \oplus x_2) \oplus (y_1 \oplus y_2) = (x_1 \oplus y_1) \oplus (x_2 \oplus y_2). \tag{16.21}$$

Figure 16.5 visualizes this simple simulation.

5. For a single *conjunction* (*multiplication*), under the same assumptions about the inputs as in feature 4, we aim at computing a share o_1 for party P_1 and a share o_2 for party P_2 that together uniquely determine the normal output $x \cdot y$ to be kept secret, i.e., in particular, the following constraint must be satisfied:

$$x \cdot y = (x_1 \oplus x_2) \cdot (y_1 \oplus y_2) = o_1 \oplus o_2. \tag{16.22}$$

This goal can be achieved by employing another sophisticated subprotocol.

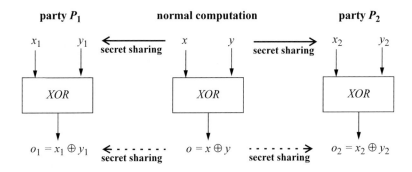

Fig. 16.5. Computing shares of a secret XOR value from shares of the secret arguments

6. Suppose that, first, party P_1 randomly selects a value o_1 as its own share. According to (16.22), party P_2 must then obtain the share

$$o_2 = x_1 \cdot y_1 \oplus x_1 \cdot y_2 \oplus x_2 \cdot y_1 \oplus x_2 \cdot y_2 \oplus o_1. \qquad (16.23)$$

Now, party P_1 knows the values x_1, y_1 and o_1 but not the values x_2 and y_2 of party P_2, and vice versa. However, there are only four possibilities $[i,j]$ for the values of party P_2, and for each of them party P_1 can determine the resulting value $o_2[i,j]$ by evaluating the respective expression using only its own values:

$$
\begin{aligned}
o_2[0,0] &= x_1 \cdot y_1 \oplus x_1 \cdot 0 \oplus 0 \cdot y_1 \oplus 0 \cdot 0 \oplus o_1 & &= x_1 \cdot y_1 \oplus o_1, \\
o_2[0,1] &= x_1 \cdot y_1 \oplus x_1 \cdot 1 \oplus 0 \cdot y_1 \oplus 0 \cdot 1 \oplus o_1 & &= x_1 \cdot y_1 \oplus x_1 \oplus o_1, \\
o_2[1,0] &= x_1 \cdot y_1 \oplus x_1 \cdot 0 \oplus 1 \cdot y_1 \oplus 1 \cdot 0 \oplus o_1 & &= x_1 \cdot y_1 \oplus y_1 \oplus o_1, \\
o_2[1,1] &= x_1 \cdot y_1 \oplus x_1 \cdot 1 \oplus 1 \cdot y_1 \oplus 1 \cdot 1 \oplus o_1 & &= x_1 \cdot y_1 \oplus x_1 \oplus y_1 \oplus 1 \oplus o_1.
\end{aligned}
$$

As a result, party P_1 obtains a sequence over values from $\{0,1\}$ of length 4 of the form

$$(o_2[0,0] , o_2[0,1] , o_2[1,0] , o_2[1,1]).$$

Only party P_2 can select the pertinent value, but in doing so, for the sake of secrecy, P_2 may not learn the remaining three values.

7. Imagine that a suitable trusted third party H_{ot} mediates the needed functionality of *oblivious transfer*:

– P_1 sends the full sequence of values to H_{ot};
– P_2 sends the required index $[x_2, y_2]$ to H_{ot};
– H_{ot} returns the wanted value $o_2[x_2, y_2]$ to P_2.

8. Finally, under appropriate assumptions about *pseudorandomness* and *one-way functions*, the trusted third party H_{ot} can be simulated by a two-party computation of P_1 and P_2, while preserving all secrecy requirements.

By carefully elaborating these features and extending them to $n > 2$ parties, one can construct a simulation of any Boolean function with a fixed number of inputs that satisfies (a suitable variant) of the correctness and secrecy property sketched.

16.6 Design and Verification of Cryptographic Protocols

The preceding sections indicate the overwhelming complexity of dealing with cryptographic protocols, regarding both their security requirements and the actual mechanisms. In the following, we roughly summarize some of the aspects that we have treated:

- Cryptographic protocols are *composed* from more elementary components, some of which are *repeatedly* applied.
- *Attacks* originate from "inside"; some parties deviate from the anticipated behavior, either only *passively* by *local computations* to gain knowledge not intended for them (they are *honest-but-curious* or *semi-honest*), or, additionally, *actively* by sending *unexpected messages*.
- In most cases, an *attacker* is modeled by considering *any* (probabilistic polynomial-time) algorithm that might *replace* the anticipated algorithm.
- Some attacks are inevitable, even if an imagined *trusted host* with (ideally secure) *private channels* is employed for providing critical functionality. Accordingly, the *security requirements* refer to a trusted-host model as the best possible accomplishment.
- For the trusted-host model, typically the *correctness properties* are expressed by *equations between terms* that describe the anticipated honest behavior based on some *secrets*. More specifically, some equations between terms should have a unique solution from the point of view of the holder of the pertinent secrets. For example, the correctness of decryption as the inverse of encryption is expressed by the equation (12.2), saying $Dec(dk, Enc(ek, m)) = m$. More specifically, one requires that the equation $Dec(dk, Enc(ek, m)) = x$ has a *unique solution* for x given m, ek and dk, and that this solution equals m. Complementarily, the *secrecy properties* say that the equations considered have many solutions from the point of view of an intruder who does not know the pertinent secrets and thus cannot identify the "intended solution". This kind of expression of fundamental security requirements is known as setting up a *Dolev–Yao model*. Any further security aspects are simply postulated by putting full *trust* in the host, imagined to be completely protected (within the Dolev–Yao model) against unspecified outside activities.
- A *refinement* is then given in the form of an implemented *mechanism* that uses distributed protocol executions consisting of *local computations* and *message transmissions* over an actual *network*. This mechanism should (*reactively*) *simulate* the behavior of the trusted host and the private channels such that the resulting effects are "essentially the same" as for the trusted host, i.e., the effects of the trusted host on the one hand and the distributed simulation on the other hand should be *computationally indistinguishable*.
- Moreover, the actual simulation uses *concrete mechanisms* as *refinements* of each of the components the protocol is *composed* of. Supposing that each individual concrete mechanism adequately simulates the corresponding individual abstract component expressed within the equational term framework of a

Dolev–Yao model, substituting the abstract components by the concrete mechanisms should again make no "essential difference".

These aspects suggest a fairly general methodology for designing and verifying cryptographic protocols, exploiting the wanted *compositionality* of the *refinements* and *compositions* employed, as discussed more generally in Subsection 1.5.1. Unfortunately, however, these ambitious goals cannot always be achieved, and thus the methodology often needs adjustment and modification for individual examples.

16.7 Bibliographic Hints

The overall success of cryptography in enforcing security in computing systems depends crucially on applying advanced protocols. Accordingly, several textbooks cover at least some aspects of protocol design and verification. For example, Stinson [470] concentrates on protocols for identification, key management, secret sharing and copyright protection, covering examples of zero-knowledge proofs as protocol components and leaving protocol verification mainly implicit; Goldreich [226, 228, 229] thoroughly investigates the foundations, theory and application of zero-knowledge proofs (seen as a fundamental technique), including covert commitments, and expands deeply on multiparty computations, leaving the engineering aspects mainly implicit. Our presentation is very much inspired by these publications, which contain much more material and many more references. Selected literature dedicated to the topics of this chapter can be found as follows.

Protocols for covert commitment are often reported as parts of more comprehensive protocols, for example by Even [195] for contract signing and Blum [90] for coin flipping. Halevi/Micali [245] and Naor [361] describe general constructions based on conjectures about pseudorandomness and one-way hash functions. The simple examples presented in this text originate from the textbook by Schneier [437].

Shamir [442] invents threshold secret sharing based on linear equations derived from polynomial interpolation; Blakley [86] does the same independently. Karnin/ Greene/ Hellman [290] introduce a simpler approach, which we use for our presentation of simulating Boolean gates. Brickell/Davenport [103, 104], Stinson [468, 469], Ito/Saito/Nishizeki [270] and Simmons [449] investigate alternative approaches. Chor/Goldwasser/Micali/Awerbuch [134], Pedersen [387], Stadler [459] and others treat verifiable secret sharing to protect against active attacks.

Goldwasser/Micali/Rackoff [233] pioneer the basic concepts of zero-knowledge proofs. Bellare/Goldreich [39] and Goldreich/Oren [225] clarify the definitions further and explore advanced properties. Goldreich/Micali/Wigderson [223] prove the existence of zero-knowledge proof systems for all NP-complete languages. Naor/Ostrovsky/Venkaesan/Yung [362] present alternative constructions. Blum/ De Santis/Micali/Persiano [92] study non-interactive variants of zero-knowledge proofs. Feige/Fiat/Shamir [200] consider applications to proofs of authenticity.

Yao [507] and Goldreich/Micali/Wigderson [222, 223] introduce the basic concepts of multiparty computations. Canetti [115] elaborates these concepts, emphasizing the aspect of compositionality. Cramer/Damgard/Nielson [145, 151] base multiparty computations on homomorphic threshold encryption. Rabin [400] introduces oblivious transfer, Bellare/Micali [38] study a protocol based on ElGamal functions, and Kilian/et al. [291, 249] discuss the impact of oblivious transfer on multiparty computations. Beaver [35] considers the impact of zero-knowledge proofs. Du/Atallah [177] survey applications of multiparty computations.

The design and verification of cryptographic protocols have been studied from various points of view. Dolev/Yao [174] propose algebraic term models, known today as Dolev–Yao models. More recently, Canetti/Dodis/Pass/Walfish [115, 116, 117] and Backes/B.Pfitzmann/Waidner [25, 26, 27, 28] study the possibilities and limits for achieving compositionality of refinements and composition. Further work examines additional aspects; for example Küsters/Truderung [302, 303] explore the impact of recursion and infinite domains, and Meadows/Escobar/ Meseguer [190, 346] treat protocol analysis by means of algorithmic inference systems such as theorem proving and model checking. Abadi [5] surveys and examines many approaches.

Part Four
Implementations

17 Design of Selected Systems

In this final chapter, we briefly review some selected implementations of security services. In particular, we show how basic and composed security mechanisms, as described in the preceding chapters, have been put together to meet the architecture and the requirements of specific applications. Taking suitable abstractions of UNIX, Oracle/SQL, CORBA, Kerberos, SPKI/SDSI and PGP as examples, these applications include an operating system, a database management system, middleware systems, with distributed client–server systems as a special case, and a file and message system.

The selected examples are not meant as recommended systems. We intend, rather, to demonstrate how system designers have dealt with the specific functionality offered by the layer under consideration in order to achieve a limited level of security. Therefore, we refrain from describing concrete products but concentrate on conceptual issues. Even where details are given, they are often abstracted from the actually available running systems, and thus the details may differ in syntax and minor aspects of semantics from a concrete version of the system the reader might be able to access.

17.1 UNIX Operating System

UNIX is an *operating system* that, among many other features, supports participants both in using their own workstation for their specific application tasks and in cooperating with colleagues in server-based local networks for joint projects. Accordingly, a participant can manage his own computing resources at his discretion, either keeping them private or making them available to other particular participants or even to everybody. Therefore, the prominent interests of a participant aim at *confidentiality* and *integrity* (in the sense of unmodified state) on the one hand, and *availability* and *accountability* on the other hand.

Basically, the UNIX security mechanisms enforce the virtual *isolation* of *identified*, previously *registered* users, thereby also enabling the deliberate *sharing* of resources. The mechanisms are closely intertwined with the basic functional concepts of files and processes, which are managed by the UNIX kernel. Accordingly, the kernel also acts as the central *controller* and *monitor* of all security-relevant accesses, whereas each participating user can autonomously specify the permitted and prohibited *operational options* of users concerning the resources that the participating user *owns*. However, the expressiveness for specifying such *access rights* is rather limited, and, additionally, owners might be too careless to fully exploit the restricted possibilities. Moreover, an owner's specification can nearly always be overruled by the *system administrator*, and the enforcing kernel might be vulnerable to several kinds of attack.

The first UNIX version was developed by D. Ritchie and K. Thompson about 30 years ago. Since then, numerous versions and extensions have appeared, which are in widespread use under acronyms such as BSD/OS, SunOS, Linux, AIX and Solaris. In the following, we outline a simplified design of only the basic features concerning control and monitoring, often abstracting from the real versions (which tend to share many commonalities while deviating in the details).

17.1.1 Basic Blocks

UNIX exploits the following basic blocks of control and monitoring (which also include a concept of cryptography):

- *Identification* of registered users as participants.
- *Passwords* for user *authentication* at login time.
- *A one-way hash function* for storing password data.
- *Discretionary access rights* concerning *files* as basic objects and three funda-mental *operational modes*, read, write and execute.
- *Owners*, as autonomous grantors of access rights.
- Owners, *groups* and the full community of all users, as kinds of grantees.
- *Right amplification* for temporarily increasing the operational options of a user.
- A *superuser*, as the most powerful system administrator, capable of overriding the specifications of owners.
- *Access control* concerning the commands and the corresponding system calls that constitute the basic operating system functionality.
- *Monitoring* of the functionality.
- *Kernel*-based implementation of control and monitoring.

17.1.2 Conceptual Design of the Operating System Functionality

UNIX provides a *virtual machine* that offers an external *command* interface with the following fundamental features: identified *participants* can *master processes* that *execute* programs stored in *files*, as roughly modeled in the white part of Figure 17.1; the processes, in turn, can operate on files, in particular for reading and writing (not shown in Figure 17.1).

A little more specifically, a previously *registered participant* can start a *session* by means of the `login` command, whereby the system assigns a *physical device* for input and output data to him and starts a *command interpreter* as the first process mastered by that participant. Afterwards, the participant can issue *commands*, which may possibly generate additional processes that are also mastered by him.

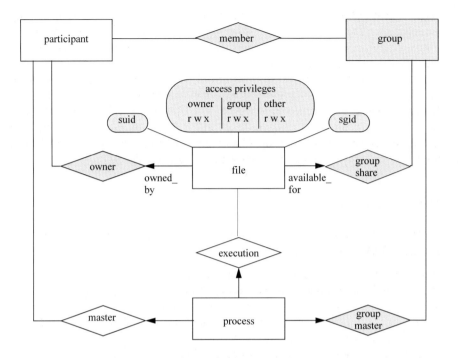

Fig. 17.1. Simple ER model of the fundamental functional features of UNIX (white boxes), together with the basic constructs for permitted operational options (gray boxes)

The commands invoke *system calls* that serve for process management, signaling, file management, directory and file system management, protection, and time management.

Processes are the essential *subjects* acting in the system. Among other things, a process can

- *execute* (the program contained in) a file, and in doing so
- *read* or *write* in (usually other) files,
- *create* new files and *remove* existing ones, and
- *generate* new (child) processes.

Each process has a *lifespan,* starting with its generation by a father process and ending with a synchronization with the pertinent father process. Accordingly, the processes actually running constitute a *process tree*, the dynamic behavior of which is visualized in Figure 17.2. When the UNIX system is started, an initial process *init* is generated. Recursively, an already running (*father*) *process* can generate new (*child*) *processes*. Figure 17.2 shows a typical example situation, where, as descendants of the initial process, a child process has been generated for each physical device, and then, using one of these physical devices, a user has entered the system by means of a login command, resulting in a new process for the *com-*

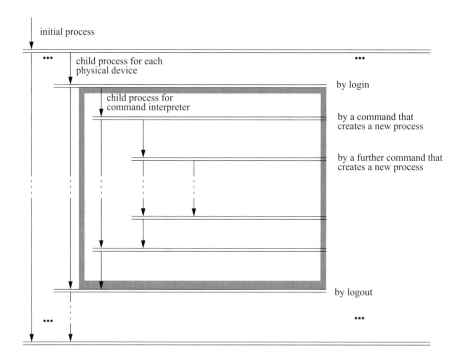

initial process

child process for each
physical device

by login

child process for
command interpreter

by a command that
creates a new process

by a further command that
creates a new process

by logout

Fig. 17.2. Growing and shrinking of the dynamic UNIX process tree (the gray part refers to the processes of a participant's session)

mand interpreter, from which, in turn, further processes originate. Each process finally synchronizes with its father and then ends; in particular, the logout command cancels the user's present process for the command interpreter.

A (father) process generates a new (child) process by invoking the system call fork. At the beginning, the father and the child are nearly exactly the same; in particular, the content of the child's address space is a complete copy of the content of the father's address space, resulting in the father and the child executing the same program. However, the two processes have different process identifiers, and each of them knows its status as father or child, respectively. Afterwards, by invoking a guarded system call of the form exec(command_file), the child typically exchanges the content of its address space, thereby loading the program that is contained in the file specified by the parameter command_file. Subsequently, the instructions of this program are executed for the child. Thus, in general, the father and the child then execute different programs. Finally, the father and the child can synchronize, by the father invoking the system call wait, and the child invoking the system call exit. On a successful synchronization, the child is ended, whereas the father continues. The typical lifespan of a (child) process and its interactions with the father process are shown in Figure 17.3.

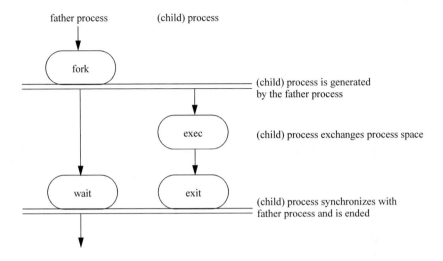

father process   (child) process

(child) process is generated
by the father process

(child) process exchanges process space

(child) process synchronizes with
father process and is ended

Fig. 17.3. Typical lifespan of a process

Whereas processes are the active subjects of the UNIX system, *files* are passive *objects* that are uniformly managed by the system using a file tree:

- A file is identified by its *path name* within the file tree.
- A file that constitutes a branching node in the file tree is a *directory* listing other files.
- A file that constitutes a leaf in the file tree is a *plain file* containing data, which might be considered as an executable program.

17.1.3 Conceptual Design of the Security Concepts

The basic security concepts refer closely to the fundamental features of the operating system functionality, as roughly modeled by the gray part of Figure 17.1: participants can be gathered into *groups*; each file has an *owner*, and is made available for a *group share*; for each file, *access privileges* are specified concerning the operational modes **read**, **write** and **execute**, with the owner, the group members and all other participants as possible grantees.

A little more specifically, a participant can act as the *owner* of the files created by him, thereby determining the degree of isolation from or sharing with other participants. The system administrator can assign participants as *members* of a *group*. A group typically comprises those participants that are entitled to jointly work on a common task and, in doing so, to share files. Accordingly, an owner can make a file *available* for a group to *share* it. Hence, for each file, the owner implicitly specifies three *disjoint* participant classes:

- himself as *owner*;
- the members of the pertinent *group*, except the owner if applicable;
- all *other* participants.

The owner of a file can *discretionarily* declare *access privileges* for each of these classes – more precisely, as described in detail below, for the processes mastered by the respective class members – by permitting or prohibiting the operations belonging to an operational mode. There are three *operational modes*,

- *read*;
- *write*; and
- *execute*.

The mode `mode(op)` of an operation `op` is determined according to its impact on a plain file or a directory. Table 17.4 gives some typical examples. In concrete systems the operations might be denoted differently, and the rules may be more sophisticated, also expressing requirements for the full path of the operand.

Table 17.4. Some operations with commands and their operational mode

Operation with command on plain file	Operation with command on directory	Operational mode
open file for reading: `open( ,o_rdonly)` read content: `read`	open directory for scanning: `opendir` read next entry: `readdir`	*read*
open file for writing: `open( ,o_wronly)` modify content: `write` delete content: `truncate`	insert entry: `add` delete entry: `remove` rename entry: `rename`	*write*
execute content as program: `execute`	select as current directory: `cd`	*execute*

For each of the nine combinations of a kind of participant class, `class`, and an operational mode, `mode`, a permission is represented by the truth value `true` or the digit 1, and a prohibition by the truth value `false` or the digit 0, denoted in the following by a path expression of the form `file.access_privileges.class.mode`. In Figure 17.1, the nine values (truth values or digits) of `file.access_privileges` are shown as `rwx|rwx|rwx`.

Normally, a user is the *master* of the command interpreter process that he has started, and of all its descendants. Additionally, the (primary) group of that user is said to be the *group master* of all those processes. If a process requests an operation `op` on a file `file`, then the access privileges `file.access_privileges` are inspected according to the masterships of the process in order to take an access decision.

For each file, the owner can additionally set two *execution flags*, suid and sgid, that direct its usage as a program, or as a directory, respectively:

- For a plain file containing an executable program, the flag impacts on the *mastership* of an executing process.
- For a directory, the flag impacts on the *ownership* of inserted files.

17.1.4 Refined Design

Figure 17.5 shows a refined (but still simplified) ER model of the functional features and the constructs for permitted operational options, also indicating the corresponding internal data structures.

First, we consider participants and groups. The informal notion of a *participant* is differentiated into the following semantic levels:

- a *human individual*;
- the *physical device* from which that individual issued his last login command and, subsequently, all further commands;
- an abstract *user*, which represents the previously registered human individual within the system: as a result of a successful login command, the abstract user is *connected* to the physical device from which the command was received; an abstract user is uniquely identified by a *username*, and the system maintains further administrative data such as the user's *password* data, its *full name*, (the path name of) its *home directory* in the overall file tree and (the path name of the file containing) its *command interpreter* (*shell file*);
- a *user identification*, i.e., a cardinal number *uid*, which serves as a *surrogate* for an abstract user, preferably though not necessarily in a unique way.

In order to achieve overall security, it is crucial that the system maintains the relationships between the differentiated notions of a participant, as it would be expected by an informed individual. Any failure may potentially result in security violations; for example, a stranger maliciously issuing commands at an unattended physical device, a cheating login procedure with a stolen password, or an unintended unification of abstract users by a single user identification.

The human individual who is acting as the *system administrator* is typically registered as a distinguished abstract user whose username is *root* and whose surrogate is superuser_id (in general, represented by the cardinal number 0). This distinguished abstract user *root* enjoys nearly unrestricted operational options, and consequently so does any human individual who succeeds in being related to *root*.

Besides users, there are *groups*, each of which is represented by its *group identification, gid*. Each abstract user is a *primary member* of one group, and can be a *member* of any further groups.

Second, we address the refinements concerning files and processes. All their relationships with participants or groups are now interpreted as relationships with user identifications or group identifications, respectively. Moreover, the *master* and

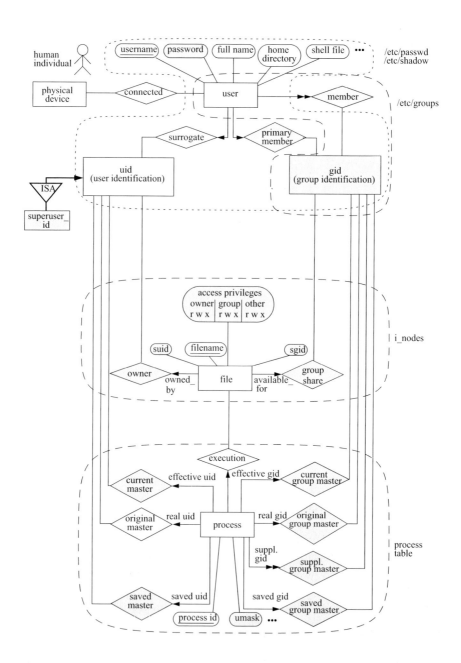

Fig. 17.5. Refined ER model of the fundamental functional features of UNIX (white boxes) and the basic constructs for permitted operational options (gray boxes), also indicating the corresponding internal data structures

the *group master* relationships are further differentiated in order to enable dynamic modifications, in particular for right amplification.

A user identification *uid* – i.e., the surrogate of a user connected to a physical device from which a human individual has issued a `login` command – is seen as the *original master* of the command interpreter process generated during the login procedure and of all its descendants; these processes are also said to have this *uid* as their *real uid*. Correspondingly, a group identification *gid* – i.e., the surrogate of a group of which that particular user is a primary member – is seen as the *original group master* of these processes, which are also said to have this *gid* as their *real gid*. Normally, the original masterships are intended to determine the access decision when a process requests an operation on a file.

However, in order to distinguish between normal and exceptional cases, an additional *current mastership* (an *effective uid*) and an additional *current group mastership* (an *effective gid*) are maintained and actually employed for access decisions. The current mastership and the current group mastership of a process are automatically manipulated according to the execution flags `suid` and `sgid` of the executed file:

- Normally, if the flag is *not* set (i.e., it equals `false` or 0), then the current mastership is assigned the original mastership, and the current group mastership is assigned the original group mastership, respectively.
- Exceptionally, if the flag is set (i.e., it equals `true` or 1), then the current mastership is assigned the user identification of the owner of the file to be executed, and the current group mastership is assigned the group identification for which that file has been made available, respectively.

The typical use of the exceptional case is *right amplification*, i.e., to dynamically increase the operational options of a process while it is executing a file with a flag set. In a sense, the owner of that file allows all "participants" that are permitted to execute the file at all to act thereby as if they were the owner himself. If the owner is more powerful than such a participant, then the operational options of the participant are temporarily increased. In particular, if the owner is the nearly omnipotent abstract user *root*, then such a participant can temporarily access files that normally are protected for the exclusive purposes of the system administrator.

The current masterships and current group masterships can also be manipulated by special, suitably protected commands, as explained below. For this option, the additional *saved mastership* and *saved group mastership* are used to restore the original situation.

17.1.5 Components of Local Control and Monitoring

In Section 7.2, we introduced a general model for *local control and monitoring* based on authenticated identities. We now review the design of UNIX by showing how the components of the general model are implemented in UNIX.

Identification and Authentication

An individual can act as a participant of a UNIX installation only if the system administrator has *registered* him in advance as *user*, thereby assigning a *username* to him. This assignment and further user-related data are stored in the files /etc/ passwd and /etc/shadow. Later on, the usernames serve for *identification* and for *accountability* of all actions arising in the system. In particular, whenever an individual tries to enter the installation by use of a login command, the system

- checks whether the username is *known* from a previous registration and
- evaluates whether the actual command can be seen as *authentic*.

The *knowledge* of the username is decided by inspecting the file /etc/passwd: if the username is found, it is considered as known, and otherwise as unknown. Concerning this inspection, the system relies on appropriate registrations on the one hand and on the integrity of the file /etc/passwd, in particular its write protection, on the other hand. The *authenticity* is evaluated by a *password* procedure: if the individual can input the agreed password, then the command is seen as authentic, and otherwise as not authentic, in which case it is rejected. Concerning this evaluation, the system relies on appropriate password agreements, the individual's care in keeping his password secret, and the integrity and confidentiality of the file /etc/shadow. The confidentiality of this file is supported by several mechanisms:

- Passwords are not stored directly, but only their images under a *one-way hash function*. On any input of the password, the system immediately computes its *hash value* and compares that hash value with the stored value.
- The hash values are stored in a specially protected file /etc/shadow: a write access to an entry, i.e., a password modification, is allowed only if the request stems from *root* or from the pertinent user, as authenticated by the current password; a read access to an entry is allowed only for authenticity evaluations. This kind of protection is far stronger than for other files. In particular, the restricted read access is necessary in order to avoid systematic *password probing*.
- The *transmission path* for the password from the physical device to the component that computes the one-way hash function must be *trusted*. This goal may be achieved by physical isolation or by cryptographic means (but, unfortunately, such mechanisms are rarely fully effective). Furthermore, the transmission of the password and the computing of its hash value must be confined; in particular, they must be memoryless and without any side effects. This includes the requirement that a typed password is not mirrored on the screen.

Access Decisions

The kernel has to take *access decisions* concerning a *process* as an active subject, a *file* as a controlled passive object and a requested *operation*. Thus, given a triple (process, file, operation), the kernel has to decide whether the process identified by process is allowed to actually execute the operation denoted by operation on the file named file. Two cases are distinguished according to the effective user identification of the process, process.current_master:

- If process.current_master = superuser_uid, then nearly everything is considered to be allowed. Accordingly, the parameters file and operation mostly do not have an impact on the access decision.
- Otherwise, the following procedure determines the access decision:

```
function decide(process, file, operation): Boolean;
if      process.current_master = file.owner
then    return file.access_privileges.owner.mode(operation)
else
   if   process.current_groupmaster = file.group
        OR
        EXISTS process.supplementary_groupmaster:
        process.supplementary_groupmaster = file.group
   then return  file.access_privileges.group.mode(operation)
   else return  file.access_privileges.other.mode(operation).
```

Knowledge Base on Permitted Operational Options

Figure 17.5 shows both a conceptual ER model of the *knowledge base* of *permitted operational options* and its implementation. The implementation exploits the fundamental functional features of UNIX as follows:

- Data about *users* and *groups* is stored in the special files /etc/passwd, /etc/shadow and /etc/group. Table 17.6 shows the types of the main entries. These files are owned by the system administrator, who has the user identification superuser_id. The access privileges for these files are given by r--|r--|r--, rw-|---|--- and r--|r--|r--, respectively, and, additionally, modifications of the files /etc/passwd and /etc/group are specially restricted to processes with the effective uid superuser_id.
- Security relevant data about *files*, like all other administrative data, is managed in *i-nodes*.
- Security-relevant data about *processes*, again like all other *runtime data*, is maintained in the *process table*.

Table 17.6. Main entries of the administration files for users and groups

/etc/passwd	/etc/shadow	/etc/group
username	username	groupname
reference to /etc/shadow	hash value of password	group password
user identification (uid)	date of last modification	group identification (gid)
gid of primary group	maximum lifetime	usernames of members
full name, comment	date of expiration	
path name of home directory		
path name of shell file		

Modifications of the Knowledge Base on Permitted Operational Options

Participants can modify the knowledge base on permitted operational options by commands and the resulting system calls. In the following, we give a simplified and incomplete introduction to the most important possibilities.

The commands useradd, usermod and userdel manipulate the entries for *users* in the files /etc/passwd, /etc/shadow and /etc/group. These commands are only executed for a process whose effective user identification is superuser_uid.

The commands groupadd, groupmod and groupdel manipulate the entries for *groups* in the file /etc/group. These commands are also only executed for a process whose effective user identification is superuser_uid.

The command passwd modifies an entry of a user in the file /etc/shadow. This command is only executed for a process whose effective user identification is superuser_uid or is equal to the user identification of the user whose password is requested to be changed.

The command login first tries to identify and authenticate the issuer. On success, the issuer is recognized as a known registered user. Then, by a system call fork, a new process is generated for that user. That process, in turn, by use of a system call exec, starts executing the shell file of the user as a command interpreter. The masterships and group masterships of that process are determined as follows:

- The real uid, effective uid and saved uid are all assigned the user identification of the user, i.e., user.surrogate.
- The real gid, effective gid and saved gid are all assigned the primary group of the user, i.e., user.primary_member.
- The supplementary gid is assigned the set of elements of user.member.

Subsequently, this process is treated as the original ancestor of all processes that are generated during the session started by the login command. Normally, these processes inherit their masterships and group masterships from their immediate ancestors, unless the file executed has an execution flag suid or sgid set, or some explicit command modifies the implicit assignment.

The system call create(filename, access_privileges, suid, sgid) creates a new file as follows:

- The owner and the group share of the file are assigned the effective uid and the effective gid, respectively, of the creating process.
- The access privileges and the execution flags suid and sgid are assigned according to the respective parameters of the call, possibly modified according to the mask umask. This mask specifies nine truth values, one for each value contained in the parameter for the access privileges: each mask value is complemented and then the conjunction with the corresponding parameter value is taken. Thus, in particular, a mask value true (or 1) is complemented into false (or 0) and thus always results in the corresponding access privilege being set to false (or 0), thereby expressing a *prohibition*.

In general, individuals are strongly recommended to prohibit write access to files with an execution flag suid or sgid set. This precaution aims at avoiding unintended or malicious modification of the program contained in the file. Such a modification might result in unwanted effects in later usages of the file with right amplification.

The system call umask(new_umask) modifies the current nine truth values of the mask umask into the values specified by the parameter new_umask. As explained above, during a file creation, a mask value true always converts a *permission* into a *prohibition*, and thus it can prevent unintended permissions. Typically, this command is called by scripts for logins or for environment declarations, which are written by a participant at his discretion. The mask is treated as a property of processes, and accordingly a (child) process inherits the mask from its father process.

The system call fork generates a new process, and a subsequent system call exec(command_file) exchanges the content of its address space, thereby loading the program that is contained in the file specified as the parameter command_file, whose instructions are then executed. The masterships, group masterships and the mask umask of that process are determined as follows:

- Normally, if the execution flags suid and sgid of the file command_file are *not* set (i.e., they equal false or 0), then the new process inherits all masterships and group masterships from its father process.
- Exceptionally, if the flag suid is set (i.e., it equals true or 1), then the effective uid and the saved uid are assigned to command_file.owner. Correspondingly, if the flag sgid is set (i.e., it equals true or 1), then the effective gid and the saved gid are assigned to command_file.group share.
- The mask umask is inherited from the father process.

The system call setuid(uid) assigns the masterships real uid, effective uid and saved uid the parameter value uid. This call is only executed for a process that satisfies the following precondition: the effective uid equals superuser_uid, or the real uid equals the parameter value uid (i.e., in the latter case, the original situation after the login command is restored).

The system call seteuid(euid) assigns the current mastership effective uid the parameter value euid, which might be the real uid or the saved uid. Thereby, while executing a file with the execution flag suid set, a process can repeatedly change its effective uid: the process can select the uid of that user who has generated the original ancestor, or the uid of the owner of the file executed.

The system calls setgid(gid) and setegid(egid) manipulate the group masterships, similarly to the way the corresponding calls for masterships do.

The command /bin/su - changes the effective uid of the currently executed process into superuser_uid. This command is only executed if the issuer is successfully authenticated with the agreed password for the system administrator with username *root*. In the form given, with the parameter "-", the command additionally transfers the environment of the process into a state that is normally selected by the login command issued by *root*. By employing the command /bin/su -, the system administrator can acquire the mastership of any process whatever, another source of the system administrator's omnipotence and of the related risks. The form of the command given specifies the full path name in order to ensure that the intended file with the instructions for the command is used, and not a maliciously modified file.

The command chown changes the owner of a file. This command is only executed for a process that satisfies the following precondition: the effective uid equals superuser_uid or it equals the current owner of the file.

The command chmod changes the access privileges of a file. This command is only executed for a process that satisfies the following precondition: the effective uid equals superuser_uid or it equals the current owner of the file.

Knowledge Base on Usage History

Basically, UNIX does not maintain an explicit *knowledge base* on the *usage history* for taking *access decisions*, except for keeping track of process generations. But most UNIX versions offer log services for *monitoring*. These log services produce *log data* about actually issued commands and executed system calls, and store that data in special *log files*. Examples are the following:

- The file lastlog contains the date of the last issuing of a login command for each of the registered users, whether successful or failed. The dates of previous attempts are lost.
- The file loginlog contains entries about all failed issuings of a login command, i.e., about repeated inputs of a wrong password. The entries comprise the username employed, the physical device used and the date.
- The file pacct contains entries about all issued commands, including their date.
- The file sulog contains entries about all successful or failed attempts to issue the critical su command. For each attempt, success or failure, the username employed, the physical device used and the date are recorded.
- The files utmp or wtmp contain entries about the currently active participants. Besides the username employed, several further pieces of data are recorded, such as the physical device used and the process identification of the original ancestor process that was started by the login command to execute the user's command interpreter.

Additionally, some UNIX versions offer unifying *audit services*. Basically, log services send their log data as *audit messages* to an audit service that, in turn, unifies and prepares that data for persistent storage or further monitoring. As an example, the audit service syslog works on audit messages that are sent either by the kernel, exploiting /dev/klog, by user processes, exploiting /dev/log, or by network services, exploiting the UDP port 514. The audit messages consist of four entries:

- the name of the *program* whose execution generated the message;

- a *classification* of the executing process into one of a restricted number of event sources, called *facilities*, which are known as *kern, user, mail, lpr, auth, daemon, news, uucp, local0, …, local7* and *mark*;
- a *priority level*, which is one of *emerg*(ency), *alert, crit*(ical), *err*(or), *warning, notice, info*(rmational), (from) *debug*(ging) and *none*;
- the actual notification of the *action* that has occurred.

The system administrator can configure the audit service using the file /etc/syslog.conf, which contains expressions of the form facility.priority destination. Such an expression determines how an audit message that stems from an event source classified as facility and has the level priority should be treated, i.e., to which destination it has to be forwarded. In this context, destination might denote the path name of a file, a username, a remote address, a pipe or the wildcard *, standing for all possible receivers.

Overall Architecture

The components for control and monitoring, including identification and authentication, are part of the operating system kernel. Basically, the *kernel* realizes the system calls offered by UNIX, some of which serve the purposes of security mechanisms, as explained above. A *system call* is treated roughly as follows:

- The kernel checks the operator and the parameters of the call, as passed from the calling process, and then deposits these items in dedicated registers or storage cells.
- A software interrupt or trap dispenses the calling process.
- The program determined by the specified operator is then executed with the specified parameters, either by the kernel itself or by some other part of the operating system.
- If applicable, return values for the calling process have to be deposited.
- Subsequently, the calling process can be resumed.
- Usually, when control is switched from the calling process to the kernel and vice versa, the scheduler of the operating system is involved, such that some latencies might arise.

From the point of view of security, this procedure for system calls needs special hardware support, including *storage protection, processor states (modes), privileged instructions* and *process space separation*. In particular, the processor should distinguish at least a "user mode" for application processes and a "kernel mode" for executing the kernel instructions, and the privileged instructions for enforcing security should be executable exclusively in the kernel mode. More generally, the security-related parts of (the operating system) kernel should be designed and implemented as a carefully evaluated *security kernel*.

Today, most UNIX installations are part of a network. We have refrained from presenting the various features used for securing the connections to remote participants and the interactions with them, though they are highly important in practice.

17.2 Oracle/SQL Database Management System

Oracle is a commercially available relational *database management system* that supports participants in *storing*, *processing* and *sharing* their application data in a unified manner. In particular, Oracle implements the standardized *Structured Query Language (SQL)*. Among many other features, SQL offers commands for *declaring* the structural aspects of data, and for manipulating *structured* (or at least semi-structured) data instances (extensions) by *inserting* new entries, by *deleting* or *updating* stored items, and by *answering queries* expressed in a declarative, set-oriented style.

In most applications, diverse data is maintained for various users, to be selectively shared according to the administrative principle of *need-to-know*, and to be *hidden* otherwise. In this way, the database management system can serve as a virtually centralized and selectively shared repository of all the data an institution needs to process, and thus as a communication tool like a blackboard, offered to all members of the institution. Moreover, these services might be discretionarily provided to external participants as well, either individually or by establishing federations with other systems.

When we see data as important assets of an institution, the main security interests that arise are the selective *availability* of the data, the selective, partially conflicting *confidentiality* of the information content of the data, several aspects of the *integrity* (*correct content, unmodified state* and *detection of modification*) of the data, and the *accountability* of acting users. Moreover, the *interest holders* are manifold as well: in particular, they comprise the (representative of the) institution as a whole, the (representatives of the) departments and more finely granulated units of the institution, and the individual members, possibly as well as business partners, for example with respect to *cooperation data* and *contract data*, and other affected individuals, with respect to their *personal data*, to be processed in accordance with *privacy acts* or related *legal rules*.

The *relational model* for databases was propagated by E.F. Codd more than 30 years ago. Since then, several research prototypes and commercial products have been implemented. Today, relational database management systems, and extensions of them capturing *object-orientation, semi-structured data*, active components such as *triggers*, and many further features, are in widespread use. Prominent implementations include Oracle, Sybase, IBM DB2, Microsoft SQL Server and PostgreSQL. In the following we outline a simplified design of a fragment of the Oracle/SQL functionality, abstracting from many subtle details and ignoring differing versions.

17.2.1 Basic Blocks

Oracle/SQL provides not only the core database functionality but also a full *application environment*. Accordingly, among other features, Oracle/SQL exploits the following basic blocks of *control and monitoring* (which also include concepts of *cryptography* and of *certificates and credentials*):

- *Identification* and *authentication* of registered users as participants.
- Linking via a supporting operating system or another external system, or via a network environment based on *credentials*.
- Declaration of *integrity constraints* to enforce common aspects of the integrity (in the sense of correct content) of data instances (extensions) under modification.
- Declaration of *triggers* and *stored procedures* to enforce application-dependent aspects of the integrity of data.
- *Fault-tolerant protocols* as part of the *transaction* management, which maintains *recovery copies* and use them to restore corrupted data instances.
- Scheduling that enforces serializability as part of the *transaction* management, which virtually *isolates* concurrently active users.
- Finely granulated *discretionary access rights* concerning the basic system structures, the declared application structures and their data instances (extensions), with respect to *operational modes* of highly differentiated operations for modifying and querying the structures and instances.
- *Content-dependent* access rights concerning querying, inspecting and possibly modifying a preliminary result before returning a final answer.
- *Collectives* as grantees, in the form of *roles*.
- Database *administrators* and *owners* as grantors.
- A proprietary variant of *mandatory security levels*.
- *Right amplification* for temporarily increasing the operational options of a user.
- *Access control* concerning the commands that are expressed in a declarative, set-oriented style.
- Options for *encrypting data*, for the sake of confidentiality, and for producing *exhibits* as *hash values*, for the sake of detecting (unwanted) modifications, which can secure connections between remote users, acting as clients, and centralized servers.
- *Monitoring* of the functionality.

17.2.2 Conceptual Design of the Database Functionality

Oracle/SQL offers an *application environment* with a rich external interface comprising, in particular, a *data definition language* and a *data manipulation language*. Using the data definition language, designated participants known as *database administrators* can declare the structural aspects of the data to be managed, including built-in or application-specific *integrity constraints*. The conceptual aspects of the declarations are gathered together in an application (*database*) *schema*, whereas the more operational aspects concerning storage allocation and supporting data structures such as *hash functions* or *search trees* are maintained in a *data dictionary*. Using the data manipulation language, participants can generate, alter and query stored data *instances* (*extensions*) that fit the structural declarations. Moreover, the application schema and the corresponding content of the data dictionary are understood as data instances of a *meta-schema*, and, accordingly, this *metadata* is manipulated very similarly to the *application data*.

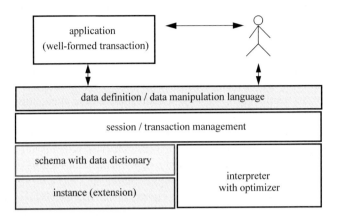

Fig. 17.7. Simplified architecture of a database management system

Any connection of a participant to the system is handled as a *session*, which deals, in particular, with the *transaction* management for *fault-tolerant computing* and virtual *isolation* of concurrent users. Within a session, the SQL declaration and SQL manipulation commands are executed by an *interpreter* that operates on the metadata and the application data, exploiting all available information for automatic *optimization* to ensure sufficient efficiency even for very large amounts of data, up to many gigabytes or terabytes. Figure 17.7 shows the overall architecture. In the following, we sketch some more details of the interface languages.

Sessions. A participant starts a *session* by means of a command of the form con-nect ..., specifying which database he intends to use, either directly and interactively from his workstation, or indirectly by a call from an application program that is executed on behalf of that participant and contains *embedded* SQL commands. Until the end of the session, which is requested by the command disconnect, all activities are attributed to an *internal representation* of the participant, and the pertinent (virtual) *connections* for sending *request messages* and *reaction messages* back and forth are handled as if they were being handled by a (general-purpose) *operating system*. In fact, a database management system duplicates part of the functionality of operating systems in a more refined, application-oriented layer.

Transactions. Within a session, several commands can be grouped into a *transaction*, syntactically expressed by an initializing instruction begin transaction and a closing instruction end transaction. There are several semantic effects, often referred to as the *ACID properties* (atomicity–consistency preservation–isolation–durability).

First, the grouped commands are treated like a single *atomic* operation: virtually, either all commands are completely and successfully executed, or none of them are executed, where the cases can be explicitly distinguished by guarded instructions containing either the command commit or the command abort, respectively. In particular, the latter case can be employed to restore an instance after some failure has been detected, for the sake of the *integrity* and *availability* of the data. For the purpose of restoring, the system automatically generates and maintains appropriate *recovery copies* of the data instances.

Second, if some of the grouped commands request that the instance is modified, then the *consistency* of the data instances is maintained, basically in two ways. On the one hand, declared *integrity constraints* are automatically checked, for example *key constraints* (or, more generally, *functional dependencies*) or *foreign key constraints* (also called *referential constraints*, or, more generally, *inclusion dependencies*) reflecting some commonly appearing aspects of the meaning of the data in the "real world". If there is a violation, some repair operations are executed or the transaction is aborted, for the sake of integrity in the sense of *correct content*. On the other hand, nearly arbitrary, more application-specific checks regarding "correct content" can be discretionarily performed, on the basis of declared *triggers* that initiate the execution of declared *procedures*, again for the sake of *integrity*.

Third, concurrent transactions are virtually *isolated* in order to ensure that they interfere only in a semantically acceptable way. In this context, acceptability is defined in terms of an appropriate notion of *serializability*, requiring that the overall effect of executing several transactions virtually concurrently, i.e., some interleaving of the commands of the transactions, is the same as if the transactions as a whole were executed in some sequence. The main challenge is to manage various *versions* of the data instances such that each transaction reads data from that version which has been written virtually most recently.

Finally, *durability* is aimed at ensuring that the effects of a successfully committed transaction remain effective for the future, unless explicitly discarded by another successfully committed transaction. Moreover, even in the latter case, *recovery copies* are kept for a while, for the sake of *availability*.

Although we have presented the ACID properties as a fundamental functionality, they nevertheless substantially contribute to the enforcement of security interests as well. In fact, the ACID properties strongly support the overall security of an application-oriented computing system, as far as security is understood as a comprehensive property and it is mainly *accidently* occurring violations that are considered. The protection against *maliciously* performed attacks needs complementary, additional mechanisms, some of which are sketched in Subsection 17.2.3 below.

Definitions (Declarations). Oracle/SQL provides a rich *data definition language* to declare the structural aspects of the internal objects to be managed. Unlike an operating system such as UNIX, which uniformly treats all objects as generic files and distinguishes only plain files and directories, a database system offers the ability to explicitly refer to the intended usage of objects, and to deal with structural relationships between objects and with specializations of object classes. Figure 17.8 visualizes some of the options and their properties (see also Figure 9.5).

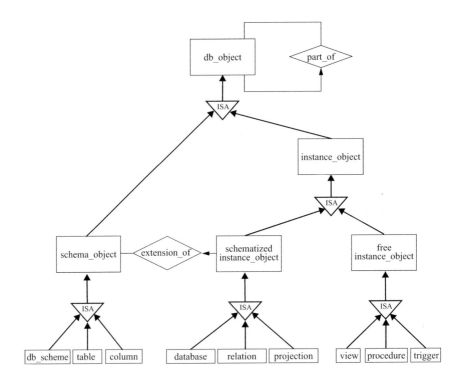

Fig. 17.8. Simplified ER model of some structures of the fundamental functional features of Oracle/SQL

Basically, the abstract object class `db_object` has two specializations, `schema_object` and `instance_object`. The objects of the former class constitute the application (database) schemas, where each `column` object is `part_of`-related to a `table` object, which in turn is `part_of`-related to a `db_scheme` object. For example, a database table is declared by the SQL command

```
create table ...,
```

together with the pertinent columns (attributes), their domains (types), applicable integrity constraints and some further specifications.

The objects of the latter specialization are seen as the "application data"; most of them are seen as data instances (extensions) of the corresponding "metadata", i.e., `extension_of`-related to the pertinent schema object, and again `part_of`-related accordingly. For example, a `relation` object *rel* is `extension_of`-related to a `table` object *tab*, and a `part-of`-related `projection` object *pro* is `extension_of`-related to a corresponding `column` object *col* that is `part_of`-related to *tab*. The operational aspects of such objects, including directions for storage allocation and access methods such as hash functions or search trees, can be declared and initialized by the SQL command

```
create tablespace ....
```

There are various options for declaring further "application data" that is not schematized and is called "free". For example, using the SQL command

```
create view ...,
```

an administrator can refer to a specific fragment of an application schema or to an object derived from the schema, in order to make solely that fragment or derived object available to other users, while hiding the rest of the schema, for the sake of *confidentiality*. Further examples include the SQL commands

```
create procedure ...  and  create trigger ... on ...
```

to declare active features, for the sake of *integrity* as explained above or for any other purpose.

Manipulations. The *data manipulation language* provides means to employ the previously declared objects within transactions. On the one hand, a participant can insert, delete or update "application data" by referring to the pertinent schematized object and supplying the specific data values, using a corresponding SQL command of one of the following forms:

```
insert into ... values ...,
delete ... from ... where ...,
update ... set ... where ....
```

On the other hand, using an SQL command of the basic form

```
select ... from ... where ...,
```

a participant can retrieve and query stored "application data" in a highly sophisticated, declarative way, employing appropriate search and qualification conditions (in the `from` clause and the `where` clause), and constructors for the returned answer data (in the `select` clause). Basic commands can also be composed into complex commands, and enriched with additional features such as standard arithmetic operations, tabular calculations, and sorting and grouping of results. Furthermore, when commands are executed, declared procedures can be called, and declared triggers can cause the execution of further commands.

These and many further functional concepts qualify an application based on Oracle/SQL to process data in a semantically meaningful way. Accordingly, the security concepts have to deal not only with the rich operational options but preferably also with the real-world meaning of the data.

17.2.3 Conceptual Design of Access Rights

Besides the mechanisms implemented for the ACID properties, Oracle/SQL also provides security concepts for *access rights*, both in a *discretionary* form, including *roles*, and in a *mandatory-like* form.

Discretionary Access Rights. Regarding the discretionary form, the SQL operations are classified as either system operations or object operations. The *system* *operations* may be employed only by designated *database administrators*, who are known under reserved usernames such `sysdba` or `sysoper`. These operations mainly serve to initialize, configure and maintain a *database application* together with its *users*. More specifically, an administrator is permitted to generate, modify and delete database objects and to register and unregister users, by issuing an SQL command of one of the following forms:

```
create ...,
alter ...,
drop ....
```

Furthermore, an administrator is perceived as the unique *owner* of the objects generated by him and, accordingly, he is permitted to perform the *control operations* for the management of discretionary access rights regarding object operations on existing owned objects and registered users (and declared roles, see below), by issuing an SQL command of one of the following forms:

```
grant ... to ...,
revoke ... from ....
```

The owner is also permitted to perform the object operations on his objects himself.

For example, such *object operations* are requested by SQL commands of the following forms:

```
alter ...,        delete ...,      execute ...,
index ...,        insert ...,      read ...,
reference ...,    select ...,      update ....
```

The concepts for *discretionary access rights* for *object operations* are partly visualized in Figure 17.9 and can be roughly outlined as follows (refer also to Section 9.1). The basic notion is a relationship class *granted*. A relationship (*grantor, grantee, object, mode*) denotes the following fact: the *grantor* has specified a permission that the *grantee* might exercise the privilege (*object, mode*), i.e., access the (*db_)object* by performing an SQL (object) operation belonging to the operational mode *mode*. Such a specification can be qualified further:

- If the Boolean qualification *grantable* is set, the grantee is permitted to grant the received privilege (*object, mode*) further.
- The qualification *issue time* indicates when the privilege was granted.
- If the Boolean qualification *cascade* is set, the *revocation semantics* demands the following: if a revoker explicitly revokes a privilege previously granted to a grantee, then the system determines a privilege distribution that would have been produced if the revoker had never granted the explicitly revoked privilege (for details, refer to Section 9.4). This goal can be achieved by *recursive revocation* of access rights according to the recorded issue times.

Basically, there are two ways to qualify as a *grantor*: with respect to the object concerned, he may be either the owner, or a grantee of a preceding, non-revoked granting (a `granted` relationship) that has been marked as *grantable*.

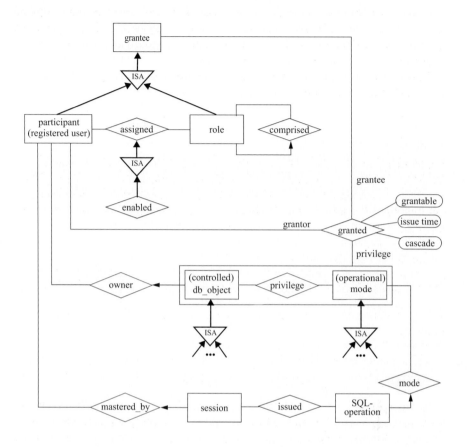

Fig. 17.9. Simplified ER model of the fundamental functional features of Oracle/SQL (white boxes) together with the basic constructs for discretionarily permitted options for object operations (gray boxes)

There are two kinds of *grantee*, individual *participants* that are *registered* as *users*, and *collectives* in the form of *roles*. For the former kind, a granted permission can be employed directly by the individual grantee. For the latter kind, some indirection is necessary: First, since a role cannot act by itself, a participant can be persistently *assigned* to one or several roles, with the intent that the participant might inherit the permissions granted to one of these roles whenever he dynamically *enables* the usage of a specific assigned role. Second, a role might *comprise* a another role as a *subrole*, with the intent that the (*super*)*role* inherits the permissions granted to the subrole. Hence, during a session, an individual participant can employ all permissions that have been granted to him directly or are inherited from the role enabled and all its transitive subroles.

Oracle/SQL offers a rich set of *operational modes* for object operations. Basically, for each object operation listed above, restricted to an applicable specialization of objects, there is a corresponding operational mode, called in Oracle/SQL an *object privilege* (not in accordance with the terminology used in this monograph). A similar property holds for the system operations, yielding a rich variety of *system privileges* too.

Furthermore, within a framework referred to as a *virtual private database* (*VPD*), Oracle/SQL provides options for content-dependent or context-based *modifications* of an issued command or of returned *query* results, respectively.

For example, a modification on the basis of rows (tuples) can be achieved by declaring a *VPD policy* for a table or view. Such a policy demands that a `where` clause is tacked on to any query that reads from the respective table or view, that another conjunct is added to an existing `where` clause, or that the call of a stored procedure is triggered to filter the accessed tuples of the respective table or view.

Mandatory-Like Access Rights. Regarding the *mandatory* or *organization-oriented* approach to *access rights*, Oracle/SQL suggests that a somewhat proprietary form of *labels* (*security levels*) is instantiated, as partly visualized in Figure 17.10, which can be roughly outlined as follows (refer also to Section 9.8). Basically, only a *security officer* is permitted to perform the general instantiations and to declare the concrete assignments of labels. For each instantiation, the labels are taken from a *product lattice* with a domain $Rank \times \wp\, KW \times \wp\, Org$ that can be defined as follows:

- *Rank* is a finite set (with cardinality up to 10 000) of *sensitivity rankings*, which are mutually comparable with respect to some *linear order* $\leq_{Rank}$, intended to express the *relative trustworthiness* of a participant or the *relative sensitivity* of an object.
- *KW* is a finite set of *keywords* (with cardinality up to 10 000), called *compartments* or *categories* in this context, intended to describe concepts such as *information content* or *intended usage*.
- *Org* is a finite set of identifiers (with cardinality up to 10 000), called *groups* in this context, intended to denote concepts such as *organizational* or *geographical units*. Moreover, an *inheritance hierarchy* (partial order) $\leq_{Org}$ can be imposed on the set *Org*, where $org_1 \leq_{Org} org_2$ means that the organizational unit denoted by org_1 is seen as a *subunit* of the organizational unit denoted by org_2.

On the one hand, such a label is statically assigned to each *user* and dynamically formed for the user's *session* as a *clearance*. The ranking component might be split into a *minimum ranking* and a *maximum ranking*, enhancing flexible employment of the clearance during a session. Besides the gain in flexibility, the maximum ranking serves to enforce confidentiality by *always* denying a *read* access for all objects classified strictly higher; similarly, the minimum ranking serves to enforce confidentiality by *always* denying a *write* access for all objects classified strictly lower, thereby prohibiting the downgrading of information beyond the minimum ranking.

Additionally, in a user's label, each keyword and each organizational unit that occurs is given a Boolean `write` *flag* to indicate whether the respective clearance

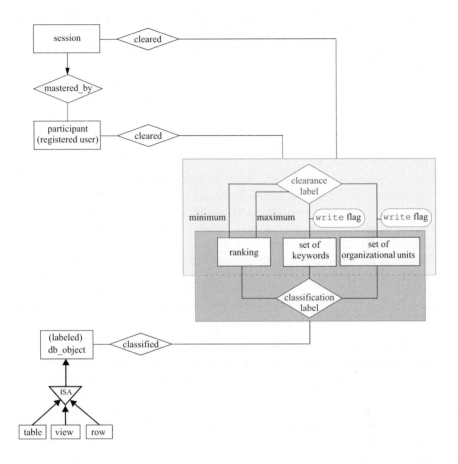

Fig. 17.10. Simplified ER model of the basic constructs for operational options permitted by mandatory-like access rights

applies either for reading only or for writing as well, and the respective flags are copied when a session label is formed.

On the other hand, such labels are attached to the *tables* (relations), the *views* and, additionally, in a more finely granulated way, even to their *rows* (tuples), as *classifications*.

Whenever, during a session, a user requests to access a labeled object for either *reading* or *writing*, the actual clearance label of the session, with the additional Boolean write flags, is compared with the declared classification of the requested object. The comparisons are performed componentwise and in a mandatory-like way, regarding the *linear order* on *Rank* and the *partial order* defined by the *set inclusion* on the *power set lattice* ℘*KW* of keywords, and there is checking for nonempty intersections in the *power set lattice* ℘ *Org* of organizational units. On the basis of the results of the comparison, an *access decision* is taken, as explained in more detail in Subsection 17.2.4 below.

However, there are also special mechanisms to *exempt* a user's session from the strict rules underlying the mandatory-like access decisions. These exemption mechanisms are based on special *label security privileges* that are grantable to a user and permit him one of the following:

- unrestricted *reading*, as if the mandatory-like access control was not present;
- unrestricted *reading* and *writing*;
- *reading* and *writing*, where the comparisons regarding *organizational units* are skipped;
- *changing* the *dynamic label* of a user's *session* to the label statically assigned to a different user, thereby becoming as powerful as that user;
- *changing* the *ranking* entry of row labels, by either *raising* or *lowering* (*downgrading*) them within the user's assigned maximum or minimum ranking, respectively;
- *changing the keyword entry and organizational-unit* entry of row labels.

Furthermore, the framework of "virtual private databases" can also be employed in the mandatory-like approach, to require a label-based filtering of rows (tuples) when a table is accessed.

17.2.4 Components of Local Control and Monitoring

In Section 7.2 we introduced a general model for *local control and monitoring* based on authenticated identities. We now show how some of the components of the general model are implemented in Oracle/SQL. In doing so, we shall not repeat considerations of the operating system functionality that have already been presented for UNIX.

Identification and Authentication

An individual can act as a participant of an Oracle/SQL database system only if the database *administrator* has *registered* him in advance as a *user*, thereby assigning a *username* to him. The following SQL commands serve for the administration of users:

```
create user ...,    alter user ...,    drop user ....
```

Later on, a registered user can *link* to the Oracle/SQL system in basically three ways, subject to a successful *proof of authenticity*:

- Directly: an agreed *password* is required as an exhibit.
- Via an underlying *operating system* or another *external system*: the external system's successful proof of authenticity is accepted by the Oracle/SQL system as well.

- Via a network environment: suitable *credentials* are required as exhibits, either issued by trusted third parties employing, for example, DCE, Kerberos or SES-AME, or provided by a proprietary public key infrastructure.

Having successfully linked to the system, a user can start a session and dynamically enable one of his persistently assigned *roles*. The selection of the *enabled role* should conform to the general *construction* and *administrative principles*.

Additionally, and following the same principles, a *session label* is formed in order to select a *dynamic clearance* for the anticipated informational activities of the user. Basically, the user might either act with his statically declared clearance, transferring his maximum ranking, his full set of keywords and his full set of organizational units to the session label, or he might want to appear less powerful, using a dynamic ranking between the minimum and the maximum, and possibly by deleting some members from his full set of keywords and from his full set of organizational units. During the *lifespan* of the session, the mastering user can repeatedly change the session label.

Access Decisions

As outlined above, the very rich syntax of SQL commands enables one to express a large variety of operations. In general, when submitting a command, a participant specifies both the wanted SQL operation and the object affected or, if applicable, several objects. The interpreter then determines the pertinent pairs of the form (object, operation) and submits the corresponding requests, of the form (participant, object, operation), to the *access decision* component.

As far as only *discretionary access rights* are concerned, in standard cases the decision is taken by the following, grossly simplified procedure, which uses the basic constructs shown in Figure 17.9:

```
function decide_discret(participant, object, operation): Boolean;
return
  participant = object.owner
  OR
  [ EXISTS granted:
    granted.privilege.mode = operation.mode
    AND
    granted.privilege.db_object = object
    AND
    [ granted.grantee = participant
      OR
      [ EXISTS role_1, role_2:
        granted.grantee = role_1
        AND  transitively_comprised(role_1, role_2)
        AND enabled(participant, role_2)
      ]
    ]
  ];
```

Among several other particularities, however, this simplified procedure does not reflect the special treatment of a request to *execute* a *stored procedure*. Similarly to the option of *amplifying access rights* by setting the execution flag `suid` for an executable file in UNIX, Oracle/SQL offers the possibility to declare a procedure in such a way that during an execution, the session acts with the access rights of the procedure's owner (rather than with the access rights of the calling participant).

Furthermore, after a positive discretionary access decision, the demands of declared *VPD policies* are taken into account while requested operations are actually being performed.

If *mandatory-like access rights* are employed, each request must *additionally* pass the pertinent mandatory-like access decision, which is based on comparing the current session label, considered as a clearance, with the object's label, considered as a classification. As a prerequisite, each possible operation is seen as working either in the operational mode `read` or in the operational mode `write`. In the following, we exemplify the decision rules for a request to access a row (tuple), where the basic constructs shown in Figure 17.10 are used.

Regarding operations with the operational mode `read`, basically, the three parts of the *session label* ($rank_{sess}, kws_{sess}, orgs_{sess}$) are compared with the *classification label* ($rank_{row}, kws_{row}, orgs_{row}$) of a row (tuple) object requested to be read. In order to obtain a *positive access decision* for reading, the conditions listed below must be met; otherwise, the processing of the row being inspected is skipped without a *notification*, and the next row of the table under consideration is processed:

- The session's clearance *rank* must *dominate* the row's classification rank, i.e.,

  $rank_{row} \leq_{Rank} rank_{sess}$.

- The session's clearance *set of keywords* (*compartments* and *categories*) must *contain* the row's set of classification keywords (where, by default, an undeclared set of keywords is interpreted as the empty set $\emptyset$), i.e.,

  $kws_{row} \subseteq kws_{sess}$.

- Provided that the row's classification set of organizational units has been declared, the session's clearance *set of organizational units* (*groups*) must have a *nonempty intersection* with the row's classification set of organizational units, after the explicitly declared sets have been *expanded* by using the *inheritance hierarchy* $\leq_{Org}$ (where, by default, an undeclared set of organizational units for the session is interpreted as the empty set $\emptyset$), i.e.,

  $expansion(org_{row}) \cap expansion(org_{sess}) \neq \emptyset$.

Regarding operations with the operational mode `write`, a *positive* access decision for writing requires the conditions listed below, which are similar to but somewhat more elaborate than those for reading; if the conditions are not met, the processing of the row being inspected is handled as for reading:

- The session's *rank* must provide a *clearance for reading* and thus *dominate* the row's classification rank, i.e.,

  $rank_{row} \leq_{Rank} rank_{sess}$.

- Additionally, the mastering user's minimum rank $rank_{user}$, with $rank_{user} \leq_{Rank} rank_{sess}$, must provide a *clearance for writing* and thus be dominated by the row's classification rank, i.e.,

$$rank_{user} \leq_{Rank} rank_{row}.$$

- Provided that the row's classification set of keywords has been declared, the session's clearance *set of keywords* (compartments and categories) must *contain* the row's set of classification keywords, i.e.,

$$kws_{row} \subseteq kws_{sess}.$$

Furthermore, if the row's classification set of organizational units has *not* been declared, then the containment must even hold for the session's clearance subset of keywords that have the `write` flag set, i.e.,

$$kws_{row} \subseteq \texttt{write\_restriction}(kws_{sess}).$$

- Provided that the row's classification set of organizational units has been declared, the session's clearance *subset of organizational units* (groups) that have the `write` flag set must deliver a *nonempty intersection* with the row's classification set of organizational units, after the explicitly declared sets have been *expanded* by using the *inheritance hierarchy* $\leq_{Org}$ (where, by default, an undeclared set of organizational units for the session is interpreted as the empty set $\varnothing$), i.e.,

$$expansion(org_{row}) \cap expansion(\texttt{write\_restriction}(org_{sess})) \neq \varnothing.$$

For both kinds of operation, the access decision rules given above can be partially or completely bypassed if suitable *label security privileges* have been granted.

Summarizing, if all features for access control are employed, the central control component decides on an access request on the basis of various features that have been defined earlier by several, mostly independently acting participants. These features include the following:

- ownership and discretionary grantings by the owner;
- enabled further grantings by grantees;
- assigned roles;
- comprised roles;
- declared VPD policies;
- the definition of rankings, with their linear order; keywords; and organizational units, with their hierarchy;
- the requestor's clearance concerning the ranking, set of keywords and set of organizational units, together with the `write` flags;
- the requested object's classification concerning the ranking, set of keywords and set of organizational units;
- the requestor's label security privileges (for bypassing mandatory-like rules);
- dynamic selections for the actual session.

Knowledge Base on Permitted Operational Options

The basic constructs for the conceptual *knowledge base* on *permitted operational options* are shown in Figure 17.9 and Figure 17.10. Basically, these constructs are implemented by *system tables* (relations) that are managed in more or less the same way as the *application tables* (relations); in particular, querying and updating are performed quite similarly.

Modifications of the knowledge base arise mainly from the following activities, listed without specifying further details:

- creating, altering or dropping an item, for example a user, role or object;
- discretionarily granting or revoking object privileges or system privileges;
- discretionarily assigning roles;
- assigning labels in a mandatory-like way as clearances and classifications;
- granting label security privileges;
- declaring VPD policies;
- dynamically selecting options for a session.

Knowledge Base on Usage History

Oracle/SQL does not maintain an explicit *knowledge base* on the *usage history* for taking access decision. However, the system does care about its dynamic evolution regarding the following aspects:

- selected options for a *session*;
- scheduling data for achieving *serializability* of transactions;
- recovery copies for guaranteeing the *durability* of transactions;
- log services for *monitoring*.

Basically, the *log services* produce *log data* about all of the kinds of activity described above. The log data is written into dedicated system tables, and an administrator can inspect the log data by means of several predefined views. Moreover, the log data might also be forwarded to the underlying *operating system*, to be evaluated there or in a connected *intrusion detection system*.

Securing Client–Server Connections

An Oracle/SQL application can be designed as a *distributed system*. In this case users act as remote *clients* for one or more *servers* that maintain the shared meta-data and application data. Additionally, users might keep local *materialized views* of the common data, i.e., suitably refreshed, stored answers to predefined queries; and servers might be connected to external data sources. In these and related cases, the connections between the remote participants can be appropriately *end-to-end* protected by applying built-in standard cryptographic security mechanisms:

- for the sake of *confidentiality*, encryption of data;
- for the sake of *integrity*, exhibits in the form of hash values;
- for the sake of *authenticity*, integration of various mechanisms, ranging from biometrics to certificates and credentials.

17.3 CORBA Middleware

CORBA (*Common Object Request Broker Architecture*) specifies a middleware system that manages a distributed federation of *locally autonomous* object systems. An implementation of CORBA supports participants in *sharing* the objects of the federated systems in a unified, interoperable manner. In particular, among many other features, CORBA wraps objects in order to prepare for mediating *method invocations* at remote *objects*, making the needed *message* sending and receiving transparent.

Regarding security, first of all CORBA enhances the *availability* of local objects within a larger federation. In doing so, it protects both the objects themselves and the messages exchanged between them, for the sake of *confidentiality* and *integrity*. Moreover, the *authenticity* and the *non-repudiation* of messages are enforced as well. The objects are protected by *controlling* the messages for method invocations twice, first at the site of the sending object, and second at the site of the receiving object, where each site can follow its local *security policy*. Such a policy specifies the permitted and prohibited *operational options* for participants at the fine granularity of *privileges*, each of which refers to an instance (object) of a *class* and a method declared for this class. This applies to each application class, and thus a *security officer* can tailor application-specific security policies that refer directly to the functional semantics encoded in the method declarations. In order to achieve scalability, options for a more coarsely granulated policy specification are offered too. The messages are protected by securing the *connection* with standard cryptographic mechanisms.

The CORBA specification was originally developed by the *Object Management Group (OMG)*, a consortium of leading IT companies, about fifteen years ago, and since then has been further enhanced and updated to the present version. There are several commercial implementations which cover substantial parts of the specification. In the following, we outline an abstract, simplified view of the specification.

17.3.1 Basic Blocks

Among other features, CORBA exploits the following basic blocks of *control and monitoring* (which also include concepts of *cryptography* and of *certificates and credentials*):

- *Identification* and *authentication* of local and remote principals.
- *Fault-tolerant protocols* for invoking a method (calling a procedure) at a remote object and returning the result.
- Finely granulated *access rights* permitting *method invocations* on *objects*.
- The option of assigning one of four coarsely granulated *operational modes* to a method.
- *Collectives* (of participants), defined by customized *granted security attributes* at a client.
- *Collections* (of objects), considered as *domains* at a server.

- Representation of access rights and other security attributes in *credentials*.
- Different modes of credential *delegation* for mediated method invocations.
- Two-sided *access control* by intercepting *outgoing request messages* at a client and *incoming request messages* at a server.
- Options for *encrypting messages*, for the sake of confidentiality, and for producing *exhibits*, for the sake of detecting (unwanted) modifications and achieving *non-repudiation*, which are used to secure *connections* between a client and a remote server.
- *Monitoring* of the functionality.

17.3.2 Conceptual Design of the Client–Server Functionality

In grossly simplified terms, a distributed CORBA-based system consists of a federating *Object Request Broker* (*ORB*) that serves many distributed *components*. Each component manages a population of *objects*, generated as instances of previously declared *classes*. The components might be located at different sites. A *participant* (also called a *principal*), i.e., a *human individual* or some *system entity*, can access a component and then act by means of that component.

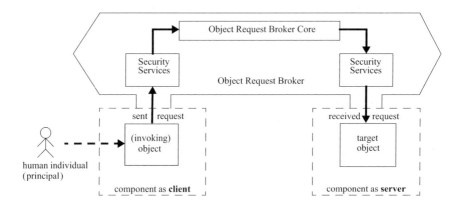

Fig. 17.11. CORBA secure method invocation for a client on behalf of a principal via the Object Request Broker at a remote target object of a server

Abstractly, as visualized in Figure 17.11, a basic action is obtained by letting an object *invoke a method* at an(other) object. A little more concretely, for any specific method invocation, the former object's component is treated as a *client*, seen as addressing the latter object's component as a *server*. First, the invoking object acts as an *activator* by forming a message containing the invocation request and sending this message to the target object. Then, the ORB *mediates* and *transports* this message to the target object, whatever component it resides at. In doing so, the

ORB employs several auxiliary services in order to enable and supervise the actual delivery of the message by the *Object Request Broker Core*. The *Security Services* complement the more functionally oriented services. Finally, the target object acts as an *executor* by receiving the requesting message, interpreting the request according to the pertinent class declaration and executing the corresponding method implementation. Moreover, if required, the ORB also handles the passing of return values.

17.3.3 Conceptual Design of the Security Concepts

We now outline the design of the security concepts according to the introduction to the functionality given above. In particular, in the following and in Figure 17.12, we describe the static structures on which basic actions operate.

Principals. After *registering* at some component, a *human individual* is assigned a *local name*, and can then access the component after a successful *identification* and *authentication*, where a *proof of authenticity* is enabled by some appropriate local *authentication information*. A system entity is introduced similarly. A registered individual or system entity is then referred to as a *principal*.

Clients. A principal acts by means of the pertinent component, which is seen as a *client*, and, conversely, this client acts on behalf of one of its principals. Blurring the distinction between a principal and the pertinent client, we also speak about an *active entity*. The security-relevant properties of an active entity, including its permitted operational options, are expressed by *security attributes*. Since security attributes have to be communicated to other components, they are represented in *credentials*, i.e., digital documents that must be digitally signed by the issuer for the sake of authentication. An exception applies for *unauthenticated attributes*, for example the predefined attribute `public` assigned to any entity by default.

An *authenticated attribute* might signify a (more) *global identifier* to be presented at a server, or it might be a *granted attribute* expressing some other *property* of the holder that potentially qualifies him to have some request permitted at a server. The format of a granted attribute may vary considerably: the essential requirement is that an addressed server is able to interpret its intended meaning. We list the following examples:

- A granted attribute can be an elementary, discretionary *privilege*, i.e., a (reference to an) object together with a (reference to a) method declared in the class the object is an instance of, where the holder, as authenticated in the representing credential, is seen to be permitted to invoke the method.
- A granted attribute can signify a *collective*, i.e. a *role* (identifier) or a *group* (identifier), where the authenticated assignment of the role or the authenticated group membership might result in the privileges of the denoted role or group, respectively, being acquired.
- A granted attribute can be a mandatory *security level*, where the authenticated assignment is interpreted as a *clearance* of the holder.

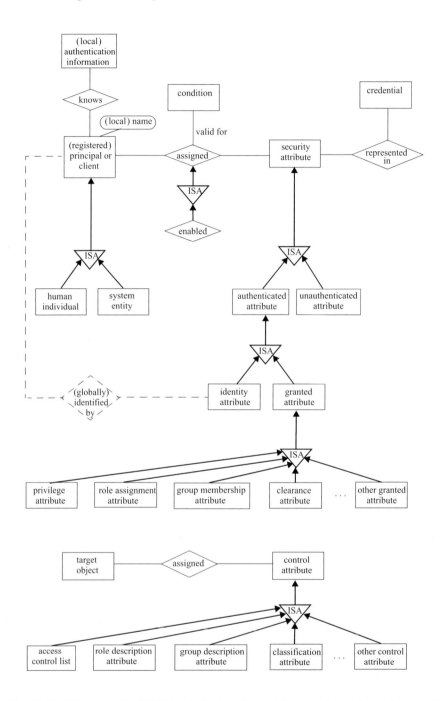

Fig. 17.12. ER model of a CORBA principal or client with assigned security attributes and of a CORBA target object with control attributes, and their correspondences

Servers. Complementarily, on the server side, a *target object* is assigned *control attributes* expressing which principals are permitted to invoke which of its methods. Again, the format of the control attributes may vary, but the format must have a useful interpretation for taking access decisions about requests that are accompanied by shown authenticated attributes of a requestor. We list the following examples:

- A control attribute can be a discretionary *access control list*, i.e., for any of the target object's declared methods, a list of (global identifiers of) those principals who are permitted to invoke the method.
- A control attribute can *describe a collective*, i.e., for any of the target object's declared methods, it can be a *role* (identifier) or a *group* (identifier), expressing that a principal who has enabled this role or is a member of this group, respectively, is permitted to invoke the method for the target object.
- A control attribute can be a mandatory *security level*, where the assignment is interpreted as a *classification* of the target object, expressing that a principal is permitted to invoke the target object's method only if the principal's shown clearance qualifies for the operational mode of the method – reading or writing – according to the access decision rules for mandatory access control.

Scalability. A CORBA system can comprise an overwhelming number of objects that are instances of a sophisticated class system, where each class defines many methods. In such a case, specifying access rights at the *granularity* of single privileges, i.e., pairs of an (instance) object and a method, might be too cumbersome. Accordingly, several concepts for achieving *scalability* are offered. First, principals that share some specific access rights can be gathered into a *collective* such as a *role* or a *group*, and objects that share some specific protection needs can be collected into a *domain*.

Second, each declared method of a class can be characterized regarding its intended usage by assigning *operational modes* to it. The following operational modes are defined:

- The mode *get*, **g**, applies to methods that return a value to an invoker; thus this mode is related to the operational mode `read` used by other systems.
- The mode *set*, **s**, applies to methods that change the internal state of an object; thus this mode is related to the operational mode `write` used by other systems.
- The mode *use*, **u**, applies to methods that trigger some outside effects; thus this mode is related to the operational mode `execute` used by other systems.
- The mode *manage*, **m**, applies to methods that are reserved for dedicated users such as system administrators or security officers; thus this mode is related to the *control modes* such as `grant` or `revoke` used by other systems.

Complementarily, on the side of a client, a granted attribute might specify one or more of these modes, expressing that its holder qualifies for invoking the methods characterized accordingly. Hence, rather than stating long lists of permitted methods, only a short term for the permitted operational modes needs to be attributed.

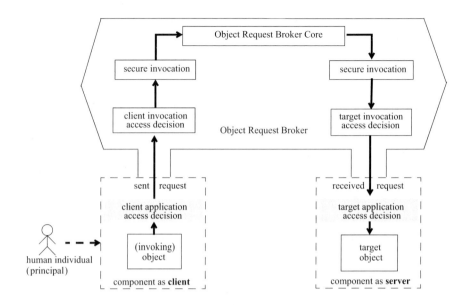

Fig. 17.13. Refined CORBA secure method invocation with additional access control by the application

Method Invocation. To prepare method invocations, the activating principal first *enables* suitable assigned security attributes by selecting the representing credentials. In order to actually invoke a target object's method, the selected credentials are attached to the outgoing request message formed. For the first control, on the client side, the request message is intercepted and subjected to a *client invocation access decision*.

If the invocation request is permitted, the *secure invocation* employs a *security association*, existing or established on demand, between the activator and the prospective target object to forward the request message. This security association is configured according to a *security context* that specifies the required quality of the end-to-end connection between the communicating objects, mainly with respect to the interests in mutual authenticity, non-repudiation, confidentiality and accountability; it also provides appropriate certificates for the underlying cryptographic mechanisms.

For the second control, on the server side, a received request message is intercepted and subjected to a *target invocation access decision*, which is based on the activator's shown security attributes and the target object's control attributes. Though, in principle, the two access decisions are independent, the access decision at the server supposes a common understanding of the shown security attributes.

These two controls apply to all method invocations between objects wrapped by the CORBA mechanisms, independently of the security *awareness* of the federated object systems. If applications running a federated object system already perform their own controls, they can continue to use them to take additional *client applica-tion access decisions* or *target application access decisions*. The overall processing of a method invocation is visualized in Figure 17.13.

Delegation. In the basic case, a client – acting as an activator – sends an invocation request for an object's method to a server, where the request shows the needed cre-dentials, and the addressed object – acting as an executor – performs the requested activities completely on its own. In more advanced cases, however, the directly addressed object might call further methods at other objects to accomplish the overall requirement. Such iterated invocations might also occur repeatedly, leading to a chain of *mediated invocations*, originating from the *initiator*, passing through one or more *intermediates*, to a final *target object*, as exemplified in Figure 17.14.

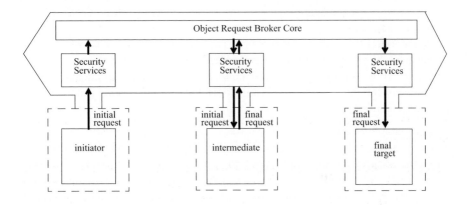

Fig. 17.14. CORBA secure method invocation at a remote target object, assisted by an intermediate

When preparing the initial invocation with accompanying credentials, the initia-tor can declare how the intermediates may use the initiator's shown credentials. The CORBA specification proposes the following *delegation* modes:

- *No delegation*. The intermediate is *prohibited* to use the *shown* credentials for iterated invocations, which then have to be accompanied by the intermediate's own credentials. Accordingly, the next site sees only the intermediate's creden-tials and thus cannot gain information about the initiator on the basis of the received credentials.
- *Simple delegation*. The intermediate is *permitted* to use the *shown* credentials for iterated invocations, but is *prohibited* to accompany them with the interme-diate's *own* credentials. Accordingly, the next site sees only the initiator's cre-dentials and thus cannot gain information about the intermediate on the basis of the received credentials.

- *Composite delegation.* The intermediate is *permitted* to use both its *own* and the *shown* credentials for iterated invocations. Accordingly, the next site can gain information about both the intermediate and the initiator on the basis of the received credentials.
- *Combined privileges delegation.* The intermediate is *permitted* to form new credentials that represent a combination of its *own* security attributes with granted attributes extracted from the *shown* credentials, and to use these new credentials for iterated invocations. Accordingly, on the basis of the received credentials, the next site might possibly gain information about both the intermediate and the initiator, depending on the new credentials actually formed.
- *Traced delegation.* The intermediate is *permitted* to act as in the case of combined privileges delegation, subject to obeying the following additional obligations: the initiator must have shown a credential with an *identity attribute*, and the intermediate must represent both the extracted identity attribute of the initiator and its *own identity attribute* by the newly formed credentials. Accordingly, on the basis of the received credentials, the next site gains full information about the chain of objects involved in the iterated invocations so far.
- Moreover, the initiator can require a *time restriction* on the declared delegation mode concerning his forwarded credentials, limiting the period of time of usage and the number of usages of them.

In general, however, this proposal raises several concerns regarding the employment of shown credentials and the formation of new ones. Most importantly, a receiving subsequent site might want to *challenge* the intermediate to provide exhibits in relation to its permission to use the forwarded credentials on behalf of their actual holder, and this site might wonder about its *trust* in the issuer of the newly formed credentials. Leaving these and related issues open, the site of an intermediate (or a target object) processes a request as follows:

- it verifies the received credentials;
- if applicable, it checks time restrictions;
- it extracts the security attributes represented in the verified credentials;
- it takes an access decision on the basis of the extracted security attributes;
- if permitted, it executes the requested method;
- if applicable and permitted, it forwards the received or its own credentials for further method invocations;
- if applicable and permitted, it creates new credentials representing the extracted and its own security attributes for further method invocations.

17.4 Kerberos

Kerberos was designed to support participants who are offering and using services in a *distributed* computing system. The participants may be unknown to each other before interacting, either as a (functional) server or as a client. Nevertheless, the servers aim to specify and enforce a *security policy* that describes the permitted and prohibited *operational options* with respect to potential clients. And both servers and clients want to initialize and maintain secure *end-to-end connections* that achieve mutual *authenticity* and enforce *confidentiality*. Evidently, without any preparatory provisions, it is impossible for participants who are completely unknown to each other to meet these goals. As a solution, however, *Kerberos* proposes the use of a *trusted third party*, known as a Kerberos server, to dynamically act as a *mediator* on a request from of a client, on the basis of statically agreed relationships between the participants and the Kerberos server.

The overall security achievements are founded on the *trust* that the participants assign to the Kerberos server. Among other things, each of the participants and the Kerberos server have to initially exchange a *secret* (*key*) for enabling symmetric authentication, and a server has to permanently delegate the granting of permissions to the Kerberos server. Basically, however, within Kerberos, permission granting is degenerated to allow accesses whenever proper authentication has been achieved. On the basis of these prerequisites, for any ad hoc client–server cooperation, each of the participants concerned can enforce his own interest in *authenticity* with respect to his supposed partner, and the participant acting as the server can protect his resources; in most cases, this concerns the interests in *confidentiality* and *integrity* (as unmodified state).

The original Kerberos versions 1–4 were developed at MIT. Subsequently, various commercial products have started to exploit Kerberos. Kerberos 5 aims at extending previous versions and overcoming known weaknesses. In the following, we outline the design of Kerberos 5 in a somewhat simplified form.

17.4.1 Basic Blocks

Kerberos exploits the following basic blocks of cryptography on the one hand and of control and monitoring on the other hand:

- *Symmetric encryption*, first of all for evaluating the authenticity of messages on the basis of the possession of a secret symmetric *key*, and additionally for enforcing the confidentiality and integrity of messages.
- *Passwords*, used as substitutes for the secret symmetric key agreed between a particular participant and the Kerberos server.
- *A one-way hash function* for dynamically regenerating a key from the substituting password.
- *A random generator* to generate symmetric *session keys*, to be used for a secure *end-to-end connection* during a client–server interaction.

- *Timestamps*, used as indications of the *freshness* of messages.
- *Nonces* (random bit strings), used as *challenges* to be included in responses.
- *Tickets*, which are a special kind of *credential* that encode *privileges* granted to a client as a grantee and are shown to a server as a (self-protecting) controlled object.
- *Validity* specifications for tickets.
- *Access decisions*, taken by a server on the basis of shown tickets.
- *Delegation* of the issuing of tickets by the Kerberos server on behalf of a server.

17.4.2 Conceptual Design

The basic blocks are used as follows by a central *Kerberos server* (one for each realm) and other participants, which seek dynamic cooperation either as a *client* or as a *server*. These usages rely on appropriate structures, which are visualized in Figure 17.15.

Basically, the Kerberos server consists of two components, the *authentication server AS*, and the *ticket-granting server TGS*. Both components can access the tables *Keys*, *Granted* and *Attributes*.

A participant P, as well as the Kerberos server and its components, is uniquely known by an identifier Id_P, and he receives messages under his network address Add_P. To take advantage of the Kerberos system, a participant registers in advance at the Kerberos server. The registration includes agreeing on a secret symmetric key K_P for a symmetric encryption method. Accordingly, the Kerberos server maintains a table *Keys*, with columns *Ident(ifier)* and *Sym(metric)K(ey)*, that contains the identifier Id_P and the key K_P of each registered participant P, as well as further administrative data. A participant, in turn, has to store the agreed key in his local table *Keys*, referring to the identifier Id_{Ker} of the Kerberos server. Figure 17.15 shows a situation after a client identified by Id_{Cl} and a (functional) server identified by Id_{FS} have been registered.

However, in contrast to the simplified visualization and exposition given so far, for a human individual acting as a client, the secret symmetric key is not directly generated and then permanently stored in the *Keys* tables. Instead, the individual can choose a secret *password*, from which the symmetric key can be repeatedly computed by use of a *one-way hash function*. On the client side, neither the password nor the corresponding secret key needs to be persistently stored: if the key is required as a parameter for encryption or decryption, the individual is asked to provide his password, which then can be used in a confined way to generate the requested cryptographic key. However, on the side of the Kerberos server, the agreed secret still has to be persistently stored under appropriate protection.

For its own purposes and on behalf of the registered functional servers, the Kerberos server conceptually maintains a second table *Granted*, with columns *Subject* and *Privilege* (or some more sophisticated mechanism), that represents the *permissions* that have been granted to clients to access services. There are two kinds of entry:

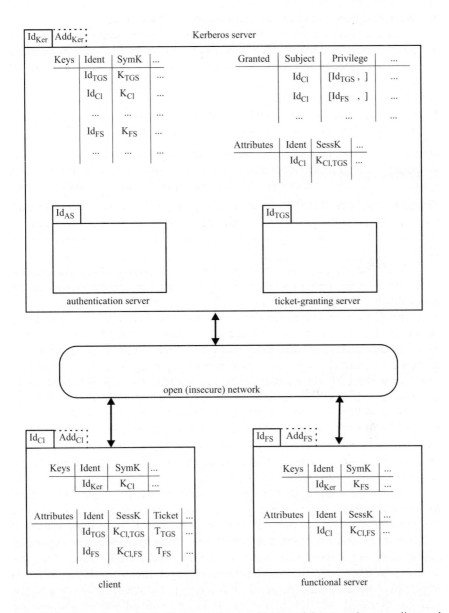

Fig. 17.15. Structures used by a Kerberos server and two participants acting as a client and a functional server, respectively

- An entry of the form (Subject: Id_{Cl}, Privilege: $[Id_{FS},]$) means the following: the participant identified by Id_{Cl} is permitted, as a client, to access the services offered by the functional server identified by Id_{FS} (where, for the sake of simplicity, the operational mode has been suppressed in the privilege $[Id_{FS},]$).

- Correspondingly, an entry of the form (Subject: Id_{Cl}, Privilege: [Id_{TGS},]) means that the participant identified by Id_{Cl} is permitted, as a client, to access the service of the ticket-granting server, which is identified by Id_{TGS} and is a component of the Kerberos server.

The permissions of the client Cl for accessing the services of the ticket-granting server TGS and the functional server FS are shown in Figure 17.15.

Kerberos does not specify any conditions for granting permissions. Rather, the concrete security policy concerning permitted operational options is left to the discretion of the Kerberos server's administrator, who in turn is supposed to act according to the interests of the functional servers' owners. In fact, in the case of granting permissions to any known client, Kerberos basically reduces to a pure *authentication support system*.

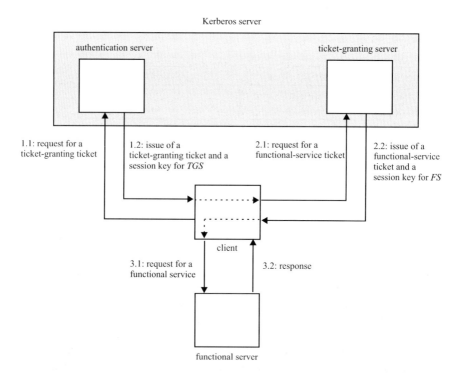

Fig. 17.16. Messages between a client, a Kerberos server and a functional server

As roughly indicated in Figure 17.16, the *Kerberos protocol* has three rounds, each being initialized by a client and having two messages. The first round is executed once per client session and can be integrated within a login procedure. The main function of the first round is to authenticate the client for the later process of obtaining and exploiting a reusable *ticket* that expresses a *privilege* for a service.

The second round is performed once for each functional server that is contacted during a client session. The main purpose of this round is to actually grant the privilege to the client. Finally, the third round is repeatedly called for each actual *service invocation*, i.e., the purpose of this round is to exploit the granted privilege. The six different *Kerberos messages* are intended to express the following rough meanings:

1.1: a client requests a ticket-granting ticket from the authentication server;
1.2: the authentication server issues a ticket-granting ticket for the client, together with a session key for a secure end-to-end connection between the client and the ticket-granting server;

2.1: a client requests a functional-service ticket from the ticket-granting server;
2.2: the ticket-granting server issues a functional-service ticket for the client, together with a session key for a secure end-to-end connection between the client and the functional server;

3.1: a client requests a service invocation from the functional server;
3.2: the functional server responds to the client.

If, as a result of the last round, as explained below, the client and the functional server have been mutually *authenticated*, then additional secured messages might be exchanged between the client and the functional server while the requested service is actually being performed. However, at least conceptually, the functional server has to take an *access decision* on the request before sending message 3.2. But, within pure Kerberos, the decision is based merely on a successful authentication of the client.

In each round, the protocol aims to guarantee that only the intended participants can exploit the exchanged messages in the expected way. In particular, honest participants are to be protected against messages that have been forged or intercepted and then replayed. The proposed solution is based on the secret symmetric (encryption and decryption) keys that are agreed in advance between the Kerberos server and each of the participants.

A client key K_{Cl} is used to protect messages (of kind 1.2) from the authentication server to the pertinent client, and, correspondingly, a functional-server key K_{FS} is used to protect the submessages (included in messages of kind 2.2) that the ticket-granting server directs to the pertinent functional server via the requesting client. These messages contain dynamically generated *session keys* $K_{Cl,TGS}$ and $K_{Cl,FS}$ to protect the respective follow-up messages (of kinds 2.1 and 2.2 between the client and the ticket-granting server, and of kinds 3.1 and 3.2 between the client and the functional server). The Kerberos server and the participants store the distributed session keys and the corresponding identifiers in the columns *Sess(ion)K(ey)* and *Ident(ifier)* of the their respective *Attributes* tables, as shown in Figure 17.15.

More specifically, the *distribution* of the two session keys proceeds basically as follows. In each case, the distributor of the session key (the authentication server or the ticket-granting server, respectively) has agreed beforehand with each of the two intended receivers of the session key (the client and the ticket-granting service, or the client and the functional server, respectively) on a secret symmetric (encryption and decryption) key. The distributor uses the appropriate key to encrypt a copy of the new session key, together with other items. The cryptogram devoted to the client is sent directly to the client; the cryptogram devoted to the ticket-granting server or the functional server, respectively, is understood as a *ticket* for the client, who in turn has to forward it in the next round (indicated in Figure 17.16 by the dotted lines in the client box). In all cases the distributor tells the respective receiver who the second receiver is, and the distributor also adds a *validity* specification *Validity*, as originally requested by the client.

The messages of kind 1.2 or 2.2, respectively, not only give a session key to the client but also contain the pertinent *ticket* for the client. This ticket also provides the pertinent session key, together with the identifier and the network address of the client and the validity specification. If, afterwards, in the next round, the client shows a valid ticket to the server (ticket-granting, or functional, respectively), then, with some further precautions, the server assumes that the client is eligible for the requested service. For repeated usage, the client stores his tickets in the *Ticket* column of his *Attributes* table.

All encrypted messages are tentatively *authenticated* in the restricted sense that the receiver can successfully decrypt such a message if and only if the message has been encrypted by use of the expected encryption key. In the positive case, and under some assumptions, including assumptions concerning the trust assigned to the Kerberos server and that the pertinent key has been kept secret by the second intended holder, the receiver can reason that the message was *originally generated* by that holder. Unfortunately, without further provisions, the receiver cannot determine when the message generation took place and whether the message just received was actually sent by the key holder, or by someone else who has *intercepted* a previous sending and has now maliciously *replayed* the message.

Therefore, the client initializes the needed provision for more *advanced authenticity* by adding an event-specific *nonce* (a random bit string) as a *challenge* in the first two rounds, and by constructing and sending an accompanying *authenticator* in the last two rounds. Basically, the authenticators encrypt the client's identifier together with a recent *timestamp*, which is also used as a *challenge* in the last round. The respective responder, in turn, includes the challenging nonce in his own message or, in the last round, the challenging timestamp.

Kerberos 5 also includes some additional options, which, among other things, provide for *renewal* and *revocation* of tickets, a *client-chosen cryptographic key* and *sequence numbers* for the messages exchanged between the client and the functional server while the service is being performed, and authentication across several *realms*.

17.4.3 Simplified Messages

We now describe and annotate the structure of Kerberos messages in some more detail, but still in a suitably simplified form:

Message 1.1. The client *Cl* requests a ticket-granting ticket from the authentication server *AS*, to be shown to the ticket-granting server *TGS*; the client also adds the wanted validity specification $Validity_1$ and includes a nonce $Nonce_1$:

$$Id_{Cl}, Id_{TGS}, Validity_1, Nonce_1. \tag{17.1}$$

Message 1.2. The authentication server *AS* issues a ticket-granting ticket $Ticket_{TGS}$ to the client *Cl*, to be shown to the ticket-granting server *TGS*. The authentication server also attaches a session key $K_{Cl,TGS}$ for a secure end-to-end connection between the client *Cl* and the ticket-granting server *TGS*, the wanted $Validity_1$ and the received $Nonce_1$, where the attachments are encrypted with the client's secret key K_{Cl}:

$$Id_{Cl}, Ticket_{TGS}, Enc(K_{Cl}, [K_{Cl,TGS}, Validity_1, Nonce_1, Id_{TGS}]). \tag{17.2}$$

In more detail, the ticket-granting ticket $Ticket_{TGS}$ contains the session key $K_{Cl,TGS}$ for a secure end-to-end connection between the client *Cl* and the ticket-granting server *TGS*, as well as the client's identifier Id_{Cl} and the client's network address Add_{Cl}. The ticket-granting ticket also includes the wanted $Validity_1$ and is encrypted with the ticket-granting server's secret key K_{TGS}:

$$Ticket_{TGS} = Enc(K_{TGS}, [K_{Cl,TGS}, Id_{Cl}, Add_{Cl}, Validity_1]). \tag{17.3}$$

Message 2.1. Showing the ticket $Ticket_{TGS}$, the client *Cl* requests a functional-service ticket from the ticket-granting server *TGS*, to be shown to the functional server *FS*; the client adds the wanted validity specification $Validity_2$ and includes a nonce $Nonce_2$. The client also attaches an authentificator $Auth_{Cl,TGS}$ that encrypts the client's identifier Id_{Cl} and a timestamp TS_3; the authentificator is encrypted with the session key $K_{Cl,TGS}$ (which is made available to the ticket-granting server by the ticket $Ticket_{TGS}$):

$$Id_{FS}, Validity_2, Nonce_2, Ticket_{TGS}, Auth_{Cl,TGS}, \text{ where} \tag{17.4}$$

$$Auth_{Cl,TGS} = Enc(K_{Cl,TGS}, [Id_{Cl}, TS_3]). \tag{17.5}$$

Message 2.2. The ticket-granting server issues a functional-service ticket $Ticket_{FS}$ to the client *Cl*, to be shown to the functional server *FS*. The ticket-granting server also attaches a session key $K_{Cl,FS}$ for a secure end-to-end connection between the client *Cl* and the functional server *FS*, the wanted $Validity_2$ and the received $Nonce_2$, where the attachments are encrypted with the session key $K_{Cl,TGS}$:

$$Id_{Cl}, Ticket_{FS}, Enc(K_{Cl,TGS}, [K_{Cl,FS}, Validity_2, Nonce_2, Id_{FS}]). \tag{17.6}$$

In more detail, the functional-service ticket $Ticket_{FS}$ contains the session key $K_{Cl,FS}$ for a secure end-to-end connection between the client *Cl* and the functional server *FS*, as well as the client's identifier Id_{Cl} and the client's network address Add_{Cl}. The functional-service ticket also includes the wanted $Validity_2$ and is encrypted with the functional server's secret key K_{FS}.

$$Ticket_{FS} = Enc(K_{FS}, [K_{Cl,FS}, Id_{Cl}, Add_{Cl}, Validity_2]). \tag{17.7}$$

Message 3.1. Showing the ticket $Ticket_{FS}$, client Cl requests a service invocation from the functional server FS. The client also includes an authentificator $Auth_{Cl,FS}$ that encrypts the client's identifier Id_{Cl} and a timestamp TS_4; the authentificator is encrypted with the session key $K_{Cl,FS}$ (which is made available to the functional server by the ticket $Ticket_{FS}$):

$$Ticket_{FS}, Auth_{Cl,FS}, \text{ where} \tag{17.8}$$

$$Auth_{Cl,FS} = Enc(K_{Cl,FS}, [Id_{Cl}, TS_4]). \tag{17.9}$$

Message 3.2. The functional server FS responds to the client by sending back the received timestamp TS_4, encrypted with the session key $K_{Cl,FS}$:

$$Enc(K_{Cl,FS}, TS_4). \tag{17.10}$$

17.5 Simple Public Key Infrastructure (SPKI/SDSI)

SPKI/SDSI (*Simple Public Key Infrastructure/Simple Distributed Security Infrastructure*) is aimed at supporting the specification and enforcement of *authorizations* in a *distributed* computing system. In such a system, a participant is represented by an *asymmetric* public/private *key pair* (possibly selected from a collection of such key pairs), and, accordingly, each resource *owner* autonomously specifies permissions to access a service in terms of the *public keys* whose legitimate holders qualify as grantees. Consequently, for the sake of *authenticity*, a remote requestor of a service has to provide *exhibits* for being a grantee by proving to be the holder of the *private key* matching a privileged public key.

More technically, resource owners issue digitally signed digital documents in the form of *certificates* and *credentials* that contain *formal statements* regarding public keys. The issued documents might be stored in dedicated places or delivered to the participants represented. Accordingly, requestors refer to issued certificates and credentials in order to apply for an actual access to a service.

Finally, an *access decision* is taken basically by verifying the documents referred to, i.e., by testing the pertinent digital signatures, proving the authenticity of the requestor, typically by performing a challenge–response protocol, and then attempting to derive a permission from the statements extracted from the accepted documents; as a default, if at some stage a failure occurs, the requested access is prohibited.

A resource owner may also *delegate* the power to make formal authorization statements to other participants, and such delegations might be iteratively granted to further participants. Moreover, when issuing a document and thereby making formal statements regarding public keys, a participant might employ *names* to implicitly denote an intended set of public keys, where *name definitions* are specified independently, by the issuer himself or by different participants.

When an access decision is taken, the issue of *trust* arises in several forms:

- First, SPKI/SDSI presupposes an appropriate infrastructure for using *asymmetric authentication* in the form of *digital signatures*, including the management of public *key certificates*, often based on *trusted third parties* (TTPs).
- Second, the SPKI feature of *delegation* raises a concern about who may legitimately *speak for* whom, and what kind of trust in delegatees is presupposed or is expressed by delegations. This concern is complicated further by iteratively granted delegations.
- Third, the SDSI feature of autonomous *name definitions* created by diverse participants raises several concerns, including the *trustworthiness* of definers, the scope of definitions, the control of the interaction of definitions, and the interoperability of definitions across security domains.
- There are further issues of trust, including the *validity conditions* and *periods* of certificates and credentials, and the management of their *revocations* and *revalidations*.

The development and analysis of SPKI/SDSI started about ten years ago, when R.L. Rivest and B. Lampson proposed the SDSI component, which dealt with *name certificates*, and C. Ellison and others designed the SPKI component, which handled *authorization credentials*. At present, an RFC specification, some research prototypes and substantial foundational research on the semantics are available.

17.5.1 Basic Blocks

SPKI/SDSI exploits the following basic features of certificates and credentials, which are an amalgam of control and monitoring with cryptography:

- *Asymmetric authentication* in the form of *digital signatures* for digital documents.
- *Public verification keys* for asymmetric authentication in the form of *digital signatures*, for denoting *principals*, i.e., formal representations of participants of a computing system.
- A *one-way hash function*, applied to public keys, for alternative denotations of principals (not treated further below).
- *Threshold subjects*, considered as special principals, for dealing with *separation of privileges* or related issues (not treated further below).
- (Name) *certificates* to assign (free) properties to principals.
- *Collectives* such as *groups* or *roles*, as examples of *characterizing properties* expressed by name certificates.
- More generally, *linked names* for autonomous local assignment of *characterizing properties* to principals at the discretion of resource *owners* or *trusted agents*.
- (Authorization) *credentials* to assign bound properties as *permissions* to principals.
- *Delegation* of the power to assign permissions.

- *Access control lists*, formed by (unsigned) authorization credentials issued by a resource owner on behalf of himself, locally denoted by *Self*.
- Implicit *property conversion* of free properties into bound properties.
- *Access decisions* taken on the basis of shown, verified certificates and credentials employing *chain evaluations*.
- *Validity specifications* for certificates and credentials.
- *Revocation* and *revalidation* of certificates and credentials.

17.5.2 An Application Scenario

The SPKI/SDSI approach is generic, without emphasizing any particular application. Nevertheless, in order to indicate the motivation behind the formal concepts, we first outline a possible application scenario. We assume a (more or less) open, distributed, interoperable computing system which is operated within a distributed, layered organizational environment. The computing system deals with data, information and services of various kinds. We abstract from all details and consider a system dealing with *objects* and the *methods* that can be executed on these objects. From a functional point of view, an object o together with a method m can be seen as an *interface* (o, m). From the point of view of access control, a corresponding expression of the form $[o, m]$ can be used as a *capability*, i.e., in a suitable context, $[o, m]$ can be interpreted as a *permission* to use the denoted interface.

Each object and thus each interface belongs to a unique *owner*. Objects may be gathered into *collections* to offer several services in the computing environment. We call such a collection of objects an *organizational entity*. Each organizational entity is administered by a unique *controller*, while the objects within an organizational entity may belong to different owners. Organizational entities contain at least one object and can be both overlapping and nested. Accordingly, a single object can be related to several controllers, namely one controller for each organizational entity that the object is a member of. The controller declares the access requirements of his organizational entity by specifying sets of *grantees*, who are permitted to access the objects. The controller explicitly states grantees or implicitly states them with the help of *trusted agents*, which we call *assigners*.

Furthermore, acting as a *verifier*, the controller regulates the actual access requests concerning his organizational entity. He might act as the verifier himself or charge another trusted agent with this task. A participant using the computing system, i.e., a *user*, can access an object as follows. He identifies and selects an organizational entity of which the object is a member, and then submits the access request to the controller administering this organizational entity. Acting as a verifier, this controller then decides on the request, whereby the decision is based on the access requirements and the corresponding explicit or implicit specifications of grantees.

Each participant might act in any of the roles sketched above. In a somewhat simplified form, Figure 17.17 summarizes these roles together with their relationships.

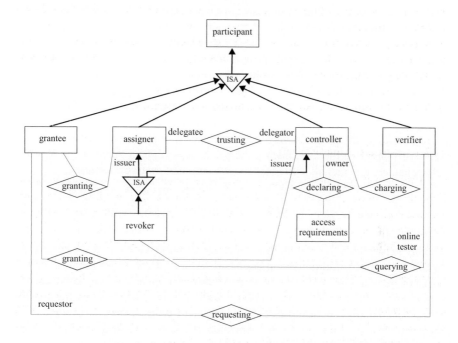

Fig. 17.17. ER model of the relationship classes for various (role) specializations of the entity class for participants

17.5.3 Certificates and their Semantics

In the following, we set out the basic formal concepts of SPKI/SDSI in a somewhat simplified version:

- *principals* for denoting participants of the computing environment,
- *name certificates* for defining local name spaces of principals,
- *authorization credentials* (*certificates*) for specifying permissions, and
- *certificate chain discovery* based on chain reduction for taking access decisions.

A *principal* denotes any participant of the computing environment, including controllers of organizational entities, assigners and grantees. A principal is characterized by an *asymmetric* public/private *key pair*. The *public key* is used for representing the principal in certificates and credentials, and the *private key* is used for digitally signing certificates or common messages. With some misuse of language, a principal is often identified with his public or his private key, depending on the context.

A SPKI/SDSI *name certificate* is a digital, digitally signed document of the form

$$(\textit{Key}, \textit{Name}, \textit{Subject}, \textit{Validity})_{\textit{IssuerSignature}},$$

consisting of a body of four components and a signature. *Key* represents the issuing principal, who certifies the body with the signature *IssuerSignature* (which will be dropped in the following for the sake of simplicity). *Name* is any identifier the principal has chosen in order to form a local name of the syntactical form *Key Name*. *Subject* specifies a new, additional meaning of this local name by giving a term that is either a principal, i.e., some public key $K_{SomePrincipal}$, another local name, for example $K_{SomePrincipal}$ *SomeName*, or an extended name, for example $K_{SomePrincipal}$ *SomeName*$_1$ *SomeName*$_2$ ... *SomeName*$_l$.

In each case, the given *Subject* can be evaluated to a set of principals. Given a set C of (name) certificates, each principal K determines a *name space* $N_C(K)$, which gathers together all associated *local names* and *extended names*:

$$LocN_C(K) = \{ K\ N \mid \text{there exist } S, V \text{ such that } (K, N, S, V) \in C \},$$
$$ExtN_C(K) = \{ K\ N_1\ N_2...N_l \mid \text{there exist } S, V \text{ such that } (K, N_1\ N_2...N_l, S, V) \in C \},$$
$$N_C(K) = LocN_C(K) \cup ExtN_C(K).$$

Validity expresses some condition to be checked before employing the certificate. In SPKI/SDSI, the traditional conditions are validity dates, for example, stated in terms of *from* and *to*. Additionally, three kinds of *online test* are proposed: *certificate revocation lists (CRLs)*, *revalidations* and *one-time validity*. A certificate revocation list contains certificates that should not be used any longer. A revalidation is the positive version of a certificate revocation. A one-time validity serves to ensure that a certificate is used only once.

As indicated above, principals (public keys), local names and extended names can be evaluated to a set of principals (public keys) by some evaluation function Val_C, which takes a set of name certificates C as a parameter. The evaluation function Val_C is inductively defined for *keys*, *local names* and *extended names* such that the following properties minimally hold:

- $Val_C(K) = \{ K \}$

  returns just the singleton set containing the specified key, i.e., each key K denotes itself, independently of the certificates in C considered.

- $Val_C(K\ N) = \bigcup_{(K, N, S, V)\, \in\, C} Val_C(S)$

  returns the keys which are denoted by the specified local name $K\ N$ by gathering together the meanings of all name certificates in C issued for this purpose.

- $Val_C(K\ N_1\ N_2\ ...\ N_l) = \bigcup_{K'\, \in\, Val_C(K\ N_1)} Val_C(K'\ N_2\ ...\ N_l)$

  returns the keys which are denoted by the specified extended name $K\ N_1\ N_2\ ...\ N_l$ by first determining the keys denoted by the local name prefix $K\ N_1$, and then inductively evaluating the resulting reduced names.

Within our application scenario, typically, the issuer of a name certificate is supposed to be an assigner, who is trusted by the controller of some organizational entity. By issuing a name certificate for a local name, the assigner states that the subject *should* be a grantee with respect to some object(s), as often indicated (but *not* formally enforced) by the mnemonics for local names.

An *authorization credential*, or in SPKI/SDSI terms, an *authorization certificate*, is a digital, digitally signed document of the form

$$(Key, Subject, Authorization, Delegation, Validity)_{IssuerSignature},$$

consisting of a body of five components and a signature. *Key* represents the issuing principal, who certifies the body with the signature *IssuerSignature* (which will be dropped in the following for the sake of simplicity). For the purpose of modeling an entry in a local access control list, the issuer is denoted by the reserved word *Self*. *Subject* denotes the grantees of the authorization. Syntactically, *Subject* must be a public key, a local name, an extended name or some other suitable term, for example a "threshold subject", in each case a term that can be evaluated to a set of principals, as defined above. *Authorization* specifies the permissions the issuer is granting in some suitable but not standardized syntax, i.e., the final effectiveness of the permissions depends on an agreed understanding of the syntax employed. *Delegation* is a Boolean flag. If the flag is set, then the authorization certificate allows each grantee to forward the permissions to other principals. As with name certificates, *Validity* expresses some conditions to be checked before employing the certificate.

Within our application scenario, typically, the issuer of an authorization certificate is the controller of an organizational entity. A controller declares his access requirements regarding the objects within his organizational entity by defining an access control list, seen as a list of (unsigned) authorization certificates. Besides declaring the access requirements, a controller may also issue and publish or distribute signed authorization certificates.

A controller, acting as a verifier, always takes an *access decision* with respect to a set C of name certificates and authorization certificates. Roughly outlined, when a principal K_{User} requests to use an interface (o, m) at a verifying principal $K_{Controller}$ of an organizational entity that the object o is a member of, then the verifier basically calls a suitable algorithm to answer a *query* about whether the certificates considered express a permission. For example, the *certificate chain discovery algorithm* tries to find and to reduce chains of delegations and local name meanings, respectively, in C such that an unsigned authorization certificate of the form

$$(Self, Subject, [o, m], true, now)$$

is generated, where $K_{Controller}$ is locally a synonym of *Self* and the principal K_{User} is an element of $Val_C(Subject)$. In most cases, the reduction is such that *Subject* is just equal to K_{User}. Such algorithms might be extended to provide hints about missing certificates in cases of failure, and there are also algorithms for answering other queries of interest.

17.5.4 Certificate Chain Discovery

As sketched above, the aim of certificate chain discovery is basically that *Self* obtains an answer to a *query* about whether a principal K_{User} may access a resource, given a set C of name certificates and authorization certificates. Roughly outlined, to compute the answer, the documents in C are seen to define structures on the set of terms (keys, local names and extended names):

- The first structure is defined by *name certificates*. A name certificate (*Key, Name, Subject, Validity*) defines a *link* from the term *Key Name* to the term *Subject*, denoted in simplified form (by ignoring the validity component) by

$$Key\ Name \rightarrow Subject.$$

- A further class of structures is defined by *authorization certificates*. An authorization certificate (*Key, Subject, Authorization, Delegation, Validity*), where *Delegation* is either *true* or *false*, defines a *tagged link* from the term *Key* to the term *Subject* with *Authorization* and *Delegation* as tag parameters, denoted in simplified form (by ignoring the validity component) by

$$Key\ [\ Authorization\ ,\ true\ ] \rightarrow [\ Authorization\ ,\ Delegation\ ]\ Subject.$$

Any of these structures might contain *chains*, in the simplest form just link paths from one term to another. Intuitively, answering the access decision query requires one to find two appropriate, related chains. The first is a tagged chain from *Self* to some *Subject* such that (1) the authorization tag parameters occurring match each other and the requested interface (o, m), and (2) the delegation tag parameters occurring are *true* along the chain (possibly except for the final *Subject*). The second is a non-tagged chain from *Subject* to K_{User}.

More algorithmically, the *operational semantics* of certificates can be defined by *reduction rules* that operate on the denotations of the two kinds indicated or, equivalently, directly on certificates. An access decision query is then evaluated by generating new denotations or, equivalently, certificates from the given ones in C by applying the reduction rules (while, additionally, verifying signatures and respecting validities), with the goal of producing the permission denoted by

$$Self\ [\ [\ o\ ,m\ ]\ ,\ true\ ] \rightarrow [\ [\ o\ ,m\ ]\ ,\ .\ ]\ K_{User}$$

whenever possible. Essentially, the reduction rules are designed to combine the denotations or certificates of two appropriate adjacent links into the denotation or the certificate of a resulting *transitive* link with the pertinent tag. In the following, we shall only present and discuss a simple example, illustrated in Figure 17.18.

Consider an organizational entity containing a *dir(ectory)* with some *file*, where some capabilities refer to the operations *r(ead)*, *w(rite)* and *e(xecute)*, and permissions on the collection *dir* are inherited by the element *file*. The principal $K_{Controller}$ acts as the owner, controller and verifier. Let $K_{Controller}$ wish to delegate the granting of permissions to exploit *dir* in *r*-mode and *e*-mode to $K_{Assigner}$. To do so in

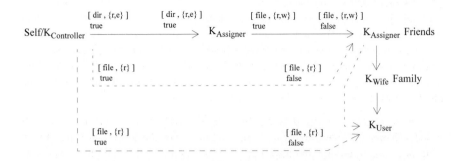

Fig. 17.18. An example of chain reduction (without treating validities)

SPKI/SDSI, $K_{Controller}$ must also grant this permission to $K_{Assigner}$. Accordingly, he inserts the (unsigned) authorization certificate

(*Self* , $K_{Assigner}$, [*dir* , {r,e}] , *true* , *from* 06-08-25 *to* 07-08-25)

into his local access control list. This certificate can be rephrased roughly as

"I, myself, as owner, state that
I grant to $K_{Assigner}$
the permission to perform on *dir* both *r* and *e*, and that
I trust $K_{Assigner}$ to grant this permission on behalf of me to further principals,
from 06-08-25 to 07-08-25".

Independently and at any time, in principle, possibly even earlier than $K_{Controller}$, the principal $K_{Assigner}$ expresses his wish to grant permissions to exploit *file* in *r*-mode and *w*-mode to a collective of grantees denoted by the local name $K_{Assigner}$ *Friends*. To do so, he may, for instance, issue and publish the (signed) authorization certificate

($K_{Assigner}$, $K_{Assigner}$ *Friends* , [*file* , {r,w}] , *false* , *from* 06-08-01 *to* 06-12-31),

which can be rephrased roughly as

"I, represented by the public key $K_{Assigner}$, state that I
grant to the collective $K_{Assigner}$ *Friends*
the permission to perform on *file* both *r* and *w*,
from 06-08-01 to 06-12-31".

Standing alone, this authorization certificate is not effective at all. However, the SPKI/SDSI *reduction rule* for authorization certificates, when applied to the two authorization certificates, generates the following new (unsigned) authorization certificate

(*Self* , $K_{Assigner}$ *Friends* , [*file* , {r}] , *false* , *from* 06-08-25 *to* 06-12-31).

This new, reduced authorization certificate combines the delegation expressed by $K_{Controller}$ with the granting expressed by $K_{Assigner}$, where the resulting authorization is determined as the *intersection* (suitably defined in this context) of the given authorizations and the resulting validity as the *intersection* of the given validities. Thus, in more general terms, we need some kind of algebra on authorizations and validities.

The reduced authorization certificate is still not effective, since the collective denoted by $K_{Assigner}$ *Friends* has not yet been defined. To add such a definition, $K_{Assigner}$, among other things, also issues and publishes the (signed) name certificate

($K_{Assigner}$, *Friends*, K_{Wife} *Family*, *from* 06-08-01 *to* 06-12-31),

which can be rephrased roughly as

"I, represented by the public key $K_{Assigner}$, say that
the collective $K_{Assigner}$ *Friends* should comprise the collective K_{Wife} *Family*
(whatever meaning of *Family* is provided by the principal K_{Wife}),
from 06-08-01 to 06-12-31".

We still need an action of the principal K_{Wife}. Let this principal, again independently and autonomously in principle, issue and publish the further (signed) name certificate

(K_{Wife}, *Family*, K_{User}, *from* 06-09-01 *to* 06-12-31),

which says roughly that the principal K_{Wife} sees the principal K_{User} as a member of the collection K_{Wife} *Family*.

Now, the SPKI/SDSI *reduction rule* for name certificates, when applied to the two given name certificates, generates the following new (unsigned) name certificate

($K_{Assigner}$, *Friends*, K_{User}, *from* 06-09-01 *to* 06-12-31).

Finally, if on October 1, 2006, the principal K_{User} requests to access *file* in *r*-mode, showing the published certificates, then $K_{Controller}$ inspects the shown certificates together with his access control list and applies the chain reduction algorithm. This algorithm can generate the two reduced certificates and, applying a third SPKI/SDSI *reduction rule* for combining an authorization certificate with a name certificate, the following new (unsigned) authorization certificate

(*Self*, K_{User}, [*file*, {*r*}], *false*, *from* 06-09-01 *to* 06-12-31),

suggesting a positive access decision (which, however, does not comprise a permission for further grantings).

The example presented indicates both the formal operational semantics, by applying syntactic reduction rules, and the intended intuitive meanings. The latter comprise the notion of *trust* and *modalities* such as "stating", "saying" and "(granting) on behalf of", and thus raise the question of whether they are appropriately reflected by their formal counterparts. There are at least partial answers, obtained by employing formal semantics based on *modal logics* and *first-order logic* and proving equivalences between operational and logic approaches.

Besides the structural reduction of certificates, the semantically appropriate handling of the authorization validity tags constitutes a challenging subproblem. Further semantic issues stem from the SPKI/SDSI design decision to treat only permissions in a monotonic way, i.e., adding new certificates can never invalidate the usability of previously issued ones. However, there are applications where we might want to deal with explicit *prohibitions* expressed by *negatively used* certificates. Clearly, we would have to ensure that a requestor could not prevent such certificates actually being considered when an access decision is required. Thus the revocation lists commonly used to invalidate a single certificate should be complemented by something like a "blacklist" of prohibitions that must be inspected for each request.

We note finally that the roles of participants, as discussed in Subsection 17.5.2 and summarized in Figure 17.17, do not correspond precisely to the formalisms of SPKI/SDSI. This observation suggests that we need to develop more sophisticated application scenarios, with appropriate guidelines for the proper usage of SPKI/SDSI certificates. Moreover, the controllers, acting as *administrators* analyzing the *control state*, i.e., the consequences of issued certificates, in particular regarding delegations and local name definitions, might want to obtain algorithmic answers to queries that are more sophisticated than an access decision query.

17.6 Pretty Good Privacy (PGP)

PGP (*Pretty Good Privacy*) supports participants of a distributed computing system in autonomously enforcing their security interests in *confidentiality, integrity* as *detection of modification, authenticity* and *non-repudiation* by technical mechanisms. This support applies particularly in the case of a non-expert *enduser* administering his personal computer and communicating with friends and partners via email.

Basically, PGP provides a user-friendly interface to the cryptographic mechanisms of *encryption* and *authentication* in the form of *digital signatures*, to be employed explicitly by means of a simple command language or transparently embedded into some appropriate application software such as a file manager or an email tool. Depending on the application, PGP may serve to protect *files* on a local computer or to ensure *end-to-end security* in a global environment. Furthermore, PGP assists participants with the necessary *key management* for the underlying cryptographic mechanisms. This includes the assessment of claims that a public key belongs to a specific partner of a participant or, more specifically, assessment of the *trust* in the respective issuers of such claims.

Starting around 1990, PGP was designed, implemented and promoted by P.R. Zimmermann, who emphasized everybody's need and fundamental right to employ cryptography at their own discretion (even if governmental institutions such as police forces or secret services might prefer to intercept plaintexts rather than ciphertexts). Early versions were publicly available, as is a basic current version. More advanced versions are also being marketed nowadays.

17.6.1 Basic Blocks

Essentially, PGP bundles the following features and basic blocks of cryptography together under a user-friendly interface; in particular, it offers suitable protocols that compose these blocks according to common needs:

- *Symmetric encryption* by a *block cipher*, extended into a *stream cipher* by use of the *cipher block chaining* (*CBC*) mode. For use as a block cipher, besides the originally employed IDEA, further options such as Triple-DES and AES are available. The symmetric encryption is applied to plaintexts, which may be either files to be stored or messages to be sent, and to private asymmetric (decryption or signature) keys.
- *Asymmetric encryption*. In particular, the RSA and ElGamal mechanisms are available. Within a protocol for *hybrid encryption*, the asymmetric encryption is applied to secret session keys for symmetric encryption.
- *Authentication* by *digital signatures*. In particular, the RSA and ElGamal mechanisms are available.
- A *one-way hash function*. In particular, MD5 is available. The hash function is employed to generate a message digest from an original message or to generate a symmetric key from a passphrase.
- A *random generator*. For instance, randomness may be generated by exploiting measured peculiarities of key strokes or other non-reproducible events. The random strings produced are used as symmetric session keys. *Pseudorandom generators* might also be used.
- *Data compression*, for reducing the redundancy of plaintexts.
- *Passphrases*, for generating symmetric keys that are used to protect private asymmetric (decryption or signature) keys for secure end-to-end connections or to protect the user's own files.
- *Key management* by means of a *private key ring* and a *public key ring*, for storing the user's own private asymmetric keys and for storing, assessing and selecting the public asymmetric keys of the user's partners, respectively.

17.6.2 Conceptual Design of Secure Message Transmission

In this subsection, we outline the conceptual design of PGP from the perspective of a participant who wants to securely communicate some plaintext to a remote receiver. Basically, as shown in Figure 17.19, PGP asks the participant for the wanted parameters, retrieves the pertinent cryptographic keys and converts the plaintext stepwise into a digitally signed, compressed and encrypted *message* that is ready for transmission.

More specifically, PGP expects four parameters:

- *SelfIdent*, denoting the participant acting as a sender;
- *passphrase*, as an exhibit for a proof of authenticity of the sender;
- *PartnerIdent*, denoting the intended receiver;
- *plaintext*, to be communicated from the sender to the receiver.

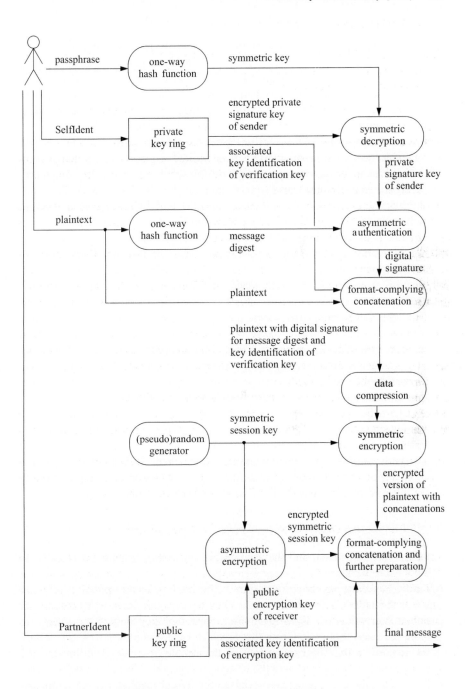

Fig. 17.19. Design of PGP for signing, compressing and encrypting a plaintext

Given these parameters, PGP proceeds roughly as follows:

- The specified *plaintext*, which might be arbitrarily long, is condensed into a *message digest* of a fixed short length (e.g., 128 bits) by applying an appropriate one-way hash function. Subsequently, for the sake of authenticity and non-repudiation, the message digest is treated as a representative of the original plaintext and, accordingly, the digest is digitally signed by a method of asymmetric authentication, delivering a *digital signature* of the sender.
- The needed *private signature key* of the sender is retrieved from the private key ring of the sender or, more precisely, from the key ring associated with the specified *SelfIdent*. However, to protect the distinguishing secret, the key ring stores the signature key in encrypted form using a symmetric block cipher. Thus, initially, only the *encrypted private signature key* of the sender is returned, together with an associated *key identification* of the matching verification key.
- To recover the private signature key, the pertinent *symmetric key* for encrypting and decrypting the signature key must be delivered. This symmetric key will have been determined as the hash value of the passphrase under a one-way hash function. Accordingly, this symmetric key is regenerated from the given *passphrase*.
- The *digital signature* produced and the *key identification* are then concatenated with the original *plaintext*. These three items are to be sent to the intended receiver with suitable provisions for ensuring confidentiality, i.e., for enabling only the intended receiver to gain the information contained.
- As prerequisite, the concatenated items are compressed in order to reduce their potential redundancy. Then, the three compressed items are encrypted by a hybrid method as follows.
- The hybrid method employs a symmetric encryption by means of a block cipher that is extended into a stream cipher by use of a block mode for dealing with arbitrarily long items to be communicated to the intended receiver. The symmetric encryption needs a *symmetric session key*, which has to be communicated to the intended receiver as well. For the sake of confidentiality, the symmetric session key is sent in encrypted form using an asymmetric encryption.
- Accordingly, a (pseudo)random generator produces the needed *symmetric session key* and delivers it to both the symmetric encryption mechanism (applied to the compressed items) and the asymmetric encryption mechanism (applied to the key produced).
- Furthermore, the asymmetric encryption mechanism needs a *public encryption key* that matches a private decryption key held by the intended receiver. This public encryption key is retrieved from the public key ring of the sender or, more precisely, from a key ring that associates the specified *PartnerIdent* with the required public encryption key of the denoted partner. Additionally, the associated *key identification* of the retrieved encryption key is returned as well.
- Finally, the three components relevant to the hybrid method, (1) the symmetrically encrypted compressed items (the plaintext, the digital signature of the message digest, and the key identification of the verification key), (2) the

asymmetrically encrypted session key for the first component and (3) the key identification of the second component, are suitably concatenated and prepared for transmission to the intended receiver.

On receipt of the transmitted data, the receiver can employ PGP to recover the original plaintext and to verify the digital signature. Basically, PGP performs the corresponding inverse operations in the reverse order, whereby the two asymmetric keys needed are retrieved from the receiver's key rings by means of the transmitted key identifications.

17.6.3 Key Management

The cryptographic effectiveness of services for secure message transmission and, similarly, for secure file management, depends crucially on appropriate *key management*. Accordingly, PGP also provides user-friendly assistance for this task. As can be seen from the outline of secure message transmission and as discussed further below, only the keys for the asymmetric mechanisms are stored persistently, whereas a secret key for any symmetric mechanism employed is generated or recovered only when it is actually needed, and afterwards the secret key is immediately destroyed.

Regarding the *symmetric secret keys*, the two cases listed are treated differently, depending on the need for authenticating the participant on whose behalf the key is used. In the first case, of using a symmetric secret key for *securing an asymmetric private key*, authentication is strongly needed, since the owner of the secured private key is distinguished among all other participants. PGP aims at authentication by demanding a passphrase. Moreover, the secret key is directly derived from the passphrase by a one-way hash function, and thus the secret key is never stored persistently but is always dynamically regenerated whenever it is required. Consequently, the task of keeping secret information is reduced to the burden of handling the passphrases, and thus is mainly shifted to the users of PGP in diminished form.

In the second case, of using a symmetric secret key as a *session key* for the *hybrid method*, the symmetric secret key is generated on the fly by a (pseudo)random generator, used only once for encrypting content data by means of the block cipher employed, and then itself asymmetrically encrypted for later use when the content data must be recovered. Accordingly, on the side of the participant acting as the encryptor, there is no need to keep the secret key, and on the side of the participant acting as the later decryptor, the secret key is held in encrypted form. When the non-encrypted form of the secret key is recovered, the first case applies, since authentication is strongly needed.

Regarding the *asymmetric keys*, PGP maintains two key rings on behalf of a user. The *private key ring* contains the user's own key pairs, each of which consists of a *private signature key* and the matching *public verification key* or a *private decryption key* and the matching *public encryption key*. Each private key is stored in encrypted form. Moreover, in addition to some further administrative data, a *timestamp*, a derived *key identification* for referencing the key pair, and an *identification* of the owner are stored for each key pair. As explained before, the access to a private key is secured by a passphrase that the owner selected when he issued the PGP command to generate and store a key pair. The passphrase serves to generate a symmetric secret key for encrypting and decrypting the respective private key.

The public key ring contains the *public verification keys* and *public encryption keys* of the owner's communication partners. In each case the key is complemented by further administrative data, a *timestamp*, a derived *key identification*, an *identification* of the partner, and some further entries to be used to assess the public key.

17.6.4 Assessment of Public Keys

Before a particular public key is employed to encrypt a message addressed to a specific participant or to verify a message claimed to originate from a specific participant, the fundamental challenge is to *assess* whether the public key considered is actually owned by the specific participant, i.e., whether that participant is the *legitimate distinguished holder* of the matching private key. This challenge can also be described as follows: the user has to inspect the *trustworthiness* of the public key, on the basis of his decisions about *trust* in other participants involved in the generation and distribution of the considered public key.

The PGP approach to assisting the user in solving the challenge relies on two independent conceptual relationships between participants and a third derived relationship. An instance of such relationships regarding a single public key is depicted in Figure 17.20 and explained in the following:

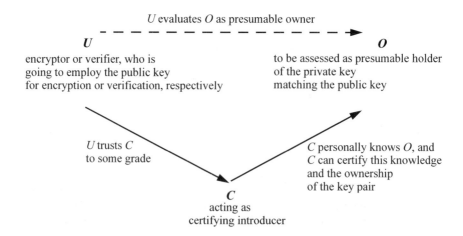

Fig. 17.20. Relationships between three participants regarding an assessed public key

- As a basic relationship, one participant *C(ertifier) personally knows* another participant *O(wner)* such that *C* can certify that a public key *k* belongs to *O*, i.e., that the participant *O* is the legitimate owner of the pertinent key pair and thus the actual holder of the matching private key. The participant *C* confirms such an ownership by issuing and digitally signing a *key certificate*, also known as an *identity certificate*, which is a digital document basically consisting of an identification *OIdent* and the public key *k* together with the pertinent digital signature. In the context of the anticipated application, the identification *OIdent* must uniquely denote the participant *O* within the collection of all potential participants. The certifying participant *C* is also perceived as the *introducer* of *O*.
- As another independent basic relationship, one participant *U(ser)*, willing to encrypt or to verify a message, may *trust* another participant *C(ertifier)* to various degrees to issue correct key certificates. PGP suggests four *trust grades*, namely *unknown*, *untrusted*, *marginally_trusted* and *completely_trusted*, but more sophisticated grades could readily be used instead.
- Then, as a derived relationship, the participant *U(ser) evaluates* another participant *O(wner)* as the presumable owner of a public key *k*, on the basis of successfully verifying the digital signature of a key certificate of the form $(OIdent, k)_{signature}$, issued and digitally signed by some introducer *C(ertifier)*. The grade of the evaluation of *O* is derived from the grade of the trust in the introducer *C*.

Figure 17.21 shows an extended model of the particular (and not totally convincing) PGP perspective of the general situation as an entity–relationship diagram, where the point of view of a single user denoted by *Self* is taken and all other *participants* are seen as *partners*. Each participant is formally denoted by a unique *identification*, whereas the relationship to a *represented* unique (real-world) *human individual* remains outside the scope of the technical treatment.

The user *Self generates* his own *key pairs*, each of which consists of a *private key* and a *matching public key*. For the purpose of referencing, a *key identification* is *derived* from the *public key*. Basically, the *private key ring* provides a data structure to formalize the relationship class of key generation or, more specifically, the path in the ER model from *identification*, through *Self* and *key pair*, to *key identification*.

Regarding *partners*, the user considered assigns each of them a *trust grade*. Moreover, the user stores the *public keys* of his partners or, more specifically, the key *certificates* of those public keys. Each such certificate is modeled as a ternary relationship between a public *key*, the (*identification* of the) *owner*, and the *digital signature* of the *issuer* acting as the *introducer*. To enable verification, each *signature* is complemented by the unique *key identification* of the key employed for *signing*. Basically, the *public key ring* provides a data structure to formalize the entity class of partners and the relationship class of certificates.

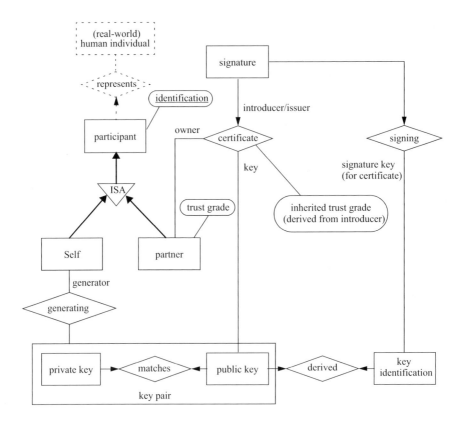

Fig. 17.21. ER model of participants, asymmetric keys, signatures and their relationships

17.7 Bibliographic Hints

For each of the systems that we have selected, there are also alternative and competitive systems, and there are many further systems for other security services. We refrain from giving bibliographic hints for systems not treated in this chapter. Furthermore, for the systems presented, we provide only some basic hints that do not cover the wide range of the literature.

Regarding the UNIX operating system, the basic sources are provided by its inventors Ritchie/Thompson [407, 408]. Among other publications, the textbooks by Tanenbaum/Woodhull [473, 474, 475] and Silberschatz/Galvin/Gagne [447] present introductions. Garfinkel/Spafford [216] treat practical security aspects of UNIX, and, for example, McKusick/Bostic/Karels/Quarterman [341] and Handschuch [247] deal with specific versions of UNIX.

Regarding the Oracle/SQL database management system, the seminal paper by Codd [137] on the relational model of data and the first attempts at prototype implementations, for example by Astrahan/et al. [19] for System/R, mark the start of a very large development process. Among other publications, the textbooks by Date [152], Ullman/Widom [489] and Elmasri/Navathe [188] present introductions. The various versions of the ISO standard for SQL, for example [267], also define the security features. Actual commercial implementations might show variations and proprietary additions. The documentation of the many versions of Oracle, for example [380], describes the specific situations. Theriault/Newman [479] treat application security using Oracle.

Regarding the CORBA middleware, the fundamental specification is developed by the Object Management Group [378, 379]. Ben-Natan [41] provides a broad survey. Blakley [87] provides an introduction to the security concepts of CORBA.

Regarding the Kerberos authentication and authorization system, the original versions are developed at MIT by Miller/Neuman/Schiller/Saltzer/Steiner/Ts'o [353, 464, 369]. Kohl/Neuman/Ts'o [298] treat modifications and extensions. The textbooks by Stallings [462] and Schneier [437] present introductions.

Regarding the SPKI/SDSI public key infrastructure and trust management system, the basic specification is provided by Ellison/Frantz/Lampson/Rivest/Thomas/Ylonen [184, 185], complemented by the work of Clarke/Elien/Ellison/Fredette/Morcos/Rivest [136] on certificate chain discovery based on term reduction, and of Li/Winsborough/Mitchell [317] for chain discovery in the distributed case. The formal semantics of SPKI/SDSI and the operational consequences have been studied from several points of view. On the basis of fundamental work by Abadi/Burrows/Lampson/Plotkin/Wobber [1, 309] on distributed authorization, Abadi [4], Howell/Kotz [259] and Halpern/van der Meyden [246] explore a modal-logic approach; Jha/Reps [279] relate the question to pushdown systems and exploit algorithms for model checking; and Li/Mitchell [319] advocate a first-order logic approach. Biskup/Wortmann [76] aimed at applying and extending SPKI/SDSI to implement compound access control policies that include "negatively used" parts.

Regarding the PGP cryptography application system, its designer Zimmermann [509] provides a full description; see [215] for a public version. Among other publications, the textbooks by Schneier [436, 437] and Stallings [462, 463] present introductions.

Appendix

In this appendix, we briefly summarize some concepts from selected fields of computer science that we have used without further explanation throughout the monograph. Basically, we assume that the reader is familiar with these concepts but might want to recall some notation or basic facts.

We have often employed *conceptual modeling* in order to visualize the material presented in the text. For this purpose, we have used classical *entity–relationship diagrams*, the basic concepts of which are treated in Appendix A.1. Readers who are acquainted with UML can easily transform entity–relationship diagrams into UML class models, essentially just by considering a conceptual entity class as an (object) class, and by treating relationship classes as associations or aggregations. We have also used all kinds of other diagrams for illustration, usually hoping that the graphical notations would suggest an appropriate interpretation.

Whenever we reason about information, information flow, the knowledge of a participant or related concepts, we could aim at formalizing important aspects within some formal logic, often preferably within *first-order logic*, and sometimes we have actually done so, by means of examples. Appendix A.2 repeats the elementary notation.

However, classical two-valued logic does not capture many more advanced features of information, which go beyond assuming that a statement either holds or not. In particular, for this purpose and many others as well, *random variables* that are essentially specified by *probability distributions* provide a worthwhile descriptive and analytical means. Appendix A.3 presents an introduction.

Many cryptographic mechanisms rely on results about appropriate *finite algebras*, most of which are based on *number theory*. Appendix A.4 and Appendix A.5 give some basic definitions and fundamental insights.

A.1 Entity–Relationship Diagrams

In this monograph, we have employed fragments of *entity–relationship diagrams* for *conceptual modeling*. Mostly, the diagrams have been appropriately simplified in order to visualize only the main aspects of the concrete concepts presented in the text. The concrete concepts are meant to be instantiations of the (abstract) *concepts* that are summarized in Figure A.1. In the following, we briefly explain these concepts and refer to Figure 17.5, which exhibits fundamental features of UNIX, as an example.

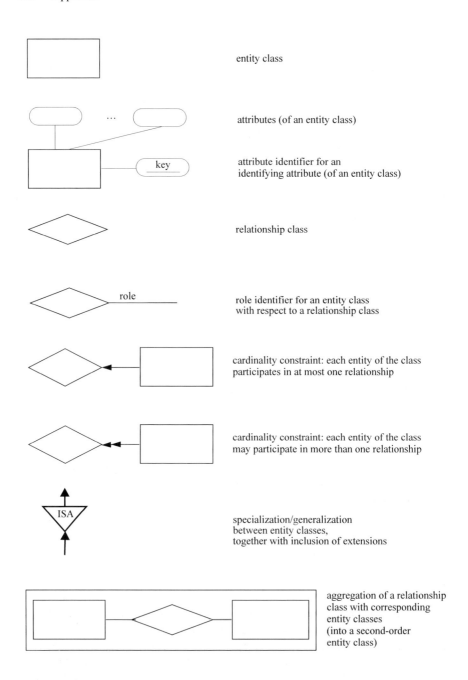

entity class

attributes (of an entity class)

attribute identifier for an
identifying attribute (of an entity class)

relationship class

role identifier for an entity class
with respect to a relationship class

cardinality constraint: each entity of the class
participates in at most one relationship

cardinality constraint: each entity of the class
may participate in more than one relationship

specialization/generalization
between entity classes,
together with inclusion of extensions

aggregation of a relationship
class with corresponding
entity classes
(into a second-order
entity class)

Fig. A.1. Basic concepts of entity–relationship diagrams

For any (programming) application, we first have to identify the basic *entities* we are going to deal with. For an operating system such as UNIX, for example, we consider *users*, *files* and *processes* and, additionally, *physical devices* and *user identifications*. In each case, when performing modeling, we are interested in the *class* of all (potential) entities that share the pertinent properties rather than in the individual entities; for example, we consider the *entity classes* of users, files, processes, physical devices and user identifications, respectively. Basically, an entity class is described by the attributes that apply to the members of the class, and by relationship classes that members of the class can participate in.

Attributes are characteristics of an individual entity belonging to some entity class. In UNIX, for example, a user (entity) is characterized by its specific values for its (internal) *username*, the (currently agreed) *password*, a *full name* (for external communication), a *home directory* (that specifies the user's subtree of the file system), the *shell file* (to be executed on a login command) and several other attributes. An attribute (or set of attributes) is specified as *identifying* or a *key* (attribute) if the attribute value(s) are required to always uniquely identify an entity within its entity class.

A *relationship class* describes the (potential) relationships between individual entities belonging to some specified entity classes. In UNIX, for example, there is an *execution* relationship between a process (entity) and a file (entity) iff the process (currently) executes the program code contained in the file, and there is a *connected* relationship between a physical device (entity) and a user (entity) iff any input generated in the physical device is (currently) attributed to the user and any output on behalf of the user is (currently) directed to the physical device. Whenever appropriate, in particular for disambiguation, the specific participation of entities in relationships can be annotated by a *role*.

Quite often, a designer wants to explicitly model the condition that any particular entity of some entity class may *participate* in relationships of some relationship class only within a predetermined range of numbers. As a special case, an entity may be *constrained* to participate at most once. In UNIX, for example, a process (entity) should (currently) participate in (at most) one execution relationship with a file (entity), whereas a user (entity) may participate in more than one member relationship with a group identification (entity).

An entity class is a *specialization* of another entity class, whereby the latter class is then said to be a *generalization* of the former, whenever all properties, i.e., attributes and relationships, of the generalization also apply to the specialization, whereas the specialization might have further attributes or be involved in further relationship classes. Additionally, one might want to specify that the (current) extension of the specialized entity class is *included* in the *extension* of the generalized entity class, i.e., the set of all (individual) entities belonging to the specialization is required to be a subset of the set of all (individual) entities belonging to the generalization. In UNIX, for example, the *superuser_id* entity class is a specialization of the *user identification* entity class.

Usually, a designer has some freedom to decide what he sees as an atomic entity. In particular, in some specific context, a designer might prefer to deal with (composed) relationships as if they were (atomic) entities. In that case, a relationship class, together with the corresponding entity classes, can be abstracted into an *aggregation* that can be interpreted as some kind of a second order entity class.

A.2 First-Order Logic

First-order logic is a powerful tool for making a field of reasoning completely formal and – subject to some important restrictions – also algorithmically tractable. The syntax of (an instance of) first-order logic with equality provides the basic vocabulary of the field considered and the connectors for expressing more advanced features. More specifically, the *syntax* is given as follows:

- For each arity $n \in \mathbf{N}$, a (recursive and infinite) set of *function symbols Fun_n*; the 0-ary function symbols are seen as *constant symbols*.
- A (recursive and infinite) set of *variables Var*.
- A set of *terms*, inductively defined by the following rules:
  - each constant symbol and each variable is a term;
  - if f is an n-ary function symbol and $t_1,\ldots,t_n$ are terms, so is $f(t_1,\ldots,t_n)$.
- For each arity $n \in \mathbf{N}$, a (recursive and infinite) set of *predicate symbols $Pred_n$*; the 0-ary predicate symbols are seen as *propositional symbols* (or *atoms*).
- A dedicated binary *equality symbol* $=$.
- A set of *formulas*, inductively defined by the following rules:
  - if p is an n-ary predicate symbol and $t_1,\ldots,t_n$ are terms, then $p(t_1,\ldots,t_n)$ is an (*atomic*) formula;
  - if a and b are formulas, so are the *conjunction* $(a \wedge b)$, the *disjunction* $(a \vee b)$, the *negation* $(\neg a)$, the *universal quantification* $(\forall x)\, a$ and the *existential quantification* $(\exists x)\, a$, where x is a variable.

Where convenient, we use only a *complete subset* of connectors, for example disjunction, negation and existential quantification; or we might employ additional derived connectors, for example the *exclusive disjunction*, often denoted by XOR. Moreover, constant symbols and variables on the one hand and positions of function symbols and predicate symbols on the other hand might be suitably *typed* in order to restrict the occurrences of the former items in the latter.

The *semantics* is defined in terms of interpretations and variable assignments, which specify a possible *meaning* of the vocabulary and thereby determine truth values for *sentences*, i.e., those formulas that do not contain any free occurrence of a variable. More specifically, an *interpretation* $\delta = (uni, mean)$ is given as follows:

- *uni* is a nonempty set called the *universe*.
- *mean* is a mapping of function symbols to functions over *uni*, and of predicate symbols to relations over *uni*, i.e., if f is an n-ary function symbol, then $mean(f)$: $uni \times \ldots \times uni \to uni$, and if p is an n-ary predicate symbol, then

$mean(p) \subseteq uni \times ... \times uni$, where the Cartesian product has n components; $mean(=)$ is the identity relation.

A *variable assignment* for an interpretation $\delta=(uni, mean)$ is a mapping $\beta: Var \rightarrow uni$, which is canonically extended to all terms by the following rules:

- if t is a constant symbol, then $\beta(t) := mean(t)$;
- if t is composed, of form $f(t_1,...,t_n)$, then $\beta(t) := mean(f)(\beta(t_1),...,\beta(t_n))$.

Finally, the *validity* of a formula a under an interpretation $\delta=(uni, mean)$ and a variable assignment $\beta: Var \rightarrow uni$, denoted by δ,β `model_of` a, is inductively defined by the following rules:

- δ,β `model_of` $p(t_1,...,t_n)$ iff $(\beta(t_1),...,\beta(t_n)) \in mean(p)$;
- δ,β `model_of` $(a \wedge b)$ iff δ,β `model_of` a and δ,β `model_of` b;
- δ,β `model_of` $(a \vee b)$ iff δ,β `model_of` a or δ,β `model_of` b;
- δ,β `model_of` $(\neg a)$ iff   not δ,β `model_of` a;
- δ,β `model_of` $(\forall x)a$ iff   for all variable assignments β' that agree with β on all variables except (possibly) on x, δ,β' `model_of` a;
- δ,β `model_of` $(\exists x)a$ iff   there exists a variable assignment β' that agrees with β on all variables except (possibly) on x such that δ,β' `model_of` a.

For a sentence q, the validity depends only on the interpretation δ, which justifies the notation δ `model_of` q for *truth values*.

On the basis of these definitions, many further concepts can be defined and then investigated, for example the following:

- A sentence q is *satisfiable*   iff   there exists an interpretation δ with δ `model_of` q.
- A sentence q is *universally valid* iff   for all interpretations δ we have δ `model_of` q.
- A sentence q_1 *logically implies* a sentence q_2 iff   for all interpretations δ with δ `model_of` q_1, we have δ `model_of` q_2.

In general, we cannot express these declarative definitions in purely algorithmic terms: *unsatisfiability* is known to be a nonrecursive (undecidable) but still recursively enumerable (semi-decidable) concept. There are various practical algorithmic *proof systems* (automatic *theorem provers*) that are guaranteed to recognize any unsatisfiable sentence but may fail to deliver a result for some satisfiable sentences. Accordingly, there are algorithmic proof systems for logical implication between sentences, since q_1 *logically implies* q_2 iff $q_1 \wedge \neg q_2$ is *unsatisfiable*.

There are several known *fragments of first-order logic* where the concepts discussed are still decidable, though they often require high computational complexity. Most notably, *propositional logic* deals only with propositional symbols and the connectors for conjunction, disjunction and negation such that interpretations can be identified with mappings of propositional symbols to Boolean (truth) values. Propositional satisfiability is then a prototype of an *NP-complete* concept. Given a satisfiable propositional sentence, a nondeterministic polynomial-time recognition procedure just guesses a satisfying interpretation for the finitely many propositional symbols occurring in the sentence, and then verifies the satisfiability by evaluating the sentence as a Boolean expression.

Furthermore, there are numerous variations of the above concepts, obtained, for example, by considering only *finite interpretations*.

A.3 Random Variables and Entropy

A.3.1 Random Variables and Probability Distributions

In this monograph, we have employed *random variables* only in the following special form, where a random variable is specified by two items:

- a finite set of *events* X, often identified with the random variable, and

- a *probability distribution* $Prob_X : X \rightarrow [0,1]$ such that $\sum\limits^{x \in X} Prob_X(x) = 1$.

A random variable X is *equally distributed* iff its probability distribution assigns the same probability $1/\text{card } X$ to each event $x \in X$, i.e., $Prob_X(x) = 1/\text{card } X$.

Given an application with two (or, similarly, more) random variables X and Y, we can consider a further *product* random variable X, Y. For this random variable, the joint events x, y are taken from the Cartesian product $X \times Y$, and the product probability distribution $Prob_{X,Y}$ describes the probability of a joint occurrence of an event x together with an event y, according to the application. The original *marginal* distributions are related to the *product distribution* by the equations

$$Prob_X(x) = \sum^{y \in Y} Prob_{X,Y}(x,y) \quad \text{and} \quad Prob_Y(y) = \sum^{x \in X} Prob_{X,Y}(x,y). \quad \text{(A.1)}$$

In such a context, the random variables X and Y are *stochastically independent* iff

$$Prob_{X,Y}(x,y) = Prob_X(x) \cdot Prob_Y(y) \quad \text{for all } x \in X \text{ and } y \in Y. \quad \text{(A.2)}$$

Furthermore, for a product random variable X, Y, we define the *conditional probabilities* of the event x under the condition y and of the event y under the condition x by

$$Prob_{X|Y}(x|y) = \frac{Prob_{X,Y}(x,y)}{Prob_Y(y)} \quad \text{and} \quad Prob_{Y|X}(y|x) = \frac{Prob_{X,Y}(x,y)}{Prob_X(x)}, \quad \text{(A.3)}$$

respectively, provided the pertinent condition occurs with a positive probability. These definitions immediately imply *Bayes' Theorem*, which relates the original marginal probabilities to the conditional probabilities by the equation

$$Prob_{X|Y}(x|y) \cdot Prob_Y(y) = Prob_{Y|X}(y|x) \cdot Prob_X(x).\tag{A.4}$$

For each $y \in Y$ with a positive (marginal) probability, we obtain a derived *conditional random variable* $Prob_{X|y}$, defined by $Prob_{X|y}(x) = Prob_{X|Y}(x|y)$.

A.3.2 Entropy

Given a random variable X that is interpreted as some kind of experiment, the *uncertainty* (if seen *before* the experiment) or *information content* (if seen *after* the experiment) of an event $x \in X$ is measured by $-\text{ld } Prob_X(x)$. The *logarithm functions* have been shown to be the only reasonable candidates for measuring information on the basis of probabilities. The *base* of the logarithm, namely 2, is selected here for normalization, assigning the value 1 (one "bit of information") to an event that has probability 1/2, for example a random coin toss. The (average) *information content*, or *entropy*, of a *random variable* X is defined as the weighted average of the information contents of its events, i.e., by

$$H(X) = - \sum_{\substack{x \in X \\ Prob_X(x) > 0}} Prob_X(x) \cdot \text{ld } Prob_X(x).\tag{A.5}$$

For any random variables X and Y, the following properties hold:

$$H(X) \leq \text{ld card } X;\tag{A.6}$$

$$H(X) = \text{ld card } X \quad \text{iff} \quad X \text{ is equally distributed};\tag{A.7}$$

$$H(X) = 0 \quad \text{iff } X \text{ has a certain elementary event } e \text{ with } Prob_X(e) = 1;\tag{A.8}$$

$$H(X, Y) \leq H(X) + H(Y);\tag{A.9}$$

$$H(X, Y) = H(X) + H(Y) \quad \text{iff } X \text{ and } Y \text{ are stochastically independent.}\tag{A.10}$$

Furthermore, the *conditional entropy* of a random variable X under the condition of a random variable Y is defined as the weighted average of the entropies of the random variables $X|y$, for $y \in Y$, where the probabilities $Prob_Y(y)$ are taken as weights:

$$H(X|Y) = \sum_{y \in Y} Prob_Y(y) \cdot H(X|y)\tag{A.11}$$

$$= - \sum_{\substack{y \in Y \\ Prob_{X|Y}(x|y) > 0}} \sum_{x \in X} Prob_Y(y) \cdot Prob_{X|Y}(x|y) \cdot \text{ld } Prob_{X|Y}(x|y).$$

The following properties hold:

$$H(X, Y) = H(X) + H(Y|X);\tag{A.12}$$

$$H(X|Y) \leq H(X); \tag{A.13}$$

$H(X|Y) = H(X)$ iff X and Y are stochastically independent.   (A.14)

A.4 Number Theory

Computing systems are built in vertical layers. The virtual objects of higher layers are ultimately represented as *bit strings* in the hardware layer, and, accordingly, all operations on virtual objects have to be translated into operations on the bit strings that represent them. Vice versa, we can assign additional meaning to raw bit strings by interpreting them as representations of virtual objects, and then exploit such an interpretation for specific purposes. The latter approach is used in major parts of cryptography: messages, sent and received as bit strings by communicating participants, are suitably interpreted as *numbers* in order to take advantage of the rich algebraic structures on numbers and the related computational aspects. In the following, we provide a short introduction to these structures and some related algorithms.

A.4.1 Algebraic Structures Based on Congruences

The elements of $\mathbf{N} = \{0,1,2,3,\dots\}$ are called the *natural numbers* or *cardinals*. The most basic operation on $\mathbf{N}$ is the unary *successor* function, $+1$, and the most basic relation on $\mathbf{N}$ is the binary *less-than* relation, $<$. The commutative *addition* (function) and the commutative *multiplication* (function) are fundamental, too. Concerning these functions, the first two natural numbers play a special role: 0 is *neutral* with respect to addition, and 1 is *neutral* with respect to multiplication.

In order to convert the additive structure $(\mathbf{N},+,0)$ into a group, i.e., to allow inversion of addition and unique solvability for x of equations given in the form $a+x=b$, *negative numbers* are introduced: $\mathbf{Z} = \{\dots,-3,-2,-1,0,1,2,3,\dots\}$ is the set of *integers*, forming the *additive group* $(\mathbf{Z},+,0)$; in this group, the above equation is solved by $x=(-a)+b$, where $(-a)$ denotes the additive inverse of a.

Converting the multiplicative structure $(\mathbf{N} \setminus \{0\},\cdot,1)$ into a group requires us to introduce rational numbers (fractions). In this context, however, we do not treat rational numbers but follow a different approach that is based on integer division. We say that a cardinal $n > 1$ (an *integer*) *divides* an integer a, $n|a$, iff there exists an integer q with $a = q \cdot n$. More generally, given an integer a as a dividend and a cardinal $n > 1$ as a divisor, we can uniquely determine an integer q as an *integer quotient* and a cardinal r as a *residue* or *remainder* such that $a = q \cdot n + r$ and $0 \leq r < n$. Thus we have two functions, the *integer division* div and the *residue* function mod, such that $q = a$ div n and $r = a$ mod n.

For any cardinal $n > 1$, called the *modulus*, the integer division $\mathrm{div}\ n$ and the residue function $\mathrm{mod}\ n$ give rise to an equivalence relation on the integers: two integers a and b are defined to be *congruent* modulo n,

$a \equiv b \bmod n$ iff n (integer) divides $a-b$ (with remainder 0); equivalently,
                iff $a \bmod n = b \bmod n$.

For each residue $0 \le r < n$, there is a corresponding *residue class $\underline{r}$* that is the equivalence class consisting of all integers yielding that residue when integer-divided by n, i.e.,

$$\underline{r} = \{\, x \mid x \in \mathbf{Z}, \text{ and } r \equiv x \bmod n \,\} = \{\, x \mid x \in \mathbf{Z}, \text{ there exists } q \in \mathbf{Z} \text{ with } x = r + q \cdot n \,\};$$

in particular, $\underline{0}$ contains all (integer) multiples of the modulus n. For example, if the modulus is $n=3$, then there are the following three residue classes:

$\underline{0} = \{0,3,6,9,\dots\} \ \cup \{-3,-6,-9,\dots\}$,
$\underline{1} = \{1,4,7,10,\dots\} \cup \{-2,-5,-8,\dots\}$ and
$\underline{2} = \{2,5,8,11,\dots\} \cup \{-1,-4,-7,\dots\}$.

A fundamental algebraic operation *op* on integers *induces* an operation $\underline{op}$ on the residue classes as follows: first, the integer operation *op* is performed on any representatives of the argument classes, and then the residue class of the integer result is returned. It can be shown that the class returned is always independent of the representatives selected, and thus the relation $\equiv$ is also a *congruence relation* concerning addition and multiplication (and any suitably derived operation).

In this way, for each cardinal modulus $n > 1$, addition and multiplication on integers induce an algebraic structure on the residue classes modulo n. Following a common convention, this structure is denoted as $(\mathbf{Z}_n, +, \cdot, 0, 1)$, where $\mathbf{Z}_n$ is represented as $\{0, 1, \dots, n-1\}$ for short. In this context, all operations are implicitly understood to be done modulo n, i.e., all operations deliver the residue after integer division of the normal arithmetic result by the modulus n. Furthermore, with some misuse of language, in this text we often do not distinguish carefully between the notation for the residue function and that for the corresponding congruence relation.

$(\mathbf{Z}_n, +, \cdot, 0, 1)$ is always a *finite ring*; in particular, its *additive structure* $(\mathbf{Z}_n, +, 0)$ is always a *group*. Its *multiplicative structure*, however, forms a group only if the modulus n is a *prime number*, in which case it yields even a *finite field*. More generally, concerning multiplication modulo n, a residue class x, $0 < x < n$, has a *multiplicative inverse* iff it is *relatively prime* to n, i.e., the *greatest common divisor (gcd)* of x and the modulus n equals 1. The set of multiplicatively invertible elements is denoted by $\mathbf{Z}_n^{\ *} = \{\, x \mid 0 < x < n, \text{ and } gcd(x,n) = 1 \,\}$; the multiplicative (sub)structure $(\mathbf{Z}_n^{\ *}, \cdot, 1)$ is always a *group*.

A.4.2 Finite Fields Based on Prime Congruences

If a modulus under consideration is a *prime number*, then that modulus is commonly denoted by p. The corresponding structure $(\mathbf{Z}_p, +, \cdot, 0, 1)$ is a *finite field*. In particular, both the *additive structure* $(\mathbf{Z}_p, +, 0)$ and the *multiplicative structure* $(\mathbf{Z}_p^*, \cdot, 1)$ are *cyclic groups*, where the underlying residue classes are represented as $\mathbf{Z}_p = \{0, 1, \ldots, p-1\}$ and $\mathbf{Z}_p^* = \mathbf{Z}_p \setminus \{0\} = \{1, \ldots, p-1\}$. The elements of $\mathbf{Z}_p^*$ can be generated by selecting a *primitive element* g and then performing repeated multiplications of g with itself, i.e., by computing the *exponentiations* g^e of g for $0 \leq e < p-2$, yielding $\mathbf{Z}_p^* = \{g^0, g^1, g^2, \ldots, g^{p-2}\}$, where $1 = g^0 = g^{p-1}$.

In general, only some of the non-unit elements of $\mathbf{Z}_p^*$ are primitive, but each non-unit element h *generates* a subgroup $\{h^0, h^1, \ldots, h^{m-1}\}$ of $\mathbf{Z}_p^*$ with $1 = h^m$, of *order* (cardinality) m such that $m \mid p-1$. Conversely, for any factor of $p-1$, there is a corresponding subgroup.

For some applications, we need a multiplicative substructure such that all of its members are generators of the substructure. This requirement can be met, for example, as follows. Select the prime modulus p such that $p-1 = 2 \cdot q$, for some prime number q, and consider the subgroup of $\mathbf{Z}_p^*$ that has order q, denoted by G_q. This subgroup G_q has no further nontrivial sub-subgroups, since otherwise the order of such a sub-subgroup would be a nontrivial factor of the prime number q.

We now exemplify the concepts described in this subsection for $p = 11$ and $q = 5$ as follows. The *residue classes* are given by the sets $\mathbf{Z}_p = \{0, 1, \ldots, 10\}$, and $\mathbf{Z}_p^* = \{1, \ldots, 10\}$. The *multiplication* $x \cdot y$ mod 11 in $\mathbf{Z}_{11}^*$ is specified in Table A.2. The *exponentiation* of elements h of $\mathbf{Z}_{11}^*$ with cardinals e such that $1 \leq e < 10$ and, additionally, such that $e = 10$ (which always results in the neutral element 1) is shown in the Table A.3, together with the order of each element.

The exponentiation table indicates that the full multiplicative group $(\mathbf{Z}_p^*, \cdot, 1)$ has only four *primitive elements* (of order 10, i.e., *generators*), namely 2, 6, 7 and 8. The exponentiation table also shows that there are four elements of order 5, namely 3, 4, 5 and 9, each of which generates the subgroup G_5 given by $\{1, 3, 4, 5, 9\}$.

Table A.2. Multiplication modulo 11

$x \cdot y$ mod 11	1	2	3	4	5	6	7	8	9	10
1	1	2	3	4	5	6	7	8	9	10
2	2	4	6	8	10	1	3	5	7	9
3	3	6	9	1	4	7	10	2	5	8
4	4	8	1	5	9	2	6	10	3	7
5	5	10	4	9	3	8	2	7	1	6
6	6	1	7	2	8	3	9	4	10	5
7	7	3	10	6	2	9	5	1	8	4
8	8	5	2	10	7	4	1	9	6	3
9	9	7	5	3	1	10	8	6	4	2
10	10	9	8	7	6	5	4	3	2	1

Table A.3. Exponentiation modulo 11, and the orders of the elements of $\mathbf{Z}_{11}^{*}$

h^e mod 11	1	2	3	4	5	6	7	8	9	10	order
1	1	1	1	1	1	1	1	1	1	1	1
2	2	4	8	5	10	9	7	3	6	1	10
3	3	9	5	4	1	3	9	5	4	1	5
4	4	5	9	3	1	4	5	9	3	1	5
5	5	3	4	9	1	5	3	4	9	1	5
6	6	3	7	9	10	5	8	4	2	1	10
7	7	5	2	3	10	4	6	9	8	1	10
8	8	9	6	4	10	3	2	5	7	1	10
9	9	4	3	5	1	9	4	3	5	1	5
10	10	1	10	1	10	1	10	1	10	1	2

A.4.3 Algorithms for Operations on Residue Classes

Cryptography exploits heavily the algebraic structures of the residue classes modulo some cardinal n, i.e., the corresponding finite ring or finite field $(\mathbf{Z}_n, +, \cdot, 0, 1)$ and the pertinent substructures. Basically, many cryptographic mechanisms employ two features of the operations in these or related structures:

- On the one hand, the fundamental operations of *addition* and *additive inversion* (*subtraction*), *multiplication* and *multiplicative inversion* (*division*), and *exponentiation* are efficiently computable, roughly in linear, quadratic and cubic time, respectively, in the length of (the binary representation of) the modulus n. Thus even if the operands are "very long", say given by 1024 bits or even more, these operations can be computed in practice. Clearly, since the standard arithmetic units of the commonly used processors deal only with 32 or 64 bits, some additional special hardware or appropriate software solutions for *long-term arithmetic* must be provided. Below, we briefly sketch the most basic algorithms, which allow many further enhancements.
- On the other hand, some specific operations are considered to be *one-way functions*, i.e., the inversion of them is widely believed to be computationally infeasible. The most prominent prototypes of an intractable inversion are *factorization* (of a cardinal into its prime factors, which is the inversion of the multiplication of factors to obtain a product) and the *discrete logarithm* (of a residue class with respect to a primitive element as the base, which is the inversion of the exponentiation of the pertinent base). Some further details are given in Chapter 12.

For the exposition of the basic algorithms for the fundamental operations, we have always assumed that a residue class $\underline{r}$ is represented by its least cardinal member r. Basically, we can then reuse well-known algorithms that operate on cardinals and integers, applied to the representatives, and additionally integer-divide and

determine the residues whenever it is required or preferable for obtaining intermediate or final results.

The simplest example is *addition* modulo n. First, using the school method, the
operands are added bitwise with a carry, treating the bits from right (coefficients of
lower exponents of the base 2) to left (coefficients of higher exponents of the base
2). The resulting sum in the cardinals is guaranteed to be less than $2 \cdot n$. Thus, we
additionally simply check if this cardinal sum is greater than the modulus n, and if
this is true we subtract the modulus n from the cardinal sum; otherwise, we can
directly take the cardinal sum as the result of the addition.

Additive inversion modulo n is simple, too. Given the operand x, we just have to
compute $n-x$ in the cardinals, since, obviously, $x + (n-x) \equiv 0 \bmod n$.

Multiplication modulo n first uses a variant of the school method for cardinal
multiplication. Roughly, from right to left, the bits of the second factor determine
whether an intermediate term has to be added to a suitably adjusted (shifted) copy
of the first factor; after at most length(n) additions, we obtain the product of the
cardinals, which is guaranteed to be less than $n \cdot n$. An additional integer division
by the modulus n, again basically reusing the school method and requiring appropriate subtractions, yields the residue as the result of the multiplication.

The *multiplicative invertability* modulo n and, if applicable, the *multiplicative
inverse* are determined by exploiting the *extended Euclidean algorithm*. This algorithm computes the *greatest common divisor* $gcd(a,b)$ of two cardinals a and b by
returning two integers u and v such that $gcd(a,b) = a \cdot u + b \cdot v$. Roughly, given an
operand x, to multiplicatively invert x we aim at solving the equation $x \cdot y \equiv 1 \bmod n$;
if there is a solution, then y, denoted by x^{-1}, is the result of the inversion. The specified equation is solvable exactly for the elements of $\mathbf{Z}_n^* = \{ x \mid 0 < x < n,$ and
$gcd(x,n)=1 \}$. Hence, we first compute $gcd(x,n) = x \cdot u + n \cdot v$ by the extended
Euclidean algorithm and then check whether $1 = gcd(x,n)$. If this is the case, then
$1 = gcd(x,n) = x \cdot u + n \cdot v \equiv x \cdot u \bmod n$, i.e., the returned integer u and the wanted
solution y are congruent modulo n; by finally converting u into the standard representative of its residue class, we obtain the result of the inversion.

For example, let $n = 11$ and $x = 7$. In this simple situation, we can look up the
multiplicative inverse of 7 modulo 11 as $7^{-1} = 8$ in Table A.2, by finding the neutral element 1 in row 7 and column 8, and we can confirm the result by calculating
$7 \cdot 8 = 56 \equiv 1 \bmod 11$. Exploiting the extended Euclidean algorithm for the
$gcd(7,11)$, we first iteratively integer-divide the last divisor by the last residue,
starting with 11 and 7, respectively:

$$11 = 1 \cdot 7 + 4,$$
$$7 = 1 \cdot 4 + 3,$$
$$4 = 1 \cdot 3 + 1.$$

We then solve the resulting equations for the respective residues, namely 1, 3 and
4, and, starting from the last equation, we substitute the residues by the respective
solutions:

$$
\begin{aligned}
1 &= 4 &-& \quad 1 \cdot 3 \\
&= 4 &-& \quad 1 \cdot (7 - 1 \cdot 4) = -7 + 2 \cdot 4 \\
&= -7 &+& \quad 2 \cdot (11 - 1 \cdot 7) \\
&= 7 \cdot (-3) + & & 11 \cdot 2 \quad \equiv \quad 7 \cdot (-3) \bmod 11 .
\end{aligned}
$$

Finally, we convert the returned integer $u = (-3)$ into the standard representative:

$$
7^{-1} = 8 \equiv (-3) \bmod 11 .
$$

The *exponentiation* modulo n takes advantage of the binary representation of the exponent and exploits the following recursive equation:

$$
h^{k \cdot 2 + i} = \begin{bmatrix} h^{k \cdot 2} = (h^k)^2 & \text{if } i = 0, \\ h^{k \cdot 2} \cdot h = (h^k)^2 \cdot h & \text{if } i = 1. \end{bmatrix}
$$

Thus an exponentiation $h^e \bmod n$ can be calculated iteratively by a *square-and-multiply* method, where all intermediate results are immediately converted into their standard representatives. For example, to calculate $6^5 \bmod 11$, we use the binary representation $(101)_2$ of the exponent 5, and iteratively obtain the following:

$$
\begin{aligned}
6^{(1)_2} &= 6 , \\
6^{(10)_2} &= (6^{(1)_2})^2 = 6^2 \equiv 3 \bmod 11 , \\
6^{(101)_2} &= (6^{(10)_2})^2 \cdot 6 = 3^2 \cdot 6 = 54 \equiv 10 \bmod 11 .
\end{aligned}
$$

A.4.4 Randomized Prime Number Generation

Several cryptographic mechanisms require the *generation* of a large random *prime number*. A naive approach would proceed basically as follows:

- Generate a random bit string of sufficient length and interpret that string as the binary representation of a cardinal.
- Test that cardinal for primality. If the cardinal is prime, then return it; otherwise, iterate from the beginning.

Besides the number of iterations needed, the crucial point of this approach is the *primality test*, which has been investigated since ancient times. Ignoring computational complexity, there is a straightforward primality test: given a cardinal n, just determine the complete factorization of n into its prime factors, say by iteratively exploring all cardinals $1 < x < n$ as potential integer divisors of n. If some divisor q is found, then q is a witness against the primality of n.

Concerning complexity, this test needs exponential time in the length of the candidate n, and thus it is considered to be computationally infeasible. Moreover, the underlying argument of the test shows immediately that the set PRIMES of all prime numbers is in the problem class co-*NP*, i.e., the complement of PRIMES is recognizable in nondeterministic polynomial-time. It has been demonstrated that PRIMES is in *NP* as well and, more recently, PRIMES has even been proven to be in the problem class P, i.e., PRIMES can be decided in (deterministic) polynomial time. However, for practical purposes, more efficient *randomized* test algorithms are preferred.

As an example, in the following we sketch the efficient randomized technique of the *Miller–Rabin primality test*, which attempts to either find a witness against the primality of a given candidate n or to conclude that there is none, with an adaptable, small error probability. Furthermore, we indicate how the Miller–Rabin test fits into the overall approach for prime number generation.

Basically, given a candidate cardinal n generated in the first part of the overall approach, three methods for finding a *witness against primality* are exploited:

- Consider all members p of some "small" precomputed table of prime numbers, and test whether $p|n$ by an integer division of n by p: if the residue is 0, then p is an integer divisor of n and thus a *direct witness* against the primality of n.
- Consider a "small" randomly selected sample of cardinals less than n, and for each member a, compute the greatest common divisor $gcd(a,n)$ by the *extended Euclidean algorithm*: if $gcd(a,n) \neq 1$, then $gcd(a,n)$ is an integer divisor of n and thus a is considered as a *Euclid witness* against the primality of n.
- For each member a of the sample that has proved not to be a Euclid witness, perform the following:
  - compute the maximal s such that $2^s|(n-1)$ and set $d = (n-1)/2^s$;
  - check the condition
    "$\neg(a^d \equiv 1 \bmod n)$, and for all $r \in \{0,1,\dots,s-1\}$: $\neg(a^{2^r \cdot d} \equiv -1 \bmod n)$";

  if the last check is positive, then a is considered as a *Miller–Rabin witness* against the primality of n.

The following theorems justify the third method (together with the second one).

Theorem A.1   [correctness of Miller–Rabin witnesses]

Let n be a prime number. Define s as the maximal number such that $2^s|(n-1)$, and then set $d = (n-1)/2^s$. Furthermore, let $a \in \{2,\dots,n-1\}$ and $gcd(a,n) = 1$. Then

- either $a^d \equiv 1 \bmod n$ or
- there exists $r \in \{0,1,\dots,s-1\}$ such that $a^{2^r \cdot d} \equiv -1 \bmod n$.

Theorem A.2   [randomized completeness of Miller–Rabin witnesses]

Let $n \geq 3$ be a non-prime number. There then exist at most $(n-1)/4$ cardinals a in $\{2,\dots,n-1\}$ such that both $gcd(a,n) = 1$ and a is not a Miller–Rabin witness.

Summarizing, the naive approach for generating a large random prime number is refined by the *Miller–Rabin algorithm*, with the following parameters:

- the length k for the prime number to be returned,
- a precomputed table of all prime numbers less than some cardinal B,
- a repetition number t for assuring randomized completeness.

The algorithm is as follows:

1. Generate a random bit string $x_{k-1}x_{k-2}\dots x_1$ of length $k-1$.
2. Append $x_0 = 1$.
3. Set a cardinal n to the binary-number interpretation of the string $x_{k-1}x_{k-2}\dots x_1x_0$.
4. For each member p of the precomputed table of all prime numbers less than B:
   if $p \mid n$ [direct witness against the primality of current n found]
       then goto step 1.
5. Compute the maximal s such that $2^s \mid (n-1)$ and set $d = (n-1)/2^s$;
   repeat t times:
       randomly (with equal distribution) select $a \in \{2, \dots, n-1\}$;
       if $gcd(a, n) \neq 1$ [Euclid witness against the primality of current n found]
           then goto step 1;
       if a is a Miller–Rabin witness, i.e.,
       $$\neg(a^d \equiv 1 \bmod n) \text{ and for all } r \in \{0, 1, \dots, s-1\}: \neg(a^{2^r \cdot d} \equiv -1 \bmod n),$$
       then goto step 1.
6. Return n [claimed to be a prime number].

The achievements of the Miller–Rabin algorithm can be sketched as follows. Suppose that in step 3 of some iteration, the variable n is set to a prime number. Then, by the correctness of the various kinds of witness, all subsequent tests in steps 4 and 5 are passed without going back to step 1, and thus n is correctly returned.

Conversely, suppose that in step 3 of some iteration, the variable n is set to a non-prime number. If neither a direct nor a Euclid witness against the primality of n has been found, then for each repetition in step 5 the event "a is not a Miller–Rabin witness" occurs only with a probability of (about) $1/4$, according to the randomized completeness of the Miller–Rabin witnesses. Hence, after t repetitions, the probability that no Miller–Rabin witness has been found is only $(1/4)^t$. Thus, n is falsely returned as a prime number only with an adaptable, small error probability.

A.5 Finite Algebras

Cryptography, like many other fields in science, relies on appropriate algebraic structures, in particular finite groups, rings, fields and vector spaces. We briefly review the basic definitions and some fundamental insights; from here onwards, it is implicitly assumed that all underlying sets are finite.

A *group* $(\mathbf{G}, \bullet, u)$ is given by the following items and properties:

- an underlying (*carrier*) set $\mathbf{G}$;
- a binary (*group*) operation $\bullet : \mathbf{G} \times \mathbf{G} \to \mathbf{G}$;
- a *neutral element* $u \in \mathbf{G}$;

- the group axioms, which require *associativity* of the operation •, *neutrality* of the element u and *invertability* of all elements, i.e.,

  – $(x•y)•z = x•(y•z)$ for all x, y and z in $\mathbf{G}$;
  – $x•u = u•x = x$ for all x in $\mathbf{G}$;
  – for all x in $\mathbf{G}$, there exists an *inverse element*, denoted by x^{-1}, such that $x•x^{-1} = x^{-1}•x = u$.

A group is *commutative* if, additionally, the following property holds:

  – $x•y = y•x$ for all x and y in $\mathbf{G}$.

As an immediate consequence of the group properties, each *equation* $x•y = z$ has a *unique solution* regarding the "unknown variable" y given x and z, and regarding the "unknown variable" x given y and z. The unique *solutions* are determined by $y = x^{-1}•z$ and $x = z•y^{-1}$, respectively.

A nonempty subset $S \subseteq \mathbf{G}$ forms a *subgroup* with the pertinent restriction of the operation • and the neutral element u if, for all x and y in S, the element $x•y^{-1}$ is in S as well. If S forms a subgroup of $\mathbf{G}$, then card S (the number of elements in S, also called the *order* of S) divides card $\mathbf{G}$.

Each group has at least two subgroups, namely the group itself and the *trivial subgroup* $(\{u\}, •, u)$. For any two subgroups of a group, the *intersection* of their carrier sets forms a subgroup as well. Furthermore, for any two groups $(\mathbf{G}_1, •_1, u_1)$ and $(\mathbf{G}_2, •_2, u_2)$, the *Cartesian product* $\mathbf{G}_1 \times \mathbf{G}_2$ of their carrier sets forms a group with the componentwise-defined operation. The original group $(\mathbf{G}_1, •_1, u_1)$ is isomorphic to the subgroup of the *product group* that is formed by the pairs that have the neutral element u_2 as the second element, and a corresponding isomorphism exists for the original group $(\mathbf{G}_2, •_2, u_2)$.

Given a group $(\mathbf{G}, •, u)$, we can define an *exponentiation* as a derived operation by the induction $x^0 = u$ and $x^{e+1} = x^e • x$. For each x in $\mathbf{G}$, the set $\{x^0, x^1, x^2, \dots\}$ forms a subgroup whose cardinality (or order) is given by the least $e > 0$ minus 1 such that $x^e = u$. If the group has an element g whose exponentiations yield the full group, then the group is called *cyclic*, and each such element is called a *generator* of the group. Each subgroup of a cyclic group is cyclic as well. For a cyclic group with a generator g, we can define the *discrete logarithm* of an element y as the smallest cardinal e such that $g^e = y$.

Sometimes, we are interested simultaneously in two related structures on the same carrier set, where, traditionally, the first one is denoted in an additive style and the second one in a multiplicative style. More specifically, a *ring* $(\mathbf{G}, +, •, 0, 1)$ is given by the following items and properties:

- $(\mathbf{G}, +, 0)$ is a *commutative group*, with the neutral element denoted by 0;
- $(\mathbf{G}, •, 1)$ is a *semigroup*, i.e., the binary operation • on $\mathbf{G}$ is associative and has the element denoted by 1 as a neutral element, always yielding $x•1 = 1•x = x$;
- the multiplicatively denoted operation • is *distributive* with respect to the additively denoted operation +, i.e.,

  – $x•(y+z) = x•y + x•z$ for all x, y and z in $\mathbf{G}$, and
  – $(x+y)•z = x•z + y•z$ for all x, y and z in $\mathbf{G}$.

A ring is *commutative* if its multiplicatively denoted operation is commutative. A ring is called a *field* if $0 \neq 1$ and $(\mathbf{G} \setminus \{0\}, \bullet, 1)$ is a group. Accordingly, in a field, both the additive *equations* of the form $x + y = z$ and the multiplicative *equations* of the form $x \bullet y = z$ have *unique solutions.*

In order to treat more complicated systems of equations, we can also view a field as a *vector space* (over the field), where the additively denoted operation applies to elements, which are seen as *vectors*, and the multiplicatively denoted operation is treated as a *scalar multiplication*. This view offers the possibility to employ the well-understood theory of *systems of linear equations*. In particular, a system of m linear equations with n "unknown variables" x_i, of the form

$$a_{1,1} \bullet x_1 + a_{1,2} \bullet x_2 + \ldots + a_{1,n} \bullet x_n = b_1$$
$$a_{2,1} \bullet x_1 + a_{2,2} \bullet x_2 + \ldots + a_{2,n} \bullet x_n = b_2$$
$$\ldots$$
$$a_{m,1} \bullet x_1 + a_{m,2} \bullet x_2 + \ldots + a_{m,n} \bullet x_n = b_m,$$

admits a unique solution iff $m = n$ and the equations are consistent and *linearly independent*, i.e., none of them can be expressed as the sum of the remaining ones.

References

[1] Abadi, M., Burrows, M. Lampson, B., Plotkin, G., A calculus for access control in distributed systems, ACM Transactions on Programming Languages and Systems 15(4) (1993), pp. 706–734.

[2] Abadi, M., Lamport, L., Composing specifications, ACM Transactions on Programming Languages and Systems 15 (1993), pp. 73–132.

[3] Abadi, M., Gordon, A.D, A calculus for cryptographic protocols: The spi calculus. In: *Proc. 4th ACM Conference on Computer and Communications Security*, CCS 97, ACM, 1997, pp. 36–47.

[4] Abadi, M., On SDSI's linked local name spaces, Journal of Computer Security 6 (1998), pp. 3–22.

[5] Abadi, M., Security protocols: Principles and calculi. In: *Proc. Foundations of Security Analysis and Design IV*, FOSAD 2006/2007, Lecture Notes in Computer Science 4677, Springer, Berlin etc., 2007, pp. 1–23.

[6] Abiteboul, S., Hull, R., Vianu, V., *Foundation of Databases*, Addison-Wesley, Reading, MA, etc., 1995.

[7] Adam, N.R., Atluri, V., Bertino, E., Ferrari, E., A content-based authorization model for digital libraries, IEEE Transactions on Knowledge and Data Engineering 14(2) (2002), pp. 296–314.

[8] Adams, C., Farrell, S., Internet X.509 public key infrastructure certificate management protocols, 1999, IETF RFC 2510, http://www.ietf.org/rfc/rfc2510.txt.

[9] Adams, C., Cain, P., Pinkas, D., Zuccherato, R., Internet X.509 public key infrastructure time stamps protocols (TSP), 1999, IETF RFC 3161, http://www.ietf.org/rfc/rfc3161.txt.

[10] Ahn, G.J., Sandhu, R., Role-based authorization constraints specification, ACM Transactions on Information and System Security 3(4) (2000), pp. 207–226.

[11] Altenschmidt, C., Biskup, J., Flegel, U., Karabulut, Y., Secure mediation: Requirements, design and architecture, Journal of Computer Security 11 (2003), pp. 365–398.

[12] Alur, R., Grosu, R., Lee, I., Sokolsky, O., Composition modeling and refinement for hierarchical hybrid systems, Journal of Logic and Algebraic Programming 68 (2006), pp. 105–128.

[13] American National Standards Institute, *American National Standard for Data Encryption Algorithm (DEA)*, ANSI X3.92, 1981.

[14] Amoroso, E., *Fundamentals of Computer Security Technology*, Prentice-Hall, Englewood Cliffs etc., 1994.

[15] Amoroso, E., *Intrusion Detection: An Introduction to Internet Surveillance, Correlation, Traps, Trace Back, and Response*, Intrusion.Net Books, Sparta, NJ, 1999.

[16]   Anderson, R., *Security Enginering: A Guide to Building Dependable Distributed Systems*, Wiley, New York etc., 2001.

[17]   Andrews, G.R., Reitman, R.P., An axiomatic approach to information flows in programs, ACM Transactions in Programming Languages and Systems 2(1) (1980), pp. 56–76.

[18]   Arbaugh, W.A., Farber, D.J., Smith, J.M., A secure and reliable bootstrap architecture. In: *Proc. IEEE Conference on Security and Privacy*, IEEE, 1997, pp. 65–71.

[19]   Astrahan, M.M., Blasgen, M.W., Chamberlin, D.D., et al., System/R: A relational approach to data base management, ACM Transactions on Database Systems 1 (1976), pp. 97–137.

[20]   Avizienis, A. (ed.), *Fault-Tolerant Computing*, Special Issue FTCS-25 Silver Jubilee, IEEE, Los Alamitos etc., 1995.

[21]   Avizienis, A., Laprie, J.-C., Randell, B., Landwehr, C., Basic concepts and taxonomy of dependable and secure computing, IEEE Transactions on Dependable and Secure Computing 1(1) (2004), pp. 11–33.

[22]   Axelsson, S., Intrusion detection systems: A survey and taxonomy, Technical Report 99-15, Chalmers University of Technology, Göteborg, 2000.

[23]   Axelsson, S., The base-rate fallacy and the difficulty of intrusion detection, ACM Transactions on Information and System Security 3(3) (2000), pp. 186–205.

[24]   Bace, R.G., *Intrusion Detection*, Macmillan Technical Publishing, Indianapolis, 2000.

[25]   Backes, M., Pfitzmann, B., Waidner, M., A general theorem for secure reactive systems. In: *1st Theory of Cryptography Conference*, TCC 2004, Lecture Notes in Computer Science 2951, Springer, Berlin etc., 2004, pp. 336–354.

[26]   Backes, M., Pfitzmann, B., Waidner, M., Symmetric authentication in a simulatable Dolev–Yao-style cryptographic library, International Journal of Information Security 4(3) (2005), pp. 135–154.

[27]   Backes, M., Pfitzmann, B., Relating symbolic and cryptographic secrecy, IEEE Transactions on Dependable and Secure Computing 2(2) (2005), pp. 109–123.

[28]   Backes, M., Pfitzmann, B., Waidner, M., Limits of the BRSIM/UC soundness of Dolev-Yao models with hashes. In: *Proc. 11th European Symposium on Research in Computer Security*, ESORICS 2006, Lecture Notes in Computer Science 4189, Springer, Berlin etc., 2006, pp. 404–423.

[29]   Bacon, J., Moody, K., Yao, W., A model of OASIS role-based access control and its support for active security, ACM Transactions on Information and System Security 5(4) (2002), pp. 492–540.

[30]   Barker, S., Stuckey, P.J., Flexible access control policy specification with constraint logic programming, ACM Transactions on Information and System Security 6(4) (2003), pp. 501–546.

[31]   Bass, T., Intrusion detection systems and multisensor data fusion, Communications of the ACM 43(4) (2000), pp. 99–105..

[32]   Bauer, F.L., *Decrypted Secrets: Methods and Maxims of Cryptology*, 2nd edition, Springer, Berlin etc., 2000.

[33]   Bauer, F.L., Wössner, H., *Algorithmische Sprache und Programmentwicklung*, 2nd edition, Springer, Berlin etc., 1984.

[34]   Beauchemin, P., Brassard, G., A generalization of Hellman's extension to Shannon's approach to cryptrography, Journal of Cryptology 1 (1988), pp. 129–131.

[35]   Beaver, D., Secure multiparty protocols and zero knowledge proof systems tolerating a faulty minority, Journal of Cryptology 4(2) (1991), pp. 75–122.

[36]   Bell, D.E., LaPadula, L.J., *Secure Computer Systems: Mathematical Foundations and Model*, MITRE Corporation, Bedford, MA, 1974.

[37]   Bell, D.E., LaPadula, L.J., *Secure computer systems: A mathematical model*, Volume II. Reprinted in: Journal of Computer Security 4(2/3) (1996), pp. 229–263.

[38]   Bellare, M., Micali, S., Non-interactive oblivious transfer and applications. In: *Proc. Crypto 89*, Lecture Notes in Computer Science 435, Springer, Berlin etc., 1989, pp. 547–557.

[39]   Bellare, M., Goldreich, O., On defining proofs of knowledge. In: *Crypto 92*, Lecture Notes in Computer Science 740, Springer, Berlin etc., pp. 390–420.

[40]   Bellare, M., Kilian, J., Rogaway, P., The security of the cipher block chaining message authentication code, Journal of Computer and System Sciences 61(3) (2000), pp. 362–399.

[41]   Ben-Natan, R., *CORBA: A Guide to Common Object Request Broker Architecture*, McGraw-Hill, New York etc., 1995.

[42]   Berlekamp, E.R., *Algebraic Coding Theory*, McGraw-Hill, New York, 1968.

[43]   Bertino, E., Samarati, P., Jajodia, S., An extended authorization model for relational databases, IEEE Transactions on Knowledge and Data Engineering 9(1) (1997), pp. 85–101.

[44]   Bertino, E., Buccafurri, F., Ferrari, E., Rullo, P., An authorization model and its formal semantics. In: *Proc. 5th European Symposium on Research in Computer Security*, ESORICS 1998, Sept.1998, Lecture Notes in Computer Science 1485, Springer, Berlin etc., 1998, pp. 127–142.

[45]   Bertino, E., Buccafurri, F., Ferrari, E., Rullo, P., A logic-based approach for enforcing access control, Journal of Computer Security 8 (2000), pp. 109–139.

[46]   Bertino, E., Ferrari, E., Atluri, V., The specification and enforcement of authorization constraints in workflow management systems, ACM Transactions on Information and System Security 2(1) (1999), pp. 65–104.

[47]   Bertino, E., Catania, B., Ferrari, E., A nested transaction model for multilevel secure database management system, ACM Transactions on Information and System Security 4(4) (2001), pp. 321–370.

[48]   Bertino, E., Bonatti, P.A., Ferrari, E., TRBAC: A temporal role-based access control model, ACM Transactions on Information and System Security 4(3) (2001), pp. 191–233.

[49]   Bertino, E., Catania, B., Ferrari, E., Perlasca, P., A logical framework for reasoning about access control models, ACM Transactions on Information and System Security 6(1) (2003), pp. 71–127.

[50]   Bertino, E., Ferrari, E., Squicciarini, A.C., Trust-χ: A peer-to-peer framework for trust establishment, IEEE Transactions on Knowledge and Data Management 16(7) (2004), pp. 827–842.

[51]   Bertino, E., Sandhu, R., Database security – concepts, approaches and challenges, IEEE Transactions on Dependable and Secure Computing 2(1) (2005), pp. 2–19.

[52]   Beth, T., Jungnickel, D., Lenz, H., *Design Theory*, Bibliographisches Institut, Mannheim etc., 1985.

[53]   Biba, K.J., Integrity considerations for secure computer systems, Technical Report ESDTR-76-372 (MTR-3153), MITRE Corporation, Bedford, MA, 1977.

[54]   Bieber, P., Cuppens, F., A logical view of secure dependencies, Journal of Computer Security 1(1) (1992), pp. 99–130.

[55]   Bishop, M., Snyder, L., The transfer of information and authority in a protection system. In: *Proc. 7th Symposium on Operating Systems Principles*, 1979, pp. 45–54.

[56]   Bishop, M., Conspiracy and information flow in the take-grant protection model, Journal of Computer Security 4 (1996), pp. 331–359.

[57]   Bishop, M., *Computer Security: Art and Science*, Addison-Wesley, Boston etc., 2003.

[58]   Biskup, J., Some variants of the take-grant protection model, Information Processing Letters 19 (1984), pp. 151–156.

[59]   Biskup, J., Brüggemann, H.H., The personal model of data, Computers & Security 7(6) (1988), pp. 575–597.

[60]   Biskup, J., Privacy respecting permissions and rights. In: Landwehr, C.E. (ed.), *Database Security: Status and Prospects*, Elsevier Science (North Holland), Amsterdam etc., 1988, pp. 173–185.

[61]   Biskup, J., A general framework for database security. In: *Proc. 1st European Symposium on Research in Computer Security*, Toulouse, Oct. 1990, pp. 35–41.

[62]   Biskup, J., Sicherheit von IT-Systemen als "sogar wenn – sonst nichts – Eigenschaft". In: Weck, G., Horster, P. (eds.), *Proc. GI-Fachtagung Verläßliche Informationssysteme*, VIS 93, DuD Fachbeiträge 16, Vieweg, Wiesbaden, 1993, pp. 239–254.

[63]   Biskup, J., Eckert, C., About the enforcement of state dependent security specifications. In: *Proc. DBSec 1993, Database Security, VII: Status and Prospects*, North-Holland, 1994, pp. 3–17.

[64]   Biskup, J., Bleumer, G., Reflections on security of database and datatransfer systems in health care. In: Brunnstein, K., Raubold, E. (eds.), *Proc. 13th World Computer Congress 94*, Volume 2, Elsevier Science (North Holland), Amsterdam etc., 1994, pp. 549–556.

[65]   Biskup, J., Technical enforcement of informational assurances. In: Jajodia, S. (ed.), *Database Security XXII: Status and Prospects*, Kluwer, Boston etc., 1999, pp. 17–40.

[66]   Biskup, J., For unknown secrecies refusal is better than lying, Data & Knowledge Engineering 33 (2000), pp. 1–23.

[67]   Biskup, J., Flegel, U., Transaction-based pseudonyms in audit data for privacy respecting intrusion detection. In: *Proc. 3rd International Symposium on Recent Advances in Intrusion Detection*, RAID 2000, Lecture Notes in Computer Science 1907, Springer, Berlin etc., 2000, pp. 28–48.

[68]   Biskup, J., Flegel, U., On pseudonymization of audit data for intrusion detection. In: *Proc. 1st International Symposium on Privacy Enhancing Technologies*, PET 2000, Lecture Notes in Computer Science 2009, Springer, Berlin etc., 2000, pp. 161–180.

[69]   Biskup, J., Bonatti, P.A., Lying versus refusal for known potential secrets, Data & Knowledge Engineering 38 (2001), pp. 199–222.

[70]   Biskup, J., Leineweber, T., State-dependent security decisions for distributed object-systems. In: *Proc. DBSec 2001, Database and Application Security XV*, Kluwer, 2002, pp. 105–118.

[71]   Biskup, J., Leineweber, T., Parthe, J., Administration rights in the SDSD-System. In: *Data and Applications Security XVII: Status and Prospects*, Kluwer, 2004, pp. 149–162.

[72]   Biskup, J., Karabulut, Y., A hybrid PKI model: Application to secure mediation. In: Gudes, E., Shenoi, S. (eds.), *Research Directions in Data and Applications Security*, Kluwer, Boston etc., 2003, pp. 271–282.

[73]   Biskup, J., Karabulut, Y., Mediating between strangers: A trust management based approach. In: *Proc. 2nd Annual PKI Research Workshop*, Gaithersburg, MD, USA, April 2003, pp. 80–95.

[74]   Biskup, J., Bonatti, P.A., Controlled query evaluation for known policies by combining lying and refusal, Annals of Mathematics and Artificial Intelligence 40 (2004), pp. 37–62.

[75]   Biskup, J., Bonatti, P.A., Controlled query evaluation for enforcing confidentiality in complete information systems, International Journal of Information Security 3(1) (2004), pp. 14–27.

[76]   Biskup, J., Wortmann, S., Towards a credential-based implementation of compound access control policies. In: *Proc. 9th ACM Symposium on Access Control Models and Technologies*, SACMAT 04, Yorktown Heights, 2004, pp. 31–40.

[77]   Biskup, J., Parthe, J., Optimistic anonymous participation in inter-organizational workflow instances. In: *Proc. 2nd International Conference on Information Systems Security*, ICISS 2006, Lecture Notes in Computer Science 4332, Springer, Berlin etc., 2006, pp. 86–100.

[78]   Biskup, J., Bonatti, P.A., Controlled query evaluation with open queries for a decidable relational submodel, Annals of Mathematics and Artificial Intelligence 50 (2007), pp. 39–77.

[79]   Biskup, J., Embley, D.W., Lochner, J.-H., Reducing inference control to access control for normalized database schemas, Information Processing Letters 106 (2008), pp. 8–12.

[80]   Biskup, J., Lochner, J.-H., Enforcing confidentiality in relational databases by reducing inference control to access control. In: *Information Security Conference*, ISC 07, Lecture Notes in Computer Science 4779, Springer, Berlin etc., 2007, pp. 407–422.

[81]   Biskup, J., Weibert. T., Keeping secrets in incomplete databases, International Journal of Information Security 7(3) (2008), pp. 199–217.

[82]   Biskup, J., Wiese, L., Preprocessing for controlled query evaluation with availability policy, Journal of Computer Security 16(4) (2008), pp. 477–494.

[83]   Bjorner, D., *Software Engineering 1–3*, Springer, Berlin etc. 2006.

[84]   Blackburn, P., Rijke, M., Venema, Y., *Modal Logic*, Cambridge University Press, Cambridge, 2001.

[85]   Blake I.F., Mullin, R., *The Mathematical Theory of Coding*, Academic Press, New York etc., 1975.

[86]   Blakley, G.R., Safeguardings cryptographic keys. In: *AFIPS Conference Proceedings 48*, 1979, pp. 313–317.

[87]   Blakley, B., *CORBA Security: An Introduction to Safe Computing with Objects*, Addison-Wesley, Reading, MA, etc., 2000.

[88]   Blaze, M., Feigenbaum, J., Ioannindis, J., Keromytis, A.D., Decentralized trust management. In: *Proc. IEEE Symposium on Security and Privacy*, IEEE Computer Society, 1996, pp. 164–173.

[89]   Blaze, M., Feigenbaum, J., Keromytis, A.D., The KeyNote trust management system version 2, RFC 2704, IETF, 1999.

[90]   Blum, M., Coin flipping by telephone. In: *Proc. Crypto 81*, University of California Santa Barbara, Dept. of Elec. and Computer Eng., ECE Report No 82-04, 1982, pp. 11–15.

[91]   Blum, M., Micali, S., How to generate cryptographically strong sequences of pseudo-random bits, SIAM Journal on Computing 13 (1984), pp. 850–864.

648   References

[92]   Blum, M., De Santis, A., Micali, S., Persiano, G., Non-interactive zero-knowledge proof systems, SIAM Journal on Computing 20(6) (1991), pp. 1084–1118.

[93]   Bonatti, P.A., Kraus, S., Subrahmanian, V.S., Foundations of secure deductive databases, IEEE Transactions on Knowledge and Data Engineering 7(3) (1995), pp. 406–422.

[94]   Bonatti, P.A., De Capitani di Vimercati, S., Samarati, P., An algebra for composing access control policies, ACM Transactions on Information and System Security 5(1) (2002), pp. 1–35.

[95]   Bonatti, P.A., Samarati, P., A uniform framework for regulating service access and information release on the web, Journal of Computer Security 10(3) (2002), pp. 241–272.

[96]   Bonatti, P.A., Samarati, P., Logics for authorization and security. In: *Logics for Emerging Applications of Databases* [outcome of a Dagstuhl seminar], Springer, Berlin etc., 2003, pp. 277–323.

[97]   Bolle, R.M., Connell, J.H., Pankanti, Sh., Ratha, N.K., Senior, A.W., *Guide to Biometrics*, Springer, New York, 2003.

[98]   Börger, E., Grädel, E., Gurewich, Y., *The Classical Decision Problem*, Springer, Berlin etc., 1997.

[99]   Brachman, R.J., Leveques, H.J., *Knowledge Representation and Reasoning*, Elsevier, Amsterdam etc., 2004.

[100]   Brands, S.A., Untraceable off-line cash in wallets with observers (extended abstract). In: *Proc. Crypto 93*, Lecture Notes in Computer Science 773, Springer, Berlin etc., 1994, pp. 302–318.

[101]   Brands, S.A., *Rethinking Public Key Infrastructures and Digital Certificates*, MIT Press, Cambridge, MA, 2000.

[102]   Brewer, D.F.C., Nash, M.J., The Chinese Wall security policy. In: *Proc. IEEE Symposium on Security and Privacy*, 1989, Oakland, pp. 206–214.

[103]   Brickell, E., Some ideal secret sharing schemes, Journal of Combinatorial Mathematics and Combinatorial Computing 9 (1989), pp. 105–113.

[104]   Brickell, E., Davenport, D., On the classification of ideal secret sharing schemes, Journal of Cryptology 4 (1991), pp. 123–134.

[105]   Brickell, E., Camenisch, J., Chen, L. Direct anonymous attestation. In: *Proc. 11th ACM Conference on Computer and Communications Security*, CCS 04, pp. 132–145.

[106]   Brodsky, A., Farkas, C., Jajodia, S., Secure databases: Constraints, inference channels, and monitoring disclosures, IEEE Transactions on Knowledge and Data Engineering 12(6) (2000), pp. 900–919.

[107]   Bruss, D., Erdelyi, G., Meyer, T., Riege, T., Rothe, J., Quantum cryptography: A survey, ACM Computing Surveys 39(2) (2007), Article 6 (27 pages).

[108]   Buchmann, J., *Introduction to Cryptography*, Springer, Berlin etc., 2002.

[109]   Bull, H.P., *Datenschutz oder Die Angst vor dem Computer*, Piper, Munich, 1984.

[110]   Bundesverfassungsgericht, Urteil vom 15. Dezember 1983 zum Volkszählungsgesetz 1983, Bundesanzeiger 35,241a, 1983 (see http://www.datenschutz-berlin.de/sonstige/volksz.html).

[111]   Burrows, M., Abadi, M., Needham, R.M., A logic of authentication, ACM Transactions on Computer Systems 8(1) (1990), pp. 18–36.

[112]   Büschges, R., Kesdogan, D., Privacy enhanced intrusion detection. In: *Multilateral Security in Communications*, Addison-Wesley, Munich etc., 1999, pp. 187–204.

[113] Butler, M., Jones, C., Romanovsky, A., Troubitsyna, E. (eds.), *Rigorous Development of Complex Fault-Tolerant Systems*, Lecture Notes in Computer Science 4157, Springer, Berlin etc., 2006.

[114] Camenisch, J., Better privacy for trusted computing platforms. In: *Proc. 9th European Symposium on Research in Computer Security*, ESORICS 04, Lecture Notes in Computer Science 3193, Springer, Berlin etc., 2004, pp. 73–88.

[115] Canetti, R., Security and composition of multiparty cryptographic protocols, Journal of Cryptology 13 (2000), pp. 143–202.

[116] Canetti, R., Universally composable security: A new paradigm for cryptographic protocols. In: *42nd IEEE Symposium on Foundations of Computer Science*, FOCS 2001, pp. 136–145.

[117] Canetti, R., Dodis, Y., Pass, R., Walfish, S., Universally composable security with global setup. In: *4th Theory of Cryptography Conference*, TCC 2007, Lecture Notes in Computer Science 4392, Springer, Berlin etc., 2007, pp. 61–85.

[118] Castano, S., Fugini, M., Martella, G., Samarati, P., *Database Security*, Addison-Wesley, Wokingham etc., 1995.

[119] Chaitin, G.J., *Exploring Randomness*, Springer, London etc., 2001.

[120] Chaum, D., Blind signatures for untraceable payments. In: *Proc. Crypto 82*, Plenum, New York, 1983, pp. 199–203.

[121] Chapman, D.B., Zwickey, E.D., *Building Internet Firewalls*, O'Reilly, Cambridge etc., 1995.

[122] Chaum, D., Untraceable electronic mail, return adresses, and digital pseudonyms, Communications of the ACM 24(2) (1981), pp. 84–88.

[123] Chaum, D., Security without identification: Transaction systems to make Big Brother obsolete, Communications of the ACM 28(10) (1985), pp. 1030–1044.

[124] Chaum, D., The dining cryptographers problem: Unconditional sender and recipient untraceability, Journal of Cryptology 1(1) (1988), pp. 65–75.

[125] Chaum, D., van Antwerpen, H., Undeniable signatures. In: *Proc. Crypto 89*, Lecture Notes in Computer Science 435, Springer, Berlin etc., 1990, pp. 212–216.

[126] Chaum, D., Zero-knowledge undeniable signatures. In: *Proc. Eurocrypt 90*, Lecture Notes in Computer Science 473, Springer, Berlin etc., 1991, pp. 458–464.

[127] Chaum, D., van Heijst, E., Pfitzmann. B., Cryptographically strong undeniable signatures unconditionally secure for the signer. In: *Proc. Crypto 91*, Lecture Notes in Computer Science 576, Springer, Berlin etc., 1992, pp. 470–484.

[128] Chaum, D., van Heijst, E., Group signatures. In: *Proc. Eurocrypt 91*, Lecture Notes in Computer Science 547, Springer, Berlin etc., 1991, pp. 257–265.

[129] Chaum, D., Pedersen, T.P., Wallet databases with observers. In: Proc. *Crypto 92*, Lecture Notes in Computer Science 740, Springer, Berlin etc., 1993, pp. 89–105.

[130] Chen, L., Pedersen, T.P., New group signature schemes. In: *Proc. Eurocrypt 94*, Lecture Notes in Computer Science 950, Springer, Berlin etc., 1995, pp. 171–181.

[131] Cheswick, W.R., Bellovin, S.M., *Firewalls and Internet Security*, Addison-Wesley, Reading, MA, etc., 1994.

[132] Chin, F.Y., Security in statistical databases for queries with small counts, ACM Transactions on Database Systems 3(1) (1978), pp. 92–104.

[133] Chin, F.Y., Özsoyoglu, G., Auditing and inference control in statistical databases, IEEE Transactions on Software Engineering 8(6) (1982), pp. 574–582.

[134] Chor, B., Goldwasser, S., Micali, S., Awerbuch, B., Verifiable secret sharing and achieving simultaneity in the presence of faults. In: *26th IEEE Symposium on Foundations of Computer Science*, 1985, pp. 383–395.

[135] Clark, D.D., Wilson, D.R., A comparison of commercial and military computer security policies. In: *Proc. IEEE Symposium on Security and Privacy*, 1987, Oakland, pp. 184–194.

[136] Clarke, D.E., Elien, J.-E., Ellison, C., Fredette, M., Morcos, A., Rivest, R.L., Certificate chain discovery in SPKI/SDSI, Journal of Computer Security 9(4) (2001), pp. 285–322.

[137] Codd, E.F., A relational model of data for large shared data banks, Communications of the ACM 13 (1970), pp. 377–387.

[138] Coetzee, M., Eloff, J.H.P., Towards web service access control, Computers & Security 23(7) (2004), 559–570.

[139] Cohen, E., *Strong Dependency: A Formalism for Describing Information Transmission in Computational Systems*, Dept. of Computer Science, Carnegie Mellon University, 1976.

[140] Cohen, E., Information transmission in computational systems. In: *Proc. 6th Symposium on Operating Systems Principles*, 1977, pp. 133–139.

[141] Common Criteria Editorial Board, *Common Criteria for Information Technology Security Evaluation*, Version 1.0, Jan. 1996; Version 2, May 1998 (see http://csrc.nist.gov/cc).

[142] Coppersmith, D., The Data Encryption Standard (DES) and its strength against attacks, IBM Journal of Research and Development 38(3) (1994), pp. 243–250.

[143] Coulouris, G., Dollimore, J., Kindberg, T., *Distributed Systems: Concepts and Design*, 4th edition, Addison-Wesley, Wokingham, 2004.

[144] Cramer, R., Damgard, I., Schoenmakers, B., Proofs of partial knowledge and simplified design of witness hiding protocols. In: *Proc. Crypto 94*, Lecture Notes in Computer Science 839, Springer, Berlin etc., 1994, pp. 174–187.

[145] Cramer, R., Damgard, I., Nielsen, J.B., Multiparty computation from threshold homomorphic encryption. In: *Proc. Eurocrypt 01*, Lecture Notes in Computer Science 2045, Springer, Berlin etc., 2001, pp. 280–300.

[146] CRAMM, *UK Government's Risk Analysis and Management Method*, http://www.cramm.com.

[147] Cuppens, F., Gabillon, A., Logical foundation of multilevel databases, Data & Knowledge Engineering 29 (1999), pp. 259–291.

[148] Cuppens, F., Gabillon, A., Cover story management, Data & Knowledge Engineering 37 (2001), pp. 177–201.

[149] Damgard, I., A design principle for hash functions. In: *Proc. Crypto 89*, Lecture Notes in Computer Science 435, Springer, Berlin etc., 1990, pp. 416–227.

[150] Damgard, I., Pedersen, T.P., Pfitzmann, B., On the existence of statistically hiding bit commitment schemes and fail-stop signatures, Journal of Cryptology 10(3) (1997), pp. 163–194.

[151] Damgard, I., Nielsen, J.B., Universally composable efficient multiparty computation from threshold homomorphic encryption. In: *Proc. Crypto 03*, pp. 247–264.

[152] Date, C.J., *An Introduction to Database Systems*, 8th edition, Addison-Wesley, Reading, MA, etc., 2004.

[153] Davis, D.W., Price, W.L., *Security for Computer Networks*, 2nd edition, Wiley, Chichester etc., 1989.

[154] Dawson, S., De Capitani di Vimercati, S., Lincoln, P., Samarati, P., Minimal data upgrading to prevent inference and association attacks. In: *ACM Symposium on Principles of Database Systems*, 1999, pp. 114–125.

[155] Dawson, S., De Capitani di Vimercati, S., Samarati, P., Specification and enforcement of classification and inference constraints. In: *Proc. IEEE Symposium on Security and Privacy 1999*, pp. 181–195.

[156] Daemen, J., Rijmen, V., *The Design of Rijndael: AES – The Advanced Encryption Standard*, Springer, Berlin etc., 2002.

[157] Debar, H., Dacier, M., Wespi, A., Towards a taxonony of intrusion-detection systems, Computer Networks 31 (1999), pp. 805–822.

[158] De Capitani di Vimercati, S., Samarati, P., Jajodia, S., Policies, models, and languages for access control. In: *Proc. 4th Workshop on Databases in Networked Information Systems*, DNIS 2005, Aizu, Japan, Lecture Notes in Computer Science 3433, Springer, Berlin etc., 2005, pp. 225–237.

[159] Delfs, H., Knebl, H., *Introduction to Cryptography: Principles and Applications*, Springer, Berlin etc., 2002.

[160] Denning, D.E., A lattice model of secure information flow, Communications of the ACM 19(5) (1976), pp. 236–243.

[161] Denning, D.E., Denning, P.J., Certification of programs for secure information flow, Communications of the ACM 20(7) (1977), pp. 504–513.

[162] Denning, D.E., Denning, P.J., Schwartz, M.D., The tracker: A threat to statistical database security, ACM Transactions on Database Systems 4(1) (1979), pp. 76–96.

[163] Denning, D.E., *Cryptography and Data Security*, Addison-Wesley, Reading, MA, etc., 1982.

[164] Denning, D.E., Schlörer, J., Inference controls for statistical databases, IEEE Computer 16(7) (1983), pp. 69–82.

[165] Denning, D.E., An intrusion-detection model, IEEE Transactions on Software Engineering 13(2) (1987), pp. 222–232.

[166] Denning, D.E., Akl, S., Heckman, M., Lunt, T., Morgenstern, M., Neumann, P., Schell, R., Views for multilevel database security, IEEE Transactions on Software Engineering 13(2) (1987), pp. 129–140.

[167] Department of Defense Computer Security Center, *Trusted Computer Systems Evaluation Criteria* ("Orange Book"), CSC-STD-011-83, Fort Meade, 1983.

[168] Diaz, C., Claessens, J., Preneel, B., APES – Anonymity and privacy in electronic services, Datenschutz und Datensicherheit (DuD) 27 (2003), pp. 143–145.

[169] Diaz, C., Claessens, J., Preneel, B., et al., *Anonymity and Privacy in Electronic Services* (APES), Technical reports, K. U. Leuven, 2001–2002.

[170] Dierstein, R., The concept of secure information processing systems and their basic functions. In: *Proc. IFIP/SEC 90*, Espoo (Helsinki), Finland.

[171] Diffie, W., Hellman, M.E., New directions in cryptography, IEEE Transactions on Information Theory IT-22(6) (1976), pp. 644–654.

[172] Dittrich, K.R., Hug, K., Kammerer, P., Lienert, D., Mau, H., Wachsmuth, K., Protection in the OSKAR operating system – goals, concepts, consequences. In: *Proc. IEEE Symposium on Security and Privacy*, Oakland, 1982, pp. 46–56.

[173] Dobbertin, H., Cryptanalysis of MD4, Journal of Cryptology 11 (1998), pp. 253–271.

[174] Dolev, D., Yao, A.C., On the security of public key protocols, IEEE Transactions on Information Theory 29(2) (1983), pp. 198–208.

[175] Dolev, S., Ostrovsky, R., Xor-trees for efficient anonymous multicast and reception, ACM Transactions on Information and System Security 3(2) (2000), pp. 63–84.

[176] Domingo-Ferrer, J., Advances in inference control in statistical databases: An overview. In: *Proc. Inference Control in Statistical Databases*, Lecture Notes in Computer Science 2316, Springer, Berlin etc., 2002, pp. 1–7.

[177] Du, W., Atallah, M.J., Secure multiparty computation problems and their applications: A review and open problems. In: *Proc. New Security Paradigms Workshop 2001*, ACM, 2001, pp. 13–22.

[178] Dworkin, M., *Recommendation for Block Cipher Modes of Operation: The CCM Mode for Authentication and Confidentiality*, National Institute of Standards and Technology (NIST), PUB 800-38C, 2004.

[179] Ebbinghaus, H.-D., Flum, J., *Finite Model Theory*, Springer, Berlin etc., 1995.

[180] Eckert, C., *IT-Sicherheit: Konzepte–Verfahren–Protokolle* (4. Aufl.), Oldenbourg, Munich/Vienna, 2006.

[181] Eckmann, S.T., Vigna, G.., Kemmerer, R.A., STATL: An attack language for state-based intrusion detection, Journal of Computer Security 10(1–2) (2002), pp. 71–104.

[182] ECRYPT – Network of Excellence in Cryptology, Information Societies Technology (IST) Programme of the European Commission's Sixth Framework Programme (FP6), contract number IST-2002-507932 (see http://www.ecrypt.eu.org).

[183] ElGamal, T., A public key cryptosystem and a signature scheme based on discrete logarithm, IEEE Transactions on Information Theory 31 (1985), pp. 469–472.

[184] Ellison, C.M., Frantz, B., Lampson, B., Rivest, R.L., Thomas, B.M., Ylonen, T., Simple public key certificate, http://world.std.com/~cme/html/sdsi.html, July 1999.

[185] Ellison, C.M., Frantz, B., Lampson, B., Rivest, R.L., Thomas, B.M., Ylonen, T., SPKI certificate theory, http://world.std.com/~cme/html/spki.html, Internet RFC 2693, September 1999.

[186] Ellison, C.M., Schneier, B., Ten risks of PKI: What you're not being told about public key infrastructure, Journal of Computer Security 16(1) (2000), pp. 1–7.

[187] Ellison, C.M., Dohrmann, D., Public-key support for group collaboration, ACM Transactions on Information and System Security 6(4) (2003), pp. 547–565.

[188] Elmasri, R., Navathe, S.B., *Fundamentals of Database Systems*, 3rd edition, Addison-Wesley, Reading, MA, etc, 2000.

[189] Eloff, J.H.P., Labuschagne, L., Badenhorst, K.P., A comparative framework for risk analysis methods, Computers & Security 12(6) (1993), pp. 597–603.

[190] Escobar, S., Meadows, M., Meseguer, J., A rewriting-based inference system for the NRL Protocol Analyzer and its meta-logical properties, Theoretical Computer Science 367(1–2) (2006), pp. 162–202.

[191] European Commission, Directive on the protection of individuals with regard to the processing of personal data and the free movement of such data, 1995 (see http://europa.eu.int/eur-lex/en/lif/dat/1995/en_395L0046.html).

[192] European Commission, Towards a European framework for digital signatures and encryption, Communication COM (97) 503, Oct. 1997 (see http://www.ispo.cec.be/eif/policy).

[193] European Commission, Directive on a framework for the use of electronic signatures, Proposal COM (98) 297, May 1998 (see http://www.ispo.cec.be/eif/policy).

[194] European Communities, *Information Technology Security Evaluation Criteria* (ITSEC), Version 1.2, Luxembourg, 1991.

[195] Even, S., Protocol for signing contracts. In: *Proc. Crypto 81*, University of California Santa Barbara, Dept. of Elec. and Computer Eng., ECE Report No 82-04, 1982, pp. 148–153.

[196] Fabry, R.S., Capability-based addressing, Communications of the ACM 17(7) (1974), pp. 403–412.

[197] Fagin, R., On an authorization mechanism, ACM Transactions on Database Systems 3(3) (1978), pp. 310–319.

[198] Fagin, R., Halpern, J.Y., Moses, Y., Vardi, M.Y., *Reasoning About Knowledge*, MIT Press, Cambridge, MA, 1995.

[199] Farkas, C., Jajodia, S., The inference problem: A survey, ACM SIGKDD Explorations Newsletter 4(2) (2002), pp. 6–11.

[200] Feige, U., Fiat, A., Shamir, A., Zero-knowledge proofs of identity, Journal of Cryptology 1 (1988), pp. 77–94.

[201] Feistel, H., Cryptography and computer privacy, Scientific American 228(5) (1973), pp. 15–23.

[202] Feller, W., *An Introduction to Probability Theory and Its Applications*, Volumes 1 and 2, Wiley, New York, 1968 and 1971.

[203] Ferguson, N., Extensions of single-term coins. In: *Proc. Crypto 93*, Lecture Notes in Computer Science 773, Springer, Berlin etc., 1994, pp. 292–301.

[204] Ferraiolo, D.F., Sandhu, R., Gavrila, S., Kuhn, R., Proposed NIST standard for role-based access control, ACM Transactions on Information and System Security 4(3) (2001), pp. 224–274.

[205] Ferrari, E., Adam, N.R., Atluri, V., Bertino, E., Capuozzo, U., An authorization system for digital libraries, The VLDB Journal 11 (2002), pp. 58–67.

[206] Feustel, E.A., On the advantages of tagged architecture, IEEE Transactions on Computers C-22(7) (1973), pp. 644–656.

[207] Fiedler, H., Informationelle Garantien für das Zeitalter der Informationstechnik. In: Tinnefeld, M.-T., Philipps, L., Weis, K. (eds.), *Institutionen und der Einzelne im Zeitalter der Informationstechnik*, Oldenbourg, Munich/Vienna, 1994, pp. 147–158.

[208] Flegel, U., Pseudonymizing UNIX log files. In: *Proc. Infrastructure Security Conference*, InfraSec 2002, Lecture Notes in Computer Science 2437, Springer, Berlin etc., 2002, pp. 162–179.

[209] Flegel, U., Biskup, J., Requirements of information reductions for cooperating intrusion detection agents. In: *Proc. International Conference on Emerging Trends in Information and Communication Security*, ETRIX 2006, Lecture Notes in Computer Science 3995, Springer, Berlin etc., 2006, pp. 466–480.

[210] Flegel, U., *Privacy-Respecting Intrusion Detection*, Springer, New York etc., 2007.

[211] Focardi, R., Gorrieri, R., A classification of security properties for process algebras, Journal of Computer Security 3(1) (1995), pp. 5–33.

[212] Focardi, R., Gorrieri, R., Classification of security properties (Part I: information flow). In: Focardi, R., Gorrieri, R., (eds.), *Foundations of Security Analysis and Design*, Lecture Notes in Computer Science 2171, Springer, Berlin etc., 2001, pp. 331–396.

[213] Foley, S.N., A universal theory of information flow. In: *IEEE Sympsoum on Security and Privacy*, Oakland, 1987, pp. 116–122.

[214] Forrest, S., Hofmayr, S.A., Longstaff, T.A., A sense of self for Unix processes. In: *Proc. IEEE Symposium on Security and Privacy*, 1996, pp. 120–128.

[215] Free Software Foundation, The GNU Privacy Guard, Version GnuPG 1.4.5, 2006, http://gnupg.org.

[216] Garfinkel, S., Spafford, G., *Practical UNIX and Internet Security*, 2nd edition, O'Reilly, Sebastopol, CA, etc., 1996.

[217] Gathen, J. von zur, Gerhard, J., *Modern Computer Algebra*, 2nd edition, Cambridge University Press, Cambridge, 2003.

[218] Gerla, G., *Fuzzy Logic: Mathematical Tools for Approximate Reasoning*, Kluwer, Dordrecht etc., 2001.

[219] Gilbert, E.N., MacWilliams, F.J., Sloane, N.J.A., Codes which detect deception, Bell System Technical Journal 53(3) (1974), pp. 405–424.

[220] Goldreich, O., Goldwasser, S., Micali, S., On the cryptographic applications of random functions. In: *Proc. Crypto 84*, Lecture Notes in Computer Science 263, Springer, Berlin etc., pp. 276–288.

[221] Goldreich, O., Goldwasser, S., Micali, S., How to construct random functions, Journal of the ACM 33 (1986), pp. 792–807.

[222] Goldreich, O., Micali, S., Wigderson, A., How to play any mental game – a completeness theorem for protocols with honest majority. In: *Proc. 19th ACM Symposium on the Theory of Computing*, 1987, pp. 218–229.

[223] Goldreich, O., Micali, S., Wigderson, A., Proofs that yield nothing but their validity or all languages in NP have zero-knowledge proof systems, Journal of the ACM 38(3) (1991), pp. 691–729.

[224] Goldreich, O., Krawcyzk, H., Luby, M., On the existence of pseudorandom generators, SIAM Journal on Computing 22 (1993), pp. 1163–1175.

[225] Goldreich, O., Oren, Y., Definitions and properties of zero-knowledge proof systems, Journal of Cryptography 7(1) (1994), pp. 1–32.

[226] Goldreich, O., *Modern Cryptography, Probabilistic Proofs and Pseudorandomness*, Springer, Berlin etc., 1999.

[227] Goldreich, O., Cryptography and cryptographic protocols, Distributed Computing 16 (2003), pp. 177–199.

[228] Goldreich, O., *Foundations of Cryptography I: Basic Tools*, Cambridge University Press, Cambridge, 2001.

[229] Goldreich, O., *Foundations of Cryptography II: Basic Applications*, Cambridge University Press, Cambridge, 2004.

[230] Goldschlag, D.M., Reed, M.G., Syverson, P.F., Onion routing, Communications of the ACM 42(2) (1999), pp. 39–41.

[231] Goldwasser, S., Micali, S., Probabilistic encryption, Journal of Computer and System Science 28 (1984), pp. 270–299.

[232] Goldwasser, S., Micali, S. Rivest, R.L., A digital signature scheme secure against adaptive chosen-message attacks, SIAM Journal on Computing 17(2) (1988), pp. 281–308.

[233] Goldwasser, S., Micali, S. Rackoff, C., The knowledge complexity of interactive proof systems, SIAM Journal on Computing 18(1) (1989), pp. 186–207.

[234] Gollmann, D., *Computer Security*, 1st edition, Wiley, Chichester, 1999; 2nd edition, 2006.

[235] Goloubeva, O., Rebaudengo, M., Rorda, M.S., Violante, M., *Software-Implemented Hardware Fault Tolerance*, Springer, New York, 2006.

[236] Gong, L., Java2 platform security architecture, Chapter 4 of JDK 1.4.2, `http://java.sun.com/j2se/1.4.2/docs/guide/security/spec/security-spec.doc4.html`, 1997–2002.

[237] Goguen, J.A., Mesequer, J., Security policies and security models. In: *Proc. IEEE Symposium on Security and Privacy*, 1982, Oakland, pp. 11–20.

[238] Goguen, J.A., Mesequer, J., Unwinding and inference control. In: *Proc. IEEE Symposium on Security and Privacy*, 1984, Oakland, pp. 75–86.

[239] Gray, J.W., III, Toward a mathematical foundation for information flow properties. In: *Proc. IEEE Symposium on Security and Privacy*, Oakland, 1991, pp. 21–34.

[240] Gries, D., *The Science of Computer Programming*, Springer, Berlin etc. 1981.

[241] Griffiths, P.P., Wade, B.W., An authorization mechanism for relational database systems, ACM Transactions on Database Systems 1(3) (1976), pp. 242–255.

[242] Grimaldi, R.P., *Discrete and Combinatorial Mathematics*, 3rd edition, Addison-Wesley, Reading, MA, etc., 1994.

[243] Groß, M., Vertrauenswürdiges Booten als Grundlage authentischer Basissysteme. In: *Proc. GI-Fachtagung Verläßliche Informationssysteme*, VIS 91, Informatik-Fachberichte 271, Springer, Berlin etc., pp. 190–207.

[244] Haigh, J.T., Young, W.D., Extending the noninterference version of MLS for SAT, IEEE Transactions on Software Engineering 13(2) (1987), pp. 141–150.

[245] Halevi, S., Micali, S., Practical and provably-secure commitment schemes from collision-free hashing. In: *Proc. Crypto 96*, Lecture Notes in Computer Science 1109, Springer, Berlin etc., 1996, pp. 201–215.

[246] Halpern, J.Y., van der Meyden, R., A logic for SDSI's linked local name spaces, Journal of Computer Security 9 (2001), pp. 105–142.

[247] Handschuch, T., *Solaris 7 – Systemadministration*, 2nd edition, Springer, Berlin etc., 1999.

[248] Hankerson, D., Menezes, A., Vanstone, S., *Guide to Elliptic Curve Cryptography*, Springer, New York etc., 2004.

[249] Harnik, D., Kilian, J., Naor, M., Reingold, O., Rosen, A., On robust combiners for oblivious transfer and other primitives. In: *Proc. Eurocrypt 05*, Lecture Notes in Computer Science 3494, Springer; Berlin etc., 2005, pp. 96–113.

[250] Harrison, M.A., Ruzzo, W.L., Ullman, J.D., Protection in operating systems, Communications of the ACM 19(8) (1976), pp. 461–471.

[251] Harrison, M.A., Ruzzo, W.L., Monotonic protection systems. In: DeMillo, R.A., et al. (eds.), *Foundations of Secure Computation*, Academic Press, New York, 1978, pp. 337–365.

[252] Härtig, H., Kühnhäuser, W.E., Kowalski, O.C., Lux, W., Reck, W., Streich, H., Goos, G., Architecture of the BirliX operating system, German National Research Center for Computer Science (GMD), 1990.

[253] Härtig, H., Kowalski, O.C., Kühnhauser, W.E., The BirliX security architecture, Journal of Computer Security 2 (1993), pp. 5–22.

[254] Hennessy, J.L., Patterson, D.A., *Computer Architecture: A Quantitative Approach*, 3rd edition, Morgan Kaufmann, San Francisco, 2003.

[255] Hess, A., Holt, L., Jacobson, J., Seamons, K., Content-triggered trust negotiation, ACM Transactions on Information and System Security 7(3) (2004), pp. 428–456.

[256] Hoffman, D.G., Leonard, D.A., Lindner, C.C., Phelps, K.T., Rodger, C.A., Wall, J.R., *Coding Theory: The Essentials*, Marcel Dekker, New York, 1991.

[257] Hoffman, L.J., *Modern Methods for Computer Security and Privacy*, Prentice-Hall, Englewood Cliffs, 1977.

[258] Hopcroft, J.E., Motwani, R., Ullman, J.D., *Introduction into Automata Theory, Languages, and Computation*, 2nd edition, Addison-Wesley, Reading, MA, etc., 2001.

[259] Howell, J., Kotz, D., A formal semantics for SPKI. In: *Proc. 6th European Symposium on Research in Computer Security*, ESORICS 2000, Lecture Notes in Computer Science 1895, Springer, Berlin etc., 2004, pp. 140–158.

[260] Hsiao, D.K., Kerr, D.S., Madnick, S.E., *Computer Security*, Academic Press, New York etc., 1979.

[261] Huang, M.-Y., Jasper, R.J., Wicks, T.M., A large scale distributed intrusion detection framework based on attack strategy analysis, Computer Networks 31(23–24) (1999), pp. 2465–2475.

[262] Hughes, D., Shmatikov, V., Information hiding, anonymity and privacy: A modular approach, Journal of Computer Security 12 (2004), pp. 3–36.

[263] Iheagwara, C., Blyth, A., Singhal, M., A comparative experimental evaluation study of intrusion detection system performance in a gigabit environment, Journal of Computer Security 11 (2003), pp. 1–33.

[264] Ilgun, K., USTAT: a real-time intrusion detection system for Unix. In: *Proc. IEEE Symposium on Security and Privacy*, 1993, pp. 16–29.

[265] Ilgun, K., Kemmerer, R.A., Porras, P.A., State transition analysis: A rule-based intrusion detection approach, IEEE Transactions on Software Engineering 21(3) (1995), pp. 181–199.

[266] ISHTAR Consortium, *Implementing Secure Healthcare Telematics Applications in Europe*, Studies in Health Technology and Informatics 66, IOS Press, Amsterdam etc., 2001.

[267] ISO (International Organization for Standardization), IEC (International Electrotechnical Commission): Joint Technical Committee ISO/IEC JTC 1 on Information Technology, *Database Language SQL* (final committee draft for 4th edition), ISO/IEC FCD 9075, 1997.

[268] ISO (International Organization for Standardization), IEC (International Electrotechnical Commission), *Information Technology – Security Techniques – Message Authentication Codes (MACs) – Part 1: Mechanisms Using a Block Cipher*, ISO/IEC 9797-1, 1999.

[269] ISO (International Organization for Standardization), IEC (International Electrotechnical Commission), *Information Technology – Security Techniques – Message Authentication Codes (MACs) – Part 2: Mechanisms Using a Dedicated Hash-Function*, ISO/IEC 9797-2, 2002.

[270] Ito, M., Saito, A., Nishizeki, T., Multiple assignment schemes for secret sharing, Journal of Cryptology 6 (1993), pp. 15–20.

[271] Jacob, J., Categorising non-interference. In: *Proc. Computer Security Foundations Workshop*, Franconia, NH, 1990, pp. 44–50.

[272] Jaeger, T., Tidswell, J.E., Practical safety in flexible access control models, ACM Transactions on Information and System Security 4(2) (2001), pp. 158–190.

[273] Jajodia, S., Sandhu, R.S., Towards a multilevel secure relational data model. In: *Proc. ACM SIGMOD Int. Conference on Management of Data*, May 1991, pp. 50–59.

[274] Jajodia, S., Samarati, P., Subrahmanian, V.S., Bertino, E., A unified framework for enforcing multiple access control policies. In: *Proc. ACM SIGMOD Int. Conference on Management of Data*, May 1997, pp. 474–485.

[275] Jajodia, S., Samarati, P., Sapino, M.L., Subrahmanian, V.S., Flexible support for multiple access control policies, ACM Transactions on Database Systems 26(2) (2001), pp. 214–260.

[276] Jajodia, S., Atluri, V., Keefe, T., McCollum, C.D., Mukkamala, R., Multilevel secure transaction processing, Journal of Computer Security 9 (2001), pp. 165–195.

[277] Jalote, P., *Fault Tolerance in Distributed Systems*, Prentice Hall, Englewood Cliffs, 1994.

[278] Javitz, H.S., Valdes, A., The SRI IDES statistical anomaly detector. In: *Proc. IEEE Symposium on Security and Privacy*, 1991, pp. 316–326.

[279] Jha, S., Reps, T., Model checking SPKI/SDSI, Journal of Computer Security 12 (2004), pp. 317–353.

[280] Johnson, D., Menezes, A., Vanstone, S., The elliptic curve digital signature algorithm (ECDSA), International Journal on Information Security 1(1) (2001), pp. 36–63.

[281] Jones, A.K., Lipton, R.J., The enforcement of security policies for computation. In: *Proc. 5th Symposium on Operating System Principles*, Operating Systems Review 9(5) (1975), pp. 197–206.

[282] Jones, A.K., Liskov, B.H., A language extension for controlling access to shared data, IEEE Transactions on Software Engineering 2(4) (1976), pp. 227–285.

[283] Jones, A.K., Liskov, B.H., A language extension for expressing constraints on data access, Communications of the ACM 21(5) (1978), pp. 358–367.

[284] Josang, A., A subjective metric of authentication. In: *Proc. 5th European Symposium on Research in Computer Security*, ESORICS 1998, Lecture Notes in Computer Science 1485, Springer, Berlin etc., 1998, pp. 329–344.

[285] Josang, A., Ismail, R., Boyd, C., A survey of trust and reputation systems for online service provision, Decision Support Systems 43(2) (2007), pp. 618–644.

[286] Joshi, J.B.D., Bertino, E., Shafiq, B., Ghafoor, A., Dependencies and separation of duty constraints in GTRBAC. In: *Proc. 8th ACM Symposium on Access Control Models and Technologies*, SACMAT 03, June 2003, Como, Italy, pp. 51–64.

[287] Julisch, K., Clustering intrusion detection alarms to support rot cause analysis, ACM Transactions on Information and System Security 6(4) (2003), pp. 443–471.

[288] Karger, P.A., Schell, R.R., Thirty years later: Lessons from the Multics security evaluation. In: *Proc. 18th Annual Security Applications Conference*, ACSAC 02, IEEE, 2002, pp. 119–126.

[289] Kallenberg, O., *Foundations of Modern Probability*, Springer, New York etc., 2002.

[290] Karnin, E.D., Greene, J.W., Hellman, M.E., On secret sharing schemes, IEEE Transactions on Information Theory 29(1) (1983), pp. 231–241.

[291] Kilian, J., Basing cryptography on oblivious transfer. In: *Proc. 20th ACM Symposium on Theory of Computing*, STOC 88, ACM, 1988, pp. 20–31.

[292] Knorr, K., Dynamic access control through Petri net workflows. In: *Proc. 16th Annual Computer Security Applications Conference*, ACSAC 00, New Orleans, Dec. 2000, pp. 159–167.

[293] Knuth, D., *The Art of Computer Programming – Volume 2: Seminumerical Algorithms*, Addison-Wesley, Reading, MA, etc., 1981.

[294] Ko, C., Ruschitzka, M., Levitt, K., Execution monitoring of security-critical programs in a distributed system. In: *Proc. IEEE Symposium on Security and Privacy*, 1997, pp. 175–187.

[295] Koblitz, N., Elliptic curve cryptosystems, Mathematics of Computation 48 (1987), pp. 203–209.

[296] Koch, M., Mancini, L.V., Parisi-Presicce, F., Decidability of safety in graph-based models for access control. In: *Proc. 7th European Symposium on Research in Computer Security*, ESORICS 2002, Oct. 2002, Lecture Notes in Computer Science 2502, Springer, Berlin etc., 2002, pp. 229–243.

[297] Koch, M., Mancini, L.V., Parisi-Presicce, F., A graph-based formalism for RBAC, ACM Transactions on Information and System Security 5(3) (2002), pp. 332–365.

[298] Kohl, J.T., Neuman, B.C., Ts'o, T.Y., The evolution of the Kerberos authentification service. In: Brazier, F., Johansen, D. (eds.), *Distributed Open Systems*, IEEE Computer Society Press, 1994, pp. 78–94.

[299] Kolmogorov, A.N., Three approaches to the concept of "the amount of information" [in Russian], Problems of Information Transmission 1 (1965), 3–11.

[300] Kowalski, O.C., Härtig, H., Protection in the BirliX operating system. In: *Proc. 10th Int. Conf. on Distributed Computing Systems*, IEEE, 1990, pp. 160–166.

[301] Kruegel, C., Valeur, F., Vigna, G., *Intrusion Detection and Correlation: Challenges and Solutions*, Springer, New York, 2005.

[302] Küsters, R., Simulation-based security with inexhaustible interactive Turing machines. In: *19th IEEE Computer Security Foundations Workshop*, CSFW-2006, IEEE Computer Society Press, 2006, pp. 309–320.

[303] Küsters, R., Truderung, T., On the automatic analysis of recursive security protocols with XOR. In: *24th Annual Symposium on Theoretical Aspects of Computer Science*, STACS 2007, Lecture Notes in Computer Science 4393, Springer, Berlin etc., 2007, pp. 646–657.

[304] Lai, X., *On the Design and Security of Block Ciphers*, ETH Series in Information Processing 1, Hartung-Gorre, Konstanz, 1992.

[305] Lai, X., Massey, J.L., A proposal for a new block encryption standard. In: *Proc. Advances in Cryptology*, EUROCRYPT 90, Lecture Notes in Computer Science 473, Springer, Berlin etc., 1991, pp. 389–404.

[306] Lamport, L., Time, clocks, and the ordering of events in a distributed system, Communications of the ACM 21(7) (1978), pp. 558–565.

[307] Lamport, L., Concurrent reading and writing of clocks, Transactions on Computing Systems 8(4) (1990), pp. 305–310.

[308] Lampson, B., A note on the confinement problem, Communications of the ACM 16(10) (1973), pp. 613–615.

[309] Lampson, B., Abadi, M., Burrows, M., Wobber, E., Authentication in distributed systems: Theory and practice, ACM Transactions on Computer Systems 10, 4 (1992), pp. 265–310.

[310] Lane, T., Brodley, C.E., Temporal sequence learning and data reduction for anomaly detection, ACM Transactions on Information and System Security 2(3) (1999), pp. 295–331.

[311] Laprie, J.-C. (ed.), *Dependability: Basic Concepts and Terminology*, Springer, Berlin etc., 1992.

[312] Lee, W., Stolfo, S.L., A framework for constructing features and models for intrusion detection systems, ACM Transactions on Information and System Security, 3(4) (2000), pp. 227–261.

[313] Leiss, E.J., *Principles of Data Security*, Plenum Press, New York, 1982.

[314] Levin, L.A., Randomness and non-determinism, Journal of Symbolic Logic 58 (1993), pp. 1102–1103.

[315] Lewis, P.M., Bernstein, A., Kifer, M., *Database and Transaction Processing: An Application-Oriented Approach*, Addison-Wesley, Boston etc., 2002.

[316] Li, N., Mitchell, J.C., Winsborough, W.H., Design of a role-based trust-management framework. In: *Proc. IEEE Symposium on Security and Privacy*, 2002, pp. 114–130.

[317] Li, N., Winsborough, W.H., Mitchell, J.C., Distributed credential chain discovery in trust management, Journal of Computer Security 11 (2003), pp. 35–86.

[318] Li, N., Grosof, B.N., Feigenbaum, J., Delegation logic: A logic-based approach to distributed authorization, ACM Transactions on Information and System Security 6(1) (2003), pp. 128–171.

[319] Li, N., Mitchell, J.C., Understanding SPKI/SDSI using first-order logic, International Journal of Information Security 5 (2006), pp. 48–64.

[320] Libkin, L., *Elements of Finite Model Theory*, Springer, Berlin etc., 2004.

[321] Lidl, R., Niederreiter, H., *Finite Fields*, 2nd edition, Cambridge University Press, Cambridge, 1997.

[322] Lindgreen, E.R., Herschberg, I.S., On the validity of the Bell–LaPadula model, Computers & Security 13 (1994), pp. 317–333.

[323] Lindquist, U., Porras, P.A., Detecting computer and network misuse through the production-based expert system toolset (P-BEST). In: *Proc. IEEE Symposium on Security and Privacy*, 1999, pp. 146–161.

[324] Lipton, R.J., Snyder, L., A linear time algorithm for deciding subject security, Journal of the ACM 24(3) (1977), pp. 455–464.

[325] Lipton, R.J., Budd, T.A., On classes of protection systems. In: DeMillo, R.A., et al., (eds.), *Foundations of Secure Computation*, Academic Press, New York, 1978, pp. 281–298.

[326] Lochovsky, F.H., Woo, C.C., Role-based security in data base management systems. In: Landwehr, C.E., (ed.), *Database Security: Status and Prospects*, Elsevier Science (North Holland), Amsterdam etc., 1988, pp. 173–185.

[327] Lockmann, A., Minsky, N., Unidirectional transport of rights and take-grant control, IEEE Transactions on Software Engineering SE-8(6) (1982), pp. 597–604.

[328] Lundin, E., Jonsson, E., Anomaly-based intrusion detection: Privacy concerns and other problems, Computer Networks 34(4) (2000), pp. 623–640.

[329] Lunt, T.F., Denning, D.E., Schell, R.R., Heckman, M., Shockley, W.R., The SeaView security model, IEEE Transactions on Software Engineering 16(6) (1990), pp. 593–607.

[330] Mantel, H., Preserving information flow properties under refinement. In: *Proc. IEEE Symposium on Security and Privacy*, 2001, Oakland, pp. 78–91.

[331] Mantel, H., On the composition of secure systems. In: *Proc. IEEE Symposium on Security and Privacy*, 2002, Oakland, pp. 88–101.

[332] Mantel, H., *A Uniform Framework for the Formal Specification and Verification of Information Flow Security*, Ph.D. thesis, Universität des Saarlandes, Saarbrücken, 2003.

[333] Marchette, D.J., *Computer Intrusion Detection and Network Monitoring: A Statistical Viewpoint*, Springer, New York etc., 2001.

[334] Martin-Löf, P., The definition of randomness, Information and Control 9 (1966), pp. 602–619.

[335] Massias, H., Serret Avila, X., Quisquater, J.-J., Timestamps: Main issues on their use and implementation. In: *8th Workshop on Enabling Technologies: Infrastructure for Collaboration*, WETICE 99, IEEE, 1999, pp. 178–183.

[336] Maurer, U., Modelling a public-key infrastructure. In: *Proc. 4th European Sympo-sium on Research in Computer Security*, ESORICS 96, Lecture Notes in Computer Science 1146, Springer, Berlin etc., 1996, pp. 325–350.

[337] McCullough, D., Noninterference and the compositionality of security properties. In: *Proc. IEEE Symposium on Security and Privacy*, 1988, pp. 177–186.

[338] McCullough, D., A hookup theorem for multilevel security, IEEE Transactions on Software Engineering 16(6) (1990), pp. 563–568.

[339] McGraw, G., Felton, E.W., *Securing Java: Getting Down to Business with Mobile Code*, Wiley, New York etc., 1999.

[340] McHugh, J., Testing intrusion detection systems: A critique of the 1998 and 1999 DARPA intrusion detection system evaluation as performed by Lincoln Laboratory, ACM Transactions on Information and System Security 3(4) (2000), pp. 262–294.

[341] McKusick, M.K., Bostic, K., Karels, M.J., Quarterman, J.S., *The Design and Imple-mentation of the 4.4BSD Operating System*, Addison-Wesley, Reading, MA, etc., 1996.

[342] McLean, J., A comment on the "Basic Security Theorem" of Bell and LaPa-dula, Information Processing Letters 20 (1985), pp. 67–70.

[343] McLean, J., Reasoning about security models. In: *Proc. IEEE Symposium on Security and Privacy*, 1987, Oakland, pp. 123–131.

[344] McLean, J., Proving noninterference and functional correctness using traces, Journal of Computer Security 1(1) (1992), pp. 37–57.

[345] McLean, J., A general theory of composition for a class of "possibilistic" security properties, IEEE Transactions on Software Engineering 22(1) (1996), pp. 53–67.

[346] Meadows, C., Ordering from Satan's menu: A survey of requirements specification for formal analysis of cryptographic protocols, Science of Computer Programming 50 (2004), pp. 3–22.

[347] Menezes, A.J., van Oorschot, P.C., Vanstone, S.A., *Handbook of Applied Cryptogra-phy*, CRC Press, Boca Raton etc., 1997.

[348] Meier, W., On the security of the IDEA block cipher. In: *Proc. Advances in Cryptol-ogy*, Eurocrypt 93, Lecture Notes in Computer Science 765, Springer, Berlin etc., 1994, pp. 371–385.

[349] Merkle, R.C., Protocols for public key cryptosystems. In: *Proc. IEEE Sympsium on Security and Privacy*, 1980, Oakland, pp. 122–134.

[350] Merkle, R.C., A fast software one-way hash function, Journal of Cryptology 3 (1990), pp. 43–58.

[351] Michael, C., Ghosh, A., Simple state-based approaches to program-based anomaly detection, ACM Transactions on Information and System Security 5(3) (2002), pp. 203–237.

[352] Millen, J.K., Security kernel validation in practice, Communications of the ACM 19(5) (1976), pp. 243–250.

[353] Miller, S.P., Neuman, B.C., Schiller, J.I., Saltzer, J.H., Section E.2.1: Kerberos authentification and authorization system, *M.I.T. Project Athena*, Technical Report, Cambridge, MA, 1987.

[354] Miller, V.S., Uses of elliptic curves in cryptography. In: *Proc. Crypto 85*, Lecture Notes in Computer Science 218, Springer, Berlin etc., 1986, pp. 417–426.

[355] Mills, D., Improved algorithms for synchronizing computer network clocks, IEEE/ ACM Transactions on Networks 3 (1995), pp. 245–254.

[356] Minsky, N., An operation-control scheme for authorization in computer systems, International Journal of Computer and Information Sciences 7(2) (1978), pp. 157–191.

[357] Minsky, N., Ungureanu, V., Law-governed interaction: A coordination and control mechanism for heterogeneous distributed systems, ACM Transactions on Software Engineering and Methodology 9(3) (2000), pp. 273–305.

[358] Mitchell, J.C., *Concepts in Programming Languages*, Cambridge University Press, Cambridge etc., 2002.

[359] Mounji, A., Charlier, B.L., Zampunieris, D., Habra, N., Distributed audit trail analysis. In: *Proc. ISOC 95 Symposium on Network and Distributed System Security*, 1995, pp. 102–112.

[360] Myers, A.C., Liskov, B., Protecting privacy using the decentralized label model, ACM Transactions on Software Engineering and Methodology 9(4) (2000), pp. 410–442.

[361] Naor, M., Bit commitment using pseudorandomness, Journal of Cryptology 4(2) (1991), pp. 151–158.

[362] Naor, M., Ostrovsky, R., Venkatesan, R., Yung, M., Zero-knowledge arguments for NP can be based on general assumptions, Journal of Cryptology 11 (1998), pp. 87–108.

[363] National Bureau of Standards, *Data Encryption Standard*, NBS FIPS PUB 46, 1980.

[364] National Bureau of Standards, *DES Modes of Operation*, NBS FIPS PUB 81, 1977.

[365] National Institute of Standards and Technology, U.S. Department of Commerce, *Advanced Encryption Standard*, NIST Federal Information Processing Standards Publication 197, 2001.

[366] National Institute of Standards and Technology, U.S. Department of Commerce, *Secure Hash Standard*, NIST Federal Information Processing Standards Publication 180-2, 2002.

[367] National Institute of Standards and Technology, U.S. Department of Commerce, *Digital Signature Standard*, NIST Federal Information Processing Standards Publication 186-2, 2000.

[368] Nerode, A., Shore, R.A., *Logic for Applications*, 2nd edition, Springer, New York etc., 1997.

[369] Neuman, B., Ts'o, T., Kerberos: An authentication service for computer networks, IEEE Communications 32(9) (1994), pp. 33–38.

[370] Neumann, P.G., *Computer Related Risks*, Addison-Wesley, Reading, MA, etc., 1995.

[371] Neumann, P.G. (moderator), *The Risks Digest: Forum on Risks to the Public in Computers and Related Systems*, http://catless.ncl.ac.uk/risks.

[372] Ning, P., Xu, D., Learning attack strategies from intrusion alerts. In: *Proc. 10th ACM Conference on Computer and Communications Security*, CCS 03, ACM, 2003, pp. 200–209.

[373] Ning, P., Cui, Y., Reeves, D.S., Xu, D., Techniques and tools for analyzing intrusion alerts, ACM Transactions on Information and System Security 7(2) (2004), pp. 274–318.

[374] Ning, P., Jajodia, S., Wang, X.S., *Intrusion Detection in Distributed Systems: An Abstraction-Based Approach*, Kluwer, Boston etc., 2004.

[375] Oberschelp, W., Vossen, G., *Rechneraufbau und Rechnerstrukturen*, 9th edition, Oldenbourg, Munich/Vienna, 2003.

[376] O'Halloran, C., A calculus of information flow. In: *Proc. 1st European Symposium on Research in Computer Security*, Toulouse, Oct. 1990, pp. 147–159.

[377] Olivier, M., von Solms, S.H., A taxonomy for secure object-oriented databases, ACM Transactions on Database Systems 19(1) (1994), pp. 3–46.

[378] OMG (Object Management Group), *Common Secure Interoperability*, OMG Document orbos/96-06-20, July 1996.

[379] OMG (Object Management Group), *CORBA Security*, OMG Documents 96-08-03 through 96-08-06, July 1996.

[380] Oracle Corporation, *Oracle 9i – SQL Reference*, Release 2 (9.2), March 2002.

[381] Organick, E.I., *The Multics System: An Examination of its Structure*, MIT Press, Cambridge, MA, etc., 1972.

[382] Osborne, S., Sandhu, R., Munawar, Q., Configuring role-based access control to enforce mandatory and discretionary access control policies, ACM Transactions on Information and System Security 3(2) (2000), pp. 85–106.

[383] Park, J.S., Sandhu, R., Gail, J.A., Role-based access control on the Web, ACM Transactions on Information and System Security 4(1) (2001), pp. 37–71.

[384] Parker, D.B., Restating the foundation of information security. In: *Proc. IFIP/SEC 92*, Singapore, pp. 159–171.

[385] Patterson, D.A., Hennessy, J.L., *Computer Organization and Design: The Hardware/Software Interface*, 3rd edition, Morgan Kaufmann, San Francisco, 2004.

[386] Pearson, S. (ed.), Balacheff, B., Chen, L., Plaquin, D., Proudler, G., *Trusted Computing Platforms: TCPA Technology in Context*, Prentice-Hall, Upper Saddle River etc., 2003.

[387] Pedersen, T.P., Non-interactive and information-theoretic secure verifiable secret sharing. In: *Proc. Crypto 91*, Lecture Notes in Computer Science 576, Springer, Berlin etc., 1992, pp. 129–140.

[388] Pedersen, T.P., Pfitzmann, B., Fail-stop signatures, SIAM Journal on Computing 26(2) (1997), pp. 291–330.

[389] Pfitzmann, A., *Diensteintegrierende Kommunikationsnetze mit teilnehmerüberprüfbarem Datenschutz*, Informatik-Fachberichte 234, Springer, Berlin etc., 1990.

[390] Pfitzmann, A., Pfitzmann, B., Schunter, M., Waidner, M., Trusting mobile user devices and security modules, IEEE Computer 30(2) (1997), pp. 61–68.

[391] Pfitzmann, A., Hansen, M., Anonymity, unlinkability, unobservability, pseudonymity, and identity management – a consolidated proposal for terminology, http://dud.inf.tu-dresden.de/Anon_Terminology.shtml.

[392] Pfitzmann, B., *Digital Signature Schemes: General Framework and Fail-Stop Signatures*, Lecture Notes in Computer Science 1100, Springer, Berlin etc., 1996.

[393] Pfitzmann, B., Sadeghi, A.-R., Coin-based anonymous fingerprinting. In: *Proc. Eurocrypt 99*, Lecture Notes in Computer Science 1592, Springer, Berlin etc., 1999, pp. 150–164.

[394] Pfleeger, C.P., *Security in Computing*, 2nd edition, Prentice-Hall, Englewood Cliffs etc., 1997.

[395] Pieprzyk, J., Hardjono, T., Seberry, J., *Fundamentals of Computer Security*, Springer, Berlin etc., 2003.

[396] Pless, V., *Introduction to the Theory of Error-Correcting Codes*, Wiley, New York etc., 1989.

[397] Popek, G.J., Farber, D.A., A model for verification of data security in operating systems, Communications of the ACM 21(9) (1978), pp. 737–749.

[398] Pottier, F., Skalka, C., Smith, S., A systematic approach to static access control, ACM Transactions on Programming Languages and Systems 27(2) (2005), pp. 344–382.

[399] Preneel, B., van Oorschot, P.C., On the security of iterated message authentication codes, IEEE Transactions on Information Theory 45(1) (1999), pp. 188–199.

[400] Rabin, M., How to exchange secrets by oblivious transfer, TR-81, Aiken Computation Laboratory, Harvard University, 1981.

[401] Raghavarao, D., *Constructions and Combinatorial Problems in Design of Experiments*, Wiley, New York etc., 1971.

[402] Ramanathan, P., Shin, K., Butler, R., Fault-tolerant clock synchronization in distributed systems, IEEE Computer 23(10) (1990), pp. 33–42.

[403] Rannenberg, K., *Zertifizierung mehrseitiger IT-Sicherheit: Kriterien und organisatorische Rahmenbedingungen*, Vieweg, Braunschweig/Wiesbaden, 1998.

[404] Ray, I., Ammann, P., Jajodia, S., A semantic-based transaction processing model for multilevel transactions, Journal of Computer Security 6 (1998), pp. 181–217.

[405] Ray, I., Chakraborty, S., A vector model of trust for developing trustworthy systems. In: *Proc. 9th European Symposium on Research in Computer Security*, ESORICS 04, Lecture Notes in Computer Science 3193, Springer, Berlin etc., 2004, pp. 260–275.

[406] Reiter, M.K., Rubin, A.D., Crowds: Anonymity for web transactions, ACM Transactions on Information and System Security 1(1) (1998), pp. 66–92.

[407] Ritchie, D.M., Thompson, K., The UNIX time-sharing system, Communications of the ACM 7(7) (1974), pp. 365–375.

[408] Ritchie, D.M., *The Evolution of the UNIX Time-Sharing System*. In: *Proc. Symposium on Language Design and Programming Methodology*, Lecture Notes in Computer Science 79, Springer, Berlin etc., 1979, pp. 25–36.

[409] Rivest, R.L., Shamir, A., Adleman, L.M., A method for obtaining digital signatures and public key cryptosystems, Communications of the ACM 21(2) (1978), pp. 120–126.

[410] Rivest, R.L., The MD4 message digest algorithm. In: *Proc. Crypto 90*, Lecture Notes in Computer Science 537, Springer, Berlin etc., 1990, pp. 303–311.

[411] Rivest, R.L., The MD5 message digest algorithm, Network Working Group RFC 1321, 1992.

[412] Robinson, A., Voronkov, A. (eds.), *Handbook of Automated Reasoning*, Volume I + II, Elsevier Science, Amsterdam; MIT Press, Cambridge, 2001.

[413] Rogers, H., *Theory of Recursive Functions and Effective Computability*, McGraw-Hill, New York etc., 1967.

[414] Rueppel, R.A., *Analysis and Design of Stream Ciphers*, Springer, Berlin etc., 1986.

[415] Rushby, J. Noninterference, transitivity, and channel-control security policies, Technical Report CSL-92-02, SRI International, 1992.

[416] Ryan, P., Mathematical models of computer security. In: Focardi, R., Gorrieri, R. (eds.), *Foundations of Security Analysis and Design*, Lecture Notes in Computer Science 2171, Springer, Berlin etc., 2001, pp. 1–62.

[417] Sailer, R., Zhang, X., Jaeger, T., van Doorn, L., Design and implementation of a TCG-based measurement architecture. In: *Proc. 13th USENIX Security Symposium*, San Diego, The USENIX Association, 2004, pp. 223–238.

[418] Sailer, R., Zhang, X., Jaeger, T., van Doorn, L., Attestation-based policy enforcement for remote access. In: *Proc. 11th ACM Computer and Communications Security Conference*, CCS 04, ACM Press, New York, 2004, pp. 308–317.

[419] Salomaa, A., *Public-Key Cryptography*, 2nd edition, Springer, Berlin etc., 1996.

[420] Saltzer, J.H., Protection and the control of information sharing in Multics, Communications of the ACM 17(7) (1974), pp. 388–402.

[421] Saltzer, J.H., Schroeder, M.D., The protection of information in computer systems, Proceedings of the IEEE 63(9) (1975), pp. 1278–1308.

[422] Saltzer, J.H., Reed, D.P., Clark, D.D., End-to-end arguments in system design, ACM Transactions on Computer Systems 2(4) (1984), pp. 277–288.

[423] Samarati, P., De Capitani di Vimercati, S., Access control: Policies, models, and mechanisms. In: Focardi, R., Gorrieri, R. (eds.), *Foundations of Security Analysis and Design*, Lecture Notes in Computer Science 2171, Springer, Berlin etc, 2001, pp. 137–196.

[424] Sandhu, R.S., The schematic protection model: Its definition and analysis for acyclic attenuating schemes, Journal of the ACM 35(2) (1988), pp. 404–432.

[425] Sandhu, R.S., The demand operation in the schematic protection model, Information Processing Letters 32 (1989), pp. 213–219.

[426] Sandhu, R.S., The typed access matrix model. In: *Proc. IEEE Symposium on Security and Privacy*, 1992, Oakland, pp. 122–136.

[427] Sandhu, R.S., Jajodia, S., Polyinstantiation for cover stories. In: *Proc. 2nd European Symposium on Research in Computer Security*, ESORICS 92, Lecture Notes in Computer Science 648, Springer, Berlin etc., 1992, pp. 307–328.

[428] Sandhu, R.S., Lattice-based access control, IEEE Computer 26(11) (1993), pp. 9–19.

[429] Sandhu, R.S., Samarati, P., Access control: Principles and practice, IEEE Communications Magazine, Sept. 1994, pp. 40–48.

[430] Sandhu, R.S., Workshop summary. In: *Proc. 1st ACM Workshop on Role-Based Access Control*, RBAC 95, 1995, pp. I1–I7.

[431] Sandhu, R.S., Coyne, E.J., Feinstein, H.L., Youman, C.E., Role-based access control models, IEEE Computer 29(2) (1996), pp. 38–47.

[432] Sandhu, R.S., Bhamidipati, V., Role-based administration of user-role assignment: The URA97 model and its Oracle implementation, Journal of Computer Security 7(4) (1999), pp. 317–342.

[433] Santen, T., A formal framework for confidentiality-preserving refinement. In: *Proc. 11th European Symposium on Research in Computer Security*, ESORICS 06, Lecture Notes in Computer Science 4189, Springer, Berlin etc., 2006, pp. 225–242.

[434] Saunders, G., Hitchens, M., Varadharajan, V., Role-based access control and the access control matrix, Operating Systems Review 35(4) (2001), pp. 6–20.

[435] Schnorr, C.P., A uniform approach to the definition of randomness, Mathematical System Theory 5 (1971), pp. 9–28.

[436] Schneier, B., *E-Mail Security: How to Keep Your Electronic Messages Private*, Wiley, New York etc., 1995.

[437] Schneier, B., *Applied Cryptography*, 2nd edition, Wiley, New York etc., 1996.

[438] SEISMED Consortium, *Data Security for Health Care – Volume I: Management Guidelines; Volume II: Technical Guidelines; Volume III: User Guidelines*, Studies in Health Care and Informatics 31–33, IOS Press, Amsterdam etc., 1996.

[439] Sejong, O., Seog, P., Task-role-based access control model, Information Systems 28(6) (2003), pp. 533–562.

[440] Sehti, R., *Programming Languages: Concepts and Constructs*, 2nd edition, Addison-Wesley, Reading, MA, etc., 1996.

[441] Serjantov, A., Dingledine, R., Syverson, P.F., From a trickle to a flood: Active attacks on several mix types. In: *Proc. 5th International Workshop on Information Hiding*,

2002, Lecture Notes in Computer Science 2578, Springer, Berlin etc., 2003, pp. 36–52.

[442] Shamir, A., How to share a secret, Communications of the ACM 22 (1979), pp. 612–613.

[443] Shannon, C.E., A mathematical theory of communications, Bell System Technical Journal 27 (1948), pp. 379–423, 623–656.

[444] Shannon, C.E., Communication theory of secrecy systems, Bell System Technical Journal 28(4) (1949), pp. 656–715.

[445] Sicherman, G.L., de Jonge, W., van de Riet, R.P., Answering queries without revealing secrets, ACM Transactions on Database Systems 8(1) (1983), pp. 41–59.

[446] Siewe, F., Cau, A., Zedan, H., A compositional framework for access control policies enforcement. In: *FMSE 03*, Oct. 30, Washington, DC, pp. 32–42.

[447] Silberschatz, A., Galvin, P.B., Gagne, G., *Operating System Concepts*, 6th edition, Addison-Wesley, Reading, MA, etc., 2001.

[448] Simmons, G.J., Authentication theory/coding theory. In: *Advances in Cryptology*, Crypto 84, Lecture Notes in Computer Science 196, Springer, Berlin etc., 1985, pp. 411–432.

[449] Simmons, G.J., An introduction to shared secret and/or shared control schemes and their applications. In: Simmons, G.J. (ed.), *Contemporary Cryptology: The Science of Information Integrity*, IEEE Press, New York, 1992, pp. 441–497.

[450] Simmons, G.J., A survey on information authentication. In: Simmons, G.J. (ed.), *Contemporary Cryptology: The Science of Information Integrity*, IEEE Press, New York, 1992, pp. 379–419.

[451] Smid, M.E., Branstad, D.K., The Data Encryption Standard: Past and future. In: Simmons, G.J. (ed.), *Contemporary Cryptology: The Science of Information Integrity*, IEEE Press, New York, 1992, pp. 43–64.

[452] Snyder, L., Theft and conspiracy in the take-grant model, Journal of Computer and System Sciences 23(3) (1981), pp. 333–347.

[453] Snyder, L., Formal models of capability-based protection systems, IEEE Transactions on Computers C-30(3) (1981), pp. 172–181.

[454] Sobirey, M., Fischer-Hübner, S., Rannenberg, K., Pseudonymous audit for privacy enhanced intrusion detection. In: *Proc. IFIP TC11 13th International Conference on Information Security*, SEC 97, Chapman & Hall, London etc., 1997, pp. 151–163.

[455] Solworth, J.A., Sloan, R.H., Security property based administrative controls. In: *Proc. 9th European Symposium on Research in Computer Security*, ESORICS 04, Lecture Notes in Computer Science 3193, Springer, Berlin etc., 2004, pp. 244–259.

[456] Soshi, M., Safety analysis of the dynamic-typed access matrix model. In: *Proc. 6th European Symposium on Research in Computer Security*, ESORICS 2000, Lecture Notes in Computer Science 1895, Springer, Berlin etc., 2000, pp. 106–121.

[457] Soshi, M., Maekawa, M., Okamoto, E., The dynamic-typed access matrix model and decidability of the safety problem, IEICE Transactions on Information and Systems 87-A(1) (2004), pp. 190–203.

[458] Stadler, M., Piveteau, J.-M., Camenisch, J., Fair blind signatures. In: *Proc. Eurocrypt 95*, Lecture Notes in Computer Science 921, Springer, Berlin etc., 1995, pp. 209–219.

[459] Stadler, M., Publicly verifiable secret sharing. In: *Proc. Eurocrypt 96*, Lecture Notes in Computer Science 1070, Springer, Berlin etc., 1996, pp. 190–199.

[460] Stajano, F., *Security for Ubiquitous Computing*, Wiley, New York etc., 2002.

[461] Stallings, W., *Operating Systems*, 5th edition, Prentice-Hall, Upper Saddle River etc., 2005.

[462] Stallings, W., *Network and Internetwork Security: Principles and Practice*, Prentice-Hall, Upper Saddle River etc., 1995.

[463] Stallings, W., *Cryptography and Network Security*, Prentice-Hall, Upper Saddle River etc., 2003.

[464] Steiner, J.G., Neuman, B.C., Schiller, J.I., Kerberos: An authentication service for open network systems. In: *Usenix Conference Proceedings*, Dallas, Texas, 1988, pp. 191–202.

[465] Stinson, D.R., Some constructions and bounds of authentication codes, Journal of Cryptology 1 (1988), pp. 37–51.

[466] Stinson, D.R., The combinatorics of authentication and secrecy codes, Journal of Cryptology 2 (1990), pp. 23–49.

[467] Stinson, D.R., Combinatorial characterizations of authentication codes, Designs, Codes, and Cryptography 2 (1992), pp. 175–187.

[468] Stinson, D.R., An explication of secret sharing schemes, Designs, Codes and Cryptography 2 (1992), pp. 357–390.

[469] Stinson, D.R., Decomposition structures for secret sharing schemes, IEEE Transactions on Information Theory 40 (1994), pp. 118–125.

[470] Stinson, D.R., *Cryptography: Theory and Practice*, 1st edition, Chapman & Hall/ CRC Press, Boca Raton etc., 1995; 3rd edition, 2006.

[471] Sutherland, D., A model of information. In: *Proc. 9th National Computer Science Conference*, 1986, pp. 175–183.

[472] Tanenbaum, A.S., *Structured Computer Organization*, 4th edition, Prentice-Hall, Englewood Cliffs, 1999.

[473] Tanenbaum, A.S., *Modern Operating Systems*, 2nd edition, Prentice-Hall, Upper Saddle River, 2001.

[474] Tanenbaum, A.S., *Computer Networks*, 4th edition, Prentice-Hall, Upper Saddle River, 2003.

[475] Tanenbaum, A.S., Woodhull, A.S., *Operating Systems: Design and Implementation*, 3rd edition, Prentice-Hall, Upper Saddle River, 2006.

[476] Tanenbaum, A.S., Mullender, S., van Renesse, R., Using sparse capabilities in a distributed operating system. In: *Proc. 6th International Conference on Distributed Computing Systems*, IEEE, 1986, pp. 558–563.

[477] Tanenbaum, A.S., van Renesse, R., van Staveren, H., Sharp, G., Mullender, S., Jansen, J., van Rossum, G., Experiences with the Amoeba distributed operating system, Communiations of the ACM 33(12) (1990), pp. 46–63.

[478] Tanenbaum, A.S., van Steen, M., *Distributed Systems: Principles and Paradigms*, Prentice-Hall, Upper Saddle River, 2002.

[479] Theriault, M., Newman, A., *Oracle Security Handbook*, McGraw-Hill, New York etc., 2001.

[480] Tilborg, H.C.A. van, *Fundamentals of Cryptology: A Professional Reference and Interactive Tutorial*, Kluwer, Boston etc., 2000.

[481] Tilborg, H.C.A. van (Editor-in-chief), *Encyclopedia of Cryptography and Security*, Springer, New York, 2005.

[482] Ting, T.C., A user-role based data security approach. In: Landwehr, C.E. (ed.), *Database Security: Status and Prospects*, Elsevier Science (North Holland), Amsterdam etc., 1988, pp. 187–208.

[483] Traub, J.F., Yemini, Y., Wozniakowski, H., The statistical security of a statistical database, ACM Transactions on Database Systems 9(4) (1984), pp. 672–679.

[484] Trusted Computing Group, *TCG Specification Architecture Overview*, Revision 1.2, 2004, https://www.trustedcomputinggroup.org.

[485] Trusted Computing Group – Infrastructure Working Group, *Reference Architecture for Interoperability (Part I)*, Version 1.0, Revision 1, 2005, https://www.trustedcomputinggroup.org.

[486] Trusted Computing Group, *TPM Main Part 1, Design Principles*, Version 1.2, Revision 85, 2005, https://www.trustedcomputinggroup.org.

[487] Trusted Computing Group, *TPM Main Part 2, TPM Structures*, Version 1.2, Revision 85, 2005, https://www.trustedcomputinggroup.org.

[488] Trusted Computing Platform Alliance, *Building a Foundation of Trust in the PC* (White Paper)/*TCPA Main Specification*, 2000–2003, http://www.trustedcomputing.org.

[489] Ullman, J.D., Widom, J., *A First Course on Database Systems*, Prentice-Hall, Upper Saddle River, 1997.

[490] Viega, J., McGraw, G., *Building Secure Software*, Addison-Wesley, Boston etc., 2001.

[491] Vigna, G., Kemmerer, R.A., NetSTAT: A network-based intrusion detection system, Journal of Computer Security 7(1) (1999), pp. 37–71.

[492] Waidner, M., Unconditional sender and recipient untraceability in spite of active attacks. In: *Proc. Eurocrypt 89*, Lecture Notes in Computer Science 434, Springer, Berlin etc., 1990, pp. 302–319.

[493] Wallach, D.S., Felton, E.W., Understanding Java stack inspection. In: *Proc. IEEE Symposium on Security and Privacy*, Oakland, May 1998, pp. 1–12.

[494] Wang, L., Li, Y., Wijesekera, D., Jajodia, S., Precisely answering multi-dimensional range queries without privacy breaches. In: *Proc. 8th European Symposium on Research in Computer Security*, ESORICS 03, Lecture Notes in Computer Science 2808, Springer, Berlin etc., 2003, pp. 100–115.

[495] Wang, X., Feng, D., Lai, X., Yu, H., Collisions for hash functions MD4, MD5, HAVAL-128 and RIPEMD, Cryptology ePrint Archive, Report 2004/199, 2004, http://eprint.iacr.org/2004/199.

[496] Wegener, I., *Complexity Theory: Exploring the Limits of Efficient Algorithms*, Springer, Berlin etc., 2005.

[497] Weikum, G., Vossen, G., *Transactional Information Systems*, Academic Press, San Diego/London, 2002.

[498] Wespi, A., Dacier, M., Debar, H., Intrusion detection using variable-length audit trail patterns. In: *Proc. 3rd International Symposium on Recent Advances in Intrusion Detection*, RAID 2000, Lecture Notes in Computer Science 1907, Springer, Berlin etc., 2000, pp. 110–129.

[499] Wijesekera, D., Jajodia, S., A propositional policy algebra for access control, ACM Transactions on Information and System Security 6(2) (2003), pp. 286–325.

[500] Wijesekera, D., Jajodia, S., Parisi-Presicce, F., Hagström, A., Removing permissions in the flexible authorization framework, ACM Transactions on Database Systems 28(3) (2003), pp. 209–229.

[501] Winslett, M, Smith, K., Qian, X., Formal query languages for secure relational databases, ACM Transactions on Database Systems 19(4) (1994), pp. 626–662.

[502] Wulf, W., Cohen, E., Corwin, W., Jones, A., Levin, R., Pierson, C., Pollack, F., HYDRA: The kernel of a multiprocessor operating system, Communications of the ACM 17(6) (1974), pp. 337–345.

[503] Wulf, W.A., Levin, S.P., Harbison, S.P., *Hydra/Cmmp: An Experimental Computer System*, McGraw-Hill, New York, 1981.

[504] Xu, D., Ning, P., Privacy-preserving alert correlation: A concept hierarchy based approach. In: *Proc. 21st Annual Computer Security Applications Confernce*, ACSAC 2005, IEEE, 2005, pp. 537–546.

[505] Yao, A.C., Theory and application of trapdoor functions. In: *23rd IEEE Symposium on Foundations of Computer Science*, 1982, pp. 80–91.

[506] Yao, A.C., Protocols for secure computations. In: *23rd IEEE Symposium on Foundations of Computer Science*, 1982, pp. 160–164.

[507] Yao, A.C., How to generate and exchange secrets. In: *Proc. 27th IEEE Symposium on Foundations of Computer Science*, 1986, pp. 162–167.

[508] Yu, T., Winslett, M., Seamons, K.E., Supporting structured credentials and sensitive policies through interoperable strategies for automated trust negotations, ACM Transactions on Information and System Security 6(1) (2003), pp. 1–42.

[509] Zimmermann, P.R., *The Official PGP User's Guide*, MIT Press, Boston, 1995.

Index

Printing: Krips bv, Meppel, The Netherlands
Binding: Stürtz, Würzburg, Germany